Eric Hobsbawm

Eric Hobsbawm

A Life in History

RICHARD J. EVANS

OXFORD
UNIVERSITY PRESS

Oxford University Press is a department of the University of Oxford.
It furthers the University's objective of excellence in research, scholarship,
and education by publishing worldwide. Oxford is a registered trade mark of
Oxford University Press in the UK and certain other countries.

Published in the United States of America by Oxford University Press
198 Madison Avenue, New York, NY 10016, United States of America.

Library of Congress Cataloging-in-Publication Data
Names: Evans, Richard J.
Title: Eric Hobsbawm : a life in history / Richard J. Evans.
Description: New York : Oxford University Press, [2019]
Identifiers: LCCN 2018051780 | ISBN 9780190459642 (hardback)
Subjects: LCSH: Hobsbawm, E. J. (Eric J.), 1917–2012. |
Historians—Great Britain—Biography. |
Communist college teachers—Great Britain—Biography. |
Communism and intellectuals—Great Britain—History—20th century. |
Jews, German—Great Britain—Biography. |
BISAC: BIOGRAPHY & AUTOBIOGRAPHY / General. |
BIOGRAPHY & AUTOBIOGRAPHY / Historical. |
HISTORY / Europe / Western.Classification: LCC D15.H63 E38 2019 |
DDC 907.2/02—dc23 LC record available at
https://lccn.loc.gov/2018051780

Printed by Sheridan Books, Inc., United States of America

1 3 5 7 9 8 6 4 2

Contents

Preface

At the time of his death in 2012, at the age of ninety-five, Eric Hobsbawm had for some years been the best-known and most widely read historian in the world. His passing merited front-page headlines not only in the United Kingdom but also in countries as far apart as India and Brazil. His books were translated into more than fifty languages. Almost all of them have been continuously in print ever since their first publication, which in some cases dates back to more than half a century ago. Millions of readers have found their combination of analytical rigour, stylistic brilliance, interpretative brio and entertaining detail impossible to resist. In Brazil alone, sales of his books totalled almost a million, and his *Age of Extremes* topped the bestseller lists for weeks. His work was not only very widely read, but also exercised an enormous and lasting influence on historical thinking, as he came up with a whole series of novel concepts ranging from the 'general crisis of the seventeenth century' and 'the invention of tradition' to 'social banditry' and 'the long nineteenth century'. Debates on his work, from the standard of living in the Industrial Revolution to the origins of nationalism, continue to inspire new historical research many decades after he set them in motion.

Eric Hobsbawm's huge reputation and global influence as an historian would alone be sufficient justification for devoting a biography to him, but he was also a public intellectual and influential spokesman for the Left, and not just in Britain. In the 1980s and early 1990s he played a key role in the political debates behind the rise of New Labour, a role that towards the end of his life he came to regret. Lula da Silva, who became President of Brazil in 2003, explicitly acknowledged Eric's impact on his thinking, as did his predecessor Fernando Henrique Cardoso. Eric's influence on the Left was equally notable in India and Italy. Not for him the quiet life of a scholar shuffling between the study, the library and the lecture hall. For many years, his political activities were regarded as dangerous enough to attract surveillance by MI5.

This book is subtitled 'A Life in History' because Eric was not only an historian by profession but was also present at major moments in the history of the twentieth century, beginning with the Nazi seizure of power in Berlin in 1933, and continuing through the first celebrations of Bastille Day after the election of the Popular Front in France in 1936, the Spanish Civil War in the same year, the outbreak of the Second World War in 1939, the war itself and on to the Cold War and beyond. His unpublished diaries and letters and the many other sources available to tell the story of his life give a vivid impression of Berlin, London, Cambridge and Paris in the 1930s, the British Army in the early 1940s, the McCarthyite atmosphere of the late 1940s and early 1950s, the crisis of Communism in 1956, the jazz scene in Soho in the late 1950s, the upheavals that convulsed Latin American politics and society in the 1960s and 1970s, the rise of 'Eurocommunism' in Italy around the same time, the political debates within the Labour Party in the 1980s, and the intellectual politics of France's cultural elite in the 1990s.

This is a very long book not least because Eric Hobsbawm lived for a very long time. He remained active, intellectually undiminished and politically committed, into the second half of his tenth decade, writing and publishing all the time. But the book is also long because I have tried to let Eric tell his story as far as possible in his own words. He was a compelling and engaging writer, not just in his chosen field of history, but in many other genres as well. His immense output included short stories, poems, descriptions of the natural world, travelogues, political tracts, personal confessions, and much more besides. He knew how to tell a good story, not only about the past but also about his own life. Although his historical works sold millions of copies in scores of languages across the world, much of his other writing remains little known. A good deal of the material presented in this book has never been published before; much of it is brilliant and deserves to be widely read.

Any biographer who attempts a life of Eric Hobsbawm has to confront his own autobiography, *Interesting Times*, published in 2002. The book was, he said, more about the story of the public than the private man.[1] His friend Elise Marienstras noted on reading that there were 'very few personal things' in it.[2] And indeed, as Stefan Collini has observed, *Interesting Times* is 'that curious hybrid, an impersonal autobiography. One learns from it rather more about the society and politics of the 20th century than about the inner life of Eric Hobsbawm.'[3] This biography, therefore, while not neglecting Eric's intellectual and political development, focuses above all on his personal experiences and indeed on his inner life. There are good reasons for this. He viewed his life, not as shaping anything very much in the wider scheme of things, but as being shaped by the times he lived through.[4] As he later said, however, he was 'psychologically an unsystematic, intuitive, spontaneous historian, disinclined to plan'.[5] This book will show how his intuition as an historian was shaped not just by the political and historical context in which he lived but also by his personal circumstances, commitments and passions. I have tried to avoid overlap between this book and *Interesting Times* as much as I can, but inevitably, it has not always been possible, especially for the early part of his life. Still, Eric's autobiography is above all a work of memory, while this biography is based overwhelmingly on sources contemporary with the thoughts and actions they describe. It does not in any way seek to replace *Interesting Times*, which can be read with profit and enjoyment alongside it.

I knew Eric not intimately, but for a fairly long time; to tell the truth, I was too much in awe of him to become a close friend, for I knew that on almost any subject on which we might converse, he would know infinitely more than I did. Not that I agreed with him on everything, far from it; I have always been a social democrat in my political convictions. I could never accept the fundamental premises of Communism, least of all after seeing at close quarters what they produced in the grim, grey and joyless dictatorship of Communist East Germany when I got to know it during the researches I carried out for my doctorate in the early 1970s. But the task the historian has to fulfil above all others is to enter into an understanding of the strange and often alien world of the past, not to condemn it on the one hand or identify with it on the other. What I have tried to do in this book is to present Eric Hobsbawm to twenty-first-century readers and let them make up their own minds about what he said, did, thought and wrote.

Although he became embroiled in many arguments and controversies, Eric was as far as I can tell entirely without malice or ill will. Unlike so many historians and academics, he was never a 'good hater'. He was kind, generous and loyal to a fault. Eric was a man who loved life and lived it to the full, as I hope the following pages will show. The more I have read his writings – and I have read the vast majority of them – the more I have come to admire and respect him not just as an historian but as a person, and wish I had got to know him better when he was alive.

In researching and writing this book I have incurred many debts. My first and most important is to Marlene Hobsbawm, who has been wonderfully supportive all the way through, and has supplied information and material I could not otherwise have obtained. I hope she is pleased with the result. I would not have embarked on this project had the Modern History Section of the British Academy not asked me to write the 'biographical memoir' that all Fellows receive after their death; a visit to Eric and Marlene's Hampstead house, where a vast mass of personal papers awaited me on the top floor, convinced me that there was enough material to write a full-length biography. Alaric Bamping, Eric and Marlene's son-in-law, kindly guided me through them and supplied at intervals further documents as they were discovered.

Most of Eric's papers are now in the Modern Records Centre at the University of Warwick, and the staff have been unfailingly helpful and efficient during my many visits there. I am also indebted to the staff at the BBC Written Archives Centre, Caversham; the Harry Ransom Center at the University of Texas, Austin; The National Archives; King's College Archive Centre, Cambridge; Churchill College Archive Centre, Cambridge; the British Library of Economic and Political Science at the London School of Economics; the University of Manchester Archive; the Labour History Archive and Study Centre, People's History Museum, Manchester; Cambridge University Library; Bristol University Library Special Collections; the David Higham Associates literary agency; Little, Brown archive; Weidenfeld & Nicolson archive; the US Department of Justice (Freedom of Information requests); the Archivio della Scuola Normale di Pisa; US Holocaust Memorial Museum Collections, Washington, DC; the Archives Fondation Maison des Sciences de l'Homme, Paris; the Centre des Archives Diplomatiques de Nantes; the Archiv der israelitischen Kultusgemeinde, Vienna; the Archiv der Fichtnergasse-Schule, Vienna; the Wiener Stadt- und Landesarchiv, Vienna; and the Dokumentationsarchiv des österreichischen Widerstandes, Vienna. Because this book is based largely on unpublished archival material, I have dispensed with a bibliography. I have also tried to keep the notes to a minimum. All translations from French and German are mine; from Italian by Grazia Schiacchitano, and from Portuguese by Antonio Kerstenetzky. Material is still being transferred from the family to the Modern Records Centre at Warwick; references to the Hobsbawm Family Archive may need checking with the Centre.

The Leverhulme Trust kindly awarded me an Emeritus Fellowship which allowed me to obtain research assistance, saving me an enormous amount of time: I am particularly grateful to Anna Grundy at the Trust for her support throughout the project. For help with the research I owe an enormous debt of gratitude to Roberto Asmat Belleza, Fiona Brown, Stephanie Chan, Daniel Cowling, Charlotte Faucher, Victoria Harris, Yannick Herbert, Antonio Kerstenetzky, Rafael Kropiunigg, Johanna Langenbrink, Holly McCarthy, Mary-Ann Middelkoop, Emma Notfors and Grazia Schiacchitano.

*

I am deeply indebted to the following people who kindly agreed to be interviewed or supplied information: Judith Adamson, Peter Archard, John Arnold, Neal Ascherson, Maurice Aymard, Joan Bakewell, Logie Barrow, Henri Berghauer, Fernando Henrique Cardoso, Youssef Cassis, Geoff Crossick, Roderick Floud, Eric Foner, Roy Foster, Patrick Fridenson, Judith Friedlander, Marcus Gasparian, Edward Glover, Andrew Gordon, Lise Grande, Marie-Louise Heller, Angela Hobsbaum, Andy Hobsbawm, Julia Hobsbawm, Marlene Hobsbawm, Anthony Howe, Bruce Hunter, Joanna Innes, Nick Jacobs, Martin Jacques, Ira Katznelson, Gioietta Kuo, Daniel Lee, Geoffrey Lloyd, Fritz Lustig, Alan Mackay, Jeremy Marchesi, Robin Marchesi, Elise Marienstras, Patricia McGuire, Alan Montgomery, Andrew Morris, Doug Munro, Michelle Perrot, Richard Preston, Stuart Proffitt, Richard Rathbone, Garry Runciman, Donald Sassoon, Pat Stroud, Pat Thane, Romila Thapar, Keith Thomas, John Thompson, Claire Tomalin, Lois Wincott and Chris Wrigley. My apologies to anyone I have failed to interview; I am sure there are many.

I am grateful to Bruce Hunter and Chris Wrigley, Eric Hobsbawm's Literary Executors, for permission to quote copyright material in what follows. At the outset of the project, David Cannadine provided some sage and essential advice on biographical research. Rachel Hoffman, Bruce Hunter, Marlene, Julia and Andy Hobsbawm and Chris Wrigley have read the typescript and done a great deal to help improve it, as has my indefatigable editor at Little, Brown, Tim Whiting. To him, Zoe Gullen, Zoe Hood and Linda Silverman of Little, Brown, as well as Richard Collins, Daniel Balado and Christine Shuttleworth, I also extend my thanks for making the process of publication a smooth and enjoyable one.

I began working on this book at Wolfson College, Cambridge, and completed the first draft in the leafy, tranquil surroundings of the University of Richmond, Virginia, and I am grateful to both institutions for supplying me with the facilities, the time and the space with which to write. Many friends have listened patiently to me as I have talked to them about the project, and I am particularly grateful to Niamh Gallagher, Bianca Gaudenzi and Rachel Hoffman for their support. I owe more than I can say to Christine L. Corton, who read the early drafts, checked the proofs with a professional eye, and helped sustain me throughout the process of writing and research. When she first met Eric, in the early 1990s, she told me I would one day write his biography, and, as with so many other things, she has eventually been proved right.

Barkway, Hertfordshire, August 2018

1

'The English Boy'

1917–1933

I

Throughout his life, whenever he filled in one of the many forms that required him to enter 'place of birth', Eric Hobsbawm was obliged to write down the unlikely location of the city of Alexandria, in Egypt. For a man who believed that very little in history happened by chance, it was ironic that so many of the circumstances preceding and attending his birth were strikingly accidental. At the same time, as he liked to point out later in life, he would not have been born where or when he was, without the multiple intersections of some very major events in world history.

The first of these was the troubled relationship between Imperial Russia and the area known in the nineteenth century as 'Congress Poland', whose sovereign was the Russian Tsar. Following an unsuccessful nationalist uprising in 1863, Congress Poland was ruthlessly incorporated into the Russian Empire, its separate identity and institutions obliterated. It was the home to a large and impoverished community of Jews, whose rights and freedoms were heavily restricted by the Russian government in St Petersburg. The Jews lived in the poorest parts of Poland's towns and cities, forced to eke out a living in miserably paid and overworked artisan trades. Unsurprisingly, increasing numbers of Jews began to emigrate to England and America from the 1860s onwards. The threat of conscription into the Russian army, especially when war with the Ottoman Empire threatened in the mid-1870s, concentrated the minds of young Jewish men in particular. Those who found their way to London began to form a distinct community among the East End poor. Nine hundred of them were counted living there in the UK census of 1861, and 4500 in the census of 1881.[1]

Among the new arrivals from Poland in the mid-1870s was David Obstbaum, a cabinetmaker. Born in or around 1838, he had, according to family legend, walked from Poland to Hamburg when he was threatened with being conscripted into the Tsarist army.[2] From there he came to London with his second wife Rosa, née Berkoltz, like him a native of Warsaw. She was considerably younger, born in about 1852. The couple brought with them two children: Millie, born in 1866 to David's first wife, now deceased, and Louis, born in 1871 to Rosa. The name 'Obstbaum', meaning 'fruit-tree' in German (or, more probably, Yiddish, the language most commonly spoken by Jews in Congress Poland), was something of a tongue-twister for the English. On David's registration as an immigrant in London, a Cockney immigration officer misheard his name, added what he must have assumed was a silent 'H' to the beginning, and dropped the unpronounceable 't' so his name became Hobsbaum.[3]

The couple settled down to a steady if modest existence in their new home country. A second child, Philip, was born in Manchester on 12 May 1874; his grandson, also Philip Hobsbaum, born in 1932, became a well-known poet, critic and academic.[4] Their third son, Aaron, known as Ernest, was born in London in 1878; his daughters Edith and Margarite became two further victims of British officialdom's inability to deal with foreign names and were registered at birth with the name Hobsburn. A daughter, Sarah, known as Cissy, was born in 1879; in 1909 she married Louis Prechner, another man of Central European origin: their son Denis was born on 16 November 1916 in Stoke Newington, a district on the northern edge of London's Jewish East End. In due course he became a prominent jazz critic and record producer. He was to play a significant role in Eric's life.[5]

Altogether there were twenty-two members of the Hobsbaum cousinhood in Eric's generation. Only a very few of them had any real contact with him, however, scattered as they were across various parts of the globe. 'Ours', as he later remarked, '... is not a very close-knit family.'[6] The two uncles who were to play the most important part in Eric's life were Solomon (Sidney), born in Dalston, in north-east London, on 25 April 1889, and Henry, generally known as Harry, born on 9 July 1888, whose son Roland became Eric's closest friend during his adolescence. All in all, the fact that seven out of David and Rosa Hobsbaum's nine children reached adulthood speaks to a certain physical resilience in the family's genetic constitution, though none of them survived into what we would now regard as old age; only Millie, David's daughter by his first wife, escaped this fate, dying in 1966 at the age of ninety-nine, sixty years after she had emigrated to America with her husband. All of Eric's first cousins, apart from Louis, who was born in Warsaw and therefore like his parents was naturalised as a British citizen, were born British and remained so throughout their lives; all of them were native English-speakers and all of them adapted quickly to English culture and English life; in fact, they were passionately ambitious to become 'English in name, politics and culture', as Eric later noted. They were mostly craftsmen or clerks: there was no record of rabbinical learning or business wealth in the family, and many of them had very little formal education.[7]

Eric's own father, Leopold Hobsbaum, generally known as Percy, was born in Whitechapel, in the heart of London's Jewish East End, on 8 September 1881, the fifth child of David and Rosa. While the two oldest sons of David Hobsbaum, Louis and Philip, followed in their father's footsteps and became cabinetmakers,[8] the others, including Percy, perhaps benefiting from the introduction of compulsory primary education between the ages of five and ten in Britain in 1880, made the social ascent into the ranks of the lower middle class. Ernest became a telegraphist, later graduating to a position as a schoolmaster. Harry was also a telegraphist, and his sister Sarah became a schoolmistress; Isaac trained as a chemist and later as a mining engineer. Sidney was a businessman in a minor way, though never, as it turned out, very successfully. So far, therefore, the story of the family following its establishment in London in the 1870s was not untypical of the social history of the Jewish immigrant community of the day. As relatively early arrivals, the Hobsbaums benefited from the liberal immigration policies of the Victorian era, enjoyed a head start over later arrivals from Eastern Europe, and were able to escape the dire poverty that characterised the everyday life of East End Jews in the 1890s and 1900s.[9]

It was around the time that Percy reached adulthood that a second major aspect of world history impacted upon the Hobsbaums. Britain in the early twentieth century was at the centre of a vast global empire that included, though not in a formal sense, countries of South America such as Chile, where Eric's uncle Isaac emigrated with his wife and children, inaugurating a long family connection with the country. Since 1869 a key element in the maintenance of the British Empire had been the Suez Canal, which shortened the route to India for seaborne traffic by seven thousand kilometres. To protect the canal, Britain had effectively taken over the administration of Egypt by force from the Ottoman Empire in 1882. By the 1890s the country's major institutions were being run and staffed by the British, offering opportunities for employment to those who wished to make a career for themselves abroad.[10]

Percy's brother Ernest moved to Cairo some time before the end of the nineteenth century, where at first he lectured to the Free Popular University and then managed to secure employment with the British-run Egyptian Postal and Telegraph Service; later on, he wrote novels about his experiences (*Cross and Crescent* and *Draper's Hall*), though they were not very successful. When Percy reached the age of majority, Ernest suggested to him that he might find congenial employment in the same institution. So Percy moved there to join his brother. In doing so, he also joined the multinational, largely French-speaking expatriate community in Cairo and Alexandria. Social life was very active, and in 1913 Ernest married Jeanne Claeys in Cairo: their two daughters, Edith and Margarite, were born in the same city respectively in 1914 and 1915.

It was also in 1913, in one of Alexandria's central expatriate social institutions, the Sporting Club, that Percy Hobsbaum met the eighteen-year-old Nelly Grün, one of three daughters of Moritz Grün and his wife Ernestine, née Friedmann. Her family lived in Vienna. Moritz and his wife were registered as members of the Jewish faith, and were engaged mainly in the jewellery business. They were relatively well off. Born on 7 April 1895, Nelly had just graduated from secondary school, still an unusual achievement for a Viennese girl. Moreover, she had passed with distinction.[11] So, as a reward, her parents had decided to give her a holiday somewhere outside Austria. They chose Alexandria as a suitable destination because her uncle Albert, a successful merchant, had based himself there, running a well-stocked retail outlet. Percy and Nelly fell in love and decided to marry. They got engaged and started making plans for their wedding.[12]

As their plans advanced, however, world history intervened again, this time in the shape of the First World War, which broke out in August 1914, with Austria-Hungary, Germany, Turkey and Bulgaria lined up on one side, and Britain, France and Russia, joined later by Italy and Romania, on the other. Nelly worked for a time as a nurse in a military hospital while she and Percy decided what to do. Since Nelly was Austrian and Percy was British, it would have been unwise for them to marry or indeed even meet in either of their respective native countries, as that would have resulted in the one or the other of them being interned as an enemy alien. They got married, therefore, in Zurich, in neutral Switzerland, on 1 May 1915, with the British Consul officiating, aided by a special permit personally signed by the British Foreign Secretary, Sir Edward Grey.[13] After a brief honeymoon in Lugano, in southern Switzerland, the couple made their way to Naples and then to Rome, in still-neutral

Italy (it was not until 23 May 1915 that the Italians entered the war, on the Allied side, despite their formal alliance with the Germans). From there they sailed to Alexandria, where Percy had his job in the Postal and Telegraph Service waiting for him and both he and his wife, now a British citizen by marriage, had relatives living.[14]

It was here, in the Sporting District of the city, situated between the seashore and the open spaces of the golf links and racecourse of the late Victorian Sporting Club, that Eric came into the world on 8 June 1917. The British Consul, Mr D. A. Cameron, not only got the date wrong (he registered it as 9 June) but also misspelled Eric's surname when registering his birth on 12 June: in English, 'au' at that time was pronounced 'or', and not 'ow', in the German manner, as it commonly is now, and so the Consul misheard the name, which presumably Eric's parents failed to spell out, and put a 'w' instead of a 'u'. Thus he became Eric John Ernest Hobsbawm. He derived his first name from a cousin born the previous year as the second son of Isaac Hobsbaum ('Berk'), the uncle who lived in Chile. He was given the middle name 'Ernest' after the uncle based in Egypt.[15] The rest of the family continued to be spelled 'Hobsbaum' with a 'u', except for those few members whose names were spelled, whether deliberately or accidentally, in some other way, like the Hobsburn sisters or Harry's son Roland (Ron), whose school name tags gave his surname as 'Hobsborn' even though his official name at school was still Hobsbaum.[16]

Eric remembered little or nothing about his time in Egypt, 'except, possibly, a cage of small birds in the zoo at Nouzha, and a corrupt fragment of a Greek children's song, presumably sung by a Greek nursemaid'.[17] Within a few months of his birth, the stalemate of the First World War was broken by the October Revolution in Russia, when Lenin and the Bolsheviks seized power in St Petersburg. The fact that Eric was born in the year of the Bolshevik Revolution was, on the face of it, a mere coincidence, but none the less, one that somehow stood as a symbol for the political commitment he was to gain later on.

II

In November 1918 the war came to an end. The rapid rise of nationalism in Egypt, which was to culminate in a revolution in 1919, followed by independence three years later, was making the country uncomfortable for expatriates. So as soon as she could, Nelly sailed to Trieste, which the peace settlement had transferred from Austria to Italy. She travelled in comfort on the first ship out of Alexandria, the steamer *Helouan* of the Lloyd Triestino Line, the two-year-old Eric in tow; Percy joined them in the early autumn.[18] Nelly's father was waiting on the quayside at Trieste and took his daughter and grandson on the Southern Railway to Vienna to live with him and his wife Ernestine in a second-floor flat in the western suburbs, at Weissgerberstrasse 14. Visiting it for the first time since then, for a television documentary made in the mid-1990s, Eric pointed out the spare room to which his parents moved with him on their arrival. 'Hasn't changed much', he commented, looking at the solid stone building from across the street. He did not accept the television director's invitation to step inside.[19]

Some months after the family's arrival in Vienna, Eric's father, flush with inflation-proof sterling from his years in the British Postal Service in Alexandria, rented a first-floor flat in the Villa Seutter, which stood on a hill in the Hacking district of Vienna. It dated from the 1880s, when Carl, Baron Seutter von Loetzen, had built it as a family home. It was a rather grand edifice, crowned with a four-sided dome and possessing extensive grounds in which Eric played with the children of the Gold family, who lived on the ground floor; Nelly became close to their mother, sharing an interest in literature and culture.[20] Post-war hyperinflation had forced the once-wealthy Seutter family to rent out the villa, and it took some time for their fortunes to recover so that they could repossess it: the building remains the family's property to the present day. This was perhaps the most prosperous and certainly the most tranquil period of Eric's childhood, although he was suffering at the time of the move there from a broken nose. 'Eric was very ill with it – he had a high temperature', his mother remembered some years later, 'and when we moved to Hacking in May, he was still bandaged. It was not pierced, it broke by itself, and perhaps that is why it took so long.'[21]

The large family group in which Eric spent his early years in Vienna centred on two married couples. First there were his mother Nelly and her husband Percy. In 1921 they were joined by his uncle Sidney, who, remarkably, on 14 December 1921 married Nelly's younger sister Grete Grün, usually known as Gretl (born on 21 September 1897). Their son Peter came into the world on 30 July 1926.[22] For much of the 1920s Sidney and Gretl lived in Vienna, where Sidney pursued various business interests, until they moved to Berlin towards the end of the decade.[23] While they were in Vienna, Eric became close to his aunt, as in 1925 he was sent for a short while to a sanatorium in the Alps to recover from an illness, and was looked after there by Gretl, who had also been sent there under medical advice.[24] Then there were the Grün grandparents and assorted, more distant Grün cousins with whom this core group met from time to time. The third and oldest of the Grün sisters, Marianne or Mimi (born on 23 February 1893), was more distant but still in contact with the family.[25] Nelly's relatives on her mother's side, the Friedmanns, were also part of the wider family circle. There were other relatives in England. 'If there was anything specifically Jewish about them', Eric wrote later of the members of his family, 'it was the assumption that the family was a network stretching across countries and oceans, [and] that shifting between countries was a normal part of life.'[26]

During the 1920s, Eric grew up in the social world of the Viennese bourgeoisic, though distanced from it to a certain degree because he, his parents and his sister, Nancy (born on 5 November 1920), were British by background and citizenship.[27] Still, to the end of his life when he spoke German it was with 'a slight hint of an antediluvian Viennese accent', as he confessed later, 'that perhaps still lets itself be heard in my German after more than seventy years'.[28] National identity was weak in the

First Austrian Republic, the residual, German-speaking part of the former Habsburg Empire left over when the 'successor states' of Yugoslavia, Czechoslovakia, Hungary and Poland became independent after the war. Reminders of the empire were everywhere: Eric later remembered a Slovenian child-minder who told him tales of werewolves from her home country; his relatives lived in or came from towns now in Poland, Romania or the Czech Republic; and the apartment building supervisors were almost certainly Czech. Thus, quite apart from his father's English background, and his own first years in Alexandria, Eric grew up in a milieu that was cosmopolitan almost by definition. At the same time, the invariable medium of communication for the middle classes was German, which gave the Viennese bourgeoisie, including the highly acculturated Jewish population, an unshakeable sense of superiority over other national minorities.[29]

Vienna was deeply scarred by the anti-Semitism of a strong minority among the bourgeoisie, encouraged by Karl Lueger, the pre-war mayor. The two hundred thousand people of Jewish descent in the city – 10 per cent of the population, including those who, like the Hobsbaums and Grüns, were not religious – could not escape from it. Austrian law required all citizens to be registered as members of a religion, and, although Percy described himself as 'without a confession [konfessionslos]', all official documents concerning him and his family described them as Jewish (mosaisch) by faith.[30] Thus when Eric was in secondary school in Vienna, he was excused Christian religious instruction and sent instead to an afternoon class for Jews in another part of Vienna, where he was taught Jewish religious customs and learned to read Hebrew script, an accomplishment that he had, however, forgotten by the time he reached adulthood.[31] He attempted to declare himself officially as not belonging to any religion the moment he was legally entitled to do so, at the age of thirteen, but his mother prevented him from carrying out his intention. Faced with hostile prejudices and negative stereotypes, Eric's mother told him firmly when he was ten: 'You must never do anything, or seem to do anything, that might suggest that you are ashamed of being a Jew.'[32] He always remembered this injunction, and, he confessed towards the end of his life, always did his best to live up to it.

Family life in the Villa Seutter consisted of the usual routines. 'I discovered Eric painting a picture for your birthday', Nelly wrote to her sister Gretl in August 1924. 'Even he didn't think it was very good.' Her main worry was the inadequacy of their maid-of-all-work. 'Her capabilities have been much exaggerated', she wrote. The girl was eventually dismissed, and Nelly fretted about doing without a servant during the winter.[33] In the spring of 1925, she travelled to England to nurse her sister Mimi, who had fallen seriously ill, leaving Percy and her mother to look after the children.[34] Eric was given three weeks off school to go and stay with his aunt Gretl in Berlin.[35] The family could have managed without a servant, but although it might have been less stressful than actually having one, to employ a domestic in 1920s Vienna was a mark of bourgeois status that Nelly Hobsbaum did not want to abandon. 'Try not ever to admit that you could do without a maid!!' Nelly told her sister: 'A maid is just as much a necessity as food or a roof over your head.'[36]

Neither the Hobsbaums nor the Grüns were well off. Such savings as the Grüns had accumulated disappeared in the massive inflation that followed the end of the First World War in Austria as well as Germany, and Percy's reserves of sterling brought from Alexandria soon ran out. Vienna after the end of the war was no place for a man who answered the question 'What are you best and worst at?' with the words 'Missing opportunities. Grasping them.'[37] Vienna was full of highly educated and well-trained civil servants who had once run the Habsburg Empire but were now thrown out of their jobs because they had nobody left to administer beyond the six million inhabitants of the rump of German-speaking Austria. Propelled into economic misery along with them were all the shopkeepers, lawyers, manufacturers and tradespeople who had depended for a living on the patronage of the now-vanished Habsburg Imperial Court and administration. In this dire economic situation, Percy Hobsbaum did not stand a chance.[38] Nelly earned some money by translating fiction from English into German, but it was by no means sufficient to keep the family going.[39] On 13 May 1926 the family was forced by economic necessity to move from the expensive Villa Seutter in the leafy suburb of Hacking to a cheap second-floor flat at Einsiedeleigasse 18, in the less fashionable district of Ober St Veit.[40]

The move meant that Eric had to change to a second primary school in the precinct where the new flat was situated. He seems to have done well there, for he arrived at his first secondary school with top marks from his previous school in everything except for the neatness of his work. His secondary school reports for 1928 gave him a 'very good' grade in divinity, natural history and singing, 'good' in German, history and geography, as well as gymnastics, and 'satisfactory' in mathematics, drawing and writing. He was evidently a model pupil, since the report described his behaviour as 'very good'. His teachers recommended him in their report of June 1928 for progressing to the next class above. Yet the instability of his schooling affected Eric's education, throwing him back on his own intellectual resources. He began reading intensively from around the age of ten and never stopped until his dying day eighty-five years later.

He devoured books and magazines on prehistory and the natural world and became an enthusiastic and discerning bird-watcher: in 1927, on holiday in the village of Rettenegg, in the wooded Styrian hills, he 'saw, for the first time in my life, the great black woodpecker, all one-and-a-half foot of it under the vivid red helmet, drumming against a stump in a clearing like a mad miniature hermit, alone under the stillness of the trees'.[41] He also went to the theatre with his parents, and watched Charlie Chaplin films at the local cinema. He read popular detective stories, and mastered gothic German handwriting. In his spare time, he collected stamps, which showed him, he later remembered, 'the contrast between the unchanging continuity of George V's head on British stamps and the chaos of overprints, new names and new currencies elsewhere'. His sense of instability was deepened by his registering in Austria of 'the changing coins and banknotes of an era of economic disruption'. He learned about 'war, breakdown, revolution, inflation' from the adults around him.[42] What intellectual stimulation Eric received at this time came not from his father, whose collection of books focused on adventure stories, including Kipling's, which Eric 'read without understanding', and a volume of poetry by Tennyson, but from his mother, and from school.[43]

'He is fine at school', his mother reported in January 1929, 'but his behaviour leaves something to be desired', a criticism which, however, she failed to substantiate with any details.[44] He was doing well in most subjects, though his struggling family sometimes baulked at the requirement to purchase textbooks, notably an expensive school atlas, which Eric persuaded his mother to buy despite the 'sense of crisis' her reluctance to buy it conveyed.[45] 'Eric's report was very good', his mother wrote at the beginning of February 1929, 'he did well in all the main subjects, only a "good" in History (I don't know why) and in Maths.'[46] In Maths, he only scored 'satisfactory' in his first half-yearly report for 1929. He continued to gain grades of 'very good' in Divinity, German, Geography, Natural History and Singing. In history he was just 'good', though he made up for this in the second half of the year with a string of 'very good' marks, as he did in every other subject, including the new one of Latin, but with the continuing exceptions of mathematics, gymnastics and handwriting, where his performance was deemed to be 'satisfactory'. Overall he was recommended as 'outstanding' for progress to the next class.[47]

Nelly clearly put a great deal of effort into encouraging Eric to read and to work hard at his lessons. She also gave him love and affection, providing him with emotional as well as intellectual stimulation. Indeed, Eric was far closer to his mother than he was to his somewhat unsympathetic father. A passionate anglophile, she spent a good deal of time correcting and improving Eric's written and spoken English and made sure that only English was spoken at home.[48] His school report for 1929 put down 'English-German' in the box denoting his 'mother tongue'.[49] He was, in other words, bilingual, a native speaker of English as well as of German. His mother 'dreamed', Eric later remembered, 'that I might one day find myself in the Indian Civil Service – or rather, since I was so obviously interested in birds, in the Indian Forestry Service, which would bring me (and her) even closer to the world of her admired *Jungle Book*'.[50] Her example as the author of novels and short stories surely had some influence in determining his later choice of career as a writer and laid the foundation for his mastery of English as well as of German prose style later in life.

Eric's relationship with his father seems to have been far from easy. He later described him as 'intelligent, agreeable, musical and a fine all-round sportsman as well as a lightweight boxer of championship standard'.[51] Percy had been crowned amateur lightweight boxing champion of Egypt twice, in 1907 and 1908. He remained in Eric's memory (or perhaps from photographs) 'a medium-sized sinewy man in rimless pince-nez, black hair parted in the middle, with a horizontally lined forehead'. In a self-assessment album of the sort fashionable at the time, Percy wrote that he valued physical strength more than anything else in a man.[52] It was not surprising that he was often impatient with his bookish, dreamy son. Percy took him to football matches, sang English music-hall songs to him, employed him as a ballboy in mixed-doubles tennis and tried, without success, to teach him boxing.[53]

Eric recalled many years later an incident, when he was about nine or ten years old, that summed up the sharp contrast in character between himself and his father:

He had asked me to fetch a hammer to knock in some nail, possibly something that had come loose from a deck-chair. I was at that time passionately into prehistory, possibly because I was in the middle of reading the first volume of the trilogy *Die Höhlenkinder* (The Cave Children) by one Sonnleitner, in which a couple of (unrelated) Robinson Crusoe orphan children in an inaccessible Alpine valley grow up to reproduce the stages of human prehistory, from palaeolithic to something like recognizable Austrian peasant life. As they were reliving the stone age, I had constructed a stone-age hammer, carefully lashed to its wooden handle in the proper manner. I brought it to him and was amazed at his furious reaction. I have since been told that he was often short-tempered with me.[54]

The family's income was boosted by an advance on a novel Nelly received from a publisher early in 1929, but the improvement this brought about was only marginal.[55] During a cold spell at the beginning of February 1929 the family could only afford to heat a single room in their apartment. 'I usually haven't got a single shilling in the house', she confessed. She avoided paying bills as far as possible, but knew a catastrophe could hit the family at any time.[56] She had fallen behind with the rent for the apartment in the Einsiedeleigasse and started to run up debts to tradesmen: towards the end of 1928 their landlord had threatened to cut off the gas and then given them notice to quit.[57]

III

Before the notice became final, however, a sudden and completely unexpected tragedy struck the family. On 8 February 1929 Nelly went to answer a knock on the apartment block door, and, when she opened it, Percy Hobsbaum's workmates, who had been carrying him home from work, put him down on the path, insensible, and left.[58] Within a few minutes he was dead. He was only forty-eight. Nelly remembered with horror his groans as he lay dying on the path, calling out to her. Recalling the catastrophe a few years later, Eric felt that his own tears were false. 'You cry just because it's expected of you.'[59] However distant he felt from his father, however, there was no doubting the profound impact the disaster had on his life. The cause of Percy's death was given as 'heart trauma'. He was buried in the New Cemetery in Vienna, in grave number 16, row 8, number 27, on 11 February 1929.[60] Eric and his sister were now dependent entirely on their mother for their survival.

Nelly never recovered from the blow. 'What I have just

been through has really torn me apart', she wrote a week later. 'Something has broken inside me.' It was perhaps some consolation that Percy had been spared the further deterioration of their financial situation. 'It wouldn't have got better in the future, only worse', she wrote. And she took some comfort in the fact that 'the children, especially Eric, were very kind, Eric like a little man'.[61] 'You have no idea what a really wonderful little lad that boy is,' Nelly wrote to her brother-in-law Sidney Hobsbaum in a reply on his behalf to a letter of condolence he had sent Eric: '– if only his Daddy could see him.' Sidney did not stop at condolences: he also sent Nelly a cheque. It would, she gratefully acknowledged, 'keep me another month'.[62] Well before the end of March 1929, however, she was forced to admit: 'I will *very* soon have no more money.'[63] They had to move out of their flat on 11 March into an even cheaper one, at Untere Weissgerberstrasse 45, in the Third District of the city.[64] The move did not greatly improve their fortunes. 'Eric is more kind, good and charming a boy than I can say', she told her sister Gretl: 'But for the moment my attempts to get us by have met with very little success.'[65] When Eric's shoes needed replacing – they let in the snow and ice in the winter ('I remember crying with the pain of it on the Ringstrasse', he later wrote) – Nelly was obliged to procure footwear for him from a Jewish charity.[66]

She visited Berlin briefly to stay with Sidney and Gretl and their young son Peter in the hope that a change of scenery would help restore her spirits, and returned to Vienna in April 1929; appended to her letter of thanks to Sidney and Gretl is a brief note from the eleven-year-old Eric, in English, in an undeveloped schoolboy hand, the first piece of his writing that we have:

Dear uncle,

I'm very sorry that I forgot your birthday. Many happy returns! I hope you are not angry because I write to you too late. Are you all well? Mummy has told us so much about the little boy and about you all. How he (Peter) always goes to the Tiergarten and how he plays there etc. etc.

Mummy came home yesterday, just after we had eaten our lunch and had washed. She will write to you as well. We are all well and quite happy. Aunti Mimi wrote to Grossmama yesterday in the morning.

How are Otto and Walter?

Many happy returns of the day and keep well! Kiss all from your Eric.[67]

Eric wrote again in June, no doubt, once more, at his mother's command, this time the obligatory thank-you letter after his birthday, for which Sidney and Gretl had sent him 'the book "The ancient Mariner"' and ten marks. 'I don't know yet what I will do with the 10 Marks', he added: 'I'll probably keep it for England.'[68]

Eric's aunt Mimi had offered to put him up for the summer and he travelled to England at the end of the school term to stay with her.[69] On the way there, at Koblenz, on the confluence of the Rhine and the Moselle, a German in a coupé pointed out to him the tricolour flying from the great Napoleonic fortress of Ehrenbreitstein across the river, advertising the French military occupation of the area that had begun after the First World War and was to end just over a year later, in June 1930.[70] From there Eric travelled to the French coast, across the Channel, and to London, where he stayed with his uncle Harry and his wife Bella. Here he met their son Roland, who preferred to be called Ron or Ronnie, though to his family he was known as 'Hobby'. Born on 21 July 1912 in Wanstead, on Essex's border with east London,[71] Ron was five years older than Eric. He took him round London on a bus to see the sights. It was the beginning of a close and important friendship for the two boys.[72]

After a couple of days, Eric travelled north by train to Southport, on Merseyside, where he stayed at the boarding house run by his aunt Mimi. Here he discovered boys' weekly adventure magazines such as *The Wizard*. These were far more exciting than the improving books his relatives had sent him from England, and he 'read them hungrily, spent all my pocket money on them, and took a collection back to Vienna'.[73] This was his first common experience with English boys of his age. And for the first time, he kept a diary, which Mimi sent to his mother. She forwarded it to Gretl, but added: 'I won't send you his letter as its appearance is awful. I am really ashamed of it.'[74] 'The boy is having a very good time', she wrote, 'and I am most grateful to Mimi.'[75] The Boy Scouts' World Jamboree happened to be taking place near Mimi's boarding house, from 29 July to 12 August, at Arrowe Park, in Upton, Merseyside. The movement had been founded before the First World War as a way of training young men to build up their physical fitness and to engage in practical activities out of doors that would prepare them for the role of independent military scouts later in life. Though not a Scout himself, Eric spent a good deal of time at the Jamboree. Indeed, he conceived such an enthusiasm for the Scouts that he signed up with them immediately on his return to Vienna: the first disciplined, close-knit milieu he joined, one consisting mainly of middle-class Jewish boys like himself. It supplied the identity, stability and sense of belonging that he surely must have craved after the insecurity of the Vienna years and the sudden death of his father. 'I was a passionately enthusiastic Scout', he wrote later. He even recruited a number of his friends. He obtained a copy of *Scouting for Boys*, the manual penned by the Scouts' founder before the First World War, Lord Baden-Powell, though, he confessed, he was 'not much gifted either for fieldcraft or group life'.[76] His school also provided him with a circle of friends, though none of them was very close, and took him on outings, including his first experience of skiing, but it was the Scouts that really aroused his enthusiasm.[77]

Meanwhile, Nelly got by financially by giving private English lessons, though many of these were to friends or their children and were really a way in which they subsidised her without damaging her self-respect. Eric was roped in as well: the first money he ever earned was by teaching English to the daughter of one of his mother's friends, to help her pass the entrance test to the local high school.[78] This saved Nelly from having to pay him pocket money. Some more funds came from Percy's brother Harry, in London. Nelly began translating fiction from English into German for the publisher the Rikola-Verlag, which had brought out her novel based on her time in Alexandria. Her knowledge of English gained her employment with the textile firm Alexander Rosenberg, based in Vienna and Budapest.[79] The family's situation seemed at last to be improving. But in November 1929 Nelly began experiencing 'strange turns'[80] and, a few months later, shortness of breath, high temperatures and growing physical weakness.[81] Her parents came to the flat to help out. Soon she was unable to do any work.[82] The doctors diagnosed tuberculosis, perhaps hastened by her frequent visits to her husband's grave, where she stood for lengthy periods in the winter cold and wet without adequate protection against the elements. She began spitting blood, and was admitted to a sanatorium in the alpine village of Weyer an der Enns for treatment.[83]

Since Nelly was now unable to look after the children, Eric and Nancy went to live with their great-uncle on his mother's side, Viktor Friedmann, and his wife Elsa, whose son Otto, ten years older than Eric, was boarding with Eric's uncle Sidney and aunt Gretl in Berlin, thus creating something of a reciprocal obligation on them to look after Eric. Eric also got to know their daughter Herta, born in 1911 and still living with her parents, while he was to encounter Otto in person when he visited Berlin. Meanwhile, Eric commuted from the Friedmanns' apartment in the Seventh District of Vienna to his school in the Third District, across the centre of the city. Nelly made little progress at the sanatorium, however.

In April 1930 the doctors collapsed and reflated a lung, a common treatment for pulmonary tuberculosis at the time, but there was no cure: antibiotics would not make their mark for another two decades.[84] The therapy required a lengthy period of convalescence.[85] Fortunately the socialist municipality of 'Red Vienna' met the costs through its advanced social insurance programme, which applied to Nelly because she had regular paid employment.[86] By early May Nelly had been lying in bed in the sanatorium for six weeks without a break.[87] Eric and his sister joined his aunt Gretl and her son Peter in Weyer an der Enns, near the sanatorium where his mother was staying. Here he made friends with Haller Peter, the son of the family's landlord in

Vienna, and since Haller's father was a railwayman and therefore a 'Red', his son followed his example. Eric, as he wrote later, 'also concluded that I wanted to be one'.[88]

Nelly's treatment in the sanatorium did no good, and she was still there in September 1930.[89] As she wrote to her sister Mimi, 'I have not rediscovered the bridge back to life, and doubt I ever will.'[90] On being told by a consultant that she had little hope of recovery, she wrote: 'The tragedy is that this confounded illness does not kill one – there does not seem the slightest hope of that at the moment.'[91] She experienced a relapse and became so weak that she began to worry about what would happen to the children if she died, especially since she had been obliged to resign from the textile firm at the end of 1929 and was subsisting mainly off her translation work.[92] Towards the end of the summer holidays she sent the children to stay for a brief visit with their uncle and aunt in Berlin. 'It seems that Eric could not have found it better', she reported later.[93]

Gretl and Sidney travelled with the children back to Vienna for the new school term and looked after them for a while. 'I am much better now', Nelly wrote to Nancy optimistically from her bed, 'and I hope to be quite better soon. I will be happy to have you and Eric with me again. You are both good children and I am very proud of you. Keep well and fit, that is all I want.'[94] But Eric's aunt and uncle had to return to Berlin, and with Nelly's agreement they took Nancy with them. Nelly now advertised for someone to give Eric bed and board, since she could not manage to look after him herself. She received '90 replies altogether'. In sorting them out, she reported, 'I first looked for people who had a garden as Eric hates town as much as I do.' Eventually he lodged with a Frau Effenberger, a widow who put him up in return for a modest payment to cover Eric's living expenses. The main requirement was for Eric to give English lessons to her eight-year-old son Bertl, who already spoke a little of the language but wanted to learn it properly.[95] Frau Effenberger's apartment was at Herbeckstrasse 12, in the north-western suburb of Währing, the location of the main Jewish cemetery and a district with a high proportion of Jewish people among its inhabitants.[96] Eric had to change to another secondary school, the Federal Gymnasium XVIII, since his previous school was too far away.[97]

Eric was well looked after, Nelly reported on 19 September 1930,[98] but his inexperience and the irregularity of the lessons caused Frau Effenberger to complain that her son was making little progress. Eric redoubled his efforts. 'Now everything is all right, I mean with Mrs. E.,' he eventually reported. 'I give my lessons daily now', he wrote, 'and Mrs. E. has said that I do it much better now.' He had no worries about his school exam results. 'Mine will be all right, thank goodness', he wrote confidently. He was still a committed Boy Scout ('we sing and play and learn').[99] He wrote long letters to his mother, one of which annoyed her by reporting that he had bought a suit and a pair of shoes; he meant well, she said, but she preferred to buy whatever he needed herself.[100] But he was already starting to become independent. 'I hear only good news about Eric', Nelly wrote to Gretl on 20 October 1930, 'even Mama says she finds him changed for the better.' He was made a monitor at school. He had a circle of friends, but they could not provide a substitute for his damaged family life. He later remembered 'sitting alone on a swing in the garden of Mrs. Effenberger, trying to learn by heart the song of the blackbirds, while noting the variations between them'. He had become solitary, and 'lived without intimacy'.[101] 'The boy lives his own, very intense life, and none of the rest of us have any place in that at all', his mother reported.[102]

'I am still the same', she wrote to Gretl and Sidney on 12 December 1930, 'in bed and feeling generally rotten – and what with my work and all I am in a pretty bad fix'.[103] By early December she was making plans for Eric to move to Berlin and live with his uncle and aunt.[104] She worried that they would spoil him:

I have not heard how Eric reacted to your invitation, but I can rather imagine it and I'm looking forward to hear from him. Only, for Heaven's sake don't you go and buy him Xmas presents on top of it all! What are you thinking of? Obviously, he is getting his heart's dream, a Scout equipment, and he really

does not need anything else – Berlin is far far better than any
present would be. So please do me the favour and do *not* buy
him a camera or anything. As regards a camera, in any case I'm
afraid it would come too expensive in the long run.[105]

Eric visited her shortly before Christmas 1930, but she had a
high fever, felt miserable and was not in much of a condition to
receive him.[106] He spent the holiday with his aunt and uncle and
sister Nancy in Berlin. 'I was very touched with his last letter', his
mother wrote shortly after he had departed for the German capital: 'he wrote and said he would prefer to spend Xmas with me, if
I'd like him to or if I come to Vienna before then he would not go
because he would have to fetch me from the station! At the same
time', she added, 'Mama wrote and told me how delighted he was
at the thought of going to Berlin.'[107]

A tubercular swelling in her neck now convinced the doctors
that she had to go to Vienna for treatment.[108] In the first week
of the new year she was moved to a hospital in the suburb of
Währing, fortuitously near where Eric had been lodging with
Frau Effenberger.[109] 'I'm going to Vienna with very little hope', she
wrote.[110] Gretl returned there from Berlin with Eric, who resumed
his position with Frau Effenberger and her son. Nelly made the
best of her situation in hospital – 'It really is quite wonderful here,
food & nursing excellent and everything tip-top'[111] – and she
experienced a brief respite in May 1931: 'I feel that I am, indeed,
beginning to get stronger. I no longer sleep all day, actually
have the courage to take a few steps again, read the papers etc.
Naturally I am still coughing etc., but I am no longer quite so out
of breath.'[112] But this was the last time she felt any improvement.
Realising the end was near, the medical authorities transferred
her, as Eric noted,

to a garden sanatorium in Purkersdorf, just west of Vienna,
where I saw her for the last time shortly before going to camp
with the Scouts. I can remember nothing of the occasion except
how emaciated she looked and that, not knowing what to say

or do – there were others present – I glanced out of the window and saw a hawfinch, a small bird with a beak strong enough to crack cherry stones, that I had never seen before and for which I had long been on the lookout. So my last memory of her is not one of grief but of ornithological pleasure.[113]

From May onwards, Nelly's letters to her sister Gretl became ever more infrequent and then ceased altogether. Her decline was now swift, and she died on 15 July 1931 at the age of thirty-six. The kindly officiating doctor certified the cause of death as 'lung cancer' combined with 'ineffectiveness of the heart', to avoid the social stigma that still attached to consumption, but there was no doubt in fact that the real cause was tuberculosis.[114] Eric was called back from the Scout camp to attend her funeral. She was buried in the New Cemetery in Vienna on 19 July 1931 in the same grave as her husband.[115] At the age of just fourteen, Eric was an orphan.

IV

Eric's closeness to his mother is revealed by the affectionate letters she wrote to him while he was away in England and later, when she was in hospital.[116] Looking back, he concluded that her influence on him had been mainly moral, exerted through her transparent honesty; politically, she was an enthusiast for European unification, inspired by the writings of an early pioneer of the cause, Count Coudenhove-Kalergi; left-liberal rather than socialist, she discouraged Eric from taking much of an interest in politics because she thought he was too young to understand the issues.[117] More important than any of this, perhaps, was the fact that she had belonged to the world of literature, as a short-story writer, a novelist and a translator. In April 1935 Eric arranged to have a crate with his mother's work sent over to London, where he was now living, from Vienna. He was keen to discover 'whether Mama was really a genius, or merely talented, whether she had written great things or simply good ones'. When the crate arrived in June, he reread some of his mother's letters. They prompted in him the sad thought that since her death no one had called him 'darling'.[118] Only much later did he read her novel, which he admired for its 'elegant, lyrical, harmonious and carefully considered German'. But he did not think she was a 'writer of the first class'.[119] After reading poems she had written when she was his age, seventeen, he found the influences of Heine, Eichendorff and other German poets insufficiently digested, but was amazed at the breadth of the material she assimilated, and moved by her expression of 'a kind of homesickness for the unknown, to a degree a flight from today', by her sensitivity, and by her need for tenderness. She was at her best, he thought, in descriptions of nature. He wanted to take everything he could from the poems because they expressed so much of the feelings of the mother who had died when he was only fourteen; as he wrote, 'I want to get to know mama'. And yet, he did not want to do so in any sentimental way. 'If I have to reflect on my mother, I have to judge her as coldly as possible. What was she as a person, a writer, a mother. Oleaginous outbursts of feeling will not get me much further.' His aunt Gretl was shocked by the critical directness of this verdict. But it was only a literary judgement in the end: Eric kept alive his feelings for his mother in his private memories.[120]

Eric's sense of loss was palpable.[121] As he matured, he began to worry that his memory of his mother was fading: she was becoming a 'phantom with dark eyes and an expression on her face that I can't describe'.[122] Her death, coming on top of his father's, but far more serious than his in its emotional impact on Eric, was a devastating blow. He dealt with the 'trauma, loss and insecurity' he suffered in these terrible family tragedies partly by plunging himself into reading and intellectual enquiry, partly by engaging in solitary activities such as building a crystal-set radio. He developed, he later recalled, 'like a computer, ... a "trash" facility for deleting unpleasant or unacceptable data'.[123] This was to help him considerably in later life. The break-up of his family deepened the insecurity of his circumstances. Nelly left no property or indeed any possessions of any value. Three thousand Austrian shillings had been invested in 1929 in an account for Eric, and one thousand for Nancy, but they would not have access to the funds until they came of age. They had no means of support. Before going to live with Frau Effenberger, Eric had lodged temporarily with his grandmother, Nelly's 'mama', Ernestine Grün, though, as the police authorities noted disapprovingly, he had not registered the move as the law required. But there was no choice for Eric and Nancy except to go and live with Sidney, who was officially appointed their guardian.[124] Identifying from the start, and identified by others, as English, Eric had no regrets about leaving Austria: 'It was not', he remarked many years later, 'it had never been my country.'[125]

On 28 July 1931, Eric was sent off to join his sister in Berlin, where Sidney had secured a job with Universal Films, a Hollywood studio run by a German expatriate, Carl Laemmle.[126] Sidney was put in charge of organising location shoots in Germany and promoting movies such as *Frankenstein*, starring Boris Karloff, whose reputation he tried to use in the Polish market by claiming his real name was Boruch Karloff (in fact, it was Pratt). A procession of unlikely figures marched through the Hobsbaum household, including a member of one of the expeditions of Alfred Wegener, who explained to Eric his leader's theory of continental drift, and told him how he had lost all his toes to frostbite on a winter journey in Greenland.[127] Up to this point, Sidney had rented an apartment from an elderly widow at number 6, Aschaffenburgerstrasse, in Wilmersdorf, a western suburb some distance to the south of the Zoological Garden. Eric remembered the flat as light, with walls thin enough for him to hear the dinner conversations of his uncle and aunt and their guests through his bedroom wall.[128] But now the salary from Universal Films enabled the family to move to a house in Lichterfelde, a bourgeois suburb a short distance to the southwest. Eric remembered that the house next door, which belonged to a musician, had its own swimming pool.[129]

Sidney and Gretl enrolled him in the Prinz-Heinrichs-Gymnasium just around the corner from their first flat, and within easy cycling distance of their grander living quarters in Lichterfelde. The school was located in the Grunewaldstrasse.

Eric described it later as 'a perfectly conventional school in the conservative Prussian tradition ... Protestant in spirit, deeply patriotic and conservative'. It had been founded in 1890 and was named after the Kaiser's younger brother.[130] It was established as a 'humanistic grammar school' in the classic mould, a state boys' school with a strong emphasis on the classics, on Latin and Ancient Greek, as the foundations for a broad, cultivated education and, more specifically, as preparation for university. As in the case of almost all other German schools, there was no uniform, though the students could if they wanted to purchase and wear a cloth cap in the school colours with a leather peak, into which the student could insert a coloured ribbon to denote the class he belonged to.[131]

The senior teachers were university-trained scholars, some of them with academic publications to their credit.[132] Eric thought they were 'almost caricatures of German schoolmasters, square, with glasses and (when not bald) crew-cut ... All of them sounded like passionate conservative German patriots.'[133] The English teacher Dr Paetzel routinely referred to France as Germany's 'hereditary enemy' in his lessons, while the Latin teacher, Balduin Fischer, who had been a naval officer in the war and reputedly commanded a U-boat, was accustomed to restore order in the classroom by barking out the words 'Silence on board!'[134] Eric learned, with his fellow pupils, to sidetrack the Greek lessons of Emil Simon by getting him to reminisce about the Great War. Much of the teaching was tedious in the extreme. Karl-Günther von Hase, a classmate of Eric's who became West German ambassador to Britain many years after the end of the Second World War, remembered that history lessons focused mostly on the ancient world and never went into the twentieth century.[135] Eric admitted later:

I learned absolutely nothing in the history lessons given by a small, fat old man, 'Tönnchen' ('little barrel') Rubensohn, except the names and dates of all the German emperors, all of which I have since forgotten. He taught them by dashing round the form pointing a ruler at each of us with the words: 'Quick, Henry the Fowler – the dates.' I now know that he was as bored by this exercise as we were.[136]

Rubensohn was in fact a distinguished classical scholar, archaeologist and papyrologist, but his teaching turned Eric off history, at least for the time being.[137] Balduin Fischer, as Fritz Lustig, a pupil in the school at the same time as Eric, remembered, 'dictated notes to us for hours on end on Latin writers', which made his lessons 'extremely boring and completely ineffectual'.[138] Only a few of the teachers were widely respected for their dedication, notably Dr Arnold Bork, who taught history and Greek and had the ability, according to Fritz Lustig, 'to awaken and sustain our interest in the material'.[139]

Yet the impression of dull conservatism Eric conveyed in his later account of the school was not quite correct, for the school was undergoing a transformation at the time he joined it. The Prussian government in the Weimar Republic, the first democratically elected administration in the state's history, was dominated by the Social Democrats, and they were determined to wrest the educational system from its roots in the monarchical, conservative world of Wilhelmine Germany and turn it into one of the foundation stones of a modern democracy. In 1925 new guidelines were issued for Prussian schools with this aim in mind,[140] and in 1929, on the retirement of the long-standing Director of the Prinz-Heinrichs-Gymnasium, Dr Sorof (a man who according to Fritz Lustig 'looked very much like Bismarck and was very upright and unapproachable'), the government appointed a member of the Social Democratic Party to take over. This was Dr Walter Schönbrunn, a 'smallish man with sharp eyes behind rimless glasses and a receding hairline', who immediately began to institute significant reforms.[141]

Schönbrunn introduced modern works to the literature syllabus, supplementing the traditional Goethe and Schiller with Büchner, Nietzsche, Thomas Mann, Ibsen and Strindberg. He replaced the Monday morning *Andacht*, a religious meeting, with a secular assembly at which a teacher addressed the pupils on moral issues and there was a musical performance by a teacher or some of the pupils. He dropped the school play performed in Ancient Greek and put on instead a modern English drama, *Journey's End*, by R. C. Sherriff, known in German translation as *Die andere Seite* ('The Other Side'), whose portrayal of the Great War as a human tragedy marked a radical departure from the celebratory patriotism inculcated by Schönbrunn's predecessor and a number of the teaching staff. The school library, as the school's annual report for 1930–31 proudly reported, was finally provided with 'really modern works'. These included the writings of Communist authors such as Bertolt Brecht and Ludwig Renn. New science labs were constructed and equipped. More dramatically, Schönbrunn also introduced class newspapers edited and written by the pupils and set up elected pupil committees and even a pupil court to deal with matters such as compensation for damage to pupils' property.[142] He celebrated the Weimar Republic's Constitution Day with a speech to the school that made it clear he believed that things had changed for the better since the Kaiser's forced abdication, 'a completely novel thought in our red-brick building', as a former pupil recorded.[143] Small wonder, as Fritz Lustig recalled, that 'most of the teachers disapproved of him because he was left-orientated and they were right-wing'.[144] Several of the teachers openly criticised the introduction of pupil committees in front of their classes.[145]

Schönbrunn was particularly keen on hiking for the pupils, and even wrote a book extolling its educational virtues. The school organised five large hiking expeditions in 1931 alone, and another eleven in 1932, to the countryside around Berlin, the Mark Brandenburg, and to Mecklenburg, further north. The boys camped out or stayed in youth hostels. Such expeditions, communing with nature, were a central tradition in German secondary education, and played a key part in the youth movement in which many middle-class children were socialised in the early decades of the century. Eric took part in them, though he disliked the boys' obsession with sex, their obscene conversation in the evenings and their taste in popular music.[146] He preferred bird-watching.

He later recalled cycling from Lichterfelde to the Riemeisterfenn, a marshy area to the west of the city, to watch birds and photograph them. Leaving his bike in a meadow, he waded into the mere. 'Here and there I heard ten, twenty metres away, the water splashing and the rustling of a duck. When it quacked I felt great. I was modest in the demands I made of nature.'[147] Partly for this reason, Eric also enjoyed the school rowing club, because it was not competitive but allowed the boys from different years to meet on equal terms. The club had

> a meadow, known as '*unser Gut*' (our estate) on the small fishery-protected Sacrower See, accessible only by special permission through a narrow waterway. Groups of friends made up crews to row there or meet there at weekends, to talk, look at the summer skies, and swim across the green waters before returning to the evening city. For the first and only time in my life I could see the point of a sports club.[148]

Apart from a limited amount of training and rowing, the boys could also explore the interconnecting lakes on the western side of Berlin, and spent a good deal of time on the meadows playing volleyball, or sitting around and talking.[149]

In the early thirties there were some 477 pupils and twenty-nine teachers at the Prinz-Heinrichs-Gymnasium, including its annexe, a technical school or *Realgymnasium* where Latin was taught but not Greek, and where the emphasis was on the sciences. The vast majority of the pupils – 388 – were Protestant; there were forty-eight Catholics, thirty-five adherents of the Jewish religion and a handful of others. Eric was classified as a Jew, but in fact he was invariably referred to as *der Engländer*, 'the English boy'.[150] The pupils called him 'Hobsbaum' (the 'au' pronounced 'ow'); Fritz Lustig remembered wondering why 'the English boy' had 'a name which did not exactly sound English'.[151] Thanks to the influence of some of the teachers, notably Dr Bork, there was no discernible anti-Semitism in the school even after Hitler became Reich Chancellor in January 1933.[152] When Schönbrunn was dismissed at the end of the academic year 1932–3, for political reasons, by the Nazis, who had seized power in the spring, his replacement was a Nazi. The new head was treated with general contempt by both teachers and pupils. They called him 'Jolanthe', after a pig which was the central figure in a popular comedy of the day by August Hinrichs, *Krach um Jolanthe* ('Trouble with Jolanthe').[153] When the much-respected Jewish maths teacher, Salomon or 'Sally' Birnbaum, was dismissed on racial grounds in 1933, the pupils organised a petition to keep him on, and, when that failed, they visited him at home to express their sympathy. The entire lower first form went to see him in the winter of 1936–7 and individual former pupils kept in touch with him long afterwards, even during the war, when Otto Luther (later a well-known writer under the pseudonym Jens Rehn) made the trip from Rotterdam, where his U-boat was undergoing repairs, to see him. Not long after this visit, Birnbaum was arrested by the Gestapo. He was sent to Auschwitz on the thirty-sixth and final trainload of Jews taken from Berlin in the so-called 'factory action' and murdered in the gas chamber at Birkenau.[154]

The pupils of the Prinz-Heinrichs-Gymnasium were drawn from the families of the educated middle classes – the *Bildungsbürgertum* – and included many whose fathers were civil servants. They were mostly moderately conservative, like their parents, insofar as they took a political stance at all. The teachers' war experience and post-war resentments at the Treaty of Versailles must certainly have had an influence on their views.[155] Eric remembered only one committed Nazi among the pupils, 'the unusually dense son of a man who was Hitler's Gauleiter of Brandenburg'.[156] The friends Eric made at the school were not particularly political – indeed, he did not remember the boys discussing politics at all, not even on the school hiking expeditions where they talked long into the night.[157] He was particularly close to Ernst Wiemer, a keen member of the rowing club, and Hans Heinz Schroeder, a musical boy who played the flute and was known as 'the classroom poet'. With Wiemer he mostly discussed 'the nonsense poetry of Christian Morgenstern and the world in general'. Schroeder was an admirer of Frederick the Great and collected model soldiers of his armies, but this did not stop them from being friends. Eric lost contact with both boys after he left the school. Many years later he discovered that after the Nazi seizure of power, his friend Schroeder had joined the SS: he played in a military band rather than joining in the genocidal activities of the organisation, but Eric was shocked none the less. Schroeder was eventually killed fighting on the Eastern Front during the war.[158]

V

When he arrived in Berlin in the summer of 1931, Eric immediately encountered the massive impact on Germany's teeming capital city of the world economic crisis sparked by the Wall Street Crash two years before, with banks defaulting on their payments, unemployment hitting more than a third of the workforce and the total collapse of capitalism seemingly just around the corner. During his life up to this point he had experienced capitalism as failure; now he experienced it as catastrophe: 'we were on the *Titanic*', he wrote later, 'and everyone knew it was hitting the iceberg'.[159] This was a very different milieu from that of the late 1920s and early 1930s in Britain, where the political and economic impact of 'the slump' was mild in comparison. In Berlin, the economic catastrophe must have seemed like the end of the world. Under the enormous strain of the Depression, Germany experienced an upsurge in political violence and a rapid destabilisation of the political system. The Weimar Republic, founded in 1919, had managed to weather the early storms of riot, assassination, putsch attempts from Right and Left, and hyperinflation to an almost unprecedented degree, and had found a modicum of stability and prosperity after 1924. But the Depression altered all this. The Grand Coalition government led by the Social Democrat Heinrich Müller collapsed, its constituent parties unable to agree on how to deal with the situation. It was succeeded by a 'cabinet of experts' led from 30 March 1930 by the conservative Catholic Centre Party politician

Heinrich Brüning. The new government, increasingly using the power of rule by decree accorded to the elected President by the Constitution, imposed savage austerity measures to reduce government expenditure. These only exacerbated social tensions, and soon the middle-class liberal and conservative parties collapsed, their votes going to Hitler's Nazi Party. Up to the outbreak of the Depression the Nazis had been on the fringe of politics and their leader Adolf Hitler an obscure figure on the margins of national life: in the elections of 1928 they failed to win the support of more than 2.6 per cent of those who voted. But from this point onwards, their popularity increased by leaps and bounds. In the summer of 1930 over four million people cast their ballots in their favour, and in the July elections of 1932 the Nazis gained over 37 per cent of the vote. The democratic political system was in meltdown, with the national legislature, the Reichstag, barely meeting any more, as the opposing parties were unable to agree on anything apart from shouting each other down. Brüning's government was replaced at the end of May 1932 by an overtly reactionary ministry led by the aristocrat Franz von Papen, which deposed the Social Democratic government in Prussia by force. As Papen began to seek mass support through a deal with the Nazis, many on the Left, dismayed by the Social Democrats' failure to offer firm resistance to Papen's coup, saw in the Communists the best chance of staving off fascism.[160]

When he came to Berlin, Eric encountered for the first time a mass Communist movement, visible everywhere, on the streets, in legislative assemblies, in newspapers and magazines and not least in the pubs and bars in Berlin frequented by some of its most solid and committed supporters. The economic slump drove increasing numbers of the unemployed into the ranks of the Communist Party, whose nationwide membership grew from around 125,000 in the summer of 1929, just before the crisis struck, to more than 245,000 by late 1931 and 360,000 a year later. It increased its national vote in every election up to and including the November 1932 national poll, where more than six million voters put a hundred Communist deputies into the Reichstag, while the Nazis lost substantially in comparison to the polls of the previous July. The Communists were well organised, dynamic and hyperactive: they exercised a special appeal to the young. In the central district of Berlin, for example, nearly 60 per cent of members who joined between 1929 and 1933 were under thirty, with the under-twenty-fives predominant. The Party's mass meetings and demonstrations, not to mention its paramilitary wing, the uniformed 'Red Front-Fighters' League', attracted thousands upon thousands of workers onto the streets to champion the Communist cause and defend it against its enemies.[161]

Soon the Nazis, under the local direction in Berlin of the talented propagandist and ruthless political tactician Joseph Goebbels, locked horns with the Communists, in constant street battles, bar-room brawls, and rowdy, violent political meetings. Hundreds of thousands of brownshirts and stormtroopers, armed with clubs, truncheons and knuckle-dusters, flooded onto the streets, above all in the capital city, in the febrile and crisis-ridden atmosphere of the last years of the Weimar Republic. The total polarisation of the political system was blocked only by the Social Democrats, who had lost much of their credibility by supporting the austerity politics of Weimar's last governments, and the Catholic Centre, which had little support in Protestant Berlin.[162] In this highly politicised atmosphere, it was perhaps hardly surprising that Eric soon became interested in the Communist cause ('Had I stayed in Austria', he remarked later, 'I would probably have become a socialist, because the social democrats were the biggest opposition party and they were clearly Marxists. But in Berlin, where the Social Democrats were the party in power, the Communists were the biggest force in opposition').[163]

He came across the brilliant poems of Bertolt Brecht, a leading Communist writer, in an anthology of contemporary German writing in the school library. These led him to declare naively that he, too, was a Communist; one 'exasperated master', Willi Bodsch, told him 'firmly (and correctly): "You clearly do not know what you are talking about. Go to the library and look up the subject."'[164] The book he discovered there was the *Communist Manifesto*, and a reading of it helped anchor Eric, at the age of fifteen, in his new-found identity.[165] The first real Communist Eric met was his cousin Otto Friedmann, 'tall, handsome, successful with women', who made a considerable impression on him.[166] Eric began 'the initiation ritual of the typical socialist intellectual of the twentieth century, namely the shortlived attempt to read and understand Karl Marx's *Capital*, starting on page one', with an older boy, Gerhard Wittenberg, also Jewish in origin, and a committed Social Democrat. They did not get very far, and Eric sympathised neither with Gerhard's moderate brand of socialism nor with the growing Zionist conviction that led him to emigrate to a kibbutz in Palestine after the Nazi seizure of power.[167]

Hearing of an English boy in the school who had begun describing himself as a Communist, one of the older pupils, Rudolf Leder, 'dark, saturnine and with a taste for leather jackets', an active and committed Party member, recruited him for the Socialist School Students' League (it has a better ring in German, *Sozialistischer Schülerbund*), a Communist front organisation aimed specifically at secondary school pupils, the vast majority of whom came from a bourgeois background. Leder had himself been expelled from another, less tolerant Berlin grammar school for writing politically radical articles for the organisation's newsletter, *Der Schulkampf* ('The School Struggle'), shortly before Eric arrived. He supplied Eric with Soviet novels from the 1920s, none of which painted a particularly rosy picture of life after the Bolshevik Revolution, but when Eric suggested that Russia's economic and social backwardness posed problems for the attempt to create a Communist society, 'he bristled: the USSR was beyond criticism'. He also obtained a collection of revolutionary songs. Through Leder, Eric bought a volume commemorating the fifteenth anniversary of the October Revolution. He wrote on the flyleaf a quotation from Lenin's *Left-wing Communism: An infantile disorder*, the first recorded evidence of his political commitment, as he later recalled.[168]

Leder himself belonged to the youth movement of the Communist Party, a rougher, more proletarian organisation altogether than the School Students' League. Eric never saw him again; but later in life Leder reinvented himself as Stephan Hermlin, a poet and author who won a leading position in the literary establishment of Communist East Germany. His autobiographical work *Abendlicht* ('Evening Light'), much praised for the richness and beauty of its language, was subsequently attacked for its alleged invention of a past, including service in the Spanish Civil War and imprisonment in a concentration camp, that had never happened; however, it was explicitly written not as a factual account of the author's life, but a novel, a fiction, charting the life of a Communist writer who bore some resemblances to Hermlin himself, but was not identical with him.[169] Eric wrote to Hermlin in 1965, when he realised he was the Rudolf Leder he had known at school, but received the disappointing reply that 'your name, to be honest, awakens a vague memory – no more. I have been forced to roam around too much and have seen too much.'[170] According to Karl Corino, whose criticisms of *Abendlicht* had begun the controversy, 'it was anyway a very characteristic reaction of Hermlin systematically to block any attempt to contact him by people from his youth, like you tried to. He wanted nothing to do with inconvenient witnesses of his dubious past.'[171]

Eric's attraction to Communism reflected among other things the starkness of the political choices that faced the young in early 1930s Berlin. It would in any case have been impossible for him to join the Nazis, since as an English boy he could not subscribe to their radical German nationalist spirit, and as a Jew he could not support their rabidly anti-Semitic ideology. The internationalism of the Communist movement must have held an obvious attraction for him, along with its dynamism and its promise to solve the catastrophic economic and social problems into which capitalism had led the world in general and Germany, and Berlin, in particular. The German Communists were devoted to extolling the virtues of the Soviet state and society, and proclaiming their central aim of creating a 'Soviet Germany'. It was not simply that almost any way of organising economy and society had to be better than the capitalism that had brought so much misery and desperation to Germany: what the Soviet Union seemed to offer was a bright, promising future, a positive and, it seemed, attractive alternative. Many leftish Western

European intellectuals became enthusiastic supporters, not only during the depths of the Depression but also afterwards. For Eric, fifteen years old and living in the political hothouse of late Weimar Berlin at a time when the German Communist Party was emphatically on the up, the attraction must have been irresistible.[172]

Quite apart from the impact of these more general factors, Eric's decision to identify with Communism also had roots in his personal experiences. As he wrote soon afterwards, he had for a long time been ashamed of his family's poverty. Already in Vienna he had experienced acute embarrassment on 'receiving my mother's birthday present – a very cheap second-hand bike ... since its frame was visibly both repainted and bent'.[173] The shame only deepened when he used it to travel to school in Berlin ('I would arrive half an hour early at the bike-shed and sneak out late, afraid of being seen on it').[174] The other boys with whom he mixed, at the grammar schools he attended in Vienna and Berlin, mostly came from well-to-do or at least comfortably-off families, even in the depths of the Depression, his own family had long lived hand-to-mouth, even while his father was alive. His family's deprivation had made him ashamed. 'Only by turning this completely around and becoming proud of it did I conquer the shame.' Becoming a Communist meant embracing poverty as a positive virtue instead of feeling embarrassed by it. This was surely a key psychological impulse behind his growing self-identification as a Communist; indeed, he thought that most people who developed a 'proletarian class consciousness' did so for similar reasons, so as not to be ashamed of the fact that they were poor.[175] Unlike most of them, however, Eric, emotionally adrift after the death of his parents, also found in the Communist Party a substitute family, giving him a sense of identity that was to prove over the long run a central part of his emotional constitution. It also turned his outsider status, as an English boy in a Berlin school, into something positive: the Communists gloried in their outsider status in German politics and society, and, by identifying with this, Eric could gain a sense of belonging that was far more than compensatory.

So he became an active member of the Socialist School

Students' League. The movement numbered among its members the children of Russian exiles who had left the Soviet Union because of Stalin's growing persecution of socialist dissidents. The organisation was open to both sexes, and as one member recalled,

> after the conclusion of our studious meetings we usually adjourned to a near-by café for extended socializing. These informal get-togethers also provided an opportunity to get to know members of the opposite sex, of which there were several attractive representatives. We also organized occasional Sunday excursions into the surrounding countryside.[176]

But as the political situation deteriorated in 1931–2, and Nazi violence on the streets became more pervasive, this rather gentle lifestyle took on a more serious tone. The members met in each other's homes, sometimes in a nearby bar in Halensee, then part of the western district of Wilmersdorf.[177] The group had an *Orglei* (organisational leader) and *Polei* (political leader) and sent reports in to *Der Schulkampf*, which by late 1932 was roughly typed, duplicated and stapled together for circulation. What was probably the final number, issued in the autumn of 1932, pilloried the 'reactionary' school system and the authoritarian philosophy of the government of Franz von Papen, attacked cuts in the school medical and dental services in the name of austerity ('savings are made at the cost of our health!'), and criticised the political campaign for the restoration of the German overseas colonies mandated to other nations in the peace settlement of 1919. Then there were individual reports, targeting 'reactionary common rooms' in a number of secondary schools, though not the Prinz-Heinrichs-Gymnasium.[178]

Such activity was possible because, like other German schools, the Prinz-Heinrichs-Gymnasium had a school day that only lasted from eight in the morning until one or one thirty in the afternoon, so there was plenty of time for pupils to devote to extra-curricular pursuits. While still engaging in normal school activities, notably the hiking club, reading widely and continuing with his studies, Eric therefore found it relatively easy to take part in the activities of the

Communist Party. His uncle Sidney had run into financial difficulties after the German government, some months before the Nazi seizure of power, passed a law designed to alleviate unemployment by forcing companies to ensure that at least three-quarters of their employees were German. As a British citizen, Sidney was obliged to leave Universal Films and, like millions of others in Germany in the early 1930s, found himself without a job. He began looking for other opportunities, but in the depths of the Depression these were not readily available. So in the autumn of 1932, he departed with Gretl and their son Peter for Barcelona, leaving Eric and Nancy in Berlin to continue their schooling. They moved in with their aunt Mimi, who had come to Berlin after her various enterprises in England had left her deeply in debt ('we have too few debts to make bankruptcy worth while', she told Eric, 'and just have to carry on'). She sublet an apartment in the Friedrichsruherstrasse, near the S-Bahn railway track at the western end of the Kurfürstendamm, and took in paying guests, making a bit of extra money by teaching German to the English ones.[179]

With Sidney and Gretl out of the picture for several months, and Mimi preoccupied with her own affairs, Eric was left at something of a loose end. He travelled by tram with Nancy to their separate but neighbouring schools, remembering 'the endless footslog during the dramatic four-day Berlin transport strike of early November'.[180] Nancy and Eric continued to grow apart during this time, despite his quasi-paternal attempt to tell her the facts of life when she reached the age of twelve. They played cards together and chatted with Mimi about palmistry, fortune-telling and her other interests, but Eric's real attention, when not occupied with reading, was increasingly taken up with politics.[181] He spent many evenings in the back rooms of Communist pubs debating the desperate political situation. He read Party material, though he did not engage with Marxism at any intellectually serious level – looking back on his political beliefs in Berlin a mere three years later, he found them naïve and half-formed; more a Romantic rebel than a true intellectual, he thought.[182]

He took part in the Communists' last public demonstration in

Berlin, on 25 January 1933, mounted as a response to a provocative mass march staged by ten thousand Nazis three days before. The Nazi march had been led by Hitler himself, and passed in front of the Communist Party headquarters at the Karl Liebknecht House on the Bülowplatz on its way to the nearby cemetery where the Nazi hero Horst Wessel, shot dead by Communists three years before, was buried. An estimated 130,000 Communists marched past the same building on 25 January, accompanied by brass bands, singing songs and shouting slogans, and raising their fists to the Party leader and former presidential candidate Ernst Thälmann, who stood in front of the building for five hours despite a temperature of minus fifteen degrees Celsius.[183] The next day, the Social Democratic journalist Friedrich Stampfer reported on the demonstration, admitting against his better judgement that it had made a deep impression on him:

> Even the most critical verdict on the policy of the Communist Party leadership cannot detract from the admiration that these masses have earned. Through biting frost and cutting wind they processed for hours in dingy coats, in thin jackets, in tattered shoes. Tens of thousands of pasty-pale faces that expressed not only their poverty but also their willingness to sacrifice themselves for a cause that they believed was the right one. Their rough voices spoke out their hate, a hate that was justified a thousand times over, for a social system that had condemned them to poverty and misery, and their protest against the grotesque insanity, the screaming injustice of our social circumstances. You would not be a socialist if you did not empathise with this protest.[184]

With its songs, chants and marching, the Communist demonstration, like the Boy Scouts before it, gave Eric a strong, even ecstatic sense of identity: 'We belonged together.' He remembered in particular the songs they sang, keeping the tattered song-sheet until the end of his days.[185] Already in 1932, however, he had sensed that the Weimar Republic was doomed. Five days after the great demonstration, Hitler was appointed Chancellor. Eric often recalled later in life seeing the banner headlines on the newspaper stands the following day announcing the appointment, as he walked home from school with Nancy 'on the cold afternoon of 30 January 1933, reflecting on what the news of Hitler's appointment as chancellor meant'.[186] The circle of conservatives around President Paul von Hindenburg had put him into power as head of a coalition government in an attempt to provide mass support for their plans to dismantle Weimar democracy. Franz von Papen was made Vice-Chancellor, and there was a conservative majority in the cabinet, which thought it would be able to manipulate the Nazi minority and box Hitler into a corner. A general strike called by the Communist Party had little or no effect; at a time when millions were unemployed, it was a futile gesture. Armed resistance was out of the question: the Party was unprepared and lacked the necessary arms and ammunition. Instead, it readied itself for the elections Hitler had called for 5 March.[187] For the time being, despite the escalation of Nazi violence on the streets, a full-blown dictatorship still seemed some way off.

Eric tried to convey the situation of young Communist activists in these final days of the Weimar Republic, in the last days of February 1933, in a short story he wrote during the Second World War, clearly based on personal experience.

I do not know about Chicago, but Berlin was a windy city in those days. The wind blew sleet through the wide spaces between the modern apartment blocks and in the district where we lived, clogged the tramlines with soaked brown leaves. It used to blow through my blue mackintosh and make me clench my hands in the pockets. We put in some old lining from one of my father's raincoats, which buttoned into the mac. That made it better. The wind blew across the lakes, through the sandy plantations of firs, making the water shiver and leaving only single coots and wild ducks on the gusty river. The forests and the town were wide-meshed like fishing-nets.[188]

Eric and a friend whom he calls Max in the story went into

a department store on their way home from school, seeking the warmth and perusing the shelves of the book department. His friend was annoyed when Eric mentioned he had a copy of *Scouting for Boys* at home. 'Boy scouts are no good', he said: 'How often have I told you they are reactionary?' Eric objected that he 'liked the boy scouts when I visited the Birkenhead Jamboree in 1929 . . . Camping and tracking is first-class stuff.' But it was the ideology of the Scouts to which his friend was opposed, and since 'he instructed us at meetings in political economy, out of Marx's *Value Price and Profit*', Eric did not feel able to argue the point with him. At a tube station they met another friend, who discreetly showed them a knuckle-duster: 'The Nazis came round our way last night and look – one of them leaves this.' Max told him not to use it: 'It's individual terror' – Lenin had polemicised against the use of individual rather than mass terror and so it was not Communist.

At six o'clock they met other members of the Socialist School Students' League. 'Don't let's stand about like a public meeting', said Max. 'It's not like 1932 any more.' They divided up, half the group taking one side of the street, the other half the other, and pushed Communist pamphlets through the letter boxes on each floor of the apartment blocks. They heard a bell ringing. Supposing someone had called the Nazis? They climbed up the stairs to the fourth floor.

> We should be cut off here. Where would we go? Ring a bell and say 'Mrs Mueller, why, they told me definitely Mrs Mueller lived on this floor.' By god we would stall them. 'This girl? Why, she is my sister Lisa. We came here to see Mrs Mueller my aunt.' I am scared to hell, but Lisa does not look scared. I bet that girl is a better Bolshevik than I am.

Back on the street they met 'Karbo', a notoriously tough member of the group. He showed them a revolver he had bought. It would come in handy after the election, he boasted. '"Put that damn gun away", said Max. "Put the bloody thing away." Karbo grinned.

"You might want a bodyguard." "Sure we might", said Max. "And you'd get us out of the black Maria and you'd beat up the bulls [cops] and the S.A. and maybe the S.S. too. You might even go and beat up Hitler.'" A girl in the group asked what would happen. Hitler wouldn't last for ever, Eric said. The people would rise up against him. In any case, he continued,

> I only half wanted to talk about Hitler. I wanted to talk, expan-
> sively and sentimentally, about the lakes and boats. Preferably blue
> folding-boats and birds ... We were middle-class kids. We did not
> know a great deal about the people ... We were communists in
> the way in which, in other places, we should have read each other
> poetry; attracted into a profound and complex movement because
> it had superior magnetic powers for intelligent bourgeois children
> who revolted against their families. We circled round the fringes
> of this movement doing sometimes useful, sometimes senseless
> things. We could sing the definitions of revolution and understand
> them in this way. In prose we could not grasp them yet.

The people, however, did not rise up, and Hitler lasted far longer than anyone expected. As for 'Karbo', the story ends by informing readers that he went over to the Nazis not long afterwards.

Eric was recruited to distribute campaign material for the 5 March elections. He later remembered stuffing leaflets into post-boxes in apartment blocks, fearing all the while the tread of a stormtrooper's boots on the staircase.[189] On another occasion, he found himself alone in a streetcar with two Nazi stormtroopers, terrified they might beat him up if they saw his Communist Party badge.[190] On the evening of 27 February 1933 he asked his twelve-year-old sister Nancy to take a bundle of Communist Party election leaflets to a friend in a northern part of Berlin after they got home from school, while he took some to other young Communists in the southern districts. Shortly after nine o'clock in the evening, as she was cycling back towards their home through the Brandenburg Gate in the centre of town, she noticed flames coming out of the Reichstag, the national parliament building. Fire engines were rushing towards the scene. She pedalled on, remembering the dramatic scene to the end of her days.[191]

For the destruction of the Reichstag, set on fire by a lone Dutch anarcho-syndicalist, Marinus van der Lubbe, marked the real beginning of the Nazi dictatorship in Germany. Using the emergency powers accorded to Reich President Hindenburg by the Weimar Constitution, Hitler suspended freedom of the press, assembly and association, and provided measures for police detention in 'protective custody', phone-tapping and the interception of mail without a court order and for an indefinite period of time, on the pretext that the Communists had burned down the Reichstag as a prelude to a violent revolutionary uprising. Soon afterwards, surprisingly perhaps, the 5 March elections failed to deliver the Nazis an overall majority despite the fact that other parties were prevented from campaigning. The Communists had still garnered 4,800,000 votes, but any Communist elected to the Reichstag was immediately arrested, while many leading members of the Party fled the country.[192] The Socialist School Students' League stored its duplicating apparatus under Eric's bed for a while, believing it was safe with a foreigner, though no leaflets were produced on it while it was there.[193]

With their 8 per cent of the vote in the March elections, together with the Nazis' 44 per cent, Hitler's nationalist coalition partners acquiesced in Hitler's destruction of civil liberties and the step-by-step introduction of a dictatorship. He quickly began to outmanoeuvre them, engineering the resignation of some, and outnumbering the rest by bringing hardcore Nazis into the cabinet. Within a few weeks, Hitler's brownshirts, enrolled as auxiliary police, had begun rounding up Communists, starting with four thousand members of the Party apparatus, abusing, torturing and sometimes killing them in improvised concentration camps. It had become extremely dangerous to belong to any opposition party, but the Communists were particularly singled out for persecution. Even the official figures recorded over six hundred political murders in the first six months of 1933, and the real total was undoubtedly higher. Well over one hundred thousand Social

Democrats and Communists had been arrested and incarcerated in the new concentration camps by the summer of 1933, while all the political parties apart from the Nazis were banned or forced to dissolve themselves.

During the 5 March elections and for some time afterwards, the Communist Party of Germany, following instructions from the Communist International in Moscow, stuck to its previous ideological line, namely that the rise and triumph of Nazism was nothing more than the final convulsion of a dying capitalism, a desperate and doomed attempt to stave off the inevitable Communist revolution. The Social Democrats were condemned as 'social fascists' who were 'objectively' serving the interests of capitalism by sucking working-class voters away from their true representatives, namely the Communists. There should therefore be no attempt to form a united front between the two working-class parties, although taken together they had actually won more votes than the Nazis in the elections of November 1932. A long history of bitterness between the Communists and the Social Democrats, going back to 1919, when the Communist leaders Rosa Luxemburg and Karl Liebknecht had been brutally murdered by the troops of the Social Democratic national government, had been deepened if anything by the massacre of Communist protesters by the police controlled by the Social Democratic government of Prussia in the 'Bloody May' demonstrations of 1929. As late as the end of 1933, a leading Communist Party official in Germany, Fritz Heckert, declared that the Social Democrats were the Party's 'main enemy' because they were the 'principal bulwark of the bourgeoisie'.[194]

This was an unrealistic and self-destructive set of beliefs, as Eric soon came to realise. 'I grew up at the most sectarian point of the socialist-communist split', he said later. 'It's now clear to everyone that that was a disaster. It was my most formative political experience.'[195] The enthusiasm of the young militants of the Communist Party was directed towards the positive goal of bringing about a Communist revolution, not towards the much duller, less inspiring purpose of preventing a fascist seizure of power.[196] For the orphaned fifteen-year-old Eric, Communism offered the sense of identity and belonging that he so craved, combined with a way of overcoming his embarrassment at his poverty, threadbare clothing and rickety bicycle, and dosed with a heady admixture of political adventure and excitement. Had he stayed in Berlin, there was every chance that he, too, in the end would have been picked up by the Gestapo and at the very least beaten up, and quite possibly thrown into a concentration camp for a while. The fact that the Nazis would have regarded him as Jewish would only have made the situation worse for him. He might have been killed.

But chance circumstance intervened in his life, neither for the first time nor for the last. Towards the end of March 1933, as Hitler's grip on the country was tightening and violence against the Communists was reaching new heights, Eric's uncle Sidney, his venture in Barcelona having failed, came back to Berlin with Gretl and Peter and declared he was going to move the family to London. Eric's aunt Mimi, who was also in serious financial dif-ficulties, joined them, opening a cosmopolitan boarding house in Folkestone, Kent. Although his uncle must have already noted the violent anti-Semitism that the Nazis were pushing onto Berlin's streets, the first great outbreak of hatred towards the Jews, the government-organised boycott of Jewish shops and businesses, on 1 April 1933, did not happen until after the family had left. Thus Eric was not a political or any other kind of exile from Nazi Germany: he was a British citizen who moved to Britain from Germany with his family for financial reasons coincidentally just as the Nazis were in the course of seizing total power for themselves.[197] As he later remarked, 'I came not as a refugee or emigrant, but as someone who belonged here; although it is difficult to convince the compilers of data about emigrant intellectuals from Mitteleuropa and their contribution to the cultures of the various receiving states that I do not belong into their files.'[198] His time in the over-heated political atmosphere of Berlin had seen the beginnings of a Communist commitment that quickly became central to his sense of identity. But it was only with his move to London that it gained intellectual as well as emotional depth.

2

'Ugly as Sin, but a Mind'

1933–1936

I

When he arrived in London in the spring of 1933, Eric was enrolled as a pupil in St Marylebone Grammar School for boys. Originally founded as the Philological Society in 1792, the school had become a state grammar school in 1908. It was located at Lisson Grove, a relatively genteel area of north London bounded by Lord's cricket ground to the north, Paddington Station to the south and Regent's Park to the east. In order to be close to the school, Eric lodged with his uncle Harry in Elgin Mansions, in Maida Vale, a nearby area dominated by Edwardian and late Victorian apartment blocks, while Sidney was looking for somewhere suitable for the family to live. Born on 9 July 1888 in Bethnal Green in London's East End, Harry was later described in a Metropolitan Police report 'as a sneering, critical type of person, harsh of speech, half Jew in appearance, having a long nose, thinning hair and blue eyes. He has always been extremely left wing in politics.'[1] Anti-Semitism was clearly alive and well and living at Scotland Yard when these sentences were written.

Harry's son Ron had recently been a pupil at the school, and so, Eric thought, 'it seemed a natural place to try, and I stuck to it after we found places of our own to live in London, which gave my leg-muscles plenty of exercise as later I had to cycle daily from areas

as remote from Lisson Grove as Upper Norwood and Edgware'.[2]
Probably because of Ron, Eric was referred to as Hobsbaum
rather than Hobsbawm throughout his time at St Marylebone
Grammar School.[3] Uncle Harry worked as a telegraphist in the
General Post Office in London, and Ron worked at the Natural
History Museum as an attendant. This was a civil service post, so
it offered him a steady income and a good deal of security. He soon
became Eric's closest friend, and in August 1933 the two of them
boarded a train to Folkestone and then walked all the way back to
London, taking almost a week (26–31 August) to do so, emptying
their backpacks of their tents and equipment every evening and
camping overnight in fields.[4]

The family milieu into which Eric moved on his arrival in
London was left-wing; Harry eventually became the first Labour
Mayor of Paddington. Eric found him 'often rather boring and
occasionally pompous'.[5] There was nothing elitist about the social
stratum from which St Marylebone Grammar School drew its
pupils. It was not, Eric recalled later, a particularly academic
establishment; very few pupils indeed went on to university, and for
most of them the sixth form, covering the ages sixteen to eighteen,
was the final stage of education before they went into business or
trade: 'I don't believe that in my time', Eric later wrote, 'it was even
designed to produce gentlemen.' He was treated leniently when he
'was discovered selling copies of an anti-war broadsheet in class,
which I had collected during the lunch break from the bookshop
in the Communist Party headquarters in King Street, Covent
Garden'. The school clearly made a lot of allowances for him, most
likely in view of his patent academic brilliance.[6]

Under its headmaster Philip Wayne, always known as 'Dickie',
the St Marylebone Grammar School modelled itself on the English
'public schools', or in other words independent, fee-paying secondary boarding schools, whose educational ethos was still essentially
Victorian. There were uniforms for the pupils, 'houses' on the
model of Oxbridge colleges (though it was not a boarding school)
to encourage team spirit and competitiveness, a strong Christian
ethic (the school had its own specially printed prayer book for

use in morning assemblies), an emphasis on traditional English public school sports (rugby in the winter, cricket in the summer) and corporal punishment for boys who infringed the rules (Eric was never beaten, though the headmaster was said to use his cane on the younger pupils 'rather too freely'). Eric found most of this extremely strange after the experience of Prussian secondary education in Berlin. Speaking to the old pupils' association of the school in October 2007, more than seventy years after he had left St Marylebone, he confessed that he came 'to the school as a sort of extra-terrestrial' who knew little or nothing of its customs: 'I had never in my life been on a cricket pitch or seen an oval ball, and so I was consequently quickly written out of the Marylebone sporting script after a few thoughtful hours at longstop. I didn't much mind, though I regret that cricket is still an impenetrable mystery to me, in spite of going to school in the shadow of the M.C.C.'[7] He was not even really 'aware of the marked Christian atmosphere of the school, which should have needled a devoted teen-age atheist'. He enjoyed the headmaster's 'efforts to make us appreciate classical music in hall, but I was not much into classical quartets at the time', he confessed. He acted in one school play but then dropped out of the drama society. The aspect of the school he found most objectionable was the uniform. 'When I was at SMGS I hated the tie and especially the cap more than even the principle of wearing uniforms', he said many years later. So 'at the ages of 16–18 I waged a persistent guerrilla war against the school's headgear'. But, in general, he experienced 'much of the effort to apply the public school model at Lisson Grove as funny rather than sinister', unlike his fellow pupil the later jazz musician and journalist Benny Green, who detested it and loathed the pretensions of the headmaster.

What Eric really valued, and profited from, was the academic education the school gave him. It was very different in style and content from the schooling he had gone through in Berlin. To begin with, 'when Dickie Wayne first interviewed me in the panelled headmaster's study, he told me with regret that I couldn't go on studying Greek as I had been doing in Austria and Germany, since the school did not teach it'. In the end, after Eric had left, he did manage to appoint a teacher of Ancient Greek, but by that time it was already in decline as a subject. As compensation, however, 'Wayne pressed on me a volume in German of the philosopher Immanuel Kant, and of William Hazlitt, which led me to treat him with definite respect from then on.' Wayne, appointed in 1923 and destined to lead the school until 1954, was, as his gift to Eric indicated, knowledgeable about and fond of both English and German culture. He was also ambitious for the school, and sought to raise its standards not only through applying the model of the English public school but also by appointing what Eric, looking back, recognised as 'a teaching team of premier quality'. 'It was in no sense a second-best education', he realised.

Immediately after being admitted to the school, Eric had to spend the summer term of 1933 preparing for the General School Certificate examinations that would qualify him to enter the Sixth Form the following September:

> I had, in the course of a term, to get through an examination on subjects I knew absolutely nothing about in a totally strange syllabus and in a language I had never used for school purposes. Of course I worked like crazy, but I couldn't possibly have done it without these old, experienced schoolmasters, enormously competent at the job of knocking knowledge into unprepared young heads, like the English master Frisby or the Maths master Willis, the Physics master L. G. Smith, or Snape, or Rowlands, and the French master A. T. Q. Bluett, of whom I have a particularly fond memory. Let me just note in passing that none of them ever talked about what they'd done in the Great War, unlike the masters in Berlin, who talked about little else.

Eric passed the examination in December 1933, gaining a Distinction in English, History (English and European), Latin and German ('with Special Credit in the oral examination'), and a pass with Credit in Arithmetic, Elementary Mathematics and French (again 'with Special Credit in the oral examination'). The regulations required a pass in mathematics, which Eric achieved, but he had no real interest in the subject, and was clearly best at languages and history.[8] He had in fact already entered the Sixth Form for the autumn term of 1933. Very soon he came under the wing of the English teacher, Mr Maclean, who was a student of the hugely influential Cambridge English don F. R. Leavis. Guided by Maclean, Eric read through the classics of the 'New Criticism', including *Fiction and the Reading Public* (1932) by Q. D. Leavis, wife of F. R. He took their criticism of middlebrow authors like John Galsworthy to be an attack on the 'spiritual emptiness and banality, or even more irritating, the petty-bourgeois nature of general reading', 'opium for the people', as Marx had said (of religion, but it applied even more to the novels and stories of people like Rudyard Kipling, in Eric's view).[9] Next came *Practical Criticism* (1929) by I. A. Richards (he thought it 'good'),[10] which he liked because it linked literary criticism to other branches of learning such as psychology.[11]

By the autumn of 1934 he was reading the literary criticism of T. S. Eliot, another favourite of Leavis.[12] Inspired by his Leavisite teacher, who introduced him to a whole new set of ideas and a whole new area of literature, Eric took to reading the novels of D. H. Lawrence (whom Leavis considered the greatest of modern English novelists because he was the most morally serious).[13] In his *New Bearings in English Poetry* (1932) Leavis made a strong claim for Eliot as one of the great poets, so Eric read as much Eliot as he could, including his long poem *The Waste Land* (1922). 'Like Byron', he thought, 'he has comprehensively expressed the mood of the intellectual in a particular era.' However, 'only here and there does he write something really great'. Eric preferred the poems of Gerard Manley Hopkins, another Leavis favourite.[14] Shakespeare was a central part of the English curriculum, and Eric went with a school party to see a performance of *King Lear* at the Westminster Theatre in 1934. It starred the twenty-two-year-old William Devlin, one of the youngest ever actors to play the part; like the professional critics, Eric found his performance mesmerising: 'He was excellent in most of his speeches, brilliant in parts, and touched genius at times.'[15]

Although he shunned many of the school's organised activities, he did play a part in the school Debating Society, whose committee he soon joined.[16] His cousin Ron had won the annual debating cup a few years before, and Eric was keen to emulate him.[17] He spoke in a debate for the first time on 18 July 1933, in favour of the motion 'That property is a nuisance'. Eric was duly chosen as the winner of the debating cup from among the seven speakers by a committee chaired by the Headmaster after an oration that must have been spoken from the heart, since it chimed so closely with his political beliefs. This launched his career as the school's leading debater. On 25 January 1934 he led the proposers of the motion 'That this House would Welcome a woman Prime Minister', a very advanced proposition for the time.[18] Returning to the Debating Society on 1 October 1934, Eric spoke from the floor in favour of the motion 'That this House approves of Russia's entry into the League [of Nations]', winning by a wide margin.[19] On 20 September 1935, Eric seconded the motion 'That in no circumstances should Great Britain intervene on behalf of Abyssinia'. His reasoning was doubt-less influenced by the Communist International's preference for concerted action through the League of Nations and its suspicion of British motives.[20] He was to be disappointed: in the end, no action was taken, and the League's failure to stop the Italian invasion sounded the death-knell for collective security.[21] The motion was lost by fifty-five votes to eleven, testifying to the sympathy among the boys, as in the British public in general, for the dignified behaviour of the Emperor Haile Selassie of Abyssinia, a potentate whom Eric doubtless, and with some justification, would have considered a relic of the feudal system.[22] At the end of the Spring Term 1936, in his final debate, Eric proposed the motion to the Debating Society 'That we dare not trust Hitler now'. The political complexion of the school and its pupils, generally conservative, was revealed by the fact that the motion was defeated by twenty-two votes to twenty.[23] Despite this, Eric came to discover a small core of half a dozen pupils in the Sixth Form who sympathised with the Left – 'a gratifying sign', he thought.[24]

Almost as soon as he arrived at the school, in the autumn term of 1933, he joined the editorial board of the school magazine, *The*

Philologian, and contributed to its Spring Term issue for 1935 a clever fictional fantasy about the return of Shakespeare, 'the news of the century'. At first, the spoof report went, everyone lionised the resurrected playwright ('Exclusive interview with Professors Dover Wilson and Bradley'). 'Baconians gnash their teeth in impotent rage. Oxford Dons look forward to the solution of the problem of how old Lady Macbeth's child was.' Before long, Shakespeare was invited to Hollywood.[25] The essay was precocious in its wit and imagination, revealing as it did a familiarity not only with Shakespeare but also with his editors and critics.

Eric's career at the school, exceptionally brilliant though it may have been for St Marylebone Grammar, was typical enough of the 'swot', the bright boy who worked hard but whose participation in school life did not go far beyond writing for and editing the school magazine and taking part in political debates. He was House Secretary of Houseman House, a role he did not take very seriously, writing the briefest possible reports on the House's activities for the school magazine.[26] He won the Abbott Essay Prize in 1934 and was even made a school prefect for 1935–6, his final year.[27] This prompted the reflection that he now 'had the right to mete out punishment to little boys. This gives me direct experience of the feelings and desires which authority and power bring along with them', reminding him of the admirable character of the Duke of Parma in the Stendhal novel he had just finished reading.[28] But in fact, however, as he later admitted, except for the teaching, 'the school was fairly marginal to my life'.[29] 'The kind of conversations which were familiar to fifteen-year-old schoolboys in Berlin – about politics, about literature, about sex – did not take place in English schools. I was a bit bored and I spent a great deal of my time reading.'[30] What really mattered to him, apart from his schoolwork, was the intellectual and cultural life he led outside the school, in the Marylebone Public Library (where he spent most of his free periods during school time), at home and in and around London.[31] This, and deepening the commitment to the Communist cause he had first espoused in Berlin, where the Prinz-Heinrichs-Gymnasium, he later thought, had in the end exercised an influence on him far greater than that of St Marylebone Grammar School.

He was taught history by Harold Llewellyn Smith, who was eventually to succeed Wayne as Headmaster. Llewellyn Smith 'was not one of those teachers who reveal and inspire', Eric recalled: 'I think he was morally rather than intellectually interesting. I never felt I had a real personal relationship to him.' Nevertheless, he became the most important of the school's teachers for Eric. 'Handsome and socially assured', he was the son of Sir Hubert Llewellyn Smith, an economist at the Board of Trade who had made a reputation with detailed social investigations of a number of working-class trades in the late Victorian and Edwardian eras. Harold Llewellyn Smith lent Eric some of his books on social questions and labour history; 'he knew all the surviving reformers and radicals. In fact he showed my essays to Sidney and Beatrice Webb. So Harold was both an ideal master and a personal introduction to the history of the labour movement for a teen-age leftist historian.'[32] It was out of a sense of social duty that he taught at St Marylebone rather than at a major public school, though he certainly had the ability to do so. 'Of course,' Eric added, 'working with boys was also an attraction, but there was none of that *History Boys* groping about him. Nobody ever even hinted at misbehaviour. On the contrary, he had the reputation of being repressed and straitlaced, and when he took boys to the theatre he always made sure there was a chaperon.'[33]

Although Eric later claimed that Llewellyn Smith 'gave me my original field of research: British labour and socialism from the 1880s to 1914', this was not immediately the case, for he was to embark on an entirely different subject for a brief time when he began research, and did not come to British labour history until after the end of the Second World War, and then for reasons that were more pragmatic than intellectual. Llewellyn Smith might have laid the seeds of this interest, and it was most probably his inspiration that prompted Eric to write an essay on 'The Battle of the Slums' around this time, but this was contemporary rather than historical social analysis. Eric later claimed that he already 'became conscious of being a historian at the age of sixteen',[34] but this, too, is doubtful. On the contrary, he thought of himself potentially as an imaginative writer. 'I have had a vision,' he wrote in November 1934. 'No joking. I'm not mystical. But I've had one.' He saw as in a flash soldiers celebrating the end of the war in 1918. The vision lasted no more than a second. 'It was desolate, dark, chaotic, cruel, petty ... I made a poem out of it. Feeble, of course. Can I become a poet or writer? If I think poet, and what I've achieved, and what is necessary, it seems to me that I'm con-demned to be an eternal dilettante (in the poetic field).' In the end, 'my future lies with Marxism, in teaching, or in both'. Poetry was not the most important thing for him but then it wasn't for many poets either, he reflected: most of them made their living in other ways. There was not the slightest hint that he intended to become a professional historian.[35]

With Llewellyn Smith what he enjoyed most was discussing not historical but economic topics, to which Eric brought a Marxist approach that his teacher clearly found interesting.[36] History did not figure very much in Eric's private thoughts or private read-ing. As he later remarked, 'I got all my historical interests from or through Marx, except my interest in labour history and social movements.' Marxism gave him 'an interest in the great macro-historical question [of] how human societies evolved', especially the transition from feudalism to capitalism.[37] The conventional school history textbooks, he thought, were mostly useless, though occasionally they provided insights:

While I read and listen, I put what is useful into my mental apparatus. Gradually I see – very gradually – how a picture of history is crystallizing out of it all. At the moment I just see individual contours – in some instances cornerstones, in others just simple rows and groups of bricks. The longer I study, the more I hope to enlarge my picture. Of course, you never put it together completely, but perhaps one day I'll have all the cor-nerstones there. Thanks to the dialectic, I'm on the right way.[38]

If he read history at all, it was Roman history, and mostly in order to write school essays.[39] Here too, however, he brought his Marxist reading to bear, noting that ancient philosophy and culture provided clear examples of how everything was dependent on the relations of production. Roman history from 276 BCE to 14 CE – the period he was required to study for his university matriculation – provided 'a true and typical example of the transition from one system to another', a thought that foreshadowed his preoccupation later in life with the transition from feudalism to capitalism. In the Roman case, he discerned the beginnings of feudalism as the Republic gave way to the Empire and an oligarchy of landowners became dominant, bringing with it key elements of Greek culture to replace the old animistic religion of the primitive countryfolk. Thus went the argument of Eric's school essay on the origins of Hellenism in ancient Rome. Yet, self-critically, he was conscious of the fact that he had written nothing about the plebs or about trade and industry, which surely belonged somewhere in the picture. Nevertheless, his teachers must have been startled to read essays on ancient history written from the standpoint of historical materialism, and Llewellyn Smith in particular found Eric's work both fascinating and original.[40]

II

His new home country might have been a safe haven for Eric and his sister Nancy, his uncle and aunt and their son Peter, but in most other respects he was unimpressed by his initial experience of the United Kingdom:

> Britain was a terrible let-down. Imagine yourself as a newspaper correspondent based in Manhattan and transferred by your editor to cover Omaha, Nebraska. That is how I felt when I came to England, after two years in the unbelievably exciting, sophisticated, intellectually and politically explosive Berlin of the dying Weimar Republic ... For my first years in Britain I

felt I was just marking time, waiting till there was a chance to carry on the conversation where it had broken off in Berlin. Of course for my older relatives from Central Europe, the fact that Britain was provincial, boring and predictable, that nothing much happened here, was one of its major attractions. Happy the country, they said, where the headline: 'Crisis' was about Test Matches, not the collapse of civilization. But that's not the way I felt at 16.[41]

Neither his uncle Sidney nor his aunt Gretl had much interest in politics or culture, though Gretl did appreciate and know something about classical music; and at home Eric sometimes suffered from 'gigantic boredom' as a result.[42] Indeed, when his uncle found him reading Sterne's eighteenth-century comic novel *Tristram Shandy*, he took it away from him.[43] In culture as well as politics, therefore, Eric had to make his own way. As for his sister Nancy, his attempts to engage her in discussion of these topics were a complete failure. 'We are all amazed', he wrote, referring most probably to himself, his uncle and his aunt, 'at how mediocre she is, even typically mediocre.' His parents had been far more interesting, and his relatives in London, his uncle Harry and cousin Ron, were people he could talk to. Not so Nancy, who shared none of his interests and occupied herself with the typical, ordinary enthusiasms and occupations of a normal English girl in her early teens. Sometimes he would play cards with her or go to the cinema – in May 1934, for instance, they went with their cousin Peter to see *Tugboat Annie*.[44] But though Nancy was intelligent, she was not academically inclined, she did not share his reading habits and she was not interested in politics. He considered her over-sensitive and prone to lie when she was anxious about something. He had no idea how to relate to her. As her brother, of course, he wanted to look after her. 'I want to do my best. Can I?'[45] He was unsure. 'In politics,' he concluded resignedly, as in other areas of life, 'I have already realized that the average human being makes up 95% of humanity as a whole.'[46]

We can reconstruct Eric's private thoughts on this and many

other topics because once he had settled down in London he began
to keep a diary, starting to write it in April 1934 'out of boredom',
he noted, and for practice in writing in German. 'Those are just
excuses', he added later: 'In reality I began it because I wanted,
as the saying goes, to pour out my heart.' After a while, it became
'a kind of trash-can or rummage-room where I could dump all
kinds of thoughts and feelings'. Rereading it in the spring of 1935
he found it rather sentimental. There was too much self-analysis,
not enough description: 'I'm just not really like Pepys.' Apart from
this, as aspiring adolescent diarists often do, he also used it for
experiments in written style. On one occasion, for example, he
devoted a long passage to describing the furniture in Sidney and
Gretl's dining room. He was trying to find a style that allowed him
to express his feelings without becoming maudlin.[47] He wrote it in
German, probably because this came most naturally to him as his
personal, intimate language; he was to revert to it in the diaries
he wrote years afterwards at a moment of emotional crisis in his
life. Certainly there is no sign that he needed to use the language
in order to practise it.

Eric began his diary by recording his regret at the move to
London, unavoidable though it was. 'In Berlin I had friends ... I
was on the best path to becoming an active Communist. Illegality
would only have strengthened my views.' And he would, he
thought, have deepened his knowledge of Marxist theory: 'It was
also from a theoretical perspective a pity that I left Berlin.'[48] It
was in Britain that he first began seriously to read the Marxist
classics. Marylebone Public Library did not stock copies of them,
so he had to buy them, a factor that imposed unwelcome limita-
tions on his reading. He 'used to go down from school in the lunch
break to Covent Garden, when the CPGB had a little bookshop
in King Street, with Jack Cohen, who became the student organiser, who was serving in there. I used to buy all those little books:
the Little Lenin Library, and also German elementary Marxist
texts.'[49] On 15 May 1934 he noted in his diary that he had bought
Marx's *Critique of the Gotha Programme* and some essays by Lenin,
but regretted that he had not managed to read more. Up to this

point he had only managed to get through *Capital*, volume one, *The Critique of Political Economy*, *The Poverty of Philosophy*, *Marx-Engels Selected Correspondence*, *The Eighteenth Brumaire*, *The Civil War in France*, *Anti-Dühring* and Lenin's *Materialism and Empiriocriticism*.[50] Just over a month later, he recorded reading Lenin's *Imperialism*, Engels's *The Development of Socialism from Utopia to Science* along with speeches by Lenin and the German Communist Wilhelm Pieck, and an early work by the American Communist Farrell Dobbs.[51] He read Engels's *The Origin of the Family, Private Property, and the State*[52] as well as less demanding texts such as George Bernard Shaw's *The Intelligent Woman's Guide to Socialism* ('very good').[53] One has to remind oneself that at this point he had only just turned seventeen.

Two years earlier, he reflected in July 1934, he had agreed with 'Mussolini's dictum, that men make history'. But 'that was still before I had read the *Communist Manifesto*. Since that time I have surely made some progress ideologically.'[54] Yet a few weeks later, he was castigating himself for his intellectual superficiality. 'Which of your books', he asked himself in the privacy of his diary, 'have you really and thoroughly read? And you call yourself a Marxist? Your nice excuse: I want to educate myself. Don't make me laugh!'[55] Yet for all his occasional dissatisfaction with the progress of his intellectual mastering of Marxism-Leninism, there could be no doubt about the depth of his emotional commitment. He went on a pilgrimage to Karl Marx's grave in Highgate cemetery, then, as he described it, 'a simple little grave with a big glass box of roses on it from the USSR' (it was only in 1954 that Laurence Bradshaw's monumental bust replaced it).[56] He read the Soviet propaganda magazine *Russia Today*[57] He repeatedly stressed his desire to immerse himself totally in Marxism-Leninism. 'I hope I will grow so far into dialectical materialism that I don't come out of it'; 'drown yourself in Leninism. Let it become your second nature.'[58] After reading twelve pages of Lenin he noted: 'Astonishing how that cheers me up and clears my mind. I was in a total good mood afterwards.'[59] This is not the feeling that most people have after ploughing through Lenin's theoretical works. He often felt a euphoric sense of confidence in the future Marxism predicted for human society: 'Thus I can listen calmly when people laugh at me and my ideas, and listen and see how the capitalists are still suppressing us. I <u>know</u> that it will come. Sooner or later. *Dies irae, dies illa.*'[60]

The Marxism Eric imbibed in this formative period of his intellectual life was the Marxism of the classical tradition established through the apostolic succession of Marx, Engels, Plekhanov, Kautsky and Lenin: the doctrine of 'historical materialism' or 'scientific socialism', founded on supposedly proven certainties that pointed towards the inevitable triumph of socialism in a future revolution that was thought not to be far away. In this version, the differences between Marx and Engels's thought vanished, and the Hegelian elements disappeared from the former in favour of the simplistic Darwinism of the latter. Eric admired both Lenin and Stalin. Both were among 'the great statesmen of this century' because they possessed principles and knew exactly what they wanted, but were flexible in the means they chose to obtain it. Great statesmen combined the virtues of the man of principle and the opportunist. 'Lenin and Stalin were such, Trotski was not.'[61] In fact, however, Eric's intellectual formation owed little to Stalin, and most of all to Marx and Engels, as interpreted by Lenin. Thus he took the view that intellectuals and political activists should form the vanguard of the proletariat, leading them onto the revolutionary path, rather than, say, the more passive interpretation of Karl Kautsky, the chief theoretician of the moderate pre-1914 German Social Democrats, who thought that economic developments would do the job for them.[62]

Eric's schoolfellows, some of whom supported Oswald Mosley's British Union of Fascists, then reaching the height of their success,[63] thought 'that I am biased, narrow-minded, fanatical, blinkered, and shut myself off against the dictates of reason'. Marx's *Capital*, they argued, was 'not to be treated as a Bible'. Everything, after all, was relative: 'there was no absolute objectivity'. It was difficult, he thought, to discuss such matters with non-Marxists.[64] Yet it was clear that 'Fascism is on the advance, war comes closer every day, and with it civil war and revolution ... I see it, like Cassandra, I

know.'[65] Hitlerism would surely crumble. 'If we consider the history
of the labour movement, we will see that in all countries where a
strong revolutionary movement developed, this only happened
under conditions of great terror.'[66] 'To be a socialist means to be
an optimist.'[67] And, indeed, he felt that 'we are living in a time of
overwhelming, inexhaustible, incomprehensible interest. No other
period of world history can be compared to ours.'[68] 'Perhaps fascism will bring some good – it will be the school through which the
proletariat passes, then to emerge victorious under the leadership
of the C.P.'[69] – a belief typical of the disastrous 'third period' of
the Communist International, when Communists everywhere welcomed the demise of 'bourgeois democracy' because they thought
it would bring revolution nearer.

Eric's faith in the Soviet Union had all the uncompromising
absolutism of an adolescent crush. Press reports of a famine in
Ukraine, then part of the Soviet Union, he dismissed as 'Lies of
the Whites' (the Russian counter-revolutionaries). He grasped
eagerly for Walter Duranty's book *Duranty Reports Russia* (1934), a
collection of articles for the *New York Times*, subsequently widely
criticised for suppressing the truth about the famine. 'Duranty', he
noted, naming other apologists of a similar kind, 'is one of the few
bourgeois who . . . honestly try to understand the Soviet Union.'[70]
'The Soviet Union today is living in a state of war,' he wrote after
visiting an exhibition of Soviet propaganda posters. Clearly, it was
necessary to use art for political purposes. 'All available forces must
devote themselves to the S.U. "Pure" art in this light is a cul-de-sac.
Art is subordinated to politics', he noted, with evident approval.[71]
This belief was strengthened by a viewing of one of the earliest
talking pictures made in the Soviet Union, Nikolai Ekk's *The Way
to Life* (1931), which used a variety of cinematic techniques to trace
the rescue of Russian street urchins and their transformation into
solid Soviet citizens. It was 'the best film I've seen in my life', he
enthused. Here was art not only subordinated to politics but inex-
tricably fused with them.[72]

His political view of art did not prevent him, however, from
undertaking systematic expeditions to the major London galleries

and museums in order to learn something about the visual arts, including the National Gallery,[73] the Victoria and Albert Museum, the Imperial War Museum and the Tate Gallery, where he looked at pictures by Cézanne, Matisse, Picasso and others and was particularly impressed by the passionate post-Impressionist art of Vincent Van Gogh.[74] He began to wrestle intellectually with the classic Marxist concepts of 'base and superstructure', according to which politics, culture and society reflected the fundamentals of the economic system: feudalism produced one kind of culture, capitalism another. Eric was too intelligent to fall for the simplistic version of this model purveyed by the Stalinists. 'Even as a schoolboy', he wrote many years later, 'I remember being outraged by a piece in *Left Review* which derived the great tragedies of Shakespeare from the harvest-failures and famines of England in the 1590s, and maybe I even wrote a letter protesting against this simplistic interpretation which was never published.' Half a century later he was still preoccupied with the problem.[75] Even in 1935 he dreamed of 'a Magnum Opus, and that's a Marxist analysis of culture – the solution to the PROBLEM', meaning the problem of the relationship between base and superstructure in the arts: of imperialism in the writings of Lawrence of Arabia, religion in the poetry of François Villon, decadence in Botticelli, of the factors underlying the taste of an era.[76]

In the school magazine, Eric wrote an essay on another exhibition he had been to, 'On Seeing Surrealists', explaining to his readers that 'what the surrealists want to do is to get into art the powerful effect of irrational experiences – dreams for instance – or the strangeness of the conjunction of quite incongruous concepts'. The humour of the surrealists was engaging, but 'when you see this same trick repeated a dozen times you get bored'. Only three of them were good: Chirico, Ernst and Picasso. Eric did not much like Miró, who 'seems to be degenerating into exercises in blots and white spaces'. Apart from these, along with Masson, Man Ray and a few others, including Henry Moore, all they produced was 'bunk, cliché, modern-modern stuff'. They were 'people who are too lazy to co-ordinate their impression, study incoherence and hide behind

Freud'.[77] He preferred another exhibition, of Chinese art, where he found the Sung work 'fascinating. It crystallises in its perfection much of what our own civilisation wants to do and can't, though it excludes so many people, because it is so aristocratic.'[78] Eric's views were clearly informed by his politics, but his appreciation of art went far beyond this. He filled the pages of his diary with lengthy analyses of Italian Renaissance art, trying to work out the balance between the individual painter and his social context.[79] By the time he left school he had a good, broad knowledge of art, both historical and contemporary.

III

Thus politics was not all, nor did Eric himself view art solely from a political perspective. He developed a strong love of the English countryside. For someone brought up in big cities – Vienna, Berlin, London – getting to know the world of nature was a particularly intense experience. 'I go into the countryside to relax', he wrote, after a family holiday in Teignmouth and on Dartmoor. 'I want to know as little as possible of the big city and big-city culture.'[80] He especially enjoyed camping at Forest Green, a country area in Surrey, near Horsham, donated in 1930 to Marylebone Grammar School by a former pupil, the press magnate and sometime backer of Mosley's British Union of Fascists, Lord Rothermere. The camp was essentially organised along the lines Eric would have been familiar with from his all too brief time in the Boy Scouts. The boys slept in large canvas tents, six to a tent. They were divided into teams, and took part in competitions, games and expeditions, including a cross-country run. There was a hike through Holmbury Hill and Crossharbour. A swimming pool was available for use at any time. The emphasis was very much on physical activity.[81] He also began to cycle into the countryside around London at weekends with his cousin Ron. On one trip in the summer of 1934, more ambitiously, they cycled to North Wales and climbed Cader Idris.[82] And in April 1936 they spent two weeks camping in

Snowdonia, cycling there and back, sleeping in tents and climbing the snow-covered mountain massif of Carnedd Dafydd, the third-highest peak in Wales.[83]

Nature was important to Eric. Sitting at home at his desk in London early in 1935, in his blue knitted sweater and flannel trousers, he felt a sudden, ill-defined

> longing. For what? Perhaps for the fields, strong, red, deep fields and broad, warm meadows. Or for the dead-silent woods at night. Or for the great sea, soft, lightly swelling with its weight, shining benignly red and silver in the evening. I want to lie down peacefully, very softly, under the great sun. In the wondrous, deep sun. I want to be still, completely still, and lie there until I fall asleep, in the sun, in the warm grass.[84]

He undertook another cycling tour of Devon and Dorset with Ron in the spring of 1935. By this time, his cousin had begun to take evening classes in economics at the London School of Economics, which helped him pass the examination for entry into the Administrative Grade of the civil service, where he could take part in the formulation and implementation of policy. From January 1935 he was employed in the finance department of the Ministry of Labour, based at Kew.[85] With his increased salary, Ron had purchased a drop-handlebar bike made by the recently established firm of Claud Butler, and by this time Eric had dumped the old bicycle which had so embarrassed him in Vienna and Berlin and managed to obtain one good enough to take him on long rides.[86]

These induced in him an almost ecstatic feeling of communing with nature, as he wrote during a tour of the West Country:

> It is morning, and I am lying in the tent, eyes half-closed and lazily watching a chaffinch on the sprig of a thorn-tree above me. The sprig is delicate, and the pale sun tinges its greyish-brown with light, and lends form to the buds just about to become leaves. The chaffinch is singing against the sky, against

the constant, recurring sound of the sea ... I am fascinated by the sea, and I turn my head to see it swaying slowly round the cliff, with a light, broken swell, green like the glass of broken bottles, glinting silvery along the path of the sun, and with the moving shapeless shadows of clouds squatting on it ... I am not even thinking. I merely feel it all ... we are astonished, exultant, and half afraid. Cliffs, trees and the seagulls and clouds, the dazzling iridescent, complex whirl of colour and form, centres in us, and wheels around the white tent.[87]

Ron had what Eric later described as 'a passion for the sea'. Already at their first encounter, he had proudly showed him 'his elaborate drawings of three-masters in full rig'.[88] For Ron, a large part of the point of cycling to the seaside was to get an opportunity to sail.

At Ron's prompting, the boys spent a night on board a coastal trawler from 'Brixham, Devon, with two ancient mariners slowly pulling us past the reddish sails and hanging nets of fishing smacks and the gleaming white of regatta craft to the place where our ship was moored'. The trawler

chug-chugged out of the harbour into the deep blue waters of Tor Bay. The sun burned on the dark red cliffs, and the sea gleamed like a shield of polished steel. The coast crept past; harbour, mole, cliffs; in the background, like a spider, Torquay and Paignton. Gulls float by, troops of diver-birds duck rhythmically ... Little shadows begin to show beneath the wavecrests, or rather, in the dells between the ripples, for the sea is calm. Bolt Head rises broadbacked against the sky. The red and yellow between the clouds deepens, and throws a quivering image on the sea.

As the net was cast, the boys sat on fish-boxes drinking tea and eating chocolate. It grew dark. Torquay shone like a 'great glow-worm ... The lighthouse sends out regular beams – two flash, pause, two flash, pause. The sea is phosphorescent. In our wake luminous bubbles rise and float slowly. Green sparks shoot from our sides.' The men hauled in the net. 'A pull, it is open, and a glittering mass of fish writhes on the boards.' They sorted out the catch and threw overboard what they could not use. 'It is a hard life', Eric reflected as the fishermen worked. 'Every night, spring, summer and autumn, they go out, and every day in winter.' And they had 'to sell their goods themselves, by auction, in an open market. That they are at the mercy of dealers and auctioneers we were to see later.'[89]

It seemed natural enough to Eric to link nature to ideology with their common intertwining in an all-embracing whole. Marxism to him seemed a system that fitted together just as the universe and all its parts fitted together:

A world-view (*Weltanschauung*) is something wonderful. It's so great, and perfected, all-embracing: like one of the lofty steel scaffoldings in new buildings: just as strong and complete in form, or like one of the great trees that stand alone in English parks – eighteenth century, even, short-cut, green lawns below, and then the broad, shining crown in the sun. And the trunk, with its tattered bark or smooth silver rind – the roots stretching out, the upward striving branches – the harmony of the whole, 'the achievement of the mastery of the thing!' – nay, even greater, scarcely to be measured in ordinary comparisons. It's like the all-embracing cosmos, the depths of the universe, from the dark distance to the floating masses of stars, through the entire, endless, deep, satin black sphere to where the bundle of white rays emerges from space . . .[90]

In the end, he broke off the passage because, he conceded, he lacked the poetic ability to describe Marxism in this way.

Despite his preference for nature and the countryside, Eric appreciated the mysteriousness of the great fogs that descended on London from time to time during the winter months, blanketing the city and the land for miles around it with a thick, acrid vapour, sometimes white, sometimes yellow, sometimes brown, which it was scarcely possible to penetrate.[91] On Monday 19 November 1934 it occasioned one of his earliest pieces of experimental creative writing:

The fog was thick. Lay over everything. One is isolated. Here am I, is my world, ten metres' circumference. Beyond that, whiteness that sucks everything up. One is thrown back onto oneself and one's impressionability enlarges and deepens itself. – I walk through Hyde Park, e.g. All the trees are motionless, turned to stone like Niobe, stretching out their branches. Ghosts. The fog drives past my feet in little shreds, the breathy exhalation of the asphalt, cigar-smoke. Beyond, at Marble Arch, shines a red cell of light, dull, dull and spongy. Lanterns dance. Cars emit geometrically deep, penetrating shafts of light, but the naked power of their headlights is melted and sucked away. Side- and rear-lights like ghostly glow-worms (it is getting dark). Shadows, ghostly suggestions of houses. Clearer air on Park Lane Grosvenor, Dorchester? Who knows? The arc-lamps float stiffly, unmoving, like gyroplanes, or wooden falcons, casting a hail of light downwards. Golden rain, avalanches of light, pyramids, film studio lamps. Everything statuesque. The fog wells up before me, sucking, shutting everything off, above, everywhere: white sleep. Shadows. Perhaps the fog is also Ixion and Juno the earth. But that is bourgeois. À la pastorale. And then Gypsy Hill station: visible in the half-dark (I am standing on the open platform) the station roofs, massive, immense, whale's backs, and a stretch of railway line with shards of fog. My feet. On the platform thin and greenish lights glow, and vague blocks raise themselves mechanically. Behind them a soft light (station hall). On the other side of the tracks lies the white wall, a spot of light in the middle (signal box). One is again in the centre of one's private cosmos, ten metres' radius. Those out there are starry blots. The tracks and the straight lines of the platform are the only certain things that one can hold on to. It is dark. The train is coming. It rumbles in the distance, like thunder. Or like beer-barrels that one rolls down into the beer-cellar. It rushes nearer, and the fog changes it from a machine, mighty, bulky, precise and wonderful in its massive, perfected symphony, harmony of the mechanical, into a dark, deformed mosasaurus. The windows spew out light like fountains, and it tumbles down in a parabola.[92]

Eric did not try any more elaborate descriptions of this sort, but it was good practice for writing.

In the privacy of his diary, Eric also began to experiment with poetry, written, like his essay on London fog, and indeed everything he put into the diary, in German. His poetry at this point was little more than agitprop sloganising. He wrote a number of different versions of what he called an 'Ode to Capitalists', though it was less an ode than a series of phrases listing the evils of the capitalist system, followed by a 'Jeremiad' in which the capitalist spokesman proclaim: 'war is beautiful, wonderfully beautiful', 'beat the Jews', 'National Britain' and other slogans, while the workers declared 'civil war. A red flag will fly. Alone.'[93] He wrote another poem after reading *The Babbitt Warren: A Satire on the United States* (1927) by Cyril Joad, who taught at Birkbeck, London University's evening college for part-time students. Joad was a pacifist and a left-wing Labour supporter, but he was not left-wing enough for Eric, who found the book good in parts, but overall 'typically bourgeois'. He appreciated Joad's insight that 'men don't make history, rather the reverse, history makes men'. The poem, however, was piece of political sloganising: it had the bourgeoisie proclaiming: 'We drive hundreds of thousands into death. But progress has left us.'[94] It was only at the end of November 1934 that he essayed some verses which were not exclusively devoted to celebrating the coming revolution: nature, he wrote, was buried on the Western Front during the First World War, at Passchendaele and Verdun. 'We can't sing of flowers any more.'[95]

His voracious reading encompassed a wide range of literature in English and German, including Macaulay's essays, Lewis Carroll's *Alice in Wonderland* and the nineteenth-century German comic writer and cartoonist Wilhelm Busch, though he found him 'crude' and lacking in the sophistication of another comic writer, the poet and versifier Christian Morgenstern. Eric felt that he would have got to know German literature better had he stayed in Berlin.[96] But his personal library included editions of German poetry by Heine, Hölderlin and Rilke and English poems by Shakespeare, Donne, Pound, Keats, Hopkins, Shelley, Coleridge and Milton. He read volumes of poetry by Auden, Day-Lewis and Spender as well as the seventeenth-century religious poets George Herbert and Richard Crashaw. His French was already good enough for him to work his way through a volume of Baudelaire.[97] His taste in prose fiction was very much focused on contemporary writing. He purchased a volume of short stories by the prolific T. F. Powys, and he read Lion Feuchtwanger's great anti-Nazi saga of the downfall of a German Jewish family, *The Oppermanns* (1933), though he found it 'oh so bourgeois!' He devoured experimental novels such as Virginia Woolf's *The Waves* (1931) and Alfred Döblin's *Berlin Alexanderplatz* (1929), which he compared to the work of John Dos Passos, an American socialist writer popular at the time.[98]

Was he really a Communist, then? He worried about having 'waverings and doubts. To doubt,' he added solemnly,

> is no doubt a sign of high intellect. Intellectuals will even tell you that dogmatic Communists are not as spiritually fine as themselves (the intellectuals). Possibly. But the dogmatic Bolsheviks do something ... I will admit: I have doubts, uncertainties ... I am an intellectual through and through. With all the weaknesses of an intellectual – inhibitions, complexes etc.[99]

Intellectuals, after all, were the one part of the bourgeoisie that were capable of becoming socialist.[100] (Shortly afterwards, on re-reading this passage, he exclaimed: 'God, how conceited I am!')[101] Defining himself as an intellectual was unusual for anyone in England, let alone a boy still in his teens. But he felt it was problematic. A large part of the problem was his inability to put into action the fundamental Marxist-Leninist principle of the unity of theory and practice. He felt that he was posing as an intellectual in order

to conceal his 'un-Bolshevik' behaviour and his adherence to bourgeois convention. He confessed that he 'cannot reach a decision to
undertake something. What will I do, when rapid and immediate
action is required of me? When I am alone without a superior or a
better informed person on whom I can rely?' What would he do, in
other words, when the revolution came? The answer, he decided,
reaching for the motto he had imbibed during his time as a Boy
Scout, was: 'Be prepared!'[102]

IV

Many evenings spent discussing such matters with his cousin Ron
Hobsbaum, who, like his father, supported the Labour Party, did
not solve the key question: how was the revolution to be brought
about? Eric did not see much hope in the British Communist
movement, which never became much more than a tiny sect on
the fringes of politics. Moreover, being a Communist in Britain
was not in any way difficult or dangerous.

> The Communist in Germany has rubber truncheons and con-
> centration camps to fear, but he has comrades; the Communist
> here has nothing to fear and has none. In Germany people say:
> Marx is a power, so we will put you in a concentration camp.
> The Communists drew new strength from this recognition of
> their power, proudly feeling themselves to be truly oppressed.
> But here Marx is an old economist whom Jevons already
> refuted.[103]

Communism really meant something in Germany, Eric felt.
The strength of his commitment to the cause derived to a very
considerable extent from the fact that it was in Berlin in 1932–3
that he had been politicised, not in Britain. In contrast to the
mass movement of German Communism, which won one hundred seats in the Reichstag in the last free elections of the Weimar
Republic, the Communist Party of Great Britain had no seats at

all in the House of Commons at this time. Moreover, the British Communists rejected the idea of becoming a mass party, and insisted instead on every member being an active militant, a role Eric was neither willing nor able to assume. He was, after all, still at school, focusing on his studies. There was no chance of joining the movement, a conclusion he reached on the basis 'partly of the condition of the Croydon cell itself, partly of the C.P.'.[104]

The only mass movement around in which Eric saw the possibility of participating was the Labour Party, which at this time was going through a period of almost total ineffectiveness after losing the 1931 General Election heavily to the national government, led by the former Labour Prime Minister Ramsay MacDonald but consisting largely of Conservatives. At least the Labour Party would not demand of him the total commitment he was unable to make. But it was 'reformist through and through'.[105] And the dispirited and disillusioned state of the movement was illustrated for him by the May Day parades of 1934. He saw 'Mayday as the biggest festival of the year, with the exception, perhaps, of the anniversary of the October Revolution', and he marked the occasion not only by listing in his diary the greatest battles of the class struggle across the world during the previous year ('a fine series: "workers of the world, unite!"'), but also by making his way to the parade itself. It left him 'deeply saddened. On the first of May, on the festive day that the workers of the world have so passionately appropriated for themselves, scarcely a thousand find themselves ready to demonstrate.'[106]

More immediately, however, he decided to infiltrate his local Labour Party in order 'to make communist propaganda'.[107] 'I am not going to join the C. P., but the Labour Party', he declared. 'Like Karl Liebknecht in the army, like the Bolsheviks in the Duma, I will go into the L. P. and do my best to make propaganda.' Eric signalled his intransigent position by quoting the clenched-fist slogan of the Communist paramilitaries in Germany before the Nazi seizure of power: 'Three cheers for the Red Front!'[108] His tactical decision was reinforced by the defeat of the pacifist and socialist activist Fenner Brockway, the candidate for the breakaway, left-wing Independent Labour Party, in a by-election in Upton, east London, a few days later. Eric criticised the local Communist and ILP members for having fought against the Labour Party instead of staying 'in the monster's belly'. 'One cannot construct mass movements simply by shouting. The C.P. and the I.L.P just shouted.'[109] It was clear, he concluded, that 'The Labour Party must be radicalized'. Otherwise Britain might become fascist (Oswald Mosley's British Union of Fascists had just made headlines with a mass rally at the Olympia Stadium in London, heavily propagandised by the *Daily Mail*). If this happened, then 'an armed general strike must be prepared'.[110]

Eric concealed his 'aim in life', to be a Communist intellectual, from his uncle and aunt.[111] But the Labour Party was not much better as far as they were concerned. When the Norwood branch of the Labour Party sent a letter to him confirming his membership, its contents were noticed by Sidney and Gretl, and they were not pleased. Eric told them that he was going to a meeting of the local branch, but they forbade it.[112] The venue was too far away and he would come back too late at night.[113] A major crisis followed, amidst a series of violent family rows. Gretl had already expressed 'the hope that I would grow out of my Communism', though he had rejected this idea with some scorn.[114] Now his aunt made it clear that he was to focus above all on his schoolwork and not be distracted by a political movement of which she strongly disapproved. Eric told himself that he had 'to decide between family and Marx. But I have already decided. Family ties, even the most sentimental, are bourgeois conditions.'[115] The gap between politics and his family was unbridgeable. 'It's funny that I want to wish uncle well as an individual but as a Communist I have to oppose all capitalist enterprises', and his uncle of course was a businessman, a capitalist by profession.[116]

As the conflict deepened, he went to the local public library to consult the literature on the rights of guardians over their wards. He was under the age of majority (twenty-one at the time) and the information was not encouraging; he would have to wait until he reached the age where he could legally be independent.[117] 'Either

I stay here and enjoy freedom to read and talk as I please or, if I become politically active, I leave home.'[118] Could he support himself with a job in the civil service and live with friends until he found a flat, he wondered? After all, leaving home would be following the example of the young men who left their homes to go to war in 1914.[119] On the other hand, he did not want to hurt his uncle and aunt. 'Aunt Gretl has cried, because of me – she must not cry!'[120] He was held back by 'my respect for Aunt Gretl and Uncle Sidney. No, not that: my weakness of character. What is it? Love or cowardice? Both?' Was Communism not worth the sacrifice? But he did not want to hurt his uncle and aunt. 'Oh God, God', he agonised.[121]

As the conflict reached its climax on the evening of the party meeting, 'Uncle Sidney became furious. Started to strike out around himself.' There was 'pandemonium'.[122] As the row continued, time passed, and it was soon too late to go to the meeting anyway. For the next week, the atmosphere in the house was tense. Sidney did not speak to Eric until he broke silence to congratulate him on his seventeenth birthday, on 8 June 1934. Eric was moved by the gesture, but blamed himself once more for his weakness and lack of commitment to the cause.[123] 'Oh damn, damn, damn! Why am I such an intellectual, such a petty-bourgeois?' he lamented.[124] 'Cowardly, yes, cowardly!'[125] He had behaved like a 'cad' towards the working class by failing to take part in political activity on their behalf.[126] But he appreciated the faith his uncle and aunt put in his academic abilities. Sidney, he conceded, 'believes in me', and Gretl was 'so motherly'.[127] In the end he had made his decision: family came before politics after all.[128]

It would be easy to dismiss these agonisings as little more than the product of adolescent emotionality; but for Eric they were a major milestone along the road to becoming a committed intellectual rather than a dedicated party activist. Sidney and Gretl did not persuade him out of his commitment but at the same time the episode constituted another piece of pressure restricting his commitment to the realm of thought alone. Some time later, indeed, he congratulated himself on remaining a Communist, even if he was a 'Bourgeois Bolshevik', despite eighteen months of breathing in political 'poison gas' at home.[129] And in any case, before long, Eric did indeed manage to go to a Labour Party meeting, at which an exiled Austrian socialist was speaking; he concealed this from his uncle and aunt by announcing that he was visiting his cousin Denis 'after (non-existent) sport' at school.[130] He was not impressed with what he saw. 'So this is the Labour Party,' Eric wondered after attending his first meeting. 'A collection of elderly ladies and old men.' From the perspective of a boy still at school, they may have been old, but most likely they were no more than middle-aged. 'Parliamentary forms and formulae' were 'adhered to with the utmost strictness, even if the topic of discussion was unimportant.' He was scathing in his verdict. 'Oh', he exclaimed sarcastically, 'vanguard of the proletariat. Master-builders of socialism.' He was more impressed by the speaker, who urged an armed uprising against the clerico-fascist dictatorship that had taken control in Austria in four days of violent clashes with the socialists earlier in the year, and proclaimed the need for the socialists to rule with the bayonet once they had seized power.[131]

Towards the end of October 1934, Eric noted that the Comintern had abandoned its previous intransigence and officially backed the policy of collaboration with socialist parties in a Popular Front. The British Communists agreed not to put up parliamentary candidates where the Labour Party candidate was 'sufficiently socialist'. Eric was undecided on the merits of this policy.[132] He had applied to join the Norwood branch of the Communist Party.[133] If he did become a member, there is no evidence that he ever did anything for it or even attended its meetings. But he took on a helping role in the Labour campaign during the local elections in Borough on 1 November 1934, aided perhaps by the fact that in the meantime he had learned to drive. 'I'm driving a car for the Labour-party people. Another new experience: an election. Not as important as I thought . . . One takes cripples to the polling station, knocks on doors [of Labour supporters] and asks if they've already voted', inviting them to do so if they had not.[134] He did not feel he was very successful at this task. In Church Place he ran up against a particularly obdurate voter, or, rather, non-voter:

We knocked: Have you voted already? 'No.' Why not, then? 'Don't want to.' But how come? 'Too tired. If the vote was tomorrow, then yes.' But there's no voting tomorrow. Come on anyway! 'Don't want to.' It only takes five minutes. The car is comfy. 'Don't want to.' But, Good God, once more, you vote to your own advantage! (N. B. my companion was speaking: I was just sitting in the car). 'Don't want to.' Sure? 'Don't want to.' You can draw your own conclusions from this. Class-conscious workers have to be created out of this. Out of tired, dull, contrary mules. It's going to last a long time.[135]

Not only the Labour Party but also the entire working class, insofar as he encountered it, seemed ill prepared for the revolution Eric's understanding of Marxism predestined it to undertake. In the event, at least the outcome of the local elections was a triumph for the Labour Party, which won 457 seats in London, gaining control of eleven councils and holding on to four. In Southwark, to which Borough belonged, Labour gained fifty-two seats, all but one from the anti-socialist Ratepayers' Association: only one non-Labour seat remained, and it was not the one in which Eric had campaigned.[136]

V

Visiting him on 5 May 1934, his cousin Denis told him, rather brutally, that he was as 'ugly as sin, but a mind'.[137] At seventeen, like most boys of his age, Eric was beginning to think about girls. 'One day – if my ugly mug should permit – I'll fall in love. Then I'll be in one of my dilemmas again.'[138] The same choice that faced him between loyalty to his family and loyalty to the cause would, in other words, confront him again if and when he got a girlfriend. But he was somehow 'desperately trying to fall in love – without success, of course'.[139] After coming to England, he had 'almost forgotten that there are intelligent and energetic women, men even, modern women and men – to say nothing of socialists'.

He was overwhelmed when one such 'modern woman' visited the family.[140] But any young woman he saw on the street gave him a good feeling, whether sexual or just of a general nature.[141] However, he had what he himself called an 'inferiority complex' about his looks. 'I am ashamed of my appearance. That sounds stupid and it is too. Nevertheless it's true.' Even in Vienna he had looked in a shop window framed by mirrors and seen his profile for the first time: 'Was I as unattractive as that?'[142] Things would be different 'if my appearance was different'. So he admitted 'that I repress my sexual feelings'.[143]

It was all the more disturbing, then, when some months later, as he was walking across Hyde Park late one night, he was approached by some prostitutes looking for custom. The park was a notorious haunt of street-walkers in the 1930s, and arrests for solicitation were common.[144] 'You will forgive me', he told his diary's imaginary reader an hour and a half or so after the incident, 'if, as an inexperienced and innocent youth of seventeen who hasn't ever so much as touched a woman, I write about it':[145]

If I were not so childish and naïve, I would not have taken it so seriously. But it was odd all the same: a dull excitement, a hesitation as I wavered between the desire to speak with her and go with her, and the consciousness that I didn't have any money and – deep in the background – didn't want Syph[ilis], a feeling between great fear and enormous triumph, that made me shiver. My eyes are shining, I know that. I just remember dimly that I am ugly. I want to speak, and I know that instead of the intended 'aloof' irony what will come out are very hesitant words, as though I were afraid, ... and say in a voice that sounds beery in its artificial nonchalance, quavering, and hidden desire, that I'm afraid I don't have any money and my pockets are empty ... And hardly have I got away, than I realise that I should have taken hold of her right away before I told her I didn't have any money, so that I could at least enjoy it a little bit, and I tremble at the thought that here there are women who – even if only for money – I could have (Comme c'est triste, la jeunesse, says Flaubert).[146]

He felt rather absurd after this encounter, noting how the incident brought out his inferiority complex and how, on reflection, he could regard it coldly and ironically as 'an interesting phenomenon' rather than arouse in him any sympathy for the women or any reflections on the nature of their trade: he was, in the end, simply too young and in this field at least too ignorant for that. But none the less, the experience had clearly disturbed him, releasing desires he was trying to repress.

So much so, indeed, that he went again along the shadowy paths of the park, 'so as to taste the pleasure of hearing "Hello dearie" again – how banal the whores are, they can't even arrange for love without the movie-romantic "lonesome tonight"?'[147] The problem was, he concluded, that his intellectualism stopped him from releasing his instincts – although he noted at the same time that the whole episode had left him sexually excited. As he left the park, stepping into the light of the street-lamps, he felt a sense of relief as he moved among ordinary people once more. He got into a train at Victoria, made his way into a compartment and began to read Bossuet's *Oraison funèbre de très haut et très puissant prince Louis de Bourbon*, a seventeenth-century sermon on the death of the Prince of Condé. 'Wordsworth's "emotion recollected in tranquillity" has a lot going for it', he reflected when considering this incident later, adding: 'Really I'm hugely naïve.'[148]

So he filled his head with Marxism. It would become a substitute for sexual love, something he had not yet experienced in any case.

One must live intensely. Life is too short, whether it lasts for twenty years or eighty, not to pack in as much as possible ... I do my best to live intensely, and with success. So I am training myself to get as much as possible out of my limited personal experience – aesthetically and otherwise – and to enlarge my small experience through books ... My life is too short to squander it on inessentials. I have my 'essential' – let's call it Marxism. And I want to dedicate myself to it. I want to dive into it as into the sea, and drown in it. I want to love it, passionately ... and yet spiritually. Like one loves a woman.[149]

He felt that he was turning his repulsive appearance into a virtue by becoming a Marxist intellectual. 'My neglectfulness in external things is just the psychological reaction to my realization that I'm ugly.' Yet at the same time he tried not to be ashamed of the way he looked. 'I deliberately turn it around and try to be proud of my appearance.' He made a conscious effort actually to look like an intellectual. By focusing on the life of the mind he was conquering his embarrassment, just as he had conquered his shame at being poor by becoming a Communist. He knew he was intelligent, though he also knew he was inexperienced in the world. Thus he posed as a cool, unemotional, cerebral person, an observer without emotion.[150]

Occasionally, of course, there were diversions from reading and schoolwork. In October 1934 his uncle Sidney, who had been in the movie business in Berlin, took him to the Isleworth Studios near Hounslow, a short way from London, to the west, where, in the coming years, technically accomplished films such as *Things to Come* (1936), *The Third Man* (1949) and *The African Queen* (1951) would be made. He noted the contradiction between the studio scenery – a full-scale mock-up of a Spanish inn – and the microphones, floodlights and cameras, with the incongruous sight of a copy of the *Daily Express* lying around on the studio floor. Filmmaking was, he thought, 'a kind of parasitism', fastening on reality and exploiting it, 'without a firm basis' in it. Still, it was 'fascinating'. By contrast, the world of left-wing politics in Britain seemed dull and unimaginative. In the end, politics in Central Europe were more exciting than politics in the United Kingdom. Eric noted with interest the news of Hitler's arrest and execution of the leading brownshirts in Germany, along with some of his former rivals, at the beginning of July 1934 in the so-called 'Night of the Long Knives'. To begin with, at least, he accepted the Nazi propaganda line that the brownshirts had been preparing a putsch, although he found it hard to believe that two of Hitler's victims, former Reich Chancellors Schleicher, who was shot, and Papen, who was packed off to become ambassador in Vienna, had been involved. He did not make the mistake of some Communists in thinking this heralded the end of the Nazi regime.[151] Indeed, he was becoming clear-sightedly pessimistic about the political situation in Europe. The new Popular Front government in Spain, he thought, might equally lead to revolution or to civil war. 'No second Austria!' he hoped, referring to the clerico-fascist coup that had crushed the labour movement in a brief civil war the previous February.[152]

Living in terrible times, with violence and death breaking out all over Europe, one great war in the recent past and, most likely, another in the near future, revolutions and counter-revolutions everywhere, the only moral course, he thought, was to devote oneself to making a better future.[153] He visited with his cousin Ron the home of a young Communist who worked in a left-wing bookshop, his wife, a secretary, and their baby. Their shabby apartment made him realise how modestly most people lived: 'How plutocratic we are in comparison, I thought, and I was ashamed. I should really do twice as much as any proletarian for the cause.'[154] He worked himself into a 'Bolshevik fanaticism' over the next few days. The cause, surely, was all. But in his heart of hearts he knew he would never follow it to the exclusion of everything else. The only hope for the future lay in Communism, so if one did not 'devote oneself completely to the destruction of capitalism, one is therefore a traitor. Conclusion: I am a traitor.'[155]

In the meantime, he continued his reading of the Marxist classics, and in January 1935 bought Karl Marx's *Das Kapital: Volume I* and took it home with a strong feeling of pride, to add to his growing personal library.[156] 'I use Marx etc. both as a textbook,' he wrote, 'and as a kind of logarithmic table. I.e., when something comes up that I want to analyse, and I don't want to take the trouble to think the whole thing through dialectically, I look up the place in Marx and I have a complete and brilliant analysis to hand.'[157] At the age of seventeen, he still lacked the capacity to think critically about Marxism that he developed later in life. Apart from these works of Marxist theory, he amused himself by reading detective stories, and in February 1935 he also focused on drama, taking in plays by Aeschylus, Beaumont and Fletcher, Chapman, Chekhov, Dekker, Dryden, Ford, Heywood, Jonson,

Marston, Massinger, Middleton, Marlowe, O'Neill, Sophocles, Strindberg and Webster, as well as tackling Sterne's *Tristram Shandy* on the side (despite his uncle's attempts to stop him). Webster's *The White Devil* prompted Eric to reflect that the decaying society the playwright depicted had its parallels in his own time.[158]

He was aided in his understanding of early modern English drama by the essays of T. S. Eliot, 'a man who is valuable as a critic every time'.[159] But when it came to obligatory reading, he was repelled by the writings of the 'bourgeois authors (literature excepted)' he was required to read at school. They were all, he declared, a 'waste of paper. That's what they are. Worse still: capitalist propaganda', dull, biased, feeble. Of course, he conceded, there were 'many bad communist books'. 'Even Stalin is no great author compared to Marx' – a verdict that anyone reading the two authors side by side would agree with, but few convinced Communists of the mid-1930s would have dared to pass. Bourgeois writing was only valuable if it 'led the mind onto paths where it could proceed further'. He thought Shaw had this, Plato, Aristotle, Wordsworth and Shelley's prose works, the historian Vinogradoff, and a handful of others. By contrast, even a dull writer like Stalin had something to teach the reader directly because he was applying the Marxist method.[160]

Eric subscribed to the conventional left-wing pantheon of heroic rebels, beginning with Spartacus, who led a slave rebellion in ancient Rome, going on to the medieval English peasant protesters Wat Tyler and John Ball, the Cossack leader Stenka Razin, the Levellers, Irish rebels such as Wolfe Tone, the Chartists, Sinn Fein, striking workers in many countries, and the anarchists Sacco and Vanzetti, executed in the USA in 1927 amidst worldwide demonstrations protesting their innocence of the murder charges on which they had been convicted. His German heroes included the Protestant Anabaptists in Münster, Karl Liebknecht and Rosa Luxemburg, the leaders of the Bavarian Soviet Republic in 1919, and Max Hölz, the ultra-left guerrilla fighter in Saxony in the early 1920s. But heroes, he noted, were to be found all over the world, from India and China to Mexico and Namibia: 'Millions!

Hundreds, thousands of millions. Is this not greater than fretting about your own wants and desires?' One only had to imagine all of the oppressed uniting across the globe to build a better future. 'Man, what a sight! Ah, I'll not likely witness it. Although – I'm seventeen. I give myself to live until I'm forty. That's nearly twenty-three years. More likely thirty to thirty-five. No, I'm not likely to experience the world revolution.'[161]

How, he fantasised, would the revolution come about? The experience of Ireland from 1916 to 1921 had shown how a small, compact, well-organised and well-equipped group enjoying the passive though not the active support of the mass of the population could fight a successful guerrilla war of liberation. It was necessary therefore ('now!') to assemble a group of revolutionaries, train them in sports clubs and similar venues, set up weapons caches, create an effective intelligence network guaranteed free of traitors, and make a list of important buildings and installations to be stormed. And since a revolution could only succeed if it had the mass of the workers on its side, it was necessary to win the proletariat over in advance so that a *coup d'état* could be mounted after the proclamation of a general strike. The railway lines had to be blown up to prevent the government moving troops to the key flashpoints. London had to be cut off from the rest of the country:

Blow up the Great North Road, the Edgware Road, the Great Western, the Southampton, the Croydon, the A20, the Hastings and Eastbourne [roads]. Blow up the railway lines – or occupy them. Blow up some railway bridges and seize the Thames crossings. Blockade the Thames upstream and throw groups [of fighters] into the side-streets to provide backup. At the same time get control of the radio or shut it down, and use your own. Build barricades in all the slum districts (as in Hamburg in 1923, Paris in 1871, Wedding [Berlin] in 1929), and attempt to secure the factories and storm the banks and public buildings. Cut the telegraph and electrical cables if it's impossible to seize the power stations. If there's no other way, blow them up. Blockade the bus and tram lines and as many streets as possible using the transport workers. Of course, that will not stop the soldiers coming to or fro, but it will make it more difficult for them.[162]

The same operations, Eric considered, would have to be carried out in other British cities.

It was possible, of course, that significant parts of the army might defect to the revolutionaries. But even if that did not happen, the armed forces were not going to destroy major public buildings, factories, banks and the like just because they had been occupied. In the end, an effective general strike would cut off the soldiers' supplies and starve them into surrender. 'That might seem unnecessarily bloodthirsty', Eric conceded as he came to the end of his adolescent fantasy of a Bolshevik revolution in the UK, 'but honestly, I have not written this out of a childish delight in adventure. I wanted openly to understand how a successful revolution would take its course, and thereby as far as possible use the experience of other revolutions.' If he had thought for a moment of the fate of the Paris Commune in 1871, destroyed by military force from outside, or the barricades of Hamburg in 1923 and Berlin-Wedding in 1929, dismantled by police, he might not have been quite so boyishly enthusiastic. Years later, when he returned to this subject in a more pessimistic mood born of decades of observation of right-wing military coups, it was the officer corps who appeared to him to be the most likely initiator of a violent seizure of power, though he still thought that it could be defeated by a well-organised popular democratic movement.[163]

As these scenarios suggested, Eric felt his life had degenerated into a routine. 'I read, eat, think, sleep,' he wrote in March 1935. 'Buy books, – Daydream quite a lot. And why not? A little wish-fulfilment – does it hurt? Maybe.'[164] He felt he was 'unable to do anything for school. God knows how the termly exam will fall out.'[165] Like a typical teenager, he felt aimless, uncertain whether to plunge himself into some activity or retreat into an ivory tower. He was dissatisfied with his life and yearned for something different without knowing what it really was. 'I am intelligent, very intelligent, and must my intellectual gifts simply rot away in private use?' He took some solace in the reflections of Vincent Van Gogh, whose feelings, expressed in the letters Eric was reading, were, he felt, similar to his own. But he was frustrated by the knowledge that he could never be an active revolutionary.[166] The poet Arthur Rimbaud made him feel inferior, since he had produced some of his greatest works at the age of eighteen, while Eric felt he had done nothing remarkable by this stage of his life.[167] Meanwhile he continued with his reading, polishing off half a dozen Shakespeare plays in early March along with Coleridge's *Shakespearean Criticism* as well as Chaucer's *Canterbury Tales*, Fielding's *Tom Jones* and *The Satyricon* by Petronius.[168] His list of books read in the last week of March and the first week of April 1935 included Proust, *À l'ombre des jeunes filles en fleurs*, Thomas Mann's *Königliche Hoheit*, the first four books of Milton's *Paradise Lost*, the first fifteen chapters of Boswell's *Life of Dr Johnson*, poems by Wilfred Owen, Donne, Housman, letters by Dryden and Pope, and works by Jean-Paul, Gotthold Lessing, Maupassant and others. Proust, he thought, was difficult because of the individualistic and subjective viewpoint he adopted. He read works by the philosopher David Hume, he read popular biographies of Lenin and he read travel sketches by Dos Passos, clearly thinking of himself when he excerpted the sentence. 'I was a writer, writers are people who stayed on the sidelines as long as they could.'[169]

After several months of concentrating on his schoolwork and examinations, augmented by his private reading, Eric decided to become politically active again. But he did not want any more family rows. He told his uncle and aunt he was visiting his cousin Denis, and whiled away the hours after school by attending a performance of *Hamlet*, starring John Gielgud, who, he thought, was 'very good', though he laid too much emphasis on the character and not enough on the verse.[170] He sat for a while in a teashop, and then made his way towards a late evening Labour Party meeting. It was all very cloak-and-dagger:

I went through the back streets towards Tulse Hill and asked myself whether Aunt Gretl and Uncle Sidney might have been able to spot me through some kind of coincidence. I thought the matter over once again, and again decided logically that my behaviour was absolutely and in every respect justified. Even so, I had a dull, vague feeling that it wasn't right. In the end one has to have a healthy relationship with one's parents or guardian – it doesn't matter which. Certainly it's not difficult to lie to them, and I don't blame myself at all for lying to them, but I would prefer it if I could say to them openly: Listen, I'm going to a meeting, or to a house and garden or something. – Perhaps I was a bit downcast, because I was feeling hot and shaking a bit when I got to the hall.

Eric's experience of the Labour Party at this meeting was no better than at the previous one he had attended. The ward, he noted, was ruled with a rod of iron by Mrs Anstey, 'a nice old lady, with a rosy appearance, and very jovial, but no socialist'. As she read out the list of new members she laid great stress on the need for them all to subscribe to the Labour Party's principles and rules, 'so that no hotheads come into the party'. Otherwise he found the members 'very sympathetic'. It was clear that not much could be done to radicalise them, however. When he got home, his deception had gone unnoticed. He did not go again.

Despite his resentment at the hostility Sidney and Gretl exhibited towards his yearnings for political activism, Eric knew that he lived in a relatively liberal and tolerant household. This, he believed, had a negative as well as a positive side. His aunt, he thought,

suffers from the decline of convention. Not brutal enough systematically to maintain the Victorian atmosphere, too uncertain to grasp for a modern way of bringing us up, she is suspended between the old and the new. She thinks regretfully of her own childhood but doesn't make any systematic attempt to apply the methods used in those days to bring up children. So we don't have an upbringing. The strict background of convention is lacking. It's dead, and we are living in an age of disintegration. Of course we have little respect for the individual. Thus it happens that Nancy and Peter are growing up on their own. Maybe later they'll bring themselves up. Probably not Nancy.

There was something helpless about Sidney and Gretl, Eric felt; they could not work out why they were so unsuccessful. They would have fitted in to society better had they lived forty years earlier.[171]

VI

On Sunday 31 March 1935 Eric set off with his sister, his uncle and aunt, their son Peter and a Czechoslovakian cameraman his uncle knew, on a trip along the south coast, taking in Bognor, Arundel, Littlehampton, Worthing and Brighton. They paddled in the sea at Brighton, where Eric was fascinated by the motion of the waves falling upon the beach.[172] He wanted again to go on a cycling tour with Ron a few weeks later, in the Easter vacation of 1935, but Sidney and Gretl thought it selfish, since none of the rest of the family would be taking a holiday at that time. Moreover, it was going to cost them a good deal of money, especially since this wasn't even his main holiday, only an extra one. Eric pointed out that they had known about the planned holiday for months, so why were they leaving it till the last minute to object? They could treat the sleeping bag they had bought him for £1 as an advance on his birthday present for June. Easter was the only possible time for Ron to take time off work, and they were welcome to treat it as Eric's principal holiday, too, and leave him at home when they went away for a summer break. The kernel of the dispute lay, however, in the fact that Eric was receiving a scholarship worth £8 a term from the school, which he was putting into a post office savings account and regarded as his own. Sidney and Gretl wanted him to save it all up and not draw from it to spend on holidays. It would be essential if he was to go to university, and would lessen the financial burden this would impose on them. Such a small sum, Eric countered, would go nowhere near to covering his expenses at university: he needed another scholarship, preferably a substantial one. Taking out a couple of pounds for a holiday was neither here nor there. He was not going to give up buying books with his modest pocket money either. Eric remained unrepentant. In the end, they let him go.[173]

The boys set off to the South West, reaching Salisbury on 18 April, then Shaftesbury and Sherborne, and so to Yeovil and Crewkerne, in pouring rain. There was hardly any traffic but by the time they arrived at their seaside campsite at Dunscombe Manor in Sidmouth they were wet through. They spent the next few days lazing around (Eric reading, of course) or undertaking short trips. Sidney and Gretl must have relented, for on Easter Saturday, 20 April 1935, they drove down to visit the boys with Nancy and Peter. The weather improved, and when the sun shone Eric and Ron walked along the coast, clambered around on the cliffs, or lay on top of them looking at the sea. When it rained they lay in the tent talking, or reading: Eric worked his way through the metaphysical poets, Marvell, Donne, Herbert and others. 'Ron was always asking questions about farming, about share-fishing, about road building, about everything' and 'about England and life'.[174] Towards the end of their holiday Ron again managed to persuade some fishermen to take them out in their boat. At dawn they made their way to the flinty village of Beer, embarking at six in the morning. At first Eric was seasick, but the sea was calm, and the boys spent an idle day sunning themselves, chatting with the fishermen and eating the rations the men gave them.

Two days later they were cycling back. During their afternoon break they talked about Thomas Hardy, Dostoevsky, Gogol and Shakespeare's *King Lear*, they discussed whether preparations were being made for war, and, travelling along what was obviously a Roman road, they compared Roman civilisation with medieval. Eric was excited to discover Tolpuddle, the site of the famous nineteenth-century dispute that had created the 'Tolpuddle martyrs', heroes of the labour movement. At Eric's prompting they made a detour through the New Forest, reaching its borders at midnight, the road lined with huge trees. Following Ron, Eric thought he looked like Mephisto with his bicycle cape and the yellow glow of his dynamo lamp before him. Occasionally a car would come towards them, and they dismounted so as not to be dazzled by its headlamps. By one in the morning they were out of the forest. 'The night had lost much of its beauty.' They were tired and in a bad mood. At half past two they finally gave up, went into a nearby field, unfurled their groundsheets and fell asleep. Woken two hours later by the dawn chorus, they ate some sausage ('never has a breakfast tasted worse') and made their way onwards. 'At six in the morning', Eric remarked, 'Winchester looks very nice.' A few miles further on, they found a field, unrolled their sleeping bags and fell fast asleep. Waking at eleven, they cycled onwards, the next day smelling the smoke and petrol of London. 'Proud of our tan', Eric wrote at the conclusion of his narrative, 'we arrive at Uncle Harry's.'[175]

Eric was lucky that nothing had gone wrong with the bicycles. A few months later, he was on a ride with his cousin Ron through Amersham and Great Missenden, admiring the rolling hills of the Chilterns, when his chain came adrift and could not be put back on again. Luckily two schoolfriends (George and 'Bilge') came past by chance on a motorbike, stopped and fixed it. 'I have always hugely admired mechanical skill. They came to us like guardian angels or literally a *Deus ex machina*.'[176] The impractical nature that had already annoyed his father stayed with him throughout his life. Using up almost every spare minute in reading, he did not fit in well to the household of his uncle and aunt. He loved and admired them both, but there were frequent rows, and he was finding it 'actually almost impossible to live peacefully with U[ncle] S[idney]. I've really made an effort not to offend these past few days but it simply hasn't worked.' Tiny things caused by his clumsiness, like dropping a spoon, led to one row after another. It would be better, he felt, if he lived on his own and only visited them occasionally. In harbouring such thoughts he was in the end not very different from many eighteen-year-old boys. Nor did he get on with his sister Nancy, and found it best they kept out of each other's hair. For her part, Nancy resented the fact that her brother's reputation as a brilliant student made people expect great things of her as well. She was not interested in academic subjects and frequently missed school to go to matinées at the local cinema, chain-smoking and eating sweets instead of studying.[177] Eric had just as little to do with his cousin Peter, Sidney and Gretl's son, who also lived in the house. By his late teens his interests – artistic, literary, intellectual, academic, political – had created a gulf between his world and the more conventional one inhabited by Nancy and Peter that would never be closed.[178]

As he cycled to school every weekday he saw the workers streaming into the factories or cycling to work alongside him, railwaymen on their way to begin the day. On a Saturday afternoon, as he passed along Praed Street, near Paddington Station, he had the opportunity to observe the working class in its leisure time: the young men in their cheap suits, their girls, powdered and with permed hair, the older men coming in and out of the pubs, children in dirty clothes playing in the sooty alleys, teenage boys trying their first cigarette, young men arm-in-arm with their girls, in their cheap dresses with their cheap jewellery on their way into cheap cinemas. 'Rough, brutalized by their milieu, undernourished and weakly, they are still – and I'm not speaking politically – more "human beings" than the people I know.' The bourgeoisie of his acquaintance were, he felt, artificial, stilted: the proletariat was more direct, more genuine. It was strange, he felt, that he had built his political views on a class of which he had not the slightest personal experience and not one of whose members he actually knew. Years were to pass before Eric was to encounter real English proletarians, and, when he finally did, he found their culture and morals rather shocking.

VII

On 10 May 1935 Sidney and Gretl rented a house at 25 Handel Close, Edgware, in north London.[179] The move to Edgware meant that Eric had to give up his membership of the Norwood branch of the Labour Party. He joined the Edgware branch instead, which was full of 'labour aristocrats who live on the council estates'.[180]

He remained, however, very much the detached intellectual. 'Intellectuals', he decided, 'are the chorus in the great drama of class struggle.'[181] Their role was not to take part in the action, but, as in a play in ancient Greece, to comment on it, even if from a standpoint that was far removed from neutrality: more Euripides than Aeschylus, perhaps. Yet while the chorus in a Greek play was powerless to affect the action, the intellectual in the twentieth century was not. It was his role to give a voice to those who engaged directly in the class struggle. Above all, it was important to defend the Soviet Union. As the world's only socialist state, it had to be preserved so that eventually it could spread revolution across the globe. For this, 'one must forgive the Comintern a great deal'.[182] Revolutionaries, he felt, had to be 'totally unscrupulous and outrageously flexible' in their tactics. This meant among other things allying with other political movements so far as necessary.[183] At this time, Eric was still very much rooted in Party orthodoxy. In 1935 he gave his cousin Ron a copy of Stalin's *History of the Communist Party of the Soviet Union (Bolsheviks) Short Course* for his birthday, with the dedication: 'To Ron from Eric. With luck, you and I will see this kind of story written in the same terms about England. In the hope that it may not be too long and help you make the waiting shorter. Eric, 20 July 1935'. Ron remained unconvinced – the book is not annotated and was not even faintly dog-eared – and stayed a lifelong supporter of the Labour Party.[184] Their discussions and debates were not all politics, however: along with the *Short Course*, Eric also gave Ron the collected works of Harold Monro, one of the so-called Georgian poets of the early twentieth century whose lyrical verses often breathed a strong sense of nostalgia. 'For remembrance', Eric wrote as a dedication: 'for looking forward. If possible, the latter – I don't think we can afford very much of the first. But if we do take the luxury – well, let's commit the great sin and be sentimental for a while. Hoping you will not follow the advice.'[185]

At the same time, however, Eric was developing a new interest alongside his incessant, prodigious reading, his love of nature and his self-fashioning as a Communist intellectual. In 1934 he had been introduced to jazz by his cousin Denis. Born on 16

November 1916, so only a few months older than Eric, Denis had been brought up by his mother, since his father had abandoned him and his sister when he was very young. At the time he met Eric he had left school and was earning money by playing the viola, in which he had professional tuition, but he was something of a drifter and spent much of his time listening to and thinking about jazz, following an enthusiasm first kindled when he attended a Louis Armstrong performance in London in 1932. Denis was, in Eric's words, a young man of 'medium height, black over-lacquered hair, a half-cheeky smile, a vertical line between his eyebrows, large mouth, broken tooth ... excessively bitten nails'. He lived in Sydenham, south London, 'in an attic room in the blackish house of his mother ... It was furnished with a large bed, some Victorian chairs and various occasional tables and containers made from packing-cases, over one of which he had pasted a gallery of photographs', mostly of jazzmen. 'The gramophone stood on a small barrel and we kept our spirits up by emptying tins of sweetened thick condensed milk and [eating] fish and chips.'[186]

Denis came round to the house in Norwood frequently. They discussed with Gretl who was the best classical violinist in the world – the experienced Fritz Kreisler or the youthful prodigy Yehudi Menuhin.[187] Sidney and Gretl's house in Edgware was equipped with a radio, on which Eric listened to jazz music when he could; it would drive him crazy, he thought, if he didn't have such a thick skin.[188] Denis brought round jazz records which they played on an old gramophone, pushing a rolled-up pair of socks down the amplifying horn so as not to disturb the rest of the house at night, listening to Louis Armstrong while drinking condensed milk and smoking cigarettes.[189] At the same time, however, Eric did not neglect classical music. He listened to Mozart and found his music reached the depths of his soul.[190] Music in general, he thought, was the most abstract and perhaps also the purest of the arts, speaking to the emotions more directly than literature.[191]

In March 1935 Denis took Eric to hear Duke Ellington at the Palais de Danse in Streatham. Ellington's tour of Britain in 1933 had been an outstanding success, his concerts attended by the social elite, including the Prince of Wales.[192] So the Streatham show was an eagerly anticipated event. As Eric and Denis arrived,

> people were streaming in to it from all sides (though it was late) but though many of them may have been jazz enthusiasts we preferred to think they weren't, because it is pleasant to have one's passion for hot music not shared by too many others. We walked through the men and the girls (it was the first time I'd ever been to a Palais de Danse which seemed like a cheap reprint of Babylon) with contempt in our hearts. I daresay we were romanticising the nice South London girls and their partners, who were not unusually depraved ... We clapped the Duke and his combination as they came out on to the stage. We clapped steadily and blindly, getting ourselves ready to accept the rhythm of the music, which is a silly way to listen to jazz incidentally; but we knew no better. We followed every one of the players, whose names and peculiarities we knew, watched them sit down, it almost made us hold our breath with hero-worship. When they began to play we stamped our feet rather deliriously, our eyes hooked to the soloists.[193]

For his part, Denis declared to Eric that he would like to learn Marxism. Eric had his doubts. 'If there's anyone who's absolutely un-Marxist, it's D. He'll be an emotional socialist all his life, or somesuch. But at the same time as he's a Marxist and wants to strengthen his command of theory, he also wants to climb into the upper classes ... Oh you, my Marxist!'[194] But even if Denis failed to become a Marxist, he had succeeded in kindling in Eric what was to be a lifetime's enthusiasm for jazz.

Eric's books were stored in the garage but he managed to unpack a volume of Baudelaire, whose poetry he liked not only because of its technical mastery of the French language but also because it dealt with urban life rather than with nature, even though it was the negative aspects of big city society that were brought out in these verses. 'The cult of prostitutes is a very bourgeois-intellectual thing', Eric noted, perhaps thinking of the fascination he had felt during his nocturnal encounters in Hyde Park.[195] On 20 May he unpacked all the books, ruthlessly foisting those he did not want any more on Nancy and Peter, who doubtless had little or no interest in any of them. He ordered his personal library under four headings: politics and history, literature and criticism, natural history and miscellaneous.[196] He read Chekhov's letters, which made him 'forget that I'm living in the year 1935; that Hitler gave a speech yesterday; that the English Parliament has tripled the size of the Royal Air Force; that Italy is threatening to swallow up Abyssinia'. His reading at this time consisted almost entirely of French literature; there is little mention of Marxist texts, and none at all of history books except for Lytton Strachey's *Eminent Victorians*. When not reading, he went for walks by the Edgware lake, where he saw a large owl, and Regent's Park, where he admired the tulips; in the summer he swam in the lake, which he found rather cold.[197]

By June 1935 Eric had moved on from French literature to the Romantics, notably the radical poet Percy Bysshe Shelley and the German fabulist E. T. A. Hoffmann. At the same time he was also reading Stendhal's *La Chartreuse de Parme* (*The Charterhouse of Parma*, 1839). School books had to be bought, and he purchased editions of Cicero, Virgil, Gibbon's *Decline and Fall of the Roman Empire*, volume 1, plays by the Restoration writers Congreve, Vanbrugh, Farquhar and Wycherley and the letters of the seventeenth-century Marquise de Sévigné, but he also worked his way through the selected correspondence of Marx and Engels.[198] Thus at more or less the same time, at the age of seventeen, he was reading intensively in English, French, German and Latin. The catalogue continued after his eighteenth birthday with Goethe's letters, Villon's poems, verses by the obscure Austrian poet Georg Trakl and plays by the rather better known Austrian dramatist Johann Nestroy, a history of Italy, and a bit of Dante.[199] He was pleased to return to German poetry, and covered page after page of his diary with reflections on it. Within a few weeks he was also tackling the first volume of Proust's huge novel sequence *À la recherche du temps perdu*, Machiavelli's *The Prince* and Thomas Hobbes's *Leviathan*.[200] George Bernard Shaw, Gerard Manley Hopkins, Edward Thomas and

Thomas Hardy were added to the list by late July.[201] As a Marxist he felt that 'every work of art is a social document', but this did not stop him enjoying poems, plays and novels as works of art in themselves.[202] Political and literary interests merged when he came to read Mikhail Sholokhov's 1934 novel *And Quiet Flows the Don*, 'absolutely one of the most important novels of the twentieth century'. It was 'the first example known to me of a successful socialist novel'.[203] By September 1935 he was reading *Seven Pillars of Wisdom*, T. E. Lawrence's account of his part in the Arab revolt against the Ottomans during the First World War, as well as continuing with Stendhal and sampling French poets such as Rimbaud and Villon.[204] In mid-November he bought more Stendhal as well as the moralist Sainte-Beuve and poems by Rilke and Walther von der Vogelweide.[205] He read Elizabeth Bowen's *The House in Paris*, published in 1926, and found it 'watered-down Proust, absolutely nothing original'.[206]

In early December 1934 Llewellyn Smith, impressed by Eric's abilities, had already advised him to apply for a scholarship to Balliol College, Oxford.[207] Eric had agreed, although he was already irritated by the fact that he was treated at school as 'a kind of miraculous animal, so that people point to me and say "Well, he knows a lot more than the others", etc. etc.' Still, he wrote, 'I already see myself in Oxford. How childish, and yet how agreeable, these fantasies are.'[208] In July 1935 he took the Higher School Examination, in which a pass was required in order to proceed to university. He gained a Distinction in history and another in Latin, a solid pass in English, and a pass in French 'with Special Credit in the oral Examination'.[209] He decided to take history at university because it was clear he was good at it. Llewellyn Smith guided him through the practicalities of the application process which, as Eric noted later, 'was vital for a boy from a family that had never sent anyone to university, and for whom Oxbridge was as unknown as Tibet; actually more unknown, because I had read some books by a Swedish explorer about Tibet'.[210]

But, for reasons that are unclear, it was not Balliol College, Oxford, but King's College, Cambridge, for which he sat the

entrance examination in history, in December 1935: if Llewellyn
Smith thought in the end that the well-known liberal atmosphere
of King's would suit Eric better than the stuffy conservatism of
Balliol, then he was right. Eric spent much if not most of his time
in October and November revising for the exam; during these
weeks the previously regular and imposing enumerations of the
French novels and poems on his 'reading chronicle' (*Lesechronik*)
disappeared from his diary though he still managed to read
Hemingway's *A Farewell to Arms*, about the Italian front in the First
World War, Horace McCoy's novel *They Shoot Horses, Don't They?*
about dance marathons in the Depression in the USA, Michael
Fessier's gothic *Fully Dressed and in His Right Mind*, a bit of Karl
Kraus and various detective novels, all much lighter fare than he
was used to consuming.[211] With examinations looming, Eric began
to include history books on his reading lists, though he disliked the
element of learning facts and dates by rote and approached the
subject more as a Marxist than as an historian: 'It doesn't matter
much if I know one date more or less, so long as I'm clear about
the main stages of development.' Even at school he was starting to
map out the principal features of the transition from feudalism to
capitalism, a problem that would become a lifelong obsession.[212]
He had perforce to learn at least some basic historical facts. His
schoolwork demanded he read Lord Acton's *Lectures on Modern
History*, put together by his students from the notes of the great
but little-published Oxford historian from his lectures, the French
Revolution specialist J. M. Thompson's *Lectures on Foreign History*,
and works about Luther and Calvin.'[213] Of Acton he said: 'that is
exactly the kind of history that is no good'.[214]

   But at this stage he had no thought of becoming a professional
historian. 'I see myself in future – Hobsbawm the fiery orator. E.
J. H. the celebrated author. E. J. H. the cold-blooded, energetic
organiser, the philosopher. Then I'm embarrassed because I'm
so childish and let my imagination run away from me.' It did not
run in the direction of history or academia.[215] By November he
felt confident that he had expanded his knowledge of English and
European history and was well prepared for the examination.

'I'm ready to roll.'[216] He went to Cambridge in December, sat the entrance examination and was interviewed by Christopher Morris, a lifelong Kingsman and expert on Tudor political thought. Morris was famous for the close attention he paid to his students, even sending candidates lengthy lists of the books they needed to read in preparation for the scholarship examination. A notorious contrarian himself, he was also well known for appreciating undergraduates with unconventional views, and clearly thought very highly of Eric, who was awarded a Foundation Scholarship worth £100 a year, roughly half the average national wage for the time, and more than enough to live off as a student, to start in October 1936. Oxford and Cambridge were still sufficiently influential in British life for *The Times* to publish a list of those who had won scholarships every year, and, true to form, Eric's name was included in the list as 'E. J. E. Obsbawm'.[217]

Even before he took the examination, Eric was outgrowing the Hobsbaum household. In September 1935 he recorded in his diary his frustration at being treated like a child, his uncle's nervousness and the tedium of home life.[218] He was looking forward to building his own life. 'You are a person of the second rank', he told himself: 'You are above normal, below genius level. You're talented, no more than that.' The consciousness of being little more than 'an average person' rather than a hidden genius was deeply frustrating.[219] Only by striking out on his own could he become truly more than average. At the same time, Eric decided to stop writing his diary. He no longer felt any need for it. Rereading it, he found some entries not bad at all, but others were soppy (*kitschig*) and immature. 'I chucked my feelings onto this rubbish bin partly in order to get rid of them, partly in order to strike a pose.'[220] He no longer needed it now that he had won a scholarship to Cambridge and could look forward to at least three years of freedom. Perhaps, too, he did not need to confide in his diary because for the first time he had 'an acquaintance I made myself rather than pulling him parasitically out of other people's pockets'. This was Kenneth Syers, a young left-winger he had evidently met when they were up for interview at Cambridge, where their shared political beliefs, unusual among candidates for entry, obviously forged a bond between them. Their acquaintance was to come back to haunt Syers during the war.

For all these reasons Eric was feeling optimistic about the future. He was now no longer going to live 'second-hand' but would experience life directly, for himself. Of course, he warned himself, 'I am in the 20th century and know nothing is certain. And I don't otherwise have such a hopeful disposition. As hard as it is, I won't harbour any illusions.' But if, he told himself, he 'remorsefully returned and scribbled again your mess of tirades, stylistic exercises, criticisms and catalogues then you know you'll look ridiculous'. He signed off as 'Eric John Ernest Hobsbawm, a tall, angular, slim, ugly blond chap eighteen and a half years of age, with a gift for quick understanding, extensive if also superficial general knowledge', a 'Poseur' who occasionally revealed his sensuality in the appreciation of art and nature, 'egoistical, deeply unsympathetic to some people, simply laughable to others, the majority. He wants to become a revolutionary but for the moment doesn't have any talent for organization; he wants to become a writer but has neither the creative strength nor the energy. He has hope but not so much faith.' Eric knew his faults well enough. He told himself that he was 'vain and conceited. He is a coward. He loves nature very much. And he is forgetting the German language.' He did not know if he would ever keep a diary again, but until then it was goodbye. 'E. J. E. ends how he began: second-hand (very). FOR THE MOMENT (very much) THAT'S IT.'[221]

VIII

A year before he went up to Cambridge, in the late summer of 1935, Eric's uncle Sidney asked him if he would like to accompany him to Paris for a few days while he pursued his business interests there.[222] They took the boat train from Victoria on Monday 2 September, returning on Sunday 8 September. While Sidney was busy attending business meetings and working dinners, Eric embarked on a vigorous round of sightseeing.[223] Writing in his school magazine after his return to London, he described going for a walk up the rue de la Gaité, in Montparnasse, where he

> looked into the art dealers' shops, and felt very pleased with myself whenever I guessed a painter correctly. There were art dealers everywhere, and between them grocers' stalls with dirty young men in berets yelling out the price of bananas. It was all very narrow and dirty and picturesque, and I felt quite romantic and had to stop myself from becoming too much so. So this is Montparnasse, I said to myself, and thought how nice it would be to live here.[224]

On second thoughts, however, the dirt was off-putting: 'there were bugs', he had been told. So he walked on, to the Jardin du Luxembourg, where he sat down and watched the nannies talking and the children playing. At the Sainte-Chapelle he looked up at the arches and pillars: 'They were slim and reached for the sky like plants growing in the dark, and the saints stood stiff and glowing, red, green and yellow, in the great blue stained-glass windows.' In Montmartre he admired the Church of the Sacred Heart, 'gleaming like soft gold in the morning, pale, with the whole town at its feet, gaunt, grey, irregular blocks of flats with the shadows playing scales in between, and somewhere in the mist, the Seine'. On his way, a man in the Metro tried to speak to him, 'but I couldn't understand and was very embarrassed'. Montmartre was already a tourist trap in the 1930s, 'and the cinemas were very dear, much dearer than in England'. The clothes sold there were 'cheap, shoddy'. Travelling out of Paris by bus, he found Versailles another tourist trap, but admired the palace, 'the Hall of Mirrors and the King's bedroom, in spite of the Americans'. 'They charged a ridiculous price there for a glass of orangeade', he complained.

But he left a good deal out from his essay in the school magazine. After the excursion to Versailles, Eric returned to Paris and made his way to a well-known music hall, the Casino de Paris, where he had high expectations of the variety show, having read about the Folies Bergère, as he confided to his diary:

I expected wit and humour, and I expected naked women (mostly because of the sexual stimulation). I was disappointed. The showiness of the scenery and costumes too often exceeded artistic tastefulness. There was almost no wit, because the show was mainly designed for people from the provinces. The naked women were what I was most curious about. But there wasn't much new there. Nothing obscene exhibited in the Casino de Paris came close to the ordinary obscenity we were familiar with from American films. Of course every now and then 'you got a thrill'. In the really big numbers it was almost impossible to think of such things, however. I used to think the male body more beautiful than the female. I've changed my mind. I've never seen anything so beautiful as the nude number. For fifty minutes I was able to study the female body in all its poses – and it was more beautiful than the finest statue.[225]

Of course, Eric was aware of the fact that he had little real opportunity to experience the seamy and immoral side of Paris, for which the city was so famous. He did, however, enjoy watching the women walking along the boulevards, and admired the sophistication of their make-up, while regretting 'the lack of beautiful legs'. He wandered around the shabbier parts of town after dark, observing the girls standing at the street corners, the glimmering gaslights, the dimly lit staircases visible through half-open doors leading onto the street. 'Except for the romantic painter, sad, dreary and boring for everyone else, not repulsive, just tedious.'

Paris was more agreeable than London, he concluded, however, even if London was more imposing. He fell in love with the city. From now on, cycling holidays with Ron were over. Eric made every effort to return to Paris in the summer months. The city was also politically exciting for him. Paris had the only labour movement outside the Soviet Union that gave cause for optimism. In May 1936 the Popular Front struck what Eric and many others thought of as a massive blow against the advance of fascism, winning elections in both France and Spain and forming a strongly left-wing government in both countries. This triumph had been accompanied by a wave of euphoria on the Left, seeming to many to herald the coming of a real social revolution. Two months later Eric was able to experience the excitement for himself when he went to Paris for three months on a grant from London County Council to improve his French, before he went up to Cambridge.

His reasons for going were most likely mixed. Apart from the ostensibly academic purpose of the visit, the activity helped him overcome the depression into which he had sunk back at home over the Christmas vacation and which recurred at intervals again over the next few months. His depression was caused by the fact that his aunt Gretl, to whom he was very close, had developed a stomach tumour 'as big as a fist' early in 1936. It was diagnosed as inoperable. She died in June that year. 'Sidney took me to see her corpse in bed in the old Hampstead General Hospital', Eric wrote later. 'Hers was the first dead body I had ever seen.' He had been able to talk to her about his problems, even about sex, and she had given him the motherly love he had so badly needed after the death of his parents. Life at home was not the same without her. Paris, where he arrived shortly after Gretl's death, would distract him from his grief, or at least so he hoped.[226]

'I'm in a country', he wrote to his cousin Ron on 5 July 1936, shortly after he reached Paris,

where the capitalists really hate and fear the Communists, and where the Communists, Socialists and the other Leftwingers are looking forward – really looking forward, mind you, not just theoretically – to socialism. Need I insist on how refreshing this atmosphere is for a would-be Marxist who through goodness knows how many months – three years and a quarter to be exact – has done his best to hang on to his Communism in a country where there still exists no adequate translation of 'Capital'?[227]

Twelve days into his stay, he told Ron, he had spoken to a variety of people, including 'a Communist unemployed, an old Communist gardener, a stay-in striker, a worker, a Communist at the cinema, a radical-socialist student, a croix-de-feu [fascist] student, my landlady, her husband, her son (all of the Right)', and his uncle's agent, who was a Communist. He had observed a small demonstration of the Croix-de-Feu and noted that 'the Right has its flats beflagged and wears cocaides [*sic*]'. He had noted placards and posters and read a range of newspapers from the Communist *Humanité* to the far-right *Action Française*. He warned Ron, however, that all this was a very small sample, and he was to tell him if he started to indulge in sweeping generalisations about French politics on the basis of such slender evidence.

Eric found the political atmosphere in Paris extremely heady in these early weeks of the Popular Front government. The political frustrations of the previous years had vanished and the danger of a fascist coup, most clearly evident in right-wing disturbances in Paris in 1934, had receded. 'The Communists are very confident', he told Ron, 'shockingly so. Of course they recognise very great difficulties, but they are quite certain – those I've met haven't even bothered to grow passionate about it – that their day is coming. "We've waited long enough", as the young unemployed told me.' A general strike launched immediately after the election had resulted in major legislative improvements in conditions of work, known as the Matignon Agreements, but even in July some people still had not returned to work. The Popular Front was putting into effect many imaginative schemes of social welfare and cultural reform. Eric found it encouraging that 'the small bourgeoisie is definitely ranged with the working-class', an assertion for which he found evidence in his conversation with the gardener, who had amended the nineteenth-century radical Pierre-Joseph Proudhon's famous dictum 'property is theft' to the more petty-bourgeois '*la grande propriété, c'est le vol*', 'big property is theft'. It was in other words 'monopoly capital' that aroused his ire and that, Eric supposed, of the rest of the lower middle class. As for the fascist leagues, 'as far as I can judge by the tricolour buttonholes and rosettes they are almost exclusively of the upper classes', perhaps, he thought, 45 per cent of them students, 35 per cent upper-class women, 7 per cent school-boys, 12 per cent businessmen, and maybe 1 per cent workers. The socialist press had estimated that 55 per cent of the flats in Neuilly ('the posh suburb, society lives there') hung fascist flags out of their windows. There were very few in the working-class districts.

There were, of course, other dangers. There were some elements in the Socialist Party that wanted to expel the Communists from the Popular Front ('bloody fools') and on the other hand there were the 'revolution-mongers of the Trotsky gang who find nothing better to do than to try to provoke risings & riots among strikers'. The fascist leagues were 'well-armed and in possession of key posts in the Services'. In this situation the Communists needed the petty-bourgeoisie. If the French Communists started agitating for the creation of soviets, the abolition of private property and the estab-lishment of collective farms, 'we'd have a successful fascist coup in a couple of months' time'. Avoiding this line was 'a model exposition of Marxist tactics, which may, if we're lucky, come off', as it had done in the end after all the twists and turns of Bolshevik tactics in Russia in 1917. Eric was reassured by the young unemployed man that there was no danger of a military coup, since France's conscript soldiers were all workers, too, a fact which prompted him to think that conscription was on balance a good idea. As for the threat of war, Eric confessed, 'I still think the war-danger is as great as ever, but here one is not very anxious'.

On 13 July 1936, Eric went to a rally in the Buffalo Stadium (a velodrome in Paris) to hear the Communist leader Maurice Thorez advising the workers not to ask for too much too soon, or they would frighten off the bourgeoisie, as they had done in 1848. It was raining all the time, but the eighty thousand people present did not seem to mind.

> They sat in tiers all around the stadium, it was getting dark, and the loud-speakers gave out revolutionary songs. Then they would stop for a little and you would hear, through the dusk, on the other side of the stadium, a crowd shouting 'les Soviets partout', but it sounded like whispering, after the loudspeakers. And then another crowd, a little further on, would take up the slogan, and then another, and it would be thrown from one to

another, and suddenly more than half the stadium would be shouting 'les Soviets partout'; then it would change to 'Liberez Thälmann', or to 'Doriot au poteau' – Doriot is the renegade Communist who has founded a 'Popular Party' supported by big money. There was no discipline. People would leave their seats and go out on the lawn to watch the dances or the orators at close range, and then they would stream back again. They had built a large platform on which the spotlights played and the rest of the stadium was like a large bowl, the sides of which were plastered with a vaguely moving dark mass. Someone from the Opera gave a recital of songs of French Revolutions and when he came to the Carmagnole everyone started singing too, very softly. Suddenly on the lawn some people joined hands and formed a circle and began to dance round. Soon others joined and in a few minutes there was a huge circle of men, women and children whirling and swaying round in the dusk while the crowds on the tiers sang louder and louder and the beams of the search-lights lit up the singer on the platform and then a vague silvery glow over the heads of the people who stood round in a compact mass. And by the time the singer came to the bit 'Ça ira, ça ira, les bourgeois à la lanterne ou leur cassera la gueule' ('we'll knock their heads in'), the whole seventy-odd thousand were yelling for all they were worth and the dancers in the circle were whirling at a wild speed.[228]

Then the music stopped and everyone returned to their seats. Thorez spoke, there were pageants, and there were brief talks on the great revolutionary names of French history (would the English Left ever sing songs about Milton or Tom Paine, Eric wondered), and then there were more songs until the band struck up the Internationale, the hymn of international socialism since the late nineteenth century, and the whole crowd yelled out the words with fists raised and clenched.

Eric and other comrades on their way home from the rally carried on singing revolutionary songs in the Metro until everyone in the carriage took up the refrain 'and we all yelled and grinned at each other and shouted slogans and gave cheers for the Communist Party and the Young Communists and the Popular Front. At the stations we could hear the songs from the other cars.' By contrast, the tradition of dancing in the streets on the night of 13–14 July seemed to Eric rather tame, as couples gyrated listlessly and without enthusiasm to the music of small bands ensconced in little booths at key crossings and junctions. Perhaps it was because the weather was bad, or because it was late (Eric thought it was a vulgar error to think that the French stayed up later than the English).

Naturally, a Parisian street looks much more lively than one in London, but even so, by midnight there are only comparatively few people about, a few prostitutes who have not found a client, a few latecomers from theatres, a few late strollers and one or two people finishing their coffee or drink in or before the cafés ... The more I see of people here the more I am convinced that this is a perfectly normal town with a large majority of perfectly ordinary and on the whole very sympathetic people ... Whenever at dusk I see all the concierges and small shopkeepers take a chair and sit on the pavement before their house or shop to watch the sunset and to chat with their neighbours I think with a shudder of our own suburban streets and slums and the nightly pilgrimage to the pictures.

English cinema, he added in parenthesis, was 'more like a kind of dope than a form of entertainment'. Still, for all the let-down after the event, the rally at the velodrome was a heady, intoxicating political experience for a nineteen-year-old. Nothing like it was to be found in Britain. It filled Eric with a hope and enthusiasm he had not been able to find at home.

Uncle Sidney had come on business to Paris and Eric had gone in the evening to view the dancing in front of the Comic Opera, then the Stock Exchange, the Porte St Denis and finally the rue Montmartre. The bands playing in each square 'were just as tinny and enthusiastic as was necessary', bunting was strung across the streets along with red, white and blue light bulbs, and people from every social background were there, all dancing with one another. Eric had a go. 'In practice, as I found, a knowledge of the steps was unnecessary. All you had to do was to go up to anyone you liked and ask her and then step in vague rhythm and leave the rest to luck.' The whole formed a 'swaying mass of many colours, like a field of flowers with wind over it. On the outskirts they danced singly, men and girls. They stepped in rhythm and swung their arms and their hips and laughed quietly and the others stood around and beat the time on the pavements and on the backs of chairs and smiled too.' By the time he had extricated himself the last metro had gone and he had to walk home, which took about an hour, stopping to dance again at the Louvre. On the way he fell in with a group of American students, 'delightful fellows, college-boys' who asked him what to do on 14 July 'and I – quite the old Parisian – told them'. He finally reached home at half past two in the morning.[229]

The next day, Bastille Day, saw, in Eric's words, 'the most aston-ishing, the finest, the greatest and the most impressive afternoon of my experience'. His uncle Sidney's friends arrived at his hotel and bundled them into a taxi, then after a quickly consumed lunch they got onto a lorry, equipped with a ciné-camera (somehow Sidney and his friends had managed to get themselves appointed as the official camera unit of the Socialist Party). 'Can you imagine', Eric asked Ron, 'a million people on the streets quite crazy with joy? Absolutely dead drunk with the consciousness of their unity and their strength?' They sang the Carmagnole and shouted anti-fascist slogans, particularly at a fascist sitting on his balcony with a 'faded but majestic banner' hung over the edge, like a Roman senator contemplating the barbarians as they invaded the Imperial capital. Elsewhere red flags were hanging from the balconies alongside the tricolour as the crowd went by, 'hundreds of thousands of them, with red flowers in their buttonholes or red ties or Phrygian bonnet badges or soviet stars. 'A train passed on the elevated way and the driver leant out and raised both fists and the conductor hung out and the passengers hung out ... of the windows and held up their fists and yelled themselves delirious.'

Perched on the lorry, Eric, Sidney and their friends 'had the best view of all'. They filmed the march of the trade unions, from transport men to civil servants, and 'the miners in their blue blouses and leather hats', 'some shuffling, some marching, none in step', as they passed holding banners aloft and singing the Internationale, the songs overlapping with one another, 'their fists stretched up till the joints ached'.

> The ex-servicemen came and the organisations of officers and N.C.Os in reserve, in uniforms, with their chests streaked and plated with decorations marching in step and saluting solemnly when the crowd clapped them and sang the song of the 17th regiment (which, some twenty-odd years ago, refused to charge strikers). Some raised their fists. They all marched in step, little puckered men with brown skins like the bark of trees and big oxen of men with shoulders like bulls and very solemn. The 'mutilés de la guerre'[230] came pushing before them a bathchair with a man who was blind and maimed and who held up a withered arm with a hand which was brown like parchment and dry and twisted as though he had touched a high-tension wire. Not a fist, just a twisted web of skin and bone which stuck out incongruously at an angle of thirty degrees from under his blanket as though he was holding a cigarette.

> Then came the Moroccans, Tunisians and Algerians in factory groups, holding up the red flag with Muslim green in one corner, marching 'with little fierce steps', shouting 'les soviets partout', men of all colours from pasty white to dark brown, wearing little berets or paper fezzes, raising their fists jerkily and staring with 'wildly fanatic eyes. I have never seen anything like them. If anywhere on that day there were people who were in deadly earnest it was the 5000 or so North Africans.' There were Young Communists and Socialists, women, provincials, workers' sports societies, even 'intellectuals and lawyers'. All of them marched past the tribune where the Socialist Prime Minister Léon Blum, the Communist leader Maurice Thorez and other leading members of the Popular

Front stood, and raised their fists as Blum spoke, his 'voice full of passion and the others followed and the million and more on the streets were quite mad with joy'. Apart from those guarding the tribune, there were no policemen to be seen. Eric eventually got home at a quarter to four in the morning. He had not experienced such euphoria since marching with the Communists in Berlin early in 1933. The occasion was marred only by the news of the attempted coup by General Franco and the Spanish army that began the Spanish Civil War.[231]

IX

While he was in Paris, Eric had met an American girl who was interested in art (no, he told Ron, it wasn't what he thought), and seemed to have some kind of role in the art world of New York. Together they went to visit the surrealist artist Richard Oelze to try and obtain from him a drawing for a forthcoming exhibition of 'Fantastic Art, Dada and Surrealism' at the Museum of Modern Art in New York. Oelze had trained then taught at the Bauhaus before he went to live first in Ascona then in Berlin, leaving for Paris in 1932, where he became acquainted with Salvador Dalí, Paul Éluard, Max Ernst, André Breton and other surrealists. But Oelze had fallen on hard times. When Eric and the American girl reached his flat on the sixth floor of an apartment block in Montparnasse, they found him looking like 'a death-head', clearly malnourished, without a penny. After drinking a glass of wine with him, they took him to a Russian restaurant to try and get some food inside him. It proved to be a bad choice. Eric incautiously drank a glass of vodka, which he had never tasted before and thought would be something like a strong liqueur, and soon began to feel drunk. They managed to get the American girl home ('I walked reasonably straight') and then Eric went with Oelze to the Dome café, a well-known haunt of intellectuals, and especially of English and American visitors, in Montparnasse, for a coffee.[232]

While Eric sobered up, Oelze started to drink white wine. He was, he said, waiting 'for two negresses who danced in the cabaret two doors away and always came in for a drink. Sometimes he seemed to want to sleep with one of them, but mostly he just had a vague desire to see them. Every three quarters of an hour he disappeared for a few minutes, I guess to pump himself full of dope.' By now it was half past two in the morning. 'The flower of artists of Montparnasse were there to get boozed up, and selected Lesbians and some whores.' Nobody seemed to have any money. The company was very mixed: a drunken Norwegian who kept quoting Shakespeare, Russians, a German artist, fat and jovial, getting drunk on Pernod, who assured Eric he was not an agent of the Gestapo, a girl with a monocle who said she was a sculptress, a hunchbacked Swiss, 'two drunk Canadians who were immediately snaffled by the least attractive of the whores', Americans, and many more. Oelze still 'wanted to wait for his negresses' when the milk carts began to arrive, and he said it was too late now to go to bed and he was too drunk anyway. Eric left the painter with the girl sculptor with the monocle and got home at half past five.

Thinking about the evening's encounters the next morning, he came to a gloomy conclusion about the German artist and his disorderly lifestyle, a lifestyle not untypical of the artistic community in Paris in the 1930s, even if it was a rather extreme version of it:

Oelze is a terrible case – the happy Bohème at its logical conclusion. He is thirty six. I should be surprised if he lives to be forty-three. Either he'll starve; likely though he'll die of dope and booze. He is so doped that he can't even paint any more, because his Surrealist stuff is not good. Occasionally it's frightening – that this is not unexpected. He can draw. He has fine slim hands. But he is too lazy to work and when he isn't he is so full of morphine that he can't draw anything but Surrealist stuff; things which are sheer exercises in technique of drawing – imitations of the effect of a photography, or such, things which have no future. And Oelze will starve unless he happens to find an American or an art-dealer who will take him up. He makes the excuse of all lazy men and says he is looking for a woman who will understand him, poor sod; and in the meantime he hasn't got the twenty-five francs for a Montparnasse whore and just looks at the women with strained eyes.

In fact, when he met Oelze, the artist had just finished what was to become his best-known work, *Expectation*, which showed a group of a dozen or so men and a few women, all in hats and beige raincoats, gathered on a hillside, seen from behind, staring across a gloomy landscape into a dark and cloudy distance. The Director of the Museum of Modern Art in New York had bought it off Oelze during a tour of Parisian studios in 1935, reporting that he had not been able to get a single word out of the artist, who had simply put one picture after another up against his studio wall until the American found one he liked. Against all expectations, however, Oelze lived to the age of eighty, after returning to Germany, serving in the war, participating in the *documenta* exhibitions in Kassel, winning several major cultural awards, including the Max Beckmann Prize and the Lichtwark Prize, and being elected to the Berlin Academy of Arts.[233]

X

Just before his encounter with the drunken surrealist, acting on the spur of the moment, Eric had bought a lottery ticket. To his surprise, it turned out to be a winner. It provided him with enough money to take a train to the Pyrenees, with the help of cheap fares introduced by the Popular Front government, one of their many reforms designed to help the working classes. 'I think it's too good a bargain to be missed', he told his cousin Ron, '140 francs return', less than two pounds in English money.[234] 'I always wanted to go to the South of France', he wrote in his journal. He travelled by train all the way to the south-western corner of France. On the train, he listened to the Toulousain who was proud to show strangers the sights of his district, the lunatic asylum, the level-crossing and the poison gas factory. Someone said: 'There they are' and we piled across the windows to catch sight of the Pyrenees in a thin pale-blue line behind the morning mist. And at 7 a.m. a young Englishman in flannels and a khaki shirt, with a rucksack which was far too heavy and a stick bought for 2.75 francs at the Samaritaine, and two Michelin maps, got out at Montréjeau station, sat down on a bench and wondered what to do next.[235]

He had discovered the cheap return ticket very late in the day ('decidedly the French have yet to learn what good publicity is') so had not had the time to make elaborate plans, or even buy a guidebook. He made his way on foot to Lourdes, a town that lived off the healing powers attributed to its waters ever since the Virgin Mary had appeared there in the nineteenth century to a young girl subsequently canonised as Saint Bernadette. Lourdes, Eric remarked caustically, 'lives off its Saint just as Cambridge lives off its university or Grimsby off fish'. It was completely commercialised. Crammed with French and foreign tourists, row upon row of shops selling Marian souvenirs and cinemas showing devotional movies, the town put on a nightly torchlit procession where the ill and the disabled said constant Hail Marys to try and effect a cure. 'Terribly sincere, of course, but not necessarily religious.'

Staying at youth hostels or camping, he walked in a southerly direction to the Pyrenean town of Cauterets. As he trudged along, he caught up with 'an old peasant in an old panama hat', who thought he was a pilgrim or an unemployed Spaniard from across the border, until he managed to explain he was an Englishman. 'I was feeling very miserable. I was a fool, I told myself, why the hell did I let myself in for this, tired and hungry and thirsty, chiefly thirsty. Parched.'

About four in the afternoon I came to a village. One of those southern villages with a long cornering chalky road and small ugly whitewashed houses with deep black short shadows and peasants siestaing sitting on the ground in those powerful shadows. No windows, or very small ones, like loop-holes. Big, elaborate wrought [iron] gates leading into farmyards; and the sun pouring light over everything and making it look as unreal as a cinema studio. And at the same time, there was nothing unreal about it at all. At last I discovered a dilapidated notice saying 'Auberge'. I wanted a drink badly. It was dark inside and very cool. There were half-a-dozen people sitting at the table. I looked round. There was a trestle-table in the room and two benches: there was the big fire-place and the pot stewing on it, the innkeeper's bed and a st[r]ay dead chicken on the cover. The Byrrh advertisement in the odd corner, the calendar of the Tarbes grocery, the fly-spots. There were chickens and little pigs running about and it was dark.[236]

After a while conversing in the local patois, the men turned to Eric and addressed him in French. A conversation began. He asked them about Spain. 'They told me', he reported with disappointment, 'that they didn't care about politics and would go with whoever was the strongest.' He found himself explaining the system of landownership in England. 'Of course it's different here, we each have our little plot of land, but actually what's the good of owning it? We have too little to be prosperous and too much to go begging outright. We might as well be on the dole.' One of the men gave him a place to sleep in a haybarn, and because they did not have permission to take in guests, they asked him to write down his details for the local gendarme.

Halfway through the fortnight he met a young Czech who introduced him to the art of hitch-hiking. In the 1930s, when motor vehicles were still a relative novelty, this was much easier than it later became, and many if not most drivers were happy enough to give people lifts. It was very easy, he remembered later, 'especially after I discovered that middle-class French car drivers could be kept from expressing their detestation of Léon Blum and the communists by well-timed enquiries about what they thought about Napoleon – a subject which kept them talking for up to

200 kilometres'.[237] The Pyrenees were disappointingly unlike the Alps, green and lush instead of snowy and majestic. Even the high mountains had 'not got that hysterical ruggedness which used to be the joy of our Romantics'. They were more like the hills of Wales, though made beautiful by gorges and waterfalls and emerald-green pools and meadows with little flowers of 'an incredible intensity of whites, yellows, purples and pinks in the grey-yellow space of the mountain-slope'. The weather stayed bright and sunny ('I should not have been fool enough to cross the Col d'Aubert (8250 ft.) ... if it had not been fine, because there is only a more or less clearly marked track across and my experience even of harmless mountains is small'). As soon as he reached the eastern Pyrenees, however, the landscape became more dramatic, with mountain chains stretching far into the distance towards the south, and the sky shimmering in the heat. The little houses were white, the roads dusty, the grass ochre and the mountains dusty blue. He passed 'a large cart with two big, white ugly oxen who walk as though they had thorns in their feet, and creaking wood, incredibly slow'. The people spoke Catalan not French and the whole area had a feel more Spanish than French. It was so hot that he could not walk or hitch-hike between eleven and five, and, in any case, everybody took a siesta during these hours. He was not impressed by the country to the south of Carcassonne, a shapeless jumble of fields and trees, the colour sucked out of it by the sun. Yet he saw beauty in the dark green cypress groves on the hillsides, and in the avenues of plane trees along the roads, with the sun shining through their leaves onto the road. The little villages with their red-tiled roofs and square little churches on the hilltops each formed a harmonious, compressed whole, seemingly impenetrable from the outside until one drew near to them.

The medieval walled town of Carcassonne he found 'too good to be true ... far too complete and metaphorically glass-cased to be of any but (questionable) esthetic value to an ordinary traveller with average curiosity like myself'. It had indeed been 'restored' more than comprehensively in the nineteenth century by the architect Viollet-le-Duc, who added many incongruous features to make it seem more authentically medieval. It was all 'sham and antiquarian'. Only the people talking softly on the doorsteps in the evening 'and the smell of the dust and the filth' seemed truly authentic. Moving on, he made his way along the Pyrenees to a youth hostel at Cerdagne, near the Mediterranean side of the Spanish border, and stayed the night there. The next morning he decided to go across the border to the nearby Spanish town of Puigcerdà whose lights he had seen two miles away the previous evening. At more than 1200 metres above sea level, the town was one of many in the more remote areas of Spain that had been taken over by anarchists in response to the attempted military coup. Eric showed his passport to the French border guards, who 'let me pass; nevertheless they warned me darkly'. He proceeded further along the 'crooked white road', which then

> turned behind a clump of bushes. Ahead in the sun was a little dog which played and behind it in the middle of the road stood a group of men, some had guns. Militiamen and frontier-guards. I came closer and raised my fist and so did they. I said: 'Salut. Can one get across to Puigcerda?' The fair-haired militiaman with the shirt with zipp-fastener said 'No' and smiled. He could speak French. He explained that a written permission of the Committee was necessary. Otherwise no chance.[238]

It was a 'wash-out'. Eric walked back across the border. He hitched a lift to Bourg-Madame, a nearby commune that was also right on the Spanish frontier.

Here, however, he resolved to make another attempt to get into Spain. 'The French commissaire stamped my passport and the customs officer grinned and I touched my button-hole to feel whether the Front Populaire sign and the little sickle and hammer were there still.'

> I had to walk 300 metres straight towards the [Spanish] border post, which was guarded by some young scamps with revolvers and rifles. I walked in the sun, and there was nobody else on the

road apart from myself. I wondered what would happen if these rascals (anarchists, of course) suddenly decided to shoot me, out of pure joie de vivre, out of an exaggerated sense of duty, or God knows what motive. (An irrational fear). They would most likely have missed. Still, I was terribly afraid. The feeling of walking with open eyes towards men who could aim at me *because there was simply nobody else there*, still causes me nightmares today. Had I been able to do so without disgracing myself, I believe I would have turned back.[239] On the bridge, three or four militiamen. I told them I wanted to go to Puigcerda. They talked among themselves for a little in Spanish, then a young man with a gun took my passport and told me to accompany him. Along the avenue of trees, shady, and I felt good, I can assure you. At the Customs we stopped and I explained in detail – in French – that I was a tourist and wanted to go to Puigcerda just for the rest of the day, because I wanted to see what I could of the Spanish business. I left my ruck-sack at the Customs office, both to avoid unpacking it all and to leave a concrete proof that I was going to return the same evening. And that I was not going to go further than Puigcerda.[240]

He was allowed through and reached the town quickly. The narrow streets were festooned with washing hung on lines slung from one side to the other. The houses were ugly and dirty. It was quiet.

But there were signs of the Civil War none the less. Eric noticed the trucks parked on the market square that headed off to the front when they were filled with volunteers. The anarchists who were now in charge of the town had implemented the anticlerical policies of the Spanish left and the revolutionary government of Catalonia. The Catholic Church had supported the military coup attempt and now it was paying the price:

I arrived before the big church, which was being torn down. The door bore a notice: Property of the Generalitat de Catalunya and another: entry forbidden. They had that on all the churches and chapels of the town. The workmen were loosening the slates on the roof. While I was watching one came out of the church with a barrowful of dusty window-panes and placed them against a wall & then he wrote his name on the uppermost with his finger, I think it was Angel Lopez, and stood back to look at it and went back into the church.

As he walked on, he saw armed men wearing the black and white armbands of the anarchist trade union, the CNT, coming out of the Casino, which had been turned into a barracks. A young militiaman who spoke French directed Eric to a café on the plaza, where he could get something to eat. Eric sat down, and ordered a meal, introducing himself as 'Communista ingles'. He asked if anyone spoke French, and a customer responded, asking Eric if he really was a Communist and trying, without success, to get into an argument about Marx's great anarchist rival, the nineteenth-century Russian revolutionary Mikhail Bakunin. 'It was the time of siesta, the café was full, the sun fell down on the white plaza.' Militiamen lounged around or chatted with a girl at the newspaper stand. 'A man walked across to the kiosk and bought a large map of Spain and a furious discussion on the war was soon started.' The town was full of anarchists, Eric remarked. 'Yes,' the young man said. 'You know, nothing is easier than to be an anarchist. This is a negative movement, a reaction against hunger and tyranny. They are incredibly brave, the anarchists, but', he went on, 'they aren't a political movement, not like, say, the communists – I think they will disappear when there is nothing to fight against.'

This relaxed situation was soon brought to an end. Eric was reported by the anarchist frontier guard who had turned him away at his first attempt to cross the border, and brought before the local anarchist commissar. 'To be grilled by trigger-happy amateurs on the lookout for counter-revolutionaries', he wrote later, with considerable understatement, 'is never relaxing.' He was eventually taken back along the road to the border in the dark by an armed militiaman who kept his gun pointed at Eric's back until they made the crossing.[241] Nothing happened, however, and he got back to

France without incident, taking with him the impression that the anarchist contribution to the Republican war effort in Spain was casual and disorganised and unlikely to do much to help it to victory. Yet overall he was moved by the courage and commitment of the militiamen, all of whom were volunteers, and from all walks of life, 'ready to have themselves hacked to pieces (and to hack others to pieces) rather than give in'. The people he met in Puigcerdà impressed him deeply:

> The youngster who accompanied me to the customs, the Trotzkist militiaman who had wild discussions with the shock-haired anarchist on the nature of 'Power'; the anarchist organiser with the fair hair, lumberjack[et] and hornrimmed glasses; the young Portuguese who had joined the militia; the two workers, who ate melons and talked about revolvers and girls; the girl in black who was secretary of the Revolutionary Committee; the man in blue overalls and huge revolver who was the Kommissar sent up from Barcelona, brown face, deep black hair, extremely handsome and almost incredibly commissarish; and the militiaman who was assisting in the demolition of the big church, carrying out two dusty window panes ... the tough hardbitten brownfaced and fanatic workers frontiersmen and assault guards and the women and the girls who went to the funeral of one of the militiamen who had died in the hospital.[242]

Nobody could doubt their fighting spirit or their determination. But how could they prevail against the well-equipped, professional armed forces of the Nationalists? Logically they should already have been defeated. They had 'sheer fanaticism' and nothing else. 'I hope the miracle occurs and they win', he concluded.

In fact, the anarchist collective that ran the town fell foul not of the fascists or the military, but of local rivals. There had been reports of spying, fake passports and corruption. Known as 'the cripple from Malaga', the local mayor, Antonio Martín Escudero, had been extorting money from refugees fleeing to France, and had had a considerable number murdered after they had surrendered their valuables. Anarchist patrols used the town to smuggle stolen goods from Barcelona across the border into France. Martín was actively extending his control over other parts of the border region, subjecting them also to his depredations. The mayors of other local towns decided to put a stop to his activities and began to gather an armed force to oppose him in the small town of Bellver: Martín led an attack on the town, there was a gun battle and Martín and a number of his men were killed. Anarchist propaganda turned him into a hero and rewrote the story to make it look as if he had been killed in an attack on Puigcerdà by government forces. The entire episode was an example of the disorder that reigned in areas controlled by the anarchists. Eric's brief sojourn in Puigcerdà was even more dangerous for him than he had thought.[243]

After returning across the border, Eric got a long lift from Cerdagne after waiting for an hour in the sun, and then had to wait even longer for a lift at the next halt, 'not that the cars wouldn't stop – there simply weren't any', only two or three an hour, most of them full of children and luggage with no space for the hitch-hiker. Overall he reckoned that in the first week he had travelled two hundred kilometres, almost all by car, and in the second week 580, of which only fifteen were covered on foot. Or, to put it another way, six days of pure walking, five of pure hitch-hiking, two days of rest and one day in Spain.[244] Eventually he made it back to the railway station at Bagnères-de-Luchon, south of Montréjeau, from where he took the train to return to Paris. Here he went on 8 September 1936 to the Winter Velodrome to hear a Spanish Communist, Dolores Ibárurri, speak. Known as 'La Pasionaria', she was a famous orator, a 'big darkhaired and whitefaced woman, dressed in black', he noted: 'Her voice is fairly deep, and occasionally hoarse, occasionally clear, she speaks in Spanish and is one of the finest orators I've heard.'[245] 'Though hardly any of the audience knew Spanish,' he wrote later, 'we knew exactly what she was telling us. I can still remember the words "*y las madres, y sus hijos*" floating slowly from the microphones above us, like dark albatrosses.' He felt politically impotent, unable to do anything to help the beleaguered Spanish Republic. 'I suppose we shall have to stay in England', he told Ron, 'and get exasperated and try to keep our Marxist ideas intact and wait.' Still, 'there is no sitting on the fence; that is too exposed a position if nothing else'. In the end, 'socialism is a series of constant defeats and deep disappointments – and someday the victory'.[246]

Meanwhile, he read French writers like Mallarmé, Giono, Péguy and Céline to try and understand different aspects of French culture that were not really known to the English (unlike, say, Proust). And he read about the 1789 Revolution, including the works of the radical Jacobin St Just, 'partly in preparation for Cambridge'; it is extremely unlikely that any of his fellow prospective undergraduates read anything at all in preparation for their studies, let alone the works, in French, of French revolutionaries. Meanwhile he undertook brief sightseeing trips to the region around Paris, including Chartres, where he was 'at first disappointed – having expected the cathedral of my dreams. But in the end it practically became perfect.' He encountered an American tourist who explained his theory that the greatest contribution to culture had been Nordic or Teutonic, and amused Eric by addressing him as 'you Anglo-Saxons' and 'you Nordics'. 'Pretty well everybody takes me for an Englishman', Eric added, though 'with some exceptions. I've been taken for Belgian, Alsatian, Swiss, German and Spaniard (!) and Russian.'[247]

By the time he returned to England at the end of the month, Eric had accumulated experiences that were unusual, to say the least, for a nineteen-year-old who was just about to begin his studies at Cambridge. By now he was fluent in English, French and German. He had read enormous amounts of fiction and poetry in all three languages. He had a good understanding of the ideas and writings of Marx, Engels and Lenin. He had sampled the popular culture of Paris and spent an evening with a German surrealist. He had travelled round the south of France mixing with local people as well as with other travellers. He had visited Spain just at the time when it was plunging into a murderous civil war. And he had participated in the mass celebrations of the Popular Front. Above all, perhaps, he had studied history intensively and passed his school-leaving and Cambridge entrance examinations brilliantly. He was the first member of his family to go to university, and the first pupil from his school to gain a place at Cambridge.[248] As he packed his bags and prepared for the course he was about to take in Modern History, he expected a level of intellectual stimulation he had not experienced at any of the schools he had attended.

3

'A Freshman who Knows About Everything'

1936–1939

I

Arriving in King's College, Cambridge, in October 1936 for the beginning of the Michaelmas Term, Eric was taken aback by the novelty of his situation and the strangeness of the institution to which he now belonged. He wrote to his cousin Ron conveying his first impressions:

> Frankly, this place is incredible; it seems to unite freedom from all responsibilities and all but trivial problems with the possibility – limited only by the ten or so lectures, the one hour supervision per week and the daily 7.30 p.m. dinner – to do exactly as you like. No place I have heard of offers so little encouragement to work; so many other things to do between lunch, and term invitations: clubs, sports, societies; no place, on the other hand, has more possibilities for work: complete seclusion, if you want it and the run of three major libraries at least; and time and peace. Chiefly peace. (Mind you, it's rather an incentive to work, realising that you are definitely supposed to do the bulk of it entirely on your own and without control) . . . And it's generally a queer life. One is so far from everything actual and difficult.[1]

In many ways, he thought King's was like a monastery, cut off from the world, peaceful and secluded.

Cambridge in the mid-1930s was a small and intimate university. There were no more than five thousand undergraduates and a mere four hundred research students. Traditions such as the wearing of gowns by lecturers and students still persisted; indeed, undergraduates still had to wear a gown when they ventured outside their College.[2] Eric did not fit in to conventional undergraduate society at Cambridge. As he later wrote:

> I was an untypical student at Cambridge, a) because nobody in my family or school had ever gone to Cambridge before (or to any other university), b) because my educational and cultural background – Vienna, Berlin, a London municipal school – was very different, and c) because, as a result, I did not share some of the typical activities of Cambridge students, e.g. spending many afternoons on sports and d) because I belonged to the minority who were at the university on, and relied financially on, scholarships. Also, I already came up politicised. Cambridge was still filled essentially with the sons of the established upper middle class, who had gone to 'public schools', had allowances from their parents, and expected to go into the family business, or into one or other of the public services or professions: at worst, into secondary school teaching. (Only 10% of students were women). Most students were not expected to study much or achieve a very distinguished degree.[3]

His interests, mainly political, cultural and academic, were thus almost totally at odds with those of the vast majority of undergraduates, to whom his cosmopolitan background and his experiences must have made him seem very exotic.

The atmosphere of Cambridge life was wonderful for young men who had just come from school, lived and were treated as adults for the first time, although still living under considerable supervision (compulsory dinner in hall, wearing of gowns at lectures and supervisions, special permits to enter and exit after a certain hour, university police to control the streets etc.). Much of their activities were, as it were, playing at what real adults did later: debating politics at the Union, student drama, music-making and other clubs, student newspapers.

That it was not automatically wonderful for Eric was clear. Moreover, as this suggests, the great majority of undergraduates in Cambridge during the 1930s were not political at all, let alone left-wing, though it is often supposed that they were; if the kind of public school student Eric describes had any kind of political views, they were most probably liberal or conservative. A poll among undergraduates held alongside the General Election of 1935 produced 650 votes for the Conservative candidate, 275 for the Labour and 171 for the Liberal.[4] As a self-conscious Communist, Eric was once again in a tiny minority.

King's College numbered among its undergraduates more than the usual proportion of Old Etonians, former pupils from England's most prestigious independent school, largely because the two institutions, Eton and King's, had been joint foundations of the pious King Henry VI in the fifteenth century. Despite this, the College enjoyed, as Eric recalled later, 'a reputation for bourgeois unconventionality, a taste for the arts and intellectual pursuits not necessarily resulting in major achievements, for personal relations, non-soldierly behaviour, rationalism, music, homosexuality and a great tolerance for people's eccentricities, including their opinions'. Indeed, as he told his cousin Ron, it had a reputation for 'acute homosexuality – the "sport of Kings" is quite a byword'. The College was sometimes known as Bloomsbury on the Cam, thanks not least to the presence among the Fellows of John Maynard Keynes, the distinguished economist and member of the Bloomsbury group of writers and artists. Among his fellow undergraduates was the brilliant mathematician Alan Turing, whom Eric recalled 'as a clumsy-looking, pale-faced young fellow given to what would today be called jogging'. With its liberal and slightly bohemian atmosphere, King's was clearly the right place for Eric, who would not have fitted in nearly so well to one of the more conventional colleges.[5]

At King's, Eric, like other first-year undergraduates, was provided with College accommodation. It was not up to modern standards, even those of the 1930s. 'The domestic side of college life in the 1930s,' he recalled later, 'peeing into the sink in the "gyp room" since the nearest bathroom and toilet might be three flights of stairs, a courtyard and a basement away', was spartan.[6] He was billeted with other freshmen scholars and 'exhibitioners' – a kind of junior scholar – in 'the same slum-annex', later demolished, 'called "The Drain"'. It was located on the opposite side of the College from the Chapel, behind the main front building on King's Parade. Stuart Lyons, a student who lived there shortly after the war, described it as

> a collection of windowless cells, accessible only through an underground tunnel near to Chetwynd Court. The Drain was as damp and cold as its name. That winter, the bathrooms froze solid, and yellow ice extended three feet from the walls. We traipsed across to Gibbs' in Long Johns and dressing gowns in search of flushing toilets and a hot bath.[7]

Eric's fellow denizens of 'The Drain' were all British, including Peter Scott-Maldon, Jack Boyd (later killed in the war), Robert Vile, Jack Rice, Norman Haselgrove, John Luce and others. Eric's room was number 2, on Staircase N.[8] He and his friends stuck together as a group in their second year as well, though they had all moved to other accommodation by then. 'We spent the nights talking', Eric remembered, 'inside college, walking in the moonlight across the back lawn and onto the lawn beyond the chapel, and outside.' Intellectually and socially, this was a distinct improvement on life with the pupils of St Marylebone Grammar School. There was a curfew for undergraduates, and the College gates were locked well before midnight, but this did not deter Eric and his friends. 'I remember', Eric continued, 'climbing out with Jack after midnight to Grantchester – to swim in Byron's

Pool. It was the sort of thing one did – talking all the time. And climbing back by the side of the back gate.'[9] All that the students had to do was to make sure that they were unnoticed by the proctors and constables, the university police, who patrolled the streets to try and enforce the curfew.[10]

Eric soon became one of the best-known undergraduates of his generation. At 5 feet 11¼ inches, he was tall by the standards of the day. Slim, at around 150 pounds, and physically fit, with blue eyes and a noticeable scar on the left side of his forehead, he was a striking and instantly recognisable figure.[11] He was well liked by the more intellectual of his contemporaries, including Noel Annan, later a distinguished academic writer and administrator, who found him 'good company and humorous'.[12] A profile appeared in the student magazine *The Granta* on 7 June 1939, written in the usual facetious and slightly arch style of the student journalism of the day. The author was an undergraduate who by this time had become Eric's friend, the Sri Lankan President of the Cambridge Union Pieter Keuneman ('a large, handsome, laughing young man educated at an English public school', according to another contemporary).[13] Eric shared lodgings with him in his third year. Keuneman noted that from an early age Eric 'had a large and vulgar patriotism for England, which he considered in weak moments as his spiritual home'.[14] Modest and self-deprecating, with a strong sense of humour and 'a complete lack of personal malice even for those who have done him wrong', he was 'not easy to get to know'. His Cambridge friends called him 'the Buddha': 'As he sits cross-legged in his great chair, there is something of the condescension of the oracle gyrating on its tripod. But under the surface is the person whose friendship is intimate and valuable, and whose honesty in personal relationships one respects.'[15]

Despite the friendship evidenced in this profile, Eric was on his own estimation 'never particularly close to Pieter' and was uncomfortably aware of the way 'he wanted to impress me – he wants to impress everybody'. He was not impressed by the chaotic state of his friend's rooms. 'I did not have a very high opinion of him. He has in my opinion still, a cumbersome intelligence, which can only put together words and thoughts with uncertainty. He suffers from the inferiority complex of the Eurasian.' He was of course good-looking, 'would be "Byronic" if he was slimmer, and obviously modelled himself on the idea of a Dandy. Lazy, without much strength of will or initiative, with great charm for women, less for men. I get along with him because he is "easy going"'. Eric confessed to feeling protective towards him like a mother hen, because his little social tricks were so transparent. Eric's relations with him were complicated by the fact that he had fallen in love, or thought he had fallen in love, with Keuneman's girlfriend Hedi Simon, a pupil of her fellow-Austrian Ludwig Wittgenstein, then a professor of philosophy at Cambridge. She had become friendly with another undergraduate, the later Indian Prime Minister Indira Gandhi, identifying with colonial peoples as a result of her negative experiences as a Jew in Vienna in the early 1930s, and this had brought her into contact with Pieter. It depressed Eric to think that both Pieter and Hedi (who married in 1939) would become fat in middle age; he would lose sight of them, he feared, when they finally settled in Sri Lanka.[16]

Notoriously badly dressed, Eric did not have a lot of time for dandies; Pieter's elegant appearance would have seemed a rather negative aspect of his personality to him. He was particularly scathing about one of the best-known and most talked-about Cambridge figures of his day, George ('Dadie') Rylands, an English don at King's. A popular lecturer, Rylands delivered his texts histrionically, reading from Shakespeare or Jonson, as Eric described it,

> in a high-pitched voice, sometimes slightly husky; long passages of blank verse dialogue with marked differentiation of speakers and a rigid pattern of verse. When he is through he switches back to his ordinary voice and pauses for a moment to allow the crackling of seats and the rustling of notes to subside. Just like the end of a symphony movement. Then he snaps his mouth shut, the lower lip sticks out with a slight air of sullenness and vertical lines appear for a moment, but they vanish, and he goes on to explain.[17]

Rylands was not only a serious Shakespeare scholar but also the leading light in Cambridge's dramatic life, which centred on the Arts Theatre, established in February 1936 by Keynes. In his day Rylands was, as Eric put it, 'an Adonis, an angel, a second Rupert Brooke', with his 'exquisite *bon-mots* heard only by the women of Newnham in his Shakespeare lectures and the little boyfriends of the moment over sherry'. Eric thought he was squandering his intelligence on trivialities, and, like the other aesthetes of the day, he would leave nothing behind after he was gone, save a few anecdotes preserved in the memoirs of people who had known him.[18]

Apart from his scruffy appearance, what impressed his student contemporaries about Eric was above all the extraordinary erudition he displayed even before he had reached the age of twenty. Academically it was immediately clear that he was a genuine high-flyer. Noel Annan, who was a year below Eric at King's, considered him 'the most brilliant historian of our generation at Cambridge – and there are some not inconsiderable ones in that generation'.[19] He was 'equipped to have a view on whatever obscure topic one of his contemporaries might have chosen to write a paper'.[20] And his reputation for brilliance was far more than merely academic. As Pieter Keuneman remarked, Eric

had at his finger-tips the strangest details about the obscurest subjects and the names of all the authorities which he could bandy about with an easy familiarity ... The usual rumours started. 'There's a freshman in King's who knows about everything' were the words that got around. There was considerable difficulty about discovering what he was reading. He was at the English club asking puzzling questions about Wordsworth's parent symbolism; at the French and German societies he would let drop dicta of such profundity as might properly only come from God.[21]

Keuneman was not the only one to be impressed. 'I remember, as if it were yesterday,' Noel Annan wrote to him many years later, 'your appearances at the Political Society, totally self-assured (not conceited) totally in command of a way that enabled you, like [John] Clapham, to discuss any topic, & speaking with a fluency that we public schoolboys could not aspire to.' Indeed, between the end of dinner and the start of the meeting Annan habitually dashed to the Still and Sugarloaf pub across the road with one of the other members of the Society to gain some Dutch courage in case they were nominated to discuss the paper in Eric's intellectually intimidating presence. After a pint or two, Annan often thought he had found a winning argument, but by the time they got back to the meeting, Annan confessed, 'it had always evaporated'.[22] On one occasion, Eric provoked him into participating in a debate. As Annan wrote later: 'He defended the proposition that, given certain circumstances (which to me seemed both improbable and undesirable), the next war could be fought to save democracy.' Annan argued 'that to talk of fighting for democracy was hypocrisy. It would be a war between fascism and Chamberlain's capitalism, and we would fight for that capitalism to survive as a nation. I was quite wrong. But then so, perhaps, was he.'[23]

Life in King's could be pleasant and relaxing, but Eric found the beauty of Cambridge in the early summer thoroughly distracting. 'It is difficult to work here', he complained to Ron in May 1937:

The weather is fine and the obvious place to take a book to is the river-bank; and once you are perched there, it is quite astonishing how little you do in fact work. And then there is always the temptation to take out a punt or a canoe. Why did they fix exams in the one term when they are so obviously out of place[?] Wouldn't it be more convenient to have them at Christmas or at Easter[?] Someday when you are Commissar for Labour and I for Education we shall consider the matter deeply.[24]

An ability to wield the lengthy pole that propelled the flat-bottomed punts along the River Cam came in handy when Eric and his friends, convinced republicans all, wanted to avoid the festivities that attended the coronation of King George VI and Queen Elizabeth on 12 May 1937. 'Are you escaping from the

Coronation?' Eric asked Ron a few days earlier: 'We here shall
do our best to get as far upriver as we possibly can, so as to see
no bunting, hear no band and generally be at a distance. If the
weather is good – let's hope it will be – it ought to be quite nice.'

II

At Cambridge in the 1930s, history undergraduates were taught
by a mixture of essay-based one-to-one supervisions by College
tutors, and lectures held by academic members of the History
Faculty drawn from a range of different colleges. Eric attended
lectures by Kenneth Pickthorn, 'specialist and writer of standard
books on early Tudors, chairman of the C[ambridge], U[niversity].
Conservative association and MP.' Eric encountered Pickthorn
'vaguely attempting to find his way about the early Lancastrians
until he comes to the part which he knows blindfolded and back-
wards. Period: Constitutional History 1399–1688.'25

> Then there is Manning on Medieval European History who
> looks deliberately foolish and prepares his epigrams before-
> hand. Occasionally quite good – and [Steven] Runciman (the
> Minister's son) on the same subject. This, by the way, is the man
> who wrote the book on Byzantine Civilization which I men-
> tioned to you some time back; and he has given a good account
> of the reasons for the decline of the Roman Empire even though
> he pretends not to bother about economic factors. He does, of
> course, that is why he is useful.26

Manning was an old-fashioned Liberal as well as an ecclesias-
tical historian who published on Methodism and similar topics;
his lectures were said to present the Whig Theory of History,
according to which English history was characterised by steady
progress towards the formation of a modern constitution, in its
purest form.27

Already in his second term, however, Eric was 'becoming more &

more disillusioned about Historical Teaching in the University, and concentrate[d] on the Library'.[28] Most of the lectures he attended, more in hope than in expectation, were, he found, of little interest. A lecture on Hobbes by the literary and intellectual historian Basil Willey, author of a much-reprinted book, *The Seventeenth Century Background* (1934), was so tedious (delivered in 'a dry, exact voice and with a deprecating air about the mouth') that Eric devoted virtually the whole of a report he wrote on it to a description of the venue and the audience ('Everything about the room is precise').[29] Eric came to despise the routine of one-to-one supervisions by mediocre College tutors, though he appreciated the Socratic teaching method of one of his supervisors, the Tudor historian Christopher Morris (who had interviewed him for admission), because it allowed him to expand on the ideas he had put forward in the weekly essay he was required to read out aloud to him.[30] Like Morris, whom Eric eventually came to think of as second-rate, his other principal supervisor, the medieval economic historian John Saltmarsh, had spent his entire career at King's, having arrived as an undergraduate at the age of seventeen. Saltmarsh devoted much of his time to investigating the history of its magnificent Gothic chapel and preferred teaching undergraduates to publishing books or articles. Unlike Morris, a family man, Saltmarsh was the quintessential bachelor don: Eric respected his 'enormous learning' but found nothing inspirational about his teaching, perhaps because he did not attend his popular and influential lectures.[31] 'History', he later remarked, was taught as a 'general educational background for people expected to take part in public life',[32] so that College supervisors like Morris concentrated their efforts on getting 'average young men from a public school a decent Second in the Tripos'.[33] When he later became a supervisor himself, Eric would revise his negative opinion on the usefulness of this approach.

There were thus very few dons whom Eric respected at all. Among these, by far the most important, indeed the only one whom he truly admired, was Michael, generally known as Mounia, Postan. Lecturing on English and European economic and social history, Postan came from a background that was highly unusual for a Cambridge don at the time. Born in 1899 in Bessarabia, then a Romanian-speaking part of the Russian Empire, now located in the Republic of Moldova, he had left in 1920, after the Bolshevik Revolution. He had studied with the leading British economic and social historian R. H. Tawney at the London School of Economics and then taught there during the late 1920s and early 1930s, supporting himself through journalism and providing research assistance to the medievalist Eileen Power. Cosmopolitan and multilingual, Postan made few compromises when it came to teaching. The bibliography he supplied to his students for part of a course he taught on 'The Economic History of the Great Powers' consisted almost entirely of works in German and Russian. His lectures included a strong dose of theoretical discussion of hypotheses such as the falling rate of profit in capitalism and the immiseration of the working classes, both topics that would concern Eric in the early part of his career as an historian, after the war.[34]

In 1935, Postan moved to Peterhouse, Cambridge's oldest college, becoming Professor of Economic History in 1938 at the age of thirty-nine. He lectured on a wide variety of topics and periods. A small, red-headed man with a charismatic presence, his lectures were 'reminiscent of a Seventh Day Adventist in full spate at Hyde Park Corner'.[35] 'Every one of them, an intellectual-rhetorical drama in which a historical thesis was first expounded, then utterly dismantled, and finally replaced by the Postan version, was a holiday from British insularity.'[36] Eric began attending his lectures almost immediately and found them stimulating because they were opinionated and controversial, unlike the bland, fact-clogged courses of most of the dons. 'I have Postan', he wrote to Ron on 21 October 1936. 'He promises to become vitriolic on 19th-century simplifications. He has already been so, and has taken to referring us to articles in the various historical reviews' leaving the twenty or so freshmen who attended his lectures to fight over the relevant volumes of the recommended journal in the Seeley Historical Library.[37]

'Postan is going strong', Eric told Ron towards the end of his first year at Cambridge:

He has just given a fine lecture on the Agrarian Revolution which accompanied and conditioned the Industrial one. Needless to say it was all good Marxism, and he has the honesty to admit it. You know the sort of thing: 'Though I dislike the jargon, this is in effect what Marx did say . . . ' Still, it is an admission.[38]

Not surprisingly, though he was very far indeed from being a Marxist himself ('I've never met a man who was so allergic to the word Marxism', Eric wrote on another occasion: 'it was literally like the bull and the red rag'[39]), Postan 'attracted Marxists like flies, since he was the only don who knew about Marx . . . He is the only man among the generally mediocre bunch whose lectures we sampled, whom I gladly acknowledge as my teacher. The only other man who (unlike Postan) gave good advice was Clapham.'[40] Postan was a passionate advocate of the relevance of social science theories and methods to the study of the past, a stance that put him at odds with the vast majority of mainstream British historians in the 1930s and for many years afterwards. He saw Marx as a social scientist who applied his concepts to history and was therefore worth studying, though he is also reported to have remarked: 'I was a Communist myself when I was seventeen, but I grew out of it.'[41] He declared that 'all students of history and sociology must be reminded that they share with the Marxists a common descent from the scientific tradition' though, he added, 'I do not think it would be right to leave the Marxists in sole possession of the truth.'[42] However, 'Postan . . . knew that the young Marxists were on his side against the conservatives', Eric said many years later.[43]

As Eric noted, therefore, 'Postan's relationship with the young Marxists was curiously complex . . . like all good dons, he could not resist the bright young. I expect he thought most of them would grow out of their communism which of course proved correct in many cases.'[44] Thus, for example, Postan tried to persuade Victor Kiernan, a young history undergraduate who would be one of Eric's lifelong friends, to become his tutorial assistant in 1938, a year after he had been elected a junior Fellow of Trinity

College following his achievement of a double starred First. Kiernan did some College teaching, and soon became notorious for giving supervisions in his dressing gown and carpet slippers, but he refused to become Postan's assistant since, influenced by Mohan Kumaramangalam, an Indian Communist and another of Eric's friends, he wanted to go to India to carry out his doctoral research.[45] As Eric came to know Postan personally, however, he began to realise that 'you could not trust any of his statements without independent verification, partly because he hated to admit that he did not know the answer to a question and so made it up, partly because, at least in personal affairs, he preferred what he wanted to be true to what was true'.[46] Despite such reservations, Eric regarded Postan as a mentor and an example in the years before the war, and for some time afterwards.

Isaiah Berlin considered Postan 'a clever ill intentioned man: & the desire to do down & triumph mars his intellectual virtues'. He found it 'agreeable to conceive himself as superior to the con fusion of contemporary ideas & words by applying some "tough" materialist criterion', an accurate enough assessment.[47] It is easy to see why Eric was impressed: the two men's backgrounds were similar – Jewish but secular, cosmopolitan, European, committed to the idea of history as a social science, fascinated as much by theory as by fact, and capable of ranging across many countries and centuries in their historical interests. Together with Eileen Power, a kindred spirit whom he married in 1937 (causing something of a scandal since she was more than a decade older), Postan conceived and, after her premature death in 1940, executed the great project of the *Cambridge Economic History of Europe*, a novel and unprecedented venture with contributions from historians in a range of European countries. Postan and Power were both in contact with, and strongly influenced by, the French economic and social historians who founded the journal *Annales d'histoire économique et sociale* in 1929. The journal aimed to make history the meeting point for all the social sciences, including geography and sociology, and sought in its early years to build an international network extending to many other countries, especially through international historical congresses. The editors, Marc Bloch and Lucien Febvre, propagated the 'spirit of the *Annales*', a spirit in which nothing would be out of bounds to the historian. A key feature of the journal and its proponents was the desire to break free from the dominant historical paradigm of the nation-state, and approach the past on a comparative or transnational basis. Postan knew the journal's editors, and invited Bloch to lecture at Cambridge, and in turn Bloch had travelled to London in 1934 to enlist the help of Postan, Power and Tawney on the *Annales*, which had been founded only a few years before.[48] Postan introduced Eric to the *Annales* school, and transmitted its core ideas to him through his teaching while Eric was still an undergraduate. This was to be of crucial importance later in his career.[49]

Postan was not known to the British public in the 1930s, however; by far the most famous historian teaching in Cambridge was the great George Macaulay Trevelyan, Regius Professor of Modern History and author of widely read works on English and Italian history. Often described as the last of the Whig historians, Trevelyan was a patrician figure deeply rooted in the Liberal tradition, and espoused a literary style of historical writing that owed a great deal to his great-uncle, the Victorian Whig historian and politician Thomas Babington Macaulay. Although Trevelyan was only sixty-one when Eric first heard him lecture, in the Michaelmas Term of 1937, he seemed to him far older. Eric gave a vivid impression of how Trevelyan appeared to undergraduates at this time:

This is a working lecture. It has not that air of revivalism that pervaded Postan's nine-o'clocks in Mill Lane, or the massiveness of Kitson Clark. One couldn't think of playing noughts and crosses. One hardly likes to doodle ... Sometimes he spreads his gown over the desk and looks like a great bird; sometimes he wraps it round his elbows and looks like a still from a Fritz Lang film ... He talks in long sentences with an old voice and is very nervous. His hair is thin and white and his eyes are sunk; from a distance you hardly see that he has spectacles. He has a close-cropped moustache cut like a Turk's, corners drooping and deep lines, and he talks about the Glorious Revolution and the Constitution and liberty, which is out of fashion nowadays.[50]

Clearly Eric was not too impressed.

Eric's atmospheric profiles of lectures and lecturers became so well known among readers of the undergraduate magazine *The Granta* that a parody of them was published, the first half of it devoted, as Eric's profiles usually were, to a description of the lecture theatre, the second to Eric himself:

> He wears a long grey raincoat, buttoned firmly up the chin ... From the depths of his leather dispatch case he extracts a Spiral Notebook ('For Student or Secretary' – Woolworth's 3d.) and puts on a pair of spectacles. He has begun to observe. The noble brow creases, his jaw drops, he fixes the unfortunate lecturer with a firm, cold glare ... The lecturer, noticing a fresh face among the regular clients, glares back at our observer, who obviously has no business here – he jots down notes in *quite* the wrong places, a word here, a word there. The rest of the lecture is a duel of glances between lecturer and observer. For the busy throng, entranced by the scene, the hour flies past. We file out into the thin November rain. Turning the corner of the sneering houses we come upon a dark figure, poised storkwise on one leg. A *Times* correspondent could do no better. He scribbles furiously on the dispatch case which rests on his bent knee. Silently we leave him to his task ... We are, happily, unobserved.[51]

III

Like many freshmen, Eric joined a whole range of student societies in his first term, including the Cambridge Historical Society (on the recommendation of his supervisor), the English Society (poetry and criticism) and the Political Society, which had been founded by Oscar Browning, a Fellow of King's, in 1876 (all holders of history scholarships belonged *ex officio*). Eric read the Political Society's minute book and discovered 'with glee that Austen Chamberlain, a past member, on one occasion voted for the abolition of private property' (Chamberlain was Chancellor of the Exchequer in the last Conservative government before the First World War and later became Foreign Secretary). The society's President was John Clapham, 'whose optimism in social matters – judging by the paper he read – is at least as remarkable as his learning in Economic History', Eric noted. He also joined the Cambridge Union. He found it 'rather nice' and enjoyed drinking and socialising in the Union bar.[52] In his first term, he spoke from the floor in a debate, though not, it seems, to any great effect: 'MR E. J. E. HOBSBAWM (King's)', one report read, 'attacked the permanent staff of the Government departments. We are not altogether sure whether this speaker thinks out his speeches clearly enough before rising.' The subject of the debate was a motion on the policy of a 'United Front' of left-wing parties.[53] After this debacle, Eric gave up the Union, saving a considerable amount of money on membership fees.[54]

The society to which Eric really committed himself was the Socialist Club. With four hundred members or so, it was one of the strongest and most active student organisations in Cambridge. Given the predominance of public school boys in the student body, Eric found this fact 'astonishing'. There were even thirty or so members at King's, where he was immediately co-opted onto the Group Committee.[55] The Club was dominated by Communists. In London before he went up to Cambridge, Eric had been politically utterly on his own, unable to make contact with anyone who shared his political views. On the rare occasions on which he had been politically active, it had been on behalf of the Labour Party. Unlike its Italian, French or German counterparts, the Communist Party of Great Britain in any case had no room for intellectuals. Men and women with a 'bourgeois' background or professional occupation who found their way into the Party had to conform to the Party's working-class ethos and were denied any special standing. Middle-class recruits often tried to disguise their social origins and anyone with a 'posh' accent or a privileged educational background was likely to encounter deep suspicion from the Party activists. There was a strong element of 'donkey-jacketism' in the Party during the early years of its existence.[56]

This situation only began to change in the early to mid-1930s, with the arrival of student Communism, which emerged largely as a response to the triumph of Nazism in Germany, the alarming spread of fascism across Europe, including Britain, the growing threat of war, and, more specifically, the Jarrow hunger march, a mobile demonstration of trade unionists protesting against the poverty and unemployment that were so widespread during the Depression. In 1934 the marchers passed through many towns and cities, including Cambridge, on their way to London, attracting nationwide publicity. Communism's suddenly improved appeal to 'bourgeois intellectuals' prompted the Party to found its own student section in 1932. Four years later, the outbreak of the Spanish Civil War brought a further influx of young, educated and middle-class members into the Party, as the British Communist Party came out strongly in defence of the legitimately elected government of the Republic in its fight against the attempted coup launched by extreme right-wing army officers on 17 July 1936, while the Labour Party supported the British government's stance of neutrality and non-intervention.[57]

Late-night discussions led among other things to Eric's friends at King's, Jack Rice and Norman Haselgrove, joining the Communist Party. 'Unquestionably the Spanish War was the major influence in radicalizing people like Jack, who, at first sight, were extraordinarily unlikely recruits to the Party', with their public school background and conservative upbringing.[58] A number of Communists and others, including the writer George Orwell, went to Spain to fight for the Republic in the International Brigades. The Spanish Civil War mobilised young intellectuals because, as Eric wrote many years later, fascism 'was opposed in principle to the causes that defined and mobilized intellectuals as such, namely the values of the Enlightenment and the American and French revolutions':[59]

Anyone entering the rooms of Cambridge socialist and communist students in those days was almost certain to find in them the
photograph of John Cornford, intellectual, poet and leader of
the student Communist Party, who had fallen in battle in Spain
on his 21st birthday, in December 1936. Like the familiar photo
of Che Guevara, it was a powerful, iconic image – but it was
closer to us, and, standing on our mantlepieces, it was a daily
reminder of what we were fighting for.

In the world of student Communism, the International Brigades
enjoyed huge prestige: Eric's birthday present to his cousin Ron in
July 1937 was a short book, *Reporter in Spain*, by 'Frank Pitcairn',
the nom de plume of Claud Cockburn, a Communist journalist
who had joined the Brigades to write about the experience for the
Daily Worker. Eric inscribed the book with the dedication: 'Because
we weren't there'.[60]

There were other, similar converts. Jon Vickers, universally
known as 'Mouse' (a corruption of his schoolboy nickname 'Muse'),
a friend of Noel Annan's, scruffy, with holes in the elbows of his
jacket, was, Eric thought, too nervous to be politically effective, but
he was certainly a brilliant conversationalist:

He was the only person who I saw using all his muscles in a
discussion. He leant forward, his sharp nose, broken by boxing,
sniffed like that of a fox terrier, his spectacles shone enthusias-
tically, his somewhat shapeless lips moved up and down like a
piston. One noticed his long, thin arm muscles moving beneath
his ragged jacket – the jacket was always ragged. His ideas tum-
bled out like a waterfall. He often got on our nerves when he
repeated arguments all the time, but we often all laughed when
he made comparisons, in hackneyed phrases with unbridled
verve. 'Comrades', he said, 'the boot is, in a way, on the other
foot.' 'Comrades – we must always keep this in mind.' And then
it would suddenly come out, completely naturally, a spontaneous
insight: 'Comrades, S[talin] is right.'[61]

He was, Eric added, not without affection, 'bourgeois to his fingertips in appearance and behaviour', instantly recognisable as a product of the English public school system. Naïve, and spontaneous, he would speak his thoughts out loud without any self-consciousness, as

> when we went out one evening (1938) to a quarry in Albury and climbed up it in the dark, just for fun. It was not easy; the sand yielded, we held on and rooted about, feeling for a grip, climbing the little ravine with sand in our shirts. Now and then he said 'fine', 'brilliant', 'we'll make it'. Nothing behind it, it was just that he enjoyed life so much.[62]

As Eric pointed out, student Communists were not just 'the dissident children of the Establishment, of whom there were certainly a number in Oxbridge'. Some came from 'nonconformist-labour or liberal backgrounds (e.g. Christopher Hill, Rodney Hilton, Raymond Williams) and grammar-school formation'. Most 'were not upper middle class' at all.[63]

The Cambridge student Communists were an eclectic, cosmopolitan and international group; there were, Eric remembered in retrospect, very few Jews among them. At one point the Party told Eric to take up Jewish issues, and he and Ephraim (universally known as Ram) Nahum, a Manchester-born undergraduate, regarded by many at the time as the leader of the Cambridge student Communists, met with a delegation from the Party's Jewish Committee. 'I can see him still', Eric wrote later, 'with that squat, strong body, big nose, and quite unselfconscious and disarming aura of complete confidence – in someone less sure of himself it might have been swagger – and I can hear his voice still.'[64] But the meeting with the Jewish Committee was not a success. At least, Eric reported, it 'gave me an opportunity to make contact with the stand-up comedian style of the East End comrades', but neither he nor Nahum was really interested, so the contacts fizzled out.[65]

Among the leading lights of Cambridge Communism at this time was Margot Heinemann, the girlfriend of John Cornford.

Born in 1913, she became something of a political mentor to Eric, who later claimed that 'she probably had more influence on me than any other person I have known'.[66] But Eric's self-identification as a Communist intellectual was fixed long before he met Margot Heinemann, and, although she took him under her wing in the later 1930s, there is little evidence that she actually influenced the way he thought. Nor did she reciprocate Eric's admiration. He 'had not got the first idea of judging people', she said on one occasion.[67] A schoolteacher and part-time employee of the Labour Research Department, an independent trade union-funded organisation, she published a number of works on the coal industry, and ended her career as a Fellow of New Hall at Cambridge University. She remained a Communist to the end. She had a relationship with the scientist J. D. Bernal and bore him a daughter, but in the end no one truly managed to replace Cornford in her affections.[68]

The other leading figure in Cambridge Communism was James Klugmann. A year older than Margot Heinemann, he had won a Double First, was fluent in French and in 1934 embarked on a doctoral thesis on the French Revolution. But he abandoned his prospects of an academic career to become Secretary of the Paris-based World Student Association, a Communist-front organisation set up earlier in the thirties by the legendary German Communist media impresario Willi Münzenberg.[69] In this capacity he involved Eric in its conferences, taking advantage of Eric's knowledge of French. Ascetic, devoted entirely to the Party, Klugmann lived alone, surrounded by books. Eric did not know him well, but then, neither, it seems, did anyone else. During the war, Klugmann played a significant role in the British Special Operations Executive (SOE) in Yugoslavia, supporting the Communist partisans led by Josip Broz Tito. Doctrinaire to the core, Klugmann also acted as a secret agent for Soviet intelligence, though Eric did not know this at the time. His job was to comment on reports by other agents in Britain, and to recruit likely prospects willing to work alongside them.[70] And, indeed, Cambridge student Communism subsequently became notorious as a nursery for Soviet agents, though Eric was not among them. Like Klugmann himself, the 'Cambridge spies' – Anthony Blunt, Guy Burgess, Donald Maclean, Kim Philby and John Cairncross – were all born before the war, and had all gone down from the university before Eric came up.[71] What impelled these men to embark on their career of betraying state secrets seems to have been a belief that only the Soviet Union offered a real chance of defeating fascism at a time when the British government was not prepared to stand against it. Perhaps, too, an innate love of secrecy and conspiracy combined with a sense of class guilt were among the personal factors that drove them to become spies: neither of these traits was even remotely shared by Eric.[72] Eric subsequently confessed he would have agreed to spy for the Soviets at this time had he been asked, but he could only have done so had he worked for British intelligence, or in a relevant government department, which, unlike the real spies, he never did.[73]

The meetings of the Socialist Club were occasionally held in Eric's rooms at King's, more often at Pembroke College, where there were several Party members, including Ram Nahum, David Spencer and the Germanist Roy Pascal, one of the very rare Communist dons of the day. Its members included a number of young radicals from the colonies, not only Pieter Keuneman but also Mohan Kumaramangalam and Indrajit ('Sonny') Gupta, both of whom became prominent left-wing politicians after they returned to their native India. Eric, who was soon working closely with the 'colonial group' within the Socialist Club, thus obtained an early introduction to the history and politics of the subcontinent.[74] At the end of Michaelmas Term, when he was in his second year, Eric was elected to the committee or 'secretariat', though he was never chosen as the principal organiser because he was considered too academic.[75] The rather grandiosely named 'ministerial portfolios' on the committee were distributed at the beginning of Lent Term 1938. Eric ('Comrade Hobsbawm') was given responsibility for putting together the Club's weekly *Bulletin*.[76] Almost immediately, he tried to broaden its scope. He complained that the *Bulletin* had become nothing more than a glorified notice-board, unread by members and of no interest to outsiders; and we think this is a bad thing. Notices and exhortations are all very well, and part of the day-to-day work of the Club and ought to get the space they deserve, but that is no reason why other matters should not be published too. . . . Why was there nothing about literary questions, about problems of art, of this and that, about sex? Why were there no general, no humorous contributions? . . . This term has been desperately barren.[77]

Already at this point, therefore, Eric was demonstrating remarkable political independence of mind, as well as impatience, even perhaps disdain, in regard to the humdrum, everyday tasks which it was the lot of ordinary rank-and-file Communist Party members to carry out.

Just to get the new orientation going, Eric contributed a short critical note on a new film showing in Cambridge, *The Good Earth*, starring Luise Rainer, who won the Oscar for Best Actress for her performance, somewhat improbably, as a Chinese peasant woman. Eric dismissed the 'slightly supercilious' attitude of 'cast-iron Socialists' to Hollywood movies; the film was an important piece of political education that should show them that the problems of Chinese peasants were also their own.[78] Eric appealed again on 15 February, this time for discussion contributions on 'the gigantic international controversy that is going on about the nature of art today', in the Soviet Union, France and America, over 'questions of art and literature, Realism and Formalism'. 'Even in England individual critics, like Anthony Blunt, have given the matter a lot of thought.'[79] In the end, however, Eric's campaign to broaden the interests of the Cambridge student Communists was frustrated by the single-mindedness of Ram Nahum, who regarded art and music as unnecessary distractions from the political struggle, though he was an enthusiastic bridge player in his spare moments.[80]

IV

Largely for this reason, Eric became bored with the Cambridge University Socialist Club, whose activities he found increasingly 'trivial' compared to the great events brewing in the world at large. He was also becoming irritated by pointless discussions on Lenin at the regular reading sessions held by the 'colonial group', 'which went through every stage of scholasticism down to grammar'.[81] By the Michaelmas Term of 1937, after just a year, he declared that the Socialist Club's senior officers were guilty of 'gross inefficiency'. Their work was 'scandalously weak'. The new freshmen were more militant than their predecessors but the 'older members' of the Club were not taking advantage of their enthusiasm.[82] The leading figures in the Socialist Club felt, on the other hand, that Eric was really only interested in intellectual and cultural matters and had no real aptitude for practical politics. 'Eric knew everything', Harry Ferns commented later, 'but he seldom knew what to do. Ram spotted this weakness very early. More than once he said to me, "Damn it, Eric is making the party into a debating society."'[83] Under Nahum's influence the *Bulletin* did not really offer Eric the kind of opportunities he craved.

So very soon he began writing for the non-political Cambridge student magazine, *The Granta*. 'It was in his first term', Pieter Keuneman recalled, 'that he walked into *The Granta* office, his raincoat buttoned to the neck, and asked to be given a job.'[84] His first articles had appeared already in his second term, Lent 1937. Together with Jack Dodd he contributed a regular series of 'Cambridge Cameos', pen-portraits of local figures. They began with Briscoe Snelson, a local pawnbroker who had approached *The Granta* with a plea for help in locating the whereabouts of the three golden balls hanging above the entrance to his shop. The traditional sign of the pawnbroker, they had vanished overnight in what was obviously a student prank. 'The great appeal was launched. "Give us back our golden balls," was on every lip. Within three days a triumphant editor bore back the gleaming emblems and handed them reverently to their owner. Professional honour, public conscience, and *The Granta* vindicated.'[85]

The American-born former editor of *The Granta* Robert Egerton Swartwout, a well-known figure in the Cambridge Union debating society, was the subject of another of Eric and Jack's profiles. Evidently multi-talented, he set crossword puzzles for the *Spectator*, a London-based political weekly, he drew cartoons, and he had published a detective story, *The Boat Race Murder* (1933), as well as an imaginary biography of the late Victorian politician Lord Randolph Churchill based on the premise that he had not died in fact in 1895 but lived on into old age.[86] According to Eric and Jack Dodd, Swartwout's enthusiasm for Lloyd George had made him a Welsh Nationalist, 'and so you may see him, climbing Cader Idris on sunny days, and addressing understanding sheep in their native tongue'.[87] Two more cameos were devoted to well-known Cambridge retail outlets: a branch of the American chain store Woolworths ('nothing over sixpence'), whose manager Walter Clarke had filled the shop with royalist kitsch ready for the coronation of King George VI;[88] and the university and college clothing store Ryder & Amies, which is still in existence, though today its staff are considerably less intimidating than the manager in Eric's day, Mr Wallasey, who cut and designed College and club ties and could 'tell any of the 656 models on sight', especially if one of them was being worn by someone who had no proper claim to it.[89] 'Shop assistants and lecturers,' reported Pieter Keuneman in his profile of Eric, 'dreaded the gray figure which would slink in conspicuously and note down their foibles in a firm round hand.'[90]

By his second year at Cambridge, Eric was setting his sights higher with his personal profiles in *The Granta*, which by now, written on his own and without the collaboration of Jack Dodd, had moved on from local Cambridge people to figures of national and international significance. He succeeded in obtaining an interview with Christopher Isherwood in Tulliver's Café in central Cambridge after a talk the poet and dramatist had given about his current work. Isherwood, who had left Cambridge without finishing his degree in the mid-1920s, interested Eric not least because they had both been in Berlin at the same time, in the early 1930s. Isherwood was then finishing 'the Berlin works', the novels *Mr Norris Changes Trains* (1935), and *Goodbye to Berlin* (1939), subsequently turned into the musical *Cabaret*:

> In the room of Tulliver's Café he looks slighter and younger than he is; his eyebrows slope downwards, it gives him a worried look at times . . . Walking back through empty Petty Cury poet Isherwood addresses the Guildhall and *The Granta* interviewer. 'Tell them', he says, 'that I think the young generation is the goods.' He would have said it to the moon, or to the Milky Way, only there is no moon, and if there is, it is too much bother looking for it all over the sky. So he says it to me and walks, slight and youngish, down towards Silver Street, smiling with thin lines round the mouth and short hair, towards his lodgings.[91]

Eric found the poet 'very charming' and rather shy, and he was impressed by his commitment to the Republican side in the Spanish Civil War, though he and his fellow poet Wystan Auden had been unable to obtain a visa 'perhaps because [Foreign Secretary Sir Anthony] Eden thought they might smuggle tanks'.

More typical of Eric's usual preoccupation was a series of four political profiles of visiting speakers at the Cambridge Union which he wrote early in 1938 under the general heading 'The Stars Look Down'. The first was of Professor Harold Laski, a left-wing professor of politics at the London School of Economics.[92] Laski knew that he was a good debater, which gave 'an edge to the nasal drawl of his polished wisecracks and the precision of his labyrinthine periods'. He spoke almost completely without notes 'and with the effortlessness of a man who knows he can ride syntax like a broncho in an Arizona rodeo'. As his speech reached its climax, however, he dropped the wisecracks and became more urgent, more serious. 'He is a passionate and brilliant man, speaking for what he believes to be true.' At the time, Laski was at the height of his influence and fame; he threw it all away at the end of the war, however, with his quarrelsomeness and tactlessness (leading to the famous put-down by the Labour leader Clement Attlee – 'A period of silence on your part would be welcome'), and his writings, second-hand and derivative, have not survived. Eric was less impressed by the second speaker whose performance he reviewed, the liberal diplomat and writer Harold Nicolson, who later became best known for the voluminous diaries he kept during this period.[93] 'Here, indeed, one says, is the British upper-class: Suave, that is the word, diplomatic, cultured.' He spoke for 'a world remote from us', largely irrelevant to current concerns. Nicolson had once been a political figure of some substance, but by the late 1930s he was no longer at the centre of events. He was merely, Eric thought, a talker. 'He is as much a specialist in talking – and talking about himself – as other people are in accountancy or piano-tuning or billiards.'[94]

Eric next turned his remorseless critical eye on Herbert Morrison, an altogether more substantial figure. A leading Labour politician, Morrison was photogenic and knew how to generate good publicity.

> He is small and pugnacious. He looks much more like a bulldog than any Englishman decently ought. He stands on the platform, before a red screen, beside the table with the ritual tumbler of water and the ornamental chairman, legs astride, his one eye cocked at the audience, his eyebrows raised in the George Robey manner, now and again shutting his mouth with a snap so that strong vertical lines appear.[95]

Eric thought him a classically Gladstonian figure, speaking in orotund periods alternating with 'short, hammering statements', raising his voice to 'an almost screaming shout' before lapsing into 'the conversational and the familiar', 'rubbing his face, pointing his fingers, leaning on his suitcase and tearing a dumb heckler into little pieces with the routine of decades of public speaking'. The last subject about whom Eric wrote in his brief series of sketches of distinguished guests at the Union was the scientist J. B. S. Haldane, a famous mathematician and geneticist, professor at University College London. He was also a committed socialist. He advised the Republican government in Madrid on protection against gas attacks during the Civil War. His appearance was thoroughly unacademic: 'In his lumbering bulk he is very much like a great bear.'[96] Still, he carried enormous conviction with his exposition of the importance of science in everyday life and modern culture, a science 'which belongs to life. For that we respect him.'

Eric's main activity for the magazine was as its film critic. As he told Ron in February 1937: 'By dint of some nepotism (not too much) I have got myself a weekly free ticket for the cinema as reviewer for the Granta, and as I am saving as much as I can, that is very welcome.'[97] Apart from anything else, his appointment as the magazine's film critic provided what he later called 'a neutral territory for friends of different politics, such as the young Arthur Schlesinger Jr., whom I met there'. Schlesinger was an American who spent the academic year 1938–9 as Henry Fellow at Peterhouse and was later to become a Democratic Party speechwriter and prominent member of President John F. Kennedy's 'Camelot'.[98] Eric focused not on popular Hollywood movies or standard British cinema fare, but on foreign films, mostly French. He reviewed a French version of Dostoyevsky's *Crime and Punishment*, finding the whole very episodic and confused and the acting in general too stagey.[99] *King Kong* was showing at the Central Cinema at the time, and *Wells Fargo* at the Playhouse, but Eric ignored them both and wrote a piece instead on the French film star Sacha Guitry ('The Editors thought I was doing a note on Robert Taylor this week', he confessed, referring to a major Hollywood star with two movies on in Cambridge at the time, 'I thought it was Sacha Guitry. I apologise to anybody who was expecting Taylor'). He thought Guitry would soon be as forgotten 'as the fifth-rate French dramatists of the nineteenth century'.[100]

In subsequent issues he wrote about the great Austrian director Fritz Lang, the maestro of 'hysteria and panic' whose gifts, displayed most extravagantly in the classic Berlin crime film *M* (1931), were in danger of being smothered by Hollywood after his emigration to the United States; but also, surprisingly perhaps, about the Marx Brothers, whose overturning of convention he found both original and enjoyable in its 'perverse and, if you consider it carefully, rather frightening logic'.[101] His list of the twelve best films he had seen in 1938 included two French (*Le Quai des brumes* and *Un carnet de bal*), two Soviet (*We from Kronstadt* and *Mother*), one German (*Kameradschaft*) and one Dutch (*The Spanish Earth*), the remaining six being American. None of the movies he liked was British, though Alfred Hitchcock's classic *The Lady Vanishes* was among those released that year, a movie he probably hadn't seen. Their absence was 'just regrettable', he confessed.[102]

In January 1939, Eric was appointed editor of *The Granta*. His most spectacular contribution in this capacity was to put together parodies of other periodicals, real and imagined. On 1 February 1939 he produced *The New Statesman and Nation: The Week-End Review*, lampooning the stylistic banality, solemnity and utter lack of originality of the flagship left-wing weekly magazine. There were spoof readers' letters asking for support in obscure campaigns, for example, from the British Committee for the Emancipation of Thought, Language and Action in favour of the banning of a novel by a young Swedish writer about a young Swedish writer who succeeds in 'finding happiness in the Kamasutra' which brings him 'a varied and extensive sex-life which cannot, however, be described as obscene, as the manner of treatment is artistic in the extreme' and includes 'real-life photography'. There were requests for information from Hugh Walpole, who was writing a biography of J. B. Priestley, and from J. B. Priestley, who was writing a biography of Hugh Walpole (both were well-known English popular novelists of the day). A lampoon of the Mass Observation Project, founded in 1937, in which five hundred ordinary citizens kept diaries or answered periodic questionnaires, focused on 'the function of ticket-stubs in the capitalist economy', which concluded that 'the throbbing mass of frustrations in modern life is somehow canalized by the manipulation of ticket-stubs. It is significant that since Munich the mastication of ticket-stubs (as distinct from simple squashing) has increased 47 per cent in Britain south of the Firth of Forth. North of the Firth of Forth they are used to feed bank clerks.' The regular 'weekend competition' asked readers to paraphrase a rhyming couplet on love of one's mother and father, which yielded poor results ('in addition to their other peculiarities, readers of this journal do not love their parents'). Dr Wittgenstein had written asking what the word 'love' meant for the purposes of the competition. Damon Runyon, the New York short-story writer, came close ('Now if there is one person who has a claim on a guy's affections, apart from dolls, it surely is his mother and his pop – and then somewhat'), as did Sigmund Freud, who detected an 'ambivalent attitude, which is a basic principle of the Oedipus complex, ... due to living in Vienna', but the winner was the music-hall singer George Formby, with his lapidary 'Can you 'ear me, muvver?'[103]

This brilliant collection of parodies prompted Eric to put together a second one, this time a counterfactual but entirely plausible issue of *The Granta* to be published half a century into the future, on 8 March 1989, when a Nazi-type fascist movement had taken over Britain. Articles cleverly adapted the language of German Nazism to demand that 'the Gauleiter of Jesus College' change the College's name to 'Horst Wessel College'. The authorities should investigate other colleges named after 'a Hebrew agitator' or some similar degenerate individual, such as Christ's College or Corpus Christi. A reporter told readers that 'the antiquated chapel of King's has been removed to provide space for the rebuilding of the Central Railway and Bus Terminus'. Stormtroopers were to be billeted in the colleges to facilitate 'proper' educational work. To shouts of 'Hail Anglia' the regional Gauleiter opened an exhibition of Anglo-Saxon art at the Guildhall. A ritual murder was reported in Selwyn College (an Anglican foundation). The Calendar of events included relays of the Führer's speech from Downing Street demanding the incorporation of Anjou into the United Kingdom in conformity with the wishes of its inhabitants 'long-suffering under the brutal oppression of the French'.[104] Press parodies of the scale and ambition of those executed under Eric's editorship, were not to be repeated until the *Guardian* published a seven-page supplement on the fictitious island dictatorship of San Scrriffe on April Fool's Day 1977.

V

By the beginning of the new academic year – Eric's final one – in October 1938, the Munich crisis had just ended with Hitler's threat to invade Czechoslovakia being resolved by British Prime Minister Chamberlain's conclusion of an agreement that the country's German-speaking borderland should be incorporated into Germany. There was widespread disquiet on the Left, and as Eric noted in the *Socialist Society Bulletin,* 'Recruiting to the Club has been extraordinary in these last few days, thanks to the Crisis.' Indeed, it was 'now the largest socialist club in any University' and 'the largest political club in this University'. It set up 'actives' groups in the colleges, aiming through posters and meetings to reach a university-wide membership of a thousand by the end of term. Three hundred new members were being recruited every week, it was reported. There were ninety in Trinity College alone. Five packed meetings had condemned Chamberlain's policy of appeasing Hitler. This rapid growth was made easier by the fact that the Socialist Club was 'not a political party, nor a propaganda machine, nor even a social club for progressive people', but 'the largest section of the University Labour Federation, which has a vote at the Labour Party Conference'. Communist members would not be expected to sign up as affiliates of the Labour Party but anyone who was 'sufficiently in sympathy with the Labour Party' was urged to do so. 'Membership of a national political party, whether the Labour Party or the Communist Party, is the best way of taking undergraduates out of the rarified University atmosphere of "playing at Socialism" and bringing us into contact with the outside world.'[105]

Much of Michaelmas Term of 1938 was taken up with raising funds to send food parcels to Republican victims, especially refugee children, of the Spanish Civil War. The Club also organised a formidable list of speakers for the year, including the leading Labour politicians Clement Attlee and Stafford Cripps, the General Secretary of the British Communist Party Harry Pollitt, the poet

W. H. Auden, the author Naomi Mitchison, and the Vice-President of the Amateur Athletic Association Herbert Pash.[106] There were also Faculty Study Groups, with Eric chairing history and inviting Mounia Postan, H. J. Habakkuk (a brilliant young economic historian of English landownership) and the Marxist German literature specialist Roy Pascal to give talks, alongside a discussion evening on the question 'Did Karl Marx write good history?'.[107] But not everything went to plan. Attlee's address, delivered in the Corn Exchange to an audience of 1500 people, was disrupted by a minority of Tory supporters of the government, including 'Pitt Club boys', the equivalents of Oxford's notorious Bullingdon Club hearties, as well as 'great, big, mature, sophisticated athletes ... The Conservative Association will be sorry to hear that one of their officers, the Marquis of Granby, was distributing fireworks.' The protesters 'shouted, blew hunting horns, let off fireworks, and behaved in the traditional way of undergraduates with too much money and too weak heads for drink'. There were not only 'shouts of enthusiasm for Chamberlain' but even yells of 'Heil, Hitler' from the rowdy audience.[108]

There were other reasons for concern among Cambridge Communists. The Soviet Union was undergoing a series of political upheavals. Following the murder of the Leningrad Party chief Sergei Kirov in 1934, Stalin had turned on his former allies within the Soviet Communist Party and put them on trial for treason. Stalin's main rival for power during the 1920s, the charismatic intellectual Trotsky, had been expelled from the Party and exiled, finishing up in 1936 in Mexico, where he was to be assassinated on Stalin's orders four years later. In two major show trials held in August 1936 and January 1937, former leading figures in the Party, including Grigory Zinoviev, Lev Kamenev and Karl Radek, confessed to playing a key role in Trotsky's conspiracies and were sentenced to death; in the following months there were to be further show trials, involving other leading figures, notably Nikolai Bukharin. They were accompanied by a purge in which hundreds of thousands of lower-ranking Party members were arrested and shot or sent to labour camps.[109]

The initial reaction to the trials in the West was one of consternation but not, in general, scepticism. As the then US ambassador to Moscow wrote, 'It is generally accepted by members of the Diplomatic Corps that the accused must have been guilty of an offence which in the Soviet Union would merit the death penalty.'[110] It was only in 1938, when the accusations in the later trials reached palpable heights of absurdity, that a degree of scepticism set in. The confessions of Zinoviev and the others, it emerged many years afterwards, had been written for them by their interrogators, and were extracted above all by Stalin's promise to spare their families from execution if they co-operated in admitting their own guilt. Only in a few cases, including that of Bukharin, did the Soviet secret police use torture, but generally the unharmed appearance of the defendants convinced observers that their confessions were voluntary and therefore true. A few Communists turned against the Party, shocked by the trials; most notable among them was the Hungarian exile Arthur Koestler, who resigned from the Party in 1938, to write his classic *Darkness at Noon*, published two years later, a chilling portrayal of the mental discipline and fanaticism that he thought led committed Bolsheviks to acquiesce in their own denunciation.[111]

The leadership of the Communist Party of Great Britain applauded the trials and harboured no doubts about the reality of the conspiracies they purported to reveal. On 1 February 1937 the *Daily Worker*, the Party's flagship publication, claimed that 'everywhere in the British Labour movement the scrupulous fairness of the trial, the overwhelming guilt of the accused, and the justness of the sentences is recognized'. After the revelations in Moscow, the British Communist Party, following Stalin's lead, even diverted substantial resources of energy into combating a more or less nonexistent Trotskyist conspiracy within its own ranks.[112] Eric, writing to his cousin Ron, tried to defend the trials:

Consider: the following facts are fairly well established: the accused are people who have, at various times in the past, been in violent disagreement with the Party Line, have at various times been expelled from the party and deposed from their positions ... Second, Trotsky had for the last five years or more consistently advocated the overthrow of the USSR as a non-socialist and anti-revolutionary body ... Third, the accusations are not intrinsically impossible; that the Trotskyists should wreck seems clear (Kirov) that they should be willing to cede USSR territory is not impossible: perhaps they wanted in the end to double-cross Hitler and Japan, perhaps they just thought it a necessary if regrettable concession.[113]

Eric accepted the Soviet explanation of some minor discrepancies in the confessions (for example, an alleged meeting of one of the defendants with Trotsky in a Copenhagen hotel in 1932 that turned out to have been demolished several years earlier). He considered the methods by which the confessions had been obtained as 'open and above board', and noted that the accused had not confessed to everything, so 'only where the full evidence has been brought out will they admit to the facts'. Radek's upright behaviour in the dock had also been 'reassuring': 'He did not beg for mercy; He did not plead irresponsibly. He said: I refuse to be judged with common spies and wreckers, I am a responsible political figure; only I was wrong in my estimate of the situation.'

In the end, therefore, Eric concluded '(a) that an underground opposition existed which, being without mass backing, had to resort to terrorism and intervention. (b) that the trial was a legal and understandable affair (c) that there is nothing very improbable about the procedure of it ' Yet the trials raised the awkward question of why, if the accused men had, as they confessed, been working against the Soviet Union from the very beginning, even before the Revolution, they had none the less repeatedly been appointed to top positions in the Party. Perhaps, he thought, 'there were not enough experienced men available for the jobs in hand?'. Or perhaps they were kept on by the Party out of 'optimism', or 'sentimentality' because they were Old Bolsheviks, or out of a naïve and misplaced faith in their integrity because they were Marxists. And the reason why they had only now been arrested and put on trial was that the new Constitution of the USSR, which came into effect in 1936, earning the plaudits of Western sympathisers such as the Fabian Socialists Sidney and Beatrice Webb as the democratic blueprint of a 'new civilization', 'would give wreckers a free hand'. Thus, 'like it or not, the Soviet authorities must clean up the country thoroughly in order to make it safe for the new Constitution'.[114]

If this elaborate and unconvincing series of justifications sounded more like Eric's attempt to reassure himself than persuade Ron, there was no doubt about the strength of his commitment to the Republican cause in the Spanish Civil War. He took part in the May Day demonstration in London's Hyde Park, organised in 1937 by members of the Labour Party. It was dedicated to solidarity with the Republicans, though Labour's official policy was one of studied if sympathetic neutrality. 'It was a fine show', he told Ron, whom he had glimpsed in the crowd of marchers but had been unable to reach,

> better than most others I've seen in England. You remember a couple of years back they would all just slouch along anyhow and with only the haziest idea of how to sing or shout slogans. Well, today they're much better. And besides, today one sees quite a representative selection of normal working-class people in Left-Wing demonstrations, where before there would be a combination of intellectuals and, as often as not, Lumpenproletariat. That's what mass-basis can mean.[115]

The British Labour Party was careful in organising such events to avoid any impression of collaborating with the Communists in a UK version of the Popular Front. Given the situation in France and Spain, the omens for such collaboration did not seem propitious. In Spain in particular, as the Republicans' military situation was deteriorating, divisions between the Communists and the anarchists were beginning to emerge. Eric shared the Communist Party's distrust of the enthusiastic but disorganised anarchists of the kind he had met in his brief visit to Puigcerdà. 'Apparently these anarchists are starting troubles in Catalonia,' he wrote to

Ron in May 1937, citing a report in *The Times*. 'If they cannot wait till the war is decided – and, God knows, it is *not* decided yet – they will seriously sabotage the job of winning it.'[116]

VI

Eric went to France again in 1937 for a summer break, partly funded by his uncle Sidney. He made his way once more to the south. He left Paris on 4 August, hitch-hiking to Lyon and thence to Avignon. He got lifts on a variety of vehicles, including a breakdown van, a lorry and a variety of family cars, travelling through the night and reaching Manosque, a short way north of Marseilles, on 8 August. He was interested in the village because, as he wrote during the war, it was the home of the novelist and pacifist campaigner Jean Giono, 'whom I admired, although I am by no means surprised that he has since turned into a collaborator. A blood-and-soil complex makes for a certain richness and sexiness in style, but in the end it generally runs away with the man.'[117]

He had hitch-hiked to Manosque in the company of two German boys he had met on the road from Lyon to Vienne.

> They were brown-haired, about seventeen, with check shirts, rucksack and shorts and we looked at each other suspiciously, like dogs on the outskirts of a football crowd. After all, I thought, these boys are no doubt members of the Hitler Youth. Only professional soldiers feel at ease with the enemy. We shall have perhaps half an hour before the next car comes along, and one can hardly discuss politics. The road stretched dead straight between, I think, poplars, hardly even dipping, the countryside had begun to wear that greyish, dusty look of the south, and the dust spilled over their little socks.

They agreed to flip a coin for who would get the next lift. The Germans won. They waited some time, since Manosque was not on any major route.

The older boy stood in the road, silhouetted between the poplars like a boy scout advertisement, the younger one and myself lay down in the ditch, so as not to scare motorists by the sight of three potential passengers at once. We lay back and let our necks rest on the dusty grass, making laboured conversation in French about youth hostels, the cathedral at Vienne and various other subjects. It is a very odd feeling to talk in a language which is foreign to both of you. He had a harmonica sticking out of his breast-pocket and a camera, the ubiquitous beautiful camera of the Germans slung around his neck. Admiring it tided us over till the next car came. Then they went, and I lay in the ditch for another few minutes watching the swifts. We said Good-bye, quite unconstrainedly.

Eric had not revealed to the boys the fact that he spoke German. His Viennese accent would have given him away, and inevitably the young Germans would have questioned him as to why he was in France, and eventually discovered that he was Jewish, with possible consequences that Eric was doubtless keen to avoid.

A roadman's lorry gave him a lift into Manosque, where he found the youth hostel empty apart from the warden. She gave him a glass of grenadine. He noticed a collection of Giono's books on the common-room shelf, but the warden told him he could not go to see the writer at this time of day, in the afternoon. A girl came in, and, after she had registered, they decided to go out and find somewhere for a swim.

We walked through the town and along the Aix road with half-closed eyes because of the sun, hardly talking for the first ten minutes. She had come by bicycle from Briançon, a tough girl. There were no carts, there were no birds except for some magpies who flew round the olive trees, there was nothing except the heat and the rumble of the river Durance in the distance. I put my sun-glasses on with a feeling of vanity overcome.

Tiring of walking in the sun, they turned aside towards the river, and Eric went in for a dip while the girl sat on the bank 'with her

legs drawn up and her brown arms bracing against the embank-
ment, her feet turned slightly outward. She was rather an ugly girl
who wore her hair in an eton-crop and had slight pock-marks on
her face.' She was a German-speaking Jewish exile, with the surname Goldmann. Her first name, or at least the name she used in
her French exile, was Marcelle. Eric invited her in. 'She shook her
head and laughed.' The current began to sweep him downstream
and he came out. They discussed Giono's books while he dried
himself off with her towel. She offered him a peppermint.

> There was no special significance in lying on a bank in Basses
> Alpes with another hiker, the sort of accidental, temporary
> combination that occurs dozens of times in any summer.
> Nevertheless people who are thrown together may become
> very intimate for the short time of their acquaintance, mainly
> in order to defend themselves against the rest of the world. Was
> this likely? I looked at her and thought, most unlikely . . . Oddly
> enough we did not talk about ourselves at all on the way home,
> which was just as hot as the way out had been.

Instead, they continued to discuss Giono, but Eric, much
though he admired the novelist, was made uncomfortable by 'the
atmosphere of discipleship at the hostel', and began to voice some
criticisms. 'Then why are you here?' asked Marcelle.
    They ran into the two German boys again as they entered the
town, and 'they smiled at the girl although she looked very Jewish.
These two boys seemed to pick their way through the intricacies of
etiquette among the lesser peoples like a canoe going through ice-
floes.' They came from a small medieval town, Gera, in Thuringia,
and the ancient streets of Manosque made them feel at home so
they 'began to see the French as almost human'. There had been
grain riots in the town during the Revolution, Eric told them. Was
it like the peasant war? one of the boys asked, thinking of the war
of 1525 at the start of the Reformation. '"Like the peasant war",
said Marcelle in German. Both boys coloured deeply and the
conversation dropped till we arrived at the hostel.' An older man

in the common room, hearing the boys speak German, declared belligerently that he had been at the front in the last war. "'Were you really" said Marcelle, who appeared to enjoy the situation in an abstract fashion, as though she were taking part in charades.' Later, as they walked round the town, Eric and Marcelle discussed the two young Germans. 'I went to school with boys like that', said Eric, referring to his time in Berlin:

> There's no harm in them. They are just reacting away from a feeling of inferiority. When I was at school one day our teacher put it to us like this: Germany is down. There are two schools of getting her up again – one school wants to do it by ingratiating itself with the victors, the other, Adolf Hitler's, by rousing the German people. By itself, without foreign help the German people will throw off its shackles. That's what he said. He said which will you choose. I almost became a nationalist for the day. It seemed so logical.

They climbed up a hill outside town. Marcelle told him that her father came from Odessa. 'We stood on the hill, looking down into the Durance valley, fascinated by our assimilation. Then we lay down and, after all, I did make love. I shouldn't have done, it was probably only a gesture of solidarity against the two nazi boys who took no interest anyway.' After catching up on sleep, having a bath and eating a meal, Eric said goodbye to Marcelle. They did not see each other again. 'I suppose she has gone through hard times since,' he wrote a few years later, when Jews in France were being rounded up and sent to Auschwitz.

From Manosque he hitch-hiked to St Raphael, on the Mediterranean coast, where he stayed in the local youth hostel, meeting a variety of students, Americans, French Canadians and a Czech, taking another bath and consuming a sandwich for dinner. There were more cars and more tourists in this part of the south of France:

> The rich women have splendid figures and their Packards don't give you lifts. There is hardly a place on earth where it is more

difficult to get lifts than the Côte d'Azur. I suppose money, which can turn middle-aged women into young ones, indifferent appearance into elegance, is of more use to them than I thought at first. Halfway between Cannes and St Raphael a Buick full of men in orange shirts and women in bathing costumes drove past, with a British number-plate. I yelled after it. It stopped and after we had gone for a few minutes they said 'We thought you were English, when you called us.' How foreign do I sound? The French say 'çe grand Anglais', the English say 'you're not English', only one dumb farmer in the Pyrenees once asked me why I was walking around. For a job? I said yes. Then you are a Spaniard, he said.[118]

The group he had fallen in with consisted, in fact, of exiles and refugees from a variety of countries or, rather, as he was told, people without a fatherland. '"These people aren't émigrés", says one of the older members of the group. "They have no country at all. They are individual atoms who do not fit into any community of place, language, economics and culture."' He took a shine to a young Russian woman, Irina, as he called her in his account of the episode, and as she played a game of tennis he found himself 'looking with longing at the fragments of Irina's body that could be seen between the net and the post'. It became clear that they had 'gate-crashed the exclusive residences of the rich'.[119]

They sang songs, danced and talked politics. 'Irina wears a flowered dress and is brown all over. Her hair is brown, her eyes are brown, her skin is brown from lying in the sun. In her left hand she swings a towel, drapes it round her neck, takes it down again and swings it forward and back.' The group decided to bathe in the sea:

The water is like silk. The water is so beautiful to see and to feel that it is hard to think of anything else. When we turn round, hearing it suck gently at our shoulders, we can see the lights of the cafés on the beach and hear the, in this case a little disturbing, music. To have a fatherland means to know all about the people among whom you work; to know their little peculiarities, what fairy-tales they are told when they are small, what they do when they take girls home from the dance at night, what bad jokes the old men make, what stereotyped things they say at card-parties in the cafés, what they like to read in the magazines. What made the Czech servant-girls sing patriotic songs and the Irish labourers give nickels to the clan-na-gael? An emotion which can mobilise the politically undeveloped and give comfort even to the stateless, by proxy, cannot be overlooked.

Eric's first recorded thoughts on national identity, a topic that would concern him closely later in life, thus occurred to him while he was bathing in the Mediterranean Sea just off the southern coast of France.

They talked about politics and identity. Irina thought that politics didn't achieve anything, but Eric disagreed: 'One must talk to do things. People who sit by themselves and work out their ideas are most likely wrong. How many quires could be filled with the stenographic reports of the debates which have changed the world?' After much talking and singing they parted. 'I can now go away and think, on a holiday I fell in love with a beautiful girl but did nothing about it. On the Riviera where everybody makes love I did nothing at all about it except to walk back in a bunch of people singing not very pertinent songs.' The next day he began to make his way back to Paris.[120] After a trip to Cannes he hitched west to St Tropez and Marseille, reaching Aix-en-Provence, where his luck deserted him ('miserable – on foot', he noted tersely in his diary). He managed to find a lift to Aubenas, in the Ardèche, where he breakfasted, then hitched further north to Le Puy and then found a lorry to take him most of the way to Vichy. By 14 August he had reached Moulins, in the Allier department, where he had a meal, then went on to Avernes. Arriving at eleven o'clock at night, he found the youth hostel closed and was forced to take a 'desperate sleep in a bean plantation'. By Monday 16 August 1937 he was back in Paris.

The trip, he told Ron, 'ought to prove the possibilities of hitch-hiking as a method of travel!'. Along the way he met many different kinds of people, including some students from the London School of Economics, an Austrian Communist who had been to one of the schools Eric had attended in Vienna, the secretary to the Oxford don and prominent moderate socialist G. D. H. Cole, a man he was to encounter in very different circumstances after the war, and a friend of his French teacher at St Marylebone:

> God, have I got through a lot of things. Eating snails in Burgundy and bathing on the Riviera and making running conversations to French car-drivers, learning new songs at French youth-hostels and waiting two hours in the sun for cars, camping in a sleeping-bag and ground-sheet in pouring rain and discussing with French anarchist students. Meeting Englishmen and French, Germans, Dutch, Swedes, Canadians, Americans, Italians, Poles, Swiss, Austrians, Belgians, Spaniards, Russians and Czechoslovaks. Nothing but Czechoslovaks. Watching the local jazz-band at Manosque and the ubiquitous bowls. Getting lifts in Chryslers and Packards. Improving my French.[121]

Back in Paris he stayed at the Hôtel Ambassador with his uncle Sidney and Nancy and Peter, now teenagers, who had come to see the World Exposition, made famous by the display of Picasso's painting *Guernica*, which recorded the suffering of the Basque town of the same name during the Spanish Civil War.

Eric stayed on in Paris at the instigation of Margot Heinemann to take part in an 'International Conference of the World Student Association', held from 25 to 28 August. The delegates included Eric's friend Ram Nahum though not Eric himself. The participants discussed reports on the situation of students in a variety of countries, many of them implausibly optimistic (the German delegate, for example, reported that university students under the Nazi regime were generally unhappy and disillusioned).[122] By this time the French Popular Front was getting into serious difficulties; the economy was not recovering from the Depression, there was a run on the franc and conservatives in the Senate were blocking further reforms. The Socialists were forced out of government in June 1937, and Léon Blum resigned. A year later the Popular Front, riven by internal disputes about French policy (or lack of it) towards the Spanish Civil War, dissolved itself. The euphoria of 1936 had long since disappeared.[123] As Eric remarked, 'the political situation looks grim all round'.[124]

Eric made some money by acting at Margot Heinemann's request as an interpreter in some of the sessions. While he was there he became friendly with a Hungarian Communist in his twenties, whom he called Arpad Fekete in the reminiscences he wrote up in the form of another short story. Arpad took him to Les Macédoines, a cheap restaurant frequented by Yugoslavs, Hungarians and Bulgarians. Eric found the atmosphere rather sinister, starting with the appearance of the head waiter:

> Iron-grey moustaches shaped like aeroplane wings, a brown, heavily-lined face with a skin grown flabby from long hours of indoor work and hard black eyes like buttons: he gave the impression of being a very capable man masquerading as a seedy head-waiter for his own purposes; but this was nothing new since everybody in *Les Macédoines*, waiters and clients, gave the impression of masquerading as something unimportant and respectable. I have never met a place that smelt so much of putsches.[125]

As a Communist and a Jew, Arpad had suffered under the right-wing, aggressively anti-Communist and anti-Semitic regime of Admiral Horthy in Hungary, imprisoned and badly beaten, before he had escaped to Paris, where he was now living. Eric thought the young Hungarian was a dandy. 'Litterateur! Philanderer! Revolution-monger! Why do they pick on men like him, coffee-house Bolsheviks, Don Juans in pinstripe padded shoulder suits, to kick their genitals?' The question answered itself.

Arpad took Eric and a Russian Communist friend to a brothel off the Boulevard Sebastopol, where they ordered drinks.

> It was not the busy season. There were [a] few clients who sat moodily behind the marble-topped tables which lined the

longish, glass-roofed room . . . At one end, besides the ladies' toilet, a small band played rather half-heartedly dressed in red gypsy blouses. Now and again they stopped and came round to collect tips and the women stopped dancing heavily with each other and came round the tables offering to do obscene parlour tricks. Arpad lay back on the red plush seats and pursed his mouth with a cigarette between his lips as though he were an Alexander Blok or a Toulouse-Lautrec, very affected.

At seven francs a glass, the beer was very expensive, 'there were no good women in the room', and 'the band', Eric thought, 'was lousy'. His friends tried to get it to play a Hungarian dance but the musicians did not know any. Eric felt an ironic sense of guilt.

Look at us, three so-called communists, members of the greatest movement in the world's history, the men who have found what Archimedes was looking for, the men who will bend the earth as though it were made of tin-plate and mould it like plastic, arguing about bad dance-bands in a second-rate whore-house. Not even a classy one. Not even the tone of betraying the working-class properly.

A girl came up to them and tried to talk to Arpad, but he was too drunk to respond, and was holding his head in his hands and leaning on the table top. 'Come with me while your friend's thinking, darling', said the girl to Eric. 'Come with me and we shall have a nice time.' And they did. In his later, published memoirs, Eric revealed that his Hungarian friend's actual name was György Adam. Forgetting his earlier encounter with Marcelle, he reported: 'I lost my virginity in an establishment – I can no longer recall its address – with an orchestra of naked ladies, and in a bed surrounded on all sides by mirrors'.[126] As for Arpad, or György, Eric tried to locate him in Paris shortly before the war, but when he asked after him at Les Macédoines, he was told they had not seen him for a while. They thought he had gone to live in South America.[127]

VII

When he returned to Cambridge to begin the second year of his studies, in October 1937, Eric felt rather more at home than he had done the year before. He was now living in better accommodation than 'The Drain', namely in room 8, Staircase U, a late Victorian building extended in the 1920s, located on the far side of the College away from the Chapel and overlooking a small lawned area next to the river. Rooms here were much prized by the students. Eric's was on the top floor of the building, reached by six flights of broad wooden stairs, but the view of the river and the meadows across the other side was peaceful, the tranquillity broken only by punters as they glided along the river in the summer months, and so he stayed in the room in the following year, 1938–9, as well.[128]

He had not managed to spend much time with his cousin Ron, who had graduated from the LSE with First Class Honours and the Gonner Prize in Economics the previous summer and was still working in Kew, at the Ministry of Labour; he married his girl-friend shortly before the war.[129] But they continued to correspond frequently. After he had moved in, Eric explained to Ron:

> Up to now I enjoy this term more than any of the others. You know, the first, one comes up not knowing a soul and not wanting or daring to get in touch with anyone and unable to adjust oneself to the new conditions. The second and third one gets used to it, but has a lot of academic work and exams, and besides, has not quite shed the awkwardness of the first. This term now is really the first one really spends 'in Cambridge': Not that Cambridge does not get on one's nerves often. Sometimes one wants to kick some of the people. And it's so very parochial; refuses to recognise that the rest of the world is anything but a place whence ex-presidents of the Union come to give political speeches.[130]

Eric was feeling in high spirits, as he had done, he told Ron, 'since I went to France early in August'. He found this surprising, since he was prone, he said, to 'fairly regular fits of depression every now and again. I expect they'll come pretty suddenly sometime round January at the latest.' Eric and some of his keener contemporaries tried to remedy this situation in the Michaelmas Term of 1937. 'We have managed – in our faculty', he told Ron, 'to set joint unofficial meetings of dons and representative students and extension of discussion-classes and suchlike. For a medieval university like ours this is quite an advance.'[131] But like so many other such initiatives, it ran into the sands of donnish indifference. It was not only Oxford that was the home of lost causes.[132]

At the end of 1937 he found the international situation 'pretty appalling', though the Labour Party at least had 'started doing something about Spain'.[133] Prime Minister Neville Chamberlain was 'completely pro-fascist' and not likely to do anything to upset Hitler, Mussolini or Franco. Yet his foreign policy was not universally popular. Differences between the Prime Minister and Foreign Secretary Eden led to the latter's resignation, over issues including the Spanish Civil War, on Monday 21 February 1938, creating a sense of national crisis over foreign policy. In Cambridge, the Socialist Club sprang into action:

We called an emergency meeting of C.U.S.C. on the Monday of Eden's resignation and well over 200 of our members turned up. Then we got an emergency session of the Peace Council which decided to hold a meeting on the Wednesday. On Tuesday morning CUSC distributed 6000 leaflets calling for Resignation [of the government] and we held a poster-parade of about 40 people all over the town. On Tuesday afternoon we had a joint committee of the Liberals, Socialists and Democratic Front which issued a joint statement and organised the Tuesday lobby of MPs. All the time we organised the sending of telegrams to MPs – we got about 600 off by Wednesday. Wednesday we had the Peace Council meeting to which so many people turned up that many had to be turned away – 500 I should say. Thursday we lobbied, and this week it goes on.[134]

Two hundred students, a hundred of them from Cambridge, sixty from Oxford and forty from London, attended the lobby of MPs and received wide coverage in the press, including conservative dailies. Eric confessed to Ron: 'I've spent a good deal of time on political work and I'll have to cram during the vac to make up leeway.'

There were other distractions, too. As in previous years, he spent some weeks every vacation reading in the library of the London School of Economics, which he found 'a good place to work. It was full of central Europeans and colonials, and therefore markedly less provincial than Cambridge, if only by its commitment to social sciences such as demography, sociology and social anthropology, which were of no interest on the Cam.' Often going to Marie's Café, which occupied a corner on the main frontage of the LSE, he made many new friends, including the later historian John Saville (who at the time still called himself by his original Greek name, Stamatopoulos), his girlfriend and later wife, Constance Saunders, the 'bushy-haired charmer' Teddy (Theodor) Prager, an Austrian student and left-wing economist, and many others. The girls he met there included Muriel Seaman, whom he was to encounter again when the LSE relocated to Cambridge during the war. Among the café's habitués was a 'silent lone Central European rather older than ourselves', who turned out to be the great sociologist Norbert Elias; his book *On the Process of Civilization* was about to be published, in German, in Switzerland, but remained unsold and unregarded until the 1960s, when it became one of the most widely read and influential socio-historical texts of the late twentieth century.[135]

But in February 1938 Eric also found the environment in Cambridge 'pretty good', especially in King's College. 'The crocuses have come out on the avenue behind the river and at night the air is mild and the river quiet and fairly fast. We always walk by the Chapel at night. I'm at last beginning to appreciate the real beauty of architecture, living with it all the time.' His personal life, however, was rather dull in comparison with the excitement of France the previous summer. Congratulating Ron on getting his 'personal affairs' into a 'satisfactory' state, he commented gloomily: 'My own are still – shall I say fortunately or unfortunately – in as detached a state as they have been. I still get my kick out of politics and, these days, out of looking at the river, while my friends get hitched and unhitched. I really think it is time I got into line, I expect I shall sometime, but it is no use hurrying'.[136]

By the end of April he was focusing on the looming end-of-year examinations, like many other undergraduates:

> Everybody is having 'Trip[os] Fever' now, and I've never seen the University Library as crowded as it has been these last few days. All sorts of queer people worried about their exams. Actually, I don't feel so good about it either – not that I can't get a First if I try, and get sufficient work done in the next four weeks, but I would like to get a star and that looks pretty distant. Barring an extraordinary choice of questions or a windfall of some sort.[137]

He had decided to 'give politics a miss' during this period, to concentrate exclusively on revising for the exams. In the event, he did get a starred First; it had never really been in doubt, except in his own mind ('I was really pretty nervous', he wrote shortly afterwards). And he had more good news: he had been awarded a £30 grant by the University's Political Science Fund to go to French North Africa ('my own suggestion') for a two-month political study of agrarian conditions there, and another £10 from the College, 'quite a big sum', as indeed it was by the standards of the day. London County Council, who supported him at Cambridge, could not deduct it from his maintenance grant because it was for a specific purpose.[138] He did not say why he had decided on this project, but it is likely that he became interested in European colonisation as a result of discussions with his Communist friends in Paris, and he clearly felt by now that his French was good enough for him to do the research. The Professor of Political Science, Ernest Barker, furnished him with a letter of introduction and recommendation to the French Embassy in London. He made the necessary travel arrangements and set off towards the end of August.

Eric's purpose was to study agrarian conditions in Algeria and Tunisia, at that time both French colonies. He took a boat train to Paris and thence another train to the south of France, embarking on a steamer for the port of Tunis, where he arrived on 25 August and stayed in the Hôtel Capitol on the avenue Jules Ferry, as noted by a local official. He had gone 'completely unnoticed', complained the official, 'and the question of the nature of his activity had been ignored for several days'.[139] He had in fact contacted local administrative officials in Tunis, interviewing them about the economic and social condition of the colony and obtaining the necessary permissions to travel into the interior. The last night in the city he spent in a youth hostel at Sidi Bou Said, overlooking the bay, with some of the most beautiful views he had ever seen. On 31 August he left for Sfax, a city located 270 kilometres down the coast from the capital. It was, he remarked to Ron,

> one of the most unattractive towns I have yet come across. It is remarkable simply for the fact that for 50 miles around there are nothing but olive-trees in straight rows, whereas 50 years ago there was nothing at all. Both the French and the Arabs point this fact out triumphantly, the one arguing that it proves the benefits of French colonisation, the other that it proves the dependence of the exploiting French on the Arabs for the real work of development. But except for the olives, and the camels and encampments of Bedouins by the roadside, and the statue of the army surgeon who discovered the existence of phosphates in Tunisia, there is nothing thrilling in Sfax. The statue is easily the most significant thing in the town.[140]

From Sfax he travelled a little way back up the coast, then took a bus inland to Karouan, 'one of my few lapses into ordinary tourism', he noted; 'for until now I've had very little chance to see much of either Tunis or the country. It has been sheer forced labour to try to collect and absorb all about the political, social and economic structure of Tunis in the space of a week, and I'm never going to do it again.' The phosphate company, he reported, made 'incredible profits' since it produced nearly a third of the world's entire output of the mineral, and was part of the capitalist system of France's legendary '200 families' that were popularly supposed to control the Third Republic.

It took some effort to acclimatise to North Africa, he told Ron, and he 'hadn't got used to the idea of a landscape containing nothing at all apart from the occasional group of incredibly starved Bedouins' and the odd patch of scrub. He talked to 'non-official contacts' such as 'anti-fascist Italian groups, local European trade-unions etc (obtained through courtesy of Mme. Andrée Viollis and newspaper *Ce Soir*);[141] slight contact with arab students (obtained through World Student Association)'. The British Consul in Tunis spent much of his time looking after the large Maltese colony. However, Eric observed:

> There aren't many Englishmen, except for a few optimistic missionaries and a colony of retired people at Hammamet with a reputation for homosexuality both among Arabs and French. In fact I had to give a careful analysis of British morals and sexuality to some Tunisian students whose ideas had been formed by the Hammamet colony. To think that a scholar of King's should be called upon to do this![142]

On 10 September he took a train from Karouan to Algiers, a journey of twenty hours.[143] After conducting some interviews there, he went on to Tablat, in Algeria's Médéa province, and then Bou Saada, a market town 250 kilometres south of Algiers. Penetrating further into the interior he reached Fort National (known nowadays as Larbaâ Nath Irathen), nearly 1000 metres up in the Atlas Mountains. 'I spent some time in these localities with the respective administrateurs', he later wrote, 'for the purpose of seeing local administration at first hand', and he filled several notebooks with the information he gleaned from talking to them.[144]

The fruits of Eric's labours were distilled into a lengthy paper he presented to the Political Society at King's College on 28 November 1938. The subject, he told his audience, might seem 'specialised and arid', and he would focus on conveying the central points, the 'dry bones' of structures and statistics:

> My sketch attempts to present these dry bones: you must clothe them with flesh. You must imagine that they concern people, arabs, muslims, who live in their peculiar civilisation which has its art, its beliefs and misconceptions; a peasantry as picturesque and as benighted and fanatic as that of the European Middle Ages and a good deal more diseased. You must imagine the setting of French empire-builders and landowners, high royalist officials and small Corsican policemen, graft, honesty and dividends. You must picture the arid and beautiful country, and the medieval towns Europeanised by petrol and Bata shoes and football teams.[145]

It was characteristic of Eric that the first thing he should mention about the Arabs of North Africa was their art; and equally characteristic that he should write off the religion of the peasantry as fanaticism (though he was to come back to agrarian religious cults with more sympathy in the 1950s). But the bulk of his paper was devoted to the European expropriation of Arab land. In Algeria, he reckoned, the eight hundred thousand European settlers owned fourteen million hectares, while a mere eight million hectares were owned by an Arab population of six and a half million. This unequal distribution of the country's fundamental resource was 'barefaced robbery', the result of repeated military sequestrations used as punishment for rebellions. Similar though less radical processes had produced a comparable outcome in Tunisia. The result was 'the destruction or at least the weakening of the self-sufficiency of the peasants, and their increasing dependence on alternative sources of income'.[146] Government relief had become a necessity.[147] It was not only important, he said, to take such questions out of the hands of administrative and fiscal writers, 'but also to point out the essential similarity – all necessary changes made – between European history and that of backward colonial countries'.[148]

Eric's North African project was perhaps the first indication, maybe also one of the real origins, of the interest in the rural poor and dispossessed that was to bear fruit in his European research of the 1950s into 'primitive rebels' and agrarian movements. Far from being backwaters, however, these colonies were of vital importance to France itself. As he wrote in the formal report he submitted under the terms of his grant:

> From a military, economic and political point of view, the three countries of western Islam occupy a position within the French Empire corresponding to that of India within the British. Their loss would mean its disintegration. The importance of the problems of North Africa for France and therefore for world politics is obvious, though usually insufficiently appreciated in this country. North Africa is the keystone of the French Empire.[149]

From Napoleon III onwards, French governments had used colonial issues to bolster their popularity at home, he argued. In the colonies themselves, they pursued a policy of 'divide and rule', using the enfranchisement of Algerian Jews in 1870, for example, 'to divert arab political resentment into anti-Semitic channels'.[150] Unlike British colonial administrators, the French tended to apply domestic French administrative practices to Algeria rather than adapt them to the local situation, and the European colonisers played a greater role in administration than they did in the British case. Some were capable, many were corrupt. In Tunisia and Morocco — colonies Eric used more for brief comparisons with Algeria than for detailed investigation — the direct rule of colonial officials was less in evidence, given the primarily commercial aims of the occupation and the colonies' status as protectorates. In all these cases, however, the support of the local Muslim population was vital if North Africa was to resist the Italian 'fascist drive for Mediterranean domination', especially with regard to Tunisia. To avert the Italian threat was 'the affair, not of Tunisia alone but of the whole of democratic and civilised humanity'.[151]

VIII

On 27 September 1938, alighting in Marseille from the boat train from Algiers, Eric went to a café, and as he ate his plate of sausages and sauerkraut he read a newspaper report of the speech Hitler had delivered in Berlin's Sportpalast the day before, outlining his territorial demands on Czechoslovakia.[152] Eric later remembered 'the sudden panic consciousness of being completely alone and of looking into the unpredictable future. For a whole evening I was physically and mentally useless. A terrible memory.' The speech convinced him that war was coming.[153] And, indeed, the Munich Agreement over Czechoslovakia did not last very long. In March 1939, in flagrant disregard of its provisions, Hitler invaded rump Czechoslovakia and occupied Prague. British public opinion, hitherto overwhelmingly supportive of Appeasement, turned against Germany. After the destruction of Czechoslovakia, Nazi propaganda directed its fire against Poland, where, as in the Czech case, it grew increasingly vociferous in its condemnation of alleged discrimination against a substantial ethnic German minority within the state's borders. A Nazi invasion of Poland now seemed on the cards. Chamberlain issued an ultimatum to Hitler, threatening war if he marched into Poland. In the UK, the Communist Party thought it necessary to renew its arguments for a British alliance with the Soviet Union, condemning Chamberlain as insincere. Only a broad front of anti-fascist nations could stem the tide of fascist aggression.[154]

A few months before, Eric's uncle Sidney, no more successful in his business ventures in Britain than he had been anywhere else, had emigrated to Chile, taking his own son and Eric's younger sister with him. His older brother Isaac (known as 'Ike') had been living there with his family for some time, and provided a social milieu and contacts to help Sidney, Peter and Nancy settle in. They all lived in Valparaiso, and Nancy became close to Ike's youngest child, Bettina ('Betty', born in 1922). She learned Spanish, to go with her English and German, and obtained employment at the British Embassy as a typist.[155] There could be no question of Eric's going as well, in view of his impending examinations. So he waved them off at the waterfront in Liverpool and returned to Cambridge to revise for his Finals. Sidney and Nancy sent him letters reporting on their new life, 'according to which they seem to like the place and get on well with the family – but it is too early to say what business prospects there are', as Eric told Ron in June 1939. 'I shouldn't think uncle will find great difficulty in earning a living of sorts, but it may take some time and be tough on the rest of the family for a bit; you never know.'[156] Eric's regret at their departure for Chile only turned into relief when war came. 'The more I think of it', he wrote in July 1940, 'the happier I am that the family managed to get out of Europe in good time. At least I needn't be worried about Nancy and Peter.'[157] Sidney, as Nancy told him in a letter, was still in financial trouble, but the cost of living in Chile was lower than in Britain, and in any case, 'even broke, Sidney and Nancy are better off there than in an ARP post or a munitions factory respectively'.[158]

Once more, he focused on revision to the exclusion of most other activities. These included the editorship of *The Granta*, though he did not resign because, as he later explained,

> One of the advantages of being editor of *Granta* in its days as a weekly was that one could make money out of it, at any rate out of the May Week number ... I didn't actually do much work on it in the summer term, because of the Tripos, I had done most of the chores in the Lent term, when we celebrated our fiftieth jubilee (mainly with an enchanting cover from the teenage Ronald Searle), and Nigel Bicknell and I agreed to split the profits of the two terms down the middle. I needed the money, since I had no income between the end of my scholarship and the start of my studentship.[159]

By mid-June, as he told his cousin Ron, Finals were over. 'I don't know how I've done yet, though I don't suppose I have got another star, in spite of the fact that I worked solidly through this term.

On the other hand, I should be surprised if I didn't get a First.' The question papers varied: 'The special period ("Utilitarianism and Tory Democracy") was dreary beyond belief, the Modern European quite fun, the Modern Economic very tough but worth while.' 'I am bloody glad to get out of that University Library', he wrote, 'in which I stuck regularly from morning to evening every day for the first seven, eight weeks of term.' While he waited for the results during 'May Week', which in Cambridge paradoxically always falls into the first part of June, he enjoyed the 'theatre, concerts and parties – this is the first time I've really spent a few weeks doing nothing but amuse myself'. The weather was warm and sunny, and he had 'become quite competent at punting and can once again bowl a pretty wood in the Fellows' Garden'.[160]

Eric knew he wanted to research for a Ph.D., and with a First Class degree he would have no problem getting funding for it. The topic would be something in the field of French imperialism, the subject he had worked on during his study visit to Algeria and Tunisia the previous year. Unfortunately there was nobody in Cambridge, indeed in the whole of England, who could give him informed advice about it. 'I'll probably choose something like "Government Policy and Investment in French North Africa, 1890–1912" which will leave me a lot of scope to narrow it down later.' But since there was little or nothing on this topic in Cambridge University Library, he would have to use the material in the British Museum Reading Room instead. A more immediate concern was how he was going to support himself until the new academic year began in October. 'I've applied for various jobs', he wrote to Ron: 'on the *Daily Mail*, with one of the big Advertising Agencies, as travel guide, but I don't know anything definite either way yet.' His application to work for the *Daily Mail*, whose owner, Lord Rothermere, had until recently been a supporter of the British Union of Fascists, was, to say the least, surprising. In the event, however, none of his applications was successful.

He had an invitation from James Klugmann to do some translating work in Paris for the World Student Association Conference, which would bring in a bit of cash. Until then he stayed in

Cambridge, to settle his affairs, and considered hitch-hiking to Vienna, 'to get my money out and spend some of it'. There was indeed an account in his name at the First Austrian Savings Bank, worth 2332 Reichsmarks and two pfennigs. Nancy also had an account, with 1098 Reichsmarks and eight pfennigs. The money had been deposited in 1929 following their father's death. But the Nazi *Anschluss* of Austria in March 1938 had been quickly followed by the barring of accounts held by Jews, a measure reaffirmed later, in 1941, which required a court order for the funds' release. Eric eventually dropped the idea, perhaps wisely in view of the brutal repression to which the Jewish population of the city had been subjected by the Nazis since the *Anschluss* the previous year: hitch-hiking across Nazi Germany into Nazi-occupied Vienna at a time when anti-Semitism had already claimed many lives and led to thousands of Jewish men being arrested, and on the eve of the Second World War as well, would not have been a sensible idea.[161]

Instead of going to Vienna, Eric spent a week at a Communist Party Student Summer School. 'I have not forgotten the Albury camp', he wrote later, 'where I recall flirting with Iris Murdoch and being stung by a bee.'[162] He found Murdoch attractive and intelligent, though he was struck by the fact that she seemed to get on best with the daughters of other Ulster people, mostly from the upper classes.[163] In a commemorative volume of character sketches of some of the participants, Eric was portrayed in a light-hearted profile as precociously brilliant, giving lectures on Marxism to the workers in Vienna and becoming the 'star theoretician of the Sozialistische Schuelerbund, or Socialist Schoolboyband', in Berlin. In Cambridge 'the University Printers ran out of stars for his firsts, and he talked his way into the Editorship of *The Granta*. It needed strict orders from King Street [Communist Party headquarters] to stop him from issuing a supplement consisting of the untranslated works of Marx and Engels.' As for the future, the anonymous writer noted that 'he means to be a Don or a Journalist, and as either he will get into the headlines. You ask him what is his favourite book, and he will say that he hasn't written it yet ... He can, in short, do everything.'[164]

And, indeed, Eric succeeded triumphantly in gaining another starred First, taking his degree in person at a Congregation in the Senate House on 20 June 1939.[165] Shortly after the degree ceremony he departed for France, where he could 'live in what I then regarded as extreme comfort for £2 a week'. He was helped by the £50 from his earnings as editor of *The Granta*, thanks to the 'May Week' number, which always sold particularly well since it dealt with the 'May Balls' and sporting events taking place after the end of term, while the undergraduates stayed up in Cambridge waiting for their exam results. He spent some time with his Cambridge friends in Paris, notably Parvati, the younger sister of Mohan Kumaramangalam, 'slim with short rough hair and the most wonderful saris. One I remember, blue, silver and black, the whole Boul[evard] Mich[el] looked back at us for she was the prettiest, or at any rate the most stylish girl in the quarter.' Later, he subsequently learned, she returned to India and became a member of Parliament.[166]

He proof-read his last issue of *The Granta* and then stayed in Paris for another few weeks until the Third International Conference of the World Student Association, which took place from 15 to 19 August 1939. He gave a speech on the afternoon of 16 August on 'What democracy means for us. The value today of the ideas of the French Revolution'. But his main work was administrative. He was responsible for putting together the files of dossiers on the student movements of various countries that were to be presented to each of the delegates. 'Since there are about 35 major reports, all of which have to be translated into French and/or English, and duplicated in two languages', he wrote to Ron on 12 August 1939, 'you can imagine the size of the job.' The German delegate had even submitted three lengthy dossiers totalling about 100 type-script pages. 'The last few days,' Eric reported, 'we have worked, on the average, from 10 in the morning to 10.30 or 11 at night, Sundays included.' Sponsorship for the conference came from fifty university rectors and vice-chancellors, and 'an incredible collection [of individuals] from Lloyd George and the Archbishop of York to Einstein and Thomas and Heinrich Mann'.[167]

Looking back in 1955, Eric remembered:

> We prepared and translated all manner of reports (English, French, sometimes German) and duplicated them, yellow covers for the English version, blue for the French. They were about fascism, democracy and progress. From time to time we dodged the creditors who wanted the association to pay for paper, duplicating and other things. Mostly we lived in the Quartier [Latin], where a decent room could still be had for £2 a month, and ate in the small restaurants which are still there as reminders of lost youth. The French ones were normally too expensive, we stuck to the Greek and Slav ones.

There was, however, at least some time free. 'I seem to remember us playing table football in the neighbouring café', he recalled later, 'with teams of Jews vs. Asians, i.e. Ram [Nahum] and myself against some Indonesian[s] and perhaps P. N. Haksar (but I'm not sure).' Although they were anti-racists, they were above all Communists 'and concerned with the world revolution. That is what we – or at any rate I – found in the WSA: the collaboration of (Communist) students from all over the world – I think all of us who helped James [Klugmann] were in CPs for this purpose. Not the differences in colour between us.' The 'more intellectual' of the student delegates played chess.[168]

Most of the students expected war to come sooner rather than later, and

> had acquired that gentle anaesthesia of sensations which is so helpful as an alternative to terror. Very few of us expected to survive the war, though in this the Englishmen among us were mistaken. We did not even think that the world had come to an end, or regard our increasingly feverish efforts to turn back Hitler over the past few years as wasted. We simply thought that antifascist war would now follow antifascist peace.[169]

But shortly afterwards, Communists across the world had a rude shock. Concerned that a German invasion of Poland would bring Hitler's armed forces right up to the Soviet border, Stalin began to play for time until he could build up the Red Army, its munitions and its equipment, to an adequate state of readiness, after the damage caused to Soviet military preparedness by his purges of the 1930s. On 23 August 1939 Stalin's Foreign Minister Molotov and his German opposite number Ribbentrop signed a non-aggression pact between their two countries. It also included secret clauses dividing Poland between the two powers and assigning the Baltic States to the Soviets. Even the public parts of the agreement made it clear that the two countries had switched from being mortal enemies to cordial allies. With this, the Cambridge spies' belief that passing on British secrets to the Soviets was the best way of defending civilisation and progress against Nazi barbarism ceased to have any kind of validity at all, if it had ever possessed any, since British government secrets conveyed to the Russians could now be forwarded to the Germans. By this time, however, the Cambridge spies were so deeply embroiled in their life of deception that they did not trouble any more to reflect on its original purpose. In the country at large, there were many resignations from the Party. But most members accepted the Pact as a masterstroke of defensive strategy by Stalin.[170]

Eric had hoped for an Anglo-Soviet Pact.[171] But when the Molotov–Ribbentrop Pact was concluded, he did not demur. 'If there was no other proof of the correctness of the Party and the USSR than the list of people who have signed declarations etc against it', he wrote to his cousin Ron on 28 August 1939, 'it would be ample.' But it justified itself by breaking down Hitler's system of alliances. Eric listed the reasons why he thought it should be welcomed:

1. It isolates Hitler.
2. It limits (slightly) Hitler's freedom of action in whatever direction he likes to expand.
3. Since the USSR & democracies had no aggressive plans it leaves things exactly as they were with regard to them.

4. It will make it very difficult to exclude the USSR from any Round Table Conferences such as Munich.

Of course, the Pact did not isolate Hitler at all; his alliance with Mussolini was not affected, nor were his relations with friendly states such as Finland and Hungary. Eric was unaware of the secret clauses in the Pact, still less of the depths of Stalin's betrayal of international Communism which led him to deport German Communists who had sought refuge in the Soviet Union back to the Third Reich, where they were immediately thrown into concentration camps. In Eric's view the Pact made the international situation more secure. 'I don't think there'll be a war', he wrote, four days before one actually broke out, adding, 'although the danger is greater than last year.' The only thing he could think of to put against the Pact was the probability that by allying Russia with Germany it gave the increasingly conservative French government the excuse to crack down on the Communist Party, which indeed it soon began to do.[172]

IX

After his work in Paris was finished, Eric left on one of his hitch-hiking trips, this time to Brittany rather than to the south. 'There is a beautiful sense of timelessness about hitch-hiking', he wrote. 'I've only been away two days and a bit, and already it seems much longer.' He made his way along the north coast of Brittany, visiting the village of Guingamp in the Côtes-d'Armor, then cut across the peninsula, where he found the landscape 'rather like Devon in some ways ... small fields, lots of pasture, and a rainy atmosphere'. He reached Concarneau in Finistère, 'a small town in Southern Brittany and a centre of tunny-fishing', as he reported to Ron on 28 August. 'Since this is a pleasant place', he wrote, '... I think I'll stay here for a couple of days'. But he was aware of the spiralling international crisis caused by the Nazi threat to Poland and kept a wary eye on the situation. The French were already mobilising, and the 'panicky' English tourists had all gone home.[173] On Friday 1 September 1939 Hitler invaded Poland in defiance of Britain's guarantee of Polish territorial integrity. In London, Chamberlain vacillated, desperate to avoid war if he possibly could. But, as Eric wrote a few days later, 'In my opinion it was largely the revolt of the House of Commons, led by Greenwood [the Labour Party spokesman], on Saturday which forced us to stand by our obligations.'[174] Under pressure from the Commons and by the majority of the Cabinet, Chamberlain's government in London issued an ultimatum for Hitler to withdraw, and, when it was ignored, declared war on Germany on 3 September 1939. The Second World War had begun.

As soon as it had become clear that war was more or less inevitable, Eric took a train from Concarneau to Angers, from where he hoped to return to Paris. Army reserves boarded at every station, as he later remembered:

> Angers was sunny and dusty, like all French towns. Later I flagged down a woman in a sports car, she was suspicious, that I can well understand, for I must have looked like a prole in my check shirt and gaunt brown face. However, I showed her my English passport and she took me with her then. She was around thirty-five to forty-five, with henna'd hair pretty chic and good-looking and offered me some fruit. We talked about the war. I don't remember whether I already knew at that point that the Germans had marched into Poland. Was war unavoidable? She was nervous and wanted to get to Paris quickly, while single taxis and heavily laden cars were coming the other way. We stopped in Chartres and drank a glass of wine. In the hotel they were just listening to the wireless: invasion. General mobilization in France and so on. It sounded very dramatic. The people were sitting around and a woman was weeping. My chauffeuse was very upset. I thought she would have liked to faint.[175]

As they drove on to Paris, they passed long lines of cars fleeing the city – 'the French middle class was escaping *en masse* the other way with mattresses on top of their *Peugeots*'. Once there, the woman put Eric down on the corner of the Place Vendôme 'and we said goodbye in the dazed manner of people who have thought about historical moments, but find them less attractive when they occur than they had imagined, even for purposes of self-dramatization'.

Eric needed money to buy a ticket back to England, so he went to the Westminster Bank to draw some.

A crowd of English people were milling round the bank counter, their politeness considerably strained. I seem to remember standing next to Wyndham Lewis, a ferocious figure in a vast black hat, but with what looked a remarkably chinless profile, and very annoyed indeed ... The night train via Dieppe was packed, among other things by large numbers of very tall, extremely pretty and extremely untourist-like girls, who also looked distrait. They were the choruses of the various Folies and Casinos of Paris who had been paid off for the duration by the managements which, like everyone else, expected the bombs to fall immediately. They were returning to their native Accrington and Bradford. It was, I remember thinking, both a suitable ending to the peace and a promising beginning to the war. It was not. I fixed up a date with a big blonde from Brixton for the next evening, after a meditative breakfast [reading the newspapers] at the Victoria Street Lyons, but she did not turn up. Anyway, I had nowhere to live in London, except a settee in the house of friends in Belsize Park, a multinational centre of revolution. There we all saw the war in, in pyjamas.[176]

Arriving in London, Eric met up with Lorna Hay, a Scottish graduate from Newnham College, Cambridge, and the girlfriend of Mohan Kumaramangalam, who had just told her that he was going back to India to take up work as a professional revolutionary and could not take her with him (he did indeed go back, and was soon arrested for sedition, but after independence joined the Congress Party and served in the government in the 1970s).[177] Eric spent the last night of peace in the flat she shared with Mohan, and together they experienced what would soon be the regular reality of war in the capital.

> It was unbelievably dark. One hadn't yet got used to it. Thunderstorm. The searchlights threw up their beams in front of King's Cross [railway station], and one didn't rightly know if there was a raid. It poured. I can't say that I was afraid, though with its natural lightning flashes this eve of the war was much more unsettling than an actual attack, it just made me sad. I slept at Mohan's. We got up late the next morning. Someone phoned Lorna and told her war had been declared.[178]

The sirens began to wail as Eric and Lorna were on their way to Caterham, in Surrey. Above them floated thousands of barrage balloons, designed to get in the way of German air raids. An air-raid warden called to them to go inside, but they walked on, not wanting to show they were afraid.

Despite Chamberlain's equivocal position in September 1939, Eric thought 'the chances of the government's – or Chamberlain's – backing out at this stage are exceedingly slim'.[179] He felt energised by the prospect of a final showdown with fascism:

> Now we're in it, it seems to me clear that our first job is to win. This war could have been avoided a thousand times over, and lots of people said so – but now it has started, it has to be waged efficiently and rapidly. At the same time I think the most efficient way of conducting it is one which makes the smallest sacrifices of democratic rights, freedom of speech etc. There is also the point that we shall have to be immensely careful that nobody foists a new Versailles on to us; that the war does not degenerate into an anti-german hate campaign etc. And, of course, I still believe that the war won't be waged really efficiently as long as the people on top are the same as conducted the Munich policy which is so largely responsible for this present position.[180]

He did not 'like at all the prospect of hanging around with nothing definite to do for a period of anything up to two months', so he wrote to Cambridge University and to the War Office in London offering his services. But in the event, he was forced to spend not two but more than four months kicking his heels until he was called up. 'I'll be glad to get a commission or a job, or anything regular and positive to help in the war', he told his cousin Ron. 'Inactivity gets on one's nerves so.' Shortly afterwards he returned to Cambridge, where he had been sharing a small house near the Round Church with Pieter Keuneman, who had been caught by the war in Switzerland and never got back. 'I read his collection of poetry and sex-handbooks, listened to jazz records and Mahler, and ate what passed for Chinese cookery at the Blue Barn. There did not seem much point in starting research.' Remembering his responsibility for *The Granta*, whose other editor had already joined the Royal Air Force, Eric got the printers, Messrs Spalding, to issue 'a brief and rather lapidary statement to the effect that *The Granta* would await the return of civilisation'.

In the meantime, his allegiance to the Communist cause was put severely to the test by developments on the international front. On the outbreak of the war, the British Communist Party announced that it 'supports the war, believing it to be a just war which should be supported by the whole working class and all friends of democracy in Britain'. But the leadership was soon forced to reconsider its line by Comintern headquarters in Moscow. The war, the British Party was told, was 'an imperialist and unjust war, for which the bourgeoisie of all the belligerent states bear equal responsibility'. The task of the working class was 'to operate against the war, to unmask its imperialist character'. On 25 September 1939 the Central Committee voted twenty one to three in favour of the new policy, whose implications included an element of 'revolutionary defeatism' in which the defeat of any country, including Britain, would be welcome because it would bring about a revolution (the tactic followed by Lenin in Russia during the First World War).[181] The minority voting against included Harry Pollitt, the General Secretary of the British Communist Party, who remarked: 'I hate the ruling class of this country, but I hate the German fascists more'[182] and was forced to resign (to be reinstated when Germany invaded the Soviet Union on 22 June 1941).[183]

By the time of Pollitt's enforced resignation, the international situation had changed dramatically again. Taking advantage of the freedom of manoeuvre allowed him by the Nazi–Soviet Pact, Stalin had invaded and occupied the eastern part of Poland on 17 September 1939. Then on 30 November he invaded Finland, which had been part of the Tsarist Empire before 1917 but had established its independence amid bitter fighting at the end of the First World War. The 'Winter War' had begun. It turned out to be a humiliation for the Red Army. Well-prepared Finnish troops fought the invading forces to a standstill. The looming threat of the invasion had brought back Marshal Carl Mannerheim, who had led the counter-revolutionary forces of the 'Whites', backed by the Germans, in Finland's civil war in 1918. Staunchly anti-Communist, Mannerheim organised the country's defences with great effectiveness, winning the sympathy and support of the international community, which condemned the invasion and expelled the Soviet Union from the League of Nations on 14 December. The Communist International mounted a propaganda effort to put the Soviet Union's case. In Britain, *Russia Today* rushed into print on 7 December with *Finland: The Facts*, which portrayed Mannerheim as a fascist who had destroyed democracy, and lauded the Red Army for trying to bring democracy to the Nordic state through a puppet government set up by Stalin. The argument was less than convincing: although the Communist Party was indeed banned in Finland, so too were the fascists, and the regular holding of elections demonstrated that Finland was closer to Sweden in its political constitution than to the mini-dictatorships of the neighbouring Baltic States.[184]

But this pamphlet was not the only one produced by British Communists in defence of the Soviet invasion. As Eric's contemporary Raymond Williams, also a student Communist at Cambridge, later remembered, the Socialist Club, no doubt acting on instructions from Party headquarters in London, got in touch with him, asking him to collaborate with Eric in a 'rush job in propaganda':

> Eric Hobsbawm and I were assigned to write on the Russo-Finnish War, which argued that it was really a resumption of the Finnish Civil War of 1918 which had been won by Mannerheim and the Whites. We were given the job as people who could write quickly, from historical materials supplied for us. You were often in there writing about topics you did not know very much about, as a professional with words. The pamphlets were issued from on top, unsigned.

In later life, Eric said he was unable to obtain a copy.[185] But in fact it is not very hard to find; there is actually a copy among his personal papers.[186] The pamphlet, *War on the USSR?* produced by the University Socialist Club at Cambridge and published by the University Labour Federation, warned its readers that 'the British people find themselves to-day on the verge of a war with Socialist Russia' as the British government threatened to intervene on the side of Finland. Popular pressure had brought intervention in the Russian Civil War of 1918–21 to an end and must do so in this new crisis (Williams's memory was at fault here; it was this conflict, not the Finnish Civil War, which the pamphlet discussed, and he was confusing his own publication with the one produced by *Russia Today*). The pamphlet went into great detail about what its authors depicted as a military plan for a three-pronged invasion of Russia. It did not portray Finland as a fascist dictatorship, nor did it try to argue the puppet government appointed by Stalin would bring democracy to the country. Instead, it presented Stalin's policy as purely defensive, and invited readers to support it in order to preserve the achievements of the Revolution of 1917 in Russia against a possible intervention by Western forces using Finland as a base, as had happened in 1918. Neither Eric nor his fellow author was prepared to tell what they knew to be lies. Thus they managed to preserve at least some political and intellectual integrity – a remarkable achievement in the Stalinist world of international Communism at the end of the 1930s.

While he was waiting to be called up, as he knew he most probably would be, Eric lived in London, staying with uncle Harry or sleeping in friends' flats, sometimes in a spare bed, sometimes on the floor. He still had the use of Pieter Keuneman's rooms in Cambridge, but the town, the university and the colleges were now empty. He was formally enrolled as a Ph.D. student, and went through the motions of beginning his research on agrarian conditions in French North Africa, 'hitchhiking to the British Museum when necessary and when the snowdrifts of an unusually freezing winter made it possible'.[187] Meanwhile, there was little action in the war. Everyone was waiting for something to happen. This was the 'phoney war', and for several months it put Eric, like many others, into a kind of limbo. He knew that the situation was unlikely to last. With few friends left in Cambridge, and the family gone from London to Chile, he was alone, drifting, with an uncertain future.

4

'A Left-Wing Intellectual in the English Army'

1939–1946

I

Eric was drafted into the British Army on 16 February 1940 under the provisions of the National Service (Armed Forces) Act of 3 September 1939, which made all men between the ages of eighteen and forty-one liable to compulsory military service.[1] He was enlisted as a private in the 560th Field Company of the Royal Engineers, based in Cambridge, and put into a company consisting of a motley collection of mostly working-class conscripts.[2] The men were given uniforms and assembled on the grassy area in central Cambridge known as Parker's Piece. The company sergeant-major, a long-serving professional soldier, addressed the new recruits with a speech that Eric immediately afterwards noted down from memory, complete with a reproduction of the Cockney accent in which it was delivered. After telling them to stand at ease, the sergeant-major said:

> You may 'ave a smoke. Well now, your corporal 'ere, 'e will 'ave told you as ow I am the Company Sergeant Major. Now p'raps you are surprised that I should come talking to you new intake like this. Your fathers what was in the last war 'as told you about sergeant majors and ow they are bastards. I'm talkin' to you now because you're in the army now and you bloody well got to know what's what so you might learn now ... You get to stand

to attention and say 'Sir' when you speaks to me. And mind you stand to attention smartly because you're in the army now and you bloody well got to do things my way or you see what 'appens ... Because if you know it or not, I got my eye on you. You may not see it, but there I am, watchin' you out of the corner of my eye. There ain't nothing what yer sergeant-major don't see, so you might get that into yer blocks. And I bears it in mind. Yer old sergeant-major never forgets. Now there is some things you can't do when ye'r in the army. I sometimes sees a man walkin' past the Company Office with is 'ands in 'is pockets, and I don't say nothing, but I thinks to myself: 'That bugger ain't no soldier' and when 'e comes up for leave, up 'is name pops in my mind, as yer might say, and I sees to it that 'e don't get is leave. 'Put this man on fatigues' I says, ''e ain't no proper soldier.'[3]

The war of course meant that the men had to observe military regulations and keep to army discipline, even if they had been drafted straight into the army out of civilian life. If they didn't obey orders, they would be marched off to Bedford Military Prison, where, in the sergeant-major's words, the warders 'ain't got no 'eart'. But if they played the game, he assured the men, they would get on all right and he would make things easier for them. If they did not, he said, they would discover that 'I'm a real bugger I am, when you don't play square.'

The sergeant-major explained the various ranks in the army to the men, and emphasised the fact that he was in the army for life, but they were only there while there was a war on:

When peace comes, out comes yer civvy clothes and it's goodbye to the army and bugger the old sergeant-major what 'as tried to do is best by you. That's what it's like. But me and the Major, we stay 'ere. I been in the army since I was seventeen and when my day comes and you come 'ome at Victoria Station with the missis and the kids, 'oo will yer see standin' there sellin' bootlaces but yer old sergeant-major, and 'e'll say 'Spare a copper for an old sweat Sir', that's wot 'appens to blokes like me.

Following this 'heart-to-heart', as the sergeant-major called it, the men were taught the rudiments of drill ('Stand to attention son, when I talk to you ... You can't stand strite not if yer tied to a bloody eight foot picket, yer's still look like a bloody barbed wire entanglement').[4]

There was 'foot-drill in the morning, rifle-drill in the afternoon' until the movements became 'almost automatic'. Their teacher, Corporal Easter, 'repeated the sentences three times, thinking they would be understood that way'. 'We stand on Parker's Piece and present arms. The corporal explains the movement from "stand easy" to "stand at ease" pornographically. "Such a movement will come easily to you", he says, and grins.'[5] He taught the men about how to deal with poison gas attacks – a widespread fear, deriving from the First World War, when poison gas had routinely been used on the Western Front (gas was never actually used against soldiers in the European theatre of battle in the Second World War). 'The corporal', Eric noted, 'is better in practice than in theory and is no great bookworm. He reads out the bureaucratic English of the Handbook with some difficulty.'[6] 'Why must military handbooks be written in the most abstract, colourless, complicated and for the ranks incomprehensible jargon?' Eric wondered. 'It breaks your heart to see the corporal and the lads struggling with the useless expressions ... The whole educational system in the army must be completely revolutionized from top to bottom.'[7] 'Drill from morning to evening', he admitted, was 'tiring'.[8] The men learned how to tie knots and clean their rifles.[9] 'The days are so like one another that I forget from one day to the next what has happened ... the normal routine. Mornings, rifles on Parker's Piece, afternoons knots and ropes and a "test" in Christchurch Street.'[10] Finally, on 18 March 1940, the squad was 'passed out'.[11]

Eric tried to divert himself on parade by rehearsing poems by Morgenstern and Schiller in his mind, but the drill took up too much of his attention and 'it didn't work'.[12] From the very beginning, indeed, he was frustrated by the lack of intellectual opportunities in the army. On 6 March 1940, he found one solution: 'I've thought to myself that it would perhaps be worth the trouble to pick up my diary, where, so to speak, I left off at the end of 1935.' He was, after all, politically 'forced into inactivity for an unlimited period'. It might remind people in future of the great times he was living through, even though he was unlikely to make any great contribution to them himself. Perhaps it might just help people who knew and liked him to remember him in future.[13] He wrote the diary mostly in German, partly because he had written his earlier diaries in German and so it felt, presumably, more natural than English, partly perhaps because he did not want the soldiers he was now living and working with to understand it if by some chance they came across it. With intervals, he continued to keep it through the wartime years. By early July 1940 he was starting to find that 'the more I write, the more empty and boring this diary becomes'. But it showed him 'that I can write. That is, I can handle words in English and German like a carpenter handles wood or a smith iron but not, however, how an architect handles his material. I feel myself technically certain in whichever language – even in French, within the bounds of a more or less limited vocabulary.'[14]

He missed Sidney and Nancy, now located thousands of miles away, in Chile, more than ever. 'Now and then', he wrote after a few weeks in the army, 'I realize how lonely I really am.' He had no family, no 'best mate'. He did not have a neighbourhood to go back to, where people would say: 'Ah, Eric Hobsbawm has come home on leave.' For his friends, he reflected gloomily, and not without a touch of self-pity, he was 'just a brown, blond, skinny creature in a badly fitting uniform who turns up from time to time for half an hour or half a day and perhaps reminds them of certain things in the past, part of their memories, hardly any more of their daily lives'.[15] At least, he thought, trying to be positive about his situation, he was still in Cambridge,[16] living in rooms near the Round Church. He could still have a 'normal Cambridge Sunday', sitting in King's reading the papers, lunching in Lyons Café with those of his friends who were still around, and going to the cinema in the evening.[17]

He even found time for political activity, though when he

attended an event in Cambridge in early March 1940, things did not go entirely according to plan. William Rust, editor of the Communist Party's newspaper the *Daily Worker*, had been invited to speak in the Cambridge University Socialist Club's meeting rooms, but outside, as Eric noted, 'a crowd of boat club hearties, reactionary students and 30–40 RAF people had gathered in front of the building and besieged it with catcalls. Many are drunk. When I speak to them I smell the beer on their breath. Since they didn't get in, they ran up and down and threw stink-bombs.' Frustrated, the mob began to sing 'Rule, Britannia' and 'God Save the King'. 'An almost orgiastic state of mind', Eric observed. These young men had 'no brain and too much money'. They reminded him of the Free Corps and the Nazi stormtroopers, he wrote rather hyperbolically in his diary; in fact, the incident more resembled 'the sound of the British upper class baying for broken glass' in Evelyn Waugh's description of Oxford student life in his first novel, *Decline and Fall* (1928).[18]

Communism was 'an ideal wish-fulfilment' for him, he wrote, rather than practical politics.[19] Yet he was, he felt, becoming increasingly alienated from bourgeois society:

> More and more, especially now, where I find myself amid non-intellectuals, I begin to understand the mistrust of the worker and the party towards bourgeois intellectuals. This dreary sitting around with glasses of hock or gin, these sporadic conversations about nothing against the background of . . . Count Basie records, the permed hair, the cigarette fumes . . . none of it has any point.[20]

The men he mixed with in the army were very different. 'Personally', he wrote after joining his unit, 'I find myself, for good or ill, once more among people with whom to begin with I have nothing in common except the clearly formulated wish on my part, unknown to them on their part, to be with them because they are workers and soldiers.'[21] The men accepted him without any kind of hostility. He joined in singing the music-hall songs the men knew, once he had learned the words: 'There's an old mill by the stream, Nellie Dean'; 'There's an old fashioned lady in an old fashioned house'; and songs learned from westerns in the movies, such as 'Home, home on the range'.[22] He played football with the lads,[23] and found himself 'in a gym for the first time since school'. He also joined them in games of ping-pong, darts and billiards.[24] On one occasion he tried wrestling, though he had forgotten what little he knew of the techniques and had to copy his opponent by looking at him. He played pontoon and won, taking considerable risks in the process, much to the disapproval of the more cautious players, and engaged in the occasional game of cribbage, a popular card game in working-class pubs.[25] He learned chess and played it sometimes with those of the men who had mastered the rules, though he did not always beat them.[26] And he did a fair amount of boxing, which many years before his father had tried to teach him. It was categorised under the heading of 'recreational training'.[27] He was aware of the fact that he had little talent for it, after he had sparred one evening with 'Corp[oral] Peabody who knocks (or would have knocked) the hell out of me'.[28]

Eric could never resist engaging in social analysis. 'The class composition of the Engineers', he observed, 'is more uniform than that of most other regiments ... The basis is a nucleus of skilled and semi-skilled workers.' There were relatively few men from heavy industry, since these had been drafted into civilian munitions work, the ordnance corps, the navy and the Royal Air Force. 'The bulk of the men are connected in one way or another with the construction industry, as carpenters, bricklayers, painters etc.' The men came from various parts of the country, but were 'chary of using their dialect', since the other men often made fun of them when they did so ('cf. the perpetual chaffing of Norfolk men for their habit of saying "I'm now coming" "I'm now doing" and "he do" "he say"; or of Notts people for the expression "our youth" for a brother'). Typically, after a year in the unit, Eric compiled statistics of which counties he had discovered the men came from: four from Lancashire, three each from London, Norfolk, Cambridgeshire and Staffordshire, and so on.[29]

As he was to do later in life whenever he entered a world that was new to him, he made notes on words and expressions with which he was unfamiliar. He was fascinated by the Cockneys among the men, and compiled a list of rhyming slang expressions: 'oak-and-ash' for cash, 'Duke of Kent' for tent, 'Robin Hood' for wood.[30] He listed some other, less esoteric slang expressions as well: 'to be browned off – fed up', 'swing the lead – be idle in work-time', 'mush – man' (pronounced 'moosh'), 'boozer (the current word) – pub', 'flog – sell'.[31] 'Current sayings in the company,' he noted, included 'I do not care a cow's cunt' and 'Go fuck a duck'.[32] Eric found the habitual obscenity of the squaddies shocking. 'In three months', he thought, 'I will be able to write an extensive study of the sexual techniques of the English proletariat.' Fascinated as always by unfamiliar words, he compiled a list of the sexual slang he heard the men use: 'have a jump' for sexual intercourse, for example, or 'have a bit of' followed by 'skirt', 'judy', 'twat', 'quim' and so on.[33]

Even more shocking to Eric was a story related by Maurice Roberts, a young ex-carpenter in his squad, who told how before his call-up he and three male companions had raped a sixteen-year-old girl in Southend, the seaside resort at the mouth of the Thames much favoured by London East Enders. 'The little thing didn't say a word the whole time. Not one word.'[34] Eric recorded this without comment but was clearly disturbed by the story. What could he do, however? If he reported the incident, the men would simply have denied it. Eric was 'deeply shocked' in a different sense when he came across 'a case of almost total illiteracy' in his squad. Dick Fuller, he discovered, 'can neither read nor write, just his name. What is terrible here is not the retarded nature of a subnormal person, it's the weakness of a society that tolerates such a case in the most modern of capitalist countries, without feeling responsible for it.'[35] Eric did what he could to help him. Fuller was not the only man Eric came across who was more or less illiterate. Some months later, he spent 'time helping Digger to learn reading and writing: for the first time in his life he realizes the need to learn. I teach him on "The Shadow" detection mag. Never realized how much these mags are adapted for use by semi-illiterates.'[36]

II

After the squad had finished its training, life took on a greater variety. The men undertook test drives in army lorries (Eric was not very good at it), and practised digging trenches, looked upon by 'swarms of children'. Eric learned how to ride a motorbike.[37] He found this 'not really so tiring, only the left wrist gets a bit stiff'.[38] The men had to shift the quartermaster's stores, 'dusty work'.[39] Less welcome was a detail to peel potatoes. Eric escaped by cleaning the latrines – 'one has to get used to that too'.[40] A day's exercises at the quarry in the nearby village of Barrington, south-west of Cambridge, hiding behind bushes waiting for 'the enemy' to appear, reminded him of his time in the Boy Scouts.[41] But as the weeks passed, the squad became restive at the lack of leave. Eric called a meeting:

> I pull myself together, bang with a steel helmet on the door to get them quiet, and raise the question of leave. 'We've got to do something', I say. 'I propose that three men, including corporal Reggie Platten as delegate of the section, go to the commandant. We've been here seven weeks and still no leave.' They shout 'yes' and 'you're right!' Eventually it's decided that Reggie, Flanagan and myself will go.[42]

After further debate they decided at Eric's suggestion to address a petition to the commandant. But 'everything is left to me – and I bear the responsibility. There's another difficulty; every delegation stronger than one man is technically a mutiny.'[43] The men's resolve weakened, then collapsed.

They were assembled by a lieutenant who told them the section had been overspending its food budget. They would now have to tighten their belts. As they set off on a twenty-mile route march through the Gog Magog Hills to Babraham, Shelford, Stapleford and back to Trumpington and Cambridge, there was much grumbling. '"We're fighting for our country and our country can't even give us enough to eat", said Froment. "Lord Haw-Haw should hear about it", said Bill Fuller.' Eric thought it typical that the English soldier saw an enemy propaganda broadcast from Berlin by the renegade fascist William Joyce ('Germany calling!') as the best way of expressing his dissatisfaction. But the men's spirits soon lifted and they sang songs on the march, though so chaotically that sometimes three different songs were rising from different parts of the column at the same time.[44]

He was depressed that he was able to 'read so little. Almost exclusively newspapers and pamphlets. Where should I do my reading anyway? Cut off from culture, or on the way to being cut off, I cling stubbornly to it.' This led him to treasure even the kind of history he hated and despised most:

> In the [Cambridge] Union I fall upon the *English Historical Review*, read the arid notices on the new edition of the *Acta Diplomatica Danica*, the colourless reviews of books on Sicilian monasteries in the Middle Ages, the concept of the Ancient Constitution in the 18th c[entury] etc. I read them not just in order to insert a few bricks into the house of my idea of history, but mainly because all of them – even the miserable extracts from Danish church documents – are signs of civilized, creating, positive life.[45]

In late March 1940, anticipating a posting away from Cambridge, he packed away his books:

> I feel unbelievably sad and want to weep, though of course I don't, since I seldom weep, unless I experience an unexpected nervous exertion. Books are like people or trees: they grow. One can reckon their lifespan generally at three or four years. When I come back from the war and take my books out of the box, they will be lifeless. Every shelf will say: died in 1939. The books, literary, political, which were alive last year and part of my personality, will just be documents of their time … It's terrible burying good books. In the end one doesn't just read them, one lives with them. That's civilization. They have a social value.[46]

He did, however, manage to read from time to time – on one occasion '100 pages of Stendhal on the back of a lorry – a gesture of civilization'.[47]

On a visit to a friend in Cambridge, he spent time listening to records of Berlioz's *Symphonie Fantastique*, which he found very uneven, 'not so overwhelming', full of 'non-musical dramatic moments'.[48] He preferred Bach,[49] Elgar and especially Mahler, with whose music, he remembered, he had practically grown up in Vienna. Mahler's *Song of the Earth* reminded him of the 'humanistically educated bourgeoisie' of Vienna, which had acquired its values from the kind of education Eric himself, of course, had undergone. In comparison, he thought, the English middle classes lacked a broad, comprehensive cultural upbringing; the narrow education in the Ancient Greek and Latin classics to which they had been subjected was no substitute. The English bourgeoisie, he concluded, 'lacks the atmosphere of a class that carries culture in its bones and not just in its earlobes.' Gaining power in the age of religion, the English bourgeoisie regarded culture as a luxury; the German, Austrian and Russian bourgeoisie, gaining power in the nineteenth century, saw it as the central means by which the problems of life were articulated.[50]

As for the British working classes, it was 'a small triumph' when he managed to get his fellow squaddies to discuss politics. In March 1940, when the Russo-Finnish 'Winter War' was coming to its formal conclusion, he reported one such conversation:

Dick Wells ('petty bourgeois') looked at the map of the Caucasus in the mirror and said 'maybe we'll soon be fighting there'. I say: 'That means war with the Russians. I don't want to fight the Russians, what for? Who wants to fight the Russians?' – 'Me', says Les Burden. 'Stalin and Hitler are the same to me.' 'Not me', says Bill Fuller. 'I don't want to fight anyone.' Someone asks: 'Why are we fighting anyway?' 'Because we've got to', answers Bill Fuller, and this ambiguous formulation isn't challenged. 'Of course we've got to', I say, 'we're put into khaki and that's that. We don't get anything from this war.' 'No', everyone agrees. 'But there are some who are profiting from the war', I add, more or less in parenthesis. Little Langley intervenes. 'People who've got money get more, it's always the same in war.' Then we get back again to talking about the Red Army, and I try to tell Burden that the USSR isn't the same as Hitler, and give him examples from Poland without much contradiction.[51]

Eric appreciated their cynicism and 'absolute lack of enthusiasm' for the Winter War, but noted with regret that 'fundamental opposition isn't very strong'.[52] Like his fellow soldiers, he was afraid that Western backing for Finland had brought them 'perhaps 24 hours away from war with the USSR', so he was as relieved as they were when the news came through that peace had been concluded. 'Mad with joy', they went to the pub to drink to the end of the conflict.[53]

With the German invasion of Norway and the British expedition to the Norwegian coast in April 1940, the situation changed and with it the mood of the squaddies. '"Thank God, finally the decision, finally a real fight," say the lads, because it does their nerves good to get out of the monotony of the phoney war.'[54] Fifteen men (not including Eric) volunteered to go to Norway – ten were accepted. Eric thought this was 'because the English soldier's life is too boring for them, and because they don't have any relatives'.[55] As the men thought about events in Norway, their mood hardened. When one of the men in his squad opined that 'the only good Germans are dead ones', Eric felt obliged to contradict him, but all the same, he wrote, he could 'sympathise with the English side for the first time in the war, probably because Hitler's action was so overwhelming and perfectly organized, I have the bad habit of always sympathizing with the weaker side'.[56]

Before long, as the Germans advanced in southern and central Norway, beating back the Allied expeditionary forces, the feeling of patriotic enthusiasm among the squaddies waned. '"You know", says Rowling, "I can't see how we can win this war." And the others agree with him.'[57] Eric considered this showed the limits of the influence of British radio and press propaganda. The lads were, Eric felt, 'complete raw material, for us [i.e. Communism] as well as for fascism'. While they were peeling potatoes, Eric and some of his comrades fell into a conversation about the Jews, who the squaddies felt ruled England. 'One of the effects of Lord Haw-Haw', Eric commented. 'Of course I objected – and the anti-Semitism wasn't very strong anyway; but the fact that a group of ordinary soldiers should regard these ideas as commonsense is worrying.'[58] On the other hand, one of the men had been reading Robert Tressell's *The Ragged-Trousered Philanthropists* (1914), a novel set in a working-class community that portrayed in detail the oppression of its inhabitants and their efforts to assert their rights. 'My people', Eric's fellow soldier told him, '[are] all strong Conservatives, but what I've seen [in the book] makes me understand much of the socialist side.'[59]

The relatively tranquil time Eric had so far spent while his unit was based in Cambridge came to an abrupt end on 16 April 1940, when the men were marched off to an army camp at Cranwich, in Norfolk, not far from the town of Thetford, where the eighteenth-century revolutionary writer Tom Paine had been born. The countryside, much of it uncultivated heath, reminded Eric of the Mark Brandenburg, the rural area around Berlin.[60] Almost as soon as they had arrived, the men drew up a letter of complaint about their poor rations. 'At the evening meal, Sergeant Warrington came into the room with an innocent smile. "The corporals have told me you've written a petition. You can't say I haven't done everything necessary: I've summoned the captain."' But he warned them not to hand over the petition 'because of the captain: he could take it badly'. The men, terrified they would have their leave cancelled, dropped the idea immediately.[61] This was not the end of the matter, however. At breakfast the next day the men, confronted with minimal provisions, banged their plates on the table. Told there was no more bread, they stayed in their seats, calling from time to time for bread. 'You think you can get something this way?' sneered Corporal Carter 'in his unbelievably bourgeois sounding voice'. 'No bread, no work', the men replied. But they had no idea what to do next. The staff sergeant marched into the room: 'Is that the way soldiers behave?' he demanded. He ordered them 'outside in five minutes'. Summoned to the lecture room, they were told in no uncertain terms what the punishment for mutiny was. The Commanding Officer threatened to arrest them all. 'Play the game', he said.

For Eric this was all a sign that their rebellion had frightened the officers. At lunchtime, the food was markedly better than before.[62] Discipline was tightened up, however, and leave was cancelled for the slightest irregularities in the men's uniform. Eric had a 'little dispute with Lieutenant Griffiths about my buttons'. He was regarded, not without reason, as the ringleader in the protests. 'You're an educated man', Lieutenant Griffiths said to him. 'You come from a good family I'm sure. You may not know it, but people like you should set an example.' Eric mumbled an apology – 'butter wouldn't melt in my mouth', he wrote when recording the incident. But he 'had in the circumstances definitively revealed himself as an agitator', though neither a professional nor a competent one.[63] Meanwhile, life in camp at Cranwich continued much as before. One of the men who had been imprisoned for robbery before the war ('"Not a screw I aven't been. Parkhurst, Pentonville, Brixton – I bin in them all. That's me."') asked Eric if he fancied breaking into a shop ('"Not me, old cock", I said. "Thanks anyway though."').[64]

Then, at the beginning of May 1940, Eric was suddenly informed that he was to be sent on a ten-day cipher course, with a view to being transferred to Army Intelligence. Twelve of them were to go: two officers, seven NCOs and three privates. With his command of languages and his double starred First Class Cambridge degree, Eric was an obvious choice. The men were taken to a Jacobean-style house five miles or so from Norwich. Eric found it 'overwhelming' that 'we are being treated like civilized human beings. The food is good, and we eat it off china plates, with cutlery, tea in cups and not tin mugs.'[65] There was no roll-call, and there were no problems if one came in late. The officer and adjutant spoke to the men in a human manner. 'Almost heavenly.' But it was not to last more than a day for Eric:

The next morning the captain calls me in and explains that I can't do the course because my mother wasn't English. The train leaves for Cambridge at 2.20 – it's got nothing to do with me personally, I must understand? – Yes, I understand. – But you know, perhaps you're against the regime [in Germany], but a little bit of feeling for the country you half belong to's still there, you understand? – Yes, captain. – I myself don't have any kind of nationalistic feelings, I don't care what nations do as long as they behave themselves, but the Germans aren't behaving themselves at the moment. – No, they aren't. – I'll recommend you for a position as interpreter. – Yes, captain. – You understand, it's just the principle, we can't go against it. – Yes, captain.[66]

Discussion, Eric realised, was useless. 'From the army's point of view he's right. You can't be too careful where ciphers are concerned.'[67]

Upset and disoriented by these events, Eric spent the next few days feeling too dispirited even to write his diary. He tried in a desultory sort of way to learn Russian, as he had done once before, at Cambridge, but though he recorded his pride in his initial progress, he never got very far on either occasion.[68] On a brief period of leave, he punted upriver on the Cam to Grantchester for tea – 'I still "punt" really well', he noted with pride, 'though the uniform's very hot.' Gradually he recovered his spirits, meeting some French visitors in the Arts Theatre restaurant and talking politics in French.[69] Back in camp a few days later, reality returned with a crash when he was hauled before the sergeant, who bellowed at him: 'fatigues from two to nine o'clock, leave cancelled'. He and five others had fallen asleep on duty and had been woken up by a major. Eric conceded that he could not feel any great anger about the fatigues, though he did think Lieutenant Griffiths had it in for him.[70] Even more depressing was the news of the German invasion of the Netherlands. 'The Germans will win, is the general view.' 'Of course we know what we're fighting for', said one, 'but you've got to admit which army is the better.' Nevertheless, Chamberlain's resignation and replacement by Winston Churchill as Prime Minister of a national coalition government on 10 May 1940 cheered them all up.[71] Churchill was undeniably inspirational as a war leader, Eric thought: he had 'a fine ability to make rhetorical speeches and debates, a lot of stubbornness, a pliable mind and a fanatical consciousness of the side on which the British Empire's bread is buttered'. But could he recognise discontent at home and head it off with concessions? Did he have 'greatness as a political strategist and tactician, as opposed to a figurehead? I don't think so.'[72]

Eric did not have much time to continue with reflections such as these. On 11 May 1940, without any prior warning, a soldier woke Eric and his fellow squaddies at two in the morning 'and said: Parade in full kit at 4.30'.[73] The unit was transferred on a column of lorries to Langley Park, another camp located just outside Norwich. Here the men had to live in tents.[74] As one dull, routine day succeeded another, Eric felt like a 'corpse in khaki, and not a human being'.[75] On Sunday, and again on Wednesday, the squaddies obtained leave to go into a nearby village, a place where nobody knew them, and where there was nothing for them to do – 'no shops, clubs or canteens'. The men, he reported, unable to stay, felt like prisoners given half an hour's leave. 'And so they wander home in the twilight, drunk, barge into passers-by, and shout after the girls on their bikes.'[76] A girl called Brenda who served in a cigarette shop proved more biddable.

> We took turns to go out with her. She was about seventeen and I reckon she had had a man every night for the past two years . . . She came and leaned over the fence, and let her big red hand trail on our side over the dried-up hollyhocks and the stems of yellow flowers whose name I do not know, and looked with moist eyes, like a spaniel bitch, towards our hut, until someone came out. We took her for walks along the top of the railway cutting, between the fir plantation which was crossed by a belt of landmines, camouflaged, and the single track which shines like a snail's path in the full moon.[77]

Just before an old swing bridge she would lie down with whomever she was accompanying in a small hollow behind a stack of reeds. 'She was almost completely brainless, judged by ordinary standards, but a strong girl who seemed out of place behind the counter of the little shop.' She had no conversation at all, so Eric soon gave up. Exaggerated though his description might have been, this kind of thing was not really for him, even in small amounts.

Eric took his turn on guard duty, carrying a loaded rifle. They were all 'bloody jumpy, because of the Germans', who were now threatening to invade at any time. 'I wasn't scared,' wrote Eric after a spell of guard duty, but 'I don't mind admitting that I should have been, had I really believed there was danger'[78] and 'the others say that they are afraid. The rats and mice make rustling noises in the forest and you think you hear footsteps in the lane, and if I hadn't been convinced that the Germans weren't going to come that night, I'd have fired a shot.'[79] After a week Eric noted that this was 'the longest time without "good" literature for nearly four years'.[80] In preparation for a possible German invasion, the company laid mines and put explosive charges under bridges, using a pneumatic drill to make the holes; they prepared machine-gun emplacements; and they dug anti-tank trenches round Great Yarmouth.[81] There were often air-raid alarms in the middle of the night, and Eric thought he heard the sound of explosions in the woods. 'The men ran in the dark to the trenches on the edge of the forest, as the searchlights swung back and forth above.' They imagined sometimes they could hear the sound of the guns across the North Sea, where the Germans were giving the French a 'pasting'. 'It gave us a feeling of importance to be able to come back to camp and say, casually, "Pasting somebody is getting yonder." It was the nearest we got to the war.'[82]

On 8 June 1940, Eric's twenty-third birthday, he went into the village and tried to get drunk in the local pub but did not have enough money. He picked up a 'plump, full-lipped girl with brown hair who works in the pharmacy and at least looks a bit grown-up'. But although he 'said the right stupidities', he felt ridiculous and did not take things any further.[83] At least when he was sent with two other men to guard a little bridge on the flat marshland between Acle and Yarmouth, he was able to 'rediscover after such a long time that peculiar ecstatic enjoyment of nature, the feeling of complete physical relaxation and passive oneness with nature that one has after coitus'.

> I haven't been in this part of the country before. I should say it's rather like Flanders or Holland to look at, flat marshes, not much more than sea-level, innumerable stagnant, deep and slow rivers (and still no drinking-water!), the outline of windmills and cows and groups of trees here and there. A straight road flanked by willows as far as you can see, and now and again sugar-beet factories and suchlike. It is rather impressive at night. One hears a plane in the distance, and one by one the searchlights flash up and finger around the sky, meeting and jerking back again, dropping out as the plane passes further inland and a new belt of searchlights takes over.[84]

As the uneventful days at the bridge passed, however, Eric became restless, tested his nerve by climbing up onto the parapet, took long walks, wrote two poems in German ('one of them very good') and tried to write more, without completing them. The impossibility of political activity and the absence of any news got on his nerves.[85]

The enforced leisure of the days guarding the bridge gave Eric the opportunity to think about the progress of the war. If Germany was going to win, it had to be soon: 'I've always believed that the Nazi system was not capable of a long war of attrition.' 'Owing to the fantastic and utterly incredible brasshattedness of English and French brasshats, who have neither learnt nor forgotten anything, the Germans have got a chance of pulling off an 1871.'[86] Thus when Eric managed to listen to the radio on 17 June 1940 and managed to learn of the defeat of France, he was not surprised.[87] He shuddered when he thought of the mass of ordinary Germans, now ruled by a barbaric system run by 'a band of neurotics, perverts, epileptics, under NCOs with strapping thighs, short-sighted clerks with a passion for files, and aristocrats from the Polish

Mark'.[88] A 'negotiated peace' with the Nazis was neither likely nor desirable: 'a Nazi-peace would be, speaking personally, too awful for words'.[89]

The official line of the Communist Party was that the war was just a conflict between capitalist powers and needed to be brought to an end as soon as possible. However, the defeat of France prompted Stalin to change his mind. From this point onwards, the British Communist Party issued no more calls for the war to come to an end, and leading figures began to support the argument that a people's government should be formed to strengthen the fight against fascism.[90] The retreat from Dunkirk and the fall of France were decisive for Eric. 'It became clear to me that the Party line was absolutely useless.' Britain was under a direct threat from Nazi tyranny, and had to be defended.[91] Neither Eric's diaries nor his long and detailed letters to his cousin Ron mentioned the continuing Nazi–Soviet Pact directly; still less did they make any attempt to justify it. As he told Ron: 'I admire and respect more ministers in the present government for their abilities than in any other British Government since L[loyd]. G[eorge].' It was significant that Eric privately applauded the Churchill government's more efficient and more effective prosecution of the war. The defeat of Hitler was what he really wanted, a view that derived not only from his identification with Britain but also from his politicisation in the anti-Nazi movement in Berlin in the early 1930s.[92]

The defeat of France had a by-product in Eastern Europe. On 21 June 1940 the Red Army, taking advantage of the preoccupation of the Western powers with events in France, invaded and occupied the Baltic States of Estonia, Latvia and Lithuania. 'Wonderful news', Eric recorded in his diary. The three states had all been ruled for some years by right-wing nationalist dictatorships that had banned the Communist Party in their respective states. From Eric's perspective the invasion was an act of progress and liberation. Its longer-term effects were to be anything but progressive, however, as Stalin put all three countries into a Soviet-style deep freeze, with many thousands of their citizens arrested, deported and killed, and growing numbers of ethnic Russians moving in to create a new social and political elite.[93] At the same time, Stalin also annexed Bessarabia and Northern Bukovina from Romania, news that made Eric 'want to sing and dance'.[94] The effects of the takeover were similar here too, though the dictatorship of Marshal Ion Antonescu in Romania was soon afterwards to commit some of the most sadistic anti-Semitic atrocities of the entire war, leading even to complaints by the German SS.[95]

III

Eric's inner anxiety after the fall of France, one he must have shared with many people in Britain, was revealed in 'an odd, logical dream' he recorded in great detail in his diary on 24 June 1940. 'We were in Algeria, on the coast north of Constantine', in the east of the country. The Germans and Italians were invading, with heavy armour and artillery. 'The same again', he thought sadly. With obsolete equipment and hopeless tactics, his side did not stand a chance and was soundly defeated. He donned civilian clothing, worrying that his army boots would betray him, and made his way towards Algiers or Oran in order to find a ship that would take him back to England. He encountered Lieutenant Griffiths, who wished him luck. He passed a boy herding goats, and then, creeping through the bushes, he came across a house, whose inhabitants offered him a bed for the night. Proceeding further the next day through the green undergrowth, he stumbled into a clearing, where there was a ragged Jewish beggar and a large, jolly English soldier. Warned that the Prefect was hunting down vagrants, he left them in the clearing and walked on, eventually coming to an Arab village whose inhabitants were dancing wildly in some kind of festival.

He skirted its borders, passed carefully by an army camp and went on to the featureless suburbs of Algiers. A pretty twenty-something girl in a car picked him up and drove him to her place in town, 'where, I think, I slept with her'. In a newspaper he read a report that the soldier and the beggar had been arrested and had told their captors that their friend, an English soldier, 'Erico Amico', had also been apprehended. So he was safe from further pursuit. Eventually, after hiding in various hotels, he found a ship and sailed back to England. 'I will disregard the Freudian content of the dream', he concluded. 'I retell it just because I like it.' Like all dreams it presented his unconscious thoughts indirectly. Perhaps the soldier and the Jewish beggar were aspects of himself, while the dream's setting in Algeria, where 'I didn't feel hot even though the African sun was shining', expressed his desire eventually to return to the country where he was planning to research for his doctorate. In the end, it is not possible to do more than speculate.[96]

Meanwhile, he thought continually about the long-term prospects for Britain. 'Frankly', he told Ron in July 1940, 'for a historian these times are absolutely unique. Since the fall of the Roman Empire or the French Revolution there has been nothing half as fascinating. It is unpleasant to have been born in this age, but by God, I wouldn't have missed it for anything.'[97] Yet the idea of becoming a professional historian was as far from his mind as ever. Instead, he thought he would devote himself to writing 'proletarian literature' based on the method of 'socialist realism', stories written in a simple style that everyone could understand. 'I want to write so that everyone recognizes the houses and streets, smells the flowers, feels the passions.' His readers would surely see real life in his writings, though whether he was capable of composing more than short stories he doubted.[98] To be sure, thinking about the future became more difficult when Hitler was reported to have announced he expected to take up residence in London within a fortnight. 'His prestige is so great that the soldiers secretly believe he'll do it. Although on the outside they're firmly convinced that the fleet will protect us absolutely . . . This uncertainty is one of the symptoms of a war that isn't a people's war.' To his dismay, Eric was 'afraid of being infected by this blind nervousness. As long as my intellect still tells me the danger is relatively small, or that worrying about it doesn't help, I'm all right. But I'm terribly afraid I'll lose my self-control.'[99] On the other hand, after the 'phoney war' had come to such a sudden and brutal end, 'the fear of invasion is creating a national determination, even if only temporary, a conviction of the necessity of the war, an intolerance of opponents of the war, that are very remarkable'.[100]

On 25 June 1940 Eric was moved with his unit to the East Anglian seaside resort of Great Yarmouth, 'empty, desolate, with the North Sea hidden behind sandbags and barbed wire, but still, a town with houses, women, cinemas, even a bookshop – civilization'. He was billeted in a summer bed-and-breakfast establishment run by a Scottish woman.[101] Life for the moment was peaceful, with regular meals, no corporal, and plenty of free time. At the local branch of Woolworths he bought a copy of *The Good Soldier Schweik*, an anti-war novel from 1923 by the Czech satirist Jaroslav Hašek, chatting to a conscientious objector who struck up a conversation with him when he saw what he was purchasing. In July he began subscribing to a lending library, which supplied him with a wide range of fiction, including Somerset Maugham's *The Moon and Sixpence*, which he found old-fashioned in style and empty in content, and non-fiction, including Alfred North Whitehead's *Science and the Modern World* (1925), in which 'the sentences [are] three times as long, three times as abstract as necessary', though, he added, 'God, I write like that myself sometimes'.[102] Over several pages of his diary he grappled with Whitehead's ideas, which were, and are, indeed, famously obscure and difficult to decipher.[103]

Meanwhile, the unit continued making preparations for a German invasion. The men attached dynamite to a metal railway viaduct over Breydon Water in Yarmouth. Eric had to walk along the top of the viaduct, seven metres above the line and twenty above the water, to tie a charge, and suddenly experienced

an unbelievable, huge, overwhelming fear. Note: I was perfectly capable of continuing. I wasn't dizzy. It wasn't impossible for me to stand upright, as it would have been with the cross-buttresses that went from one side of the bridge to the other and were only 20 cm. wide. But I was afraid because I was expected to do it coolly, and I wasn't sure I could.

The walk to and from the spot where the charge had to be laid was 'terrifying'. In the meantime, the men's concerns about a German invasion gradually lessened as it became clear that the Luftwaffe was not succeeding in its attempt to gain command of the skies over the English Channel. 'After some initial scepticism', Eric wrote on 20 August 1940, 'I've been converted to the belief in the real superiority of the RAF, though I feel vaguely that Goering still has one or two cards up his sleeve for a real invasion.'[104]

Eric occasionally went to London when he got a weekend pass.[105] The city seemed to him 'full of soldiers in various uniforms, one feels as if one were in the old German or Austrian monarchy'.[106] In December 1940, as the German bombing 'Blitz' on London was still in full swing, he stayed on the streets for a night 'out of interest'.

A few bombs fell near me (it was a medium-sized attack). Especially incendiaries. I went for a walk in the West End, albeit with a few small glasses of whisky in my stomach, but neither drunk nor otherwise out of my normal condition. I experienced no fear at all. Absolutely none. At least not after the first quarter of an hour. That wasn't the courage of a hero; it was apathy. I said to myself: nobody's aiming at you. Nobody's taking notice of you personally. Your private behaviour has no influence on the situation: whether your nerves hold or collapse, the German pilots will carry on letting their shit fall and don't know anything about it. Your chances can be mathematically calculated and on the basis of this calculation of probabilities the nervous system will be tortured only among schizophrenics. So I walked without much effort to be courageous the three miles from the West End to the East End, as if from one side of the room to another.[107]

Such visits were rare, however. For months on end there were few distractions of any kind from the monotony of army life.

To fill the time, Eric wrote some 'English army sketches' and submitted them for publication in July 1940.[108] The sketches were returned on 15 March 1941 with a rejection slip. This made Eric 'disgruntled, more than I care to admit'.[109] He also returned to writing German poetry during the war, mainly on impulse, or out of boredom, or in reaction to events of the day, or even, more abstractly, when a particular group or series of words appealed to him, combining, as he thought, German sounds with English rhythms. Some of them dealt with army life or with the casualties and privations of war, or, more subtly, the contrast between the soldiers who wore a 'uniform of bravery' while inwardly afraid: 'We are small, the times are great.'[110] Sometimes he described soldiers taking a break as they went to the cinema or the theatre, the cooks sunning themselves in front of the canteens, the layabouts playing cards and writing their weekly letters.[111] Russia was a recurring presence in these verses, with one poem entitled 'Kaddish for a Russian Soldier', written after the German invasion of the Soviet Union in June 1941; Eric's choice of the Jewish prayer for the dead as the title, rather than a more neutral term such as 'Elegy' or 'Epitaph', showed that his Jewish sense of identity remained beneath all the accretions of the previous years.

His political verses were far more sophisticated than the agitprop sloganising he had written as a teenager. In one poem he articulated the doubts he had about his own commitment, describing himself as 'half-white, half-red', wearing the costume of 'a Pierrot of politics'.[112] He was living a life of 'theory without praxis', politically dead: 'Only in action is there strength.'[113] And he recalled with nostalgia the great demonstrations he had taken part in before the war: 'Am ersten Mai/An unsern Kleidern wieder rote Nelken./Die Augenzeugen von Geburt und Tod,/Das letzte und das erste Aufgebot.'[114] Looking across to Germany and Austria, Eric even tried to imagine Nazis enjoying the unpolitical nature of a spring before they turned nature into a wasteland.[115] One poem, 'The Munich Professors', completed on 11 July 1943, imagined the creeping conformity of German university academics to the Nazi regime and its demands. Overall, however, Eric had considerable difficulty in putting what he wanted to say into a regular, structured verse form. Most if not all of the poems were seriously deficient in metre, rhyme and other respects, often attempting imagery that was not really appropriate to the subject.

In the end, Eric was always better at writing prose than verse, and always at his best when he had a basis of fact on which to build: the radical compression, imaginative invention and artificial rhythms of poetry simply did not suit him.

Eric felt continually frustrated by the impossibility of politicising the men among whom he was forced to live: 'the unnatural, demanding Tantalus position of a left-wing intellectual in the English army'. In order to escape this situation he decided he would apply to become an officer. It would be less physically demanding, he admitted – 'my laziness and love of comfort also says "officer"' – but he also wanted a role that would make demands on his intelligence, which he was unable to use as an ordinary private. But he doubted whether he would succeed.[116] He applied for posts in the British and the Indian Army. There were rumours that all the applicants for both theatres of war were to be sent for several months' officer training in India ('I have no objection to going there at all', Eric told his cousin Ron, though 'India would mean a pretty complete waste of the languages I know').[117] But on 7 April 1941 he told Ron his application for a commission in the Indian Army had been rejected, and on 15 February he had been informed that he was not going to be an officer in the British Army either – 'news through', he wrote in his diary, 'that the commission business is off; which makes me pretty cross'.[118]

Although he was thankful for the peaceful environment of Great Yarmouth, he was frequently bored. He took what intellectual stimulation he could from using every opportunity to continue his voracious reading. As he told his cousin Ron:

I'm steadily working through the Yarmouth Public Library, while we're still here. It reminds me of the time at school, when I used to read thro' the Marylebone Library as fast as I could go. It's only now I notice how I've let my general reading – as distinct from historical and political specialization – fall back while I was at Cambridge. But it is disheartening to read, and discuss valuable things which one can't make use of at all. It makes reading as pointless as collecting stamps or buttons.[119]

The relative calm of Norfolk was not to last for long. In January 1941 Eric's unit was transferred to the Scottish Borders. He was glad of the activity he was required to undertake, spending 'pleasant if cold and wet days doing imaginary reconnaissances and building bridges across rivers full of salmon. This,' he told Ron, 'is by far the most interesting work I've done in the army since we played about with explosives early last summer.'[120] The unit was sent to reconnoitre a bridge near the border town of Yetholm, but Eric found the plans for its defence against a possible German attack 'unrealistic'.[121] After completing their reconnaissance of the bridge, the men were supposed to return to base on foot, but they hitch-hiked instead, and were punished the next day by being sent on a seven-to-eight-mile route march.[122] In another exercise, the tactical scheme revealed 'wild weaknesses from A–Z: guns on an open field absolutely without cover from any direction. Convoys parked in a long line along the road equally without cover. Battalions "wiped out" by ambushes. The worst neglect of aerial damage etc. But', he added, 'I can't judge, since my personal experience is so fragmentary.'[123]

For the second week of March the unit was transferred to Stanley, seven miles from Perth, for a week's pontoon construction over the River Tay. They spent the days 'rowing up and down the river, lifting the pontoons in the sand'. 'We do our work at a bend of the river, below some rapids, where the banks slope down easily.' Some of the time they were made to wear gas masks: 'We sweat like hell and the spittle collects in the cup below the chin and makes it wet and slippery.' Nevertheless, overall the experience of pontooning in Perthshire was 'very pleasant' and sometimes enlivened by 'mock invasions' and manoeuvres.[124] As they worked, he observed the fishermen who would 'row to and fro across the river, dragging a net, which they hand out with a winch and pull the fish out'. Occasionally swans would fly across: 'I never noticed before that their necks rippled while they flew.' In his spare time Eric read Tolstoy's *War and Peace* and one evening went with some of the men to a cinema in Perth, where they watched *Boy Meets Girl*, a comedy starring James Cagney and Pat O'Brien, which he found 'superficial' and full of 'allusions, wisecracks of fairly limited application, padded with Slapstick. Cagney tries like hell, but no.'[125]

Otherwise, there was the regular 'morning parade: rifle drill in battle order', all, Eric felt, 'fantastic and divorced from all reality. Trouble is that under the present system the best men and NCOs take too much interest in purely superfluous and ornamental drill, rather than better things.'[126] After heavy snows they were sent to clear local roads.[127] 'What did they do in peacetime,' he asked, 'when there were no gangs of soldiers? But one gets very warm. I enjoy this work, which is quite hard for a day now and again.'[128] When a regular soldier, a Corporal Carter, came to work with them, Eric was impressed: 'Quelle différence. The background of experience, apart from the personal ability of the man. Object-lesson in the behaviour (and effect) of a good experienced NCO.'[129] Much of the time he was still bored. Idleness, he complained, alongside 'soulless and aimless work depresses me intensely'. Idleness for Eric, however, was always a relative concept. 'I do bugger-all', he noted on 25 March, 'except finish *Moby-Dick*.' A fortnight later, now in charge of the unit's store room, he was still complaining. 'Nothing to write about ... Reading – Balzac, *Père Goriot*, Lewis G. Gibbon, *Cloud Howe*, Sam Butler, *Way of All Flesh*, George Douglas, *House with Green Shutters* and so on.'[130]

Eric's unit was given lectures on the use of explosives, the 'formulae for cutting bridges', the 'theory of arches', or the 'lining of [a] box girder'.[131] 'Lectures and all these lectures without demonstration are of little value', Eric thought.[132] They were mostly taken straight out of an instruction book.[133] To vary the monotony, six of the section were selected to deliver some impromptu lecturettes on a choice of subjects.[134] Eric was selected, but confessed the next day, after the trials were over: 'My own lecture's bad.'[135] In the end, he felt completely out of place. 'What in hell am I in a Field Co[mpan]y R.E. for?' he asked.[136] In the evenings, he often went out with the men to a pub to get drunk, although on occasion he had to spend an 'evening at home because I'm broke'.[137] The pay system, he complained, was 'chaotic. 60% are inexplicably in debt (70% in HQ section. I'm £1.10.0 in debt).'[138] He even had to ask Ron for money, gratefully received at the beginning of April 1941.[139] He tried to organise a 'hut committee' to raise the pay issue but 'the unity has been cracked because the worst debtors are hoping to have their cases taken up personally by the officer'.[140] Eric heard a good deal from 'the extraordinarily garrulous Scots' about a major German raid on Clydeside, an important location of the shipbuilding industry, on 13–14 March. Local people, he reported, blamed the government for underestimating the casualties, perhaps reflecting the notoriously left-wing nature of the population on 'Red Clydeside'.[141] Some of the men thought the war would end with a peace treaty between Britain and Germany, but others disagreed: 'Rather shoot yourself than live under Hitler.'[142]

In April 1941 Eric's unit was transferred south to Liverpool, perhaps, he thought, in preparation for embarkation abroad.[143] The men were billeted in the grandiose surroundings of Croxteth Hall, the country home and estate of the Molyneux family, in the suburban area of West Derby. They spent the morning on bayonet drill and were told that if they came under aerial attack from fighter planes, they should deal with it 'by standing upright in formation and pointing rifles at them'. These ludicrous instructions met with derision from the men, 'who feel sorer and sorer as they realise they are still fighting with 1917 methods against a 1941 army'.[144] Shortly afterwards Liverpool was heavily bombed in a series of German raids lasting for the whole of the first week of May.[145] 'The damage is very bad', Eric wrote to Ron, 'and made worse, as usual, by inefficient organization. No serious evacuation till too late, nothing to cope with the rush of temporary unemployment etc.' The phone exchange was out of action, making communication difficult, though gas and electricity had been quickly restored, along with water supplies. Local people were 'dazed' and 'astonished' by the raids.[146] Eric thought that such attacks would be more effectively dealt with if the government in London was in charge, rather than 'local aldermen who will believe in their miraculous immunity until the bombs actually fall'.

IV

The military and diplomatic situation was transformed on 22 June 1941 when the Nazis and their allies invaded the Soviet Union in Operation Barbarossa, thus ending the Nazi–Soviet Pact. Eric was hugely relieved at the news 'that, at last, we were – officially at least – on the right side. Since the fight had to come, sooner or later, that at any rate is a consolation . . . I do not see how Hitler is to beat the USSR.' On 2 July, after recovering from the initial shock of the invasion, Stalin had delivered a major speech over the radio, calling upon everyone in the Soviet Union to come together to defeat the Nazis. It had a huge, morale-boosting effect. 'Stalin's speech', Eric told Ron Hobsbaum on 8 July, 'means a people's war in every sense – technical and political.'[147] Within a few days, as Eric remembered many years later, he

> organized the sending of a football, signed by the entire RE company in which I then served – including the CSM – to a unit of the Red Army. I saw to it that it was sent to the *Mirror* for forwarding. A college friend, the late Lorna Hay . . . worked there at the time and got us publicity. I daresay it got to Russia eventually. The lads queued to sign: not a moment's hesitation by anyone.[148]

Eric was optimistic about the Red Army's chances of success. 'Every day they hold out, every victory they win, every plane they bring down, brings the English and Soviet people closer.'[149]

Enthused by the outbreak of war between Germany and the Soviet Union, and with plenty of spare time on his hands, Eric wrote two army sketches which he managed to get published in *Lilliput*, a pocket magazine founded in 1937.[150] The first of these two short pieces, 'Battle Prospects', published in the January 1942 issue, presented a conversation between a comically upper-class major, a captain and a lieutenant that is revealed only towards the end to be not about a military action but about a cricket match in which the Red Army supplies players for their team.[151] His second sketch, 'It Never Comes Off', was a brilliantly written monologue voiced by a member of a University Socialist Club who had promised his comrades to get 'really blind, smashing drunk' if the Soviet Union entered the war. Eric captured the essence of drunken speech perfectly:

Hooray for the glorious Red Army that beats the Germans. Hooray. Hip, hip, hooray. Who says I am shouting? You? I'm glad you're not; I was going to smash anybody who said so. Have one on me. I insist, have one on me. Are you my friend or aren't you. I ask you a plain, simple question and I want a plain, simple answer, and no backchat. Remember, I am a politically conscious guy and there is no hoodwinking me . . . Tell that man in the corner to shut up. Tell him I'll wipe the floor with him if he doesn't . . . You think I'm drunk. I can see that. But let me tell you I am not drunk, I am sober as a judge.[152]

Despite the initial German victories in the campaign, Eric was full of admiration for the fighting spirit of the Red Army troops. They did not give up as easily as the French had.

In the meantime, Eric's unit was transferred once again, this time to Bewdley in Worcestershire. However, he had begun to suffer from a septic toe, which first prevented him from taking part in bridge-building exercises and then, as his condition worsened, required medical treatment. He was sent to a hospital near Kidderminster in August 1941, 'a pleasant Georgian House, lovely surroundings, good food – obviously the thing well-meaning St Johns & Red Cross women imagined for the wounded warriors. Seems a shame to go in with nothing more martial than a septic toe.'[153] On his release he went to stay with friends in a house near Hay-on-Wye, on the Welsh borders.[154] While he was there, he was told he had been accepted for service in the Army Educational Corps, which was undergoing rapid expansion at the time. Founded in 1920, the Corps enlisted only men who possessed a university degree or a teacher-training qualification, and all of them were immediately promoted to the rank of sergeant. Its aim was above all to boost morale by providing ordinary soldiers with interesting educational courses, alongside basic skills of literacy for the most poorly educated. Many university lecturers joined the Corps, and Eric was a natural candidate for it; his officers in the Royal Engineers also, he wrote much later, may have seen his transfer as a way of getting rid of someone who was obviously unsuited for the practical work in which the regiment was engaged, and a bit of a troublemaker to boot.[155]

The transfer probably saved his life. The 560th Field Company of the Royal Engineers had already been issued with tropical gear some months before Eric left, and, soon after he had gone, the Company was embarked on a ship that took them to Canada and across the North American continent to Singapore, where the British forces surrendered to the Japanese on 15 February 1942. The men Eric had got to know in the army spent the rest of the war in captivity, many of them working on the notorious Burma Railway, where a very high proportion of them died from ill-treatment, starvation and disease.[156] In the meantime, back in the UK, Eric was sent for training in early September 1941 at the Army School of Education in Wakefield, Yorkshire, a small town that Eric described as 'smoky, full of sharp fog and crowds of mill-girls in overall suits and clogs; uninspiring to look at, but I think preferable to nondescript towns like Bury St Edmunds or Yarmouth, or cities too large for their industry, like Liverpool'.[157] The move marked a change in his life in more than one respect. Shortly after his arrival, Eric wrote excitedly to Ron: 'The man who writes now is not a sapper, nor a lance corporal, nor even a corporal, but a genuine sergeant, acting, admittedly, and what is worse, unpaid for the moment.' After twenty-one days in the unit to which he would be sent on completing the course, however, he would be paid at the usual rate for a sergeant, which he found much more satisfactory. Better still, he wrote, 'The corps itself is a pleasant surprise. The instructors lay stress on all the right things and the right techniques – and are, in regard to manner as opposed to matter, very enlightened.'

Life at the Army School of Education was agreeable, though the hours were long and the days were packed with activities of many kinds, most of them not directly educational. Eric described a typical day to Ron:

> Reveille at 6.30, a quarter of an hour's PT before breakfast; lectures and study groups from 8.30 to one, with a half-hour break; sports and games from 2 to 3.30; lectures and groups and private study from 3.45 to seven with an interval for tea – we are not allowed to go out before seven. For the afternoon sports we have the choice of swimming, road-walking or team-games – or whatever other sports they arrange ... With being cooped up in the building all day long we want it. I don't know about the others, many of whom used to be office-clerks in their units, but I'm not used to a predominantly indoor life now. Conditions are tip-top: rooms for two, classy washing arrangements, civilian servants at the tables, a good common-room.[158]

The trainees were divided into 'syndicates' or study groups of eighteen. The men in Eric's syndicate included 'a lecturer in History from the School of Oriental Studies, a PT teacher from Nottingham, three Scottish art teachers, a mild little solicitor from London, a handicraft teacher from Hackney, and an ex-student from Oxford named Michael Marmorshtein, of slightly more obscure nationality even than myself'. Otherwise the trainees were mostly from Wales or Yorkshire. 'Maybe', Eric quipped, 'they will run an eisteddfod one of these days, there are enough of them to provide bards, choir and audience, and I'm willing to bet that we have quite a few writers of harp-music and Cymric verse.'[159]

On completing his training, Eric was transferred to the Army Educational Corps attached to the 12th Field Training Regiment Royal Artillery at Bulford Camp, a large army base on Salisbury Plain, on 2 October 1941. He was put in charge of the *Sunday Times* library at the base and also taught German to paratroopers.[160] Early in 1942 he had a surprise visitor: Fritz Lustig, with whom he had been at school in Berlin in 1932–3. Lustig had managed to escape from Germany in 1939, but after Dunkirk he had fallen victim to Churchill's order to arrest and intern all enemy aliens in the UK ('collar the lot!'). On his release, Lustig had joined the Army Pioneer Corps, the only military unit at the time which German and Austrian exiles were allowed to join. It was basically a reservoir of unskilled labour for military engineering and construction projects. But he was also a talented amateur cellist, and he soon joined a small orchestra established at the Pioneer Corps Training Centre in Ilfracombe, Devon. It was given the task of travelling around giving light music concerts to soldiers.[161] When the centre was closed down, in January 1942, Lustig was transferred with the rest of the orchestra to Bulford. In typical army fashion, the players were required to clean the library because they were otherwise unoccupied in the daytime. Thus Fritz Lustig came into contact again with Eric after an interval of nine years.[162]

Their renewed acquaintance soon took on a political as well as a social aspect. As Lustig later remembered:

> I was always very interested in left-wing politics, and this was the time when the *Daily Worker* was prohibited, and I read the *New Statesman*, and the Communist Party had inserted an advertisement saying that they were publishing a newsletter, and I was interested in seeing that. So on my next London leave, I went to their office in Tottenham Court Road, and asked to be enlisted in the newsletter. And the Communist Party – this was long before computer days – were so efficient that they discovered that a member of theirs was in the same garrison as I was. And so Eric approached me in the library when I was cleaning, and took me by the side, and said 'well, you probably would be better served by the *Freie deutsche Jugend*', which was a Communist organization – which I didn't realize then – 'and they will look after your interests'.[163]

Lustig joined but found the attitudes of the other members, none of whom was in the armed forces, annoying. He thought they should have enlisted and taken part in the struggle rather than carping from the sidelines. So he resigned. In 1943 he was transferred to the Intelligence Corps and spent the rest of the war transcribing secretly recorded conversations between captured German officers.[164]

By the time Lustig arrived in Bulford, the Communist Party was starting to campaign for the opening of a 'second front' in Europe, invading France to relieve the pressure on the Red Army in the east. In the Party's view, the fight for the Second Front was political; it was opposed mainly by pro-fascists who wanted to weaken the Soviet Union.[165] 'I rather think we're getting into a ticklish period with the second front movement', Eric wrote on 3 August 1942: 'Most people I find are at bottom defeatist. Their line is, what's the use of saying we want a second front, if the government wants one we'll get it, if not we shan't.'[166] The British, he concluded gloomily, were 'too damn likely' to 'relapse into the temporary paralysis of wait and see'. As he told his uncle Harry in September 1942: 'The High Command seem to have made up their mind *not* to have a Second Front this year, and it is enough to make anyone mad. I can just imagine what the Russians are thinking. I know what we should be thinking if the boot were on the other foot.'[167] Eric began to advocate the opening of a Second Front in the wall newspapers he edited and to a large extent wrote, with official approval, for display on the camp noticeboard.[168] However, the military and civil authorities regarded such propaganda as insubordination. Propaganda campaigns among the troops along these lines could easily lead to criticism of the overall conduct and direction of the war. Eric soon learned that there were limits to what he could write, though he did not suspect that his activities had aroused the suspicion not only of his superior officers but also the political police, or in other words Scotland Yard's Special Branch, and the secret service, Section 5 of British Military Intelligence, or MI5.

V

Eric first came to the attention of British Intelligence as a result of his correspondence with the leader of the German Communists in exile in the UK, Hans Hahle, formerly commander of the 11th International Brigade in the Spanish Civil War. Hahle was trying to form a Free German Brigade in Britain, and Eric was 'anxious for him to be allowed to lecture to Army units'.[169] Eric, as Colonel Archie White reported,

> like most recent university graduates in history, is politically minded, and takes an intense interest in 'current affairs'. He has been editing a wall newspaper, which is displayed weekly in the 'Sunday Times' library at Bulford, and is censored before publication. The tone of this publication is good . . . I have come into frequent contact with Sgt. Hobsbawm, and heard him speak. I have no reason to suspect him of using his position to commit any indiscretions. He is anxious to gather and display material explaining the Russian point of view.[170]

Nevertheless, White remained suspicious of Eric, and later in the month he began to view his activities in a more serious light. As MI5 subsequently reported,

> Colonel A.C.T. WHITE, Command Education Officer at Salisbury, reported that on July 31st of that year when visiting Bulford with Brigadier MAUDE he saw a specimen of a wall newspaper conducted by HOBSBAWM which, by a misunderstanding, had not been censored before publication and contained arguments for a Second Front which was considered highly partisan, and Colonel WHITE reprimanded HOBSBAWM in the presence of the I.A.E.C. He subsequently read all available back numbers of this wall newspaper, saw Sgt. HOBSBAWM in the presence of officers and strongly reprimanded him for abuse of his position as a teacher and for

presenting current affairs in a partisan light. Colonel WHITE regarded the material as not seditious but ill-judged propaganda, and forbade HOBSBAWM to have any further contact with the teaching of current affairs.[171]

Or, as Eric put it, 'I got my balls chewed off by the colonel for putting too much second front material into my wall newspaper.'[172]

Now he couldn't even do 'the little things … which, if they didn't influence world history, certainly kept our consciences quiet'. Frustrated, he applied on 26 August 1942 for transfer to the Army Mobile Information Service. But his superior officers were now on to him, and blocked the appointment. He had, White noted, 'a tendency to produce left wing literature and to leave it lying about'. He had tried to recruit a warrant officer into the Communist Party, and it is also possible that his conversations with Fritz Lustig had been noted, along with Lustig's visit to Communist Party headquarters in London. 'I no longer', concluded the Colonel in his note to MI5 about Eric, 'trust his discretion.' MI5 agreed he was not to be trusted, since 'The *Sunday Times* Discussion Group at Bulford' had been brought to their attention 'as a centre of communist discussions'. True, this was 'not specifically in connection with Sgt. HOBSBAWM'.[173] However, Eric was most likely a leading light in these discussions since he was actually in charge of the *Sunday Times* library at the camp.

Moreover, MI5 had installed a listening device at Communist Party headquarters in London, and learned from it that Eric's presence at Bulford was regarded as presenting an opportunity for propaganda among the troops. Robbie Robson, a founder member of the Communist Party of Great Britain and now in charge of relations with Party members in the armed forces, was heard discussing the possibility of using a visiting American Communist in some capacity. He thought as Eric 'was, fortunately, a Jew, and as every Jew obviously knew someone in the States, the best idea would be that the visitor should go and see HOBSBAWM on the pretext that he was going to give him news of relatives in the States'.[174] How would the contact recognise Eric?

Robson noted that Eric was 'tallish – well, he's not so much tall as he's slim. He's not a particularly striking person ... [but] I think you would be able to pick him out if you saw him coming along making enquiries. V[isitor]: One of those tall, weedy looking, willowy types is he?'

The visit does not seem to have had any further consequences, but this was largely because Archie White ensured that Eric was transferred from Bulford with effect from 31 August 1942 to the Guards Armoured Division as a German-language teacher and banned again from giving any mention to contemporary military or political issues.[175] On 30 August Eric clambered into a bus that took him along with other servicemen to the army camp at Wincanton, in Somerset. Everywhere, he noted, was packed with the military, although the Americans had not yet arrived in the area. The local inhabitants treated the soldiers with reserve. 'One can't blame the civilians', he conceded. At first they had offered them cigarettes; later the men had to beg for them. On a train to London a few weeks previously, he remembered, he had encountered an old man who wanted to give him two shillings to buy cigarettes. 'In England, soldiers have a threefold charitable capital: as representatives of the conscripted members of all civilian families; as pariahs, and thus worthy of sympathy because they have been unwillingly expelled from society; and as the poor. But after three years even the softest hearts are hardened.' All the soldiers with whom he had to deal were Guardsmen, who spent much of the time telling dirty stories. 'The tradition of "manliness" seems to be strongly developed among the Guards.' They laid great stress on drill. 'When I say On Parade, I want to see a cloud of dust and a row of statues.'

Apart from this, he found Wincanton agreeable enough: 'The land is deep and damp, mainly cattle and dairy. Fat, green meadows, neglected hedges, little copses and curtains of mist, groups of clouds in the distance.'[176] But it bored him 'enormously'. 'I don't go to pubs much, except when I want to get drunk, the cinema is miserable, the other sergeants not very interesting either. I'm not getting myself a girl here either, because first I don't need one, and second I'd find that boring too.' Sooner or later, perhaps, he would meet someone he knew personally or politically. He reflected with regret that he found even Party members boring after a short while. He was, he concluded, a poor mixer, for which he only had himself to blame.[177] He amused himself instead by observing those around him:

> Tibbits (the officer) sits in the office like a feeble steer, his blond hair is tousled, and under the unkempt strands the back of his head is bald. If he was wearing a laurel wreath one might confuse him with Nero. His face is fat, sly, and ruddy, his little eyes vague. He is utterly unsystematic but forgets little, least of all anything that concerns himself. He sits at the desk the whole morning, always on the telephone, adapting his voice to whomever he is speaking with (after a while you can guess from his tone whether he is talking to the general's wife, with the D[eputy] A[ssistant] A[djutant] G[eneral] or merely with NCOs), and when he's not on the phone he accompanies his work with endless monologues.[178]

As he lay relaxing on the grass in Salisbury Cathedral Close, Eric was approached by 'a little man with steel spectacles, a blue suit and rather brown hands, from which the veins stood out'. The old man explained how he had seen five wars – the two world wars, the Boer War, the Sudan War and the Zulu War. He said he had never been to school, since the first school was opened in Bromsgrove, where he grew up, only in 1879. But he possessed a fund of homespun wisdom nonetheless. 'Young man', he said to Eric, 'treat life with respect, and not just yours but others' too.'

Throughout this period, Eric remained in his own mind a committed Communist intellectual, and he reflected on what he saw as the sad betrayal of the cause by renegades such as the German-American journalist Louis Fischer, whose autobiography *Men and Politics* (1941) marked his break with Communism, and the Hungarian ex-Communist Arthur Koestler, whose *Darkness at Noon* was published in 1940. They were, Eric thought,

people for whom politics is merely a gymnasium for their conscience and culture. Real politicians possess the courage to be
without culture and to use clichés when necessary. Koestler com-
pares his relationship to Russia with love. But the creation of a
new world is not to be compared to a honeymoon. What do they
understand of the vigilance of the old functionaries, who know
what it is to make a revolution? It was at the beginning surely
not easy for Dzerzhinsky to have people shot. What keeps them
going and sustains and justifies their objective cruelty? Trust.
Belief in the proletariat and the future of the movement . . . The
boundary between revolutionaries and counter-revolutionaries
among intellectuals runs between believing in and doubting the
working class.[179]

Despite all the doubts he harboured as a result of his personal
encounters with its members, therefore, he still felt that the future
of the revolution lay with the proletariat.

The means to winning them over thus lay in propaganda and
persuasion. Still, it would not be easy. White was now reporting
on Eric regularly to the Intelligence Service. 'Care is taken', he
reported to MI5, once Eric had settled in to his new role teaching
German to the Guards, 'to see that his duties are sufficiently full
to leave him no time to proffer instruction in current affairs. No
instance of any subversive action or tendency has been noted. On
the contrary', the Colonel added in a comment that was both
patronising and wide of the mark, 'he seems to be beginning
to realize, through contact with Guards officers, that opinions
other than those he holds may be based on reading and travel
and a knowledge of affairs.'[180] Eric taught German to a variety of
interested groups from the Signals and Intelligence Corps to the
Armoured Corps but mostly the Guards, who were something of
an elite group in the British Army. He found them 'not so much
unintelligent, as trained in such a way as to make intelligence
non-operative'. He found the Scots Guards the most intelligent,
but the Welsh Guards 'a queer lot . . . The system of distinguishing
the Jones', he added, referring to what was by far the commonest

Welsh surname, 'is simple: they just add the last two figures of their army number', as '28 Jones, 38 Jones' and so on. He found it 'very fascinating'.[181]

While MI5 was spending time and energy on tracking Eric, a harmless intellectual who was doing nothing to undermine the Allied war effort – rather, he would probably have argued, the opposite, through the encouragement of a Second Front – it completely failed to notice the activities of the 'Cambridge Five', who were already engaged in betraying significant state secrets to the Russians, until 1951. After all, Blunt, Burgess, Cairncross, Maclean and Philby were men of impeccable British Establishment credentials, while Eric was not. MI5 initially tried to extend its surveillance across the entire Communist Party membership, but the rapid growth of the Party during the war, after the Soviet Union had become Britain's ally, when membership reached a total of fifty-six thousand, made that impracticable.[182] At one point, MI5 even suspected Eric's sister Nancy, cousin Ron and uncle Harry of being Communist spies.[183] In August 1941 Nancy had accepted an offer to go to Trinidad, then a British colony, with a number of other British secretaries at the embassy in Chile, to work as a censor 'with some other Anglo-Chilean girls'.[184] Here MI5 tracked her down just over a year later, reporting that she was 'employed in the Imperial Censorship at Port of Spain, Trinidad', and, worryingly from MI5's point of view, had not been put through any vetting procedure.[185] But the security services were soon reassured; there was nothing political about either Nancy or her fellow employees except for the guidelines they were obliged to follow when they were engaged in their work as censors.

Although he spent nearly all his time as a language teacher, once the army discovered he had been to North Africa before the war and had studied social conditions there, he was allowed to lecture on the state of affairs in Tunis and Algeria to the Guards Armoured Division. 'His lectures', it was reported, 'are appreciated and contain no matter calling for comment.'[186] Building on this success, Eric offered to make his knowledge available on a wider basis on 8 November 1942.[187] But the offer does not seem to have been taken up. The security services remained suspicious because it was clear that Eric belonged to a small committee of Communist Party members at Bulford.[188] However, he was almost equally distrusted by the Communist Party leadership. MI5 picked up a conversation at Party headquarters in London in which those present agreed that Eric was 'an excellent Comrade': he had 'sent in a 10 page document on Army re-organisation to the Centre, but it hadn't really contained anything new'. He was inclined to make 'wild proposals', and it was necessary 'to make HOBSBAWM a little more practical and less of an idealist'.[189] Despite these surveillance reports, on 20 December 1942 MI5 noted: 'Sergt. E. HOBSBAWM has been cleared of suspicion of engaging in subversive activities or propaganda in the army. No further action in this section necessary'. But, the report added, 'I doubt whether you would consider him suitable for I[ntelligence] Corps, should he apply for a transfer'.[190]

This heavy hint to Colonel Archie White was for the time being to frustrate Eric's plans to escape from the Army Educational Corps. He was getting bored again. Some relief from the tedium was provided by the American GIs who would, if asked, take British soldiers into the well-equipped American Red Cross Club, but it was 'boring to run around the streets to dig up a Yank'. There were no decent films on. Some pleasure could also be found in the consumption of tobacco. Like almost everyone else at the time, Eric was a heavy smoker. In 1943, in a brief fragment on his life in the army, he noted:

Very often we don't notice how we live. Suddenly the smoke from my cigarette (Capstan) gets in my eyes. I blink and wake up like a camera. Before one can draw any conclusions, one must observe and notice things quietly, so I'm noticing. I begin with the bits of tobacco on my tongue and the smoke which edges past my screwed-up eyes. I wonder will this habit of keeping the fag in my mouth stain my teeth. Probably yes. One gets used to feeling the little cylinder on the lower lip, the acrid taste on the roof of the mouth, the tap of the finger to shake off ash.[191]

Wondering what the future might hold for him at a juncture when it was still unclear which side would win the war, he conceded that he would not be of much use in the case of a full-scale military mobilisation.

> I recognize my bottomless inadequacy as a soldier, and my possibly even greater inadequacy as an 'expert' ... I'm mediocre and erratic at shooting. I don't have much élan (perhaps I'd acquire it if there were enough sympathetic onlookers); and a consignment of moral dynamite would be needed to turn me from a shy, ironic, whispering person into an NCO capable of command.

It was things he wasn't physically capable of doing that would frighten him if and when he had to do them.[192]

In January 1943 he applied to be allowed to accompany the Guards Division when it was sent abroad. 'My functions,' he told Ron optimistically, 'would be those of an intelligence nco at advanced HQ with special emphasis on the German, though no doubt in quieter periods I'd do educational stuff as well.'[193] The trouble was, he admitted, that he knew very little about the German army whose communications he would presumably be studying and whose soldiers when taken prisoner he would probably be interrogating. The matter had acquired some urgency because the Second Front would surely be opened in the spring or summer of 1943, to take advantage of what he thought would be the demoralisation of the *Wehrmacht* following the surrender of the 6th Army at Stalingrad. If the defeat of Rommel's Afrika Korps in Tunisia took much longer, however, 'it would balls us up till almost midsummer'. In fact, the Germans did not surrender in North Africa until 13 May 1943, and the Allied forces were tied up for even longer with the invasion of Sicily and then the Italian mainland, which followed soon after. There was, despite Eric's optimism, to be no Second Front in Western Europe in 1943.

In any case, Colonel White and the security services were determined that Eric should stay at home in Britain where they could keep an eye on him. In February 1943 he was told that 'probably it would be against regulations for a sergeant to go abroad unless to a static establishment'. Eric was outraged. 'Who the hell,' he asked rhetorically, 'wants to go to, let us say, an Ordinance Depot at Suez or similar assignments? I don't. I'm applying for an infantry commission, reckoning that I'd be a natural for unit Intelligence Officer (if I don't get into I-Corps).' Perhaps to boost his qualification record, on 6 February 1943 he obtained his MA from Cambridge University, where, as in the other five medieval British universities, all successful Honours graduates were entitled to the Master's degree once a certain period of time had elapsed. He was uncertain what good it would do, however, 'having forgotten 75% of what I knew as a B.A. So what.'[194]

On 19 March 1943 Eric visited Communist Party headquarters in Covent Garden, bugged by MI5. According to the transcript of the conversation, he said

> that officially he had been posted back to Salisbury Plain district, but he wished to be removed, and 'they were trying to negotiate, but he didn't know if it would succeed.' They discussed the number of troops in East Anglia now . . . Eric spoke of R[oyal] A[rtillery] C[orps] Units in Cambridge and Newmarket area – where he has been . . . Eric described a manoeuvre he had taken part in, and then they got on to the conjectures about the 2nd Front . . . Eric thought . . . they would do a few practise [*sic*] embarkations and then suddenly find it was the real thing . . . Eric told JACK about their exercise, saying 'our Armoured Brigade' was completely beaten. He took a poor view of the Canadians.[195]

Communist Party headquarters knew about the trouble Eric had got into over his wall newspapers, since one of his officers was also a Party member.[196]

None of these schemes came to anything. Eric was transferred to Bovington in Dorset in April 1943, 'back in the old rut again'. The area was not unpleasant, 'not so bleak as the usual Norfolk

Breckland or Salisbury Plain camps. A bit limited in amenities though. We have a very good wall newspaper which I'm trying to improve,' he told Ron on 18 April 1943. Through all of this, Eric had not the slightest suspicion that the security services were in control of his career. He thought the obstacles placed in the way of his transfer were just 'one of those cases of sheer red tape which do still crop up in the Army. If we'd have gone straightaway overseas I'd have gone too, and nobody would have been any the wiser. As it is, I was hauled back: A question of establishment. Can't be helped.'[197] Some months later, in November 1943, the army's resolve was strengthened when a further MI5 report confirmed that 'there is no doubt that HOBSBAWN [sic] continues to be a member of the Communist Party and ... is quite unsuitable for I. Corps'.[198]

Eric relieved the tedium by writing and publishing some brief articles in *University Forward* (the magazine of the University Labour Federation) at this time. Perhaps the most substantial of them was 'Aux Armes, Citoyens!' (on the French Revolution):

The Terror has been slandered and maligned ever since the fall of Robespierre. We, who are engaged in total war, can judge it with greater insight. But to get the true perspective, we must learn to see it, not only through the eyes of fighters for freedom of 1943, but through those of the common soldiers who, bare-foot and starving, saved their country because it was a good country to save. For them the Terror was not a nightmare, but the dawn of life.

Another article, 'No Future for Heroes?', was a light-hearted lament for what he argued was the disappearance of the hero from Hollywood. At home, he worried about the possibility of the Labour Party leaving the coalition cabinet, which would place Churchill 'at the mercy of the less victory-minded Tories'.[199] He did not think the 'Popular Front' atmosphere would survive the 'sharpening of the social situation' that was likely when the war finally ended. The Americans would swing to the right and engage in 'a red- and liberal-hunt that will make 1919 look like a picnic' – an uncanny premonition of the McCarthyite persecution of Communists, real and alleged, that began in February 1950.[200] In Britain, the opposition of the Labour Home Secretary Herbert Morrison, who had seen secret documents on the Communist Party, stopped the Party's application for affiliation to Labour.[201] Morrison, Eric concluded, was 'still the most important figure in the party', and while that was the case, the Communists stood no chance of being affiliated to Labour unless membership in the trade unions improved and the unions exerted themselves at the Labour Party Conference.[202]

VI

Eric continued to enjoy a social life with his old friends during his brief periods of furlough, though two of his friends at least had come to grief. During the night of 27–28 July 1942, Ram Nahum, the leading Cambridge student Communist before the war and a close friend of Eric's, was one of three people killed in an attack on the town by a lone German raider. A German bomb fell directly onto the house where he was staying with another member of their circle, Freddie Lambert, who had fallen in love with Nahum while 'Mouse' Vickers, her husband, was missing, presumed dead. Teddy Prager, an Austrian economics student whom Eric had got to know at the LSE, was living in the house at the back, near the Round Church (Eric had also stayed there for a time). Hearing the explosion, he rushed out and heard Freddie's screams. He got hold of an axe and tried to free her from underneath a burning wooden beam but it was no use. Thinking she was going to die, she shouted: 'I'm done for! Long live the Party! Long live Stalin! Goodbye, boys!' In fact, however, she too survived the war, became a social worker in London and lived with 'Mouse' until her death in 2006, though she never told him of her wartime affair. Prager himself, by now in a relationship with Eric's old friend Marjorie, returned to Vienna at the end of the war.[203]

In 1941 Eric began a relationship of his own, with Muriel Seaman, 'a very attractive LSE girl' to whom he had been introduced by Prager. Muriel's father was a soldier in the Coldstream Guards whose job was to look after the Crown Jewels in the Tower of London; her mother was the daughter of a Beefeater (the name given to the Yeomen Warders of the Tower). Born in the Tower of London on 29 October 1916, and so a few months older than Eric, Muriel was tall, at 5 feet 10 inches, and was described in a later report by the Special Branch of the Metropolitan Police as of 'slim build, sallow complexion, hair dark brown, eyes hazel'. She was, the police noted, 'keenly interested in extremist matters and is believed to be a member of the Communist Party'.[204] By this time Muriel was working as a civil servant in the Board of Trade. She had been a Communist but had left the Party; now she rejoined it to please Eric.[205] They met in London or Cambridge at the weekends or other times when Eric was on leave. 'When one sleeps with a girl nowadays,' Eric reflected, 'it's a relatively simple matter ... Techniques have perhaps improved [since Victorian times] (though I hardly believe much).'[206]

Contraception was indeed little more effective in the 1940s than it had been a century earlier, and on 1 September 1942 Eric received an alarming letter from Muriel:

> M. writes that she has missed her period. That's odd, because in the first place as far as I know our precautions were all right, and secondly there wasn't much danger the last time. But I could be wrong. There's a third possibility, that she's slept with someone else, but since she wouldn't have done that without taking precautions, that isn't really relevant. Anyway I don't believe she did. What should one do? Our combined funds might perhaps just pay for an abortion – if it comes to that. I wouldn't mind a child, but it would be difficult for her. I'll try to go to London this weekend.[207]

The next day Muriel wrote again, this time reassuringly, as Eric reported: 'Everything ok. She drank a skinful of gin. God', he added ruefully, 'I don't really understand much of this. If it goes on like this however I'll soon become an expert.'[208] The intermittent nature of his new relationship caused a good deal of anxiety. Moreover, he wrote on 7 September 1942 after spending the next weekend in London with Muriel, the gin didn't seem to have had its desired effect.

> I get on well with M. Although I looked forward a lot to this weekend – the consequence of village life in Wincanton – the reunion doesn't disappoint. Odd. As usual she is wearing the green outfit, which is slowly starting to bore me. We sleep at the Pragers ... The level of M.'s politics is rising, she'll soon be very good if she learns to express herself. She has the ability. God knows what happened last week, but it seems not to have worked. She's very worried about the quinine intake. She isn't much afraid of an abortion, but she's fearful of the early months of pregnancy, with their constant feeling of sickness. Bit by bit I will learn about women. But what I observe, I easily forget. Pity.[209]

In the end, it turned out to be a false alarm.

Eric was nervous about becoming too close to Muriel. 'Entre nous', he confided to his diary on 29 November 1942, 'I'm in a bad mood because I've got used to M[uriel]. Or perhaps not. Perhaps I'm in a bad mood anyway and just localise it. Perhaps. One shouldn't get used to people.' The problem was that he missed her. 'Now we've to some extent got used to each other, being away from London is getting harder.' He worried that she might find someone else. 'I have to conclude from my feelings that I'm in love. Probably she is too.' He wasn't jealous, but he feared that absence from Muriel might make him so. That might relieve his boredom, but it would be difficult too.[210] On 21 February 1943 he told Ron, 'Muriel and I will probably get married. You met her, you remember', he added:

> I suppose it is the logical outcome if you've been with the same girl for over a year. As you know I have great inhibitions about

getting tied up, but this hand-to-mouth life is a lot less fair to a woman than to a man, and I see no logical reason for not getting married. Sooner or later the question was bound to arrive, so why not sooner. Anyway by now we have, in one important respect, got used to each other: which, as you'll agree, is a big thing. I have no views at all about dates ... But no doubt it will come sooner than we think, it always does.[211]

This was hardly a ringing endorsement of the idea of marriage to Muriel. Love hardly seemed to come into it at all.

It is telling that among the love poems Eric wrote during this period, not a single one was addressed to Muriel, not even by implication.[212] A woman's arm and mouth are described – 'Arm, schoen wie die weissen Pferde ... Mund ein glaenzendes Metall' ('arm, beautiful like white horses ... mouth a brilliant metal') – but we are not told to whom these body parts belong; they seem almost abstract, disconnected from any person.[213] In one poem he imagined a girl sleeping with Trotskyists, expressing an obvious fear of betrayal, but he crossed out the word and replaced it with 'literary men'.[214] In 'Peace' he compared the mood after the war to a couple's mood after having sex: 'Nur zwischen unsern engen Koerpern lag,/Betauebend und gereizt wie junges Heu,/Der Friede, die Erinnerung, die Zukunft', but again the frame of reference was entirely impersonal.[215]

Nevertheless, the day after he had written to Ron, Eric asked Muriel to marry him. She said yes. He worried immediately about whether he had done the right thing. 'Yesterday evening', he wrote on 23 February 1943,

I was a bit depressed, and the thought of having a wife was very agreeable ... So I'll just marry her. I don't like uncertainty and yet I find it so difficult to make decisions. I hate uncertainty and welcome the *fait accompli* ... If it had been necessary I would have married her already ten months ago. And during my last leave I didn't press her and so I found out that it matters a lot to her and so I'll just marry her. Personally I don't believe it will last for ever. She's not ideal – me neither, of course – and if one waits for the ideal ... ach, I'm talking rubbish. I'm too tired to think logically and anyway, what's the point? I'll probably ring her up this evening, she'll be pleased.[216]

Once more, his doubts and hesitations were as noticeable as the lukewarm pragmatism of his decision.

His impending marriage led Eric to reflect on what he had achieved so far and what the future might hold in store for him. He concluded gloomily that he had wasted the entire period since the beginning of the war.

> I've achieved nothing serious in the war except dig holes, give lectures, and provide paratroopers ... with a few dozen German phrases. I've done nothing for the P[arty] except a good Russia action and two laughably trivial, soon terminated Org[anisational] tasks, creating a few abstract documents. I've written little and that hardly valuable. My only success has been the luxury success of making my wife fall in love with me, and I'd have gladly given that up if I could have exchanged it for Party or war work. Perhaps 'gladly' is an exaggeration. At any rate I would have given it up.[217]

The future was surely more important. There would probably be a second round of revolutions. So he made a provisional resolution to become a professional Party worker after the war. He thought he was good enough at propaganda and analysis and to some extent organisational work to do this. If he did not obtain such a post, 'then any position that has to do with propaganda – advertising, journalism or somesuch. I'll talk to M[uriel] about it.' At least he took some pride in the wall newspapers he produced for the Army Educational Corps, so 'I haven't wasted the last ten months'. He had no thought of becoming an historian but he recognised that his talents lay in writing of some kind. Just as earlier in his life he had considered becoming a poet, now he was thinking of becoming a propagandist. This was not going to bring in very much in the way of income. Nevertheless, the prospects for Eric and Muriel were improved when on 18 April 1943 she was promoted to the rank of Principal at the Board of Trade, a senior post with good prospects. Her promotion, Eric reflected, gave her '480£; taxes paid about 7£ a week, and my allowance would make that to 8.10 – enough to go on with. Particularly since she'd not be spending a lot.' They had decided to marry sooner rather than later, he told Ron, because 'there's nothing special to be gained by waiting. I think it will work out allright.'[218]

Eric's wedding to Muriel Seaman took place on 12 May 1943 at the Register Office in Epsom.[219] Ron had offered to act as witness but was still away from London and the date could not be altered. Eric and Muriel had visited Ron's parents – now Eric's closest relatives in the UK and the ones he knew best – to tell them of his intention to get married, and he told Ron, 'your father and mother were very nice about it, and, though the atmosphere was a very little bit strained to start off with, it loosened up a bit later on, I fancy. I don't know what impression M. made on them', he added, 'but no doubt they'll get used to the idea in time. I missed the South Americans though', referring to his uncle Sidney, his sister Nancy and his cousin Peter. Muriel had been living with her parents for the past two years, and she and Eric now decided to look for a flat nearer her work, in Whitehall. He would spend part of his next leave flat-hunting. 'That won't be easy, in view of the flat shortage', in part a consequence of the Blitz.[220] Despite their joint income, Eric and Muriel were still short of funds, and Ron once more sent some money to Eric.[221]

By this time, Ron had also been called up. Naturally, in view of his love of ships and sailing, he chose the Royal Navy. His initial medical assessment had ruled him unfit for service as an Ordinary Seaman because of his poor eyesight, but the navy, with the typical logic of the British armed forces, decided to train him in aircraft recognition. Ron was also married by now, to Lillian Cannon, known as 'Gun', his long-time girlfriend, also a civil servant. He went through a succession of postings, serving on HMS *Colossus*, a brand-new aircraft carrier, which sailed from Alexandria in

October 1944, calling at Taiwan, Manila, Hong Kong, Sydney and Sri Lanka, before he was finally transferred home in November 1945 after having been promoted lieutenant the previous June. It was small wonder that in their subsequent correspondence, Eric more than once had to confess he was not certain what address to send his letters to.[222] In the meantime, after getting married, Eric and Muriel found a flat to rent

in Camden Town, (round the corner from Regents' Park[)] which is convenient in many ways, not expensive, and passable, though not of course ideal. Furniture is on order and we have managed to get a lot of odds and ends (carpets, kitchen-stuff etc) from Sidney's stored things. In fact the moving-in depends entirely on the date by which the utility furniture can be delivered.[223]

On 7 August 1943 Eric reported that 'the flat is still minus furniture – till the utility stuff is delivered'. Until then the couple lived at 86 Springfield Avenue, in Wimbledon, south-west London.[224]

VII

In April 1944, Eric again fell foul of the military authorities. As MI5 noted,

The C.O. of 58th Trng. Regt. R.A.C. at Bovington reported that he had noticed that his A.B.C. and Brains Trust discussions were becoming too political and left wing views were being introduced; there was a falling off in attendance of young soldiers as they objected to the strong left wing theories produced by members of the Permanent Staff. The C.O. discovered that Sgt. HOBSBAWM was at the bottom of it and expressed the view that although he was a very capable instructor, it was felt that he was abusing his position as a senior N.C.O. and Education Instructor.[225]

Eric, his superiors noted, 'knows perfectly well that he is being watched', and he later confirmed that he knew he was under surveillance, though he thought it was by the army, not, it seems, by the security services.[226] He asked for an interview with his CO, 'and stated that he thought he was a political victim'. MI5 added: 'It is clear that HOBSBAWN [sic] is not aware that he is the object of interest in this office, but is disgruntled because he has more than once been reprimanded by his C.O.s for allowing his political views to influence his work.'[227] Following this incident, the army posted Eric to Headquarters, Isle of Wight Sub-District. He had already been there, as well as at Portland and Southampton, for a few weeks in the early summer of 1943, 'running courses for regimental officers and ncos in the best way to run their "British Way and Purpose" – the programme of education in civics which the Army has (in theory) been running ever since last November. It is an adequate programme, and it is the kind of job I like', he had told Ron.

He thought the Isle of Wight 'over-rated, and I'm glad a lot of those Victorian boardinghouses went west. Tough on the locals though', he added.[228] He found time to write some verses about the island, the black cattle on the meadows, the seagulls throwing their shadows on the grass, the narrow harbour mole stretching out to sea. He noticed 'a harbour for destroyers' and the prison at Parkhurst and listened to the air-raid sirens as they drove the gulls away in fright.[229] A year later, his brief period of service on the Isle of Wight in 1943 evidently judged a success, Eric was given a permanent posting there. MI5 was horrified. This was, after all, a major preparation and training ground for the long-planned invasion of Normandy, due to take place in little over two months. 'In view of the many secret and important operations going on in that district and the impossibility of adequately supervising the execution of his duties' they ordered Eric to be transferred once again, this time as a welfare officer in an army hospital outside Cheltenham, an elegant spa town not far from Gloucester.[230] He left the Isle of Wight on 24 May 1944 to take up his new duties.[231]

In Gloucester, as MI5 later noted suspiciously, 'he regards his position as having some possibilities, presumably for communist propaganda'.²³² On 29 August 1944 MI5 had recorded a telephone conversation between Eric and Margot Heinemann: 'M: Are you still on the same job? E: Yes. M: Any better? E: It has possibilities.'²³³ However, he had complained to Heinemann on 2 July 1944 over the phone that he was 'about as tucked away as I can possibly be!' 'That's very bad luck, I must say', she replied. 'Oh, I don't know', said Eric; at least he was away from the bombing.²³⁴ On the hospital wards, he encountered patients from a variety of different countries. He talked in German to a Polish patient with a heavily bandaged neck who had deserted from the German army: 'It feels slightly indecent to speak to a Slav in the language of Hitler, but there is no choice.' Eric chatted in French to a Moroccan soldier who had fought with de Gaulle's Free French against the Germans in North Africa from 1940 until he was invalided out in 1944. 'A small thin figure in bulging hospital blues, who looks more than ever like the consumptive monkeynut pedlars of the Boulevard Montparnasse, he has yet – and the ward recognizes it uneasily – something of the frightening detachment of the natural, instinctive warrior.' He had a 'thin high-cheeked Berber face and half-moon moustache'. With pride he showed Eric 'a silver watch, ornamented, with slightly cracked face and a few dents which he took off a German in 1940'.²³⁵

More disturbing were the patients with severe wounds. One man 'with a rather white face and hollow eyes' and a leg 'cut off just above the knee' clearly wanted to die. 'He was burned out in a tank, and the only man to escape.' He refused food and after three days was force-fed. 'Six men hold him, while he is made to swallow a pipe. The six men have their faces in ribbons of foreign skin, arms in plaster and their jaws in splints. He cries out in a hoarse indescribable manner, but one has got used to the cries of those who can't bear their pain.' He had lost the will to live because of guilt over the death of his brother, who had fought in the same tank as him and been burned to death.

There is nothing to do. Nobody can help him. Nobody can begin to help him. On the sixth day he dies ... On the table, next to the chief clerk's *Daily Telegraph* and the bundle of washing belonging to the orderly the remaining possessions of the dead man are stacked in a small box: a razor, a note block and pencil, a couple of novels, two boxes of matches and eighty cigarettes. The weekly cigarette ration which had been sent round the wards on the day before his death. That is all.[236]

Eric was struck by 'the unexpectedness of seeing people with only half a face'. 'Occasionally some one comes in whose mutilation is a shade more gruesome, and we hold our breath when we turn to him, for fear our face might give away our shocked repulsion.' It reminded him of the Greek myth of Marsyas, who was flayed alive by Apollo for daring to challenge him to a musical competition. Yet there was hope, too: 'Those who come here know, in general, that they will leave in the end as, approximately, human beings.'

On 6 June 1944 the much hoped-for Second Front finally arrived, when Allied troops landed in Normandy on the long-prepared 'D-Day'. At the Gloucester hospital, Eric noted the arrival of the first battle casualties. He encountered a group of Welsh miners

walking along the path rather like a shop stewards' deputation. Dressed in their best blue suits, a little uncertain in an unaccustomed environment ... One can tell from the blue marks on their faces what their profession is. 'Looking for anything?' 'Yes. Can you tell us where the military wards is?' ... I go some of the way with them, to the entrance of the ward. The leader, a small bald man, looks at a piece of paper. 'Can you tell us if this is the ward where Evan Thomas is?' It is. 'We are his mates from work. We had a free day, so we thought we'd come over and see how he was getting on.' I go and ask the sister whether Thomas E. can have any visitors. His mates from the pit are outside. Thomas already has some – his parents and a friend,

who are sitting by the bed in attitudes of constraint and love.
Outside the ward the miners stand in the corridor looking
at the passing nurses and soldiers, and not chatting to each
other . . . One of the soldier's visitors comes out of the ward. The
man's friends bend forward and form a small collective group.
One can hear a few words. 'Oh hello Mrs Thomas' 'How are
you Ianto Evans' and so on. There is great pathos in this small
meeting, which I cannot quite account for. Perhaps it is because
this accidental encounter crystallises all the private loyalties:
of miners as such, of the inhabitants of the valley, of friends,
of Welshmen, of healthy men faced with helplessness. I don't
know. It is very moving.[237]

But before Eric had been in Gloucester for very many months,
the question of a posting abroad came up once more. This time it
was not Eric who requested it, but the administration of the Army
Educational Corps.

On 17 November 1944 MI5 noted: 'Captain Ronald, Southern
Command, telephoned to say that HOBSBAWM had been
ordered to the School of Education before drafting overseas.
Ronald knew that, in this case, observation had ceased, but knew
we were interested in HOBSBAWM's movements.'[238] An MI5
officer, J. B. Milne, reiterated the security service's insistence that
it would be dangerous to post Eric overseas:

HOBSBAWM has twice been reprimanded by different C.O's
for introducing strong partisan views into unit wall newspapers . . . He is a keen and very active member of the Party and
well thought of at Party Headquarters, and if he were allowed
to go overseas I think it is very likely that he might cause similar
trouble . . . If he went to B[ritish] N[orth] A[frica] F[orce] he
might link up with the Benghazi Forces Parliament, which has
been formed and about which we are making enquiries, and
cause trouble similar to that which we have had in the past with
the Cairo Forces Parliament. I suggest that we should first find
out where HOBSBAWM is to be sent and then I think in any

case take steps to prevent it as I think he would be far better kept under our eye in this country.[239]

MI5 also informed Eric's commanding officer in the Army Education Corps of 'the whole facts of this case'.[240]

But on making further enquiries, MI5 learned that 'this man was only actually on the "waiting list" to go abroad ... There would be no difficulty in removing him.'[241] By 4 December 1944 Eric had indeed 'been removed from the draft' and posted back to Gloucester.[242] He was puzzled by the sudden vanishing of his prospects of being posted overseas. 'All the strings seem to have broken,' he told Margot Heinemann at the Labour Research Department, which was being bugged by the security services, on 31 May 1945 over the phone: 'All the ones that would have taken me to India or Mombasa or other places.' So he was looking for employment in the UK. 'Margot', as the transcript of MI5's wire-tap of the Department's phone reported, 'went on to say that there were plenty of useful jobs if Eric had any spare time – digging out records of Tory M.P.s etc.' Eric thought he might manage 'a bit' but did not have a great deal of time.[243] He was, after all, still in the army.

Suspicions remained. MI5 took out a surveillance order on 12 January 1945 and began monitoring his correspondence.[244] By this time, anyone in a sensitive position who was associated with him in any way was liable to have questions asked about him in MI5 or MI6. In the winter of 1944–5, the security services expressed some doubts about the loyalty of one of their officers, Kenneth Syers, who had been a contemporary of Eric's at King's College, Cambridge, and had met him when they were up for interview. Fluent in Serbo-Croat, Syers was dropped into Yugoslavia twice during the war, and then on his return was given a London post in the security services on the strength of his reports from the Communist partisan movement. He came under surveillance because he was one of a number of security service officers who were 'so far Left as to be scarcely distinguishable from Communists'. In November 1944 Syers aroused further suspicion when he became engaged to a niece by marriage of Maxim Litvinov, the pre-war Soviet Foreign Minister. Syers had met the young woman in Italy between his two postings in Yugoslavia. Asked to investigate further, Roger Hollis, who later rose to the position of head of MI5, reported that Syers was connected with 'a certain Communist in the Army Education Corps named Hobsbawm, who was before the war an undergraduate in Cambridge'. The report was passed to none other than Kim Philby for comment. Philby leapt to Syers' defence. 'Syers seems to be remarkably unfortunate in his choice of friends', he reported, referring to Eric, but he had talked to Syers and ascertained that he intended to leave the service after the war to take up journalism. It would be inconceivable, Philby argued, that if he actually was a spy, his spymasters in Moscow would allow him to do this. In any case, Syers made 'little attempt to conceal his interest in Marxism and Marxists – an attitude which is hardly consistent with sinister designs'. In the event, the entirely innocent Syers did indeed leave the service to take up journalism, while Kim Philby, the real spy, stayed on, to please his masters in Moscow, until he was eventually unmasked.[245]

Eric was kept on in the hospital at Gloucester for the whole of the rest of the year. He played an active part in the 1945 General Election, which took place on 5 July, though the count was not held until 26 July because of the time it took to get British servicemen's ballot papers back to the UK from wherever they were stationed. The result was a surprise landslide victory for the Labour Party, which won 47.7 per cent of the vote. Asked some years later about his role in the campaign, Eric wrote:

My own experience of the election was canvassing for the Labour candidate in Gloucester, where I was stationed as an Army Education sergeant, billeted with a pillar of the local Labour Party. They didn't expect to win ... I remember, as I canvassed the prosperous little houses on the outskirts of the city, being amazed at the solid Labour reactions I got. From someone used to identifying Labour streets as inner-city terrace houses with corner grocers and pubs, this was unexpected. I concluded that Labour would win (they did win Gloucester – a lawyer called Turner-Samuels, if I recall), but I can't think of many in the area – including myself – who would have confidently predicted this earlier. As for the forces vote, neither I nor anyone else in the ranks, was in the least surprised. That they would vote Labour was predictable and predicted.[246]

The Labour government now formed by Clement Attlee was in many respects 'not too hot ... I daresay the time will come when we shall have to ginger them up, but so far the programme seems ok.'[247] 'If a communist party waits long enough under capitalism', he wrote optimistically, 'it will get a chance, big or small.' Nevertheless, the leadership of the British Party was 'stale', and needed 'a general self-critical survey of our work in the war'. Democracy was largely absent from Party affairs. 'So much of what discussion there has been in our party has taken place above the membership.' The ideological tergiversations of the 1930s had shown a lack of foresight. Opposing the war in the early 1940s without any clear idea of what should be done if the Nazis invaded the Soviet Union had caused 'ideological stomach-aches'. Where was the strategic thinking 'which the really big Marxists had had?' Already, therefore, Eric's independence of mind was rubbing up against the Stalinist rigidity of the Party leadership.

At the end of the year, he found out that he was finally going to be posted abroad, long after he had ceased to wish such a transfer, and to the place where he most probably least wanted to go: the British Mandate of Palestine, which was rapidly descending into a maelstrom of chaos and violence, like so many other parts of the British Empire after the end of the war. 'Interesting country', he told Christopher Meredith, a Communist acquaintance then serving with the Royal Air Force in Italy, 'but I resent being posted to a place where the line is so god-damned obscure that hell alone knows what's right or wrong.' So early in December 1945 he applied to the Board of Research Studies in Cambridge to take up residence in the New Year as a research student.[248] On Boxing Day, his old tutor at King's, Christopher Morris, wrote him a reference,

describing him as 'a man of very great ability with every qualification for this kind of work ... just about the ablest pupil I have had
in some 15 years of teaching – abler in my opinion than another
pupil who is already a Fellow of the College'.[249] Mounia Postan
also obliged with a recommendation.[250] On 15 January 1946 Eric
formally applied for 'compassionate leave to resume his studies at
Cambridge' from 1 February and was released from the army on
6 February, being transferred to the Army Reserve on 3 April.[251]
In anticipation of his demobilisation, the military authorities had
already ceased their surveillance of his activities on 16 January.[252]
Eric could at last resume his academic career in Cambridge and
properly begin his married life in London. Neither, however,
turned out to be quite what he had expected.

5

'Outsider in the Movement'

1946–1954

I

By the time he was demobilised, early in 1946, at the age of twenty-eight, Eric had reached a decision about his future. He had, he noted later, 'scribbled since the age of fourteen, but discovered as a young adult that poetry and fiction were not for me. History, which provides plenty of scope for writing, suited me.'[1]

I became a professional historian because I studied history as an undergraduate, was extremely good at it, and was awarded a research studentship after my first degree, which in those days (1939) was not as common as it later became. If I hadn't managed to get a studentship I would probably have tried for the Civil Service exam, another conventional option for people with a first-class degree in the humanities. I also considered a job in journalism (having edited a student weekly) or advertising. In the 1930s copy-writing for ad agencies was fashionable among some intellectuals. Happily I did not choose either, since I don't have the temperament, though I've done a bit of journalism on the side. If I had not known myself to be both inefficient and not good at managing people, I would have considered becoming a fulltime political organizer for the Communist Party, in which a lot of us were then. Once again, luckily I kept out of that, though

I respected and still respect my friends who didn't. It would have eventually caused a lot of problems. I wasn't committed to becoming a professional academic until I got out of the army in 1946, though I was fairly sure I would try.[2]

He chose economic history, he added, because it was the only aspect of university-based history that fitted his interests and beliefs as a Marxist, at a time when mainstream history departments were dominated by political and diplomatic historians. He was not, in fact, he said many years later, an economic historian: he came to history via literature, and through an interest in the relations between 'base' and 'superstructure' in history and society, and economic history was the only place in the academic world where it was possible to focus on this problem.[3]

When he had graduated in 1939, he had proposed a Ph.D. thesis on French North Africa, building on the work he had already done there the previous year. But while he was in the army he was unable to access material on it, and in any case, now that he was married, he felt he should not disappear abroad for long periods of time.[4] So he looked around for a subject that he could research in the UK. He naturally turned to his old mentor Mounia Postan, who suggested he write a dissertation on the history of the Fabian Society, a group of radical intellectuals founded in the late nineteenth century, and agreed to supervise the research.[5] The Fabians took their name from the Roman general of the second century BCE, Quintus Fabius Maximus, who gained his nickname *Cunctator* ('the delayer') from the tactics he employed when faced with a superior enemy, refusing open battle and wearing the enemy forces down by continual attrition until the moment came to strike the fatal blow. This summed up the way in which the Fabians hoped to bring about socialism. With Postan's support, Eric was admitted to the History Faculty as a Ph.D. student and began his research in February 1946, as soon as he was demobbed, reading deeply in the Fabian Society's papers and publications and conducting many interviews of the surviving members.[6]

But the more Eric read about the Fabians, the more he became disenchanted by them. Previous writers had regarded them as socialists, but he could not agree ('To doubt the theories of one's predecessors', he wrote, 'is as natural for historians as to develop a rolling gait for seamen, and as useful').[7] Fabianism was, in his view, not a socialist movement in the modern sense.[8] It did not 'abandon capitalism' but aimed at 'making it more efficient and more secure'.[9] 'As socialists', he concluded, 'the Fabians' reputation rests entirely on their success in establishing the vocabulary and doctrine of a theory which repudiated Marxism, the class struggle, and the necessity of facing problems of political power.'[10] Ultimately they were not very significant.[11] After 1909, they were outflanked by the emergence of a younger generation of socialists who actually believed in the class struggle and exerted an increasingly powerful influence on the emerging Labour Party.[12] The most remarkable aspect of the thesis, in retrospect, was not, however, its highly critical attitude towards its subject, but rather its breadth of European reference, foreign to most work in British labour history at the time. Eric noted in particular Sidney and Beatrice Webb's affinity with (and perhaps indebtedness to) the ideas of the mid-nineteenth-century German apostle of 'state socialism' Ferdinand Lassalle, and their influence on German 'revisionist' thinkers such as Eduard Bernstein.[13] This was only one of its many impressive aspects. With 169 pages of text, sixty-nine pages of endnotes and six appendices, the thesis was an imposing work of scholarship.

Eric completed the thesis in first draft in the summer of 1949, but in the course of Michaelmas Term he 'found, however', as he explained to the Board of Research Studies at Cambridge, 'that in the course of that term I had to do much more serious redrafting, rewriting and revising than I had expected to have to do at that stage of the work. Even after earlier revisions, I was obliged to be busy on all parts of the dissertation until the very end of term.'[14] He finally submitted the dissertation on 15 December 1949, just under four years since he had begun it. However, the Board of Research Studies rejected it. The typist to whom Eric had entrusted it in London had typed it on foolscap paper rather than the smaller quarto size, and it had been submitted bound in soft covers. 'The dissertation is not acceptable in its present form', he was told severely: 'It should have been typed on quarto paper and at least one copy should have been permanently bound in stiff covers with the title and your name clearly inscribed on the cover, in accordance with Paragraph 20 of the Memorandum to Research Students, a copy of which was sent to you on your admission as a Research Student.'[15] Eric had to get special permission to allow the deviation of the thesis from its formal requirements. Making a virtue of necessity, Postan assured the Board that the larger format was necessary for the inclusion of statistical tables, adding that a retyping would involve Eric in substantial extra expense which he could ill afford.[16] As Eric explained in his own letter to the Board, 'the cost of research and examination fees, and of preparing a Ph.D. examination is in itself quite serious, and as you know, none of it is recoverable in the form of income tax allowances. Naturally I am reluctant to add another substantial sum to it.' Since the History Faculty's Degree Committee, which had to approve all of these details, met rather infrequently, it was not until April 1950 that the formal submission could go ahead, much to Eric's frustration. His thesis was finally sent in to the university on 30 June 1950, along with the required formal documents, including a certification from Eric that the thesis did not exceed the then upper limit of sixty thousand words.[17]

Following Cambridge practice, the Faculty appointed two examiners, one from outside Cambridge, one from inside, who were required to submit independent reports to the Faculty before conducting the viva voce examination. Nearly five more months passed while the examiners read the thesis and compiled their reports, which were sent in to the Faculty on 24 November. The external examiner was Robert Ensor, an Oxford historian and Labour Party politician who was best known for his substantial volume in the *Oxford History of England* on England 1870–1914. The internal examiner was Denis Brogan, Fellow of Peterhouse and Professor of Political Science. Ensor had no doubt about recommending the dissertation for the award of a Ph.D. He praised the research Eric had put into the thesis, as well as the clarity of the work's structure, though he thought that a small number of 'errors of grammar or syntax give the impression that English is not his native language'. His principal objection was to what he considered its 'lack of historical imagination', for instance in the failure to mention the impact of the 1906 General Election, which brought the Liberals and Left to power and prompted 'self-seekers eager to get on the band-waggon' to enter the Fabian Society, where they were disappointed by its gradualism and began to cause trouble. Eric, Ensor declared, had missed this point altogether and did not understand the nature of the rebellions that took place in Fabianism at this time.[18] Brogan concurred in the recommendation, finding the dissertation 'a real and important contribution to our knowledge of the political and, to some extent, of intellectual history of the first part of this century'. He praised Eric's research, and considered his arguments, though perhaps too severe on the Society's leaders, 'well supported and plausible': 'Standing outside the Fabian milieu, he has been able to see the society in historical perspective more than previous writers have been.'[19]

The viva duly took place, and the two examiners formally recommended the award of the degree.[20] The Degree Committee of the History Faculty voted it through, nem. con, on 1 December 1950, those voting including well-known names such as J. H. Plumb, Herbert Butterfield, Mounia Postan and Dom David Knowles.[21] Eric was formally admitted to the degree of Doctor of Philosophy on 27 January 1951.[22] It was still relatively unusual at the time for historians to obtain doctorates, and the obvious next step was for the thesis to be published. Eric submitted it promptly to the Syndics of Cambridge University Press, whose secretary obtained copies of the favourable examiners' reports.[23] However, at this point it ran into trouble again. The Syndics – academics who were formally commissioned to approve or reject book manuscripts sent in for publication – sent the thesis for a further opinion to the eminent economic historian and Christian Socialist R. H. Tawney, author of many works including *Religion and the Rise of Capitalism*. Tawney did not like Eric's thesis at all. He found it 'slick, superficial, and pretentious'. Hobsbawm was immodest and overconfident in his judgements: 'He has chosen, for some reason, to write in a somewhat patronising tone, as one possessing *a priori* authoritative knowledge of the truth and correcting the errors of lesser mortals in the light of it.' Tawney acknowledged that Eric 'writes with vivacity', but after cataloguing a lengthy series of what he categorised as 'defects of knowledge and judgement', he concluded that the thesis could not be recommended for publication. He much preferred the work of A. M. MacBriar, which was eventually published over a decade later by Cambridge University Press as *Fabian Socialism and English Politics, 1884–1918.*[24]

Tawney's rejection of Eric's thesis obviously reflected his own personal identification with Fabianism, but there was another, less creditable reason for his hostility. Eric's research had been seriously compromised by the fact that the personal papers of Sidney and Beatrice Webb were barred to researchers until the official biography had been published. The official biography had been commissioned by the Trustees of the Webbs' Estate from none other than Tawney himself. After some negotiation, he had agreed to write it at the end of 1948, and engaged an assistant to begin research. However, on discovering that Margaret Cole, one of the Trustees, was herself using the papers for a publication, Tawney, now elderly and ailing, withdrew from the project. But the damage had been done, and since the other Trustees vainly persisted over many months in trying to get him to resume his work on the biography, access to the Webb papers continued to be denied to other researchers, including Eric.[25]

Eric's critical attitude towards the Fabians caused him further problems. Christopher Morris, Eric's undergraduate supervisor at King's, had already told him in 1940 that his name was being touted for a Junior Research Fellowship at the College.[26] It was a requirement of election that candidates submit a 'Fellowship dissertation'. Eric was already far advanced enough with his Ph.D. in 1948 to feel able to submit the majority of it for the competition. However, Gerald Shove, a Fabian economics don at King's, objected 'that his memory of the Fabians bore no relation to Hobsbawm's analysis', and it was rejected.[27] Eric did not rate his chances highly if he submitted the same or similar material a second time. While he had been working in the LSE Library he had come across the printed material the Webbs had amassed for their *History of Trade Unionism*, published in 1894. This was 'a historical treasure-trove', he remembered later, which 'opened the door to a structural, problem-oriented history of the workers', far removed from conventional institutional and political narrative forms of labour history.[28] For the next ten months he used the Webb Collection at the LSE to research and write from scratch an entirely new Fellowship dissertation, 'Studies in the "New" Trade Unionism (1889–1914)'.

Typed double-spaced on 184 pages of foolscap (again), this was a substantial piece of work. Eric admitted that given the short space of time available to research and write the dissertation, it could be no more than 'a preliminary sketch'. However, it made a concerted attempt to explain why new trade unions had emerged in Britain after 1870 and had been more successful as organisations than unions had been before. A key point of the dissertation was its attempt to relate the institutional development of trade unions to the economic background, living conditions and structures of work and employment of the era.[29] As was normal practice, the Fellowship dissertation was sent out to two eminent specialists in the field for an opinion. Economic historians were few and far between in Britain at this time, so it was an almost inevitable piece of bad luck that Eric's work should once more be submitted to R. H. Tawney. The great man had a lot of good things to say about the dissertation:

> He has worked on sources, such as trade union reports and journals, which has [*sic*] hitherto been little used for the purpose of writing an account of the new unionism. He is widely read in the American, as well as the British, literature, relating to trade unionism. He has a keen eye for what is significant in his materials, and asks the right questions. Finally, as chapter 1 and the concluding section show, he has a gift for making suggestive generalizations.[30]

On the other hand, however, Tawney thought that Eric's interpretation of the history of British trade unionism rested on *a priori*
assumptions that 'require to be more effectively sustained by evidence and argument'. And the conclusion was 'much too sketchy
for so large a subject'. Clearly he had been working under pressure
of time. 'Mr Hobsbawm', Tawney concluded, ending on a positive
note, 'though inclined at times to be super-subtle, is clearly a person
of great ability and of wide knowledge in the field covered by his
researches.'

A second report was sent in by T. S. Ashton, another leading
economic historian and a specialist in the history of industrialisation in Britain. A professor at the London School of Economics
since 1946, Ashton was resolutely anti-Marxist, and used his
inaugural lecture to launch a withering attack on those who used
concepts like 'capitalism' and 'Economic Determinism'. He urged
the profession to 'cast out' the exponents of these ideas 'from the
house' of economic history altogether.[31] In contrast to Tawney,
Ashton found Eric's account of the growth of the unions 'disappointing', criticising in particular the absence of statistics. It was
'empirical rather than analytical in its approach'. It failed to refer
to the wider economic context, such as the growth of population,
the costs of production and the effects on the labour market of the
export of capital. The spread of unions was related to changes in
technology but not to changes in the trade cycle.[32] Stylistically, he
criticised Eric's 'undue use of the parenthesis, and a tendency to
prefix "of course" to statements not all of which are self-evident'.
Despite these critical remarks, Eric was elected by the Fellows
to a four-year Junior Research Fellowship with effect from the
beginning of the academic year 1950–51, probably on the strength
of Tawney's praise of his 'great ability and wide knowledge' and
their own recognition of his intelligence and promise. The post
was what would now be called a postdoctoral fellowship, entailing
light teaching duties but intended principally to provide time to lay
the foundations for a research career. It was not particularly well
paid, but it carried with it free meals and rent-free accommodation
in College.

Unlike his work on the Fabians, which turned out to lead to a dead end, Eric's research on the trade union movement of the late Victorian and Edwardian eras provided a basis on which to research and write a number of academic articles for publication in learned journals. He launched his career as a professional academic historian with 'General Labour Unions in Britain, 1889–1914', published in the *Economic History Review* in 1949. This distillation of his Fellowship dissertation was paralleled by a relatively lengthy and more overtly ideological article for the American Communist periodical *Science and Society* (in this context, 'science' meant 'scientific socialism').[33] This was followed by a similar article on 'The Labour Aristocracy in Nineteenth-Century Britain', published in a volume of Marxist historical studies produced by the Communist Party publishing house of Lawrence and Wishart in 1954.[34] The concept of a 'labour aristocracy' drew heavily on the work of Lenin, who in turn had borrowed it from the Austro-German Marxist theorist Karl Kautsky. Lenin had argued that craft-based trade unions and their members were seduced away from the idea of forming a revolutionary working-class party by being accorded a share in the status and profits of the capitalist bourgeoisie. The argument came under fire, naturally enough, and in subsequent contributions Eric conceded that any idea that the 'rough' working class was more naturally revolutionary than the 'respectable' working class was untenable in the British context. And, of course, artisans and craftsmen, like the shoemakers, were bearers of revolutionary ideas earlier in the nineteenth century. Nevertheless, this was an early example of the ability to spark fruitful historical controversy that would be one of the outstanding features of Eric's career.[35]

He also published more focused and specialised work, the best way to gain a reputation as a serious academic researcher in the small world of economic and social history. His major publication here was an article on 'the tramping artisan', a figure familiar from the *Wanderburschen* and *compagnonnages* on the Continent, but little researched in the case of Britain. Using mainly the reports and rule books of trade unions, the article traced the rise of the system

of itinerant skilled artisans or 'journeymen', and argued that its
decline from the 1860s onwards reflected the growth of labour
specialisation, the supersession of casual by permanently employed
labour, and the beginnings of unemployment benefits, to which
workers with no permanent residence were barred. Determined
that the article would not be shot down by his seniors, who would,
almost inevitably, be asked to review it for publication in the
Economic History Review, Eric sent it for informal, preliminary comment to two of the men who up to this point had proved the major
obstacles to his academic career: R. H. Tawney and T. S. Ashton.

Tawney found it 'very interesting: the subject, as far as I know,
has been almost completely neglected'. He suggested there might
be more material in the papers of the early nineteenth-century
radical Francis Place. Eric replied that these had been extensively
used by earlier historians and so he felt he could use secondary
literature here. But he tactfully noted his appreciation of Tawney's
advice to pay more attention to local peculiarities, and especially
to the role of London. Ashton was also favourably impressed and
lent his imprimatur to the article. Through this tactic, Eric ensured
that the piece would glide smoothly onto the pages of the *Economic
History Review*, as indeed it did, after the usual editorial delays, in
1951.[36] This opened the way to a more wide-ranging exploration
of the linkages between the rise of the labour movement and
the development of Britain's industrial economy in 'Economic
Fluctuations and Some Social Movements Since 1800', which
appeared in the 1952–3 volume of the *Economic History Review*. With
three research pieces published in the flagship journal of British
economic and social history, Eric's career as a serious academic
historian had now been successfully launched.

II

Not only as a graduate student but also as a Junior Research
Fellow, Eric 'felt isolated in post-war Cambridge'.[37] His old undergraduate friends had dispersed to various parts of the world, the

Sketch of Eric by an anonymous participant in the Communist Party Summer School in 1939, where Eric recalled flirting with Iris Murdoch, the future novelist; Denis Healey, who was to be Labour Chancellor of the Exchequer in the 1970s, was also there.

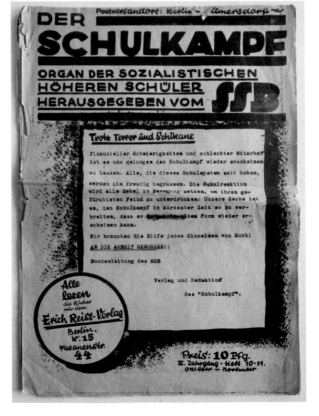

Eric's school report for 1927–8, giving his name as 'Erich Hobsbawn'. His grade in History was only 'good'. His native language was given as 'German'; later school reports marked it down as 'English/German'.

'The School Struggle: Organ of the Socialist High School Students'. Eric and his sister Nancy distributed copies in Berlin by bike in the early 1930s. On her way home from one delivery run, on 27 February 1933, Nancy saw the Reichstag in flames.

Ernst Thälmann (1886–1944), leader of the Communist Party of Germany, outside the Reichstag in Berlin. On 25 January 1933 Eric took part in the last Communist demonstration in Berlin, five days before Hitler became Chancellor.

Eric (far right) with sister Nancy, cousin Ron (far left), Aunt Gretl (minus head) and her son Peter (front), on the south coast of England, April 1935, and Eric's Uncle Sidney inexpertly wielding the camera.

Workers with raised fist at the Bastille Day Parade in Paris, 14 July 1936: Eric took part in the celebrations, enjoying the Left's euphoria after the victory of the Popular Front a few weeks before. It was not to last long.

Eric on the way down from Carnedd Dafydd, Snowdonia's third-highest mountain, which he climbed with his cousin Ron on 26 April 1936, after cycling from London on one of their numerous camping holidays in Eric's teenage years.

Editor of the Cambridge magazine *The Granta*, in 1939. Dissatisfied with the ideological rigidity of the *Bulletin* of the Socialist Club, he turned to non-political student journalism instead.

Sergeant Hobsbawm in 1943, around the time of his marriage to Muriel Scaman. He was already under the surveillance of MI5, who ensured the Army put him out of harm's way, teaching basic German to Guards officers.

Eric's sister Nancy (1921–90) in Jamaica, where she worked for the British military censorship authorities during the Second World War: 'a very straight English person'.

A sketch of Eric in 1947 by one of his pupils at a 're-education' camp in Germany for former members of the Wehrmacht, the future historian Reinhard Koselleck. 'I taught him democracy', Eric later said.

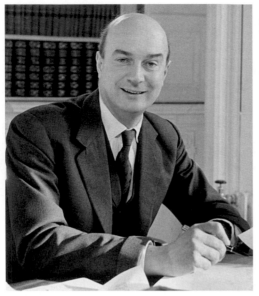

Noel Annan (1916–2000), Eric's friend since his undergraduate days, fellow-Apostle, later Provost of King's College, Cambridge, and Provost of University College, London; a quintessentially Establishment figure.

Edward Thompson (1921–93), author of *The Making of the English Working Class* (1963) and member of the Communist Party Historians' Group. He took part with Eric in a series of seminars in Paris in the late 1970s; participants noted the rivalry between the two men.

The Oxford historian Christopher Hill (1912–2003), member of the Communist Party Historians' Group and co-founder of the journal *Past & Present*, in 1965. Hill left the Communist Party in 1957 and went on to become Master of Balliol.

Joan Bakewell (b.1933), 'an ordinary little scholarship girl from a northern town', whom Eric taught Economic and Social History at Cambridge in 1953. 'It was Eric who taught me how to ask things', she later recalled.

Eric's friend Giorgio Napolitano (b. 1925), a leading Italian Communist and President of Italy from 2006 to 2015. Eric became increasingly close to the Italian 'Eurocommunists' after 1956.

Existentialist philosopher and playwright Jean-Paul Sartre (1905–80), a critical Marxist and anti-colonialist who frequented the *La Coupole* café in Paris with Eric in the 1950s. They always ate mutton curry for lunch.

Die Erwartung (*The Expectation*) painted in 1935–6 by Richard Oelze (1900–80). Eric spent a memorable evening with the dissolute German Surrealist in a Parisian nightclub in 1936, and returned to life in the cafés and bars of Paris on many occasions in the 1950s.

Eric in 1955, smoking a pipe, by Peter de Francia (1921–2012), a French-born British artist who met him at London's Geneva Club. A committed socialist, de Francia was one of the founders of the *New Left Review*.

old student Communist Party had fallen apart and there was nobody any more who had shared his political and intellectual life in the town or the university. However, there was one social group into which he fitted immediately. He had been proposed in the Easter Term of 1939 for membership in the small, exclusive and elite Cambridge Conversazione Society, whose twelve members, known as the Apostles, consisted of undergraduate and postgraduate students selected by the existing members of the club for their cleverness and articulacy from a small range of colleges, including King's. The identity of members was kept a closely guarded secret. Eric's election was confirmed on 11 November 1939.[38] 'I was', he recalled later, 'obviously suggested by John Luce, who took me to tea with Andreas Mayor at the Arts Theatre café, presumably to be vetted by Andreas, whom I did not know. He said little or nothing and I have never seen him since. He never turned up at dinners.' Eric was filled in by Leo Long, an Apostle who was also a member of the Communist Party, about the Society's folklore and conventions.[39]

Motions for discussion at the meetings varied widely but were seldom academic. The Apostolic tradition went well back into the Victorian era.[40] Perhaps because of its secrecy, the group became associated in the interwar years both with homosexuality and with the 'Cambridge spies'. Eric was at pains to deny it, but there was perhaps something to this, at least in the 1930s. On 11 March 1939, shortly before Eric joined, for example, the nine attending members discussed the question 'Would we sleep with our friends?' to which one added the gloss: '"sleep" meaning all forms of ecstatic physical enjoyment, buggery, fucking, canoodling', and another noted: 'Don't believe in women "friends" in the non-sexual sense.' Five of those present answered yes, in two cases specifying women only, in two cases either men or women, and in one case men only.[41]

As Eric later noted, there were in fact very few Communists among the Apostles by the late 1930s:

The criterion for election (relaxed perhaps only for exceptional good looks, as in the case of the climber Wilfred Noyce) was not ideology or even a good mind, but being 'apostolic' – a state more easily recognized than defined. The Society spent enormous amounts of time discussing what it was. I don't believe that even the most communist Apostle would have regarded, say, Lenin, as 'apostolic'. After the early 1930s ... I don't believe that the tone of the Society was particularly red.[42]

Nevertheless, as Eric's Cambridge friend Noel Annan later pointed out, 'of the thirty-one members elected to the society between 1927 and 1939, fifteen were communist or *marxisant*'.[43] The influence of the later radio producer and intelligence officer Guy Burgess and the art historian Anthony Blunt was obvious here. Both were regular attenders at the Society's annual dinners, where current student members mingled with former members, known as 'Angels'; both of them were homosexual, and both were later unmasked as Soviet spies, as was Leo Long. But the majority of Apostles were not Communists, and the majority of 'Cambridge spies' were not homosexual.

Eric did not find the members 'particularly distinguished':[44]

I enjoyed the meetings because I liked arguing and listening to arguments and especially to be with friends, but they contributed little or nothing to my own intellectual development. On the other hand I was enormously influenced by the apostolic style and ambiance, which, like most brethren, I absorbed and cherished ... One of the things apostolic discussions had inherited, probably from the Edwardian era, was a deliberate lightness of touch, a slight tongue-in-cheek quality, a taste for wit, deadpan jokes, a flight from 'tierischer Ernst' [deadly seriousness], even when propounding the most serious and deeply-held opinions. The other characteristic, and of course the major one, was that insistence on total honesty (or as much of it as one could face) in the presence of friends in whom one put total trust.

He was 'not the type to whom people, anyway people one is not in love with or loved by, bare their souls', but outside the meetings at least, the brethren did indeed tell him about their sexual tastes and problems, just as he did not attempt to conceal his political views, 'even in this very militant phase of my C[ommunist] P[arty] life'. Nevertheless, the Apostles did not 'criticise each other with the openness and even the brutality which I had got used to in party groups, where a different but in some ways comparable closeness existed, anyway among the Historians'.

At his first meeting, held in November 1939 in a room on Staircase D in King's College, opposite the Chapel, Eric responded to the question 'One Big Lie or Many Little Lies?' by coming down on the side of 'One Big Lie', but only one more meeting was held, on 25 November 1939, before the war intervened and dispersed the members, mostly into the armed forces. The next meeting recorded in the Society's Minute Book was a dinner at the Ivy restaurant, in London, for Apostles and Angels, on 20 June 1942, attended, among others, by the economist John Maynard Keynes, the novelist E. M. Forster, the literary critic Desmond MacCarthy, the psychoanalyst James Strachey, Anthony Blunt and Guy Burgess. Another, on 17 July 1943, was presided over by Blunt, at the White Tower restaurant, at which the author and publisher Leonard Woolf (husband of the novelist Virginia Woolf, who had committed suicide in 1941) was also present, along with MacCarthy, Strachey and Burgess. The members next met at the legendary Kettner's restaurant in Soho for their first post-war dinner on 29 June 1946. Blunt was there, as well as MacCarthy, the philosopher G. E. Moore and James Strachey. Eric, as one of only two remaining active student members in Cambridge, was appointed Vice-President at the dinner and had to deliver the after-dinner speech. He was charged by the Angels with the task of reviving the Society. 'The Society', he later noted briefly but triumphantly in the Minute Book, 'was revived.' After the first few meetings, held in the rooms of F. R. Lucas, a conservative English literature don who had made his name with a sharply critical review of T. S. Eliot's *The Waste Land*, they met in the King's College rooms of E. M. Forster.[45]

At the beginning, to make up the numbers, Angels attended as well as Apostles, and after consulting them, Eric and the English don Matthew Hodgart set about proposing new members from among the student body. It was noticeable that as reconstructed by them the Apostles contained very few homosexuals and no Communists at all.[46] The literary critic and later biographer of Forster, P. N. Furbank, who in his mid-twenties had just begun teaching English at Emmanuel College, was proposed by Hodgart, and elected on 21 October 1946. Eric recruited his friend the intellectual historian Noel Annan, now a Junior Research Fellow at King's, Michael Jaffe, a history undergraduate and one of Eric's first pupils, and the historian Jack Gallagher, now an ex-Communist, who had returned to Trinity College after war service to complete his degree. Eric proposed two more members on 3 February 1947, namely the mathematics student Robin Gandy and the future Labour Party government Minister Peter Shore. The average age of the early post-war Apostles was unusually high because several of them had seen their studies interrupted by the war, and in any case both Eric and Matthew Hodgart were, as Eric remembered, 'isolated from the undergraduates and therefore looking around mainly among research students and other contemporaries'.[47]

At the discussion on 4 November 1946, Eric took both sides on the question 'Has the period in which we live any claim to the character of a pre-eminently enlightened age?', because he thought it was enlightened but not pre-eminently so. In answer to the question 'History – written or right?' on 2 December Eric said 'right' but only 'for the sake of balance', since his vote resulted in a tie of five on each side. On the next occasion Eric said yes to the question 'Are we prepared to trust our forecast of the future?' On 17 February 1947, his work of recruiting being done, Eric resigned as Vice-President. After answering the question posed at this meeting – 'Plain or Dazzling?' – with what had by now become his trademark note of paradoxical compromise ('Plain but not without an occasional dazzle') he did not attend meetings any more until he took up his Research Fellowship, though he went to the dinners regularly.[48] However, he kept in touch, and in February 1948 he wrote to Noel Annan congratulating him on his election to the Apostles, which, he wrote, in an implicitly self-critical verdict on his own performance as a recruiter, 'thinking of past and really eminent apostles, not of the present, less impressive crop – we persist in regarding as a great honour'.[49] The Apostles did much to mitigate the loneliness that Eric felt in Cambridge as a Ph.D. student, cut off from the world of undergraduates even more than before, in a milieu in which postgraduate students were still rare beasts indeed.

III

While he was laying the foundations for his academic career, Eric was also reconnecting with his family after the separations and traumas of the war. It soon became clear that those who had stayed behind in Europe had suffered heavily from the anti-Semitic persecution and genocidal policies of the Nazis and their allies.[50] Eric's great-uncle on his mother's side, Richard Friedmann, and his wife Julie, who had owned a fancy goods store in the spa town of Marienbad in Czechoslovakia, taken over by Germany early in 1939, had been deported to Auschwitz and murdered there, as had his aunt Hedwig Lichtenstern.[51] Another great-uncle, Viktor Friedmann, and his wife Elsa, had fled to Paris from Vienna after the *Anschluss*. Eric had stayed with them in Vienna during his mother's final illness. They lived in Montmartre for a while (Eric met them there in 1939), then, following the German invasion in 1940, they fled further westwards. Arrested in Bordeaux and imprisoned separately for a while, they subsequently made their way to Nice, where they were reunited but then were arrested again on 18 November 1943, and taken to the transit camp at Drancy, near Paris, where they arrived on 19 November. The next day they were put on transport number 62, a train into which some 1200 Jews were packed, to the extermination camp at Auschwitz-Birkenau. Arriving there on 25 November, they were taken after a 'selection' to the gas chamber and were among a total of 895 deportees from transport number 62 who were murdered. Their daughter Herta, whom Eric had got to know well during his stay with them in the early 1930s, survived the war, worked for a time for the American occupation authorities, then emigrated to New York, taking the name Herta Bell and finding employment in an hotel before travelling on to the Philippines, where she vanished from the record. Her brother Otto, whom Eric had so admired when he was in Berlin in 1932–3, emigrated to Palestine, changing his name to Etan Dror, and married 'an old flame from Vienna who had followed him from Austria for love'; in 1957 he returned to live in Berlin to rebuild his life in Germany, but by this time Eric had lost touch with him as well.[52]

Other members of Eric's far-flung family had survived, if only just. Some time after the end of the war, his cousin Gertruda Albrechtová ('Traudl'), now living in Bratislava, reconnected with Eric. In 1944, when the Hungarian puppet government, under orders from the German occupying forces, began to arrest and deport Jews, Traudl reported, 'Papa and I went into the camps, Papa to Bergen-Belsen, I to Theresienstadt. My grandmother had already been deported from Vienna, 11 different camps, she was liberated in France, came here and died in 1947. Papa died of the effects of the camp in Summer 1946.' Traudl studied English and German at university, obtained her doctorate at the German-language Charles University in Prague, and married a Czechoslovak musician; they did not have children. She remembered being taken round the Tate Gallery by Eric when she had visited London in 1934 or 1935. Apart from Philip Hobsbaum, she was the only other member of Eric's family to achieve academic distinction.[53]

Eric had rather lost touch with his cousin Denis during the war, but they soon re-established cordial relations when peace came, based on their common love of jazz. Denis had married a fellow musician, Queenie Pearl, shortly after the outbreak of the war, and changed his name by deed poll from Prechner to Preston. During the war he had embarked on a career as a broadcaster of music programmes for the BBC, and was also making a living as a jazz concert promoter as well as a journalist for *Melody Maker* and *Musical Express*. Soon after the end of the war, he divorced Queenie and married Noni Jabavu, a South African from a prominent Xhosa family. By 1948 Denis was working for the Decca Record Company, signing up Afro-Caribbean musicians to record calypsos and steel drum music. His enthusiasm for jazz continued to inspire Eric throughout the post-war years. Denis and his wife met Eric regularly, often at Indian restaurants, then something of an exotic novelty, talking music and politics.[54]

Eric's uncle Sidney, meanwhile, had remarried following his relocation to Chile. His new wife, Lily Kaufmann, was a German refugee whom he had met there. The marriage did not last long; Sidney died soon after the end of the war. Eric's sister Nancy, who had been working for the British Imperial Censorship authorities in Trinidad, returned to South America after the war and got a job as a secretary in the British Embassy at Montevideo, in Uruguay. Here she met and fell in love with the dashing Royal Navy captain Victor Marchesi, illegitimate son of Sir Vincent Caillard, a business associate of the notorious pre-1914 arms dealer Sir Basil Zaharoff. Caillard's wife was a morphine addict, looked after by an Italian companion, Romani Marchesi, with whom Sir Vincent had a passionate affair. The family did not attempt to conceal Victor's parentage. He was given his real mother's name at birth and was brought up in the Caillard–Marchesi household until he entered the Royal Navy. Because he had some experience of sailing the southern oceans, he was given command of HMS *William Scoresby*, the principal vessel serving in Operation Tabarin (the name was taken from a famous Parisian cabaret, the Bal Tabarin). The operation's main aim was to establish a British presence in the Antarctic region and forestall Argentinian and other claims on these territories, thus preventing them being used as bases for German U-boats.

For three years, beginning in 1943, Victor helped set up and supply bases in the Antarctic itself, in the South Shetlands, South Georgia, the South Orkneys and the Falkland Islands, putting in for refitting and supplies for three months a year at Montevideo.

It was on one such visit that he met Nancy. They married in the Falklands in 1946.[55] But there was another, far more secret aspect to Operation Tabarin. On one occasion Victor was required to set off from the *William Scoresby* in a motor boat, towing a small barge with an open-topped cage full of sheep on its deck. When they reached a safe distance, Victor and a fellow officer lobbed a milk bottle stuffed with rags into the cage and headed back to the ship, where a team of scientists was waiting. The rags were covered in spores of the deadly disease anthrax, and the operation was an experiment to see if it could be used in biological warfare. Fortunately, perhaps, it never was.[56]

Nancy felt her government employment obliged her to distance herself from Eric, even spelling her name 'Hobsbaun', with a 'u' and 'n', before she married. Nor did she share even Eric's residual Jewish identity. As their son, Robin Marchesi, born in 1951, later recalled:

> I think she just wanted a quiet life and to forget that she was Jewish because I found out partly because of Eric publishing his books and somebody as a young man turning around to me and saying, 'you must be Jewish,' – 'Of course not' and then thought about it, 'Yeah I'm Jewish.' And when I asked my mother, I can still remember how she put her hands over her ears, burst into tears, stopped crying and went to me, 'Never say it, Robin! Never say it!' So she was really affected by obviously what happened in Germany . . . And I think her answer to it was to pretend that, and that's why she married such a straight, what she thought was a very straight English person.

Victor and Nancy moved back to England after the war because Nancy had contracted tuberculosis in Trinidad and needed treatment.[57] Her condition was not helped by the fact that she smoked up to sixty cigarettes a day. The arrival of antibiotics at the end of the 1940s probably saved her life, although Robin remembered that 'she was always wheezing'. She rented a small house in High Wycombe with Victor, who assumed responsibility for Nancy and also for Gretl's son Peter, after Sidney's death, and even paid his fees and expenses at McGill University in Montreal, Canada, from a legacy he had been left by Lady Caillard.

Eric resumed contact with his sister after she returned to England. But, increasingly, Victor Marchesi felt that his close family relationship with a known Communist was blighting his naval career. For by 1947 the wartime alliance with the Soviet Union was disintegrating. In March 1947, US President Harry S. Truman announced that the United States would seek to prevent the Soviet Union from gaining influence in countries where it did not already hold sway. Stalin responded by forcing Eastern European nations under occupation by the Red Army to establish Soviet-style political systems. The German capital, Berlin, divided into four zones of occupation, was located in the Soviet zone of occupation, and in June 1948 the Russians cut off all routes to the west, in a blockade that lasted the best part of a year. West Berlin, run by the British, French and Americans, was kept going by the celebrated Berlin Airlift until the blockade was finally lifted. In the autumn of 1949, two separate states were created in Germany – the Federal Republic, a parliamentary democracy, in the west, and the Democratic Republic, dominated by the Communists, in the east. Communists in Western countries were increasingly viewed as subversive and came under growing official suspicion.[58]

This was the start of the Cold War. Eric began to feel its impact already in 1947–8, when he became briefly involved in the post-war reconstruction of Germany. Walter Wallich, an Apostle who later became a literary translator, had written to Eric on 4 July 1945 about the possibilities of rebuilding German society after Nazism. He registered agreement with Eric's optimistic view 'that, by divorcing Nazis from their natural surroundings and getting them separate and into a civilized society, you can get somewhere with them'. 'Kick the Germans by all means', Wallich said, 'but for heaven's sake kick them in a definite direction, not just in circles.'[59] Not long after this, the Foreign Office, remembering from somewhere the fact that Eric spoke German, commissioned him to 're-educate' Germans at a hunting lodge on the Lüneburg Heath in north Germany as part of the British policy of converting teachers from Nazism. Eric gave his re-education lectures on the Lüneburg Heath for the first three weeks of August 1947.[60] 'What may these harmless-looking people not have done between 1933 and 1945?', he wondered. One of the pupils was the later historian Reinhard Koselleck – 'I taught him democracy', Eric once said to me, with a wolfish grin. Koselleck had fought with the *Wehrmacht* on the Eastern Front and had been captured by the Russians. Recognising a kindred spirit, Koselleck became friends with Eric and penned an accomplished sketch of his face, which Eric preserved among his possessions. After the many atrocities committed by the Red Army troops in their invasion of Germany, it was not surprising, Eric noted, that 'hatred and fear penetrated the atmosphere in Germany, among both the natives and the vast numbers of refugees'. 'The more I'm here the more depressed I get', he wrote. 'Hope? I can't see any.'[61] The programme was discontinued soon after. The following year, on learning that Eric was 'a member of the historical section of the Communist Party' and that his wife was a Communist, William Hayter, Chairman of the Joint Intelligence Committee of the Chiefs of Staff, a professional diplomat who later became Warden of New College, Oxford, expressed concern that there was 'a proposal to send this man on a lecture tour in the British zone of Germany' and told MI5 that he 'intends to see that he does not go to Germany'.[62] And indeed, for many years he did not return.

Eric did not write about the Nazi persecution of the Jews or the murder of his relatives in Auschwitz. Years later, responding to the left-wing American historian Arno J. Mayer, who had sent him the typescript of his book *Why did the Heavens not Darken? The "Final Solution" in History* (1988), Eric confessed: 'Since the first material on the camps came out in the early fifties or late forties, I have kept away from it. Reading these early publications – I was particularly impressed/depressed by Kogon – I have just found it too difficult to face emotionally.'[63] Eric closed the book 'still unconvinced that I understand the extermination', but pointed out that it was implied already by the demand of some Austrian anti-Semites in the early 1900s that Jews be deprived of their rights and put into camps. He remained unconvinced by the parallels Mayer drew with the Crusades or the Thirty Years War. Even in the history of barbarism, the camps such as Treblinka, devoted solely to killing Jews and nothing else, remained a special case that had still not been explained satisfactorily. Eric was not alone in his reluctance to comment publicly on the Nazi genocide of the Jews. In the immediate post-war years, hardly anything was published on the topic. Most Jews who had survived the war simply wanted to get on with their lives. In any case, the Cold War meant that governments and broadcasting institutions like the BBC were becoming increasingly reluctant to criticise the Germans at a time when their allegiance to the West was seen as vital.

IV

At the beginning of the war, Eric had applied for a job at the BBC and was due to have an interview, but when he was called up he was told by the officer commanding his unit that it was out of the question, and the interview had to be cancelled.[64] In April 1945 Eric came back to the idea and applied for release from the forces to take up a full-time position at the BBC. The job involved making educational broadcasts intended to supplement the work of service instructors in the classroom during demobilisation, and included twenty-minute lectures and discussions on history and literature. The BBC was favourably impressed:

> He has been interviewed here and considered a most suitable candidate for the Corporation's new Services Educational Unit. He has now had five years' service in the Forces during which time he has apparently had experience of almost every branch of Army Educational work and also has an excellent academic record, ie. a First Class in both parts of the Cambridge Historical Tripos.[65]

But MI5 feared that if he was appointed to the post, 'HOBSBAWM is not likely to lose any opportunity he may get to disseminate propaganda and obtain recruits for the Communist Party'.[66] The secret services ordered that 'in the event of his applying for BBC employment at a later date, his name will be referred to us for vetting before any other action is taken'.[67] 'It may seem odd to the B.B.C.', Eric's MI5 case officer J. B. Milne added on 8 May 1945, 'that we should wish to turn down an applicant for these duties who has been doing very similar work in the Army Education Corps for so long but in fact of course it did not come to our notice until HOBSBAWM was already in the A.E.C. for over a year and he would certainly have been turned down had he been vetted for it.'[68] From now on, the BBC was aware that it would not be politic to offer him any full-time or permanent employment, and a broadcasting executive noted confidentially on 14 March 1947 in a memorandum about 'E. J. Hobsbawn' [*sic*] that 'Any correspondence with this man obtaining a job in the B. B. C.' should be referred upwards, adding to the note: 'Please keep this on top' of the file.[69]

This rejection did not prevent Eric from working with the BBC on an ad hoc basis, however. On 11 December 1946 he wrote from King's to the Director of Talks at BBC Radio's Third Programme, offering a review of *Le Canard enchaîné*, a 'French satirical weekly which has, I believe, the largest circulation of any French periodical and is quite unique'. He had been prompted to do this by listening to a review of the *New Yorker* magazine on the Third Programme and thought that 'the idea of reviewing periodicals is admirable'. He added:

> As a passionate (and as far as circumstances have allowed a regular) reader of the Canard these ten years I should like to do this, if possible. I do not think the language difficulty is insuperable. In practice the 'New Yorker' is unknown to the vast majority of the Third Programme listeners except by description, and a Canard Programme would be built up in a similar way.

The detailed synopsis he appended to the letter divided the proposed broadcast into eight sections, beginning with the magazine's appearance, its writers and cartoonists, and its style and conventions (here he admitted an 'initial difficulty for Englishmen not well up in French politics'). Conscious of the fact that listeners needed to be entertained, he proposed to include a discussion of 'The beard and the Third Republic' and the 'Effect of disappearance of bearded Radical-Socialists on their most loyal tormentors', clean-shaven politicians presumably being harder to mock in cartoons than those with whiskers. He also proposed briefly to discuss 'Wine, Women and the Republic'. Finally, after talking about 'What the Canard Laughs at' and 'The Canard and the Arts', he wanted to conclude by asking why the magazine was not better known in Britain. The reason, however, was obvious enough: it was written in French.[70]

Any other British radio station might have found this proposal too esoteric to contemplate. But Eric was in luck. Created in 1946, BBC Radio's Third Programme focused on classical music and cultural and intellectual topics.[71] The Producer, Home Talks, Anna Kallin, a Russian-born, German-educated translator who had spent the war working for the BBC's European Service, was determined to maintain the highest possible standards in the broadcasts for which she was responsible. The Oxford philosopher Isaiah Berlin, who knew her through a mutual friend, described her as 'a typical Moscow intellectual, high-grade, highbrow ... a brilliant and interesting woman'. Her obituary in *The Times* in 1984 called her 'fiercely individual, having intense convictions, and intolerant of all sloppiness, whether in thinking or in execution'. Kallin came from a well-off Jewish merchant family and arrived in England in 1921, when she was in her mid-twenties, well aware of the danger she would be in as a 'bourgeois intellectual' if she stayed in Moscow. Cosmopolitan, international, European, 'an eager listener, a passionate talker', Kallin was impressed by Eric's outline and accepted his proposal.[72]

Eric reviewed *Le Canard Enchaîné* on 4 February 1947 in a twenty-minute broadcast running from 7.40 to eight o'clock in the evening.[73] He wrote to Kallin, thanking her for her 'kindness in seeing me through my first broadcast – a frightening experience, as you know'.[74] Kallin had listened to it 'with a sympathetic audience who tried to persuade me that you are a Frenchman'.[75] Encouraged by Kallin's secretary, Eric suggested further talks, beginning with one on the Austrian writer Karl Kraus, whose magnum opus, the unperformable play *Die letzten Tage der Menschheit*, 'The Last Days of Humankind', had recently been republished. 'Nobody knows Kraus here', Eric pointed out, 'though his reputation has grown vastly since he died ten years ago, and he is altogether a major figure.' The early twentieth-century French syndicalist Georges Sorel, author of the celebrated *Reflections on Violence*, would be another possible topic, as would 'British pamphleteering today', or 'Journalese' (a comparison of the language of British, American, French and Austrian journalism). Eric also suggested a 'History Survey' series, 'non-technical' in nature, dealing with 'all those developments which normally take some 30 years to percolate from the universities via the popular books and schools to the educated layman'. But the BBC was not encouraging. On the advice of the responsible executive, Peter Laslett, later a professional historian himself, the Director of Talks wrote to Eric with the news that 'we shall not be arranging a series on the lines of your note, or indeed any major historical series for some months. We are feeling our way in this matter.'[76]

His keenness to broadcast showed that even at this early stage in his career as an historian, Eric was concerned to make his work accessible and available to the wider public. Kallin responded positively to his suggestion of a talk on Kraus. 'I think', she wrote, 'I am one of the few people who do know something about him (in this country!) and I am delighted that you are interested.'[77] The talk was broadcast on 8 April 1947 between 7.55 and 8.15 in the evening.[78] Eric's piece on British pamphleteering, from 1870 to the present, followed on 24 June, though Anna Kallin made him amend it extensively, somewhat to Eric's irritation: 'There really seems to be a difference of taste between us', he wrote; 'not merely one of those questions of presentation or clarity which you are in a much better position to judge than I.'[79] Besides the excitement at launching his career in broadcasting, there was also a modest fee (usually six guineas) to be had from the BBC;[80] and Eric was engaged for ten guineas (£10 10s, in other words) as consultant for a four-month series of Friday evening talks for the BBC Far Eastern Service on 'Industrial Revolution', dealing with 'industrialisation in Great Britain, U.S.A., U.S.S.R., Japan and under-developed areas in Africa etc.'. He advised on the selection of speakers, briefed them, and coordinated their scripts.[81] Eric himself delivered a talk on 'New British Attitudes to Industrialisation in the Colonies'.[82]

Eric's further suggestions do not seem to have been taken up by the BBC, perhaps because they were too recondite – for example, book reviews of his Ph.D. examiner Denis Brogan's *The Development of Modern France* and the brief essay *Die deutsche Katastrophe* ('The German Catastrophe', on the origins of Hitler's dictatorship) by the German historian Friedrich Meinecke ('one of the last of the old pre-nazi Professors. Fascinating but rather discouraging', Eric wrote).[83] In addition, however, the Cold War was already beginning to affect broadcasting. In March 1948 guidelines were issued by the Director of the Spoken Word at the BBC on 'the treatment of Communism and Communist Speakers'.[84] Two years later, the BBC was coming under intense fire from Conservatives who thought that it should essentially be a propaganda arm of government. Lord Robert Vansittart, who had been a senior figure in the Foreign Office before the war (and an extreme, even rabid Germanophobe during it), complained in a House of Lords debate about the presence of Communists in a range of important institutions:

> I shall begin my illustrations with the B.B.C., which ought to be, but is not, the most potent weapon in the cold war. A short while ago the B.B.C. refused to cleanse itself of Communists, and consequently Communists have remained. There is no mystery about it: the B.B.C. admit their presence, and I naturally know some of the offenders ... The percentage is small but, as the Lord President has also observed, the Communists always

manage to arrogate to themselves a degree of influence out of
all proportion to their real numbers.[85]

Such pressure was bound to have an effect.

On 4 February 1953 Eric delivered a nineteen-minute talk on
'The Political Theory of Auschwitz', his only known consideration of Nazism at this time, for the English-language European
Service of the BBC.[86] He was on the Third Programme again
the following month, on 4 March, when he took part in a series of
three discussions on the Nazi seizure of power, arranged by Alan
Bullock, an Oxford don who had become famous as a member of
the BBC's regular discussion programme *The Brains Trust*.[87] But
on learning that he was to deliver this broadcast, the Controller,
Talks (Home Sound), Mary Somerville, told the series producer,
Michael Stephens: 'the fact that Hobsbawn [*sic*] is there to put the
Marxist view must be publicized, e.g. it could be worked into the
blurb'.[88] In other words he could not be presented as an objective
contributor. However, there were powerful influences behind the
programme, not least that of Oxford University.[89] Eric took part in
the broadcast series unhindered, and the series no doubt provided
welcome publicity for Bullock's large-scale biography *Hitler: A Study
in Tyranny*, published the same year.

But the situation was becoming increasingly unfavourable for
Eric as a broadcaster. One executive complained that his broadcast style was 'a little monotonous', though he was better in her
opinion than Rodney Hilton, who was 'a little schoolmasterish',
and far better than Christopher Hill, who was 'not recommended'
because he 'stammers', and in any case was not thought to be a
'sound historian'.[90] A further proposal from Eric, on the teaching
of the arts in Great Britain, was rejected by Anna Kallin ('This
kind of talk which pleads too much and is slightly didactic doesn't
come off well on the air'), though she did like his idea of a review
of what she called a 'dreary series' of broadcasts on Communist
revolutions by Hugh Seton-Watson, who was at that time building
a reputation as a rather conservative historian of modern Russia
and Eastern Europe.[91] This did not come to fruition either, and

when Eric proposed a talk on 'Religion and the British Labour Movement' early in 1954, the idea was roundly condemned by Anna Kallin's boss, J. C. Thornton:

> Its purpose is clearly to discredit religious influences in the Labour Movement. It is not very objective and does not to my mind have an authoritative ring about it. ... It is not a straightforward objective historical piece, but treats the subject controversially, and it doesn't fit in with our plans at present to deal with the subject in that way.[92]

Thornton suggested the BBC should either 'reject this talk outright' or seek further opinions. If it was broadcast, 'Hobsbawm would be billed as a Marxist'. In the end, the talk was rejected. Kallin was forced to relay the views of her superiors, telling Eric:

> I do not think you have treated the problem sufficiently objectively, not as a straightforward historical piece. There is a certain lack of documentation in it (probably inevitable in a short talk), and it would not have given the listener a full picture of a very complex situation; in fact the picture would have been a rather one-sided and not very clear one.[93]

Eric was fobbed off with a payment of '15 guineas to cover the work and time involved'.[94]

Eric reacted with courtesy and understanding, telling Kallin she did not need to apologise: 'The main thing is that the BBC paid, which is, after all, the chief purpose I had in mind in the first place.' Still, while he admitted it was perhaps 'too controversial', he had thought, he told her, that 'you wanted some necks stuck out, to make it more interesting'. He was sorry he had misinterpreted her intentions. 'As you know', he added, 'my "tour d'esprit" is to be intellectually a little outrageous – even those with whom I am in political agreement have sometimes found this so – I need not be an enfant terrible on explosive topics.' He suggested 'a return, sometime, to the safe, because relatively obscure, subjects

I used to talk about once. I still hanker after a talk on Nestroy or Giraudoux, both of whom I (and I hope you) adore.'[95] By a stroke of luck, the BBC broadcast an adaptation of a play by Nestroy a few months later, and so Eric was able to put on a twenty-minute talk about him for the Third Programme on 12 October 1954.[96] Eric was interested in Nestroy because he was 'the spokesman of the Viennese who overthrew Metternich in 1848 in a revolution which Nestroy himself approved completely, if not without scepticism'.[97] Whether the audiences of BBC Radio's Third Programme would have made much of what Eric had to say if they had not listened to the play beforehand might well be doubted.

Meanwhile, Eric had found an alternative outlet for his views on Central European literature, when he wrote for the *Times Literary Supplement* in 1951 a review of the classic Czech satire of the First World War, *The Good Soldier Schweik*, by Jaroslav Hašek, first published in 1923, and a book he had read in translation during the war. In its portrayal of authority Eric detected a clear parallel with Britain in the early phase of the Cold War: 'The detective Breitschneider, smelling out un-Austrian activities in the public bar, the police-sergeant at Putim, certain that he has caught a Russian master-spy, are no longer merely Central European extravaganzas.' The book had a 'universal appeal'.[98] But overall, Eric's time as a regular broadcaster for the BBC had run into the sands by the mid-1950s. It was only one of a number of areas in which the Cold War was beginning to impact negatively on his career.

V

Eric did not live full-time in Cambridge in the immediate post-war years. His marriage in 1943 to Muriel Seaman meant that he spent most of his time in London, which was also convenient for his work, since the LSE Library contained virtually all the source material he needed for his dissertations and his articles. The couple lived at first at 30 Gloucester Crescent, on the edge of Camden Town and within hearing of the roar of the lions in Regent's Park Zoo; cheap, central and fashionable with ex-Oxbridge intellectuals.[99] They moved in October 1947 to Flat 5 Wilberforce House, Clapham Common North Side, SW4, in south London. Their neighbours included, coincidentally, Fritz Lustig, who had been at school with Eric in Berlin and had reconnected with him in the army in 1942.[100] Eric's life in London provided the opportunity for some writing about life in the great city. The magazine *Lilliput* published a commentary by Eric on four specially commissioned colour paintings of Camden Town, in north London, by James Boswell, a New Zealand-born artist who had joined the Communist Party in 1932 and served as art editor of the magazine until 1950. The district was, Eric wrote, rather old-fashioned and nondescript: 'It has the street-crowds, the stalls of oranges, whelks, and jellied eels, the odd jobs, the smell, the music-hall gilt and the greasy soot which the LNER and the LMS spread impartially over it. It isn't as flamboyant as Shoreditch, or as grim as Canning Town. It is just ordinary.'[101] As he wrote about the Irish immigrants in the area, the pubs with their 'brass and engraved glass', the 'spivs' and the drunks, art commentary became social reportage, the atmospheric prose perfectly matching the paintings' focus on the ordinariness of everyday life.[102]

The need to spend time in London was caused not only by his need to research in the LSE Library but also by his appointment with effect from 24 February 1947 to a Lectureship in Economic and Social History at Birkbeck College, London University's centre for evening classes for mature part-time students. He owed his new job above all to his old undergraduate supervisor at King's College, Cambridge, Christopher Morris, who had written a warm and fulsome letter of recommendation for him.[103] The appointing committee must have been impressed, too, by Eric's double starred First. In some ways Birkbeck was a natural academic home for him. The evening teaching left the day free for writing and research. Eric called it 'the poor man's All Souls', comparing it to the Oxford college which, famously, had no students and did no teaching. With its mission of teaching ordinary working people,

Birkbeck naturally attracted left-wing academics. 'The mood in the small, crowded and friendly staff common room,' Eric wrote later, 'suggested that it was overwhelmingly composed of Labour voters.' The College 'provided a built-in, unforced protection against the pressures of the Cold War outside'.[104]

Eric's appointment caused some consternation in Cambridge when the Board of Research Studies, to whom Eric was answerable as a Ph.D. student, found out about it. Research students, like undergraduates, were required to be in residence in Cambridge during term-time. Those who worked away from Cambridge had to obtain prior permission. Eric had not done so. 'I have just been informed by your College', the Secretary of the Board told Eric sternly on 21 July 1947, 'that you were not in residence last Easter Term but that you were working in London.' What had he been doing?[105] His reply – that he was now a Lecturer at Birkbeck – came as something of a shock to the Board, who admonished him severely:

> You should have applied for leave to work away from Cambridge before you left Cambridge, and you should have applied, informing the Board of Research Studies that you were proposing to accept appointment as Lecturer in History at Birkbeck College, in order that they might consider whether the acceptance of that appointment was consistent with your continuing on the Register of Research Students. The Board of Research Studies will wish to know how much of your time you are required to give to your duties as Lecturer at Birkbeck College, including the time which you will necessarily spend in preparation for the lecturing you are required to give.[106]

'A highly unsatisfactory situation has been revealed', wrote the Secretary of the History Faculty's Degree Committee, the philosopher Michael Oakeshott, on 26 November 1947. It was doubtful whether Eric would be allowed to continue working for his Ph.D. under these circumstances.

Once more, Postan came to the rescue. 'Hobsbawm's thesis was virtually completed last Spring', he assured the Board of Research Studies on 29 October 1947, in a considerable overestimation of the progress Eric had made on the dissertation he had only begun the previous year. He expected it to be submitted by the end of the Easter Term. The sources he needed were in London, not Cambridge. Postan was happy to continue supervising him. His teaching commitments at Birkbeck were limited, and all were in the evening, leaving the days free for research. In any case, 'I very much doubt whether the work he does in London would at its worst make heavier demands on his time than the supervision which he and other men of his standing undertook on behalf of the colleges last year.'[107] For his part, Eric apologised to the Board for his 'discourtesy' in failing to apply in advance: 'My only excuse is that it came through at very short notice, and the work of immediately starting to lecture, and keeping abreast of my subjects, was somewhat confusing.' Altogether, he assured the Board, his commitments at Birkbeck amounted to no more than three or four hours a week of lectures, and one hour every other week for a class. Preparation took no more than two hours a week, 'increasingly less, I find, as my lectures approach the periods on which I find myself in less need of revision'. The Board relented, and renewed Eric's registration on condition that his work at Birkbeck did not exceed twelve hours a week, that Postan continue to supervise his research and that he be granted retrospective intermission of his studies for the Lent and Easter Terms of 1947, which would therefore not count towards the required period of residence in Cambridge. The Board understood that his research materials were all in London, and therefore granted him leave to work away in order to consult them.[108] Very much to his relief, therefore, Eric was not forced to decide between continuing with his Ph.D. in Cambridge and lecturing in London. Leave to work away did, however, involve surrendering his privileges at King's, including his scholarship. Still, his salary from Birkbeck compensated for this. Unusual though it was, the arrangement was in the end acceptable to all sides.

VI

Not long after he had completed his doctoral dissertation, however, Eric's marriage began to run into difficulties. In November 1950 Eric began writing his diary once more, feeling the need to reflect on these problems. As before, he wrote in German, the language to which he still turned when he wanted to express his deepest emotions in private. 'It seems that I only write diary pages when I am alone, when I am bored, when the normal material and mental routine (and would it work without it?) collapses.' Of course, he could not stop himself from describing things that happened to him and people he met. But the main purpose of this particular diary was introspective. 'In the end', he wrote, 'I'm not writing for other people, but as a private catharsis, and if all of this sounds sentimental and banal at a rereading, there's nothing can be done about it.'[109]

To refresh his memory about the early days of his marriage, Eric turned back to the diaries he had written shortly before he married Muriel. He had been 'not particularly enthusiastic' about the prospect, he noted, accurately enough: 'It won't last, I thought then (rightly). The critical point will come when we've been married for a few years – 6–7. I didn't write that down then, but I remember thinking it.' Why had he got married, then? Because he was lonely, he concluded. He was 'never genuinely in love', neither at the time nor afterwards. But 'when I got used to her and to the domestic life, when things improved in bed, when she grew more beautiful – as she did, her complexion improving markedly after 1942, even if she got a few grey hairs – then I said to myself sometimes, that's a kind of love too.' Seventeen months earlier, in June 1949, Muriel had fallen pregnant. She did not want to see it through. It was not so much that she did not want to have children; it was, rather, that she was terrified of the pain of childbirth. Until 1967 abortion was illegal in the UK, and it was common for women to procure what was known as a 'back-street abortion' from an unqualified clandestine practitioner. Muriel, however, was determined to avoid any information about her abortion leaking out. So she carried it out at home, and Eric was forced to assist. He had cared for her while she stayed in bed recovering, waiting on her, bringing her food, doing the cleaning, emptying the chamber-pot. This kind of intimacy and tenderness, he thought, might not have been genuine love, of the sort that caused heartache or made one wait trembling in anticipation by the telephone, but it was at least some kind of feeling. But the experience traumatised him and was deeply damaging to their relationship.[110]

Muriel, he concluded gloomily, had little in common with him. He had noticed, for example, that when he was carried away by the music at a concert, she did not share in his euphoria.

And then she was afraid of me intellectually, like so many. I don't know why. It remains a fact that I scare people off. Thus I was never able to give her things to read. Every time I tried it, when I'd written an article or some other piece: 'Read that, and tell me what you think: go on, criticize it.' And then these terrible moments for the both of us, while I waited, certain that she would say nothing – nothing, not one syllable; while she desperately looked for something to be able to say to me. I knew she would be able to say something to other people; so did she. But no, she was afraid of me. Until in the end I gave up.

And so talking to each other became increasingly difficult. 'What was left to us was just bed.'[111] The crisis began in March 1950, when Muriel came home to their Clapham flat from work one evening and told him their marriage was over. They were not going to have sex any more. She would look for someone else. At first Eric did not take her seriously. In June, she admitted to him that she had taken a lover, but even then he was not unduly upset: he was more concerned about the fact that the man was not a member of the Communist Party than about the fact of his wife's adultery. In an attempt to patch things up, they went for a summer holiday in Corsica. It was a disaster. They spent the time shouting at one another. When they got back, they agreed there was no hope of putting things back together.

Eric felt the need to get away from what was becoming a steadily more impossible situation. France was the obvious destination. He had already visited the country shortly after the war, travelling with Margot Heinemann and three other Party members to the first post-war celebrations of Bastille Day.[112] 'What I remember most vividly about France after the war', Eric wrote later, 'was not the destruction, with which we were after all familiar in London, but the fact that the girls wore enormously chunky shoes, sole and high-heel combined.'[113] The International Congress of Historical Sciences was held in Paris in 1950, the first since the war, and Eric decided to attend. The meeting provided not only a relief from his domestic woes but also a rare opportunity to exchange views and opinions with professionals from across Europe and, in lesser numbers, the rest of the world.[114] 'The birth of post-war historiography', he recalled later, 'took place at a section on social history.' Eric believed that 'this is when the field made its first institutional appearance'. He was put in charge of the 'contemporary' session, chairing what he thought of as an 'odd collection of anomalies and marginals'.[115] The experience left Eric determined to strengthen his contacts with colleagues abroad, and to return to the next Congress, wherever it was held.

A month or so after his return to London from the Congress, Eric came back to the flat from an evening's teaching at Birkbeck to find Muriel had changed the furniture around. 'It was a stranger's home.' She told him it would be better if he moved out right away, as soon as possible. His appointment to a Junior Research Fellowship at King's College at this precise moment came with a set of rooms large enough to live in, and he could eat his meals in the College dining hall. He did not need the Clapham flat any more. It was time to make the break final. She had been sexually unfulfilled for years, she told him brutally: she had even gone to a doctor about it. She was in the prime of life. 'She needed to be fucked all night long.' Of course she had never told him before: 'God, one doesn't talk of such things.'[116]

With one blow, Muriel had taken away his confidence in his masculinity 'and hung it like a big cloak around the other man, who is satisfying her'. He could not get the conversation out of his head. 'I know', he confessed, 'that it's true.' Eric now felt he had to fight back. 'She's plunged a dagger into my breast. I don't want to evade it, I want to go back. I want to phone her every day from Cambridge, and give her presents.' He would try to put the marriage back together again. 'So now I'm unhappy – for the first time in a long, long time.' In the past he had at times felt uneasy or upset. 'But real, frenzied unhappiness, that makes me weep and causes me sleepless nights (the first since God knows when), that's new.' 'My only maxim was: you can survive everything, you won't feel sorry for yourself. And now I do feel sorry for myself.' He wanted other people to feel sorry for him too. 'I've lost my self-respect.' 'I can't work', he wrote, 'I can't sleep and for a while I've hardly been able to eat ... because almost without knowing it I've built my private life over the past seven years almost completely around her.' He could 'not live without her soft skin and the wrinkles she has, without her sagging breasts that were always too small for my taste, without all the unbelievably boring chats we had, without everything that made our marriage impossible'.[117]

The break was neither total nor clean. As Eric confessed to his diary:

At first I did not want to see her, I wanted to leave her alone. Then I rang her up and she asked me to keep telephoning. Then we had lunch together, twice (Monday a week ago and two weeks ago), and once I took her to the theatre. It didn't go well ... We've also written each other a few letters, I to her about how afraid I am, she to me about how my changed behaviour is forcing her hand: she is going to her boyfriend in India over Christmas to 'find out if it really was only an episode'. But if it was, she still doesn't promise anything.

His depression deepened. He thought of killing himself, then abandoned the idea; but 'next week, tomorrow, I could become suicidal again'. This was 'the first time in my life that the thought had ever seriously entered my head', he wrote, but by day at least there always remained in his spirit a small grain of optimism that prevented it. At night he was plagued by dreams of Muriel. He did at least manage to finish off his two articles for the *Economic History Review*, on the tramping artisan and on economic fluctuations and social movements, that had by now become overdue because of the emotional crisis he was going through: 'Deadlines were always lucky for me.' He wondered wildly whether he should flee the scene of his unhappiness by going to the south of France, or Paris, but soon abandoned the idea. 'So just wait, wait, wait.'[118]

He had agreed that Muriel would have the flat for the time being, and he would live in the set of rooms at King's he had been allocated at the beginning of his Fellowship in October 1950, number 6 on Staircase G in the Gibbs Building. The rooms were on the top floor, reached by climbing six flights of broad wooden stairs. They were capacious, with high ceilings and large windows: the sitting room, with a magnificent view of the front of the College straight ahead and the Chapel on the left-hand side, was about 20 feet by 20 feet, then through a short passage was the study, slightly longer and narrower, looking out across a perfectly manicured lawn going down to the River Cam. From the rear window one could see the river and the meadow beyond, with cattle grazing amidst the trees. Through a small door on the inside left-hand corner of the sitting room a steep, winding wooden spiral staircase led up vertiginously to a tiny bedroom. The whole ensemble could not have been much smaller than the flat Eric had just vacated in Clapham. The major disadvantages were typical of the older Cambridge colleges: the bathroom was located down eight flights of stairs, in a dark and dingy basement, and the rooms were almost permanently cold: there was no central heating, and the small open fires, one in each of the two large rooms, both of them kept banked up in the winter by a College servant, did not give out enough heat to make much difference; the bedroom, and the bathroom in the cellar, were entirely unheated. There was running water and a basin only in the 'gyp room' on the landing outside the living room at the top of the main staircase. But with enough space for his books, room to entertain friends after dinner and the quiet and tranquillity he needed to work, Eric had no real reason to complain. He stayed in these rooms for the next three years, moving in 1953 to room 3 on the same staircase for the final year of his Junior Research Fellowship.[119]

Yet the move did nothing to raise Eric's spirits. In Cambridge, after the end of the Michaelmas Term, he found

> an empty King's, with frost on the lawn, no students, and the boring residuum of the resident dons – i.e. the bachelors round the table: the grotesque, sly, withered Provost Donald, with his courtly belly which conceals the entire essence of tact and *comme-il faut* in its exquisitely disguised folds; the old loner and misogynist Pigou, a weathered old stick; the retired bore Scholfield; and John Saltmarsh, whose quiet, superannuated bachelor life exhausts itself in anecdotes about professors from the year 1740. He tells these stories endlessly but amusingly ... That's my life.[120]

Unable to stand being in King's any longer, he spent ten days in London, from 18 to 28 December 1950. Here he was able to forget Muriel for a time while he researched in the LSE Library. When he was feeling 'very desperate' he got talking to a girl in a Lyons Corner House. But when they met again he felt completely cold and left her sitting over her coffee as he made his way to a dinner appointment at his fellow Angel Walter Wallich's home, where he got drunk on Courvoisier brandy, putting him in a 'devil-may-care' mood. A few days later, over dinner with a couple of other friends, he found out that Muriel was still in town, planning to leave for India the next day. On an impulse, he rang her up. She told him she had sent a Christmas present for him to Cambridge, a small vase. 'She seemed to have a bad conscience. I asked her to come back and hung up. Stupid, stupid, stupid!' He ordered a bunch of red carnations to be sent to her in the departure lounge at Heathrow. Once more he put himself on the emotional rack. He imagined her flight to India. 'Now she is in Rome, in Cairo, in Karachi. Now she is in Calcutta. Now he is meeting her. Now they are sleeping with each other.'¹²¹ Christmas drinks with Nancy and Victor he found tedious. It was 'awful' that Victor 'goes to Mass because it's tradition, and is bored', and 'even more awful' that Nancy went with him. 'If only I had something in common with Nancy! I couldn't even talk about M. with her . . . A disastrous Christmas, alas.'

On 27 December Eric went to have tea with Jack Tizard and his wife Barbara, both of them psychologists. They lived in Clapham, in the flat above the Hobsbawms'.¹²² 'Unfortunately', Eric wrote, 'Jack let slip that he had the key', and Eric took it and went down to have a look around. He riffled through Muriel's files and found letters from a parliamentary draftsman with whom she had clearly begun a new affair. The letters ran from 25 October to 12 December. The draftsman was a forty-year-old lawyer called Peter Sée. He seemed more intelligent than Geoffrey Brazendale, her previous lover.¹²³ The discovery of the new affair hit him 'as if I had just been run over by a bus'. He could neither eat nor drink, nor could he even speak until Jack gave him a large brandy to loosen his tongue. 'I knocked back a quarter of a bottle of brandy, and later a whisky and a large Bols, and then it was better. Thank God, there wasn't much in my stomach, so it worked.' But the shock was far greater than the news of Muriel's first affair had been. 'How terrible things must have been for her to abandon us both for a third man.' Their shared commitment to the Communist Party had been a central part of their relationship, he felt. 'If she really abandons us, then it's over . . . For us there is no life fit for a human being without taking part in a movement like ours.' It was like belonging to a church, and, with this thought in mind, Eric turned to St Augustine for consolation, finding it in the saint's affirmation of the Church that 'there is no other place to live in unto eternal life, though there be others enough to attain human glory in'.¹²⁴

Term was looming, but he found it 'difficult to write my lecture, to get on with the article, and so on'. He woke up at ten in the morning after a mostly sleepless night, with a strange dream of a South African millionaire in the Seychelles selling slices of melon to Muriel and himself. 'Then we didn't know what to do with the rind. It seemed that one was not allowed to throw things onto the street in the Seychelles.' He also remembered the singsong accent of the negroes ('yes, negroes!') who lived there. His obsession with her had even penetrated his unconscious mind. He managed to eat a little and read *Capitalism, Socialism, and Democracy* (1942) by the Austrian economist Joseph Schumpeter, whose combination of learning, rigour, logic, style and wit reminded him of Freud.[125] Eric began writing a critique of Schumpeter, and it made him feel better: he recovered his appetite and slept through the night. But he continued to be obsessed with Muriel. 'An existence like that of the last few days, since Wednesday evening, really isn't worth it', he reflected on Sunday, New Year's Eve.

He went to London again to see his old Cambridge friends Hedi Simon and Pieter Keuneman. Unable to bear the poverty-stricken life of a Communist activist with Keuneman in Sri Lanka, Hedi had returned to London at the end of the war and divorced him. Together Eric and Pieter downed 'a few glasses of whisky in the Captain's Cabin' and talked about personal matters. 'Well, one is sentimental. Hedi has run away from him, Muriel from me.'[126] Hedi had taken refuge in blissful domesticity in Hampstead with Peter Stadlen, still at this time a concert pianist (it was only later that a neurological finger complaint forced him to give up playing and focus on contributions to Beethoven scholarship).[127] Eric noticed that his library was overwhelmingly German, with a small amount of English and French literature. He was an 'attractively ugly' man, perhaps a mirror image of Eric himself. Hedi by contrast was becoming 'ever thinner, and somehow ever more lifeless'. By this time he did not think he had ever been in love with her.

He enjoyed debating with Stadlen issues such as the official Soviet criticism of 'formalist' composers such as Dmitri Shostakovich and Sergei Prokofiev in the late 1940s, and the Marxist view of art and culture. Stadlen, a learned, intelligent and forceful man, who later wrote music criticism and essays for the *Daily Telegraph*, more than held his own in argument with Eric. What could one do, Eric reflected, but make one's own point of view crystal-clear? 'If one really wants to convince people, one requires for it a combined operation of experience, of feeling and of logic; with the addition of a few strategic and tactical tricks. The unity of theory and practice. That's also a crisis I have to overcome.'[128] The argument led Eric to rehearse yet again the perennial dilemma that had haunted him ever since his teenage commitment to the cause, as a thinker but not an activist. He felt that as 'an intellectual by profession' he was limited by his attachment to the rational.

> If one is to bear one's responsibility as a Marxist university teacher, one must all the same do something useful. Good, I can convince myself that publishing my books and articles is useful. I can even convince myself that the fact that I'm (hopefully) a good historian gives the Party kudos (or could, if I were Dobb or Bernal). But isn't that an evasion? Especially nowadays? One asks oneself: isn't it at present about convincing people? Can one allow oneself the luxury of liberal academicism – e.g. the luxury of talking about the things that interest one ... ?[129]

Perhaps, he thought, he would sooner or later have to become 'a lower second-class politician or perhaps even a third-class organizer instead of an upper second-class Marxist historian'.

Still in London, on the afternoon of 4 January 1951, he wandered the streets aimlessly, popping into the bookshops to browse, before he noticed a pretty and smartly dressed girl in Leicester Square. He approached her, they fell into conversation and took tea together at the Watergate Theatre Club. She was an actress and seemed to find Eric attractive. She had come to England as a child before the war and spoke German. 'How unbelievably easy it is', he reflected later, 'for me to chat up a woman nowadays. In the first place because of the stupid, empty condition I'm in. Just the thought of not being alone is enough, the thought of a room in which a woman's clutter is scattered around, silk stockings, powder and so on.' He also found he got drunk more easily than before and so lost his inhibitions. Just one glass of whisky was enough.

Secondly, however, it's just a relief to be with a woman who has qualities that I always missed in M.; a woman who immediately excites me sexually, who's younger (though not so beautiful), with whom one has the one or the other thing in common (for example, German); and especially, who talks with one in this easy, playful, somewhat sentimental, rather tender and mocking tone, constantly accompanied by a sexual playfulness that's so soothing and comforting for me (and probably for most men).

He took a taxi with the young actress in London, and though she seemed to want to kiss him, he thought better of it. They exchanged telephone numbers. He found it reassuring that 'with my ugly mug' a good-looking young woman could still find him attractive. He met her again a few days later, but 'as always the second time', he was bored; the girl could not drive Muriel out of his mind.[130]

Back in Cambridge on 11 January 1951, Eric felt depressed again. Thinking back to Christmas 1949, he realised that Muriel's present to him, a copy of George Orwell's *Nineteen Eighty-Four*, with its bitter depiction of the crushing weight of Communism on the human spirit, had been a declaration of war. He had not appreciated how hostile she had grown towards him until told by a mutual friend. Such thoughts made it difficult to write his lectures, and he was worried that they were no good.[131] Muriel's growing estrangement had been expressed in other ways too. When his brother-in-law Victor Marchesi had stayed with Eric and Muriel in the Clapham flat and had come to breakfast from his room, he had noticed that Muriel was ostentatiously reading the *Daily Telegraph*.[132] Eric did not seem to take any notice of it. Eric recorded a dream in which Muriel not only walked away from him but also mocked him; he ran after her 'and bit her until she bled'. When he awoke, he did not feel as depressed as before.[133]

On 13 January he spent 'almost the whole day alone' in his rooms. In the evening he conversed with other Fellows of King's at dinner, but was 'too bored' to go on, as was the custom, to drink port over 'dessert' in another room. 'Why has this convention grown up in Cambridge', he wondered, 'that one doesn't talk about anything serious?'

> The High Table's ideal is neither wit (as people outside believe) nor learning, but a never-ending series of anecdotes, in which not even what is comic counts, but rather the adaptation to a certain private atmosphere, rather unworldly, rather pedantic, rather self-consciously archaic, and self-consciously superficial. The quintessence, so to speak, would be a rambling story with a decidedly bland punch-line, in which the following topics are touched upon: a) the private eccentricities of a deceased don (preferably one who died before 1840); b) the College today (preferably its architecture); c) one or two graduates of the College who have entered public life (so that one can say how much one has one's finger on the pulse of the big wide world); d) a soupçon of learning (so that one can say one's earning one's bread); e) a soupçon of art or music (so that one can demonstrate that one is not a narrow specialist). The whole perhaps spiced with a little bit of malice, and a little bit of one's own eccentricity.

If they could actually talk about their own work, he thought, then even the most boring among them ('and good God are they boring') might manage to say something interesting. Only the philosopher Richard Braithwaite, he thought, was prepared to do this, and Eric found it 'refreshing to sit next to him, and talk about God knows what, philosophy, or mathematical logic; much better than, as with today, listening spasmodically to the soft mumbling of John Saltmarsh'.

VII

Eventually, Eric began to see the pointlessness of his obsession with Muriel. He could not read these sentimental diary entries without blushing. He appeared to himself in them as limp, rudderless, lazy and weak. It was time to give up. Muriel eventually came back from India, but she did not come back to Eric. He pulled himself together and focused once more on his work. He managed to deliver his lectures for the Lent Term, and then, in March 1951, as soon as term was over, he escaped the misery of Cambridge by travelling to Spain for the first time since General Franco's victory in the Civil War. For legitimation he secured a commission to write a report for the *New Statesman*, on a general strike that had broken out in Barcelona. Though Spain was a post-fascist dictatorship, where brutal repression was the order of the day, it was also an ally of Britain and the USA in the Cold War, and any kind of Communist subversion was highly suspect to the British security services, who still had Eric on their books. Discovering his intended trip, MI5 immediately went on the alert. 'There would appear to be some secret means whereby Communists and left-wingers are enabled to go to Spain without the Spanish authorities becoming aware of them', the police told the intelligence agency.[134] But the result of their enquiries was disappointing: 'It appears that Eric HOBSBAWM visited Spain, ostensibly on behalf of the "New Statesman and Nation". And therefore went out quite legally.'[135]

As he had done on his travels in France before the war, he kept a diary of his journey. His command of Spanish was good enough to enable him to talk with 'ordinary Spaniards', beginning in Barcelona, where the strikes, one of them told him, had been 'exaggerated . . . just because it's in Spain, the world press is making a lot of it'. The disturbances had begun in early March 1951 with a successful demonstration against a fare hike on the trams. A student told Eric: 'I thought the spirit had died in the people. This has given me faith in the people once more.'[136] A barman said wages were so poor that people had to live by cheating and playing the black market.[137] 'They say we are not good patriots', said one. 'But when you don't have enough to eat, you can't be a good patriot.'[138] Visiting Tarragona, Eric was depressed to encounter beggars, young and old, a sight he witnessed in other towns as well. He had little difficulty in finding old Republicans in the bar beneath his hotel. All of them belonged to a clandestine Strike Supporters' Club. In a bar in Murcia he also came across a waiter who belonged to an illegal oppositional group that called itself the Boy Scouts ('funny, to read Scout Law in Murcia as a political manifesto'). When they were not talking politics they talked bull-fighting, and Eric actually managed to attend a bullfight, finding pathos in the moment when the bull was finally given the *coup de grâce*.[139]

He encountered one man who treated him with hostility, blaming the British for the Republic's defeat in the Civil War; but a girl who showed him the way to the hotel confessed she admired England because the women there were emancipated. Some Franco supporters assured him 'everything is improving'. Eric was depressed by 'the monotony of the meals' but at least they were cheap and hearty. 'Why shouldn't I eat myself to the full for 25 P[esetas]?' he asked.[140] Transport was chaotic ('Oh, Spanish organization!'), but he managed to find a coach to take him on the six-hour journey to Valencia.[141] Here he found 'the sights mostly disappointing, as usual' with 'the great exception' of the cathedral. Prices on the market, which he noted in detail, were low, and fruit, vegetables and eggs could be bought very cheaply. In the café, where conversation was mostly about bullfighting, the customers had 'general admiration for the Catalans', he noted. They obtained news about the strikes and in general 'the truth about Spain' not from the officially controlled media but from foreign radio stations.[142]

In another café, the locals bemoaned the fact that 'people in Spain are poorer than anywhere else in the world'. Was it better before the Civil War? Eric asked them. 'Yes', answered one man, who was sitting in the café with his family. 'Primo de Rivera was the best time', said his wife, mentioning the dictator who had held sway over Spain in the 1920s: 'since then everything's been bad, one thing like another.' People, said a younger man, were starving. One girl who worked in the hotel complained she did not earn enough to buy herself stockings. The customers generally admired the strikes, news of which had reached them via long-distance lorry drivers. 'Sooner or later it's going to break out – it can't go on like this, when people don't have enough to eat.'[143] In Murcia, as he passed a 'totally ragged beggar leaning against a wall', an acquaintance he had made in a café turned to Eric with the words: 'That represents Spain.'[144] Eric found much of Spain sunk in the depths of the past. Towards the centre of the country, people told him they were simply too backward to follow the example of the Catalans – 'they are fighters, but that's the exception'. From his hotel window in Murcia he looked down one evening on the Good Friday procession with its masked and hooded confraternities. On the streets he saw young ladies with their chaperones, a couple of bordello alleys, farmers sitting in cafés on the market square, dozens of children being shepherded around by black and white uniformed governesses, the buildings all in a baroque-rococo style. He might have been in a 'Habsburg provincial town' in the nineteenth century, he thought.[145]

Eric's trip turned out to be more of a tourist holiday than a journalistic investigation. He did not discover very much about the Barcelona general strike, which fizzled out in the end, as the Franco regime mobilised armed forces against the strikers, though mostly to intimidate them, and eventually, towards the end of March, the strike subsided, and the government released most of those arrested. The strikers did not achieve very much in terms of direct improvement in living conditions, but the action laid the foundations for the re-emergence of the labour movement in the mid-1950s, as the Spanish economy slowly began to modernise and improve.[146] Back in England, Eric organised some petitions for the release of the Spanish strikers who were still detained (he was, sneered MI5, 'a tireless (and tiresome) organizer of petitions and champion of lost causes') but otherwise had to concentrate on his work.[147]

At Birkbeck, teaching took place only between 6 and 9 p.m. on weekdays, and it was possible to cram it all into two days a week, so during term-time Eric stayed with friends in London. For the rest of the week and the weekend, he lived in his rooms at King's. As soon as the Easter Term came to an end, however, he felt the need once more to escape from his miserable personal situation and go abroad. On 27 June 1951 he wrote to Delio Cantimori, an

Italian Communist historian who was translating volume 1 of *Das Kapital*. Eric had been introduced to him by the Oxford medievalist Beryl Smalley. He was leaving England for a holiday in Italy on 12 August, he told Cantimori, and would be in Rome during the second half of the month.[148] After leaving Verona on 18 August and Perugia on the 22nd, he arrived in Rome on 23 August before moving on to Florence a week later.[149] Cantimori not only met Eric but also furnished him with more letters of recommendation, and he also carried introductions from the Marxist economist Piero Sraffa in Cambridge.[150] Eric knew little or no Italian, as he confessed in notes he made during the war.[151] But he got by with a mixture of English and French. In Rome, he met Ambroglio Donini, a history professor and member of the Central Committee of the Italian Communist Party, who aroused his curiosity by talking about rural branches of the party where Christian millenarians of one kind or another seemed to hold sway. Their discussion was in due course to lead to Eric's first published book.[152]

VIII

In the early summer of 1952, Eric's dismal personal situation finally resolved itself. He had arranged to meet Muriel at the end of the Easter Term, but instead she wrote a long letter to him on 12 June, leaving him in no doubt about the fact that their relationship was definitively over. Eric kept it in his papers for the rest of his life, as his first wife's only written explanation of the failure of their marriage:

> My dear, you've asked me several times to come back. You've been so patient & gentle that I hate myself for the pain I shall cause you by saying – as it is only fair I should say without delay now that I know where I stand on the matter – that I cannot live with you again, and that I hope you will now divorce me.
> Patience & gentleness, you see, weren't enough – even if they could have survived a second attempt to live together. There

were too many conflicts in our marriage – emotional and otherwise, between your distrust of personal relationships & my sentimentality, between the intellectual comradeship you wanted & the humdrum cosiness I looked for in marriage – and I couldn't face them again with any sort of optimism.

There is of course – as you have by now felt – another man involved, Peter Sée. You will feel, no doubt, that since he has already been on the scene for many months I must have known that I should not return to you & might have saved you a good deal of uncertainty & discomfort by saying so. But, as it happens, that is not so: though he has now been my lover for some time, it is only in the course of making up my mind about you & me that I have incidentally come to the point of determining to live with him permanently – & to marry him as soon as may be. But that decision is now a firm one, & we shall be living together from now on.

Eighteen months ago you said, fairly enough, that I didn't seem to know what I wanted. Now I do – at the expense of pretty good hell for several people – & most of all for you, my dear. I am not proud of my record – but I can only say that I've sweated a good deal myself over the past two years.

I lack the grit to tell you this to your face: (if I'd not done so – & then had hysterics – last time) you at least would have been free of all this mess two years ago. That's why I write now, instead of keeping our date for tomorrow night & telling you then. And now that I have asked you to divorce me – & if you decide to do so – I believe the drill is that we should not meet without solicitors' advice. So will you write to me and let me know what you propose? And what, incidentally, you would like me to do about your family china & so on? I have said nothing to my mother – & do not propose to until I hear from you.

That's about all there is to say on this morbid occasion. Except to say thank you for being kind & gentle & very dear – it isn't your fault that I'm too neurotic to be content with that. I hate to think of you lonely & sad. Bless you, my dear.

Muriel.[153]

Eric had no choice but to accede to Muriel's request. The days when he had hoped and believed that the marriage could be rescued were past. He agreed with Muriel that they should appoint solicitors. Eric chose Jack Gaster. A Communist since the 1930s, Gaster was a partner in a left-wing law firm in Chancery Lane, representing dockers, trade unionists and others, but he was also prepared to help members of the Party in their personal affairs.[154]

Until 1964, English divorce law required proof of a 'matrimonial offence' to have been committed before a divorce could be granted. The normal procedure in a consensual divorce such as Eric's was for the guilty party to rent a hotel room, traditionally for some reason located in Brighton, and take along a friend of the opposite sex to play the part of the 'co-respondent' in the divorce suit. The aggrieved party would hire a private detective to go to Brighton, enter the hotel bedroom and photograph the couple, usually sitting up sedately in bed together, thus providing 'evidence' of adultery, backed up by copies of the hotel receipt for a double bedroom. Since she felt herself, with good reason, to be the driving force in the break-up of the marriage, Muriel agreed to follow this procedure, and so had herself photographed in the customary compromising position in the Brighton hotel room by a detective hired by Eric. Writing to Gaster, Eric enclosed the photographs to allow him to begin the divorce suit: 'Here are the photos ... and a letter from my wife about the whole matter ... If this letter, plus any material such as hotel bills which her solicitors may be able to supply you with, is sufficient for our purpose, you might as well go ahead.'[155] He did, and the lengthy process of obtaining a divorce began. The date for the hearing was finally set for 21 January 1953, when Eric went with Jack Gaster to present his petition; a Decree Nisi was granted unconditionally.[156] On 9 March, following the mandatory six-week delay after the provisional divorce decree, he was granted a Decree Absolute, 'by reason that the Respondent had been guilty of adultery with Peter Henri Sée the Co-Respondent'.[157] He never saw Muriel again after the court hearing. Ten years later, Muriel Seaman and Peter Sée were killed in a car crash in Portugal.[158]

Eric was no longer as obsessed or depressed as he had been the year before, but the finality of Muriel's letter clearly upset him, and his students noticed his gloomy frame of mind. One of them, Tyrrell Marris, with his brothers, owned 'an elegant (but leaky) 1904 gaff cutter' in which he had learned to 'go cruising under sail'.[159] It was a single-masted, light green boat, called the *Zadig*, and Marris and his friends – three students – invited Eric to sail in it with them to Portugal and Spain. After meeting on 18 August 1952 at Salcombe, on the Devon coast, they loaded up the boat with supplies. 'We were all particularly impressed', Eric later recalled, 'by being able to buy cases of whiskey duty-free on the strength of the voyage.'[160] They set sail, calling in at Plymouth before continuing to Ushant, where they arrived on 23 August. 'Despite the rough sea', Eric noted, he was 'not seasick'. After crossing the Bay of Biscay and sailing down the coast, the engine ran into trouble, so they decided to put in to Seville for repairs. As Eric wrote in an account of the trip shortly afterwards, they 'came up the Guadalquivir with the afternoon tide between great flocks of storks, lagoon salt and cattle ranches', sliding 'through the yellow water full of eroded soil' and steering between the buoys. 'I looked at the shore through the binoculars and watched the black-and-white birds and the low windowless wattle huts in which we were shocked, and yet not surprised, to find people living who waved to us.' They waved back, ate a meal of 'spaghetti, melons and chocolate and drank whisky in honour of ourselves'. They docked in the centre of Seville, near the bullring, and stayed there for several days while mechanics came to repair the engine.

> Seville ... is dusty, sprawling, twisted and broken down like some overgrown provincial town. What binds it together as a city is not buildings or streets, but a dense and moving tissue of noises and rhythms. After a short while we became conscious of occasional threads: a few bars of rhythmic clapping overheard in a side-street, a phrase of melody sung by the labourer shoveling salt or a girl crossing the bridge to the market, the grating of

the trams by day, the sound of a guitar-player going from bar to bar in the evening.[161]

Eric was struck by the relative lack of bustle and business in the port. 'Weeds grew between the stones and bollards, except where nets were spread out to dry. There were more anglers than ships.' He read on deck in the sun while the others were in town:

> It was pleasant to lean against the cabin roof, surrounded by the mess which a boat inevitably accumulates when in port, especially when half its floor and galley are ripped out to allow the engine to be mended: towels, match-boxes, cigarette cartons, tin bowls with the remains of breakfast cereal, trousers, mugs, Frank's easel and unfinished canvas, my dictionary and phrase-book, someone's razor, someone's blankets.

The group soon became friendly with the helpful crew of a large yacht with a Belgian flag and the name *Astrid* that was moored nearby. The two young men, Domingo and Luis, had been looking after the yacht for a couple of months while its owner was away. Most nights, they told Eric, they rowed across the river to a dance-hall and brought women back to the boat. Not untypical were Marí and Salud, whom the Englishmen saw emerging from the *Astrid* one morning. Salud was a girl of about eighteen, wrote Eric, who carried herself with 'a general contour of enchantment. To say that almost any man would want to sleep with her on the spot is to miss the point. Her plump, firm, brown body was not the only thing she possessed. Still, one did want to sleep with her; at any rate I did.'[162]

Invited over to the *Astrid*, Eric sat down with the two men and their girls, drinking coffee and smoking cigarettes. Someone turned on the radio and put some flamenco music on and Salud, a dancer by profession, it seemed, began to dance, not very skilfully according to Eric, but naturally and spontaneously, falling into the traditional steps of the Mediterranean dancing-girl:

> She was unaffectedly pleased with her movements, her

high-heeled shoes, her enchanting body, the wide hips and thighs which she waggled before us, the great round breasts whose shape she emphasized with her hands, her two circular gilt ear-rings, her seven white-metal bracelets, her short black hair, and everything. She did not wish to excite anybody or get anything from anybody. While she danced she smiled to herself and hummed, and when she felt tired she threw herself on a settee and buried her head and breast in someone's lap, Luis', Mari's, whoever happened to be nearest. She had no coquetry whatever and was clearly very stupid.

Conversation was difficult because Eric's Spanish was still not very good and the others spoke rapidly with a strong Andalusian inflection. So they persuaded Marí, also a professional singer and dancer, to sing some flamenco pieces, which they accompanied by clapping, while Salud danced. The noise brought two of the students who formed the *Zadig*'s crew across, Eric supplied a bottle of gin, they began to drink wine and they danced with one another but 'without success for everybody broke down laughing, kissing and drinking after a few bars'. 'We drank toasts, clinking glasses all round.'

Marí dressed up as a man, and Domingo as a woman, complete with lipstick and make-up, and tried to dance with one another, but quickly broke down laughing. Eric thought his students, products of English public school, single sex education, were overwhelmed, 'full of gin and desire' but also 'pale-faced and awkward'. As Salud handled the situation with ease and aplomb, Eric admitted that perhaps he had 'exaggerated her brainlessness a little. I rather think we fancied ourselves in the parts of neurotic and complex intellectuals among the children of nature, latter-day Bougainvilles finding their Tahiti on the Guadalquivir.'[163] Eventually the girls fell asleep. The two Spanish men began to talk about the Civil War, which had ended just over a decade in the past. Luis said his father and uncle had been shot by the Francoists. The slightly older Domingo remembered too: 'They shot many many people in ditches ... They went round the villages, picked them out and shot them.' They were all reds in his village. 'All over Andalusia', Eric noted, 'the children who had been six or nine in the summer of 1936 remembered their murdered parents in such nights, though there had been no fighting here for fifteen years; though they should have forgotten, as one forgets things at that age.'

Eric realised that the group on the *Astrid* had run out of money and food, so the Englishmen provided a makeshift meal for them. The girls repaid them by doing the washing-up while Luis and Domingo went into town for supplies. The students showed them card tricks and tried to teach them English songs and party games. The girls were not impressed. 'A loud and uneasy schoolboy wind blew round their cotton skirts.' The atmosphere was edgy. When Luis and Domingo returned, they all went to write down their names, but they discovered Salud was illiterate. In the end she went off with Luis, while Eric disembarked to wander round the town on his own. Running into Marí, he invited her to the cinema, and then they returned to the *Astrid*, where they sat on deck waiting for the others until it grew too cold and they went into the wheelhouse and lay down on a mattress and made love. The next morning however it was clear to him that 'it was friendship and not love she wanted'. Relieved, Eric set out to find Salud. The directions he was given took him to what he realised with a shock was a brothel, with 'heavy iron grills' and a 'blowsy madam'. 'I felt ill and lost all desire to sleep with anyone, even Salud.' In any case, she was not there. 'Perhaps the gentleman would like another young lady?' Eric declined the offer. 'In most European towns', he reflected, 'one can tell prostitutes from the others, but not in Seville, where ordinary girls cannot make a living.' When he eventually found her, it was only to say goodbye. They shook hands. 'The ceremony of innocence was drowned.' Eric got onto a train out of Seville to travel onwards to Paris, and only remembered too late that he had forgotten to say his farewells to Marí. The *Zadig*'s engine now repaired, his students sailed back downriver and on to Tangier before returning to England via Brittany, where they ran aground at the small fishing village of Audierne and had to be towed off by the *bâteau de sauvetage*.[164] Overall, however, the trip had been a great success. He often recalled it fondly in later life, and it did a good deal to restore his spirits.[165]

IX

After staying briefly in Paris at the end of July 1952, Eric reached Cambridge in good time for the start of Michaelmas Term. There were very few specialists in economic and social history in the History Faculty at Cambridge, so as a Junior Research Fellow he was required to plug the gap by giving lectures and supervisions in the subject. He shocked some of his conservative colleagues by dressing casually and wearing white gym shoes when he taught, contributing to his reputation for sartorial unconventionality.[166] He was popular with the students, however, who reported that he was one of the few dons who was known for 'always being available to help students'.[167] Eric always remembered something Postan had told him. '"The people for whom you are there", said my own teacher, "are not the brilliant students like yourself. They are the average students with boring minds who get uninteresting degrees in the lower range of the second class, and whose examination scripts all read the same. The first-class people will look after themselves, though you will enjoy teaching them. The others are the ones who need you."'[168]

One such, on her own admission, was Joan Rowlands (later Joan Bakewell, the broadcaster). 'I was a modest grammar school girl with a huge hang-up about coming from Stockport with an accent', she remembered, 'surrounded by public-school toffs, who terrified me.' To her advantage, on the other hand, was the fact that she was an undeniably attractive 'girl, in a minority, with a huge male "demand" (as it were)'. Rowlands came up to Newnham, an all-female College, in 1951, and took nineteenth-century economic history with Eric. The teaching involved eight weekly essays which Eric as supervisor would criticise and then use as the basis for an hour-long, one-to-one discussion bringing in other aspects of the subject. Unlike most dons, who sat quietly while their students read out their essays to them and then opened a discussion, Eric demanded that the essay be sent to him three days before the supervision so that he could read it and make notes on it.[169]

In October 1953 Rowlands went to King's at the beginning of term to meet him, without knowing anything about him:

> I was very timid, and indeed timid confronted with him. Gibbs Building. Vast and beautiful room. And this tall, lanky figure – bounding around – and sort of filling it with his seriousness. I mean, he was very serious. He was lumbered with me. He wouldn't have chosen to teach me because I was a second-class mind. I mean, it was clear that I wasn't going to sparkle in any way. And he was very keen on brilliant people, because he asked me after several of them "do you know so-and-so? Do you happen to know so-and-so?" He wanted to know where the brainy people were, and when they were women, he was even more interested ... I felt he was lonely and looking for company.[170]

Rowlands found Eric intellectually intimidating. 'I knew he was brainy', she said, 'simply because he exuded being brainy.' But he did his best to put her at her ease:

> Eric was a good talker, I mean even to small fry like me; he didn't patronise me or anything – he talked at his level, and, you know, I found my eyes watering with the kind-of trying to keep up with him. He was a marvellously thoughtful teacher because he took in the fact that I didn't have the range or the background for the sort of level he was talking [at]. So he taught by way of asking me questions ... It was Eric who taught me how to ask things. I always remember him talking about the Luddites – and I think I must've used it as a term of contempt – and him saying 'Why do you think they were breaking frames? Weren't they – did they not – did they have a case?' ... So he led me, because I wasn't tremendously adventurous in my thinking, to go, 'Oh yes, I see, right, yes.'

The origins and growth of the trade unions were a central part of the course. Rowlands came from a Labour background; her grandparents were factory workers and the history of trade unionism was in her blood. What Eric said 'appealed to my political background, so I was very comfortable with what he was telling me. You know, I wasn't sort of thinking, "Good heavens, I'm being brainwashed into being a Marxist."'

Up to this point, Rowlands had identified with the union movement and its origins, its history and its progress up to the present. What Eric did was to make her see

> how the movement – the trade union movement – belonged in society and grew out of its background. And so he gave me a sense that history is not things that suddenly happen – and they turn for the worse, or this way, or the other – but there was an amazing, kind-of onflow of construct in history that you could identify ... I [would] sit there, and – his great limbs folded up around him, I remember – him asking me 'Why do you think?' – 'But surely' – you know. And he'd introduce me to a sort of discourse.

In the end, she felt that he was 'frankly not impressed by me ... I was an ordinary little scholarship girl from a northern town, completely awe-struck by everything that was going on.' Later in life, however, as Joan Bakewell, she enjoyed a highly successful career as a journalist, writer and radio and television broadcaster, probably better known to the British public than Eric ever was.

Eric was never rude or condescending to his students. Another of his pupils was Tam Dalyell, a Scottish Old Etonian. Dalyell remembered how, in 1952, as a nervous freshman at King's, straight out of the army, he was sent to Eric for supervisions in history. 'College gossip had it that the Communist Eric Hobsbawm will tear you to shreds. On the contrary', he told Eric many years later, 'you could not have been nicer or more constructive to a very ignorant public school boy who had done no advanced history.'[171] Very different was the experience of Neal Ascherson, another Scot and Old Etonian. Eric described Ascherson as 'perhaps the most brilliant student I ever had. I didn't really teach him much, I just let him get on with it.'[172] Not surprisingly, Ascherson was soon enrolled in the Apostles. At the time, British men had by law to do a period of service in the armed forces – National Service as it was called. Ascherson had served as an officer in the Royal Marines from July 1951 to September 1952, and was sent to Malaya, where the British were attempting to suppress a nationalist insurgency that had begun in 1948. By the time he came up to King's to read history in October 1952, he was harbouring serious doubts about his part in the anti-insurgency action. 'When you're very old, as I am', he confessed to me in his eighties, 'you feel much worse about having killed people than you do when you're eighteen years old, but none the less, that also weighed on me.' He came away from the experience with a service medal and a guilty conscience.[173]

Shortly after Ascherson arrived at King's, there was a College feast, to which the new undergraduates were invited,

and I was still trying to adjust to all this, and feeling a bit out of it, as one would ... and people were dressing up, so I thought, 'Well, *I'll* dress up.' So, very stupidly, I put on my medal – you know – from the Malayan campaign ... And there was dinner – we all drank an enormous amount, too much – and then afterwards people said, 'Oh well, whose rooms are we going to? – Let's go to Eric's', you see. So I thought, 'Well, come on!' ... Eric's room was in the Gibbs Building, and I went in there, we all drank a lot; a great deal of wine was consumed by me as well; I was quite drunkish, I think. Anyway, at one point in the evening, this sort of tall, thin man was just sort of led across to me and somebody said: 'This is Neal Ascherson', and he peered at me, and he looked at this medal. He said: 'What's that?' I said: 'Oh, this is my naval general service medal, you know, Malaya.' And he said: 'You should be ashamed to wear that' with considerable intensity, and I was sickened – absolutely rigid – partly because, looking back, subconsciously, if one believes in the subconscious, I had been hoping that somebody would say something like that, because my feelings about what I'd been doing – and that in particular – were extremely conflicted ... I walked out. I went down onto the front lawn ... I walked around it, weeping. I remember I was crying. I was rather drunk. And I walked round and round in the dark, and eventually, at one of these circuits, I just took this medal off and stuck it in my pocket, and I never wore it again.

Ascherson later looked back on this, his first encounter with Eric, as 'cathartic'. In an odd sort of way, he felt grateful to Eric for bringing his guilty conscience out into the open. They never referred to it again, but the incident marked the beginning of a close friendship that was to last a lifetime.

The encounter had a curious coda. Decades later, well after the turn of the century, by which time he had become a distinguished journalist and historian, Ascherson encountered Daniel Ellsberg, a former US government military analyst who had caused a storm in 1971 by leaking to the press a large quantity of confidential documents on American policymaking during the still ongoing Vietnam War. Their publication as *The Pentagon Papers* had led to Ellsberg being arrested and tried for espionage and theft, but the court had dismissed all the charges and he had walked free. Eric's name came up in discussion, and, Ascherson recalled, Ellsberg said: "'The trouble about Eric, well, you know, he could be *pretty cruel*.'" He said: "I was present at this incident when he talked to this undergraduate, looked at his medal, said, "You should be ashamed to wear that." "Oh, really? ... That undergraduate was me! And you were there?" "Yeah".' Ellsberg had indeed arrived at King's at the same time as Ascherson, on a one-year Woodrow Wilson Scholarship, to study economics. He had been so shocked at what he had heard Eric say that he remembered it for the rest of his life.[174]

Eric took Ascherson for economic history, which was 'not my thing': he was more interested in revolutionary political history, which was not taught at Cambridge at the time.[175] His supervisions with Eric were more like talking to an older friend. The actual supervision was not close at all. I mean, I would write an essay on some subject and show it to him. Sometimes he would have read it, and sometimes not, really – just glanced at the subject, which we'd then discuss, you know. And then it would verge off into all kinds of other interesting discussions which were nothing to do with the subject I was supposed to be supervised on ... I just remember drinking red wine with him, and talking – the way in which we digressed off.[176]

Nevertheless, however interesting the discussion, and however much red wine was consumed, Eric always brought the session to a close at the end of the allotted hour. Ascherson duly obtained a double starred First in history, and Eric naturally wanted him to go on to an academic career. 'You really ought to do research', he said to him, 'not just drift off somewhere.' But he went into journalism instead, working for the *Guardian*.

Eric mixed on easy social terms with the undergraduates at King's, as his sailing trip to Seville suggested. He did not get on particularly well with the other dons, however. He found them dull, even if not quite as dire as suggested in the jaundiced diaries of the time, which were written, after all, while he was deeply depressed. Nor did he have many contacts with the History Faculty, which was still at the time notably conservative both politically and methodologically. One exception was one of Trevelyan's pupils, J. H. (Jack) Plumb, a brilliant historian of eighteenth-century English politics who at this time was still on the political left. 'He was a man of great abilities', Eric remembered later, 'and I liked talking to him in the 50's, though I never had close contact with him after he stopped being a 1930's Red.'[177] Later, Plumb moved sharply to the right. Eric 'could never understand how he came to end up such a political reactionary'.[178]

Lonely and emotionally vulnerable, when he was in Cambridge Eric was thrown back on the resources of undergraduate sociability, helped by the fact that the dons and students at King's were not required to lunch at separate tables, as was customary in many other colleges. On his very first day in King's, in October

1951, Geoffrey Lloyd, a scholarship boy who had come up to read classics, was invited back to his rooms by Eric ('a craggy face, *jolie laide*') for coffee:

> There were a number of other people there. I can't remember their names but they started talking about just about everything – novels, jazz, films, politics ... I encountered this group of people who seemed to be able to talk about everything completely openly. I didn't know he was a research fellow. I thought this was heaven, intellectual heaven.[179]

The easy social relations between the younger dons and the students owed something to the fact that, as Geoffrey Lloyd observed, 'The generation of undergraduates that were there in King's [included] ... still some people who had fought in the war.' Girls from the women's colleges were important in these impromptu parties, but Eric did not seem to be chasing after any of them. Lloyd knew that Eric was married, but thought his wife lived abroad. They never talked about it.

The most important thing about social life at King's was the conversation. Willing to talk about anything, knowledgeable, open and unstuffy, Eric soon became a favourite at these gatherings. As Neal Ascherson later remembered:

> He came to our parties all the time. So if some of us had, you know, – nothing formal – but a few of us would decide to have a drink and play some records and settle down in a room and talk about the world and everything, Eric would roll up, or somebody would say 'Come on Eric', you know, and he would be there ... After the incident with the medal, but before I began to be supervised by him ... [there was] a lunch party with Geoffrey Lloyd in his rooms, and everybody was sitting on the floor eating spaghetti Bolognese, which was quite an adventurous thing to do in those days. And Eric was there. He was talking about Spain (he'd just been to Spain) ... I thought rather grandly, about bullfights and so on, of which he was a fan. And

he said at one point: 'And then, of course, the matador – *torero* –
puts on this red thing which you hang on the end of the sword,
and gesticulates like that – it's called a ... I don't know what
it's called.' And I said: 'It's called a *muleta*.' There was a sort of
awful silence. He looked at me like *that*. ... But I only knew that
because part of my family's in France ... so I knew how it was
done and what the names of the parts were, as it were. Anyway
that was a strange, a curious moment.[180]

Eric never liked being bested in matters of knowledge.

Besides socialising with undergraduates on this impromptu
basis, Eric also rejoined the Apostles in 1950, attending meetings
with a regularity he had not been able to attain while he had been
living with Muriel in London. The honesty and intimacy of the
Society, Eric later wrote, 'helped me most at a time when I was
unhappy'.[181] But he felt increasingly isolated by the gap in age
and experience, and he was now the only Communist among the
Apostles, which put him on a different intellectual wavelength from
the others. By this time the homosexual aura of the Society had
largely vanished, too, though Eric recalled 'a paper on buggery by
Annan, married by then but speaking from ample experience'.[182]
However, the unmasking of Guy Burgess as a Soviet spy brought
unwelcome attention for the Apostles from the security services
and the media. After Guy Burgess had fled to Moscow in 1951 to
avoid arrest, causing a sensation in the daily press, he telephoned
Eric early one morning to offer his apologies for not being able
to attend the annual dinner of the Apostles, thus, Eric thought,
'making absolutely certain that my phone would thenceforth be
bugged. His message,' Eric gleefully reported many years later,
'helped to make the dinner a great success.'[183]

X

The security services did indeed continue to keep an eye on Eric
throughout the early post-war period. A 'reliable and accurate'

source at King's College, Cambridge, who 'has had personal contact with HOBSBAWM' reported in 1951 that Eric 'has rooms in Staircase G, Gibbs Building. His rooms are full of Communist literature, and he appears to be a militant Communist, making no secret of his political views. He dresses in a slovenly way. He is believed to be married to the daughter of an ex-sergeant of the Grenadier Guards.'[184] Soon, however, they had caught up with his life and were reporting that Eric had 'recently separated from his wife and has left her in possession of the flat and contents. He relocated to Cambridge, where King's provided a free set of rooms and continued with his salary of £300 a year.'[185] 'He is reputed recently to have had an emotional breakdown.'[186] This did not make him any less dangerous in MI5's eyes, however, especially since he was in touch with Alan Nunn May, a physicist who had been jailed for passing nuclear secrets to the Russians during the Second World War.[187] In fact, the contact was completely harmless. Still, the security services remained suspicious. 'Doubtless Eric HOBSBAWM', MI5 noted sarcastically, 'will do some good propaganda work among the student body at Cambridge.'[188]

MI5's suspicions were almost wholly unfounded. Eric was anything but a militant Communist. He knew that in political terms he was living 'an odd life as an outsider in the movement'. He had always thought he was not capable of being fully committed, he was 'weak and vacillating' and he clung too much to the old conventional society to be able to devote himself to building a new one.[189] Eric's 'party autobiography', a document all members were required to write, was submitted on 2 November 1952, and was unsparing in its self-criticism. 'Most people have political differences with the Party from time to time. I've argued them out', he wrote, 'and then accepted party decisions until the line changed. How else are they to be settled? I've tried to stick to democratic centralism.' Since coming out of the army, however, he had tended 'to be rather cut off from the masses, and even from ordinary party work (when in on-University branches I've tried to do ordinary basic work, but have kept off responsible work). Moderately satisfied with trade union work.'

He was indeed Branch Secretary of the Association of University Teachers in Cambridge and had been a delegate to its Council, though he must have been aware that this was hardly evidence for commitment to the kind of industrial militancy the Party was interested in; nor was the fact that he edited and to a large extent wrote the Communist-steered Cambridge *University Newsletter* from October 1951 to November 1954, in which he inveighed against the discrimination from which Communist academics were increasingly suffering, comparing it to the exclusion of Social Democrats from university posts in the Kaiser's Germany.[190] He wanted, somewhat unrealistically, 'to have more to do with factory workers. I've considered full-time work, but don't think I'm good enough at organizing to take the idea seriously. [...] I don't feel that I've done what I might for the Party', he concluded, 'or that I've been advancing in my capacity to do so.'[191]

As far as the union and its members were concerned, Eric's main activity consisted of writing and giving lectures on the social and economic position of university teachers. On 25 September 1949, speaking to a conference organised by the Cultural Committee of the Party, he claimed, according to an MI5 report,

> that the least educated BALKAN peasant, who today is helping to construct an ordered society, is freer than are the university professors in this country. He claimed that [during] the periods in which the intellectuals have attached themselves to the people, they have performed their finest tasks. In the periods in which the intellectuals have retreated into their 'ivory tower' they have produced nothing of value due to their disassociation from the people.[192]

But by the time he went to the Association of University Teachers' annual conference at Royal Holloway College, in Egham, to the south-west of London, in December 1950, the Cold War was having an effect on the union's politics. Although he stood for the Council he was not elected and indeed thought, rightly, he never would be. He was not even asked to sign petitions or join in campaigns. All that Party members could do, he concluded, was to exert some influence behind the scenes because they were so mistrusted. 'That hurts', he wrote.[193]

He was frequently at odds with the Party in these years. British Communists faced a particular test of loyalty with the split that came in 1948 between Stalin and the Yugoslav Communist Josip Broz Tito, who had led his partisans to victory during the war and was developing a relatively liberal economic policy for his country. Yugoslavia's expulsion from Cominform, successor to the Comintern, was followed by a series of show trials of 'Titoists' across Eastern Europe. Eric knew many of the Bulgarian, Czech and Hungarian 'traitors' well from their wartime exile years in Britain, found the accusations incredible and did not believe the about-turn of the British Communist Party, which praised Yugoslavia as a close ally of the Soviet Union in 1947 and denounced it as a tool of capitalism in 1948.[194] He made it clear privately that he did not follow the orthodox Party line against Yugoslav 'revisionism'. In a letter to the *Listener* in January 1949, Eric criticised a polemical broadcast by A. J. P. Taylor on the situation, but said nothing in defence of Stalin, nor did he anywhere else.[195] In 1953 his undergraduate friends Neal Ascherson and Geoffrey Lloyd went to Yugoslavia as volunteers for a 'youth brigade' to rebuild the Bosnian railway, which was still suffering from the effects of the war. They stayed with Serbian working-class families by invitation and 'had a great time', especially since the project had been cancelled because there were no spades, according to Geoffrey. They spent a good deal of time on the Danube by Belgrade, where 'there was a nice sort of little beach kind of thing, and swimming, and girls who were sort of would-be starlets, with very hairy legs, some of whom went to Cambridge, I mean as visitors', as Geoffrey remembered. When they got back to Cambridge, Eric did not in any way upbraid them for becoming involved with 'Titoism'; he was, according to Ascherson, 'rather delighted that we'd gone to try and build this railway, you know, out of a sort of youth brigade enthusiasm of a formless non-party kind'.

To more committed Communists, Eric could seem 'revisionist'

himself. Ascherson remembered that one of his friends was a young Chinese woman, Gioietta Kuo,

> an absolutely incandescent, passionate Communist; and she was also a nuclear physicist – not only that, she was a bloody good nuclear physicist – she got terrific first-class degrees at Cambridge, and was talked about, you know. Her purpose, I think – well, really, I mean she occasionally said – was to go and build a bomb for China. So, anyway, she became extraordinarily interested in Eric ... I think Eric quite fancied her. I don't know if anything happened – probably not – she was very kind-of severe, you know, in an early Maoist way. Well, she was very attractive, and Gioietta used to upbraid him for revisionism, and being soft on this and that – for enjoying Western culture too much and not understanding how degenerate it was. And she really used to scold him – I remember hearing that several times – and Eric ... didn't put up a fight.[196]

Gioietta thought in fact that Eric was homosexual, because he never talked about women; like many other people in Cambridge, she had no idea he was married. She enjoyed going to his rooms after an exam, where she could relax as he brewed her a cup of tea and plied her with biscuits as they talked about Communism and China, where her mother was a film director. In due course she went to Birmingham to take a Ph.D. in nuclear physics, then married a Croatian and went, ironically, to live in Yugoslavia, going on to research at Oxford and Princeton and eventually heading up an institute in California.[197]

Eric also had a reputation at King's as an unorthodox Communist. As J. H. Money, an MI5 official, reported in October 1953:

> When I visited King's in June of this year I overheard one of the Fellows, named HARRIS, discussing HOBSBAWM. He said that HOBSBAWM was thoroughly out of date with his Communism and was still in the 'popular front era; that he would probably not survive if the Russians came' ... On a

previous occasion another Fellow had remarked: 'HOBSBAWM would shoot us with regret'.[198]

The Communist Party leaders in London were also well aware of the fact that Eric did not conform to their idea of what an active Communist should be. As the novelist Doris Lessing, herself a member of the Party at this time, later reported: 'The pressure on writers – and artists – to do something other than write, paint, make music, because those are nothing but bourgeois indulgences, continued strong.'[199] A Communist was supposed to write only for the Party press, for example, but Eric published in all kinds of 'bourgeois' periodicals such as *Lilliput* and the *Times Literary Supplement.* A Communist was supposed to sell copies of the Party newspaper the *Daily Worker* on street corners, but he did not appear to be doing so.

True, in 1948 he was said by MI5 to be engaged in organising 'the regular contribution of historical articles to the *Daily Worker,* and lately', it was reported to MI5, 'some articles have also begun to come into *World News* and *Communist Review*'.[200] But Eric's writings failed altogether to stick to the orthodox Party line. The Party headquarters sent him frequent letters, which he immediately binned, demanding that he behave like a proper Communist. MI5 reported a conversation, held in the bugged Party rooms in King Street, where the leadership confessed more or less to giving up on him. Dorothy Diamond, a science teacher and Party member who was Honorary Secretary of the British Council for German Democracy, and Idris Cox, a Welsh miner, former editor of the *Daily Worker,* until recently National Organiser for the Party, and Secretary of the International Department of the CPGB, gave vent on this occasion to their frustration with him:

DIAMOND asked whether there was any point in launching another attack on Eric HOBSBAWM(?). She went on to say she thought something ought to be done about it – he had just ceased to answer any letters! COX asked whether he was associated with the Cultural Committee? (The answer to this question was not clear). Following a loud burst of laughter, COX said he could make enquiries as to what his position was.[201]

But he does not seem to have done so. As before, the Party concentrated overwhelmingly on trade union activities. The non-conformity of a single intellectual was not a matter of great concern to it.

In any case, after Eric moved to Cambridge in 1950, he completely gave up taking part in orthodox Party activities, for which, he later confessed, 'I had no natural taste or suitable temperament. From then on, in effect, I operated entirely in academic or intellectual groups.'[202] He wrote the occasional letter to the press, for example condemning as illegal the United Nations Security Council resolution that triggered the Korean War ('the United Nations cannot be made a tool of the West'), or condemning French military intervention in Indochina. But his commitment, such as it was, did not extend to active campaigning or work for the Party. In 1960 he commented on media condemnations of the Soviet shooting down of an American U-2 spy plane piloted by the young airman Gary Powers ('What would have happened if a Soviet plane had been shot down over Kansas City?'), but he did not write on behalf of the Party like ordinary members did; he wrote as an independent, politically engaged academic.[203]

Eric was more active in the support of Communist Parties outside the UK. He was a member of the British-China Friendship Association.[204] He also became involved in supporting the German Democratic Republic, founded in the Soviet zone of occupation in parallel to the Federal Republic of West Germany in 1949. Many people on the Left considered that the Federal Republic exhibited too many continuities with the Nazi regime, whose civil servants, judges, businessmen and teachers were reoccupying their former positions in large numbers, so the main hope for a new beginning free from the burdens of German history lay in the East. In September 1949 Eric agreed to take over the editorship of a monthly newsletter, *Searchlight on Germany*, on behalf of the British Council for German Democracy, a Communist front organisation.[205] The administrative work was carried out by Dorothy Diamond. The circulation was about five hundred. 'Since this man has taken over the editorship', MI5 reported, 'the quality of the magazine has improved.' At the same time it had no doubt that he was a 'doctrinaire intellectual'.[206]

But both Eric and Dorothy, the Party noted, 'were not doing all the things which they ought to be doing'. The paper was in financial difficulties. At the end of 1950, Eric resigned the editorship.[207] He was living a 'half-and-half nomadic London-Cambridge life' which made it difficult for him to commit himself fully to Party work in London. 'I can't afford 3 fares a week from Cambridge to London', he told Dorothy Diamond. If meetings fell on a day when he was not teaching at Birkbeck he would have to miss them. The best he could do (with her help) was to supply Communist Party newspapers and magazines 'with the facts about Germany – properly digested etc. – and for them to write them up'.[208] He had reason to pull out anyway, at a time when East Germany was undergoing rapid and ruthless Stalinisation. Nevertheless, his activities and contacts once more aroused the suspicion of MI5. A Home Office Warrant for the monitoring of Eric's correspondence was applied for on 3 January 1952, on the grounds that he was 'a member of the British Council for German Democracy and as such, is in frequent touch with German and Austrian Communists. The object of the check is to establish the identities of his contacts, and to unearth overt or covert intellectual Communists, who may be unknown to us.'[209] However, opening Eric's correspondence was a complete waste of time. Nothing of interest emerged from it, and the warrant was suspended until further notice on 10 June 1952.[210]

Eric was also a member of the London Committee of the British-Czech Friendship League, dedicated to fostering good relations with the new Communist government of the country. He had met a number of young Czech historians at a World Youth Festival in Prague in 1947, not long after the Communist Party had won a remarkable 38 per cent of the vote in a free general election. Even after what was in effect a coup by the Communists in the country early in 1948, following a sharp deterioration in relations with the non-Communist parties, he continued to believe in the cause of political change in what had been before the war East-Central Europe's only functioning democracy. His views came out when, in 1949, he attended the annual dinner of the Apostles, held at the Royal Automobile Club, and presided over by Guy Burgess, still in Britain and still unmasked. Burgess's main contribution to the discussion was reportedly to ask those present to agree that Catholics should not be admitted to the Apostles because they would be prevented by their adherence to Church dogma from discussing matters openly and honestly (an argument whose multiple layers of irony would only become clear in retrospect).[211] One of those attending the dinner was Michael Straight, an American contemporary of Eric's at Cambridge who had been recruited as a spy by Anthony Blunt and succeeded in obtaining a position in the State Department in Washington during the war. A former Apostle who by this time had become a successful magazine publisher, he had run into Burgess by chance on the street in London and been invited by him to the dinner.

By this time Straight had become a convinced anti-Communist, and indeed a few years later he was instrumental in exposing Blunt as a former spy. His account of conversation with Eric at dinner was not flattering:

I sat by a rising historian named Eric Hobsbawm. I remembered Hobsbawm as a member of the student Communist movement at Cambridge. He made it plain that he, at least, had not given up his beliefs. I made some bitter comment about the Soviet occupation of Czechoslovakia. Hobsbawn [sic] countered with a comment about the Americans who had been imprisoned under the Smith Act. He said with a knowing smile, 'There are more political prisoners in the United States today than there are in Czechoslovakia.' 'That's a damned lie!' I cried. I continued to shout at Hobsbawm. I was aware that others were staring at me. I was not acting in a manner becoming to a member of the society.[212]

Indeed he was not. But this was an indication of the passions that the Cold War was beginning to arouse even in the normally polite surroundings of the Cambridge Conversazione Society.[213] After this, however, Eric did no more for British-Czech friendship, especially after friends he had made before and during the war fell victim to the final round of Stalin's show trials, not least because they were Jews.[214]

XI

Conventional left-wing activities in support of Communism were not the main focus of Eric's activity in the Party during these years. The overwhelming bulk of his engagement was in the Historians' Group of the Communist Party, originally established as the Marxist Historians' Group in September 1938 and reconstituted after the war. Eric later described the Group as 'at war with Stalinism' from 1946 onwards. 'In fact we were critical communists.'[215] Eric also wanted non-Communists to join, and to this end he proposed that the showing of Party membership cards at the start of each meeting should not be required. The committee rejected this request, made early in 1948, but endorsed the idea that sympathetic outsiders should be included in the meetings.[216] The moving spirit in the formation of the Group was a non-academic from an upper-middle-class background, Dona Torr, who had earned a degree in English before the First World War and worked at Lawrence and Wishart. Fluent in German, she had also translated into English the Soviet-sponsored edition of the *Correspondence of Marx and Engels* (1934), a copy of which Eric had bought and read as a schoolboy.[217] Many years later Eric remembered her as

a small old lady always with a headscarf and with very firm opinions both about the Communist Party and about Marxist history. Unlike the younger generations of political radicals from respectable middle class families she kept the family accent and manners. I have no idea how she escaped her family background ... She had a great knowledge of Labour history, particularly in the last thirty or forty years before World War I, but wrote very little ... She had a very high reputation among CP intellectuals and liked to see herself as a sort of guru and patroness to the young historians before and after World War 2.[218]

Eric was virtually the only member of the Group with a Ph.D. and therefore some experience in writing at book length, so he was less influenced by Torr than many of the others. When asked by an Austrian colleague and comrade for a reading list on the English labour movement, he felt unable to recommend her work.[219] Her role in the Group was almost purely advisory and organisational, though for some members it was very important.[220]

The Group met in London, in the upper rooms of the Garibaldi restaurant in Farringdon, or, sometimes, in Marx House at Clerkenwell Green. It aimed to mobilise history in the service of revolutionary ideas,[221] and it pursued in particular

the popularization of history throughout the Labour movement, giving historical perspective to every part of the struggle for the achievement of Socialism ... Knowledge of history must be used to strengthen the confidence of the workers in their own powers, through fuller understanding of the past achievements of their own class. Particularly important here is the development of the knowledge of history in our own Party; not only because of its importance in helping us to understand Marxism, but also because a clear understanding of the Party's historical roots in the Labour movement is one of the best ways of overcoming sectarianism and feelings of isolation.[222]

Members of the Group delivered lectures on working-class history and were planning a textbook, in which Eric was to write the eighteenth-century section; they encouraged the foundation of local history groups (in Manchester, Nottingham and Sheffield);

they held conferences; and they hoped to start a project identifying the forms of bias in conventional school history textbooks.[223]

Few if any of these aims were achieved. The Group's activities in practice were confined to seminars for its members on historical problems. 'For Marxists, at least at that time,' Eric recalled later, 'the problem of how capitalism developed was the central problem of history.' Yet 'no British, or for that matter any other Marxist [historian], had tackled this problem head-on, in the light of the most uptodate research, including that by "bourgeois" historians'. A key influence here was the work of the Cambridge economist Maurice Dobb, whose lectures were notoriously dull, and hardly attended by any students, not even by Eric, but whose book *Studies in the Development of Capitalism*, published in 1946, exercised a considerable impact on members of the Group.[224] Dobb attended a number of its meetings but generally took a back seat in the discussions.[225] The Group was divided into sections by period. Eric was a member of the nineteenth-century section. His first recorded contribution was at a conference held on 6 June 1948 on 'The impact of Capitalism on the Working People', to which he contributed a lengthy critique of what he saw as the inadequacies of the German Communist historian Jürgen Kuczynski's work on the British standard of living during the Industrial Revolution.[226] He took part in a general discussion of Leslie Morton's classic, *A People's History of England*, published in 1938.[227] He was critical of G. D. H. Cole's book *The Common People 1746–1938*, published in 1945 and co-authored with Raymond Postgate, an example, he thought, of the demerits as well as the merits 'of an advanced humanitarian, social-reforming liberal history'.[228]

The Communist Party Historians' Group held a summer school in 1947, and a general conference in 1948, but after this it began to decline, with the students' and teachers' sections having fallen into abeyance by 1951, the modern section going through 'a period of acute difficulty' and the medieval section in a state of collapse by 1953. The core members' growing professional commitments were getting in the way of regular attendance. Eric resigned as treasurer and left the committee in 1950, and his attendance at this time was far less regular than before.[229] It is hard, however, not to see this as a consequence of the deep personal crisis he was going through, for he rejoined the committee in September 1952 and indeed replaced Rodney Hilton, the medievalist, as Chairman.[230] He revived plans for a collectively written textbook on English history, and drew up an updated list of Party members' research in the field.[231] The most important consequence of Eric's re-engagement was an ambitious summer school he organised on the rise and decline of British capitalism. It was held at the rather grand Netherwood Hotel in Grange-over-Sands, in the Lake District, in mid-July 1954.[232] 'The purpose of this school', Eric declared in his opening address, 'is to get our minds clear about the history of capitalism in Britain.'[233] Eric's various drafts for his contributions ranged across the field from the role of Methodism to the role of empire. Already, he was thinking on a global scale as he put forward theses on the role of white settlers and indigenous local collaborationist elites in maintaining colonialism at a time when the imperialist metropolises were clearly loosening their grip.[234]

Summing up at the end of the meeting, Eric found that 'the growing convergence of ideas in the discussions was a sign of our growing maturity'. Characteristically, he regretted the lack of the discussion of culture, and urged 'a great improvement in our knowledge of the common people in determining and shaping history'. He suggested further summer schools for Marxist historians should be held every few years.[235] However, the 1954 summer school proved to be the Group's swansong. Some years later, the English historian Edward Thompson confessed that he missed the Group and its meetings; academic conferences were no substitute: 'too many papers, trying to be bright, and all too brief'.[236] It remained the case, however, that the members of the Group were 'formed within a certain unified cultural matrix, a certain "moment"', so that 'we must look a bit like a closed club, who share pass-words and unspoken definitions and operate within a shared problematic which today can't be entered in the same way'.[237] These shared ideas and assumptions lent the former members of the Group a distinctive profile when they began to produce their major historical works in the late 1950s and 1960s.

Eric wanted to extend the work of the Group onto the European continent. In July 1952 he wrote to Delio Cantimori, following a visit to Paris, suggesting a 'joint anglo-french meeting' of Marxist historians at the end of the year to discuss the transition from feudalism to capitalism and the previous transition, from communal society to feudalism. The French specialist on Spanish economic history Pierre Vilar was roped in to the plans.[238] The Italian Marxist historians, Eric thought, should take part as well, and he wanted more generally to establish greater collaboration between west European Marxist historians.[239] The conference took place from 28 to 30 December 1952, with Eric, Christopher Hill, Rodney Hilton, Robert Browning, Victor Kiernan, John Morris and Louis Marks, though who took part on the French side is not known.[240] But this ambitious scheme came to nothing in the longer run. At most, the Marxists met from time to time on the fringes of European or world historical congresses. The French Communist historians were too dogmatically Stalinist for a meaningful dialogue. The Communist Party Historians' Group never managed to make the leap across the English Channel.

However, four members of the Group, Eric, Christopher Hill, Robert Browning and Leslie Morton, were rewarded not long after Stalin's death in 1953 by an invitation to Russia from the Soviet Academy of Sciences during the academic winter vacation of 1954–5.[241] The group travelled by train across Europe and was warmly welcomed on its arrival. The day after Eric and his companions arrived, they were taken to the Bolshoi Theatre, where they were served vodka and caviar and saw a performance of Tchaikovsky's *Eugene Onegin*. The next day, a Wednesday, they attended a reception at the Academy and then were taken to a 'terribly old-fashioned and charming' circus, with the full Victorian panoply of lion-tamers, jugglers, acrobats, tightrope walkers and clowns. On Thursday there was a 'long session at the Institute of History', after which they were whisked off to see the embalmed corpses of the founders of the Soviet Union, getting in without much waiting because they had been placed in the 'privileged queue'. Eric found it 'pretty impressive . . . Lenin looks slighter and finer-faced than one thought, Stalin bigger'. He was particularly impressed with the grandeur of the Moscow subway, as everyone who has seen it surely must be. But he complained privately that it was very hard to get any alcohol, apart from the vodka they were served on ceremonial occasions, and almost impossible to listen to jazz. And there was no question of having anything to do with ordinary people or, indeed, everyday Russian life.

The group then went on the famous overnight Red Train to Leningrad (St Petersburg) for an historical colloquium. Eric thought the city was 'well kept & clean . . . A superb town in every sense.' He was less impressed with Russian women. Their 'hairdos are appalling' and 'their dresses could be so much better designed . . . Altogether it's sad, for though their shape is probably too plump for our tastes one could get used to it.' They visited the forbidding Peter and Paul Fortress, where so many revolutionaries had been imprisoned, and attended a performance of Tchaikovsky's *Swan Lake* at the Mariinsky Ballet, after which they were surprised when, as was the custom, the prima ballerina, still perspiring from her exertions, came into their box to be presented to them. They also visited the 'wonderful coll[ection]' of the Hermitage Museum. Eric was impressed by the 'passionate cultural interests' of the Russians, with 'queues in bookshops' as well as crowds in the theatres and concert halls. There was even a black market in literary classics that were not to be found in the Communist-censored bookshops, though people 'don't talk in private as they would in public', where they could be overheard by agents of the secret police. But overall 'the main positive impression is that of vast energy and expansion'.[242]

He found himself depressed by the remaining scars of war in Russia, and the pervasive atmosphere of secrecy in which not even telephone directories or maps were available. He was impressed by the closeness of distinguished scientists to their peasant roots, evidenced by their ability to quote Russian proverbs at will. They met hardly anyone like themselves, though the Soviet media broadcast an account of the visit, in which the British guests had apparently engaged in 'animated discussions' with Soviet colleagues on issues such as the Norman Conquest, the ideology of British workers and medieval peasant uprisings. Eric's political views were not affected by this experience. Whatever the problems and difficulties of supporting Soviet-style Communism, he continued to think that it was preferable to Western imperialism, and therefore it needed defending as stoutly as ever.[243]

XII

The most lasting product of the extensive debates and discussions held by the Communist Party Historians' Group was the publication of a journal. Discussions began on the initiative of John Morris, a member of the Group who taught Roman history at University College London. Morris visited Eric in King's on 6 January 1950 to discuss 'the new historical magazine. God knows', Eric confessed, 'the man is irritating, but I wasn't able more or less to lose my temper with him.' The ninety-minute discussion left him feeling worn out.[244] But Morris persisted, and the founding meeting took place some months later around the kitchen table at his home. Present besides Eric and Morris were Christopher Hill and Rodney Hilton. The meeting appointed Morris as the journal's editor, a capacity in which he served until 1960. Each member pledged to contribute whatever funds they had at their disposal to subsidise production costs.[245] They raised £25 between them as a startup, with Morris gifting a matching amount and three further well-wishers contributing another £8. Most of this money went on printing fifteen thousand leaflets and sending them to individuals and libraries to announce the journal's appearance. When they were asked for financial contributions, a number of Party members did, however, cough up.[246] By October 1951, 217 people had signed up for subscriptions, a number so small that the founding group considered scrapping the entire project. However, when Morris found a printer who could produce the journal cheaply enough to break even with a circulation of four hundred, they went ahead.

Morris wanted to call the journal *Bulletin of Marxist Historical Studies*, but Eric and other members of the Group thought it should cast its net far wider and focus on drawing out the significance of the past for understanding the present in a more general sense. Borrowing its title from a short-lived series of brief historical books edited after the war by the archaeologist V. Gordon Childe, the new journal was called *Past & Present*, with the uncompromisingly Marxist subtitle *A Journal of Scientific History*. The editors wrote around asking sympathetic historians to submit articles. Delio Cantimori, at Eric's request, delivered an article in January 1952.[247] Preparations for the journal's publication were going well, Eric assured Cantimori; they had secured an article from the Soviet historian E. A. Kosminsky, a respected specialist on English medieval agrarian history, and persuaded Georges Lefebvre, the great historian of the French Revolution, to become a member of the editorial board.[248] Eric consistently did his best to boost sales, asking Cantimori if he could arrange a display table for the journal at the Tenth International Congress of Historical Sciences in Rome in 1955, to be staffed by any available graduate students.[249]

Morris's managerial talents were minimal. He was said to have kept the journal's funds in a shoebox under his bed. To begin with, there were two issues a year of sixty to seventy pages each. The cover design was kept simple. Unpaid assistant editors and 'business managers' were drawn from among the Group's circle of friends and pupils. The members of the editorial board wrote the articles themselves or commissioned them from friends and colleagues. They decided not to include book reviews because they had nowhere to store the books.[250] Eric drafted an inaugural statement in December 1950, which, with additions by others, eventually became the journal's manifesto.[251] Its purpose was ambitious: nothing less than to counter the leading historiographical trends of the post-war era in Britain. It was above all due to Eric's influence that *Past & Present* saw its remit as developing a broad, comprehensive concept of history and that the editors sought out representatives of neighbouring disciplines. Eric later described the journal as 'the British equivalent of the *Annales*'.[252] The very first paragraph of the editorial introduction to issue number one paid tribute to 'the tradition of the late Marc Bloch and his associate, Lucien Febvre' of studying change in the past 'not by means of methodological articles and theoretical dissertations, but by example and fact'.[253]

Later, Eric wrote to the French social historian Pierre Goubert, whom he had met at the international historical congress in Rome in 1955, soliciting a contribution. Goubert remembered the 'long-armed, long-legged' historian, who could be found at various times in the congress talking in one or other of five or six languages; he had read some interesting articles by this 'Marxist English-style', and agreed to send something in.[254] The closeness of the journal to the *Annales* school was underlined by the contribution of the medievalist Jacques Le Goff to the one hundredth issue, in which he recalled that French historians had no idea of the political complexion of the original editorial team behind *Past & Present*. He had always, Le Goff confessed, in a rather French way, 'been a reader from the beginning, an admirer, a friend, almost (if I might say so) a secret lover'.[255]

Within a short space of time, the basic character of the journal had been established on the basis of a consensus between the Marxist and non-Marxist editors. They shared from the outset

a common hostility to 'the sort of article which would get into the English Historical Review', i.e. orthodox traditional historiography. In this sense, though less defined, we were analogous to the Annales' revolt against their own traditionalist historical tradition in the 1930s – and aware of the parallel . . . In a sense we made ourselves the spokesmen of the new postwar generation of historians for whom, Marxist or not, economic and social dimensions of history were more important than before, who were ready to break out of the orthodox archival politics-cum-institutional cage, and use new sources, techniques and ideas.[256]

Very much in this spirit, Eric's first contribution to the new journal was an article on the Luddites, the machine-breaking protesters of the early Industrial Revolution in Britain. Attacking Jack Plumb's view that Luddism was 'a pointless, frenzied industrial jacquerie', Eric argued that in some circumstances it was a rational form of industrial bargaining on the part of the workers – precisely the point he had pressed upon his pupil Joan Rowlands in their supervisions on British economic history.[257]

He followed this up with a pair of substantial articles, building on notes he had taken at a session of the Group two years earlier, on 8 March 1952, on the crisis of feudalism in the seventeenth and eighteenth centuries.[258] These were published in 1954 under the title of 'The General Crisis of the European Economy in the 17th Century'. Here for the first time the full power of his command of the sweeping generalisation, based on an astonishing breadth of reference across the European continent, was fully in evidence. Departing from his usual research territory of nineteenth-century British labour history to range across the economies of several countries, and drawing on literature published in several European languages, Eric identified a common economic crisis that led to a widespread series of rebellions and revolts, the most radical and successful of which was the overthrow of the English monarchy in the 1640s, in what he regarded as the first complete bourgeois revolution.[259]

Eric's articles were immediately discussed in the *Annales*, which picked up his contribution as an all-too-rare example of ambitious and sweeping generalisation by an English historian.[260] More generally, the articles sparked a major historical debate as the seventeenth-century specialist Hugh Trevor-Roper published a contribution focusing on the political consequences of the crisis while at the same time criticising Eric's focus on the economic transition from feudalism to capitalism. More contributions followed from a wide range of historians, and they were eventually published as a book. The debate rumbles on in the twenty-first century, with the most recent focus on the climate change of the 'little Ice Age' that underpinned the crisis, dismissed by Eric as an extraneous factor with little relevance to the human history of the time. The debate on the 'general crisis' was Eric's first contribution to historical controversy on the grand scale. It was far from being his last.[261]

Past & Present was not at first very successful. 'For some years', Eric remembered later, 'few except Marxists were prepared to write for it. Some, like the historian of Ancient Greece Moses Finley, himself a victim of McCarthyism, kept away from it for years. Others, like the art-historian Rudolf Wittkower, withdrew because they were told it wouldn't be good for their careers. The Institute of Historical Research refused even to subscribe to us for several years.'[262] Mounia Postan was representative in his disapproval of the new journal. The members of the editorial board, he told R. H. Tawney, who had rejected a request to join it, were 'nearly all Communists and fellow-travellers ... It goes without saying that they will try to get as many non-Communists to co-operate as they can, and occasionally they may even print a non-Marxist or anti-Marxist article. However, I agree with you that it's most likely to become one of the CP's satellite bodies.'[263] 'I think you underestimate the degree of suspicion that surrounds the board as at present constituted', the leftish historian of the early modern English aristocracy Lawrence Stone wrote to Eric when asked to join it. It was only after most of the Communists on the editorial team left the Party, in 1956, and then Stone and other non-Marxists joined the board in 1958, that the journal succeeded in broadening its contributor base and becoming, in due course, the most widely respected academic journal of social history in the English-speaking world.[264]

The problems faced by the journal in its early years was not the only respect in which the Cold War affected Eric's career. At King's in the early 1950s Eric was remembered as 'an embattled, slightly exotic figure'. He was generally acknowledged to be very brilliant, but 'an invisible fence seemed to stand around his prospects. Britain's version of "McCarthyism" was weak and erratic', but it was to blight his future in Cambridge and already in 1952 seemed to be making him more isolated than he had been before among the dons.[265] Overall, the years from the end of the war to the end of his Fellowship in Cambridge in 1954 had been difficult ones for Eric, despite the confirmation in 1950 of his appointment at Birkbeck as a permanent position, after the conclusion of the required three years of probation.[266] The Cold War had blocked his career as a broadcaster. He had only managed to secure a Fellowship at King's at the second attempt, and he had not been able to publish his Ph.D. thesis as a book. He had secured a permanent post at Birkbeck and managed to get his first academic articles accepted by the *Economic History Review,* but a successful career in academia still seemed a long way off. He had played the leading role in founding the new journal *Past & Present* but its closeness to the Communist Party Historians' Group was preventing it from being widely accepted in the academic world. The Group itself was falling into apathy and inaction. Eric was only too aware that he was an unsatisfactory member of the Communist Party, contributing little to its political activities. Yet his attempts to secure a position in the academics' trade union had been blocked because of his Communism. The crisis and finally the break-up of his marriage had plunged him into a deep emotional depression from which he was only slowly beginning to emerge. Life in Cambridge was unsatisfactory in the extreme and he escaped from it as often as he could, not just to London but also abroad, to Spain, Italy and above all, as we shall now see, France, which played a crucial role in his intellectual formation as well as his emotional recovery during the 1950s.

6

'A Dangerous Character'

1954–1962

I

By the mid-1950s, Eric was travelling widely and often, for reasons both professional and personal. In 1955 his friend Delio Cantimori had booked him into the Tenth International Congress of Historical Sciences, which began in Rome on 9 August. This was a vast historical jamboree, bringing together two thousand delegates from all over the world. They included for the first time historians from the Soviet bloc, among whom there were twenty-four from the USSR.[1] Eric, as he told Cantimori, was keen 'to arrange some sort of meeting with our various friends from eastern countries, as well as a meeting of progressive historians from western Europe, to meet and exchange views'.[2] However, the Congresses were still dominated by political and diplomatic historians, and despite the holding of a session on the bourgeoisie at the Rome meeting, Mounia Postan and Fernand Braudel felt impelled, against strong opposition from the Secretary of the organising committee of the Congress, to found a breakaway organisation almost immediately afterwards, the International Economic History Association.[3] Eric remembered the conference afterwards mainly for the good weather, which persuaded him to take a break from the proceedings with George Rudé, a fellow British Communist and pioneer of the history of the crowd in the

French Revolution, and go onto 'a beach in Ostia . . . with a bottle of wine and in a swimming costume'.[4]

The professional part of his visit concluded, Eric made his way via Florence to Syracuse, in Sicily, from where he boarded a steamer for Malta to visit his sister Nancy and her family.[5] Her husband Victor Marchesi had been posted by the Royal Navy to the island following two years on board an aircraft carrier during the Korean War. By this time the couple had two children, Anne, born in 1948, and Robin, born in 1951; a third, Jeremy, was born in Malta in 1957. Eric's occasional visits were keenly anticipated by the children. As Robin later remembered,

> Eric appeared, you know it was a big deal, oh you know your uncle is coming, because you know we didn't have any family and it was quite strange because everybody else had lots, big families, and I can remember thinking it was a bit odd. But that was the first time I can remember I ever met him and he bought me a copy of *The Crab with the Golden Claws*, and I've never forgotten it, because that taught me, every year he'd sent me a Tintin book and that was how I learned to read, from Tintin.[6]

On one occasion, Eric sent him a toolbox, which Robin found 'a bit silly' since he had no more interest in using one than Eric ever had. After that, Victor was posted to Northern Ireland, where the family stayed for two years before returning to the UK at the end of 1957. They subsequently followed Victor to a posting in Nigeria, before settling in Greens Norton, Northamptonshire, in 1962.

Eric also kept in touch with his cousin and teenage friend Ron Hobsbaum, known to his family as 'Hobby', now living with his family in Romford and then Shenfield, in Essex. Ron worked as an economist in the Civil Service Pay Research Unit. His daughter Angela, born in 1944, recalled their continuing friendship in the 1950s:

> I can remember Eric coming for occasional visits like Christmas or in the summer, and I just always remember Hobby and Eric

sitting down and having really long discussions about heaven knows what, probably economics or politics, definitely economics or politics, and my mother and I would scurry about doing the plates and the washing up.[7]

Eric also met fairly regularly with Denis Preston, another first cousin, to whom he was closely bound by a common love of jazz. By now Denis had become a record producer, focusing mainly on British traditional jazz. Flamboyant and successful, he drove a Mercedes and wore Savile Row suits. At the same time, although he had divorced his South African wife Noni in 1954 and remarried, Denis campaigned seriously on racial issues, and managed to get a patronisingly racist reading primer, *The Story of Little Black Sambo*, withdrawn from many school libraries.[8]

After his Junior Research Fellowship at King's ended, in September 1954, and with it his free accommodation in the College, Eric moved to London permanently, renting a capacious but rather expensive apartment at 37 Gordon Mansions, just round the corner from Birkbeck, close enough indeed for him to pop back between lectures. It was 'a large, partly dark flat', he later recalled, 'full of books and records, overlooking Torrington Place'. To cover the steep rental costs, he was obliged to share it, mostly with friends and acquaintances from the Communist Party, including Henry Collins, a member of the Historians' Group, Alick West, a Marxist literary critic, and Vicente Girbau, a Spanish refugee. At the beginning of 1956, MI5 noted that he was sharing it with Louis Marks, another historian and an active figure in the Party. There was room to put up guests as well, and a series of foreign visitors and other friends and acquaintances passed through. 'It was, to be honest, much more fun than living in a Cambridge college.'[9]

Throughout the 1950s, Eric spent most of his vacations in Paris, as he had done before the war.[10] Here he stayed with Henri Raymond and Hélène Berghauer, a married couple of about his own age to whom he had been introduced by a young Frenchwoman he had met at the previous international historical congress, in 1950.[11] The Raymonds were childless – Hélène was told by her doctor that she had little chance of conceiving.[12] Henri, born in 1921, worked for the French national railways, wrote poetry and studied sociology with the leading Marxist thinker Henri Lefebvre. He eventually became a teacher of the subject at the École nationale supérieure des Beaux-Arts, publishing a lengthy series of articles and exercising a strong influence on the younger generation of architects and urban sociologists. His wife Hélène was a painter and illustrator who made a living working at the Brazilian consulate in Paris; Jewish, and half-Polish, she had escaped from France with her family in 1941 and spent the war years in Brazil.[13] Eric described her as 'a charming and extremely attractive young woman'. As Eric did with all his Parisian friends, he conversed with them in a French that by now was well-nigh perfect.[14]

He had first stayed with the couple on his way back from Spain in July 1952. As he recalled in his memoirs, they lived in a

> rather basic working-class flat on the boulevard Kellermann . . . When they left Paris I would travel with them in their small car to wherever we agreed to go – to the Loire valley, to Italy, wherever. When they were in town I shared it with them, going round in their company, observing the passing scene from the approved cafés such as the Flore or the Rhumerie, watching out for, and passing the time of day with, acquaintances among the intelligentsia – Lucien Goldmann, Roland Barthes, Edgar Morin. When they were absent, I stayed there alone, using it as a private desert island.[15]

The Raymonds' circle of friends and acquaintances, which also included Henri Lefebvre and the novelist Roger Vailland, both former members of the wartime Resistance, consisted mainly of intellectuals who were either unorthodox Marxists or were drifting away from Marxism altogether.

The French Communist Party, like its British counterpart, adhered rigidly to Stalinist orthodoxy, and the intellectuals who followed its line, including a number of subsequently well-known historians such as Emmanuel Le Roy Ladurie, François Furet, Annie Kriegel and Alain Besançon, had nothing to do with Eric and his heterodox intellectual companions at this time. French Party officials were all too aware of Eric's nonconformity, and never dared to interview him or invite him to any meetings.[16] He also became friends with the great photographer Henri Cartier-Bresson, whose work he admired. And he spent a good deal of time in Parisian clubs, from the Club St Germain to Le Chât Qui Pêche, where the best jazz was to be found, though overall he thought it second-rate, far inferior to what was to be found even in London. Only the Paris-based jazz clarinettist Sidney Bechet met with his enthusiastic approval.[17] The legendary café Les Deux Magots was close by, and provided intellectual nourishment. The philosopher Jean-Paul Sartre was one of its habitués in the 1950s; it had been made famous as the haunt of Pablo Picasso and his fellow artists some decades earlier. There were other clubs, such as the Sigale, where Eric listened to North African popular music.[18]

He got to know Sartre quite well and met him frequently. As Eric's nephew Robin Marchesi recalled,

I bumped into Eric in Paris when I was living in Paris with my American wife – girlfriend, at the time – in '82 ... I always remember him taking us out for a meal at La Coupole. And ... always, you know, we'd had meals there before and ... always had the mutton curry. And she used to go, [in American accent] 'You must be the only person who ever comes in here and orders the mutton curry!' OK, when uncle Eric invited us to La Coupole, my ex-wife turns to Eric and goes,

'Well, when did you first come here?'

'Well, I think it was in the 1950s, and I came here and I had a lunch with Jean-Paul Sartre.'

And she goes, 'Oh my God!! What did he say?'

And Eric just looks, and he says, 'He said to me, "There's only one thing to eat here, Eric, and that's the mutton curry."'[19]

By mixing in Paris mainly with nonconformist or dissident left-wing intellectuals, Eric kept Stalinism at a distance and became familiar with a wide range of unorthodox ideas.[20]

Throughout the 1950s, the Raymonds subsidised Eric's stays in Paris. A room was permanently reserved for him in their apartment, and money was left for him there if he was expected when they were away ('Dear', said one note from Hélène, 'You'll find your money in the drawer of this same table. I put it there because the new housekeeper [is] supposed to be honest ... I hope you'll have a splendid time without me if possible. Kisses. Hélène').[21] They shared a common concern with many of the topics that concerned Communists and more generally the Left in the early 1950s, from the show trial of Rudolf Slansky and other leading Czech Communists – almost all of them Jewish – on charges of 'Zionism' and 'Titoism' in the winter of 1952–3 to the latest activities of the French Communist leader Maurice Thorez, a grimly dogmatic Stalinist. The apparent spread of anti-Semitism in France concerned Hélène.[22] They discussed books of mutual interest, movies, world affairs, her latest ventures in the art world, and of course plans to meet up, either in Paris, Cambridge or London.[23] 'Do you know', she told Eric in a letter, 'that I'm jealously guarding your gin, so if you hurry up I'll be able again to offer you more than one glass. Isn't that a reason to come?'[24]

This was no ordinary correspondence between political and intellectual comrades. Hélène's letters to Eric are full of expressions of affection and love well beyond convention, and are disarmingly open and frank. 'How are you?' she enquired in October 1952, a few months after he had stayed briefly with the Raymonds for the first time: 'And your heart?'[25] If her letters were relatively restrained in the autumn and winter of 1952, they lost all reserve after he stayed in Paris the following year. She sent him a poem about lovers ('The lovers' bedroom/all the world laughed there').[26] She ended one letter with a quotation from Elizabeth Barrett Browning's Sonnet 43 – 'How do I love thee? Let me count the ways.'[27] Her husband Henri did not seem to mind. He did not possess a faculty for jealousy, she reassured Eric when their affair began in July 1952.[28] 'How's your sex-life going?' she asked Eric on one occasion when they had been apart for some time.[29] She hoped she would always have a privileged place in his heart, she wrote on another.[30] Although after five years together with her husband she thirsted for freedom, she could never leave him, she told Eric.[31] Hélène did not hesitate to tell Eric about her own affairs when they were apart – 'I am a charming, adorable creature', she declared, and 'am conducting here a little sentimental intrigue.'[32] She did not keep her relationship with Eric secret from Henri either; sometimes indeed she included his greetings at the end of a letter. For his part, Henri also had affairs, one of which at least Hélène told Eric was 'a serious liaison. Love', she added sarcastically, 'ah, love is good.' Confronted by the end of the decade with the increasingly obvious disintegration of their marriage, she started to think of moving out.[33]

In 1957 Eric spent a holiday with the Raymonds at the seaside resort of Rodi Garganico, on the Adriatic coast of southern Italy, chosen by the Raymonds because it was the setting for their friend Roger Vailland's novel *La Loi*, winner of the Prix Goncourt that year. Eric encountered another young couple, Richard and Elise Marienstras, on the beach, 'he a tall broad-chested blond, she tiny, thin and dark', both from Polish Jewish families who had somehow managed to survive the war in the unoccupied zone of France. Richard would later become a leading Shakespearian scholar, while Elise published on the Native American resistance in the USA. The Marienstrases were about to spend a spell as teachers in Tunisia, a country Eric had got to know before the war, and they immediately plunged into animated discussions that forged a lifelong friendship. Remembering this first encounter many years later, Elise Marienstras could not disentangle the relationships between Henri, Hélène and Eric: 'Basically I didn't know whether she was Eric's former wife, or Eric's mistress, or the mistress of Henri Raymond. Their relationships remained opaque to me.' Perhaps, she thought, Hélène was still married to Eric. Hélène's refusal to take her husband's name, still very unusual in the 1950s, confused her. 'One sensed it wasn't going particularly well', Elise noticed, talking about Hélène's relationship with Henri: 'some difficult moments, and no demonstrations, really, of intimacy' even on this first encounter. The Marienstrases became firm friends with Eric, but not with the Raymonds.[34]

A common interest in Algerian independence, the major political issue in France in the mid-1950s, continued to bind them all together. Eric's pre-war involvement with North Africa, and his frequent visits to Paris, had brought him into contact with the Algerian independence movement, the Front de libération nationale, or FLN. An uprising staged by the FLN in Algeria in 1954 quickly degenerated into a violent civil war, made more complex by the opposition of many French Algerian settlers to the idea of independence. Bombings, massacres, assassinations and torture were routinely practised on both sides as four hundred thousand French troops were posted to Algeria and the conflict began to extend to metropolitan France. On 17 October 1961 French police under the control of Maurice Papon, who had arrested and deported Jews to Auschwitz during the collaborationist Vichy regime in the war, deliberately killed between one and three hundred people peacefully demonstrating in Paris for Algerian independence.[35] The French Communist Party supported Algerian independence, and in this situation, where the lives of FLN members and their active supporters were in danger, some of its members began an operation to hide them from the French police, in some cases by spiriting them across the Channel. Eric became involved in this scheme and asked Neal Ascherson if he would assist him. 'The idea was', Ascherson later remembered, 'that we would hide people – militants, who came across – how, God knows, under false names and so on – and we would then conceal them and look after them until the coast was clear, whatever it was. So I signed up for that. As it happens', he added, 'I was never called upon to hide anybody. I was married at that time, had a baby. How many other people were involved, and how many militants were concealed, I don't know.'[36] Meanwhile, beginning in April 1961, the Organisation armée secrète, or OAS, supported by many French colonists, began a campaign of bombings and outrages in France and Algeria with the aim of preventing Algerian independence. At this point Hélène Berghauer visited Eric in London, as he recalled later, informing him that she had come to buy timers for bombs to be used for a counter-campaign against the OAS. 'I asked where she would get them. "At Harrods, naturally", she said. Of course, where else?'[37]

By this time, the Raymonds' marriage was in terminal decline. Hélène moved out of the apartment at the beginning of 1962 and the couple went through a formal divorce.[38] Henri remarried, this time a woman of independent means, while Hélène continued to have affairs.[39] By 1965 she was undergoing psychotherapy for depression, sleeplessness and anxiety, and told Eric she was no longer capable even of having casual sex.[40] They lost touch, and neither met nor corresponded until Hélène wrote to Eric many years later, on 17 October 1985, to tell him she had breast cancer.[41] Her treatment was successful for a time, but the cancer returned and she died at the beginning of July 1992.[42] While their *ménage à trois* had lasted, however, it had provided Eric with what he later described as 'the closest thing to a family I had'.[43]

II

Back in England Eric continued to try and build his career as an historian. After he had published his early academic articles in the *Economic History Review* and *Past & Present*, he felt the time had come to put together his reading and his research into a book. It would tell the story of the rise of the working class in Britain from the late eighteenth century onwards. Entitled *The Rise of the Wage-Worker*, it was intended for publication in Hutchinson's University Library, previously known as the Home University Library, a successful series of short textbooks covering virtually every academic subject. Eric's synopsis, which he sent to the publisher on 17 November 1953, envisaged a work of eight parts or chapters:

As a rule the subject of each part would be arranged as a cross-section of all industrial countries, rather than a series of sections dealing with individual nations. Each part would be divided into chronological segments: early industrialism, middle industrialism, modern industrialism. (In Britain these would correspond, roughly, to 1780–1850, 1850–1900, 1900–).[44]

Eric's proposal was warmly welcomed by Ruth Klauber, the responsible editor at Hutchinson, who told Eric it 'sounds immensely interesting and exactly suitable for this library'.[45] The history section was edited by G. D. H. Cole, the left-wing historian of socialist ideas. Cole wrote to Eric on 28 November 1953. His reaction was positive, and the critical points he made about the synopsis were all minor ones.[46] After a meeting with Cole, Eric signed a contract in January 1954.[47] It took a little longer than anticipated to complete the book. Hutchinson had hoped for delivery by Easter 1955 (which would have meant publication in the first quarter of 1956), though the contract stipulated 31 July. In the event, Eric sent it in on 7 August.

'I think the length is all right', he told Ruth Klauber. 'I cut out large chunks at earlier stages and got it down to well within 60,000, but I have not made a detailed check of the final length, especially as I can't quite reckon up the length of the notes.' These would be extensive, he warned, because

> unfortunately the subject is not one which can be simply boiled down from a few larger books. I am afraid there *must* be at least that much in the way of references . . . that I have put little quotations of poetry – all from folksongs, blues, popular songs etc. – at the head of each chapter. I hope they can stay in, if necessary in small print. a) they are nice and b) they add a bit of human touch and may cheer the reader up. I don't see why one should neglect human interest in a serious book, and it might even attract one or two extra buyers.[48]

Two months later, Cole returned the manuscript to Eric informing him that it had been rejected.[49] He had sent it to a senior British economic historian – the usual procedure with academic

books, including textbooks – and had received the verdict that it
was too biased for a publication intended for use by undergraduates.[50] Eric immediately consulted his solicitor, Jack Gaster, who
had handled his divorce a few years earlier.[51] He drafted, but did
not send, a letter to Ruth Klauber asking for 'concrete suggestions
for revisions and alterations. I will then do my best to make the
required changes, provided that this does not amount to a substantial redrafting or re-casting of the manuscript. As you know',
he added, 'my view has been and is, that what you commissioned
is entirely suitable for the Hutchinson's University Library as a
whole.'[52] In further exchanges, however, the publisher alleged that
the manuscript contravened the terms of the contract signed with
Eric, which included a clause certifying that the book should contain nothing that was in the publisher's opinion 'objectionable'.[53]

Eric reminded Ruth Klauber that he had offered to make
changes to deal with this alleged problem:

> You passed on to me a report by an anonymous critic, of whose
> qualifications for the task of criticizing a specialist, indeed in
> some respects a pioneer, work of scholarship I am necessarily
> ignorant. This left me largely in the dark about what I am to do
> to please you. I submitted a rather detailed list of my perplexi-
> ties to you, as well as commenting on several points where the
> critic appeared to be mistaken. You merely answered this with
> the statement that his report ought to provide me with enough
> guidance to make changes, and if I did not make vague and
> undefined changes you won't publish.[54]

Books for the Hutchinson's University Library, Ruth Klauber
told Eric, 'must be written without any point of view'. This, said
Gaster, was a key contention, and he helped Eric draft a letter to
the publisher that placed a refutation of this point at the centre
of the argument. After reaffirming that it was the publisher, not
himself, who was in breach of contract, he told Ruth Klauber that
'to suggest that a serious work of scholarship should not reflect the
point of view of the author in the light of his research is, of course,

impossible, and I do not think you would seriously contend for this suggestion if my conclusions or views were conclusions and views with which you agreed'.[55]

Many of the books in Hutchinson's University Library, he noted, 'cannot be described as "informative without partiality"'. Allen Flanders's *Trade Unions* 'polemicises openly against the communists', for instance, while Father Corbishley's *Roman Catholicism* was 'a presentation of Roman Catholicism not by an impartial writer, but by a leading Roman Catholic. He cannot be expected to present the opposing views fairly'. 'A number of books in the section on the British Empire are also plainly written by authors with strong bias in its favour', he noted.[56] Eric insisted that his role as an academic historian could be separated from his role as a Communist:

> In proposing to write a book for Hutchinsons University Library I could not of course contemplate producing anything but an academic work. On the other hand I could neither, nor could I be expected to, write a book which did not utilize the Marxist analysis as I understand it . . . A scholar has certain obligations: to weigh the evidence and arguments and to judge both according to the criteria of scientific method. If he distorts or omits evidence, or neglects arguments, he is to be criticized. But he cannot be criticized for writing as a Marxist if he *is* a Marxist. If a publisher does not believe a Marxist writer to be capable of writing the sort of book he wants, he should not commission him. If he commissions him, he should not complain of receiving a Marxist manuscript (which should not be confused with communist propaganda).[57]

The publishers had known he was a Marxist but had still signed the contract with him. Two other publishers had rejected the proposal before Hutchinson took it on. Yet 'there was virtually no hitch'. Why had the book been so suddenly rejected?

Eric was by now thoroughly alarmed. This was, after all, the second book he had tried to publish that had been rejected on grounds of 'bias', following Tawney's intervention to prevent the publication of his Ph.D. thesis some years before. What most annoyed him was the knowledge that the 'specialist' on whose advice Cole had turned down *The Rise of the Wage-Worker* was clearly not as expert in the field as he was himself, though the publishers insisted he was. As he wrote to Ruth Klauber,

> I do not think the degree of expertise of your anonymous reader is very relevant to the difference between us, unless you wish to argue that my book is unacceptable because of inadequacies of knowledge and scholarship; an imputation which I should resent very much indeed, and which cannot in any case be substantiated. ... Your reader commented not so much as an expert, but as someone with a bias very different from my own but *not* from the point of view of 'informativeness without partiality'.[58]

It was clear, however, that Hutchinson were not going to budge. 'We have obviously reached an impasse', Eric concluded. The contract allowed disputes to be sent for arbitration, and that is now what he proposed. After Jack Gaster had written formally to the publishers, Hutchinson's lawyers (ironically, 'Birkbeck & Co.') responded by reaffirming 'that our Clients are not willing to publish the book in its present form'. Hutchinson had commissioned a second independent report and it had come to the same conclusion as the first.[59] Since they were confident that their position was legally defensible, they offered Eric compensation of 25 guineas (£26 pounds and 25 pence in modern British currency).[60] At this point, since the file Eric compiled on the dispute comes to an end, it is probable that he threw in the towel and accepted the offer, modest though it was. As Gaster told him, a lawsuit against the publishers was unlikely to win: 'You may find people to testify to your academic standing, but they will find more to testify that you are biased.'[61] Under the conditions of the Cold War, this was probably true.

Who, then, was the author of the damning report that caused the rejection of *The Rise of the Wage-Worker*? Properly enough, the publisher never let on. Nor did Eric ever publicly voice any suspicion of the author's identity. But he made his view clear by including in the dossier he compiled on the affair a copy of a letter he sent to his colleague at London University, William H. Chaloner, Professor of Economic History at University College, just down the road from Birkbeck. The two men must have met fairly frequently, at the examination board of London's federal history degree or at the Economic History Society. Eric's letter was addressed to 'My dear Chaloner', the common form of address between academic colleagues at the time. It consisted of a lengthy and detailed rebuttal of an article Chaloner had published in the popular magazine *History Today* with his customary collaborator, the Anglo-German economic historian William Otto Henderson. Both men took an overwhelmingly positive view of the Industrial Revolution. 'I have read your & Henderson's article in *History Today* with growing astonishment', Eric wrote: 'Whatever possessed you to lend your name to it? It just won't do!' Over the next several pages Eric took apart the article's attempted savaging of his own work on living standards during the Industrial Revolution. He warned Chaloner he would repeat his criticisms in public.[62] More likely than not, it was Henderson who penned the second damning report on Eric's book, since Cole, not himself an expert in British economic history, would probably have asked Chaloner to suggest a name.

The Rise of the Wage-Worker was never published, but the manuscript survives in Eric's papers. The eight chapters dealt with the division of labour, recruitment, education and training, the wage contract, conditions of living, and culture, with two final chapters on, respectively, the economic and political aspects of the labour movement, or in other words, unions and strikes, and the attitude towards them of employers and government, and the rise of organised socialism. At over 250 quarto pages (a slightly smaller format than the now customary A4), it was a substantial work of scholarly synthesis. The tone was carefully didactic, with explanations of terms and an avoidance of literary artifice, in sharp contrast to the books Eric would write from the 1960s onwards. Nevertheless, it did not mince its words about the process of industrialisation, which was 'almost certainly the most catastrophic historical change which has overwhelmed the common people of the world' (Ch. 2, p. 2). Conditions of work deteriorated through the period 1800 to 1850, an argument the book supported with statistics (gathered from a variety of European countries) of death rates, consumption, the height of army recruits and the like. Only in the more advanced stages of industrialisation did living conditions improve, thanks mainly to pressure from labour organisations. In Chapter 6, Eric turned to 'the culture of the workers', and here, as in other chapters, with the exception of a brief discussion of women workers, the focus was exclusively on men: a rural labourer would sing songs, 'he' would take part in village events, and 'the territory of his life was mapped and signposted'. The vast mass of research and publication on women workers, women in the rural community, women in family and household and similar subjects since Eric wrote in the 1950s has made this aspect of *The Rise of the Wage-Worker* more obsolete perhaps than any other.

One of the best sections in the book was a discussion of changes in popular culture, from folksong to music-hall, flamenco and jazz, and the emergence of specialist centres of urban entertainment like Vienna's *Prater* or north-west England's Blackpool. Chapter 7 turned to the rise of unionism, beginning with burial clubs and friendly societies, and moving on through workers' cooperatives and strike committees. In Chapter 8, the narrative turned to the emergence of political organisations, focusing on socialism and then communism. A concluding section discussed the reactions of the state to the rise of labour, with less intelligent governments attempting to repress it, leading in some cases (notably Russia) to revolution, more intelligent ones (particularly Bismarck, with his social policy) taking the wind out of its sails by reaching accommodation on enough issues to divert its revolutionary imperatives into reformist channels. Had it been published, the book would have been an effective teaching tool, informing students and at the same time providing them, and perhaps even more, their teachers, with fodder for arguments and debates.

A key point in Eric's dispute with Chaloner was the British standard of living during the Industrial Revolution. This was not a new subject, of course: social commentators in the nineteenth century had argued for the negative impact of industrialisation on the quality of life of ordinary people, and had been echoed by the husband and wife team of J. L. and Barbara Hammond in the twentieth.[63] A new generation of economic historians, particularly J. H. Clapham and T. S. Ashton, used statistical evidence of real wages to argue the opposite case.[64] Eric took a broader approach in an article he published in the *Economic History Review* (as he had warned Chaloner that he would) bringing in factors such as mortality and unemployment rates, and using detailed statistics of food prices and consumption to challenge the view that real wages had improved. The Australian-born Oxford historian Max Hartwell, who became editor of the *Economic History Review* in 1960, published a robust response, criticising Eric's statistics and arguing for a positive development in working-class living standards in the course of industrialisation. An increasingly acrimonious exchange of views and statistical evidence followed in the pages of the journal.[65]

Soon others were joining in, as the debate became a major focus of scholarly attention and entered university history curricula as a central topic in modern British economic and social history.[66] Among Eric's critics was, perhaps surprisingly, Edward Thompson, whose massive, groundbreaking book, *The Making of the English Working Class*, was to be published in 1963. After it had come out, Thompson confessed that in the controversy over working-class living standards, he

> didn't feel happy about simply coming down on your side. My position is ambiguous here, and I'm afraid the middle of the book shows this. If you hadn't pitched in and started this controversy (and no-one else has done much to help you, here) where would we be? . . . A hundred interesting questions would never have been raised. On the other hand, I have felt that you have fought too much on the ground which they chose, rather than on traditional (or new) grounds of our own; and (tho I am probably the last person to complain of this) I think you have

been provoked by twerps like Hartwell into an unfortunate tone (e.g. in this last bout in the EHR) which makes it appear that you have dug yourself so deeply into positions that you aren't ready to come out and discuss the evidence in a spirit of exchange, I wonder whether you have sometimes felt yourself to be more isolated than you should do?[67]

Thompson declared he wasn't really capable of statistical work, and confessed that the chapter on 'Standards and Experiences' was the weakest in his own book ('right up to galley stage I wondered about cutting it out altogether'). For his part, Eric considered Thompson's book important, but marred by 'a lack of self-criticism' that made *The Making of the English Working Class* 'excessively long, without actually being comprehensive'.[68]

Although the end result of the Hobsbawm/Hartwell debate might be viewed as inconclusive, it inspired a massive amount of research over the following decades. During this period, the scope of the debate widened almost continually: the original exchanges, for example, were widely agreed to have focused too narrowly on the real wages of male workers, neglecting the living standards of women and children. Statistics of the average height of children and adults at various ages, the impact of disease, and much more besides, brought new evidence into play. Broadly speaking, it looks now as if industrialisation did indeed have a negative effect on the living standards of the working class in Britain over a lengthy period, certainly from the late eighteenth up to the middle of the nineteenth century, but after that living standards began to improve – precisely the arguments Eric had put forward in *The Rise of the Wage Worker.*[69]

III

Almost from the very beginning, Eric was a pragmatist in politics. His Communism was never sectarian or dogmatic, not even in the first years of his adolescent commitment to the cause. He had, after all, canvassed for the Labour Party in 1935 and 1945. His loyalty was not so much to the Communist Party as to the broad cause of socialism in general. He had never done the things members of the Communist Party were supposed to do, publishing only in Party organs, selling Party newspapers on street corners, cutting himself off from 'bourgeois' society in order to keep his powder dry for the Revolution and his conscience clear for the socialist future.[70] He believed consistently in the unity of the Left, not in any kind of Marxist sectarianism. Privately he had harboured frequent misgivings about the official Communist Party line ever since the 1930s. But in the mid-1950s these misgivings were brought dramatically out into the open by events that unfolded in the Soviet Union.

As he emerged from the squabbling factions that jockeyed for power after Stalin's death in 1953, the new Soviet leader Nikita Khrushchev began to free the Soviet Union from the straitjacket imposed on it by the dictator. In 1955 he dismayed Communists everywhere by staging a public reconciliation with Tito, thus forcing them into their second reversal of policy on the issue in less than a decade. But it was on 25 February 1956, the final day of the 20th Congress of the Communist Party of the Soviet Union, that the decisive break with Stalin came. In a secret speech (soon made available to the world by the CIA) Khrushchev excoriated the 'cult of personality' that had been built up around Stalin, denounced him for numberless murders and atrocities, and distributed the confidential testament written by Lenin shortly before his death, warning his successors not to trust Stalin. For Communists all over the world, Stalin had been beyond criticism. Now it seemed his reputation had been built on lies.[71] The leadership of the Communist Party of Great Britain at first attempted to ignore Khrushchev's speech, censoring reports on it in the *Daily Worker* and reaffirming in a secret session of its annual Congress at the beginning of April 1956 its view that Stalin had overall been a force for good.[72] But it soon became clear that it was not going to be able to stifle debate for very long.

The lead in demanding an open discussion of Khrushchev's

speech was taken by Eric, Christopher Hill, Edward Thompson
and other members of the committee of the Communist Party
Historians' Group. They met on 6 April 1956 and issued a sting-
ing rebuke to the Party Congress for its failure to issue a statement
expressing the Party's regret for its 'past uncritical endorsement
of all Soviet policies and views'. Harry Pollitt, the Party's General
Secretary, responded to the resolution by saying a statement was
still being drafted. On 8 April, with Leslie Morton in the chair,
the Group met again to discuss the situation. The labour historian
John Saville condemned the British Party's 'slavish adherence'
to Stalinism.[73] On 5 May Pollitt finally reacted to Khrushchev's
denunciation of the purges, show trials and executions of leading
Communists in the 1930s. He expressed the leadership's shock at
learning 'that many of those who were represented as traitors to the
people's cause, were, in fact, devoted Communists, victims of what
are now revealed as deliberately organised violations of justice'.
Lessons had to be learned, he conceded, and it was important to
improve Party democracy and listen to all points of view.[74]

The debate got under way in the Party magazine *World News* on
19 May 1956, when John Saville complained that 'the tradition of
controversy within the Party has become much weaker in recent
years', and needed to be revived.[75] Eric weighed into the discussion
by demanding that the Historians' Group follow 'the new thinking
of Soviet historians' about the crimes of Stalin.[76] The British Party
needed to engage in a self-critical reckoning with its past as well.
It had failed utterly to grow into a mass movement in the UK.
The most successful tactic from the point of view of furthering the
cause of socialism was to support the Labour Party where the candidate was left-wing, and to seek again, as the Communist Party
had during the war, affiliation with Labour.[77] Yet open debate
within the Party on this and other issues was only possible if its
organs, principally the *Daily Worker*, the Party's daily newspaper,
did not try to censor or delay demands for change, and this was
not happening.[78]

Matters came to a head when Eric submitted another letter to
the *Daily Worker* criticising the Party for its decision to contest the

parliamentary seat of Leeds South in the next general election. The
seat was held by the Labour leader Hugh Gaitskell.

> The Party has decided to fight Leeds South in the General
> Election. Why? Do we expect to win the seat? No. Have we a
> consistent record of electoral activity and support in the con-
> stituency? I should doubt it. Would we be fighting it if it did
> not happen to be Gaitskell's seat? Well, would we? What do we
> expect to get out of the contest except the chance of making indi-
> vidual attacks on the leader of the Labour Party? Of course he is
> a right-winger and many of us believe him not to be a Socialist
> at all. But is putting up a propaganda candidature against indi-
> vidual rightwingers the best and most responsible way to set
> about getting Labour unity? It won't win us South Leeds. It will
> certainly antagonise many honest Labour supporters there and
> elsewhere. For Heaven's sake, let us think again about this type
> of electoral adventurism. Yours fraternally, E. J. Hobsbawm.[79]

George Matthews, the editor of the *Daily Worker*, summoned Eric
to a meeting and asked him if he minded the publication of the
letter being 'put off for a couple of weeks'. 'HOBSBAWM however',
as MI5, who had a listening device in the Party's London headquarters, reported, 'did not agree with this, and they continued to
argue heatedly'.[80] Eric accused Matthews of 'having too narrow
an approach'. Matthews 'retaliated by saying that HOBSBAWN
[*sic*] was not considering the Party members as a whole'. Eric left
'abruptly' and another meeting was arranged for the next day.
Matthews then told Eric that his letter could not be published 'as
it might be against the interests of the Party in the long run'. The
decision to stand against Gaitskell had been made by the local
Party, which was increasing in strength. Withdrawing the candidate would 'mean a public reversal, which would be bad for the
Party'.[81] Eric agreed to tone down the letter, and it duly appeared
in the *Daily Worker* after a lengthy delay, on 30 July 1956.[82]

Another leading member of the Historians' Group, Edward
Thompson, writing on 30 June 1956, compared the Party to the

medieval Church, with its habitual condemnation of heretics. There was a robust tradition of argument in England, he pointed out, quoting Milton, and its purpose was dialectical – 'to arrive at the truth through the clash of opposing views'.[83] This aroused an allergic reaction from Matthews, who had attended the 20th Party Congress in the Soviet Union in person. Thompson, he said, was painting 'a caricature of our Party', picking up all the clichés of anti-Communist propaganda.[84] In May 1956 the Executive Committee agreed to set up a 'Commission on Inner-Party Democracy' to try and get away from the 'dogmatism, rigidity and sectarianism' which it now conceded had characterised its behaviour hitherto. However, the commission was stacked with full-time Party officials and eventually produced a report so bland and uncritical that the reformers, led by Christopher Hill, produced a separate minority report (which was not considered by the Party at all).[85]

In July 1956 Harry Pollitt, John Gollan and Bert Ramelson from the Party leadership went to Moscow to obtain guidance from Khrushchev. On their return, it was noticeable that they took a much more cautious approach to demands for change.[86] Meanwhile, the debate on inner-Party democracy was taking up nearly half of every issue of *World News*. Eric contributed a long letter insisting that the acid test was whether policy could be changed from below. The Historians' Group of the Communist Party, of which Eric had for some time been Chairman, demanded an open and properly researched history of the Party in the UK.[87] Soviet historians were chronicling 'the past faults of omission, commission and even lying' in their own Party history, and the Historians' Group should do the same 'in case there were similar errors' in the history of the British Party. The Party needed to think about why its electoral record was so poor. It was necessary to realise that the Soviet road to socialism was not the only one.[88] Eric's initiative was met with delaying and denying tactics from the leadership; another official commission was set up, this time to prepare a history of the Party, but, like the commission on inner-Party democracy, it was effectively sidelined by the leadership, represented by James Klugmann. Eric stayed on as a member, but got nowhere with his arguments. Eventually Klugmann himself was appointed Party historian, and some years later turned in a chronicle of its early years that was entirely uncritical and celebratory.[89]

Frustrated by the situation, John Saville and Edward Thompson began issuing an independent, cyclostyled journal called *The Reasoner*, which acted as a vehicle for demands for the democratisation of the Party. The Party leadership 'instructed' them repeatedly to stop its publication. Party members, by long-hallowed tradition, did not set up rival organs to the Party's own periodical publications. They responded by threatening to resign if they were muzzled. The Executive Committee's response, announced in November, was to suspend them from Party membership for operating 'outside the Party organisation and procedure, without reference to the Party membership, and without responsibility to the Party's elected committees'. It was clear that the leading figures in the Party were doing all they could to suppress the debate.[90]

The crisis deepened in October 1956, after students and others in Budapest, prompted by strikes and demonstrations in Poland, demanded the resignation of the Stalinist Hungarian government, which had refused to react in any way to Khrushchev's revelations. The government was replaced by a new regime under the reformist Communist Imre Nagy, who had been sacked as Prime Minister the previous year on orders from Moscow for pursuing a course of liberalisation. The Soviet leadership responded on 4 November with a military invasion, followed by the execution of Nagy and the imprisonment of many other liberals, and the re-imposition of a regime led by Stalinist hard-liners. Some 2500 Hungarians and around seven hundred Red Army troops were killed in the violence, and more than two hundred thousand Hungarians emigrated.[91] 'For Communists outside the Soviet empire', Eric wrote later, 'especially intellectuals, the spectacle of Soviet tanks advancing on a people's government headed by Communist reformers was a lacerating experience, the climax of a crisis that, starting with Khrushchev's denunciation of Stalin, pierced the core of their faith and hope.'[92]

The British Communist Party declared that the Nagy regime,

backed by the reactionary Catholic Cardinal Mindszenty, had been aiming at a counter-revolution. The 'danger of fascism' and the restoration of 'capitalism and landlordism' had become 'acute', and there was a danger of Hungary becoming 'a bastion of Western imperialism and reaction in the heart of Europe' and thus a threat to the very survival of socialism, including in the Soviet Union itself.[93] This was too much for many of the advocates of democracy within the British Party. In a letter to the *Daily Worker*, Eric condemned the Party's intransigence on 9 November 1956. He was clearly concerned to leave the Party leadership room to retreat without capitulating completely, so he conceded that 'a Mindszenty regime would be a grave and acute danger for the USSR, Yugoslavia, Czechoslovakia and Rumania which border upon it. If we had been in the position of the Soviet government, we should have intervened.' On the other hand, he also pointed out

> *First*, that the movement against the old Hungarian government and the Russian occupation was a wide *popular* movement, however misguided. *Second*, that the fault for creating the situation in which the Hungarian Workers' Party was isolated from, and partly hated by, the people lay with the policy of the USSR as well as of the Hungarian Workers' Party. *Third*, that the suppression of a popular movement, however wrong-headed, by a foreign army is at best a tragic necessity and must be recognised as such. While approving, with a heavy heart, of what is now happening in Hungary, we should therefore also say frankly that we think the USSR should withdraw its troops from the country as soon as this is possible.

It was no good, he said, the Party suppressing or distorting the facts. This would only lose it support, as indeed it did.[94] The British Communist Party leadership had simply backed the Soviet invasion of Hungary without consulting the members at all.

Nineteen fifty-six opened up a major rift. A quarter of the Party's members resigned, along with a third of the staff of the *Daily Worker*.[95] The Party leadership condemned them all. They

were 'profoundly mistaken', it declared, and their actions were
being 'received with great joy by the Tories and the traditional
enemies of the working class'. It called on members to 'rally
round the Party'.[96] Meanwhile Thompson and Saville used *The
Reasoner* to attack the Soviet invasion of Hungary.[97] They urged
the immediate withdrawal of Soviet troops from Hungary and
the calling of a special Congress of the British Communist Party
to discuss the situation.[98] Eric agreed. As Betty Grant, a member
of the Historians' Group, reported to Edwin Payne, the Group's
Secretary, on 12 November 1956, 'Hungary proved the last straw
for E[ric] . . . Eric knows personally six people who have left the
Party.' Payne suggested to her that they should continue to treat
those who had left, such as Thompson and Saville, 'as members of
the Group, which shall in future be no longer (if it ever was) strictly
confined to Party members'. More broadly, he thought that with
oppositional elements leaving the Party in droves, the movement
for inner-Party democracy was being progressively weakened,
and this was perhaps what the leadership wanted; they would not
therefore mind too much about defections in the future.[99] On 15
November a telephone conversation recorded by MI5 made it
clear that Eric was seen as a leading, even radical, figure in this
campaign. 'ERIC is taking a bellicose attitude towards their leadership', one of the campaigners for Party democracy was heard
saying, ' . . . and he has put forward a proposal to the leadership
that he should be permitted to organise a National Opposition.'
Whether permission would be granted was doubtful. 'ERIC is
leaving himself out on a limb, which can be sawn off, which would
be a pity, as, quite apart from ERIC, it would weaken the case for
all of them.' There were, of course, 'moderate elements, who want
to improve things but not so drastically as ERIC', who had turned
down a draft letter to the leadership 'as not being strong enough.
He wants to call for the overthrow of the leadership and a new
policy.' Christopher Hill was even talking in terms of 'ERICism'.[100]

Eric duly signed a letter drafted by Christopher Hill and
Rodney Hilton, rejected by the *Daily Worker* and published instead
at their request in the *New Statesman* on 18 November, condemning

'the uncritical support given by the Executive Committee of the Communist Party to Soviet action in Hungary' as 'the undesirable culmination of years of distortion of fact, and failure by British Communists to think out political problems for themselves'. It went on: 'The exposure of grave crimes and abuses in the U.S.S.R., and the recent revolt of workers and intellectuals against the pseudo-Communist bureaucracies and police systems of Poland and Hungary, have shown that for the past twelve years we have based our political analyses on a false presentation of the facts.'[101] The letter was condemned as too sweeping by the Party hierarchy, and a betrayal of Communism because it was published in a 'bourgeois' magazine. In his response, Eric renewed his plea for greater inner-Party democracy, commenting that 'the test of inner-party democracy is, whether policy and leadership can be modified *from below*'. The Party rules, he argued, should be altered to allow ordinary members to take part in the *formation* of policy, not just in its discussion, and to recognize that wrong decisions, even if backed by a majority, could lead to 'members "voting with their feet"'. He demanded a 'recognition, by our leadership at all levels, that it may not always be right'.[102]

On 22 November 1956, at James Klugmann's suggestion, Eric telephoned John ('Johnnie') Gollan, the Scottish trade unionist who succeeded Harry Pollitt as General Secretary when the latter, ill, tired and feeling incapable of controlling the situation, resigned. The phone call was monitored by MI5. Gollan's reaction was not friendly. Eric, he charged, was misquoting Lenin, who, contrary to what Eric maintained, had not tolerated internal Party factions.

'We're now getting to the stage where everybody points pistols to our heads, if it doesn't go into WORLD NEWS one week it will go into the New Statesman the next week and I must say quite frankly I don't like the whole attitude. However it'll go in WORLD NEWS.' JOHNNIE sighed deeply having got that off his chest.

ERIC: 'Yes well, thanks for that anyway.'

JOHN: 'You've nothing to thank me for.'

ERIC: 'Well anyway, I expected you to put it in anyway.
             But well . . . on the other hand, I'm sorry about it.'

JOHN: 'See comrades want it both ways, they want to
             keep the fight in the Party and they want to keep
             the fight outside the Party. And you can't have it
             like that, life's not like that.'

ERIC: 'Yes, well I don't think anybody wants to take
             it outside.'

JOHN: 'Oh but they ARE, it's becoming quite legitimate
             now and also threats are being used and I must say
             I react to threats, you know. I've been fighting all
             my life and I intend to go on fighting and I don't
             like threats, and I don't like this type of attitude. I
             don't think it's particularly Communist and I don't
             think it's particularly comradely . . . But to suggest
             that we carry out what was in fact being proposed
             by TROTSKY, and that's what it was – 1921 – it's
             your whole reference to the Party crisis of 1921 and
             the situation then which is not the position here.
             And you as a historian, you ought to be telling me
             that instead [of] me, as a non-historian, telling you.
             You know more about it than I do.'

ERIC: 'Well I was merely trying to show that this was
             regarded as a perfectly legitimate way of proceed-
             ing by LENIN . . . '

JOHN: 'I don't think that's quite fair, Eric, and I don't
             think it's quite fair in your letter and it does your
             reputation NO GOOD (with emphasis). The way
             you've taken out the little bit of quotation which
             suits your purpose and then leave out the following
             words which shows that LENIN completely disap-
             proved of it. After all, you've also got yourself to
             think about.'[103]

The conversation had resolved nothing. Gollan's reference to Trotsky was a serious insult to Eric's integrity as a Communist and intended as such.

None of Eric's demands was met. Speaking in private, their conversation secretly recorded by MI5, the leading officials agreed that they could not be tolerated. John Williamson, a Glaswegian trade unionist and long-term activist who had been deported from the United States under the Smith Act the previous year, 'mentioned something written by HOBSBAWM and said that he was a dangerous character. [Reuben] FALBER thought HOBSBAWM was an opportunist.'[104] The Party leadership clearly regarded Eric as dangerous because, rather than resign, he was continuing his campaign to democratise the Party from within. He was also riding a coach and horses through basic principles of Party discipline by maintaining close relations with members who had resigned or been suspended. He had tried to form an inner-Party opposition. And he was campaigning for the removal of the existing Party leadership.

IV

The Historians' Group broke up under the strain of these events. More than half its members left in the course of 1956. Eric did his best to save it by proposing to extend it into a 'broader, independent, non-party Marxist Historians' Group' with what he hoped would be the approval of the Party leadership,[105] but opinion was too bitterly divided for him to succeed. One of the Group's members, Betty Grant, complained on 3 December 1956 that Eric's position did not represent the views of the Group as a whole. She pointed out that 'he and I had the strongest opposing views' and complained that hers were not being heeded. She had written to John Saville asking him to rejoin the Party, but all he had done in response was to send a justification of his actions. Saville had continued:

About the Historians' Group, I saw Eric for a short while some eight days ago and he told me in general terms what was being proposed, vis, that the new grouping was to be a Marxist Historians Group not affiliated to the C.P. I don't think there was any alternative because although all of us outside want very much to continue the personal, political and intellectual contacts we have developed over the past decade, we should not have been prepared to continue within a Party framework.[106]

Grant was appalled. She had done what she could to prevent Saville's expulsion and to help him in various ways, 'but there are limits beyond which one cannot go'. For his part, however, Saville, according to the Party leadership, 'was worried about the slackness of Abramsky and Hobsbawm; he had told them they would have to get a move on if they wanted to make any impression on the E[xecutive]. C[ommittee]'.[107]

Eric insisted that his proposals did not mean the severance of all connections between the Historians' Group and the Party. His views were being misrepresented by Grant.[108] However, on 10 December 1956, facing accusations of uncomradely behaviour from the Party leadership, Eric assured George Matthews, the Party's Assistant Secretary, 'that we are not a group', at least not an internal ideological faction, while asserting his right as an individual to do things the Executive Committee disagreed with. He defended appending his signature to another letter in the *New Statesman*.[109] With his co-signatories, who included the historians Robert Browning, Henry Collins and Edward Thompson, and the novelist Doris Lessing, he was treated to a lengthy diatribe by Matthews, accusing them of violating Party rules and repudiating the Party's achievements over the past years. Their letter was 'an attack on the Party itself'. In a private letter to Eric, dated 19 December, Matthews declared that the publication of the letter in a non-Party organ when it could have been discussed internally was reprehensible: 'I don't regard this as a very good example of honest, straightforward and above-board dealing between Party comrades.'[110] Behind the scenes, Matthews and the Party leadership, expressing their views in a typed memorandum on 7 December, regarded Eric and the Historians' Group as 'a clueless lot of scruffs, potentially quite dangerous from [a] nuisance value point of view. No clear idea [of] what they want except "freedoms" leading to party anarchy.' 'Who knows what other groups of this type may not be in existence at this very moment?', the leadership wondered.[111]

On 12 January 1957 Matthews waded in again with a long condemnation of a 'negative and defeatist' and 'un-Marxist' letter published by Eric and others in the *New Statesman* and *Tribune* on 1 December 1956. The signatories, he said, were ignoring the advances made by the working class as a result of Communist pressure since the war. They failed to realise that the Soviet intervention in Hungary was in the interests of the Hungarian working class. Their attitude towards the Party was 'contemptuous'. They were publishing in non-Party organs that habitually put 'vicious anti-Soviet slanders' before their readers. The historians' letter, organised by Rodney Hilton, who had since joined the Labour Party, and Christopher Hill, was 'an attack on the Party itself'. Party intellectuals also needed a 'sense of discipline' in 'combating petty-bourgeois ideas'.[112]

In response to this diatribe, Eric attacked what he called Matthews' 'monumental complacency'. Why was the British Communist Party the weakest in Europe, with the support of no more than one per cent of the electorate? 'We are in politics not just to make "correct" statements but to influence the masses. If we don't influence them, we might as well make "incorrect" or no statements, for all the difference it makes in practice.' Matthews was continuing to deny the facts about Stalin's rule in the Soviet Union, facts which the Party had failed to face for years. 'Many of us had strong suspicions about them, amounting to moral certainty for years before Khrushchev spoke, and I am amazed that Comrade Matthews had none. There were overwhelming reasons at the time for keeping quiet', he added, 'and we were right in doing so.'[113] He was presumably referring to the 1930s, when Communists believed that the defence of the Soviet Union was the only way to defeat fascism. Nevertheless, Eric was vigorously criticised by the historian and educationalist Joan Simon, who condemned his 'shamelessly opportunist standpoint', which discredited the cause he was purporting to represent.[114]

In a private conversation held on 28 January 1957, recorded by MI5, John Gollan, General Secretary of the Party, and George Matthews discussed Eric's contribution to the Annual General Meeting of the National University Staffs Committee of the Communist Party, where the main point of discussion had been the role of intellectuals in the Party: 'According to Colin [i.e. Gollan], HOBSBAWM had talked a lot of arrogant drivel, but Brian SIMON, Arnold (KETTLE) and Ron BELLAMY had "put up a good battle about this business of the intellectuals".' Eric's defence of the role of intellectuals in the Party indeed prompted an anti-intellectual campaign to enforce the Party line.[115] The debate continued up to the 25th Party Congress, held in London in April 1957, at which the desire of delegates for a massive display of orchestrated Party unity in the face of all the crises it had undergone during the past year brought discussion to an end. The Party faithful launched a series of withering attacks on what Andrew Rothstein, press officer to the Soviet mission in Britain, called 'groups of backboneless and spineless intellectuals who have turned in upon their own emotions and frustrations'. With great reluctance, Hill and several other historians resigned from the Party.[116] By the spring of the following year almost all the intellectuals had left.

Many if not most of them had joined the Party to fight fascism and Nazism, and to support the Republicans in the Spanish Civil War, seeing in Communism the only organised, determined and uncompromising opponent of the far-right racism, ultra-nationalism and militarism sweeping across the European continent in the 1930s. By the mid-1950s, however, the threat of fascism had disappeared and with it the reason for their adherence to Communism.[117] Most of the leading intellectuals, including Eric, gravitated towards a discussion group that came to be known as the New Left Club, or simply the New Left, organised around the

New Reasoner and then *Universities and Left Review*, later the *New Left Review*, founded by men, such as Raphael Samuel and the West Indian-born cultural theorist Stuart Hall, who were still in their twenties, with participants including the film director Lindsay Anderson, the historians Isaac Deutscher and Edward Thompson, and even the moderate socialist G. D. H. Cole. Eric was also on the new journal's editorial board.[118] He remained personally and politically close to his friends in the New Left, including Edward Thompson, John Saville, Rodney Hilton and many others. They had no real political differences beyond the merely symbolic one of membership in the Party, and they were engaged in a common enterprise to build a new kind of radical social and political history 'from below'. Eric tried to persuade the Party leadership to take the New Left Club seriously. 'Organisationally', he reported, 'it is a complete shambles and is virtually certain to go broke', but 'it appears to have a surprisingly firm, and lasting mass basis ... U[niversities] and L[eft] R[eview] meetings attract the same sort of public as the Left Book Club did in the 1930s: overwhelmingly middle class and intellectual/artistic people, vaguely but strongly rebellious and "progressive"'.[119] The Party, however, simply condemned it as 'petty-bourgeois'.[120]

Eric resigned as Chairman of the Historians' Group and continued in defiance of all the Party's rules and conventions to contribute to the *New Reasoner* and to argue for the inclusion of articles from it in the Party-approved bibliography of English history 'in the light of Marxism' he had proposed the previous year.[121] The Party leadership forbade this. Gollan said 'it was fruitless to spend 2½ hours arguing with ERIC HOBSBAWM as he would not be convinced'.[122] A meeting actually was held, but Eric refused to budge. It would be embarrassing, he said, if these articles were not mentioned. In further discussions, George Matthews

> said that if it provoked HOBSBAWM to leave the Party it would, in his opinion, be a good thing; he thought he had got a nerve to talk about them being embarrassed ... the New Reasoner was a vicious anti-Communist thing which started with the

particular object of dishing the Party, especially HOBSBAWM who writes for the Times [Literary] Supplement in the same way as THOMPSON did for the New Reasoner.[123]

The Party leadership seemed in general to hope that he might resign.[124]

'ERIC', concluded Bill Wainwright, Deputy Secretary of the Party, was 'a swine'.[125] His membership of the Party's Cultural Committee came under fire.[126] The leadership thought there was a 'good spirit' among the members, and 'all of them now, with the exception of ERIC HOBSBAWM, really talked like Communists at the meetings'.[127] Eric 'only had to sit in the meeting to spread cynicism, he did not even need to open his mouth'. However, Wainwright pointed out 'that HOBSBAWM had been completely isolated on the Cultural Committee. On one occasion he had been devastatingly defeated in a discussion by people he had thought were his cronies.'[128] He attracted further disapproval by writing, Wainwright complained, 'from the attitude of an outsider, and "not an insider"'.[129] And he should not have published in the *Universities and Left Review* at all.[130] Discussions about whether to expel him continued well into 1959, and he was taken off the Cultural Committee, but though he was always 'going to do just what he thought he ought to' and Wainwright declared 'that he should then not be in the Party and not stay in', Eric would refuse to quit and demand that they expel him, and Wainwright 'did not see why they should'.[131] 'He definitely wanted to keep him in the Party', he added, '. . . because he had great talent.'[132] Eric ('that young rogue who knows very well what he was doing', as Harry Pollitt described him) was hauled in to Party headquarters and told by Wainwright 'that they wanted him to remain in the Party and not do things that might put him out of it[.] ERIC had been frightfully upset[,] swearing that he never wanted to leave.'[133]

Eric wanted to have his cake and eat it. On the one hand he was wedded at a very deep emotional level to the idea of belonging to the Communist movement, but on the other hand he was absolutely not willing to submit to the discipline the Party demanded. His refusal to toe the line led to considerable frustration in the Party leadership, who knew his value but hated his lack of discipline. Eric was, Bill Wainwright complained, 'a bloke who had given them a spot of trouble now and then and was a slippery customer who still played about with these other b....y people and one could never get a really straight answer from him'.[134] In the end, the leadership decided he was better in than out, and reluctantly gave him an implicit free licence to write whatever and wherever he wanted. For his part, Eric began attending meetings of the Cambridge University branch of the Party and by November 1959, in the view of John Gollan, 'appeared to be much more optimistic altogether'.[135] Joan Simon agreed, reporting in January 1960 that 'he had been talking about the Party in a way he would not have done eighteen months ago'.[136] He was actually making noticeable financial donations to the Party.[137] From the Party's point of view, he was practically the only 'real' historian they had left.[138] However, as James Klugmann noted early in 1962, if he was 'quite all right on history' he was 'not so on politics'.[139] Even MI5 had by now come to acknowledge 'HOBSBAWM's own shaky party affiliations'.[140] He had in the secret service's view only 'partially rehabilitated himself' in the eyes of the Party by the end of the decade.[141]

'The thing I remember best about 1956', Eric wrote later, 'is Deutscher coming up to me at one of the first meetings of the *University* [sic] *and Left Review* in the aftermath of the rows and saying earnestly: "You must not leave the Party".'[142] 'I let myself be expelled in 1932 and have regretted it ever since', he added.[143] Isaac Deutscher, a long-time Trotskyist whose scholarly biographies of Stalin and Trotsky were earning widespread acclaim, was a significant figure on the intellectual Left. Eric took his advice very seriously. So in the end he decided to stay in the Party. The crucial thing was remaining loyal to the idea and inspiration of Communism, and to symbolise this membership in the Party, even at a more or less purely formal level, was vital. As for the Party itself, it did not in the end expel Eric, even though he was, in the words of Johnny Campbell, editor of the *Daily Worker*, not very 'politically committed to the Party'.[144]

V

Eric's quarrel with the Communist Party in 1956 cut him adrift from what for more than two decades had been his spiritual and political home. His relationship with Hélène Berghauer, as much intellectual and political as sexual, had in some respects been a continuation of his search for a comradely personal union, a search that had failed so dismally in his marriage to Muriel. It was a sign that he was already emancipating himself from this restricted view of marriage that he embarked on a relationship with a woman who was not a Party activist, at a time when he was beginning to be openly critical of British Communism. On 28 January 1956 he started an affair with Marion Bennathan, a married mature student who was studying psychology at Birkbeck.[145] She met him at a party, where she thought he had 'an interesting face, which looked not happy' but was 'sensitive' and 'alive'.[146] They exchanged love letters and postcards, planned assignations and talked endlessly on the phone when they were not together.

But she fell pregnant, and on 3 April 1958 she wrote to Eric telling him: 'So now you have a son', born the previous night. She called the baby Joshua, Joss for short.[147] Eric wanted her to leave her husband Esra, a German-Jewish exile who had studied economics at Birmingham University and became a professor at Bristol, but she refused to break up her marriage. She knew she would be happy with Eric, she told him, and she would never love anyone else after him. But, she went on, 'I would not leave Esra if I were certain that this would mean total ruin for him – either mental or suicide. I couldn't live with myself afterwards and you wouldn't be able to either', she wrote to Eric before the child was born. The two agonised over the dilemma for months.[148] Eric suggested they go to Italy. But Marion's decision firmed up after Joss was born. As she wrote to Eric:

The reasons why I can't leave Esra are strong & to you, unconvincing. Life with him doesn't get any better – for either of us.

I haven't time to write about this now. It wouldn't advance matters much if I did. It isn't and wasn't that I don't love you as much as I could anybody. But when I was thinking of & intending to leave him, I had to argue with myself along the lines of it only being one person that was being ruined. You haven't been ruined by my not coming to you (nor have I) and I have a fairly good idea of your immense need for me. And if you had been a weakling I wouldn't have been in love with you. I don't think I ever was with Esra. I married him out of my own strong needs at the time, he lacking the bad qualities that would have prevented my making of him what I wanted to see.[149]

They continued seeing each other through the following year,[150] but Eric's frequent travelling made meetings difficult and he became increasingly reluctant to meet her, not least because when they did he found it hard to avoid imagining what their life together might have been like had she agreed to marry him.[151] Immediately after the birth, Marion told her husband of the boy's parentage and he agreed that they should bring Joss up as if he was their own. She wrote regularly to Eric after that, but her letters were, obviously, more distant and formal once their affair was over.[152] Eric's affair with Marion Bennathan was, in the end, the product of his search for emotional stability in the years after the end of his first marriage. They had too little in common for there to have been any real chance of the relationship lasting. His sense of being adrift was no doubt made more acute by the end of his feeling of commitment and belonging in the British Communist Party. It was to be some time before he was to find complete happiness and contentment.

In the meantime, deprived of his substitute family in the Communist Party, Eric found another kind of substitute family in the world of jazz. From the mid-1950s onwards he spent far more time than before with its aficionados and practitioners, a close-knit group of people, 'a sort of quasi-underground international freemasonry', as he called them. Jazz-lovers, he thought, were a 'small and usually embattled group even among the cultural minority tastes'.[153] The jazz milieu combined a sense of intimacy and group identity with a feeling of being out of the mainstream and far from the centre of society.[154] Listening to jazz was always a form of relaxation for Eric, a complete contrast to the demanding intellectual world of history and politics. He enjoyed the nature of jazz as a form of controlled improvisation, especially in solo passages, in which musicians could emancipate themselves from classical music's rigorous confinement to reproducing the notes a composer had written down. At the same time, because they played as part of a larger group, jazzmen developed their individuality only in relation to that of the other musicians playing with them; there was no real cult of leadership even in the biggest of the big bands, something Eric appreciated as well.[155]

Eric felt that jazz offered a radical aesthetic alternative to 'the bankruptcy of most orthodox arts in our time'. Conventional art, music and literature were undergoing a threefold crisis, he believed:

> It is a formal crisis, which springs from the apparent exhaustion of certain key technical conventions such as representationalism in painting and tonal harmony. It is a technological crisis, due to industrial revolution: new materials and methods (methods of reproduction, for example) and the sheer increase in the mass consumption of the arts have transformed the creative situation. Newly invented arts, such as the photographic ones, have annexed a great deal of territory formerly in traditional hands. Lastly, it is also a crisis in the relations of artist and public.[156]

For while the audience for the classical arts consisted of passive consumers, jazz abolished the distinction between the creator and the appreciator, and embedded itself in everyday social activities in a way that the classical arts could not. It thus showed 'that there are other ways of developing a living and serious art than the one which grew up with middle-class society and is dying with it'. There were several obvious retorts to these claims: in the end, middle-class society proved more than capable of renewing itself and surviving, the contemporary visual arts turned out to be more resilient and indeed more popular in the era of modernity and abstraction than many had forecast, and post-Romantic, modernist music was still able to touch a chord with the public through the works of composers such as Britten, Shostakovich, Tavener, Pärt and others, as well as finding huge new audiences through scores written for films and, later on, video games. Perhaps therefore there was less cause for pessimism about the future than implied by Eric's gloomy vision of mass-produced cultural sludge threatening to drown producer and consumer alike in a morass of mediocrity.[157] And indeed, in time, Eric did come to appreciate at least some aspects of modern music in the classical tradition.

Eric's engagement with jazz during the late 1950s was helped by a dramatic shift in the stance taken towards it by the international Communist movement. The official Communist attitude to jazz, laid down by the Soviet Union, was very negative during the Stalin years, when many Soviet jazz musicians disappeared into the labour camps of the 'Gulag Archipelago'. In 1949 saxophones were banned by the Soviet authorities and thousands of the instruments were confiscated. 'Jazz', declared the *Great Soviet Encyclopedia* in 1952, 'is the product of the degeneration of the bourgeois culture of the USA.' After Stalin's death, however, some jazz musicians were partially rehabilitated and released from the camps, and in 1955 a cultural thaw allowed jazz bands to start up again in the Soviet Union. By 1957 one visitor to Moscow 'found more fanatical jazz enthusiasm in Russia than anywhere else I've been'. And by 1962, there was a thriving jazz community in the Czechoslovak Republic, which was planning an all-Eastern European jazz festival to be held in Prague.[158] For Communists, jazz, and especially the blues, could now be presented as the music of the oppressed black working class in capitalist America. And the cultural dictators of Communist regimes all across Eastern Europe had found another species of capitalist decadence to ban by the late 1950s – rock and roll.[159]

Not surprisingly, the status of jazz had been the subject of some controversy within the Communist Party of Great Britain. Party puritans who wanted a youth dedicated to political activity regarded dancing to jazz and swing as particularly deplorable. It was surely wrong, as one of them commented in 1948, 'to turn oneself into a slobbering savage, a drooling psychopathic horror, a jerking bundle of sensual emotions'.[160] This view was given full weight by a conference organised by the Party in London on 29 April 1951 on the supposed threat to British culture posed by 'arrogant gum-chewers' or in other words, by Americans.[161] The Party preferred folk music. It was closer to the working masses, or so it thought, though Eric was sceptical of events where 'the bevy of performers dressed in the sort of costume which nobody in Wisbech has been wearing since the last rising of the fenmen'. He noted the absence of 'revolutionism' in the folksong movement, and, a fatal flaw in his eyes, the closeness of its founder Cecil Sharp to the Fabians.[162] Jazz had become somewhat more acceptable to the Party by the mid-1950s.[163] Still, Eric was careful not to tell the leadership of the Communist Party about his writings on jazz for the press; when Bill Wainwright eventually discovered in 1959 that Eric was moonlighting as a jazz critic, he remarked disapprovingly that Eric 'must be making a "canny screw" out of all this'.[164]

Jazz gave Eric the opportunity to return to broadcasting, since it was regarded by the BBC as a safe and politically neutral area of culture. Discovering that the list of speakers and scriptwriters the BBC had sent to them for vetting included Eric's name, MI5 had not neglected to inform the BBC once more that 'HOBSBAWM continues to be an active Communist and is a member of the Society for Cultural Relations with the U.S.S.R.'.[165] Nevertheless, Eric did record a programme on 'The Art of Louis Armstrong' under his own name on 14 December 1955; it was broadcast in early February 1956.[166] He was not just going to play records, of course. 'On the whole', he told Anna Kallin, 'I think a biographical approach (or if you like, a historical approach) is best.'[167] Armstrong, Eric pointed out, was, 'by universal agreement, the greatest jazz-musician, or at any rate, the greatest soloist. Jazz', he added as a further selling point to the Third Programme, 'is now getting intellectually quite respectable, as I can observe among my undergraduate acquaintances; which pleases an old aficionado like myself.'[168]

Eric's presentation did not go down well with some jazz fans, one of whom ('a quiet, reasonable, intelligent and polite person called Mr. Horsman') phoned the BBC to criticise 'the Armstrong programme on the ground that it was too intellectual and patronising an approach to jazz. He felt that Hobsbawm neither understood jazz nor felt enthusiastic about it, and that he gave the impression of an intellectual trying to persuade other intellectuals to appreciate something rather quaint.'[169] As Eric told Anna Kallin:

To judge by the 'phone calls from newspapers after the BBC handout on my forthcoming Armstrong talk, there is more curiosity value in a don liking jazz than I thought. Do you remember the story of the Hollywood agent who advised Marilyn Monroe in her early days: When you go out, always carry a book by this guy Spinoza under your arm and when they ask you what it is say 'That's Spinoza; I'm just reading him'? I now regard myself as a sort of Marilyn Monroe in reverse.[170]

Kallin replied, reporting: 'We have had masses and masses of letter[s] about your jazz talk, and also some extremely silly suggestions on the same subject. I am so glad it was such a success.'[171] Eric indeed was 'staggered by the publicity-value of a don on jazz'. He too had been 'flooded by letters and cuttings which friends send me from as far as the New York World Telegram and the Wisconsin State Journal ... I gather my prestige among students has gone up tremendously, which means I am now supposed to write unpaid articles and give talks for them.' The 'main social function' of the broadcast, he concluded, would probably be 'to give schoolboys an unanswerable argument against fathers who think they are wasting their time on jazz-records. Altogether, a very odd affair, but entertaining.'[172]

Further talks followed, including one on 'The Art of Bessie Smith', recorded on 24 January 1957 and broadcast two months later.[173] Less successful with the BBC was Eric's attempt to broadcast a programme featuring the notoriously difficult German Marxist philosopher Ernst Bloch. In May 1962, taking advantage of a rare visit to the UK by Bloch, Anna Kallin managed to persuade the BBC to record a discussion between Eric and Bloch on 'Marxism, Philosophy and Music'.[174] Alas, it was not a success. 'Bloch's English is too bad', as a BBC executive reported; but even if it had been native-speaker standard, he added, 'I doubt whether one could have made much sense out of his – to quote Hobsbawm – passion, turbulence & confusion.' Since Bloch was, however, one of only a handful of important Marxist philosophers in existence, a talk on him by Eric ('his pupil, friend, acolyte') would still be a good idea, since Eric would be able to give his ideas a coherence they appeared to lack when the great man tried to present them himself.[175] But it did not happen. Perhaps Eric found the prospect too daunting. Jazz was a safer bet, even with the highbrow audience of the BBC's Third Programme.

VI

Having to pay the rent on a Bloomsbury flat instead of living in free lodgings in a Cambridge college, Eric needed some money on top of his modest academic salary. But the occasional fee from the BBC was in no way sufficient, even taking into account the fact that he usually shared the flat with a paying guest. So when he noticed that the novelist Kingsley Amis, who surely knew less about jazz than he did, was writing on the subject for a national newspaper, the Sunday *Observer*, he overcame his diffidence and asked Norman Mackenzie, whom he had known at the LSE, and was on the editorial staff at the *New Statesman*, to secure him the post of jazz critic for the magazine.[176] Eric got the job, and began work on the paper as its regular jazz reporter under the pseudonym 'Francis Newton' (the name of one of the very few American jazz musicians known to have been a Communist), taken because he thought, quite rightly, that it would not do his academic career much good if he wrote under his own name, and perhaps also because he did not want his work as a jazz critic to be a distraction for his students.[177] The identity of 'Francis Newton' was something of an open secret in the jazz world:

Dr E. J. Hobsbawm may be heard during day-time hours lecturing on history to the students of London University. Francis
Newton, jazz critic for the *New Statesman*, may be encountered
after dark in the cellar-clubs of the West End in the company
of musicians, cool and hot, white and coloured. Dr Hobsbawm
does not require a phial of sizzling chemical brew to slip into
the personality of Mr Newton, merely a few bars of *Back of Town
Blues*, a toot or two from Sonny Rollins.[178]

Nevertheless, Eric seems to have been able to conceal the existence of his alter ego from most of his academic colleagues.

Journalism was generally frowned on in academic circles in
the 1950s, as the opprobrium heaped on A. J. P. Taylor for his
regular writings for the popular press testified.[179] Since, as the
New Statesman's editor Kingsley Martin told him, the readers of
the magazine were mostly male civil servants in their forties and
led rather dull lives, Eric was commissioned to write his monthly
column as a cultural reporter rather than a music critic. While
he continued to go to jazz concerts and clubs, therefore, he also
frequented the Downbeat Club in Old Compton Street, 'where
musicians and others in the business like to drop in for a little
drinking, gossiping, watching the dancers – players are rarely great
dancers themselves – and perhaps sitting in with the band'.[180] One
of the 'Athenaeums of the profession', the club was 'easily recognisable by the clientele of men with instrument-cases and the hipsters
and night-people who cluster round them'.[181] According to one of
the club's regulars, the writer Colin MacInnes:

> The great thing about the jazz world, and all the kids that enter
> into it, is that no one, not a soul, cares what your class is, or what
> your race is, or what your income, or if you're boy, or girl, or
> bent, or versatile, or what you are – so long as you dig the scene
> and can behave yourself, and have left all that crap behind you,
> too, when you come in the jazz club door. The result of all this is
> that, in the jazz world, you meet all kinds of cats, on absolutely
> equal terms, who can clue you up in all kinds of directions – in

social directions, in culture directions, in sexual directions, and in racial directions . . . in fact, almost anywhere, really, you want to go to learn.[182]

In MacInnes' novel *Absolute Beginners*, the Downbeat Club, lightly disguised as the 'Dubious Club', was 'not a jazz club. It's a drinking club where some of the jazz community foregather.'[183]

The players, Eric reported later, 'accepted me as an oddity on the scene', as a 'sort of walking reference book who could answer (non-musical) queries'.[184] He also joined the notorious Muriel Belcher's Colony Room at 41 Dean Street, registering as member number 216 under the name of 'Francis Newton'. Its dingy and malodorous premises were frequented by a largely gay and determinedly alcoholic clientele, including the painter Francis Bacon, to whom the landlady referred as 'daughter'. Eric felt rather out of place there ('alcoholic camp was not my scene, nor jazz theirs') and did not visit it often.[185] However, drawn into 'the avant-garde cultural bohème', he became a participant observer of Soho life in the late 1950s, getting up late, teaching at Birkbeck between six and nine in the evening, then spending night after night in 'places where the day people got rid of their inhibitions after dark', mingling with rebels and nonconformists like the singer George Melly, the Old Etonian trumpeter Humphrey Lyttelton, the theatre critic Kenneth Tynan and the cartoonist Wally Fawkes ('Trog').[186] His explorations of Soho were also, he recognised, part of a wider phenomenon, the growing interest of at least some intellectuals, such as himself, with a netherworld of alternative culture in which they could escape from the conventions of respectability, control and bureaucracy.[187]

Eric wrote seven articles on jazz for the *New Statesman* from the start of his engagement as the magazine's jazz critic 'Francis Newton' in June 1956 to the end of the year, then roughly one a month for the next few years – 13 in 1957, 17 in 1958, 11 in 1959, 12 in 1960, 13 in 1961, 13 in 1962, 8 in 1963, and 13 in 1964. After that, his contributions fell off sharply in number, with only 5 in 1965. His last contribution as 'Francis Newton' was on 25 March

1966. He did not follow Kingsley Martin's request to focus on the bohemian lifestyles of Soho, and he wrote, not about the Downbeat Club or the Colony Room, but about the music. The sheer range of Eric's commentary was dazzling. Early in 1961, for example, he wrote a column on Hungarian gypsy music, which began with a virtuoso *tour d'horizon* of the folk scene across the world: 'On the whole popular music', he began, 'does not travel well':

> German military bands, beerhouse choirs of *Schlager* (song-hits) make no appeal except to those brought up as cultural Teutons. Since the 19th century, when the romantics took over a few folk-borrowings into the ballroom repertoire, European popular dances have been mainly left to their native practitioners. Zither players are left where they came from, except on the rare occasions when they, like the Greeks, the Malayan Chinese or the South African jive-bands, produce a novelty hit for a week or two.[188]

But mostly he wrote about jazz in the UK and USA. Some of the articles focused on individual jazz musicians, including Count Basie, whose big band he thought 'very high-class', though he disapproved of their uniforms ('the band appeared in a décor which looked like a design for a sea-lions' pool, and was supposed to symbolise its music').[189] However, new singers like the gospel-influenced Ray Charles, whose music Eric found generally second-rate, represented a retreat from protest into a world of private feeling: 'Charles is a star. But one cannot escape the thought that a world in which he is a star is an unhappy and a sick world.'[190]

Jazz was in decline, he thought. 'Since the middle Nineteen-Thirties jazz itself has, in one way or another, become a paying proposition, and audiences insist on hearing the spontaneous, felt, improvised music of good moods and jam sessions at fixed hours and on floodlit platforms; a demand which is as unrealistic as that which faces poet laureates.' The spontaneity that was at the heart of good jazz was getting lost, and public performances were 'brilliant but uncreative'. It was best to listen to jazz on record, since in the recording studio it was easier to create a mood than it was in public: 'The musicians play for themselves and one another, for their wives and girls, and perhaps for a few technicians.'[191] Added to the problem of commercialisation was 'the eclipse of the girl singer', because 'the mass public will not listen to women'. Only Sarah Vaughan came close to rivalling the great female jazz singers of the pre-war years,[192] although he also greatly admired the gospel singer Mahalia Jackson and a British jazz singer of a younger generation, Annie Ross, whose brilliance, however, still had to find public recognition.[193]

Eric thought modern as opposed to traditional jazz was a minority taste, a 'flight from mass appeal', even though he admired the dazzling virtuosity of Dizzy Gillespie.[194] The jazz produced in the 1950s was either 'parasitic on the achievements of earlier years' or produced by '"cool" experimenters indistinguishable from several dozen others'.[195] The restrained and cerebral classicism of the Modern Jazz Quartet rejected 'the old, full-blooded, spontaneous jazz . . . because it reminds them of oppression, illiteracy, of Negroes clowning to wheedle crumbs from the whites'. Their intellectualism staked a claim for African-Americans to make music of the same complexity as mainstream white classical music, but it would turn out in the end to be a blind alley.[196] They were markedly superior to that other 'cool jazz' group, the Dave Brubeck Quartet, whose music Eric found 'lifeless and superficial'.[197] The introverted trumpeter Miles Davis, much lauded by critics, was 'a player of surprisingly narrow technical and emotional range', and 'most of his records are not very good'.[198] The pianist Thelonious Monk had 'neither the technical mastery nor the staying power' of a musician like Ellington and often appeared to be disengaged, even bored, when he was playing.[199] Erroll Garner might have been the best pianist around in the early 1960s, but 'a great deal of his improvisation is mere embellishment; a great deal is highly stylized mannerism'.[200]

Eric thought jazz was now cut loose from its roots in the black working class of the southern states of the USA. In the 1950s, the big band was being displaced on the jazz scene by the small group.[201] Audiences were becoming more white, and more intellectual, especially in the clubs where the latest in modern jazz was played.[202] Surprisingly, perhaps, Eric found the avant-garde saxophonist Ornette Coleman 'unforgettable' because of the incomparable passion with which he played. Still, in time, he thought, 'the search for red-blooded jazz' would overcome the modernists, until 'the old-fashioned heat ... slowly melted the ice of even the coolest cats'.[203] On occasion, he could react strongly to the more outré experiments in jazz fusion music: he led a walkout of a concert at the Institute for Contemporary Arts in 1966 when a performance by Cornelius Cardew's AMM jazz improvisation group turned out to be a mix of random electronic sounds and instrumental noises far removed even from progressive, avant-garde jazz.[204]

'Trad jazz' of the sort performed by Chris Barber or Acker Bilk was a purely British phenomenon, he thought. It was the only form of jazz that reached a popular audience, mainly because it was 'today the basic dance-music of British juveniles'. It was, indeed, he wrote in 1960, 'a possible successor to the rock-and-roll vogue, which is, at last, thank God, fading away' (how wrong he was).[205] He especially admired the British jazz band leader Humphrey Lyttelton, whom he knew personally through the Downbeat Club. He had produced

> That rare, perhaps that unique article, a British band which genuinely 'jumps'. It was a memorable sight to see the noble artist and gentleman (in the old-fashioned sense of the term) heave himself up from his table, adjust a vast suit over a pink shirt and cuff-links in the shape of black poodles, and, diamond ring flashing from finger, kindness from under his close-shaven head, tread the platform like a hippopotamus, to give the blues as it ought to be sung.[206]

Apart from this, the superior quality of American bands was driving the British out of business, to the dismay of the Musicians' Union in the UK.[207] Much of this had to do with the commercial acumen of American concert and tour promoters, whom Eric regarded as capitalist corrupters and exploiters of vulnerable artists.[208] Only a few jazz concert managers earned his praise, such as Norman Granz, 'a grey-tweeded Beverly Hills intellectual' who organised the travelling show 'Jazz at the Philharmonic'. Granz paid and treated the artistes well, 'unrelentingly fought the colour bar', recorded players who might otherwise not have been immortalised on shellac and worked in the business out of idealism rather than a quest for profit.[209]

There was one respect in which Eric admired the British jazz scene wholeheartedly, and that was in its attitude towards race. Jazz clubs, he noted, were places where black and white people mixed on easy terms, and this at a time when racist white hostility towards West Indian immigration was becoming widespread.[210] 'There didn't seem to be any difference between white and black at the Downbeat Club', he noted later, 'and the young Cleo Laine was perfectly at ease describing herself as "a Cockney spade"'.[211] When racially motivated rioting spread across the west London district of Notting Hill from 30 August to 5 September 1958, as white youths, many of them fashionably dressed Teddy boys, began attacking West Indian homes, encouraged by Oswald Mosley's fascists, a group of jazz musicians and singers quickly wrote a pamphlet condemning the rioters, and followed it up with an educational programme, including letters in fanzines, mainly aimed at young white men.[212]

Eric's distaste for rock and roll only grew over time. When he listened to Elvis Presley he found himself 'retching slightly'.[213] Bill Haley and the Comets were among the 'phoniest' of musical groups, and 'the craze will have subsided before the rock-and-roll machine could come off the assembly line'.[214] The Beatles, he opined in 1963, when they were at the height of their fame and success, were 'an agreeable bunch of kids', and teenagers were currently buying no records except the ones they had made, but 'in 20 years' time nothing of them will survive'.[215] Nor was he very complimentary about the singer Bob Dylan, who played the Royal Festival Hall in London on 17 May 1964. His singing was 'unprofessional', his compositions lacked musicality and his lyrics were 'little more than pastiche'. 'It's clear – especially from Dylan's fairly numerous bad verses – that he comes from that *Reader's Digest* mass civilisation which has atrophied not merely men's souls but also their language.'[216] He asked rhetorically, in shocked terms, during one of his visits to Italy: 'Must the Platters, Elvis Presley, Bill Haley and the rest drive out not merely the old operatic arias (I have come across only one disc by Gigli on a juke box), but even home-grown popular music, which is reduced to about 25 per cent of the repertoire?' Italian popular culture was being swamped by 'a mass of drivel'. Only in the remoter regions of the south, including 'the small Apulian fishing-port in which I write these notes', did older forms continue, he noted.[217]

Authenticity was being driven out of popular culture by rampant commercialism. Mass civilisation, he thought, was becoming international. Visiting Tenerife in the Canary Islands in January 1964, he was dismayed to find the local culture all but obliterated by the cosmopolitan standardisation of the international tourist industry, whose hotels ensured that

> orange squash (bottled in England) may be ordered from waiters capable of understanding German and mini-golf is within reach. It is the sort of place where the Englishman can learn what a Finnish paperback looks like and what is the Swedish for laundry, but in which local food is a good deal harder to find – except by going into the native quarters – than Klaus's sausage snacks 'as mother makes them', which are readily available on the seafront.[218]

As for the music, 'local colour', he complained, was provided by nightclub performances of flamenco, which had nothing to do with local music, nor even with the genuine article, which he had come to know and love in Spain. In the hotels themselves, guests ate their Wienerschnitzels to the accompaniment of Palm Court orchestras, where Strauss and Lehár were played by those 'timelessly middle-aged fiddlers who are the world's honorary Hungarians ... This is the international culture of money, now democratised.'

The fundamental distinction Eric drew between jazz as an

urban folk music of protest aspiring to the status of high art, and
the commercialised products of the rock and roll industry churning
out industrialised pap, came out with particular clarity in October
1960, when he spoke about jazz and popular music to a conference of the National Union of Teachers in London. The topic was
'Popular Culture and Personal Responsibility', and it addressed
the influence of the mass media on children, and the emergence
of a new kind of youth culture that was clearly beginning to have
an effect on school pupils. There was an impressive line-up of
speakers, including the Home Secretary (R. A. Butler), leading
sociologists Mark Abrams and Richard Titmuss, broadcasters
John Freeman and Huw Wheldon, playwright Arnold Wesker, art
critic Herbert Read, artist Richard Hamilton, literature specialist
Raymond Williams and composer Malcolm Arnold. Over three
hundred voluntary associations were represented. Eric ('who does
not represent anything especially', as the chairman explained) was
asked to speak on jazz. The main burden of Eric's brief address
was 'the problem of the debasement of music by the mass-media'.
Pop songs were not the expression of creativity but the industrial product of big business. 'The actual pop song as it comes
out is the result of the division of labour and the actual creation
almost disappears.' 'The effects', he said, 'are appalling.' Teachers
could counter this trend by resisting it in the schools, introducing
folk music and jazz into the classroom rather than modern pop
music.[219] Needless to say, his unrealistic plea, which bore louder
echoes of the Communist line of the Stalinist years than the more
nuanced articles he wrote for the *New Statesman*, went unheeded.

VII

Eric loved jazz for itself, but he was also intrigued by the social
history of the jazz scene. He was fascinated by the fact that many
jazzmen died young, like the legendary Bix Beiderbecke. This was
a feature of the jazz scene that once more located it in the world of
the oppressed. 'The characteristic early dier among the old-style

jazzmen then did not succumb to *Weltschmerz* but to something like TB, induced by years of underpaid playing in small nightclubs. If he died of drink or over-indulgence, it was after a Rabelaisian, Falstaffian life like that of the pianist Fats Waller.'[220] 'The list of those who have never reached forty-five', he remarked, 'is abominably long.' There were many reasons for this high mortality rate: poor working conditions ('The average bar or club in which the working life of many musicians is passed, would not have got by a factory inspector in 1847'), an endless, exhausting sequence of one-night stands in one city after another, long working hours stretching into the night, and a low income, much of which was creamed off by agents and managers.[221] And then there were the drugs: 'Alcohol and marijuhana, the traditional stimuli of jazz-players', he observed, 'make men feel that what they cannot normally realise is within their grasp; the needle merely makes them abandon trying.' Modern jazz, he thought, was mostly played by junkies, who had become addicted for the same reasons that heroin abuse was so widespread in the black ghettos of America's great cities.[222]

The death of the singer Billie Holiday in 1959 at the age of forty-four prompted Eric to pen a heartfelt eulogy ('few people pursued self-destruction more wholeheartedly than she'); by the time of her death 'she had turned herself into a physical and artistic wreck' through a life of heavy drinking and drug-taking, her days of greatness far behind her, leaving behind records where one could still hear 'those coarse-textured, sinuous, sensual and unbearably sad noises which gave her a sure corner of immortality'.[223] The film director Joseph Losey, who had fallen victim to Hollywood blacklisting in the McCarthy era and moved to Europe, wrote a personal letter to Eric on 24 August 1959 about this 'brilliant and moving obituary of Billie Holiday'. Although he wrote to 'Frankie Newton' care of the *New Statesman*, he 'knew that the name under which you sign your articles is a nom-de-plume', adding that 'John Hammond [a record producer] a long time ago gave me your real name and telephone number and suggested that I ring you'.[224]

But all of this was still focused intensely on the music and the people who sang or played it. Kingsley Martin must have reminded Eric at some point that he was not fulfilling the brief he had given him to provide the *New Statesman*'s middle-aged male readers with the vicarious thrills that would keep them reading his column, for on 24 March 1961 he obliged in the most spectacular fashion, with a full-page article, more than twice his usual allotted length, on Soho's strip clubs. It bore the hallmarks of very thorough research and was a minor masterpiece of social history and reportage. 'With the disappearance of five major striptease clubs', he began, 'an epoch in the history of the affluent society may be coming to an end.' Strip clubs had grown rapidly in number between 1957 and 1960, spear-headed by Paul Raymond's Revuebar, a private club which opened at Walker's Court in Soho in 1958 and flourished despite frequent police raids that revealed that the customers were mainly men rather like the readers of the *New Statesman*, if perhaps politically more to the right.[225] For Eric, the strip club was no more than a business:

> Indeed, stripping is an ideologically purer example of private enterprise than most, since it can be defended and propagated by no other argument except the one that you can make money out of it. It produces neither goods nor services, for the only real service that is in the minds of the men who watch a strip is the one they will not get. Whether it could be art is debatable, but it isn't. 'I don't pretend', an honest and therefore sympathetic manager told me, 'that it's great art. In fact I don't say it's art at all. All I'm saying is the last time I handled art I lost £6,000.' It is not even a type of performance which requires any special and therefore scarce abilities and training. 'Any chick can do it if she's got the figure', is the view of a realistic young operator of one of the less eminent Soho clubs, 'once she makes up her mind she wants to face undressing in public.'[226]

The old Windmill Theatre before and for a time after the war had offered nude shows, a trend taken up by the surviving music-halls in order to stave off bankruptcy, but it was the discovery that the obscenity laws could (at least to a degree) be circumvented by turning public venues into private clubs that prompted the proliferation of strip joints in the late 1950s, and the growing competition between them pushed the better ones into becoming more professional in their presentation. One operator was said to have complained to the police during a raid: 'How can I be running an obscene show, I got a choreographer!'

Running a strip club was becoming an expensive business, and as Eric remarked at the beginning of his article, a number of the more ambitious establishments overspent and went under. These problems led in turn to the proliferation of more modest strip clubs where membership fees were correspondingly lower and the outlay and overheads kept within strict limits:

> They range from fairly elaborate set-ups to sleazy rooms with a few cinema seats occupied by single men who watch a succession of girls (interspersed by strip-films) taking off their clothes contemptuously to the accompaniment of one and a half records. Of late some clip-joints (where suckers are sold blackcurrant juice cordial at staggering prices until they realise they will get nothing out of the girls who press this and other disappointing drinks on them) have turned over to stripping ... At the bottom of the scale girls are offered as little as £1 for a five-minute strip. Higher up they may get £15–£25 (special acts excepted). £16 a week for 11 strips a day (the girl paying her own insurance) is the rate at one club, but managers tend to be chary of giving figures. Actors' Equity might well look into the situation which at present fills the West End with breathless blondes rushing from one club spot to the next.

It was difficult, he thought, for any one club to move ahead of the others, since the act at the centre of attention was almost always the same wherever it was shown, and this was a world of anonymous female bodies where there were no individual stars like Gypsy Rose Lee or Josephine Baker. The girls were not really dancers, and whether or not they wore G-strings made little difference in the end. Perhaps taking Kingsley Martin's instructions a little too literally, Eric recommended to his readers in particular the Nell Gwynne Club at 69 Dean Street, which he 'congratulated for building up a stable core of girls and a "head girl" who relies on movement rather than a big bust', and the Casino for its 'excellent costumes' and the relative sophistication of its shows.

Eric did not follow this piece up with further despatches from the underworld of the Soho clubs. Nevertheless, it marked a distinct change of gear in his writing for the *New Statesman*. From now on, his brief critical appreciations of individual musicians and bands gave way to lengthier general essays on aspects of popular culture. For by September 1961 Eric was beginning to weary of his employment as a jazz critic:

> The jazz scene seems to me at present to be marking time. I feel I am beginning to run out of different things to say about the same people repeating the same type of thing. Perhaps that feeling is worse in this country, where our native musicians are so few and unchanging – we don't often get anyone new on the stagnant modern scene – but from the point of view of anyone writing about it, it would be a good thing to have some real innovation that one could argue about. I'm already worrying what else there is to say about the MJQ who will be coming round again, and after them X and Y and Z, behaving just like X and Y and Z.[227]

Before the Second World War, the cultural independence of jazz had been preserved by its low social status, but once the first generations of jazzmen had developed technical mastery, stylistic individuality and musical maturity – roughly in the 1930s – they stayed where they were, not troubling to develop any further.[228] Duke Ellington, a prime example of this, was still great, of course, but, Eric thought, 'his orchestra will eventually die with him, and records alone will preserve his irreproducible works'.[229] Dispensing with rhythm and tonality, new musicians like Cecil Taylor represented a kind of cultural modernity that moved jazz far away from its origins.[230] As a consequence, jazz was in a 'serious crisis' by the early 1960s. In New York, some clubs had been reduced to opening only at weekends, excellent musicians were on the dole or serving in shops behind the counter, and jazz groups were playing to houses that were four-fifths empty. Jazz was 'in the doldrums'.[231] For nearly twenty years jazz was indeed to be eclipsed by the new trends in popular music, and, when it finally re-emerged, it was to cater for minority tastes, a musical niche, no longer a vehicle of moral and social rebellion against convention and propriety: the 'Swinging Sixties' put paid to all that, and the pop music of the day reflected the shallow rebelliousness of the affluent young, not the righteous anger of the dispossessed.[232]

Eric's declining interest in reporting on jazz concerts and club performances was in part also a reflection of the fact that he had by this time made a major statement summing up his views on the jazz world. Through his cousin Denis, he came into contact with a publishing house, MacGibbon & Kee, founded by the historian and journalist Robert Kee and the ex-Communist publisher James MacGibbon in 1949, which had already produced books by Humphrey Lyttelton and Colin MacInnes and was being bailed out of financial difficulties by Howard Samuel, a wealthy supporter of the Labour Party. They persuaded Eric to write a book about jazz, which was published in 1959 as *The Jazz Scene*, under his *New Statesman* pseudonym 'Francis Newton'.[233] They paid him a modest advance of £200.[234] Aspects of the book reflected the introductory survey intended by the publisher, notably the chapters on 'how to recognize jazz', on style, on instruments and on the relationship of jazz to the other arts, but mainly the book was a work of contemporary social history, and as such, it showed all the hallmarks of Eric's other works on more academic subjects.

As so often, when he entered a novel social milieu, he provided an appendix on 'jazz language' which explained the difference between a band and a combo, elucidated the nicknames given to jazz musicians and ran through the constantly changing designations of illegal substances like marijuana ('reefer, muggles, weed, tea, grass, muta, grefa, charge, gauge, hemp, hay, pot').[235] The book's range of reference was astonishingly broad, including, for example, a dismissive section on the influence of jazz on modern-ist composers like Milhaud and Stravinsky, and a knowledgeable discussion of the business aspects of live and recorded jazz. Like Eric's doctoral dissertation on the Fabians, it contained a statisti-cal appendix providing a social breakdown of its subject, in this case based on the card-index files for the 820 members of the National Jazz Federation (only sixty were female, and the rest were an eclectic mix of young white-collar workers and skilled artisans, 'cultural self-made men', often of proletarian origins, revolting against the respectability of their parents' generation and the world of upper-class culture). 'This was the world of the grammar school and the public library rather than the public school and university; of the teashop and Chinese restaurant, rather than the sherry party.'[236] The meat of *The Jazz Scene*, however, was in its account of the origins and rise of jazz, starting in New Orleans at the end of the nineteenth century, and drawing on a whole range of sources from African rhythms to gospel singing. It remained for Eric deeply rooted in the folk music of the black poor in the USA, the people who made it, and in Europe it became the music of 'outcasts and protesters against social convention . . . the milieu of gangsters, pimps, and prostitutes'.[237] However, Eric saw the rebellion of jazz musicians and their public not as the prelude to organised resistance to exploitation, but as a diversion from political action.

Some jazz experts inevitably found fault with one or other of Eric's judgements. 'This is a layman's book', wrote Ramsden Greig. 'The expert will know most of what is in it already.'[238] For his part, Eric considered professional British jazz critics hide-bound and conservative.[239] Another review complained that the book's 'seriousness is damn near intimidating', though 'the final five chapters' were 'the finest ever written about the jazz scene – from outside it'. The author was indeed 'THE expert on the long love affair between intellectuals and jazz'.[240] Similarly, another American, Clancy Sigal, novelist, screenwriter and sometime lover of Doris Lessing, wished that Eric could 'let himself truly relax and enjoy jazz, without having to rationalise his appreciation with a utilitarian puritanism which, at the last moment, causes him to hedge his bets'.[241] However, the book was slow to gain a readership beyond the narrowly specialised world of jazz aficionados. Penguin Books published it as a paperback in 1961, but when a postgraduate student wrote to the publisher a few years later complaining that he was unable to obtain a copy either from bookshops or from libraries, and suggesting, therefore, that it was time for a reprint, Peter Wright, Eric's editor, told him that the book 'was a notably bad seller in our list, and therefore now that it is out of print we cannot really contemplate reissuing it. This is very sad', he added, 'but we know of no way in which to make a success of books on this subject.'[242] Eric's belief that because jazz was shedding its links to black protest and 'becoming culturally more respectable', the book-buying public now wanted to read about it, was thus wide of the mark. Only after a considerable number of years did *The Jazz Scene* really gain a wide readership.[243] It was reissued in 1975, 1989 and 1993 (the last-named of these editions with the addition of a selection of Eric's essays from the *New Statesman*), but there were relatively few translations (only Czech (1961), Italian (1961), Japanese (1961) and French (1966)). After this, interest died down until the book appeared in Greek in 1988. Its most successful foreign-language edition was published in Brazil, where Eric became very well known around the turn of the century: royalties from the Brazilian edition of the book from 1997 to 2007 came to nearly £10,000.[244] It was reissued in English in 2014 by Faber & Faber. All in all, *The Jazz Scene* was perhaps the most enduring product of Eric's ten-year spell as a jazz critic; it eventually became 'indispensable to any jazz-lover's library'.[245]

VIII

An unexpected by-product of Eric's Soho years was a relation-ship he began with a young woman he met in the Star Club, in Wardour Street, in 1958, before it was shut down by the police (it later reopened as the Club Afrique). Twenty-two years old, with a young daughter, Jo (not her real name) was a part-time sex worker, raising money to pay for her drug habit and provide for her child. As so often when he entered a new social world, Eric compiled a glossary of the language and terminology of its denizens: 'lamming' was 'injecting drugs w[ith a] hypodermic [syringe]', 'charge' was 'the thrill got out of drugs', 'stoned' was 'drunk, more usually with pot or some other drug', 'hooked' was 'addicted', 'hashish' was 'smoked in joints (cigarettes)' and 'snorting' was 'sniffing' cocaine ('In a night', Eric added, 'Jackie S (who pushes it) says he can get through £60 worth if he's not careful. It makes people talk & talk'). His ignorance of sexual slang was sometimes surprising: 'a date', he noted, was 'to meet someone with whom one is to have intercourse', a definition that surely elided several intermediate stages of the actual process of going out on a date. More esoteric was 'a bunk-up' as in 'to give him a b-u' which meant 'let him have intercourse with you'. 'Taking a walk' was a reference to prostitution: 'a chick takes a w. so she can pick up a client. As against cars, or being on the blower, or suchlike'. 'Get down to' was 'get down to oral caresses of other person's genitalia'. 'Go out to work' was 'to pick up a client'. A 'trick' could earn anything between £5 and £10, enough to make a living from if several were 'pulled' each night.[246]

Jo was a jazz fan and a regular in some of the clubs Eric frequented, notably the Downbeat, where she often went for a drink before going out onto the streets, so they met each other frequently. She lived in a single furnished room, with two beds, a bay with a gas-ring and wash-basin, a telephone on the landing, 'smalls drying over the screens', in the Cromwell Road in west London, with another part-time sex worker called Maxine. It was a 'hip neighbourhood, and raffish'. Eric took the girls to the Tate Gallery to see an exhibition of paintings and drawings by Toulouse-Lautrec, whose subjects often included prostitutes (he 'got a charge out of the idea of taking a couple of hustlers to see Toulouse-Lautrec'). But he 'didn't think they thought too much of it'. 'In these situations', he added, 'I always wondered whether they thought my interest in them was qua whores or whether the fascination with whoredom showed. The answer to both questions is probably yes.' One evening in the spring of 1961, he recalled, 'as I took her out of my sitting room to the front door, having called a cab, I said by the sideboard: "You know, I'd like to make it with you sometime" and she said something like (resigned, accepting, not actually sighing) "Well, sooner or later it had to come"'. They developed a regular routine: Eric would pick Jo up at the Downbeat around seven in the evening, then they would go to the theatre or the cinema, and then had a meal at a steak or curry house. Sometimes they would go back to the Downbeat or on to Ronnie Scott's jazz club. Jo would take an overnight bag when they went out for an evening, and stay in Eric's flat.

'Heaven knows', Eric wrote in 1962, after their relationship was over, 'when we got to sleeping together ... I think we had our moment in May–June' (1961). He began taking her to social occasions, including one memorable party in Belsize Park to which he was asked when he was due to take her out on a date. Eric wondered whether he was presentable ('always worried about that sort of thing') but Jo certainly was ('she was an extraordinary looker that spring'). The party was 'a bit of a flop':

> We sit in the kitchen and eat, drink wine, then up in the loft-room where they have a sort of trad [jazz] group blowing for dancing. Mostly we sit round on cushions and so on. There is that actor Patrick Wymark (from the Aldwych) ... J. got more and more drunk, a Brechtian gamine-frech. Got a cab back home about 2, with J very pissed and very tender. The other guests wondering who she is, and me wondering whether they suppose she is a whore or just some chick that I have picked up, and concluding that it doesn't matter ... That was an evening when she was very loving, or more precisely when she showed her feelings. It may have been then that she told me in the cab going from Cromwell Road that once she'd thought me a phoney, but she'd changed her mind. About jazz that is. I said I knew f-all, but I tried to write straight. I had the impression she might be half in love with me. I don't remember whether we made love, but suspect that she was too stoned, and didn't

even have a bath, and left her coat in the front room. I led her half-asleep to bed and she fell asleep almost immediately.[247]

When Eric took her to see the Leningrad Ballet with his friend the architect Martin Frishman and his wife, Jo was 'both stoned (on pot) and very quiet and withdrawn. But of course she was always quiet with me, very unlike the bubbling, never-ending talk and joking with Maxine.'

Jo liked sitting around in Eric's flat doing nothing while he was writing, although he confessed he 'couldn't work much when she was around. If we had a Sunday together eventually I'd say, let's go out and see a movie. It was not boring, however.' But the affair could not last. As Eric admitted,

> I was scared. It was not my scene at all. I didn't think I could cope with a chick that took so much looking after: lazy, inert, incapable of looking after money, drinking like a fish, and obviously leaning heavily on me as on everybody else she got close to ... Except for a few nights, she never gave any sign of liking me physically and we only got adjusted once or twice, and even then I was afraid that I wouldn't have enough for her. She admired me and after a while made up her mind that I wasn't patronising her or just slumming or talking down. Well, I tried to be straight. And then, to tell the truth, I always felt I had to be careful about who I showed her off to. Some people would have taken her, others not. In a word, a combination of fear and avarice (she could get through a lot of money without knowing it) and a bit of snobbishness, but chiefly fear.

In the end, Eric felt, he wasn't right for her. Neither of them in any case was very good at saying what they felt. They merely compared notes, 'as between difficult and unhappy and isolated people who hang on to life by their finger-nails'. Jo quarrelled with Maxine and then moved out, staying in a series of cheap rooms, subsidised at times by Eric. She finally moved away altogether, to Brighton, with her young daughter. 'You know', she told Eric, 'at one time I thought there might be something with you. Not for good, but maybe for a year or two.' He was after all her 'best pal'. 'But', she told him, 'you never said anything. Perhaps that is why she was depressed. She wasn't in love, but she said we got on ok. It was cool. She felt relaxed. She dug me.'

Eric's narrative of this relationship is couched in an idiom which gives the impression that it is an alter ego that is writing. Clearly, 'Francis Newton' could be more than a pseudonym. It is difficult to imagine him using phrases like 'she dug me' in every-day conversation at Birkbeck. Outside the milieu of the Soho clubs he probably never called men 'cats' or women 'chicks'. The age gap between Eric, now in his mid-forties, and the twenty-two-year old Jo, lent an awkwardness to his account, as if he was pretending to belong to her world when in reality of course he could never fully enter it. This liaison was very far indeed from the imagined comradely relationship he thought he had had with Muriel. It was based above all on a mutual love of jazz. But he was not ashamed of it, and did not make any attempt to conceal it. In his lectures on British economic and social history at Birkbeck he would sometimes talk about 'my friend, the prostitute': it was not, one of his students thought, because 'he wanted to shock you', simply that he 'wasn't afraid' of mentioning people whom others might look down on.[248] Later on, he reconnected with Jo as a friend, and continued to support her with occasional funds until the end of his life as she made her way in the world.

IX

In conversations during the early to mid-1950s with Italian Communists, especially Giorgio Napolitano, many decades later President of the Italian Republic, Eric had been fascinated to hear stories of the millenarian tendencies of some of the Party's rural branches. He visited the country repeatedly over the next few years, often in the company of the Raymonds, using contacts supplied by the Cambridge Marxist economist Piero Sraffa but also taking advantage of the local scene wherever they spent their vacations. Elise Marienstras remembered walking with her husband on holiday in southern Italy in 1957, not long after she had first met Eric, along a lane cut into a hillside above

> some fields down in the plain below. It wasn't very high, and we saw two men in a field, both of them tall and thin, chatting as they walked round it. And I said to my husband, 'but look, it's Eric!' And it really was Eric, with a peasant. He was interviewing the peasant . . . Even when he was on holiday, he never forgot the things that interested him about the world of yesterday and even the world around him.

He had a unique rapport with simple people, she said. The peasant, she learned later, was telling him stories about brigands.[249] He kept notes on some of these trips, talking to as many ordinary people as he could. In Catania, Sicily, he came across an 'old man eating spaghetti in café outside [the] station. Turns out [he] is [the] owner.' 'The peasants today are like lords', the man said. He met former 'blackshirts', members of Mussolini's Fascist movement, who still cherished the memory of the *Duce*. 'Before the war', one of them said, 'nobody would have dreamed of having women dancing and meeting in public. Now look at them!' Catania, he complained, was becoming like north Italy, and he clearly did not think this was a good thing.[250] Eric's Italian at this time was 'full of errors', but he made himself understood, and he gained a reputation among academic colleagues in Italy by using it, however inaccurately.[251]

On expeditions such as these, Eric was fascinated by a form of peasant activism

> in which the politics of the 20th century somehow seemed to be embedded in the ideology of the Middle Ages. I also discovered the writings of Gramsci on the question of the so-called 'subaltern classes'. At the same time English social anthropologists were trying to explain analogous problems in movements of

colonial liberation. I was asked as a historian whether there had been any movements in European history similar to, for example, the Mau-Mau rebellion of the Kikuyu in Kenya.[252]

The question was posed at a seminar Eric attended on the topic back in the UK, and his contribution led to an invitation from the social anthropologist Max Gluckman, a fiercely anti-colonial Marxist of South African origin, to deliver a set of lectures at Manchester University. Impressed with the lectures, Gluckman suggested Eric publish them with Manchester University Press, with a few additional chapters. Eric completed the typescript early in 1958 and it was considered by the Manchester University Press Committee at Manchester on 13 February. The committee consisted of the Vice-Chancellor John Stopford (a distinguished anatomist), the Professor of History Albert Goodwin (a liberal historian of the French Revolution), the Professor of German Ronald Peacock (an expert on German poetry), the Professor of French Eugène Vinaver (who wrote on Racine and Flaubert) and the University Librarian and Press Secretary Moses Tyson.[253] They felt insufficiently expert to reach a decision and so sent the manuscript to John Plamenatz, an exiled Montenegrin political theorist and historian of ideas who was a Research Fellow at Nuffield College, Oxford, and author of studies of Utilitarianism and Marxism; among other works, he had written a short book *What is Communism?*, published in 1947. Plamenatz reported to the meeting of the committee held on 1 May 1958 and 'drew attention to some serious defects and shortcomings' in *Primitive Rebels*. Provided these could be corrected, however, he recommended publication. The committee still 'felt that they were arguing too much in the dark', and deferred a decision till the meeting held on 5 June. Tyson reported that in the meantime he had read the manuscript and found it 'quite entertaining and well written'. He was in favour of publication. Peacock, however, had tried to read it but it was 'too far removed from his field' to reach a judgement. Edward Robertson, Emeritus Professor of Semitic Languages, also attended the June meeting of the committee, as did the University Bursar, and a majority now voted in favour of publication.

Eric Hobsbawm: A Life in History

The book finally appeared the following year, 1959, as *Primitive Rebels: Studies in Archaic Forms of Social Movement in the 19th and 20th Centuries*. Relatively brief, at just over two hundred pages, it contained nine chapters, augmented by thirteen documents in which the 'primitive rebels' told their stories 'in their own voices'. Three of the chapters were devoted to Italy. Characteristically, Eric prepared himself for writing it by reading a wide range of southern Italian literature, part of what he saw as a 'meridionalist cultural revival'. He was particularly taken with collections of autobiographies of peasants, often based on interviews. 'All parts of the South', as this material showed, were 'primitive' in varying degrees, internally colonised by the more advanced Italian north. The remote Sardinian village of Orgosolo had been until recently virtually untouched by modern civilisation and continued to be plagued by violent blood feuds into the second half of the twentieth century.[254] The book also discussed the Sicilian Mafia and the millenarian movement of the Tuscan messiah Davide Lazzaretti, which lasted into the post-war era despite its leader having been shot by police in 1878.[255] Spanish anarchism, he argued in a chapter that recalled his brief encounter with it in 1936, appealed mainly to impoverished peasants and rural labourers, who turned their wrath on the government, embracing a rudimentary form of millenarianism in which the violent removal of Church and state would leave their villages to rule themselves. Disorganised, spontaneous and undisciplined, it was doomed to failure. To the Spanish and Italian studies printed in *Primitive Rebels* he added essays on religious sectarianism in industrialising Britain, and on the pre-industrial city crowd, again mostly in Britain, deriving from his earlier project on the rise of the working class.

If *Primitive Rebels*, as Eric later wrote, was part of the rethinking he was doing after the debacle of 1956, then it was also 'an attempt to see whether we were right in believing in a strongly organized party', to which the answer was 'yes'; but it was also a demonstration, or discovery, that the Communist assumption that there was only 'one way forward' was wrong, and 'there were all sorts of other things happening that we should have taken note of'.[256] Yet by consigning his subjects to the category of 'primitive', or in other words pre-political, Eric was slotting them into a Marxist teleology that did not entirely rescue them from what Edward Thompson, in a famous phrase, called 'the enormous condescension of posterity'. Underneath the surface, however, as John Roberts, a conservative historian working on secret societies and their mythologisation in nineteenth-century Europe, noted perceptively: 'Mr. Hobsbawm sometimes allows himself to sympathise for a moment with their aspirations and their fanaticism.'[257] The leading British historian of modern Italy, Denis Mack Smith, noted similarly that Eric's sympathy was especially warm towards bandits.[258]

Primitive Rebels remained Eric's favourite book. 'Why? I had a good time writing it.'[259] It introduced novel concepts into historio-graphical debate – 'primitive rebellion' and 'social banditry'. Eric was to return to these ideas later. For the moment, however, it was clear that his life among the marginal deviant and nonconformist denizens of the Soho clubs, his critical appreciation of jazz as a form of unorganised cultural rebellion, and his historical studies of bandits, millenarians, anarchists, Luddites and other 'primitive rebels', were all of a piece: his writing and his life meshed seam-lessly together, and the personal and professional were two sides of the same coin. This was a long way from his earlier focus on the rise of wage-labour and the growth of the organised labour movement, just as the very different relationships he forged with Hélène, Marion and Jo were a long way from his doomed attempt at a comradely marriage with Muriel Seaman.

In one respect, his turn to writing about deviant and marginal people brought Eric more tangible rewards. The success of *The Jazz Scene* and *Primitive Rebels* prompted the literary agent David Higham to get in touch with him on 24 November 1959, suggest-ing that 'we might be of service to you in relation to your work and especially over books', and proposing a meeting.[260] Literary agents can negotiate contracts with greater professionalism than authors can ever aspire to, and with a keen eye for the fine print and for clauses and conditions that might otherwise be overlooked. And at the time, they are generally far more active in seeking out subsidiary rights, including translations, always important for Eric, than most publishing houses. The meeting with Higham was a success.[261] With an agent, he was for the first time on the road to earning a real income from his publications.

X

In 1955 Eric became embroiled in a controversy with the formidable Hugh Trevor-Roper, an unapologetic Cold War warrior who had been involved with the CIA-funded Congress for Cultural Freedom. Trevor-Roper published a review in the *New Statesman* of a selection of letters by the nineteenth-century Swiss-German cultural historian Jacob Burckhardt. Trevor-Roper's enthusiasm for Burckhardt's work was testimony to the breadth of his sympathies, so much in contrast to the narrow focus of most British historians of the day. He described Burckhardt as 'one of the profoundest of historians', far profounder, he thought, than Marx, whose grand prophecies had never been fulfilled. Eric replied angrily, condemning his 'silly statements'. Why should praising Burckhardt involve denigrating Marx, who was after all a far better known and far more widely discussed writer?[262] Trevor-Roper, never one to avoid controversy, hit back, and the arguments continued over several issues. Isaiah Berlin weighed in on Trevor-Roper's side, asserting that Burckhardt's predictions had been 'of a startling originality and accuracy'. His method of studying history provided 'a powerful antidote to one-sided interpretations of the facts by the bigoted followers of many a fanatical creed'. Trevor-Roper conceded that Marxism had exerted a profound influence 'on all forms of historical writing', but if Marxist historians did make a contribution, he asserted, it was never as Marxists.[263]

Yet Trevor-Roper also deplored the persecution of Communists in the America of the McCarthy era. It was a modern version, in his view, of the witch-hunts of the sixteenth and seventeenth centuries about which he later wrote so scathingly. Aware of his position on McCarthyism, Eric wrote to him in 1960, somewhat diffidently, to ask for his support in applying for a visa to the USA.

'Please do not hesitate to say that you could not help me', Eric wrote: 'There are, after all, plenty of reasons, all valid, why you should wish to do nothing about what is, in any case, a slightly impertinent request, for which I apologise.' 'I shall certainly give you any help I can', Trevor-Roper, by now Regius Professor of Modern History at Oxford, replied, enclosing a letter for Eric to present to the American immigration authorities in support of his application. Eric was travelling to Stanford University in California to deliver a series of lectures he had been invited to give by the Marxist economists Paul Sweezy and Paul A. Baran, editors of the left-wing *Monthly Review*. Trevor-Roper's letter did the trick, along with the prestige provided by Stanford, one of America's leading universities. Eric's request was granted.[264] His visit was made easier by the fact that inexperienced American consular officials in London had omitted to ask about Eric's Communist Party history. 'No questions asked whatever', he told Joan Simon: 'there is a drill for exchange professors which avoids them, doubtless to the relief of everybody concerned, including the American authorities.'[265] MI5 was not impressed when it was informed by immigration officials at Heathrow that Eric had been granted a visa to enter the United States on 10 June 1960.[266] 'HOBSBAWM's visa application was not referred to us', MI5 complained, 'and the Americans are not, therefore, aware of his record.' But it was too late to do anything about it. The FBI was not to be informed unless it made a specific enquiry.[267]

In San Francisco, Eric was introduced by Baran to Harry Bridge, leader of the longshoremen's union, a left-winger whose connections with the Mafia were a major source of fascination for him. The union, it was clear, had to work with the mobsters because they controlled the east coast seaports. They managed to coexist with them by establishing a culture of mutual respect. Eric had already learned about the Mafia during his early researches on 'primitive rebels', and built on this in his discussions of the rather different context of organised crime in the USA.[268] He also, of course, used his connections in the jazz world to explore the clubs and concert venues of San Francisco (where he had a 'disastrous evening' trying to get Baran to appreciate jazz, not normally a taste of full-time Marxists in the USA, at a Miles Davis concert). He made new friends on the local jazz scene, notably the concert promoter John Hammond, who had long ago discovered Billie Holiday and was about to launch Bob Dylan onto the world, and the journalist Ralph Gleason, to whose house in Berkeley he often drove in the first car he had ever owned, a 1948 Kaiser 'bought for $100 and sold at the end of the summer quarter to a mathematical logician of world distinction for $50'.[269]

Gleason gave him an introduction to jazz contacts in Chicago, where he drove together with three Stanford students, each of the four taking turns at the wheel. He met Studs Terkel, a left-wing radio journalist who was on the way to becoming the pioneer of oral history in the USA, and through him the gospel singer Mahalia Jackson, whose agent Terkel had been. Prompted by hearing her sing, Eric attended a black Baptist church service. The songs, he wrote, 'rose and thundered into the heavy air, charged with enough longing, hope and joy to make even a saint forget the terrier-sized rats and the smell of stale garbage and decay which pervades the places where the Son of Man would lay his head if he came to Chicago'. It was all a show, he felt, timed to the minute, and even if 'a few women did become hysterical and had to be led out', they soon returned 'much refreshed. It was all a little like a whore pretending to a client that she is having sexual trans-ports.' Not even the interjections of the crowd were unprompted. Musically, it was unimpressive and unoriginal. It had nothing to do with jazz. But it was a great show none the less.[270]

Eric thus got to know America not only through its academic life, but also through its underbelly, through dissident Marxists, music promoters, trade unionists, gospel singers, jazzmen and the like: much the same kind of people he was moving among in Britain and France at the time. 'The men and women I met with or through people like Ralph Gleason and Studs Terkel', he wrote later, were not 'middle America'. He was to be described later in life as being anti-American, but the warmth with which he recorded his experiences in 1960 gives the lie to this accusation.[271]

On his way back from the USA, Eric managed to put in a visit to Cuba. The corrupt Batista dictatorship, with its links to organised crime, had recently been overthrown by young and idealistic socialists led by Fidel Castro, and one of them, Carlos Rafael Rodríguez, invited Eric, along with Baran and Sweezy, for a visit. At this time, the revolution had not yet turned Communist, as Eric quickly realised, so it was still possible to travel directly between Cuba and the USA. He arrived in Havana and found time to travel a little and improve his already competent Spanish. Writing in the *New Statesman* on 22 October 1960, he enthused about the socialisation of the factories and plantations, and quoted a friend who declared that 'this is a good revolution. There was no blood-bath ... Nobody is being tortured any more.'[272] On his return to England, Eric briefed the International Affairs Committee of the Communist Party on the state of affairs in Cuba. Castro, he said, 'began as a very muddled person', but after coming to power he had gone further than he had originally intended, above all in land reform. Communism was influential within the Castro movement but still did not dominate it. He urged visits to the island, closer trading ties and an educational effort of a non-political kind.[273]

Before long, however, US–Cuban relations had deteriorated sharply, pushed in a negative direction by the geopolitical concerns of the administration of President John F. Kennedy and the campaigning of the growing number of right-wing, middle-class refugees who were fleeing the island and taking up residence in Florida. Kennedy soon decided on direct action. On 15 April American planes bombed Cuban airfields in advance of a CIA-sponsored paramilitary group which landed at the Bay of Pigs in Cuba on the night of 16/17 April with the intention of overthrowing Castro. The invasion was a fiasco. Cuban intelligence had learned of the invasion before it took place. Within three days the incursion had been defeated. The attack prompted widespread outrage among sympathisers with the Cuban revolution. Eric wrote to *The Times* condemning the American invasion as an assault on democratic values, since Castro clearly had the support of the majority of the Cuban people.[274] In the UK, the theatre critic and writer Kenneth Tynan, whom Eric knew from the Downbeat Club, decided to launch a campaign in support of Castro.[275]

On 16 April Tynan telephoned Eric, came round to his flat in Gordon Mansions and won him over to the cause. A formal meeting was held with the actor, writer and literary agent Clive Goodwin (who, according to Eric, 'acted as Ken's Man Friday in those days'), the novelist Penelope Gilliatt, who soon afterwards married the playwright John Osborne, and the loquacious Welsh trade unionist Clive Jenkins, at Eric's flat, and a few days later, on 28 April, the British Cuba Committee was set up. The Committee's members, Eric among them, approached a series of prominent people they knew to sign protests, including the left-wing Labour MP, writer and journalist Michael Foot. They organised more meetings, held in Penelope Gilliatt's flat in Lowndes Square, and a demonstration march was assembled in Soho Square in May. As Eric remembered:

> It took place on Sunday 23 . . . [and] people came back to have drinks at my place after it. Perhaps a party Ken organized in Mount Street on the 18th helped to mobilize his friends. I remember the occasion of the demo more vividly than the date – we marched along Oxford Street and into Hyde Park, and the occasion was remarkable for the largest concentration of stunning-looking girls – [from] theatre and model agencies presumably – that I've ever seen on a political demo.[276]

The Communist Party was not involved, a fact for which an angry and disappointed leadership blamed Eric's lack of commitment to it. The MI5 bugging device installed in the Party's headquarters in London recorded one official saying: 'Well we all know HOBSBAUM [*sic*] you know and if there's any b----y reason as to – for keeping us (out?) he'll be the main man in getting this done.'[277]

Tynan followed up the demonstration by sending a strongly worded letter to the *Observer* newspaper, proposing a delegation to visit Cuba to show solidarity with the revolutionaries. After many delays, a group from the Committee, including Eric, Clive

Goodwin and the printers' union leader Richard Briginshaw (whom Eric described as 'not without an interest in foreign nooky'), decided to fly to Cuba towards the end of the year. They had to travel via Prague, since the tightening of American sanctions meant that there were now no flights to Cuba from non-Communist countries. The group was initially accompanied by Joan Littlewood, founder and director of the left-wing Theatre Workshop in Stratford, east London, but, as Eric reported, 'she made it with us to Prague but the endless delays snapped her patience. She insisted on being disembarked from the plane as it waited on the airport for another delay of unspecified length, and the last we saw of her was a small figure alone on the tarmac walking back to the terminal.'[278] The plane took off but got into difficulties and had to turn back. The flight was rescheduled for the New Year. Meanwhile, the British Communist Party discovered the composition of the delegation and succeeded in getting two more acceptable delegates, the Communist fellow-traveller and recipient in 1954 of the International Stalin Peace Prize Denis Pritt, and a member of the Party executive, Arnold Kettle, added to the group along with Eric, 'who', MI5 reported, 'is not held in high regard by the C.P.G.B'.[279]

Eric made it to Cuba in January 1962 with the rest of them apart from Littlewood and with the addition of the two Communist appointees, some assorted nuclear disarmers and left-wing activists and 'a young, fast-talking African' whom he saw as 'a black confidence man exploiting the ignorance or anti-imperialist reflexes of white progressives' (the Cubans refused to have anything to do with him). Once in Cuba, as Pritt reported to the Party leadership when they eventually got back to the UK, they had discovered that 'the interpreters had been simply dreadful, and PRITT himself had been guilty of the crack that nearly everybody in Cuba spoke English, except the interpreters! They had been compelled to use HOBSBAWM as interpreter on several occasions and he had done pretty well.' Overall, indeed, as Pritt reported with evident disappointment, 'that nasty piece of work ERIC HOBSBAWM had behaved very well'.[280] Indeed, he had translated a speech by Che Guevara, who was taking Castro's place in a meeting held at the former Hilton Hotel in Havana. Guevara, he reported, was a fine figure of a man, though he had nothing much of interest to say.[281]

One member of the delegation reported on its activities to the security services, though he had little to say about Eric, since, as the informer told MI5, Eric 'did not go around with the group much in Cuba largely because he had his own contacts which he met during a previous visit to Cuba about nine months ago'.[282] One of these contacts, the Director of a new Institute of Ethnology and Folklore, Argeliers León, showed him round the black *barrios* of Havana, where Eric did not miss out on the opportunity to sample the local musical scene. Religious tradition and African strains were still evident when ritual fraternities celebrated the anniversary of the consecration of their drums, all wearing green and yellow sashes, the colours of the Virgin of the Cobre:

> The same four drums and two hand-bells (struck with sticks) beat out the same few figures endlessly, while the dancers step singly on to the floor, to dance until possessed, until the lady of the house serves beer, coca cola and sweet cakes, or until they take their leave by kissing each drum in turn. The sound of the drums spreads across the quiet Sunday afternoon in Guanabacoa, a suburb of Havana. Across the next-door fence two tiny children are gently and separately doing the twist in a dirt yard. Down the road a mulatto girl in a yellow dress, arrested by the drums halfway on an errand, shakes her hips quietly in the sunlight. I am, I suppose, watching the ever-repeated re-birth of Cuban popular music. African rhythms once more break loose from their ritual origins, to be fused with European elements for the secular entertainment of a Cuban suburb.[283]

The revolutionary regime led by Fidel Castro had done its best to encourage such traditions of folk music alongside more commercial strains. Eric was enthused: he thought that 'the present evolutionary stage of Cuban music corresponds to that of American jazz before it left the South'.

Eric's friendship with Kenneth Tynan brought him into contact with circles far removed from the world of academia. In May 1973 Tynan invited Eric to a party he was throwing at the Young Vic for his daughter Tracy's twenty-first birthday. The guests included the comedians Eric Morecambe and Frankie Howerd, the philosopher Freddie Ayer, the singer Liza Minnelli, the film stars Peter Sellers and Lauren Bacall, the novelist Edna O'Brien, the composer Stephen Sondheim and the Marxist writer Robin Blackburn. Entertainment was provided by the pianist and comedian Dudley Moore, the satirist John Wells and ('disastrously') the music-hall artiste Max Wall. 'A wild mixture of people', Tynan exulted.[284] The eminent theatre critic ended the evening snorting coke in the wings with his daughter, whose later volume of memoirs gave a vivid account of the occasion, along with colourful details of her parents' turbulent marriage ('watching them was like watching a horror movie').[285]

XI

As Robin Marchesi remarked, his mother Nancy used to say of Eric, her brother: 'He's such an ugly man, I just can't understand why all those women are attracted to him!'[286] 'He was horribly ugly', Elise Marienstras agreed, but 'he loved women' and they were attracted to him: he was fit and physically active; it was only his face that seemed ugly.[287] Some women are in any case attracted to intelligent and knowledgeable men whatever their appearance, and Eric was also a good listener, endlessly fascinated by people and the stories they had to tell. Through the 1950s he had been engaged in a search for marital happiness and emotional stability. Although he had recovered from the break-up of his marriage to Muriel by the middle of the decade, success in the search for a long-term relationship had eluded him. In November 1961, all this changed, when Marlene Schwarz came into his life.[288] Born in Vienna in 1932 into a secular Jewish family, she was the third child of the Tyrolean-born Theodor Schwarz, a businessman in the textile industry, and his wife Louise, known as Lilly. She had two older brothers, of whom the elder,

Victor, eventually took over their father's business, while the middle child, Walter, became a well-known foreign correspondent, working for the *Guardian* newspaper. In September 1937, suspecting earlier than most that Hitler was going to invade Austria, Theodor had taken the family to London, moving to Manchester the following year.[289] Marlene had gained her school certificate at Manchester High School for Girls after the war, following a brief and unhappy period as an evacuee and then at a Quaker boarding school. Her gregarious father's circle of friends had included, among others, the historian A. J. P. Taylor, who was then teaching at Manchester University. Among Marlene's many attractions for Eric was the fact that she spoke fluent French and was well versed in French literature and culture. Her father was a great Francophile, and his influence had led to her travelling to Paris to work for a family as an *au pair* for a year, after leaving school in 1949, in order to learn French. In the mornings she took French language classes at the Alliance Française. One of the teachers asked her to live with her and her husband and look after her new-born baby, so she agreed, and for her second year in Paris she took a French literature class held by the Alliance Française jointly with the Sorbonne. She used her spare time to explore Paris with her friends and perfect her command of French.

Eric's friend Elise Marienstras found Marlene characterised 'at the same time by beauty and culture, elegance and warmth. But clearly very English.'[290] In London, Marlene had an active social life that included regular Thursday evening 'at home' occasions with her brothers and guests, listening to records and consuming simple refreshments. Among the friends she made at these events was the Vienna-born young Tom Maschler, who worked for the publisher André Deutsch and later became a distinguished publisher himself, so to a degree she was already moving in the world of literature and journalism. By the mid-1950s, she had learned a range of secretarial skills, which provided her with the qualifications for her first job, as the subscription and distribution secretary on *Pulpit Monthly*, a magazine whose principal function was to supply draft sermons to clergymen. Mariella de Sarzana, an Italian girl with whom she shared lodgings in Putney, invited her to come to Rome, and while visiting the island of Capri, Marlene fell in love with the country and decided to live there. In 1955 she obtained employment at the United Nations Food and Agricultural Organization, based in the Italian capital. She stayed for five years, using her holiday time to tour the peninsula with her boyfriend Osvaldo. Mariella was trying to get into the entertainment business, and wanted a career in Hollywood, and through her Marlene met the music-hall singer Gracie Fields and the film star Kirk Douglas, whom the two young women accompanied on a train journey from Naples to Rome, enjoying Douglas's flirtatious attentions. By the end of the period Marlene was fluent in Italian as well as French.

In 1960 a deep and violent political crisis in the Congo, which achieved independence from Belgium in June, led to the United Nations sending in a peacekeeping force that eventually numbered twenty thousand troops. Marlene answered a call for volunteers to help the mission, and after visiting her family in London, she travelled to Léopoldville (now Kinshasa), where she looked after the welfare and leisure activities of the mostly American members of the UN mission, which arrived in late July 1960. Her job involved organising supplies of books, films and sports equipment and putting on entertainment events for the troops. Marlene socialised in the evenings and at weekends with the foreign press corps. At one of their parties, in 1961, a young army officer, Joseph-Désiré Mobutu, a former aide of the left-wing nationalist Prime Minister Patrice Lumumba, who had made him army chief of staff, asked Marlene to give him English lessons, but she wisely declined (she was about to leave the country anyway); a cruel and ambitious man, Mobutu had already staged a coup with Belgian assistance in 1960 and had Lumumba murdered. In 1965 he established a military dictatorship which quickly became known for its corruption and brutality and lasted until his overthrow in 1997.

Arriving back in London from an increasingly violent and unstable Congo, Marlene obtained a position as personal assistant to Garran Patterson, European News Supervisor at the London offices of the Canadian Broadcasting Corporation. At this time her brother Walter lived with his wife Dorothy and their small children in Hampstead Garden Suburb, and often threw dinner parties for their friends and acquaintances. Dorothy was studying history part-time as a mature student at Birkbeck, and her MA thesis was being supervised by Eric, and so she invited him to one of their dinner parties in November 1961. The party was a success. Eric had far more in common with Marlene than with any of his other girlfriends, even Hélène: not just Viennese background and French culture but also a shared knowledge and love of Italy. Although Marlene was not a Communist, she was certainly on the left, and Eric found her experiences with the United Nations and in the Congo instantly fascinating. Afterwards, neither Eric nor Marlene could remember anything about the other people who had been present. Marlene was sharing her brother Victor's large West End flat in the elegant surroundings of Mansfield Street with two other young women while he was away on a lengthy foreign trip, and they decided to hold a dinner party of their own, inviting one male friend each. Marlene phoned Eric to ask him if he would come. Luck came to their aid: it was precisely at this time that the plane carrying Eric and his fellow delegates from Prague to Cuba developed an engine fault and had to turn back, leaving Eric to make his way back to London to an empty flat and an empty diary, nothing to eat and nothing to do, as he told her. Eric accepted Marlene's invitation with enthusiasm. 'What are you doing NOW?', he asked when she phoned him, consumed with interest in her. Immediately after his return from his visit to Cuba in January 1962, he started going to jazz clubs, classical music concerts, plays and films with her. Soon they were in love. Gradually he introduced her to his friends, both the bohemian ones in London and the academic ones in Cambridge, where Noel Annan's wife Gabriele later told her they were curious about her because they had thought Eric was a confirmed bachelor and unlikely to marry outside the Communist milieu: expecting to meet a severe and committed Marxist, they were pleasantly surprised to find Marlene nothing of the sort.

Eric had organised a three-month tour of Brazil, Argentina, Chile, Peru, Bolivia and Colombia to begin at the end of October 1962, sponsored by the Rockefeller Foundation, to research

'primitive rebels' in Latin America. Persuaded by Eric's application, the Rockefeller Foundation gave him the grant, and he
booked a flight to Buenos Aires for 31 October. The Cuban missile
crisis, sparked by the Soviet Union's decision to site nuclear missiles
on Cuban soil and US President John F. Kennedy's declaration
that he would resist this action by force if necessary, had broken out
in early October, and the threat of a nuclear war between the two
superpowers was reaching its terrifying height. As they watched
a performance by the George Shearing jazz quintet, which Eric
had agreed to review for the *New Statesman*, and discussed the
upcoming UK tour by Bob Dylan, Eric suddenly said to Marlene:
'I think we should get out our diaries, and find time for a wedding
before I leave.'

She agreed, and they booked a register office. Since the booking
required a three-week wait before the ceremony took place, they hur-
riedly arranged a pre-marital honeymoon, for which they travelled
to Bulgaria, going to the opera in Sofia and relaxing on the beach at
a Black Sea resort. On their return, they got married at Marylebone
Registry Office. Eric's best man was the architect Martin Frishman,
and a small reception was held at the Schwarz family home in Golders
Green. After spending a weekend on a brief second honeymoon in
Castle Combe, a quintessentially English village in Wiltshire, where
Eric drove them in a car kindly lent him by Marlene's brother Victor,
they returned, and Eric prepared to depart. Scruffily dressed as usual
(Marlene had not yet got to work on his wardrobe), Eric looked older
than his years 'Is your father going to Buenos Aires?' an official at
the airport asked Marlene, to her great amusement. 'Should things
go wrong and the US and Russia go to war', Eric said to her as they
parted, 'then get yourself a one-way ticket to Buenos Aires – there's
enough money in the bank, and I'll meet you.'[291]

7

'Paperback Writer'

1962–1975

I

Before he departed for South America, Eric had already taken his first steps towards writing serious history for a readership beyond the limits of academia. Doing this while pursuing an academic career was by no means easy, as he remembered later:

> That was a time when British academic historians would have been shocked to think of themselves as potential paperback writers, i.e. writers for a broad public. Between the world wars hardly any historians of standing did, other than G. M. Trevelyan. Many of them even shied away from writing books of any kind, hoping to make their reputations with learned articles in specialist journals and savage reviews of other colleagues unwise enough to bare themselves between hard covers. For much the same reasons they kept away from writing history for schools, which was left to schoolmasters, two of whom produced the classic send-up of secondary, as distinct from university history: Sellar and Yeatman's *1066 and all That*. All this has changed. My own generation, especially those passionate expositors and popular educators, Marxists and other radicals, wrote eagerly, both for the academic specialists and the non-specialist public. Publishers, increasingly advised by academics, soon noticed that

the learning public grew spectacularly, as higher secondary and university education expanded, and the chasm between sixth-form and college-level disappeared.[1]

This consideration was what lay behind the book that first brought him to the attention of the wider reading public: *The Age of Revolution*, published in October 1962, just about at the moment when Eric was getting married again and departing for his Latin American tour. The book was squarely aimed at 'that theoretical construct, the intelligent and educated citizen', not talking down to the public but 'only making serious thought more accessible'.[2]

The Age of Revolution owed its existence to the vision of George Weidenfeld, a Viennese-born publisher who had conceived the ambitious idea of commissioning a forty-volume *History of Civilization* covering the whole of the globe and the entirety of the past. Weidenfeld had teamed up in 1949 with Nigel Nicolson, son of the diplomat and diarist Harold Nicolson and his wife the novelist Vita Sackville-West, to form a new publishing house, Weidenfeld & Nicolson (the ampersand was in the name from the very beginning), specialising in non-fiction. Weidenfeld sold the translation rights of the books on signature to foreign publishers and used some of the money to pay the authors advances they were unlikely to get elsewhere. Advised by three Oxford grandees – the Regius Professor of Modern History at Oxford, Hugh Trevor-Roper, the philosopher Sir Isaiah Berlin and the ancient historian Sir Ronald Syme – he commissioned forty titles from a wide range of historians in a number of countries. For nineteenth-century Europe, he turned first of all, most probably on Berlin's prompting, to the Polish-Israeli historian Jacob Talmon, who had studied in France and obtained a doctorate from the LSE. Talmon was fiercely anti-Communist, and had won fame with his two-volume work *The Origins of Totalitarian Democracy* (1952, 1960), in which he traced the 'political Messianism' of the Bolsheviks back to the writings of Jean-Jacques Rousseau. However, Talmon withdrew from the commission after a few months, and so, perhaps now following a suggestion from Trevor-Roper, they turned to Eric, whose writings on the seventeenth-century crisis, the English working class and the 'primitive rebels' of Spain and Italy had demonstrated a similar breadth of knowledge to Talmon's.[3] Weidenfeld duly signed him up. This was a bold move, given the fact that Eric was a known Communist. It proved to be a canny one.[4]

Eric was already well prepared with a set of Birkbeck lectures on modern European history which he quickly used as the basis for *The Age of Revolution*, adding in other material which he also presented in lecture form as he went along.[5] His style of exposition surely derived not least from the experience of teaching Birkbeck students, all mature part-timers who had spent years away from formal education and thus constituted exactly the kind of intelligent general public to whom these books were addressed:

> As a lecturer I know that communication is also [a] form of show-biz. We are wasting everyone's time if we cannot keep the attention of audience or reader. I have tried three ways of holding it: communicating passion (i.e. the writer's conviction that the subject is important), writing that makes readers want to read the next sentence – and the right dosage of light relief and sound-bites. I have usually tried out my books first as student lecture courses because lecturing is a good way of testing whether a historian holds his audience. It also gives the writer what he or she must otherwise construct in the mind: an actual body of people to whom we address and who must understand our message. However, the spoken word is not writing, which has to be learned, and above all, practised, like an instrument – and words are the writer's instrument, his 'style' is what his 'sound' is to a musician. Journalism (i.e. good editing) has probably taught me most about the craft of writing, not least how to write non-technically for non-specialists and how much can be fitted into a prescribed length.[6]

A clear, plain style was what suited academic writing best, and in this respect modern historians were on the whole no worse than their predecessors. Indeed, Eric thought that 'we are living in something like a golden age of popularization'.[7]

Eric laid out the basis of his approach to historical synthesis in a lengthy article published in the *Times Literary Supplement* in October 1961, entitled 'A New Sort of History: Not a Thread but a Web'. A history based on a chronological political narrative like the standard textbook by Grant and Temperley, *Europe in the Nineteenth and Twentieth Century*, could 'neither be written today, nor indeed – in view of its omissions – can it be read with profit'. The encapsulation of history into discrete national components was being superseded by a transnational approach as the links between the writing of history and nation-building were being severed. It was thus entirely possible to discuss trends in history on a genuinely European basis.[8]

Eric identified three counter-currents acting against the conservative modes of writing history that had taken hold in Britain after the First World War, removing the liberal and leftist domination of the historical profession up to that point: Marxism, the *Annales* school of historians and the social sciences. 'None of comparable, or indeed of any real significance has come from the traditional branches of history.'[9]

The Age of Revolution was determinedly thematic and analytical, and threw the British tradition of political narrative overboard. It covered the whole gamut of European civilisation, not just politics but also the economy, society, culture, the arts and sciences. And it portrayed Europe in the broader context of global history in a way that was entirely new and had few imitators until the arrival of 'global history' in the early twenty-first century. The book's 'combination of analytic and synthetic history', Eric thought, 'comes straight from the Marxist inspiration'.[10] But it is also plausible to see its focus on the *longue durée*, its avoidance of political narrative and its aspiration to total history, as reflecting the influence of the *Annales* school. Indeed, some years later, Noel Annan reported that it 'was regarded by the Annalistes – and not only by them – as a contribution to history fit to be mentioned in the same breath as Braudel's history of the Mediterranean'.[11]

The Age of Revolution was not just a general survey of European history between 1789 and 1848: it was also a book with a thesis. Its intention, as Eric explained in the Preface, was to trace the impact of the 'dual revolution', the French political and ideological revolution of 1789 and the British Industrial Revolution of roughly the same time, on the world. 'If its perspective', he explained, 'is primarily European, or more precisely, Franco-British, it is because in this period the world – or at least a large part of it – was transformed from a European, or rather a Franco-British base.' Typically, and in a manner he had done so many times before in writing about other topics, Eric began the book with a list of words, 'industry', 'railway', 'liberal', 'scientist' and so on; the fact that so many concepts came into being during this period was an indication of the profundity of the changes it underwent. The age of revolution saw the foundation of the modern world. And indeed, the concept of the 'dual revolution' has had a huge influence on history writing and teaching in the last half-century and more, particularly in Germany, where, for example, it forms the central binding idea of the second volume of Hans-Ulrich Wehler's monumental *Deutsche Gesellschaftsgeschichte*.[12]

The book's structure embodied its central methodological premise, that the economy or, to use the Marxist term, mode of production determined everything else; so it began with an account of the Industrial Revolution. Already in this opening section its profound originality is evident. The global perspective adopted in *The Age of Revolution* ascribes the Industrial Revolution in Britain not to any supposed technological or scientific superiority on the part of the British, but to Britain's command of the seas, especially after 1815, which enabled it to create a virtual monopoly of cotton exports to India and Latin America. Eric's account of the French Revolution followed in most respects the standard Marxist interpretation of the day, dominated by the great French historian Georges Lefebvre.[13] The Third Estate is equated with the bourgeoisie, a 'coherent social group', driving political change when the French monarchy, plunged into a deep financial crisis following the War of American Independence, lost the support of the feudal aristocracy.[14] The *sans-culottes* whose street demonstrations and revolts radicalised the revolutionary process are described as the petty bourgeoisie, fighting back the tides of history; a proletariat would only come into existence in the nineteenth century, with industrialisation.[15] Unlike Lefebvre, Eric did not ascribe any notable role to the peasantry, a social group he considered, in the light of the studies he gathered in *Primitive Rebels*, to be 'pre-political': 'The peasantry never provides a political alternative to anyone', Eric remarked; 'merely, as occasion dictates, an almost irresistible force or an almost immovable object.'[16]

The book met with an ecstatic reception from fellow historians on the Left, who realised its achievement in bringing Marxist interpretations to a wide readership. Edward Thompson wrote congratulating Eric on his 'splendid book; your ability to say something both profound and original and *with brevity* (!) is one I should try to school myself at' (he never did).[17] The Austrian Communist literary scholar and philosopher of art Ernst Fischer particularly enjoyed the seamless way in which the book integrated economy and society, statistics and anecdotes, culture and politics. 'This is the way one should write history', he remarked. Marxism was applied without jargon: 'The innocent reader has no idea why the matter tastes so good, and digests the Marxism as if it was a stimulating spice.'[18] Eric's friend Victor Kiernan paid tribute, in a lengthy appreciation in the *New Left Review*, to the book's easy readability. 'Marxist and other socialist authors there have been who were inclined to drive and dragoon their readers, but Hobsbawm is not one of them.'[19]

In the political and historiographical mainstream, economic historians were kinder to the book than political historians were. The American economic historian Rondo Cameron, a specialist in French business history, declared *The Age of Revolution* 'a real tour de force', though he had some reservations about the 'chronological bifurcation' involved in the division of topics into the two parts of the book, between 'developments' and 'results'.[20] Jacob Talmon, the historian originally nominated to write the volume by Weidenfeld and his advisers, considered that *The Age of Revolution* showed some influence of Marxism, but it was 'revisionist' rather than orthodox. 'There is little in it that a progressive liberal or even enlightened conservative might not have said, if with more reservations and greater qualifications.' The major problem with it, he thought, was its massive underplaying of nationalism as a cause of the 1848 revolutions. This was, indeed, far from the last time that Eric was accused of misunderstanding the role of nationalism in the history of nineteenth-century Europe.[21] The political historian G. R. Potter felt the book concentrated excessively on the economy: 'George III and George IV are not mentioned, Wellington receives praise for his cook, and the Napoleonic Wars are discussed in a few paragraphs.' Clearly, this was not the sort of textbook to which Potter, editor of one of the volumes in the *New Cambridge Modern History*, was accustomed.[22]

The political writer Max Beloff was the only reviewer to spot the French influences on Eric's approach, though he commented that 'he either lacks the capacity of the French school (or has not been given the scope) to drive home the facts of demography, economics and cultural change by a more intensive and imaginative use of charts, diagrams and maps'.[23] Beloff was also right in thinking that publishers in Britain had always fought shy of including such graphic devices in books intended for the general reader. The general reader fights shy of them too. More generally, Eric's Marxism, at a point when the Cuban missile crisis had plunged the Cold War into deep-freeze once more, aroused allergic reactions in the most conservative reviewers. Irish historian T. Desmond Williams found Eric 'too often captive to the philosophy he has unobtrusively adopted'. Thus he underplayed the role of religiously motivated social reformers: 'Lord Shaftesbury, needless to say, does not figure in this world.' Nevertheless, even the conservative Irish professor had to admit that the book made history come alive, as the *New Cambridge Modern History* did not. 'This is', he wrote, in a compliment that was nothing if not backhanded, 'television treatment at its most expert and cocky.'[24]

At the same time, however, not every reviewer was convinced by the book's central thesis of the 'dual revolution' that, in different ways, brought the bourgeoisie to power. Asa Briggs, writing (anonymously, as was the journal's policy at the time) in the *Times Literary Supplement* found that 'Dr. Hobsbawm does not say how, if at all, the French and Industrial Revolutions were related to

each other.' The French Revolution did not lead to the industrialisation of France; indeed it probably helped retard it by creating
a large class of independent small farmers. On the other hand,
the British Industrial Revolution did not lead to a political revolution that overthrew the existing British constitution. This was
somewhat unfair, since the two revolutions did come together in
1848, when continental economic development under the impact
of British industrialisation merged in an explosive mix with revolutionary ideologies, including nationalism and liberalism, that
were invented, or at least given a huge boost, in France in 1789.[25]
Similar points were made by A. J. P. Taylor, the best-known and
most popular British historian of his day: Eric's account was an
exciting one, and yet 'it is all done by sleight of hand' because
the economic bourgeoisie brought to power in Britain by the
Industrial Revolution and the political bourgeoisie brought
to power in France by the French Revolution had nothing in
common. 'Robespierre and Cobden would not have hit it off ...
All Balzac knew of Lancashire was that there women die of love,
a remark which, though interesting, is not true.' 'Mr Hobsbawm',
he concluded, 'has written a most powerful historical overture to
the revolution which did not happen.'[26, 27]

At the other end of the political spectrum, the former BBC
producer, now a conservative Cambridge historian of ideas, Peter
Laslett took exception to what he saw as the book's left-wing bias:

> It is in ugly taste. Marie Antoinette is 'chicken-brained and
> irresponsible': we follow her and her *stupid* husband (he never
> seems to appear without the adjective) up to the minute of
> execution. Not a flicker of sympathy, not a note of tragedy – no
> one suffers nobly from the beginning to the end of this history
> of riot, oppression, war, and exultation. All noblemen are
> nincompoops, and all Englishmen are acquisitive, aggressive
> businessmen, except of course where they are expropriated
> peasants or exploited labourers. All artists, moreover, seem to
> be bourgeois ideologues ... Anyone who could believe in this as
> cultural history can scarcely be trusted as a scholar.[28]

Yet in finding fault with the book for not appreciating the 'tragedy' of Louis XVI and Marie Antoinette, as the Austrian Marxist historian Ernst Wangermann commented, 'how could Laslett have missed the really great tragedy with which Hobsbawm is concerned in his book – the tragedy which overwhelmed millions of ordinary people with the break-up of the traditional society that provided them with their security and livelihood?' Wangermann, a scholar of the social and cultural history of the Habsburg monarchy, declared, 'I do not know of any historical work in which this tragedy is more movingly portrayed than it is in the passages written by Hobsbawm' on the fate of the handloom weavers and the rural poor.[29]

The Age of Revolution was an outstanding success. It has remained in print continuously since its first publication and was eventually translated into eighteen foreign languages including Arabic, Farsi, Hebrew and Japanese. Some of its arguments, for example the thesis that early industrial capitalism experienced a falling rate of profit, now seem outdated, and its portrayal of political movements as direct products of social classes reductionist, but the clarity with which it expresses these views make it a continuing and fruitful source of discussion and debate for students, academics and the general reader alike.

II

By the time Eric left for South America on 31 October 1962, funded by the Rockefeller Foundation to carry out research into 'primitive rebels' in the region, the Cuban missile crisis was already over, with the Russian fleet yielding to American pressure to return to its home port carrying the missiles originally intended for placement in Cuba.[30] His departure was noted by the security services, worried about 'Communist penetration' of local peasant movements.[31] 'The Americans', an MI5 officer opined sarcastically, 'will no doubt be interested in this development.'[32] It was too late to block Eric's grant, of course; indeed, news of Eric's travel was only picked up by MI5 several weeks after he had begun his tour.[33] He started off in Brazil, where he travelled to the city of Recife, in Brazil's north-east, and found 'desperate poverty everywhere. The population looks as though nobody has had a square meal for ten generations: stunted, undersized and sick.' There were 'signs of rebellion', however, and the Peasant Leagues had learned to communicate with their target constituency. 'The potential of peasant organisation is immense.' Unlike MI5, however, he seemed unaware of the fact that the illegally operating Brazilian Communist Party was behind much of the activism of the Peasant Leagues.[34]

In São Paulo by contrast he found 'a sort of nineteenth century Chicago: brash, fast, dynamic, modern ... The skyscrapers sprout, the neon-lights glow, the cars (mostly made in the country) tear through the streets in their thousands in a typically Brazilian anarchy.' The city's onrushing industrialisation was unique in Latin America. But in the absence of stable and growing domestic and export markets it had 'the air of a pyramid balanced on its point'. Hope here lay in the growing collaboration of the labour movement and the industrial bourgeoisie, whose nationalism was bringing them together in a common struggle for 'independence from U. S. imperialism'. He visited the quarter where the popular musicians were based, which he found surprisingly similar to its counterpart in London: 'The same sharp, maudlin, slightly wolfish characters hang around the same sort of offices, overflowing with records and back copies of *Billboard* and *Cashbox*. The same mixture of lyric-writers, disc-jockeys, journalists and guitar-players fill the bars, grabbing sandwiches, telephoning and talking shop.' No wonder Brazilian popular music such as the bossa nova had achieved a global appeal, which had led to its commercialisation in the USA as a form of dance music, though in Brazil itself it remained rooted in the local population as 'a way of playing and singing. When I showed them the ball-room diagrams which US radio stations have been distributing in order to help their listeners learn the new steps, local musicians burst out laughing. For them it is no more a special dance than jazz is.'[35]

When he arrived in Peru, he found further cause for hope. 'If any country is ripe for and needs a social revolution it is Peru.' On the market at Quillabamba, 'a quiet, flat-faced, tough man' intervened in a discussion Eric was engaging in with the help of a carpenter, who spoke both Spanish and the local Indian language and was acting as an interpreter: 'You see, there are two classes. One has nothing, the other has everything: money, power. The only thing the working people can do is to unite, so that is what they do.' I ask: 'But are you not afraid of the police and the soldiers?' 'No, not now', says the carpenter. 'Not any more'. On the long train journey to Bolivia, he talked with an insurance agent, who blamed the landowners' failure to invest in their estates or help the indigenous population. 'There are the Indians walking barefoot, even in the houses of the estate owners, and sleeping on the floor while the lord blows 2 or 3,000 Soles a night on a party. There are the clubs: cards – more whisky, boy! And they are not even aware of the contrast. Now the chickens are coming home to roost.'[36]

In Colombia, Eric encountered 'the greatest armed mobilization of peasants (as guerrillas, brigands, or self-defence groups) in the recent history of the western hemisphere'. The potential for a genuine social revolution was enormous. Colombia 'can make a decisive difference to the future of Latin America, whereas Cuba is not likely to do so', he thought, thanks not least to the country's strategic location. Here too he seems not to have recognised the Communist Party's role in peasant organisation. He did, however, make the acquaintance of the great Communist poet Pablo Neruda, with whom he remained in touch afterwards.[37] Latin America, he concluded at the end of his trip, was 'the most critical area in the world'. The possibility of real social revolution might be remote in Europe or Africa or even the Indian subcontinent, but in Latin America 'the awakening of the people' had already begun.[38]

'I'm crazy about the continent', he wrote to Anna Kallin not long after his arrival in Chile, offering her a short series of broadcasts: '*Not*, however, one talk, which would have no purpose except to get me some money, which I don't particularly need at the moment' (the success of *Primitive Rebels* and *The Jazz Scene* was clearly already having a positive effect on his finances).[39] Back in the UK in March 1963, his proposal for three broadcasts met with approval from BBC Radio executives and a desire to act quickly: 'Hobsbawm must be caught still "hot" from his voyage. He is a very good speaker and writes well, with imagination and full awareness of "Kulturgeschichte" (being a good Habsburgian – no *trace* of accent though!) as well as of politics, economics, sociology.'[40] In the event, the three programmes became two. In the first, Eric noted how Latin American politics confounded normal European political categories and definitions.[41] In his second broadcast on Latin America, he described how huge numbers of migrants coming into the cities carried with them 'the mental world of the European middle ages, which is after all the world the sixteenth-century conquerors brought with them'. Nevertheless, there was clearly hope. 'The old Latin America is collapsing. Something radically new must take its place.'[42]

Eric's broadcasts did not go unnoticed by the security services. One official ('Mr. Barclay') said at a meeting on 23 May 1963 that he had been 'astonished' that Eric, a 'well-known Communist', had not only been permitted to travel to Latin America but, as indicated by his articles in the *Listener*, had even broadcast about his visit on the BBC. 'The matter should now be taken up ... with some senior official of the BBC.'[43] And indeed it was, though without any real result.[44] Official pressure on the national broadcasting service was obviously continuing. The security services could also follow Eric's views through their listening device installed at Communist Party headquarters in London, where Eric reported his findings on 1 April 1963. Eric told his listeners that what was needed in Latin America was the insertion into peasant movements of a leavening of professional Communist revolutionaries who could organise them along the lines of Mao Zedong's Red Army guerrillas in China in the late 1940s. Very little was happening in the capital cities, and one could not speak of any working-class radicalism. All in all, Eric's report could not have been experienced as very encouraging by the British Communist Party apparatchiks.[45]

Eric's interest in Latin America arose because, as Neal

Ascherson remarked, 'it was a new field in which his idea of a broad, liberating, revolutionary struggle could take place, which was non-dogmatic and exciting and romantic'.[46] Eric visited Latin America in 1969 and again in 1971. This time, he was more cautious in his political prognoses. In Colombia, for example, he thought, peasant agitation had reached its height in the years from 1925 to 1948 but thereafter had been overshadowed by a 'bloodthirsty, anarchic civil war' whose violence had pitted peasant farmers against one another and significantly inhibited the further development of peasant protest movements.[47] In Bolivia, a succession of military rulers had suppressed social change, in the process defeating a guerrilla movement led by former Cuban revolutionary Che Guevara, who was captured and executed in 1967, leaving behind a legend that would continue to inspire revolutionaries and radical students the world over.[48] Guerrilla movements in Latin America, Eric thought, were limited in their effectiveness anyway, and needed political organisation to make a real impact. As a former guerrilla from Colombia said to Eric: 'In this country anyone can start an armed band among peasants. The problem is what happens afterwards.'[49] Army officers in Peru were turning to nationalism, even taking over foreign-owned industries and sugar estates.[50] They made it clear they intended a complete transformation of society.[51] In the absence of any 'hegemonic Marxist mass movement', however, this was very much a revolution from above.[52]

The election in November 1970 of a Popular Front government in Chile led by the Communist Salvador Allende was a sign that the combination of neglect and exploitation by the USA was leading to revolution across the continent.[53] It was clear that Allende aimed at a peaceful transition to socialism. Eric regarded this as a 'thrilling prospect'. On the far-right fringe, however, he noted 'paranoiac' signs of 'bourgeois hysteria': 'terror already stalks the land, the police are supporting groups of left-wing assassins, and so on'.[54] In particular, though he failed to remark on this ominous fact, such paranoia permeated the upper ranks of the Chilean armed forces. On an earlier visit to Chile, he had poured scorn on the Chilean armed forces' inability to stage a coup, following a non-violent protest by an artillery regiment ('luckily the Chileans have no experience in this field, neither generals nor civilians ... What's the use of a military coup without even a single armoured car at a street corner?'). The country's democratic institutions seemed safe enough. Within a short space of time, events were to prove him spectacularly wrong.[55]

The mid-1970s saw a series of abrupt reversals of progressive developments in Latin America. In Chile, a US-backed military coup overthrew Allende in 1973, killing him in the process and introducing a brutal and violent dictatorship that had no qualms about torturing and murdering thousands of its opponents. In Peru, there was no direct American intervention, but the military regime, as Eric had suspected it might, took a more conservative turn in 1975, ending the period of radical experimentation.[56] The cruel and corrupt military dictatorship that had existed since 1954 in the somnolent backwater of Paraguay, under General Alfredo Stroessner, had become by the end of the 1970s more or less the norm.[57] Still, in Brazil, where a coup had brought the military to power in 1964, the early signs of a thaw in the dictatorship prompted leftist academics at the University of Campinas, in São Paulo province, to invite Eric in May 1975 to what was one of the first significant conferences to feature left-wing intellectuals in the country since the coup.

Along with the left-leaning modern historian Arno J. Mayer from Princeton, the Spanish political scientist Juan Linz, from Yale, and the Dutch historian Rudolf De Jong, Eric was there, it was reported, to teach people to 'think in a new way'. He had, however, to tread carefully, and his declaration that he was a Marxist historian was reported to have 'alarmed the public'. Eric spoke on Brazilian peasant millenarian movements, and was said to have been the star of the conference, not least because he clearly knew far more about Brazil than most of the other foreign speakers. The conference certainly played a role in opening up Brazilian cultural and intellectual life; growing popular and middle-class pressure forced the regime to issue an amnesty for political offences in 1979, and in 1985 Brazil returned to civilian, democratic rule.[58] Thanks not least to this conference, it was to be in Brazil, of all the countries in Latin America, that Eric was to achieve his greatest fame.

III

While Eric was away touring Latin America in 1962–3, Marlene had moved into Eric's flat in Gordon Mansions in Huntley Street, around the corner from Birkbeck. On his return, their married life began properly. She began to establish a domestic routine. 'If it was pasta for dinner I would put the water on, phone him and it would be ready when he arrived home.'[59] Within a couple of years they had two children, Andy (born on 12 June 1963) and Julia (born on 15 August 1964). Eric and Marlene were out with Eric's cousin Denis Preston and his wife at Bertorelli's restaurant in Charlotte Street, not far from Birkbeck, when Marlene unexpectedly went into labour with Andy; Denis had to drive them all to hospital.[60] It was not customary for fathers to attend the birth of their children in the mid-sixties, and so, when the baby was born, Marlene asked the nurse in the delivery room to tell Eric the good news. She would recognise him, Marlene advised her, if she went 'out into the corridor and find the one not pacing up and down but the one reading'.[61] The arrival of Andy and Julia put a final stop to the late-night expeditions of Francis Newton, and his contributions to the *New Statesman*. Fatherhood also slowed down Eric's writing and research. As he told Jack Plumb in August 1964: 'I am now married and with two tiny children (14 months and a few weeks), and the degree to which this diminishes productivity is quite astonishing. I dream of solid Victorian comforts when husbands didn't have to take turns with wives in feeding infants in the middle of the night etc.'[62] As this suggests, Eric did indeed play his part in looking after the children's infant needs.

In December 1965 Eric and Marlene moved from the flat at 37 Gordon Mansions, WC1, to 97 Larkhall Rise, in Clapham, SW4, a mid-nineteenth-century villa of two storeys and basement, a frontage of three windows, with generously proportioned rooms, nine steps up to the front door of the raised ground floor from the street, and a lower ground floor below, visible from the street through the front window.[63] They shared the property with the Nottingham-born playwright Alan Sillitoe (best known for his novels *Saturday Night and Sunday Morning* and *The Loneliness of the Long Distance Runner*, both turned into successful films) and his wife and child, co-existing by getting an exiled Austrian architect, Max Neuburger, to partition it into two flats. The Sillitoes had part of the raised ground floor and first floor, the Hobsbawms the lower ground floor and the rest of the raised ground floor and first floor, and the two families shared the large garden. At the time, Clapham had still not been gentrified and the neighbours found Alan Sillitoe's lifestyle difficult to understand. 'They couldn't make him out at all because he didn't go out to work. What does he do? He doesn't go out to work . . . They'd never come across somebody who was living there as a writer.' Marlene made a playroom in the lower ground floor for the children, 'and people would stand outside my playroom and it was all books and Galt toys and very middle-class and once a lady said: "What is this, a school?" – she wouldn't believe that anybody would have all these wooden toys just for her kids and it was bound to be a school.'[64]

Clapham was inconveniently far from Marlene's parents in north London, however, and while the sharing arrangement with the Sillitoes worked smoothly enough, Eric's earnings from his books were now sufficient to allow him to take out a bridging loan and then, in July 1971, a mortgage on a six-bedroom, three-storey, semi-detached Victorian house, in Hampstead, at 10 Nassington Road, just down from the Heath.[65] Marlene set to work putting the property in order. 'Marlene has completely restructured the garden at Nassington Road', Eric wrote on 11 June 1973 (his own interest in gardening, though not Marlene's garden, was minimal).[66] At Nassington Road, he established a study and a writing routine during the day, before heading down the hill to South End Green to catch the number 24 bus for an evening's teaching at Birkbeck. Not infrequently he met the left-wing Labour politician Michael Foot on the bus, and engaged in animated conversation on issues of the day, before Eric got off at Goodge Street, leaving Foot to go on to Westminster. Over the years, both became celebrities for regular passengers on route 24.[67]

Meanwhile, the house became a Mecca for Eastern European intellectuals – 'Polish intellectuals, Czech intellectuals, Hungarians', as Neal Ascherson remembered: 'They all knew about Eric Hobsbawm, you know. And the kind of, rather "lapsed" or "sceptical" Party members of these intellectual layers were well aware of him.' They had most probably read his work in English or German.

> They thought of him as . . . a revisionist . . . a guiding light out of the rigidities of Stalinism, and towards a more open, thoughtful, free-speaking . . . form [of Communism] . . . Whenever I mentioned the subject of censorship . . . with Eric, he was always absolutely contemptuous of it. He never had a moment of support for that kind of intervention by ruling parties, and instead he always had sympathy for the rebellious intellectuals, some of whom weren't quite as rebellious as he may have thought.[68]

The children remembered a seemingly endless stream of visitors coming for evening meals or staying in the house. At dinner parties, 'British intellectuals could find themselves outnumbered by German publishers, Czech historians and Latin American novelists' in what some knew as 'north London's most distinctive Central European salon'.[69] Eric 'didn't do solitude'.[70]

During the day, however, Eric 'shut himself up in his study all alone', as Elise Marienstras remembered, though he always left the door open. But 'I don't think that the children suffered from his intellectual absences', she thought, and 'he became a good father'.[71] By the late 1960s the children were attending the local primary schools. Eric, as Andy later noted, would frequently drop them off or pick them up. He

> was an older dad, so when I was at school, he was this figure with a satchel slung [over his shoulder]: the 'absent-minded

professor' dad . . . There was a certain period when you were younger when all the sporty track-suited dads would come to pick up their kids, that it was slightly embarrassing that this . . . wispy-haired, . . . absent-minded guy would sort of wander in who was a lot older than them. So I do remember that as a . . . formative moment.[72]

Later in life, Eric's children recalled him, as Andy noted, always 'absorbing and reading: head buried in the papers. Not in an exclusive sense, but it was just like who he was; and the sound of the typewriter and him being kind of buried in information.' A strong smell of pipe smoke emanated from his study. While he was working, he would always finish the train of thought he was following before responding to interruptions from the children. Julia recalled seeing him in his study,

> sitting, writing. And I could literally visualise the piles and piles of paper, the scribbled notes; he would surround himself with literally a sea of open books, and scribbles. And then, at a certain point in the evening he would stop, and we would watch . . . trash TV like *Kojak* and – d'you remember *The Golden Shot* and things like that? . . . But he had this wonderful light and dark, that he could really veg out.

Every surface in every room of the house at Nassington Road was covered in books, on which, Julia remembered, Eric would 'graze' as he passed. 'I think he couldn't quite calibrate, always, how to be with very young children', she added, sitting with Julia when she was ill, trying to do a crossword with her, when all she wanted was to be left alone. Roderick Floud, an economic historian who became a colleague at Birkbeck, thought Eric 'was very good with the children, our children. I don't think he was nearly so good with his own children.' On one occasion, when his daughter was in her early teens, 'Eric was on the 24 [bus], and Julia got onto the bus . . . and sat down next to him. And he took not the slightest notice of her . . . . didn't recognise his own daughter sitting down next to him!' He was, as always, completely absorbed in a book.[73]

When she was nine, Eric gave Julia

an impossibly grown-up academic book, *Maria Theresa* ... after he decided that the empress would be a perfect subject for a school project on 'Important Women in History'. It was published in the Prentice-Hall 'Great Lives Observed' series: a far cry from Puffin paperbacks. I still feel a shudder of resentment and recall precisely feeling stupidly useless as I hold this well-meaning present in my now adult hands.[74]

To children who were not academically inclined, he could indeed feel intellectually intimidating.

While he was not actually the kind of parent who force-feeds his children *Great Works* – he read every Tintin book aloud to us and seemed to love shouting 'Blistering barnacles!' as Captain Haddock as much as we loved hearing him exclaim it – I think he forgot sometimes that we were ordinary children, not high-minded scholars ... As a child I often felt out of my depth and out of sync with him but by adulthood he was the best a parent can be to a child: cool.

At the same time, he learned from his mistakes with the children, and tailored his reading suggestions to what he perceived they would like. Eric and Marlene took the children to exhibitions – Andy remembered in particular a Lucien Freud show at the Whitechapel Art Gallery, which, he said, 'left a real impression on me' – and it left them with an abiding appreciation of art.[75] He did not involve them in his love of jazz while they were still young. Nor did he really expect them to become intellectuals or bury themselves in books as he had as a child. 'He wasn't a father', Julia observed, 'who had an impression of how life was or how he was as a parent, or how his children were, and then retrofitted that. He really did watch how *we* were, and respond.' Nor did he try to influence their political views, though in a left-wing household they naturally gravitated towards the left as they were growing up. More profound was the sense instilled in them of the importance of social justice and fairness in society and in life.[76]

A little earlier, in 1966, Eric and his family started to stay during the summer and other times of the year in Snowdonia, in Bryn Hyfryd, a cottage at the end of a row of four located on the estate of the wealthy, eccentric architect Clough Williams-Ellis, who built the Italianate village of Portmeirion on a south-facing slope going down to the sea near Porthmadog. His own family home, Plas Brondanw, a seventeenth-century stone mansion with an elaborately designed hillside garden full of geometrically shaped yew bushes, was located a few miles further north, in the Croesor Valley. Eric had been introduced to the area by his friend and former Apostle Robin Gandy, who had whisked him away for a few days to a cottage he rented in the Croesor Valley, telling him he looked stressed and needed some relaxation amid the remote mountains of Snowdonia. The region was already popular with Cambridge people who had known Williams-Ellis and his wife, a member of the Strachey family, including the philosopher Bertrand Russell, the scientist Patrick Blackett, the historian of science Joseph Needham, and Eric's teacher Mounia Postan. Eric was bowled over by the experience, not only impressed by the wild natural beauty of the landscape but also fascinated by the post-industrial ruins of the slate-quarrying industry, with its abandoned quarries, vast slag heaps, disused narrow-gauge railways and deserted hill farms, their economic base destroyed by the collapse of the slate industry earlier in the century.[77]

He already had a connection with the area through having known Clough Williams-Ellis and his family since the 1930s, when a Cambridge friend had married Clough's daughter Susan.[78] So, he wrote, 'we asked the estate for a cottage because my wife thought the Croesor Valley one of the most beautiful places she had ever seen. Both the houses we have occupied were ruins, restored to hab-itable condition by the landlord at different times.' Indeed, another cottage in the row was still in ruins. Living arrangements were very basic; there was water and electricity but no central heating, and Eric had to install a paraffin heater to drive out the pervasive damp. He spent many hours chopping wood for a fire when it was cold. Julia thought he enjoyed staying there because the very basic nature of the living conditions reminded him of Cambridge in the thirties.[79] Marlene's brother Walter and his family joined them, renting a small gatehouse nearby. Edward Thompson and his wife and fellow historian Dorothy Thompson also had a cottage in the area. They all became known as 'the Welsh Bloomsbury set'. As Marlene recalled: 'It used to be said one could hear more typewriters clicking than birds buzzing in our valley.'[80] They sometimes visited the seaside, above all at Portmeirion, where Williams-Ellis had provided them, as he did all his tenants, with a permanent complimentary entry pass in the form of 'a letter, sort of a cross between "To Whom it May Concern" and some kind of financial bond', as Julia later recalled,[81] but mostly they went on invigorating walks, clambering along sheep tracks on the steep sides of the local mountain, Cnicht, 'the Matterhorn of Snowdonia', bathed in the lakes hidden in its folds, visited each other for meals and talked late into the night. In 1976 Eric and Marlene took out a lease on a larger and slightly more glamorous cottage, Parc Farmhouse, on the lower slopes of the mountain. The neighbouring farmer, Dai Williams, kept sheep but there were no other animals about.[82] As Julia later recalled,

> My father used to take me and my brother Andy walking to the lakes overlooking Beddgelert, where the only movement for miles would be the odd divebombing gull, a sheep dragging some grass into its mouth, and the tinkle of a clear mountain stream. We would stop on some rocks and look for our usual gap, 'The Robber's Cave'. Inside, our dad would bring out chocolate bars: Ice Breakers for us and Bourneville for him. We would sit together, cramped in the musty quiet dark with our torches and chocolate, and be happier than anyone could be.

Julia's memories of the cave were fond enough for her to take her own children there long after Eric had moved away from the Croesor Valley.

In 1973 Eric went to the cottage with the children for a week while Marlene was at a music summer school. 'It is the first time ... ', Marlene commented, 'that he has looked after the children alone for a whole week.'[83] She need not have worried, as he reported:

> The management side works ok so far: the chicken was satisfactory and for the rest we have kept going on sausages, chops and suchlike. Of course the children were very hungry today. They slept in the tent in a nearby camp of rather charming railway fanatics who are planning to rebuild a railway from Port[hmadog] to Beddgelert (Clough says it's a non-starter) with various children. There they made them work at washing up and (Andy) collecting material for the railway such as old rails and screws etc ... They invited a boy of 6 to sleep in the tent with them, who wants to marry Julia, but as the tent was pitched next to his parents', no problem ... Weather perfect, but I have trouble focussing the telescope on any stars. There seems much more empty sky than stars ... The Thompsons are here – we are going over for supper tonight ... We haven't done much: been to Votti, and to Portmeirion. But what with the railway madmen's camp, the children have been fully occupied.[84]

A mock-ruined castle-like tower built on the hillside opposite Brondanw as a folly by Williams-Ellis became a favourite place for the children's games and fantasies. 'We would run a family diary', Julia recalled, 'and it was a sheet of paper divided into four. And, you know, he would say "I chopped wood today", and Mum would say "I did this". So he was very, very family-orientated, and very affectionate.'[85] It was in Wales, indeed, that Eric was closest to his family, spending all his time with them, rather than teaching or travelling, as he did so often when he was not there.

Eric's strong family orientation also led him to keep up contact with his other relatives, including, especially, his sister Nancy.

Her husband, Victor Marchesi, had by this time retired from the Royal Navy, and after various posts, including that of captain of the *Cutty Sark*, the famous nineteenth-century sailing ship, or 'tea clipper', now a museum ship in a dry dock at Greenwich, south-east London, the couple retired to Menorca. By now, their children had grown up and left home. Nancy was still occasionally resentful of her brother's brilliance and reputation. Her son Robin: 'Another thing my mother said to me I always remember, I was fifteen, or actually I was younger. "Well, if you want to be a writer, Robin, be a REAL writer, not like your uncle Eric!!"'[86] The relative to whom Eric was probably closest, his first cousin Ron, retired from the civil service, and spent a good deal of his time with his family sailing on the Blackwater River, acquiring a small cabin cruiser which he kept moored at Burnham-on-Crouch, in Essex. Eric continued to visit him, now with Marlene, two or three times a year, especially just before Christmas, though they did not join in his nautical activities.[87]

Christmas Eve was a very special occasion, as Julia, in conversation with her brother many years later, remembered:

> Christmas Eve – we always had this funny little thing on Christmas Eve. We had a sort of middle-European Christmas . . . – it was all a bit higgledy-piggledy, but essentially we would have waifs and strays – academics who couldn't go anywhere when the British Museum [Reading Room] was closed on Christmas Day. So we'd have a very unusual type of arrangement on Christmas Day. But on Christmas Eve, it was just our family. During the day, Mum would get the house ready and Dad would take us out to exhibitions and movies before the four of us opened our presents in the Continental tradition. I used to love our Christmas Eves. And it made it – you know, because he was a remote father physically through travel, OK? It made these, you know, special milestone occasions . . . so memorable.[88]

Christmas Eve, as Marlene described it, was the most

choreographed family occasion of the year. The 'waifs and strays' had not yet arrived, so it was just Eric and the children, when they returned from their expedition, and Marlene, who stuffed and pre- pared the turkey in the afternoon while listening to the Service of Nine Lessons and Carols from King's College Chapel on the radio. Then on Christmas Day, friends and visitors arrived, especially, for many years, Francis and Larissa Haskell, who had no children and did not own a television set, Marlene's mother and her cousin Gretl, and Arnaldo Momigliano, an eminent specialist in ancient historiography who held a Chair at University College London. Usually there were around fourteen people at the dinner table as Eric carved the turkey. On Boxing Day, more guests arrived for a cold buffet, since the Reading Room at the British Library was still closed. Then, on the 27th, Eric and Marlene packed up the remaining food and drove off to Wales for the New Year. It was, Marlene recalled, 'the only thing that was run like a ritual in our household'.[89]

Eric's family also included, in a more distant way, his illegitimate son Joss Bennathan, born in 1958. Eric thought that Joss should have been told who his real father was at the earliest opportunity, but his mother Marion waited until 1972, when he was fourteen, before revealing the truth to him. Joss seems to have taken what must have been a startling revelation well, and felt some pride in being the son of a famous historian.[90] He did not see Eric very often, but as he later wrote, 'God knows how and why our blood tie is no significant and special but it is, and I am glad of our relation- ship, however we define it.'[91] His letters to Eric were already fluent and sophisticated, betraying a spirit of rebellion that he might well have inherited from his father, announcing on one occasion how he had walked out of school at the beginning of 1974, after taking his 'O' level exams, 'as a protest against the complete & utter boredom of it all'.[92] Eric's own children did not learn of the existence of their half-brother until a good deal later, but formed a strong friendship with him afterwards.

From the early 1960s onwards, then, Eric's life settled down into a kind of routine he had not known before. As Roderick Floud recalled, 'Marlene was very important in terms of ... running this very well-oiled household ... He wasn't an involved father, he was quite an old father, even by modern standards, and so I think Marlene was the absolute key to his, well to a lot of things really, to the way, to his life.'[93] 'Regarding the books', Marlene later recalled, 'I think I did help in a mysterious way, because he wrote his best stuff when we were together. Sometimes he showed me a chapter or two and I probably said certain things about them but only to do with length and clarity rather than content ... I think it helped that I pointed out what I didn't understand or that sentences were too long etc.'[94] 'I don't know', thought Elise Marienstras, 'whether this marriage and this stability really changed his life for him. In the first place, he retained his taste for travelling everywhere, a kind of practical universalism. And then, he researched more and more; he published more and more.'[95] But it surely did change his life in a number of respects, giving him a loving family and a sound and secure home. Above all, his marriage brought him happiness. Occasionally in later life, he would, in an unconscious slip of the tongue, refer to Marlene as Muriel, but she did not seem to mind; she knew it was her he really loved, however deep the scars of his first marriage.[96] From the early 1960s onwards, with the new-found stability in his life, Eric was to produce his most famous and most widely read works, establishing his global reputation as the leading historian of his day.

IV

Although Eric no longer haunted the jazz clubs and bars of Soho after his marriage, and especially after the birth of his children, he was still absent from home on two or three evenings each week during term-time, teaching part-time students at Birkbeck, which was after all for many years the principal steady source of income for the family. His undergraduate courses were deservedly popular. Pat Robinson, one of Eric's undergraduate students at Birkbeck, remembered, she told him much later, how dynamic your style of lecturing was for the Political Theory course ... the lecture on Utopias you started with quoting the 'Big Rock Candy Mountain' song of Burl Ives ... From your Birkbeck lectures I realised that history was endlessly fascinating as it involved ideas as well as facts and traversed every boundary.[97]

'Whereas most of our lecturers very obviously spoke from carefully prepared notes, sometimes prepared long before', as Alan Montgomery, who attended Eric's classes on modern European history in the early 1960s, recalled, 'Dr Hobsbawm's talks had a spontaneity and freshness which made them something to look forward to.'[98] Another former student recalled Eric 'charting the rising influence of the middle class by the spread of golf & tennis clubs or the widening impact of European culture by classic opera performances in such unlikely places as Egypt or up the Amazon. The rising height of Ligurian conscripts was, if I remember correctly, another social indicator.'[99] In an argument about the condition of labour in the 'informal economy', Eric did not hesitate to use his own children as an example:

Both my children do newspaper delivery rounds and similar jobs, which are an accepted way for middle-class kids to earn more pocket money than most parents would be willing to pay. They like it, we don't mind, and Hampstead (unlike say parts of Kentish Town) has better services in these respects. But the kids *are* underpaid and (if you include school and homework) may be overworked.[100]

Eric's lectures at Birkbeck were also open to students from other colleges of London University who were taking the federal degree in history. As the young Indian historian Romila Thapar, who attended some of them, noted, 'Even as a young lecturer he was already something of an icon among students.'[101]

Students found his lectures 'brilliant, incisive and inspirational ... An evening with Eric Hobsbawm was always an electric experience.' Edward Glover, then starting out on what was to be a successful career in the Foreign Office, recalled: 'From him I learnt to question and, when required, to be unorthodox. In short, ever since, my approach to problems is that nothing should be off-limits.' On occasion Eric could transmit a sense of belonging to history himself, as when he told the students in the course of a lecture on the Russian Revolution that he had met Alexander Kerensky, the premier of the Provisional Government in 1917, who lived on in exile in New York until 1970: 'It was as though we were able to reach out through Eric Hobsbawm to one of the most remarkable events in modern history.'[102]

He taught by a mixture of lectures and seminars, and at the latter, as Pat Stroud remembered,

> Eric would sit cross-legged on the top of the desk facing his students whilst we took turns at reading our most recent essays aloud to the group. He would listen intently whilst, for us, the most interesting aspect was his actions during the readings. As an inveterate pipe smoker, he would take his pipe out, knock the old tobacco into the adjacent waste bin, take out his tobacco pouch, and start packing his pipe afresh. In the next stage of the procedure out would come three boxes of matches, several of which had to be struck on the upturned sole of his shoe before the pipe would be lit, the used matches being tossed in turn into the bin. On one occasion, as he talked about the French Revolution, he emptied the contents of his pipe into the waste-paper basket beneath his feet, which promptly caught fire, and when he tried to stamp it out, his foot became jammed in the narrow bottom of the basket, leading to a brief tussle to free it. Throughout the whole episode, he barely ceased his comments on a student's essay.[103]

Lois Wincott, a schoolteacher and then lecturer at a teacher training college who studied part-time for a BA in history at Birkbeck from 1962 to 1967, still remembered the details of Eric's lectures on early modern Europe more than half a century later.

Always delivered entirely without notes, they succeeded in focusing the students' attention from the very beginning:

> He started the Thirty Years War, he'd start off saying it was a particularly bloody war, so he got your attention straight away ... And then he'd tell you about, you know, the Siege of Vienna [1683] with the Turks .... how the Austrian ladies baked a little crescent shape ... the origin of the croissant. But it's these little things, that somehow he made history come alive, and made you want to listen to the other things.[104]

So fascinating were the lectures, indeed, that she forgot to take notes, and so 'you'd go and start revising and you didn't have any notes!'

Wincott returned to Birkbeck in 1973 to take a two-year Master's degree in nineteenth- and twentieth-century social and economic history, a stand-alone course that Eric had recently founded. She found the course fascinating because 'you know when you're sitting in the presence of a very able person. Never made you feel inferior.' The MA course met for a two-hour seminar each week, covering topics such as the working classes in England from 1815 to 1914, and sources and historiography in British social and economic history from 1815 to 1970. Peter Archard, a sociology lecturer who took the MA in the early 1980s, remembered that 'Eric would invariably join his students for a break halfway through a two-hour seminar, to share a drink and opinions on current affairs. These occasions were hugely enjoyable and offered an insight into his thinking on a wide range of topics.'[105] 'Those two years with Eric transformed my intellectual and academic interests', he later wrote. Born and raised in Argentina, Archard decided to do a doctorate on Mexican labour history. Armed only with a backpack and a letter of recommendation from Eric, he travelled to Mexico City and knocked on the office door of the economic historian Enrique Semo. 'My unorthodox arrival and request to work under him was met with scepticism – until I pulled out Eric's letter.'[106]

Eric ran a graduate research seminar in modern economic

and social history at the Institute of Historical Research for many years. One of the participants later described the ones he attended in the early 1970s as 'the pre-eminent intellectual experience of my life ... Through them history unfolded in breadth and depth in a way that only happens once in life.'[107] And, of course, Eric supervised a substantial number of doctoral dissertations, above all in the 1970s and early 1980s, after he had become famous. As Geoffrey Crossick, who completed his doctoral dissertation under Eric's supervision in 1976, recalled:

> My choice of Eric was very deliberate – most of my contemporaries as social historians on the Left would have gone to Edward Thompson, but even then I knew that I wanted somebody whom I saw as more international in mindset and more systematic in analytical approach. It was Eric's kind of historian that I wanted to be rather than Edward's.[108]

In keeping with the normal practice of doctoral supervisors at the time, when box-ticking, regular reports and close monitoring were not yet required, Eric's method was rather hands-off. As Crossick remembered:

> My experience of Eric as a supervisor was that he saw me only very occasionally – even in my first year I doubt that I saw him more than a few times and I did seriously lose my way that year, not really focusing on the questions that would drive my thesis and identifying which sources would enable me to address those questions. I worked hard but needed more direction. And once I'd resolved those issues early in my second year, Eric still saw me only very occasionally and was a very light-touch supervisor. He took a very long time to read any chapters I gave him, and the final draft of my thesis sat with him for six months or so before he read it.

On his own admission, however, Crossick spent far too much time on participating in the anti-Vietnam War movement than was good for the progress of his thesis. Eric did not object – how could he? – and Crossick duly gained his Ph.D. in the end, going on to a distinguished career in a variety of academic posts, including the Wardenship of Goldsmiths College in London. Other Ph.D. students remembered Eric as a rather demanding supervisor. As Chris Wrigley, who started working on a dissertation on the early twentieth-century British labour movement in 1968, remembered, Eric would always return his drafts with suggestions for further reading, especially of a comparative nature. 'When I gave him some section on Lloyd George and labour, he said, "You haven't really thought about the Peruvian peasants", and I said, "No, Eric, I have not thought about the Peruvian peasants, nor am I going to!"'[109]

Eric attracted doctoral students on continental European topics as well. Donald Sassoon, the cosmopolitanism of whose background rivalled that of Eric's – a British citizen, he was born in Cairo, went to school in Paris and Milan, and had degrees from London and Pennsylvania – sought him out in 1971 because he

> had been very taken with the works of Louis Althusser and I wanted to do something on the Italian Communist Party, treating the Party as an organic intellectual, as Gramsci would have it, and I wrote to Eric at Birkbeck saying that I wanted to do a PhD with him ... [he was] someone I could trust and someone I of course thought highly of and all the rest of it. And he immediately wrote back, a fairly short, succinct letter, which was in points 1, 2 and 3. Point 1: I'm interested in the topic; Point 2 ... Birkbeck has no money and Point 3: I'm not an unconditional admirer of the works of Louis Althusser.[110]

'PhDs', Eric told Sassoon, 'don't have to be boring ... Throw in bits of factoids which are interesting but won't change the thing but which enlighten and lighten.' Sassoon was politically active, and was very taken with the theory and practice of Eurocommunism, so he asked Eric if he should join the Party. But he advised him not to: 'It's a complete waste of time! You're going to spend all your time fighting against Stalinists. There are five of them, and there are five Eurocommunists [in the leadership of the Communist Party of Great Britain]. Just don't.' Sassoon joined the Labour Party instead.

Left-wing students from many countries clamoured to work with Eric. One such was Youssef Cassis, an assistant at the University of Geneva, heavily involved in Maoist politics in the rather unpromising environment of an affluent Swiss city, and keen to do something more productive in an environment that was less provincial. Rather than follow the normal path for leftists and write a dissertation on labour history, Cassis decided to study 'the enemy', and suggested a project on the financial bourgeoisie in the nineteenth century. Eric asked around, decided it was feasible and introduced Cassis to the literature on bankers in England. Eric read and commented on his work at regular intervals, and it did not make any difference that Cassis, lacking confidence in his command of English, decided to write it in French and submit it to the University of Geneva. Eric supervised it anyway.[111]

Eric's style was in sharp contrast to the discouraging formality of the dry-as-dust Professor of History and permanent Head of Department R. R. Darlington, a small man in every sense of the word, whose main scholarly endeavours were devoted to producing editions of medieval chronicles and charters. One of Eric's former students at Birkbeck recalled his 'uncomfortable interview' with Darlington, whose teaching on Anglo-Saxon England had clearly failed to enthral him:

'Ah, Mr Sharpe, Dr Ruddock seems quite pleased with your work, as are Drs Dakin and Hobsbawm, it is only me, who has doubts about your getting a degree.' (Long pause, during which he sucked hard on a cold pipe). 'But I must remind you that all my colleagues are judging you on prepared essays; whereas I am judging you on a written examination. I must remind you that your degree will be awarded on how you perform in a written examination. Good night!'[112]

Allegedly because Eric did not use manuscript sources, Darlington blocked his promotion, though there may also have been some political animus as well. Noel Annan, who knew Darlington as a London University colleague, said that the professor always 'maintained that there were at least two others in the department superior to Hobsbawm – though research has failed to identify them'.[113] Most likely the two were Darlington himself and his senior colleague Douglas Dakin, whom he respected because he was editor of *Documents on Foreign Policy*, the sort of historical project Darlington understood. Dakin, who was also a leading historian of modern Greece, had tried to secure promotion for Eric, but Darlington was said to have replied: 'Over my dead body!'

Although his academic articles would surely have justified promotion to a Readership by the middle of the decade, Eric had stayed on the Lecturer grade through most of the 1950s. He was finally made a Reader in December 1959. The Communist Party leadership pondered whether to send him a letter of congratulations, but John Gollan, as MI5 noted when transcribing the bugged conversation about it, told the other Party apparatchiks this was not normal practice.[114] There was nothing unusual about this delay in promotion, Eric thought. Communists who had a post before the Berlin Airlift of 1948 kept it, but 'almost certainly got no promotion for ten years and no chance of moving. Those who had not got in before then, did not get jobs for about ten years ... Of course the Marxists were isolated as much as possible, both by actual discrimination and by the general, and justifiable, suspicion of the USSR.'[115] The older generation of university historians would warn their students against him. As Donald Sassoon remembered:

At University College London in the 1960s, I took a course in British economic history. The lecturer in charge (whose name I have forgotten, so undistinguished has he remained) ... warned us: '... Hobsbawm is a perfectly good historian, but be careful: he is a Marxist ... Thompson too is a good historian, but be on your guard: he too is a Marxist.' He mentioned no one else. At school I had not heard of either of them. Naturally, when the lecture was finished, many of us trooped across the road to the bookshop to acquire Hobsbawm and Thompson with the excitement of teenagers buying dirty books.[116]

The historian in question was most probably W. H. Chaloner, who had clashed so spectacularly with Eric a few years before.

Frustrated by Birkbeck's lack of appreciation of his growing public reputation, Eric looked around for other possibilities. In 1965 he applied for the Cambridge Chair of Economic History vacated by Postan on his retirement, but it went to David Joslin, an obscure figure who had written about South American banks and who died only a few years later, before he could produce a really major work. Eric applied again in 1971 after Joslin's death, and was again passed over, in favour of the business historian David Coleman, a competent enough historian but no more in Eric's league than Joslin had been.[117] This was his last chance at Cambridge, but there were other possibilities. On 18 September 1966 Eric received an informal and unofficial approach from Noel Annan, by now Provost of University College London, asking him whether he would be interested in taking up a Professorship of Economic and Social History there. His reply was positive:

> I am getting fed up with Birkbeck, partly because the future of the place is so uncertain, partly because I've been there so long, and also for local reasons. While I've been refusing chairs in various places too far away from London, I would naturally like one in London, and certainly would jump at UC now that, under you, it will be even more distinguished than before. (This distinction does not apply without qualification to the actual history department.) I had not seriously thought about it, since no chair was vacant, and I expect Cobban would be rather against me on ideological grounds.[118]

He was, he added, being considered for a chair at Sussex University, and had told Asa Briggs, the Vice-Chancellor and an eminent social historian of Victorian England, that he would be 'willing in principle to go there', but 'Marlene and I would much prefer a post in London ... I don't really want to go to Brighton, but it is just within the range I'm prepared to accept.'

He did not in the end try to go to Brighton, but Annan's initiative eventually bore fruit in an application for the Chair of French History at University College London, which had become vacant in 1968 on the death of Alfred Cobban. Proper appointment and interviewing procedures had to be followed, of course, and once more Eric found himself blocked by political opponents within the Department; the Chair went to Douglas Johnson, a specialist on nineteenth-century France, instead. The previous year, he had applied for the Chichele Professorship of Economic History at Oxford, a post tied to a Fellowship of All Souls and vacated by H. J. Habakkuk on his election to the post of Principal of Jesus College. A Board of Electors had been put together, on which Hugh Trevor-Roper, the Regius Professor of Modern History, was the dominant figure. Trevor-Roper respected Eric as an historian but detested him as a Communist and was determined to block him. The Oxford historian Keith Thomas later recalled: 'I heard Trevor-Roper at a post-seminar drink in the Eastgate [hotel] boast to the admiring throng that he had that day succeeded in keeping Eric out of the Chichele Chair of Economic History.' The successful candidate was Peter Mathias, a Fellow of Queens' College, Cambridge, whose only book was a study of the brewing industry in England from 1700 to 1830. Prudently, perhaps, Mathias delayed taking up the chair until 1969, the publication date of *The First Industrial Nation*, a history of the British economy from the eighteenth century to the twentieth, a lucid and magisterial work. As for Eric, his failure was a blessing in disguise: he would have hated All Souls, with its close ties to the Conservative Party, its deeply reactionary Fellows, and its Warden, the bibulous bibliophile John Sparrow, a lawyer best known to the general public as author of an article in *Encounter* magazine criticising the acquittal of Penguin Books of charges brought against them under the Obscene Publications Act for publishing D. H. Lawrence's *Lady Chatterley's Lover*.[119]

At the prompting of Tim Mason, a young social historian of

Nazi Germany and co-founder of the History Workshop and its academic offshoot, the Social History Group, Raymond Carr, Warden of St Antony's, a graduate college, wrote to Eric in 1969 with the suggestion that he become the Director of a proposed Centre for Social History he hoped to establish in Oxford.[120] But Carr was unable to raise the funds. After a further lengthy interval, Eric was finally promoted to a Professorship of Economic and Social History at Birkbeck in March 1970, at a salary of £4300 per annum, some way above the professorial minimum of £3780, with a London allowance of £100, all backdated to 1 January 1970. The promotion had been pushed through by the College's Master, Ronald Tress, soon after Darlington's death in 1969.[121] Welcome though all this was, the position of professor brought with it potential new and unwelcome responsibilities. In particular, Eric wanted if possible to avoid the tedium of university administration, and above all appointment as Head of Department, which would have reduced the time he needed for writing and made it difficult for him to travel, at least during term. After Darlington's retirement, the position of Head of the History Department at Birkbeck fell to Douglas Dakin, but Dakin himself was due to retire in 1974. Alarmed at the prospect of having to take over from him, Eric cast about for a means of escape.

He had got to know a young economic historian, Roderick Floud, then teaching at Cambridge and preparing his first book, on the British machine tool industry from 1850 to 1914, for publication. Floud's father Bernard had joined the Labour Party before the war and was elected as a Labour MP in 1964; denied security clearance by MI5 because he was erroneously suspected of having been a member of a Communist circle in Oxford in the 1930s, he had committed suicide in 1967. His son had evidently already acquired the reputation as a formidably efficient academic administrator that was to lead him later on to become Vice-Chancellor of London Metropolitan University. Roderick Floud later remembered:

I first met Eric in a lift at the Economic History Society meeting, it must have been in 1973 ... And we got out of the lift and he kind of drew me aside and said, would I be at all interested in applying for the chair of history at Birkbeck? ... And I was rather taken aback, really, because I was only ... thirty-two. So we talked a little bit about it and then I went away and thought about it and I talked to him again, as far as I remember, then applied. And I assume he was on the appointments committee but he was quite influential in getting me the job. So that's how I first met him and then it rapidly became clear that one of his motives for getting in myself or presumably someone else was that he didn't want the responsibility of being Head of Department or anything else, so he didn't want the job for himself. And that, I think, was a continuing characteristic of his attitude, that he wasn't at all interested in administration.[122]

Floud was duly appointed Professor of History in 1975 and guided the Department safely through the turbulent years that were to follow. While they were both at Birkbeck they would have lunch 'three or four times a week together' and then and later they met often at Eric's home: they talked about British and world politics, about College gossip, and about Floud's own work. 'But he was always extremely reticent about talking about his research, to the point that I used to feel rather foolish, because suddenly a book would appear and I wouldn't have known anything about it.' Talking about history in the end would have been too much like talking shop.

V

After publishing *The Age of Revolution*, Eric gathered together his early articles on English labour history in the nineteenth century in a volume entitled *Labouring Men*, published, like *The Age of Revolution*, by Weidenfeld & Nicolson. Although essay collections are seldom bestsellers, the book was surprisingly widely reviewed in the press, perhaps because *The Age of Revolution* had made Eric well known to book review editors. Hostile reviewers identified Eric as a 'sophisticated, slightly chastened Marxist', who was 'so unfair to the Fabians', and too fond of academic infighting, obscure detail and lengthy footnotes to exercise a broad appeal, in this book at least.[123] A more intelligent commentary was supplied by George Lichtheim, one of the leading students of Marxist thought of the time. Lichtheim regretted the absence of comparative material from the European continent, and while Eric's Leninism was in his view little more than 'residual', it sometimes got in the way of his analysis, as for example in his treatment of the labour aristocracy. With his own continental background, Lichtheim agreed that the Fabians were 'provincial and boring' but thought Eric was unable to explain why they succeeded in influencing the British labour movement while the Marxists failed. The fact that the Fabians were middle class did not mean they could not be socialists.

> The simple truth is that a Marxist movement (or any other) can establish its hold over society only if it begins by winning over the intellectual élite. This – as Mr. Hobsbawm well knows – has been the secret of Italian Communism. Inversely it explains why the British CP has always been a hopeless failure. Labouring men by themselves cannot make a revolution. Lenin knew this; so did the Fabians. Mr. Hobsbawm does too. Why does he not say so?[124]

Lichtheim had a point. Nevertheless, the book as a whole was an outstanding success. It came at a time when labour history was moving into the academic mainstream, and *Labouring Men*, which pioneered an entirely new approach to British labour history, focusing not on institutions but on contexts, had an influence on the subject that was to endure.[125]

Eric achieved a really broad student readership in the field of British economic and social history only through the publication of a general textbook survey. Already in June 1961 he had signed a contract to write the third volume in a paperback economic history of England, published by Pelican, the non-fiction imprint of Penguin Books.[126] The series, like many such enterprises at the time, was the brainchild of the Cambridge historian Jack Plumb, whom Eric had known since the 1950s. Plumb met Eric, along with the responsible editor at Penguin, Dieter Pevsner, for lunch at the Oxford and Cambridge Club in London's Pall Mall on 8 June 1961 to discuss the project following Eric's acceptance of the commission in principle the previous month.[127] The book was conceived as the companion to an early modern volume, by Christopher Hill; subsequently a medieval volume was commissioned from Mounia Postan. The original idea was for Eric to cover the period from 1750 to 1900, with a fourth volume by someone else dealing with the twentieth century, but in the event Eric carried the story up almost to the present day. The book was to be a brief one, at eighty thousand words: Eric received an advance of £400, on a royalty of 7½ per cent, and the publisher optimistically wrote in a delivery date of 31 December 1962.[128] All three books were to be published first in hardback by Weidenfeld & Nicolson, but it was clear that they were intended above all for the paperback market, since it was Penguin who had actually commissioned them.[129]

Inevitably, given his many other commitments, Eric did not manage to meet the extremely tight deadline imposed by his contract. On 17 January 1963 David Higham assured Penguin after phoning Eric that 'he will be delivering this to you by mid-year. He's been rather held up with this as he was given an unexpected Rockefeller grant and has been abroad.'[130] In July 1963, however, Eric informed his agent that 'he doubts very much that he can finish the book before the end of '63 or the end of January '64. He intends to work on it during the long vacation but feels he can't really commit himself to October.'[131] January 1964 came and went, and still there was no sign of the book. A revised delivery date of July 1964 was agreed, and Penguin brought in Jack Plumb to 'write him a note saying how disappointed you are, and how very sincerely you hope he is going to keep to this new date'.[132] But all the pressure now piling on Eric failed to achieve any result. 'Now that July has come', Pevsner wrote to Higham on the 13th of the month, 'I feel I must have some really definite [information] about

when Hobsbawm proposes to deliver this book.'[133] None was forthcoming. As Eric wrote to Penguin Books on 24 August,

> If your other authors find themselves, in the course of prepar-
> ing a book, with two tiny children on their hands (one born a
> few weeks ago) and the additional complications of buying and
> reconstructing a new house, I hope their diminution of produc-
> tivity is not as great as mine. I've been working like mad when
> I could on the Penguin, but progress has been slower than I
> thought. Another couple of months should see it through, if the
> rhythm of domestic life stabilises itself again.[134]

He also wrote to Plumb in similar terms.[135] But all the pressure
failed to achieve the desired result. Pevsner began to lose patience.
'I am beginning to develop a terrible fear', he wrote to Eric's agent
on 28 August, 'that unless we get this book finished quickly I will
go sour on Hobsbawm and everyone else connected with it.'[136] This
threat did not work either. The delivery date was postponed once
more, this time to July 1965.[137]

Eric worked hard on the book during the summer vacation,
and eventually managed to finish it by the end of December
1965.[138] However, on reading through the typescript early in 1966,
Penguin's editors were not satisfied with the twentieth-century section, which, not surprisingly in view of the pressure Eric had been
under to finish quickly, seemed to show signs of haste. Penguin's
history editor Peter Wright told Eric on 8 February:

> In general we have no comments to make at all up to the end of
> Chapter 10. After 1918, however, we at Penguins have a slight
> feeling of unease about the general balance of the book as it
> stands. There is a *lot* on the living standards etc of individuals in
> society (about 50 pages) some of which seems to us to be a little
> to[o] expanded and too verging on the peripheral ... Our own
> feeling is that Chapter 11 should be expanded somewhat and
> should particularly explain more fully such things as what did
> cause the Slump ... The only other general point which strikes

Yo

us is that in all spheres (including farming – Chapter 10), the discussion of the years after 1951 is extremely brief. As it stands we feel it would be better either to expand the discussion of the past 15 years fairly considerably or end the work as a whole in 1951.[139]

In due course, Peter Wright met Eric for lunch and went over the typescript with him. In October 1966 Eric met the publishers' criticisms by submitting a heavily revised and extended final chapter.[140] 'The new chapter', Peter Wright told him on 24 October, 'seems quite splendid to me, for which many thanks.'[141]

Still, Penguin's overall view was that the book was 'stronger on 19th century than on 20th century', though, taken as a whole, it was 'good left-wing stuff'.[142] Further delays ensued, this time occasioned by complicated negotiations with George Weidenfeld, and with André Schiffrin, of the American publisher Pantheon Books, about the hardback rights. The production process was also far from simple. Julian Shuckburgh of Weidenfeld & Nicolson complained about the 'great investment in time and effort that the Hobsbawm has involved for us'. 'Hobsbawm has been slow and inaccessible over the last twelve months and his book contains 52 complex line drawings and was (until a very recent decision) to have contained 50 or 60 photographs.'[143] Eventually, the book went into the editorial and production processes and was published in hardback by Weidenfeld & Nicolson on 11 April 1968, more than five years behind schedule.[144]

At a little over three hundred pages, *Industry and Empire* was a masterpiece of elegant synthesis and compressed exposition. The Industrial Revolution, which Eric rightly saw as 'the most fundamental transformation of human life in the history of the world recorded in written documents', took centre stage and occupied nearly a third of the book. Eric's rewriting had thus not entirely met his editor's complaints about the imbalance of coverage. What made the book so striking and original was that it took a global view of its subject, placing it in a context far broader than that essayed by previous attempts to explain why the process of industrialisation began in Britain and not elsewhere, attempts which had focused overwhelmingly on factors located within Britain's economy and society. Eric argued here, as he already had done in *The Age of Revolution*, that it was the expansion of the British overseas empire in the eighteenth century that provided the essential ingredient by acquiring new markets and suppressing domestic competition in the countries colonised. Massive sales of cotton goods in Africa and, later, India were achieved as a result, stimulating mechanisation, lowering prices and leading to a rapid accumulation of capital back in Britain.[145]

Industry and Empire had much of interest to say about social and political as well as economic history. British society – and Eric really did mean British, with space devoted to Scotland, Wales and Ireland as well as to England – was transformed socially as well as economically, with a large industrial working class providing the basis after the turn of the century for the rise of the Labour Party. Reviewers, indeed, even critical ones, recognised that the book was perhaps most significant in its insistence 'that our current predicament is inexplicable except within the terms of historical argument, that anatomies of Britain which lack this dimension are thin and insubstantial'.[146] In this sense, it was a contribution to the 'decline of Britain' debate that raged in politics and the media through the 1970s.

Eric's reputation, boosted by the publication of *The Age of Revolution* six years before, was enough to get the book widely reviewed in the quality press. *Industry and Empire*, clearly based on Eric's lectures at Birkbeck on British economic history, was perhaps more of a textbook than anything else he published. But it was still written in a style that enabled the general reader to profit from it. David Rubinstein, a left-wing American who taught economic and social history at the University of Hull, explained the originality of the book to readers of the Labour Party magazine *Tribune*:

> Economic history has been bedeviled since the war by an apparent determination on the part of its practitioners to make the subject as obscure as possible to the general reader. Concern for statistics rather than people, specialist jargon, erudite quarrels

and a view of the past as consisting mainly of production, investment and profit curves have tended to make economic history
the dismal science of the 1960s. This approach has now been
challenged by one of our outstanding historians. While Eric
Hobsbawm's prose is not always easy to follow – his argument
is closely reasoned and economically stated – he never forgets
that he is writing about people.[147]

Rubinstein picked out a number of striking epigrams from the
book. 'However strongly the winds of change blew elsewhere, as
soon as they crossed the Channel in Britain they grew sluggish',
Eric observed, for example. Such vignettes helped make the book
readable. Others agreed. A. J. P. Taylor, in a characteristically
opinionated review, agreed that while most economic history was
boring, *Industry and Empire* was not, because it consigned the economic history to statistical appendices and focused on social history
in the text. This suggested that, as so often, Taylor had not really
read the book he was reviewing.[148] More critical was the review
by Harold Perkin, whose view of the same period, expressed in
his 1969 book *The Origins of Modern English Society, 1780–1880*, and
subsequent works, was very different from Eric's. Perkin rejected
Eric's pessimistic account of working-class living standards during
industrialisation and focused instead on their steady improvement
since the 1840s. Eric's portrayal of English economic and social
history, he said bluntly, was 'as Lenin sees us'.[149]

The global impact of *Industry and Empire* was obviously limited by
its exclusive focus on British history. A German edition appeared
almost immediately, though Eric found the translation deficient in
a number of respects, from 'the stilted literal translatese' of much
of the text to the mistranslation of many technical economic terms.
He went through the typescript of the draft translation carefully,
marking it up, and urged the publisher to commission a competent
person to go over it before it went to the printers.[150] A Portuguese
translation appeared in Brazil the same year, 1969, to be followed
by an Italian one in 1972, a French one in 1976, and subsequent
translations into Farsi, Turkish, Korean and Spanish. *Industry and*

Empire secured its place as a leading textbook in the field, and, like Eric's other books, it never went out of print.

VI

Industry and Empire was followed in 1969 by a book that combined the two subjects that had absorbed Eric since the late 1940s – the impact of capitalism on society and the forms of unorganised, 'primitive' resistance to it in the countryside. This was *Captain Swing*, written jointly with George Rudé. Born in 1910, so a few years older than Eric, Rudé had made a name for himself with detailed research on the composition of the great mass revolts in Paris which had done so much to push forward the French Revolution of 1789. His dissertation, completed at University College London in 1950, and published in 1959 by Oxford University Press as *The Crowd in the French Revolution*, marked him out as one of the pioneers of 'history from below'.[151] Rudé was unable to secure a university position in the 1950s, before the expansion of the universities in the late 1960s: he thought he was too old and in any case had never taken a history degree until his doctorate. He found a position at the University of Adelaide, in Australia, an application for which, he noted, his rather conservative supervisor Alfred Cobban, whom Eric blamed for blocking his career since Rudé was a member of the Communist Party, had in fact been very helpful. Later, Rudé was appointed to a professorship at the newly built University of Stirling, in Scotland, but his wife Doreen, visiting the area, did not take to it, so he resigned before he even got there, and at Eric's suggestion, Concordia University in Montreal, where his former pupil Alan Adamson was chair of the search committee, offered him a position, which he accepted with alacrity.[152]

The origins of the collaboration lay as far back as 1962, when Rudé told Eric during one of his visits to London that he was interested in writing about the 'Captain Swing' disturbances in the English countryside in 1830 (the name derived from the fact that many letters threatening to destroy threshing machines and burn down hayricks were signed by a fictitious 'Captain Swing'). He came to it from records he had discovered in Australia of the men transported there as punishment for their part in the disturbances. 'As it happened', Eric recalled later,

> I had done some work on Swing in Wiltshire years before, for a contribution to the Victoria County History of that county which was turned down or anyway not published, and I suggested the collaboration for that reason: I'd thought about the problem, and knew about at least one county. Actually, more than one, since I also supervised a Ph.D. on Swing in SE England. So it seemed natural. He was an ideal collaborator.[153]

Responding positively to his suggestion, Rudé agreed that the book should take a long view and deal with rural industry, the Poor Law and the repression of agricultural disturbances. 'I agree entirely', he added, 'about the need to follow the day-by-day course of the rioting with the aid of maps (Lefebvre's *Grande Peur* would be a model here).'[154]

From his location in the Antipodes, Rudé would only, however, be able to research the fate of those offenders who had been transported to Tasmania; research in the English archives would have to await a period of study leave he was due in 1963 or 1964. He also had to complete a volume in the Fontana History of Europe (*Revolutionary Europe, 1783–1815*), which was published in 1964, but after that, he reassured Eric, 'I can go full steam ahead on the 1830 project and I shall certainly brood about it and complete my Aussie material long before.' The book, with most of the detailed research carried out by Rudé (except the analysis of the distribution of the riots in Chapter 9), and the background and interpretative chapters written by Eric, was published in 1969 by Lawrence and Wishart, and in America by André Schiffrin at Pantheon. *Captain Swing*, in essence, was a study of violence, especially in the face of incipient mechanisation, committed as a desperate form of collective bargaining by established and respectable workers. As such it belonged in a group of publications along these lines by other left-wing historians of the period, notably Edward Thompson's essay on the 'moral economy of the English crowd' in this period.[155] *Captain Swing*, a compelling narrative and analysis of what its authors called 'the most impressive episode in the English farm-labourers' long and doomed struggle against poverty and degradation', attracted widespread attention, and was quickly issued by Penguin Books in paperback.[156]

Like many reviewers and indeed like the authors themselves, A. J. P. Taylor paid tribute to the only previous study of the riots, by the left-wing liberal historians J. L. and Barbara Hammond, but noted that *Captain Swing* went far beyond their work in terms both of research and of understanding. It was 'a book in a thousand'.[157] Jack Plumb, however, chided the two authors for neglecting eighteenth-century popular protest and indeed the general, long-established tradition of agrarian violence, as well as the involvement of small-town radicals in it. Peasant revolts such as this, he pointed out, were often backward-looking, asserting traditional rights rather than claiming new ones.[158] Richard Cobb, an historian of popular life and popular uprisings in France during the Revolution, writing in the *Times Literary Supplement*, thought the book a perfect marriage between Rudé's skill in empirical research and Hobsbawm's 'acuteness of perception, his flair for the striking metaphor and his abundant historical imagination'. At the same time, Cobb concurred with Plumb in emphasising the naturally deferential attitudes of most of the '"Swing" men . . . These are not rural egalitarians, they accept the established order of village society and their expectations are fantastically minimal.'[159] Despite such critical voices, the book established itself as a classic of empirical research and analysis on rural reactions to the impact of capitalism and mechanisation on the English countryside and has, like Eric's other books, remained in print ever since its publication.

Despite his – and Rudé's – choice of Lawrence and Wishart as publishers of *Captain Swing*, Eric's ties to Weidenfeld at this time were close. He helped the publisher find interesting and talented new authors who could write about historical subjects in a way that would appeal to a broad readership. When Keith Thomas joined the editorial board of *Past & Present* in 1968, he encountered Eric in person for the first time. Not long afterwards, he recalled,

> in his role as talent scout for Weidenfeld & Nicolson, he asked me whether I would like to offer them whatever I was writing, which happened to be *Religion and the Decline of Magic*. Since I hadn't got round to thinking of a publisher and had some doubts as to whether anyone would want to publish it, I accepted with alacrity and it was published in 1971, very handsome with nice paper and footnotes on the page, but at a price (£8) so outrageous by the standards of the day that the TLS made it (the price, not the book) the subject of a leading article and it was followed by a correspondence in which, if I remember rightly, someone suggested that it might have been better to spend the money on taking his wife to London for the weekend and doing a show. I don't know how much Eric got for it (he was always very watchful about royalties and a fierce guardian of his copyrights), but I had a rotten deal, so that to this day Weidenfeld (now Orion) get 50% of the royalties on the Penguin paperback version. I was an innocent then.[160]

It was a rotten deal indeed: the huge book instantly became a classic and sold well for many years.

Eric felt indebted to George Weidenfeld in a number of ways, then, and at the same time as completing his contribution to *Captain Swing*, in December 1965, he agreed to write a short book on *Bandits* to Weidenfeld's new illustrated series *Pageant of History*, edited by the literary scholar and editor John Gross. The series included *Highwaymen* by the popular historian Christopher Hibbert, *Bloomsbury* by Quentin Bell, *Gladiators* by the Roman historian Michael Grant and *Nihilists* by the Russianist Ronald Hingley.[161] Eric began writing it after he completed *Industry and Empire* but soon started to have misgivings, as he wrote to David Higham on 16 November 1967:

I am getting on with the Bandits book for Weidenfeld, but am rather worried. The book is to appear in a series, of which the first 4 vols. are now out. Frankly, they rather frighten me. They look cheap and bad (I had assumed they would come out along the lines of the World Univ. Library with integrated text and illustrations), the general title is pretty awful, and indeed the whole thing now looks like a good idea which hasn't come off. George [Weidenfeld] says they will change the appearance of subsequent vols and I hope they will. As it stands the series will flop and drag all its volumes down with it. What makes it worse is that four vols. of a miscellaneous kind are published together. They have therefore been given as a bunch to the usual 'general' reviewers, which means a) that they are reviewed by ignoramuses and b) that each volume is patted on the head with an anodine line or two. This is what has so far happened. I don't want my book to come out in a way which will ruin its chances from the start. This one could do quite well, if not strangled at birth.[162]

Higham promised to talk to Weidenfeld about Eric's concerns.[163] Weidenfeld did indeed redesign the jackets and ceased publishing the books in batches of four.[164] Eric delivered the typescript of *Bandits* in early October 1968 and it was published the following year.[165]

In *Bandits* Eric built on his chapter on the subject in *Primitive Rebels* but expanded his field of vision enormously, taking in banditry across the world, from China to Brazil. This was perhaps the most purely enjoyable of Eric's books, kitted out with some fifty striking illustrations, and presenting a range of exotic information, stories, legends and biographies. Nothing like it had been published before. It brought together a mass of familiar and unfamiliar material to advance a coherent set of arguments about the whole phenomenon of banditry. The social bandit, it argued, was a representative of rural society, living on its margins and fighting on its behalf to redistribute wealth, like Robin Hood, or avenging the wrongs done to it, like the Brazilian Lampião, or mounting sporadic and unorganised resistance against the state, like the *haiduks* of south-eastern Europe who fought against their Ottoman rulers in the eighteenth century. 'Social banditry' was a pre-organisational, pre-ideological but still in a broad sense political attempt to bring about the liberation not of the industrial classes, but of the pre-industrial poor, like the other 'archaic forms of social movement' studied in *Primitive Rebels*.

It was striking in terms of the trajectory of Eric's thought that he had moved by the middle of the 1950s from writing about the rising industrial working class to writing about the dispossessed and the marginalised, from history's eventual victors, as he saw it, to history's undoubted losers. Eric's sympathy for his subjects shone through the teleological framework. Men like Francisco Sabaté Llopart, he wrote, a bandit and resistance fighter in Franco's Spain through to the end of the 1950s, were heroes: tragic, doomed heroes, but heroes none the less. Some reviewers sensed Eric's admiration for his subjects, and pointed out that living under the control of bandits could mean violence, murder and extortion and was for many ordinary countryfolk deeply oppressive. For Eric, however, the greatest compliment paid to the book was praise from a group of peasant radicals in Mexico in the 1970s, who wrote to him saying they approved of what he had written. 'It does not prove that the analysis put forward in this book is right', he wrote in the revised 1999 edition. 'But it may give readers of the book some confidence that it is more than an exercise in antiquarianism or in academic speculation. Robin Hood, even in his most tra-ditional forms, still means something in today's world, to people like these Mexican peasants. There are many of them. And they should know.'

In academic circles, the book sparked a long-running debate over its central concept of 'social banditry'. The Dutch anthropol-ogist Anton Blok, whose book *The Mafia of a Sicilian Village* would be published in 1974, considered (clearly on the basis of his own experience) that Eric neglected the links of many bandits with established power-holders.[166] But Eric knew full well that in some cases these links were close. 'The Sicilian Mafia', he wrote in 1964, 'is essentially a method of building middle-class wealth by means of extortion based on murder.' The Mafia in many cases played a key role in securing votes for the Italian government in elections. After the Second World War the Americans co-opted it into the fight against Communism.[167] The Mafia was not really a form of banditry. But even bandits who formed part of local peasant society were often violent, intimidating and blackmailing the local rural communities from which they came into providing them with funds and concealing them from the authorities. In the end, perhaps, the myth was more important than the reality, expressing as it did the deep longing of poor and oppressed peasants for a compensatory celebration of resistance to authority that may well have had only a limited basis in reality.

Bandits was serialised in the *Observer* and attracted attention far beyond the confines of academia.[168] The book's success prompted George Bluestone, an American movie producer, best known for his 1957 book *Novels into Film*, to take out an option on the film rights. The intention was to make a documentary. Eric was worried about the possibility of a vulgarisation. 'Have I the right to withdraw my name (75% of the screenwriter's credit)', he asked, 'if, say, they decide that poor Sabaté would be better material as a conservative Texan rodeo rider who sings hillbilly songs?'[169] He was more minded to go ahead with Bluestone, however, than to accept an offer from another company, David Paradine Productions, run by the television personality and entrepreneur David Frost.[170] In the end, nothing came of either offer. The book, however, continued to sell well in a growing number of languages. As late as 2009, forty years after the book's first publication in English, Eric's regular Brazilian publishers, Paz e Terra, made an offer for the Portuguese language rights.[171] And a history of banditry in Latin America published in 2015 noted that 'Eric Hobsbawm still dominates the literature on bandit theory'.[172]

The books Eric published in the late sixties and early seventies played a central part in a revolution in British historiography that took place in this period: the coming of social history. Along with the publications of Christopher Hill, Rodney Hilton, Victor

Kiernan, Edward Thompson and other former members of the Communist Party Historians' Group, it brought the English Marxist historians to international fame. Soon they were being treated by writers on historiography on the same level as the *Annales* school, pioneering what the German-American historiographer George G. Iggers called *New Directions in European Historiography*, the title of a widely influential book published in 1975.[173] Yet, social history was still an undeveloped field. It had no independent representation in university history syllabuses, no textbooks, and in Britain at least, no society of its own (the UK's Social History Society was founded in 1976, and the journal *Social History* published its first issue the same year). Social history in the old sense of the history of the 'social movement', Eric declared in a widely influential article, was being replaced by a broad-based history of society.[174] The message was heeded above all by the younger generation of British historians who came into the profession with the rapid expansion of the universities in the late 1960s and early 1970s (I was a part of this generation, taking my doctorate and getting my first job in 1972). Soon Eric's books were set reading in social history courses all over the country.

VII

In 1966 Eric was offered a six-month Visiting Professorship in the Humanities at the Massachusetts Institute of Technology, located in Cambridge, Massachusetts, on the outskirts of Boston. This time the American authorities were ready for him.[175] Eric's visa application informed the immigration authorities that among other places he had visited recently had been Cuba, Czechoslovakia, Hungary, East Germany, Bulgaria and Yugoslavia.[176] The application was referred to the FBI, who reported on 9 January 1967 that he 'has been found by the Department of State to be ineligible to receive a visa because of his membership in the Communist Party of Great Britain from 1936 to the present as well as his membership in the Society of Cultural Relations with the Union of Soviet Socialist

Republics from 1953 to date'. They put considerable pressure on MIT, resulting in a series of 'increasingly frantic transatlantic telephone conversations' with Eric as MIT tried to clarify the situation. No doubt prompted by an inadequately informed FBI, the sponsoring official at MIT asked Eric whether he was, or ever had been, Chairman of the British Communist Party (evidently they had confused the Party with its Historians' Group). He was able to say with a clear conscience: no.

Eventually the Department of State relented, and Eric was granted 'temporary admission to the United States pursuant to section 212(d)(3)(A) of the Immigration and Nationality Act; despite inadmissibility under Section 212(a)(28) of the Act'. 'The Department of State', as the FBI reported, 'has made a strong recommendation that his admission be authorized on the ground that the courses he will offer at MIT are regarded by that institution's Department of History as being educationally significant.' It was also decided 'that the itinerary proposed by the applicant is approved, no deviation therefrom or extension of stay to be authorized without prior approval by the District Director, Washington, DC'.[177] This last condition meant that Eric was required to report to the university administrator responsible for visiting professors every time he left the Boston area. 'You mean I can't spend the night in New York without your OK?' he asked her. She saw the absurdity of the demand and did not insist, though the FBI did express a strong interest in a lecture Eric gave on 9 May 1967 at the Columbia University Faculty Club in New York to a hundred people, sponsored by the American Institute for Marxist Studies jointly with the Students for a Democratic Society, a radical movement whose main activity was to protest against the draft of young men into the armed services to fight in the Vietnam War.[178] However, the FBI felt able to report later on, in response to an enquiry, that Eric had been granted a visa because on his previous visit 'his record contained nothing to indicate he acted outside the stated scope of his visits'.[179] He duly arrived in Boston with the family, and spent an uneventful semester teaching at MIT.

At no point during its monitoring of his visits did the FBI note the fact that Eric had also returned to Cuba in the meantime, and in a very public manner. In 1968 Eric attended the Cultural Congress of Havana, a gathering of some five hundred people from seventy countries, which 'symbolized in a curious way a return to the mood of intellectual commitment which was characteristic of the 1930s'. Eric found the occasion reminiscent of the Writers' Congress held in Republican Madrid in 1937. 'As Fascism united the intellectuals in the 1930s, so the United States united them at Havana.' The Congress, Eric reported, showed how a broad and heterogeneous collection of intellectuals could be mobilised in defence of movements of liberation in the 'Third World' and the civil rights movement in the USA. The variety of points of view represented reflected the Cuban government's reluctance to have much to do with old-style Communist Parties, preferring instead to link up with the New Left. The debates none the less were 'not merely unconstrained but seemed at times to verge on the anarchic'. There were neo-Dadaists, Trotskyist surrealists, Reichians arguing for the political function of the orgasm, and other representatives of 'that fringe of dottiness which is so engaging a part of the left'. Eric greeted with some scepticism calls for the participants to join guerrilla movements: 'the public activities of intellectuals cannot be confined to carrying machine-guns'.[180] Avant-garde French theorists produced the major incident of the Congress when 'old surrealists physically attacked the Mexican artist Siqueiros, who had once been associated with the plans to assassinate Trotsky, at the opening of an art show, though it was not clear how far this was on grounds of artistic or political disagreement'. A positive outcome of the Congress for Eric was making the acquaintance of the left-wing German poet and writer Hans Magnus Enzensberger, but overall he was depressed by 'the evident mess Cuba had made of its economy'.[181]

The British authorities were less tolerant of Eric's travels abroad than were their American counterparts. In 1968 he was invited to India by the leading historian Sarvepalli Gopal under an arrangement whereby Indian universities hosted two British historians every year to take part in seminars and discussions, and provided maintenance while they were there, with their travel expenses being paid by the British Council. In 1967 Richard Cobb and Keith Thomas had gone to India under the scheme. But Gopal was obliged to tell Eric that the Council was refusing to pay his air fare, clearly because he was a Marxist. Eric mobilised Noel Annan in his support. Eric had never concealed his political sympathies, Annan told the Council's Director, but

> he is, however, a pretty distinguished historian, whose books have had wide success – so much so that he was invited to go for a semester to M. I. T. and the American authorities gave him a visa. He is a cultivated man, by no means narrow and sectarian – incidentally an expert on Jazz – and, however much his fellow historians may disagree with his emphasis on this or that point, none would deny that he is a man of deserved international reputation.
>
> The refusal of the British Council to pay Hobsbawm's air fare is said to have caused considerable surprise and indeed annoyance in India – so much so that they are considering finding the money to pay his air fare themselves. Meanwhile Gopal has informed Hobsbawm that the ostensible reason given by the British Council authorities to him for the Council's refusal is that when abroad Hobsbawm is imprudent in his dealings with women. This has amused Eric Hobsbawm intensely. He regards this as exceedingly flattering, but he remains convinced in his own mind that he is being discriminated against for his political opinions.[182]

Annan told the British Council that Eric was 'happily married', and added that 'if the British Council were willing to gamble on Richard Cobb', who was a notoriously hard drinker, 'I would have thought they could take a gamble on Hobsbawm'. Putting on his most impressive official manner, Annan concluded that he doubted 'whether it was wise if under an agreement with another country the British Council was seen to be exercising political discrimination, when the other country has invited a particular scholar to visit them'. He warned that 'this matter could explode publicly' and do the Council's reputation considerable damage.

Thanks to Annan, Eric did go to India, where he stayed from 12 December 1968 to 11 January 1969. To his great surprise he was greeted on the airport tarmac by his old Cambridge friend Mohan Kumaramangalam, now a member of the Congress Party and running Indian Airlines.[183] Eric found the Moghul architecture in India 'fabulously elegant, but what really impressed me most is those cows walking up and down the streets by themselves eating rubbish'. He was struck by the variety of spectacle in the country, 'because of all this mix-up of religions, costumes, colours etc.', though taken aback by the poverty – 'I doubt whether you can get any poorer than poverty is here'. He liked the 'enchanting cycle-rickshaws all painted up with lovely Indian gods, goddesses (or maybe today filmstars) in the wildest Sicilian-type colours. The kids would dig them', he told Marlene in one of his many letters home. The better-off lived in houses 'modelled on the suburban bungalows of long-gone Indian Civil Servants, building little Wimbledons in the Empire'. He lunched with the secretary to the Prime Minister and dined with the Vice-Chancellor of Aligarh University, a Muslim institution where he had been invited to speak.[184]

Eric was already known to the younger generations of Indian historians, who were regular readers of *Past & Present* and were familiar with his books, most notably *Bandits*. The Indian historian Romila Thapar remembered later:

His presence was important for those of us who were arguing for the inclusion of social and economic history to the syllabus of most Indian universities, the existing curriculum being largely devoted to political and diplomatic history. His discussions on the Marxist approach to history also elicited much interest since this was the time when Marxist history was beginning to be taken seriously not so much in departments of history in some Indian universities but among individual historians.[185]

Eric was frustrated by what he took to be Indian inefficiency, but enjoyed the experience and liked the Indians none the less. He was able to fit in some tourism, despite all the hard work, and was pleased that he experienced 'no stomach trouble [though] I get no exercise, [and am] over-eating'.[186] He inspected the temples at Orissa and Konark, admiring, as he told Marlene,

the women in the countryside (and the men) all dressed in lovely green, purple and a sort of burnt orange, the fresh coconuts – but also the tiny, thin, undeified figures of rural India. The Indians are a bit embarrassed about the Konark temple. Plenty of guff about how all sides of life are being represented on the statues, but in fact 80% of them are purely erotic, including most of the interesting ways of sexual play and fucking one can think of, very beautifully displayed. It made me think about you even more than usual. There's only one problem: one of the positions means the man standing up & *carrying* the woman, which implies either a very big man or a very tiny woman, or both. Altogether, an enchanting form of art and a really *marvellous* kind of sculpture.[187]

He thought the Indians he met at a Christmas dinner thrown for him were 'all *terribly* English in spite of the biryani and betel nuts. The old empire survives still in their souls, even when they are Communists.' It was to be a long time before he returned to India, but from this moment onwards his reputation in the subcontinent began rapidly to grow.

The reluctance of the British Council to fund Eric's trip was followed not long afterwards by another case of official disapproval of Eric's politics. When the Director-General of the United Nations Educational, Scientific and Cultural Organization (UNESCO), René Maheu, approached Eric to ask him to attend a conference to be held in Finland to mark the centenary of the birth of Lenin in 1870, officials at the British Ministry of Overseas Development demurred.[188] A Foreign Office mandarin objected to Eric on the grounds that he 'is a leading Communist'. He urged a formal protest to the Director-General. It then emerged that Maheu had invited Eric on his 'personal authority', after having been impressed by him at a previous meeting. Upon learning this, the Ministry of Overseas Development addressed what it called a 'strong personal remonstrance' to him on the grounds that the invitation was 'liable to cause considerable damage to UNESCO's reputation in the UK' and could be seen 'as evidence of undue communist influence' within UNESCO. An official sent to meet Maheu to remonstrate with him in person about Eric's invitation did not get very far. 'When I said that he is a member of the British Communist Party', the official reported, 'M. Maheu replied "So What?"' The row fizzled out when Eric declined the invitation anyway.

His views also got him into trouble when they were broadcast on BBC Radio. He was signed up for a run of four broadcasts for BBC Radio 3 (as the Third Programme was now called) in the spring of 1972 in the series 'A Personal View'.[189] Eric's proposed four lectures were on 'The United States and Vietnam', on 13 May, 'The motives behind terrorism', on 27 May, 'Problems of excessive capitalism', on 10 June, and 'Shop stewards are a good thing for capitalism', on 24 June.[190] In the end, 'Problems of excessive capitalism' was dropped, presumably because its title was deemed by BBC executives as too polemical. The broadcast on terrorism went ahead, with Eric reflecting on the numerous political assassinations and bombings of the early 1970s. His conclusion was that terrorist attacks, however devastating, were 'gestures rather than purposeful acts'.[191] In his broadcast on shop stewards, he made a case for industrial democracy as a form of direct political participation, particularly in the intervals between parliamentary elections.[192]

His broadcast in the series on 'Why America Lost the Vietnam War', however, proved altogether too controversial for the BBC and some of its listeners. Eric made no secret of his commitment to the Vietnamese cause. He had taken part in the great demonstration against the war held in London in 1968, which ended in a violent confrontation with the police in front of the American Embassy in Grosvenor Square. 'I got there', Claire Tomalin, literary editor of the *New Statesman*, recalled, 'and there was Eric, and he took my arm, and he tucked my arm through his arm and he said "Come on!" and we sort of ran, not very fast, but you know we were all running round and round, and it gave me a marvellous sense of doing something properly and being seriously politically engaged.'[193] As he reflected on the war in his broadcast, he began: 'It doesn't often happen in world politics that the goodies defeat the baddies, especially when the goodies are small and weak and the baddies overwhelmingly strong.' Though the war was still continuing (it would last, indeed, up to the fall of Saigon in 1975), there was no doubt the Americans had lost (as they were implicitly to concede by agreeing the Paris Peace Accords in January 1973). They had been defeated by their own hubris, 'the inability of big white men to believe that little yellow ones could possibly beat them', by the folly of presidents determined on asserting their virility by displays of global machismo and by the ability of politicians to believe their own lies. 'History', he concluded, 'will not forgive those who laid waste the countries of Indo-China for a generation, who expelled, mangled, corrupted and massacred their peoples for the sake of the calculations of poker-players. Or those who gave them support, however ineffective. Or even those who kept their mouths shut when they should have cried out in outrage.'[194]

It was one of Eric's most powerful polemics. And it called forth a strong reaction from the American Embassy which pressured the BBC into commissioning a rebuttal of Eric's talk from Dennis Duncanson, a British intelligence officer who had worked for the Malayan authorities in their brutal suppression of the Communist insurgency. Duncanson branded Eric's talk the product of ignorance and credulity in the face of North Vietnamese propaganda lies. His broadcast was not very effective, however. When Duncanson pointed out to listeners that the North Vietnamese forces far outgunned those of the South, it was obvious enough to anybody who heard him that he had failed to mention the vastly superior firepower of the Americans. The Americans, he declared in conclusion, had not really lost; they could not stay indefinitely anyway, and the ongoing 'Vietnamization' of the political system in the South left the essential institutions of a market economy and open society intact (perhaps wisely, he did not claim there was a functioning democracy in the country, since there was not).[195]

Eric's troubles with the American authorities in other respects had now largely disappeared, however. He was back in the USA for a week, to attend a symposium of the American Academy of Arts and Sciences at Boston, on stratification and poverty, in June 1969, and again in October 1970, to accept Harvard's Silas Marcus Macvane Prize for European History. In December 1970 he was at the American Historical Association's annual conference, a vast gathering of several thousand professional historians, in Boston, and from late April to late June 1973 he went on a lecture and conference tour, including Chicago, Madison (Wisconsin), Rutgers (New Jersey) and New York.[196] These and subsequent visits were all logged by the FBI, but without any special precautions being ordered. Even the FBI was by now describing him as a 'noted historian'.[197]

Eric's experiences on these visits were mixed. Madison he found 'a paradise for students but probably not for professors, who must get a bit claustrophobic in this beautiful ghetto, so un-American, everything clean and works, lakes, blue sky and sun, and you can't get away from your colleagues'.[198] In Chicago he was dismayed by the corruption of Mayor Daley's administration and by the rigid racial segregation the Mayor appeared to have imposed on the city's precincts. 'In the ghetto .... empty burned-out houses and a demoralisation which is unbelievable.'[199] 'Chicago', however, was 'still the place for blues', which he experienced on the west side 'in a place called Ma Bea's where the black cleaning women have a social club and the band and singers go more for dancing ... What a marvellous thing these blues bars are. I get stoned simply by listening.' He was impressed by the latest 'male black fashions, which would send everyone on the King's Road round the bend. Right now fantastic hats are in: straw hats with great shiny metal bands, far-out berets, even women's semi-cloche straw hats. Purple jackets and shirts with great check trousers, huge crosses worn as ornaments.'[200] In New York he had dinner with Bob Silvers, editor

of the *New York Review of Books* ('a determined vegetarian').[201] The
city had changed, he thought:

> Though they've cleaned up Times Square a little bit & keep
> some cops there, the place is worse than I remember it. New
> York is running down like anything, only when one gets to odd
> bits of the East Side and among those great big glass cliffs of
> skyscrapers on 6 Avenue and Park Avenue does it still feel as
> exhilarating as it once did . . . Everybody in Manhattan seems
> to talk Spanish now – more than ever.

New York was indeed deteriorating and becoming more dangerous, and its decline was not to be reversed until the beginning
of the 1990s. He was back in the USA in August 1975, visiting
New York again as well as San Francisco.[202] By now, while Eric
was still occasionally sampling the kind of life he had experienced
in America in the early 1960s, his visits were overwhelmingly
academic in character and he mingled mainly with middle-class
intellectuals.

VIII

Eric's contacts with British Communism during the 1960s were
intermittent, and there was no sense in which he was an active
or committed member of the Party. Indeed, he harboured serious reservations, as he most likely always had, about the human
cost of Communist politics in the era of Stalin. As Isaiah Berlin
reported in 1972:

> I asked Eric Hobsbawm the other day whether he did not think
> that his party, of which he is still a loyal member – or perhaps
> disloyal member, but a member – was not on the whole respon-
> sible for a great deal more pain than happiness, and shed too
> much blood with very little to show for it, comparatively speak-
> ing, if one was to reckon these things in terms of human beings

and not of inexorable cosmic forces ... Surprisingly enough, he agreed, but what this is worth I simply do not know. I enjoyed my meeting with him very much. He is ... a very suitable acquaintance for me.[203]

The two men, indeed, became friends, recognising in each other the insatiable intellectual curiosity, cosmopolitanism, deep intelligence and breadth of knowledge that they both prized.

Whatever his misgivings about the Communist cause, Eric did continue and in some ways deepen his engagement with the writings and ideas of Marx and Engels. During the 1960s, many of Marx's writings were rediscovered or republished. Among them was the so-called *Grundrisse*, a vast, inchoate set of notebooks prepared in the late 1850s but unpublished until 1939. No English translation was even attempted until the 1970s. A significant theme of these notebooks was the transition from feudalism to capitalism, a topic that continued to seize Eric's imagination. It cannot have been easy to draw anything coherent from *Grundrisse*, but the relevant extracts had been published in East Berlin in 1952 and were now translated into English under the title *Pre-Capitalist Economic Formations*, which Lawrence and Wishart brought out in 1964. At their request, Eric provided a lengthy introduction. The crucial point that he stressed was that Marx did not posit a unilinear series of stages through all of which history marched to the present and the future. The book was of interest mainly to Marxists, but it did attract a review in the *Times Literary Supplement*, where, not for the first or last time, it was pointed out that Eric's 'prejudices are obvious enough, but he never allows them to ride rough-shod over his scholarship'.[204]

Eric's contribution to this slim volume led to his involvement in a far larger project. In 1968, in an unsigned leading article for the *Times Literary Supplement*, he marked the 150th anniversary of the birth of Karl Marx by noting the great thinker's universal appeal. 'His reputation is at present genuinely global.' It was for this reason that a new complete edition of his works was now being undertaken. This gigantic enterprise was necessary not least because the *Marx-Engels-Gesamtausgabe*, the famous and, as far as it went, indispensable edition produced under the aegis of the Marx-Engels Institute in Moscow, founded by the Old Bolshevik David Ryazanov, who had begun the monumental task of editing in 1927, had been 'cut short' (Eric did not mention the fact this was because Ryazanov had been an early victim of Stalin's purges, expelled from the Party in 1931, imprisoned, and shot seven years later). Ryazanov's standards of scholarship were impeccable, and he had brought to light many previously unknown works, but the successor edition, a far less scholarly series of forty volumes produced by the East German Institute for Marxism-Leninism-Stalinism (the 'Stalinism' was dropped shortly after Stalin's death), had many gaps and failed to publish all the different versions of Marx's writings, even though he had constantly been revising *Das Kapital* and other works.[205]

Eric joined the editorial board of this ambitious project, set up by Progress Publishers in Moscow in 1968 and published in English by Lawrence and Wishart in fifty volumes between 1975 and 2004.[206] Nick Jacobs, at that time working for Lawrence and Wishart, was appointed executive editor and in this capacity went to see Eric to get him involved. As he later remembered,

> I went into his office at Birkbeck ... He was standing, opening Air Mail envelopes with a very effective stroke of an envelope opener. And I got the impression that he didn't quite know who I was or why I was there. But eventually, he read his letters from Brazil or wherever – I'm sure they were from Brazil – and we started talking about the Marx/Engels ... He was the editor of three volumes of the correspondence. He did it for the cause, unpaid. He enjoyed seeing that Marx's and Engels's idiomatic German, and also French, found the right English idiom. For this he was the past master.[207]

The Soviet publishers financed the whole enterprise, printed it and supplied the scholarly apparatus, which Jacobs edited, negotiating with the Russians about how many quotations from Lenin he was allowed to excise. Once a volume was finished, he would cycle up Highgate West Hill to the Soviet trade delegation with the enormous manuscript ('we never copied them, I mean they were so huge, you couldn't possibly make second copies, we hadn't got the staff to do that'), leave it with the porter and cycle back to begin working with Eric on the next volume. The Soviet editors insisted that they had the last word, but on some issues at least, for example Marx's notorious *Secret Diplomatic History of the Eighteenth Century*, a short tract in which Marx gave his paranoid conspiracy theories about collaboration between Russia and Britain free rein, the English editors got their way. The Soviets had wanted to leave it out because it might damage the great man's reputation, but Jacobs and his team eventually persuaded them to leave it in.

Eric did not attend meetings of the editorial committee in London, but he did deal with the many problems that arose in relations between the British and Russian publishers and the holders of the German-language originals from which the translations had to be made. Special introductions were written for the English-language volumes, and these too became the subject of disagreements. As Eric informed the Marx specialist David McLellan on 7 November 1969: 'It looks as though the Russians ... still hanker for introductions which contain "political orientation" ... but our view is strongly that the introductions should not contain such matter.'[208] In addition, perhaps stemming from their treatment of Marx and Engels's writings as sacred texts, the Russians insisted on a painfully literal translation, no matter how unreadable it might turn out to be. A translation carried out by the Marxist sociologist Tom Bottomore was rejected for this reason. 'We can't use your text', Eric told him: 'The kind of close translation they want would completely change the character of your version. In the end there was nothing to be done. So far as I can tell there was no ideological element in their objection, but merely a fundamental disagreement about how freely the text of Marx can be translated. I happen to be on your side in this debate', he added.[209] Overall, however, the edition, despite a few flaws, was a major achievement, and Eric's part in it one of his least acknowledged contributions to scholarship.

Eric was also closely engaged in the debates, sometimes fiercely polemical, that surrounded other, later thinkers in the Marxist tradition who emerged on the scene in the 1960s and early 1970s, in particular the writings of the French Communist philosopher Louis Althusser, who had become fashionable among the Marxist student ultra-left during the 1970s. His ideas did not meet with Eric's approval, brilliant though he found them. Althusser's attempt to remove the influence of Hegel from Marx's thought meant in effect removing Marx almost completely from Althusser's definition of Marxism, though 'M. Althusser, admittedly, had always left himself considerable scope for originality by a rather pretty argument showing that the greatness of Marx consisted not in what he said, but in making it possible for Althusser to say what he meant.' Nor did Eric approve of his attacks on 'empiricism' and 'humanism' as alien importations into Marxist theory. If there were ever any qualities that distinguished Eric's own approach to history, these surely ranked high among them. A lot of what Althusser said was, for Eric, mere 'eyewash' or 'platform rhetoric, and a poor specimen of its kind'. His discussion of the Marxist theory of the state was 'infantile'. Althusser's 'waffle' was designed simply to enable him 'to explain away the body of Marx's thought which he wishes to dismiss as a petty-bourgeois survival'.[210] Eric had rumbled Louis Althusser long before Edward Thompson entered the fray with his powerful, if somewhat overblown, denunciation of the Frenchman's ideas in his tract *The Poverty of Theory* (1978). As historians, neither of the two men could follow the road away from respect for empirical evidence laid down by Althusser.

IX

British Marxist intellectuals, Eric thought, were far more isolated from politics in Britain than their counterparts in Italy or France were from politics in their own countries.[211] Only one of the younger generation, Raphael Samuel, who had been in the

Communist Party Historians' Group and now taught history at the trade-union-funded Ruskin College in Oxford, attempted to break out of the cultural and political constraints that commonly limited the influence of left-wing intellectuals in the UK. His first venture was the creation in 1958 of the Partisan Coffee House in Carlisle Street, in London's Soho, where he envisaged lively political and intellectual conversations taking place on the lines of similar institutions on the Parisian Left Bank. Eric, who was nominally Samuel's Ph.D. supervisor, agreed to become a company director of this venture. Somehow Samuel managed to raise the money to get it started, from sympathetic figures such as Ken Tynan, Doris Lessing and others, but it folded within two years, a quixotic venture that Eric regarded as symbolic of the impracticality and lack of clear purpose of most of the New Left.[212]

Samuel's next project, launched a few years later, was more successful. This was the 'History Workshop' movement, born in the late 1960s, through which sympathetic academics and students would join forces with workers who were writing their own history. The annual History Workshops were hugely exciting events with up to a thousand participants on each occasion and pioneering lectures and papers by Samuel's own students, mature men and women from working-class backgrounds. Eric described them as 'the nearest thing to a Durham Miners' Gala for militant historians, both professional and, in unusually substantial numbers, non-professional: unique mixtures of learned conferences, political rallies, revival meetings and weekend holidays'.[213] He had his doubts, however, about the vigorous but eclectic category of 'people's history' that the Workshop sought to promote:

> Its strength and weakness today is that it is largely inspirational: a recovery of ancestors, a search for the village Hampdens and mute inglorious Miltons who can be shown to have been neither mute nor inglorious, a transformation of the past, through identification, into an everyday epic . . . The problem about this kind of history . . . is that it sacrifices analysis and explanation to celebration and identification.

Eric was not the only left-wing historian to be frustrated by the chaos that surrounded Samuel, a brilliant writer who achieved less than he might have done, largely because of his disorganised way of working. He could often be seen all but disappearing under huge mounds of books and journals in the Reading Room of the British Museum, and when he gave a paper it was usually from the midst of a similar pile of notebooks and lever-arch files that he brought with him to the seminar room. After hearing him give a talk in 1969, Eric dispensed some much-needed advice:

> If you lose yourself in the contemporary material in order to recreate the past, how does this differ (except in subject matter) from the traditional type of history which we wanted to get rid of? *Get something on paper.* That talk of yours, pruned of 80% of the quotes which actually make it so bulky, would make a good article for P&P [*Past & Present*]. All you need is to make explicit the conclusions implied in it. Please don't mind my pushing you. You are so talented, and your stuff so important, that your friends don't want to see you and it wasted.[214]

'Posthumous works', he added acerbically in response to Samuel's reply, in which he had evidently tried to defend himself by claiming he was preparing a lot of books and articles, but they were taking a long time, so that they might only be published after his death (he was forty-four at the time), 'are *written* in the author's life-time, only published after his death. If the writing is postponed too long, it tends not to get done: then no works at all (cf. Acton).'[215] The late-Victorian historian Lord Acton had indeed accumulated a vast quantity of knowledge, as his heavily annotated book collection, preserved in Cambridge University Library, attests, but always felt there was more to learn and so he never did publish anything.

Eric was sceptical, therefore, when in 1976, following a series of pioneering volumes of essays drawn from the work of his students and sympathetic colleagues, Samuel launched the *History Workshop Journal*, an enterprise that soon got into financial difficulties. Asked in 1977 to make a donation to help keep it afloat, Eric was anything but sympathetic. Drawing on his experience with *Past & Present*, he told one of the journal's editors:

> I thought from the start that it couldn't work. It's too big by far – what on earth is progressive about committing oneself to regular jumbo issues which, as is evident, cannot be filled without padding? It's too cheap. It never looked like getting 2500–3000 subscribers which, with that costing, it needed *immediately*. In short, it looked like a typical Raph Samuel enterprise. I reckoned it would fold within 3 issues, and it evidently will, without outside aid.[216]

Raphael Samuel did indeed have a long record of starting projects he was unable to complete; his bibliography is littered with two-volume works of which only the first ever appeared. After his premature death in 1996 at the age of sixty-one, his friends appropriately enough produced a three-volume collection of his essays, *Theatres of Memory*, of which only two volumes were ever published.

Not surprisingly, perhaps, the History Workshops themselves became the site of increasingly acrimonious disputes between different sects of the Left as they went on, and were taken over by radical schoolteachers and left-wing academics, pushing aside the workers and trade union activists whose writing of their own history dominated the early meetings. The Workshops declined and eventually stopped altogether in the early 1990s as the unions themselves declined under the onslaught of Thatcherism. But despite Eric's gloomy predictions, the *History Workshop Journal* survived, becoming steadily more academic, keeping its financial head above water through reducing the number of pages and increasing the number of subscribers. In a witty review, David Cannadine presented the trajectory of the History Workshop movement as 'one of the most spectacular examples of *embourgeoisement* in the 1970s', as it followed 'the path already blazed by that earlier *enfant terrible*, *Past and Present*, from mutinous opposition to respectable dissent'.[217] Less successful was Samuel's abortive attempt to convert the meetings into an academic institution, the History Workshop

Centre for Social History, registered as a Limited Company at Companies House. Eric agreed to become one of its directors, but he rapidly discovered that it was so poorly managed that it failed to declare its accounts and he began to receive minatory letters from Companies House threatening him and the other company directors 'with terrible penalties'. The Centre even ignored Eric's request to be taken off the board. Eventually it was all sorted out, but there was no disguising Eric's irritation.[218]

Eric thought that other members of the New Left could also be intellectually undisciplined. Edward Thompson, for example, was, he felt, a writer of genius, but 'nature had omitted to provide him with an in-built sub-editor and an in-built compass', so that he lacked the ability to express himself with brevity, and succumbed to the temptation to be diverted into side issues.[219] The chaotic nature of the New Left was, however, only one of the reasons for its isolation and ineffectiveness in Eric's view. The main problem was that it had no organisational expression. Moreover, the basically working-class character of the Communist Party remained unaltered, and intellectuals were still barely tolerated in its ranks. Attempting to take advantage of the upsurge in left-wing student activism in the late 1960s, the Party appointed the twenty-two-year-old graduate student Martin Jacques to its executive. But as Jacques discovered,

> There was almost a wall between the generations ... I felt like a Martian on the Communist Party executive ... They would turn up in the conservative clothes of the British labour movement. I was dressed in the style of the times. I'd turn up in a sweater. I'd go to the Congress and I'd be the only man in the place not wearing a suit.[220]

Much the same could be said of the Labour Party. In terms of political organisation, there was nowhere for the New Left to go.

Yet it was far more influential than Eric sometimes claimed. This became abundantly clear in 1968, when student discontent across Europe and America erupted into a massive wave of protests and demonstrations, shaking the foundations not only of higher education but also of governments. Eric was actually in Paris himself on 8–10 May 1968, attending a conference organised by UNESCO to mark the 150th birthday of Karl Marx. During the Cold War, the organisation had naturally to pay due tribute to the intellectual interests of the Communist states of the Eastern bloc, and the conference, held at its headquarters, which were located in the French capital, was the result. The conference, Eric noted,

> was admittedly somewhat overshadowed by the events in the Latin Quarter, which Marx himself might have regarded as a more apposite reminder of his existence. The inscriptions, hastily chalked or painted on the walls of the Rue d'Ulm and the Rue Gay-Lussac, amid the reminders of barricades and the persistent irritations of tear-gas, would certainly have been to the taste of the great revolutionary: 'Vive la Commune 10 Mai' or: 'Camarades si tout le peuple ferait comme nous?'[221]

Eric was dismayed by the rigidity and dogmatism of the Eastern European participants in the conference, and found those who wanted Marx's analysis to be brought up to date more stimulating. Among them were the radical students, whose mass demonstrations on 6 May and again on 10 May marked the real beginning of the upheavals of that year.

There were, Eric observed, two stages in the 'events' of 1968 in France. First, between 3 and 11 May, the students rose spontaneously in protest against the conditions they were forced to endure in the new world of mass higher education. Secondly, from 14 to 27 May, they were joined by a general strike of Parisian workers, which again wrong-footed the government and conservative commentators and created the real possibility of a genuine political revolution. At this point, President de Gaulle, who had applied moderate repression to the student movement, resulting only in its radicalisation, called in the army. But de Gaulle's recovery of nerve, the divisions within the opposition – between Communists and socialists, workers and students – doomed the revolution to failure. The students lacked the kind of coherent political programme that only an organised party could have given them.[222] For their part, the Communists, as Elise Marienstras observed, were shocked by the outburst of youthful utopianism on the streets of Paris in 1968 and did not know how to take advantage of it.[223]

Neal Ascherson remembered hearing Eric give a lecture to students in West Berlin, at the height of the student revolt that was also sweeping across the former German capital. The students invited him,

> and he came, because of course his name came up very much when the whole student movement began in West Berlin ... His attitude to all that was fairly severe or austere. I mean, he thought it really was infantile and would come to nothing, because it wasn't founded on correct class analysis and all the rest of it, and it was frivolous – little middle-class kids dashing about ... Everybody was thinking 'is he going to say that he supports us?' and he didn't.[224]

For all Eric's scepticism, Ascherson was perhaps laying too much emphasis on the negative side of his view of 1968. As Eric remarked in July that year, nobody thought the students would create a genuine revolution, 'yet a month later 10 million workers were on strike – and *not* primarily for economic reasons either. A new situation brought out the revolutionary potentialities.'[225] It was not inevitable that these potentialities never actually materialised. Looking back on the student revolt forty years later, Eric conceded that it was a seminal experience for the young, an experience he was then already too old to share; its political legacy might have been small, but it did at least nurture a new generation of left-wing politicians who came to prominence in the ensuing decades.[226]

In the summer of 1968 another dramatic series of events unfolded in Europe, this time in Communist Czechoslovakia. Earlier in the year, the country's hard-line Stalinist leader had been ousted and the Communist Party in Prague taken over by Alexander Dubček, who with his associates began to move the regime in a more liberal, more democratic direction. Their reforms drew increasingly vehement criticism from Moscow, until eventually, on 21 August, Soviet troops, assisted by forces from other Warsaw Pact countries including East Germany (which aroused unhappy memories of the previous German invasion, thirty years before), marched into the country, arrested Dubček and the liberal Communist leadership, and reimposed hard-line Stalinist rule. It was a measure of Eric's distance from the British Party leadership by this time that he did not engage at all in the bitter debates that raged in its circles over the invasion. Ten years later, he made his support for the Dubček regime's model of democratic socialism abundantly clear in a lengthy article in *Marxism Today*, the Party's intellectual magazine.[227]

Thus Eric's ideological position by the late 1960s and early 1970s was far from simple, a fact illustrated in abundance by a collection of short, mostly non-academic pieces entitled *Revolutionaries: Contemporary Essays* published in 1973 by Weidenfeld & Nicolson. Here he distanced himself both from orthodox Communism and from the wilder theories of the New Left. In one essay, first published in 1969, he took issue with the link, drawn explicitly by Wilhelm Reich and implicitly by Herbert Marcuse, between sexual permissiveness and socio-political revolutionism, a link that was translated from theory into practice with considerable enthusiasm by the rebellious students of 1968, taking advantage of the introduction of the contraceptive pill earlier in the decade. Eric poured cold water on this idea by pointing out that most revolutions had been puritanical in their approach to sexuality. 'The Robespierres always win out over the Dantons', he remarked drawing on a similar phrase in *The Age of Revolution*. Sexual liberation had already happened in bourgeois society by the time the student rebellion began. It was an irrelevance to the issue of social revolution.[228]

Revolutionaries was widely reviewed. Some critics were put off by the political stance Eric took, more open here than in his historical works. *The Economist* considered that few readers would 'click their heels when the snarl of the commissar breaks through his felicitous

prose'. He seemed to think the politics of the student revolutionaries resembled those of the old-style anarchist movement more than
anything else.[229] Tom Kemp of the University of Hull, author of
some simplistic but useful books on French economic history, and
a member of the Trotskyist ultra-left group led by Gerry Healy,
which was to split into eight or nine different *groupuscules* after it was
revealed that Healy had been routinely abusing his young female
followers, damned Eric as a 'sophisticated apologist' for orthodox
Communism. He was, Kemp alleged, 'a prized decoration on the
tarnished blazon of British Stalinism'.[230] However, the American
sociologist David Halle thought that Eric

> obviously considers himself a Marxist, but what he wishes to
> mean by this is unclear. He rejects dogma and sectarianism
> and refuses to equate Marxism with whatever set of beliefs the
> Russian or any other Communist party holds at any time. Yet he
> implies there is something that can be called 'correct' Marxism.
> What this might be is hard to determine.[231]

Still, however unclear its precise nature as an ideology, Eric's
Communism was, as every reviewer apart from Tom Kemp
seemed to agree, highly unconventional.

The crusading anti-Communist American journalist Arnold
Beichman thought that Eric was 'the kind of Communist who, if
he were living in the Soviet Union, would either be in a lunatic
asylum repenting his deviations or seeking an exit visa to Israel'.[232]
And indeed, as Eric later noted, 'Not a single one of my books was
ever published in Russia in the Soviet period ... In Hungary, yes.
In Slovenia, yes. You were supposed to write a straightforward
line, and whatever I said did not fit in.'[233] The Oxford political
philosopher Steven Lukes similarly recognised that 'Hobsbawm's
political position is one that is distinctly, and increasingly, deviant'.[234] The Marxologist Leszek Kolakowski, whose position was
gradually shifting to the right after his flight from Poland, found
that the book brought out 'the uneasy position of anyone who tries
to combine the classic Marxist approach in historical studies, the

classic Leninist approach in political allegiances, and a determination to abide by traditional standards of intellectual conduct'.[235] In this he was surely right.

X

Following the success of *The Age of Revolution*, Eric was swamped by offers from a variety of publishers, and, flattered by the attention and persuaded by his agent, accepted more of them than he could possibly manage. He also launched time-consuming editorial schemes of his own. In 1964 Eric approached Weidenfeld with a proposal for a series called 'Epochs of England', 'a range of ten books covering the social history of the English people from the Regency period until today'. Each book was to cover a relatively short period and be no more than sixty thousand words long, with '40% of the total number of pages taken up with illustrations'. The authors were to be 'young historians and writers with a catholic background, not practising academics'.[236] As discussions with the publisher developed, the original series title was dropped and the scope widened so that it became a 'History of British Society'. The search for authors, conducted with great persistence by Eric, came up in the end with practising academics, despite his original intentions. The volumes included Geoffrey Best's successful book *Mid-Victorian Britain*. Particular trouble was caused by the volume on the Edwardians, by the young pioneer of oral history Paul Thompson. Eric himself felt it contained 'too much quoting at excessive length'[237] – a common failing of works of oral history, which at the time had a strong tendency to fetishise painstakingly recorded interviews with contemporary historical eyewitnesses. The publishers found it less useful as a textbook than the other volumes, and proposed to publish it in hardback only. Eric was outraged. 'I hear with absolute horror', he wrote to George Weidenfeld on 30 April 1975, 'that your firm has decided to issue Paul Thompson's book on the Edwardians, which is part of the social history series I edit, *only* in a hard back edition of one thousand copies at the price of £10 … It will be bought only by a handful of libraries.' Students could not afford it. A 'gross confidence trick' was being played on the authors, who thought they were writing for a student market. 'Unless this decision is rescinded', he warned, 'you really leave me no option but to resign formally and publicly from editing the series and to explain to anyone who wishes to know why I must do so.'[238] The book was duly printed in paper-back. However, as so often with such ventures, only a small number of the projected volumes eventually appeared in print.

In 1966 Eric signed a contract with Weidenfeld for a book enti-tled *History of Revolution*, with an advance of £4000.[239] But shortly afterwards he shelved this in the light of a better offer, for a com-parative study of revolutions, one of a series of twelve volumes on key aspects of history.[240] This caused some difficulty since the series ('containing some high-powered authors and rather highly paid', as David Higham noted) originated with an American publisher who expected it to be published in the UK by Jonathan Cape through the services of the literary agent Hilary Rubinstein. Eric asked George Weidenfeld if he minded this arrangement, and, as Higham reported, since Weidenfeld was Eric's regular publisher, 'George minded extremely and said so and then rang me and at this point we came into it.'[241] Cape rejected the idea of a joint pub-lication since that would look odd in the light of the fact that all the other volumes in the series of twelve were being published by them alone. Weidenfeld in turn expressed himself 'really shocked by the lack of co-operation on their part'. In the light of these dis-agreements, Eric withdrew from the series, though he still intended to write a book on revolutions in the longer term (to be delivered within four years, his agent estimated optimistically).[242] Eric's book on revolutions was now to be called *The Pattern of Revolutions*, but as David Higham noted in 1968 after talking to him on the phone, 'Hobsbawm [is] not sure he wants to do it'.[243]

Shortly afterwards Eric received another offer, from another American publisher, Prentice-Hall, who wanted Eric to write a contribution to a multi-author textbook called *Europe Since 1500*. Each part was to be the length of a short book. The aim was to recruit a leading authority on each of four broad periods in order to ensure the widest possible use in college teaching. The general editor of the book was to be H. Stuart Hughes, an historian whose writings on the history of modern thought had exerted a good deal of influence both academically and more generally. His task was 'to make sure the book hangs together as a volume and to help the British authors, if necessary, with trans-Atlantic balance'.[244] The medieval section was to be written by Richard Southern, a distinguished Oxford medievalist.[245] The sixteenth-century contribution was by the eminent historian of the English and Continental Reformation A. G. Dickens. Another contributor signed up was Maurice Ashley, a former research assistant of Sir Winston Churchill. While Southern and Dickens had already produced major works, Ashley had only written somewhat bland student texts on the English Civil War.

Eric estimated his nineteenth to twentieth section of the book would be 350 to 400 pages long, and told his agent that he would need research assistance.[246] Prentice-Hall agreed to the new sum and in addition offered to pay $1000, or more if needed, to provide Eric with a research assistant 'to improve the schedule'.[247] But on 27 August 1969 the agency informed the publisher that 'Hobsbawm's problem is really that he has two books to write before he does the Prentice-Hall book. He won't commit himself to an earlier delivery date than the end of 1973 at the moment'.[248] Nevertheless, he signed the contract in 1970 and the publisher told Eric that 'our enthusiasm for the project and our delight in having you as author remains boundless'.[249] However, Eric began to have doubts after visiting the USA in October 1970, a trip during which he called in on the Prentice-Hall offices at Englewood Cliffs, New Jersey.[250] Colleagues he met at Harvard had informed him that the $10,000 advance he had been offered was way below what he should expect or what, indeed, as Higham reported, he could earn if the book was published in the UK as a stand-alone volume because this would be 'in itself a major contribution to his personal opus'. 'Now', he continued:

Eric doesn't need immediate money – he is a very well paid academic and author indeed. The existing advance is payable in instalments, as you know. The very substantial sum he now wants Prentice-Hall to guarantee is also a sum to be paid long term. The sum he wants guaranteed is a hundred thousand dollars and he would be prepared to take it at ten thousand dollars a year.

There was a further, perhaps insuperable, difficulty. 'Of the contributors besides himself to this volume', Higham informed Prentice-Hall, 'he doesn't think much of a man called Ashley: thinks rather more of a man called Dickens. But the real point here is that both these men have delivered their portions of the book and in each case these portions are being published as separate books.' Yet Eric had not even started writing his own, which was to cover the modern period. Thus, if and when he completed it, the whole book would consist of his contribution and two others that had already appeared as books in their own right. This would, Higham said, 'seriously impair the chances of a very wide sale on which the whole of the volume was predicated'.[251]

On 22 February 1971, Prentice-Hall came back with an improved offer of $35,000.[252] Eric thought this was 'very attractive' and was minded to take it.[253] But the agency disagreed.[254] On 19 March, on Higham's advice, Eric rejected the offer of $35,000 and asked instead for $50,000, which was accepted, settling the matter for the moment.[255]

Quite apart from this, Weidenfeld was pressing him to write a sequel to the highly successful *Age of Revolution*. Another contract was duly signed. In October 1969 Eric responded to a query from Weidenfeld on his progress with 'the post-revolution book' with the news that 'I have the substance of three and a half chapters done out of about fifteen and am in fact in the middle of writing. If I had time to concentrate entirely on the book I could certainly be sure to have it ready in six months but of course in term time it will not be possible to work intensively on the m/s.' He did not feel bad about overrunning the deadline, he had to confess.[256]

The delivery date was repeatedly put off, not least by the time-consuming nature of his house move to Nassington Road, as he wrote on 19 November 1970:

> I was pushing ahead quite nicely until my wife decided to sell/ buy/reconstruct houses, which is a time-consuming business, and complex enough to have forced me to put my library into storage for a couple of months. It is only just unpacked again. I have about half the book, but won't finish by the end of 1970. I still hope to have it done by the end of March, but that's not, alas, a guarantee … I doubt whether the book can be got out before the end of 1971, especially as nobody has thought about pictures yet.[257]

In August 1971 Bruce Hunter, David Higham's assistant, assured Julian Shuckburgh at Weidenfeld & Nicolson that Eric intended to deliver the completed manuscript by the end of the year.[258] But despite repeated urgings by Hunter, who was concerned by the fact that Eric had already received most of the advance for the book and was 'supposed to have written most of it', he did not seem to be anywhere near completing the text by 1972.[259] Weidenfeld made plans for the book to be published that year, and so importunate were the editorial staff's demands, transmitted through David Higham, that Eric simply stopped answering their letters for a time.[260]

By the summer of 1971 he was clearly seriously overcommitted. David Higham was obliged to tell him on 22 July that 'Julian Shuckburgh of Weidenfeld has written asking "how he now sees his writing plans" and when may they expect to see the three books they have commissioned.' There was the Prentice-Hall contribution, then *Revolutionaries*, the book of 'political-historical' essays ('strictly to have been delivered in May') (in fact it was delivered in 1972), the sequel to *The Age of Revolution* and the general book on revolutions ('if you have any ideas about the delivery date for that, I know Shuckburgh would be glad to hear them – and so should we').[261] He was repeatedly pressed by the publishers for his manuscripts.[262] Clearly something had to give. In the end, the book on revolutions was never written, nor was the Prentice-Hall contribution, though it was not until 6 February 1987 that the David Higham agency finally deleted the contract Eric had signed in 1970. 'It is not a book', he told the publisher, 'which Eric Hobsbawm has any intention of ever doing and he would rather have the agreement definitely cancelled.'[263] And so it was.

Long before this time, Eric's success as a writer had finally brought him financial security. On 22 June 1961 he received an advance of £200 for what was to become *Industry and Empire*, and a smaller one, £75, for *Labouring Men*. The advance was in fact far too modest, for royalty cheques began to come in for *Labouring Men* – nearly £200 in June 1965, for instance, and another £234 in November the same year, with £166 coming in the following year, thanks not least to a Japanese edition; a US edition brought in £233 in 1967. The book continued to sell steadily, with 1566 copies coming off the bookshelves in 1968 alone, and 828 copies of the paperback sold in 1974: Eric was clearly benefiting from the upsurge of labour history in teaching and research during these years. He obtained an advance of £150 for *Bandits* and significant sums were already being paid on *Industry and Empire* for foreign and other subsidiary rights: in 1969, Eric earned £729 from the book in its first year of publication before his agents took their commission. It continued to sell well, thanks not least to its widespread use as an economic history textbook in the new universities that had pro-liferated across the English-speaking world in the 1960s and early 1970s. In the second half of 1972, it sold over ten thousand copies, and in the first half of 1975, 6837 copies. Eric's success as an author brought an increase in the advances he earned against royalties, reflecting publishers' growing confidence in the sales prospects for his books. André Schiffrin at Pantheon Books in New York paid $2500 for his collection of contemporary essays, *Revolutionaries*, in 1972. These may seem insignificant sums by the standards of the twenty-first century, but in the 1960s, taken together, they amounted to more than the average annual salary of a university lecturer already before the end of the decade.[264] 'The number of writers who can live entirely by their books', Eric wrote in 1964, 'would go into a single not excessively large room.' Most of them earned no more than the average typist from their works. He still needed his salary from Birkbeck to support the family. But at least he was now financially secure.[265]

All in all, the 1960s and early 1970s were a period of astonishing productivity for Eric, with a string of major books and essay collections published – *The Age of Revolution, Bandits, Labouring Men, Industry and Empire, Revolutionaries* and *Captain Swing* – as well as the Marx-Engels edition and an edited book series. Along with the other British Marxist historians, he clearly felt liberated by breaking free from the political and intellectual constraints of the British Communist movement. Eric's marriage to Marlene and the birth of his two children gave him the stability he had so lacked in the 1950s, providing him with happiness and contentment. His interests had broadened markedly, to encompass in particular the recent history and contemporary politics of Latin America. He had engaged more closely than before with the theoretical legacy of Marxism. For the first time, he was experiencing academic, personal and financial success. Along with Edward Thompson, he had begun to exert a powerful intellectual influence on the younger generation of historians who were coming into the universities as they expanded in the wake of the Robbins Report. His departure in all but formal terms from the Communist Party left him politically adrift, however, and it was not until the 1980s that he began to engage directly with British politics once more. His growing reputation, and the impact of his publications, ensured that he would be listened to with respect. But the message he was to convey was very far removed from the dogmas and doctrines of the Communist Party of Great Britain.

8

'Intellectual Guru'

1975–1987

I

Eric took a long time to complete the typescript of the promised sequel to *The Age of Revolution*. Even after it had reached the publisher, he kept sending in numerous additions and alterations. Weidenfeld & Nicolson's file on the book is full of substitute pages, crossed-out passages, amendments and alterations in pencil or green ink. Eric supplied the epigraphs that prefaced each chapter only at a very late stage.[1] His new editor, Andrew Wheatcroft, wanted a number of alterations to the early chapters, mainly to reduce overlap with *The Age of Revolution* ('I wonder', he wrote in response to an early draft, to take just one instance among many, 'if you could not start the chapter roughly at page 24 (b)').[2] With changes coming from both author and editor, it was not surprising that the book's completion was repeatedly delayed.

At some point during the process, the book's title was changed. It was originally going to be called *The Age of Steam-Power*, but by the time Eric came to correct the proofs, in June 1975, it had become *The Age of Capital*.[3] This reflected, perhaps, the book's focus on the age of prosperity and expansion in Europe from the defeat of the 1848 revolutions to the economic crash of 1873 and the ensuing depression. *The Age of Capital* was finally published in October 1975, as another volume in Weidenfeld's ambitious *History of Civilization* project. The book had an initial hardback print run of four thousand, with another two thousand to be published by Scribner's in New York. The advance on royalties was £2000 for the UK edition and £2350 each for the American, Italian, French, German and Spanish editions. It was published in paperback on 20 October 1977 by Sphere and garnered for Eric an additional advance of £500.[4] The royalties were relatively high, at 12½ per cent for the first four thousand copies, rising to 15 per cent to ten thousand and 17½ per cent thereafter.[5] These were generous terms for the time, reflecting the success of *The Age of Revolution*.

Like its predecessor, the new work was aimed at the general reader; students could quarry it for ideas, but some reviewers thought that they still needed an old-fashioned narrative textbook for basic orientation.[6] The American economic historian Herbert Kisch, at Michigan State University, agreed: how could his middle-class, midwestern students be expected to grasp the book's many cultural allusions and insights from their background of apolitical cultural ignorance?[7] They would need to do some serious background reading to sort out in their minds what happened when, before they came to tackle the book. And, indeed, it had the same determinedly thematic structure as *The Age of Revolution*, with the sixteen chapters divided into two parts, 'developments' and 'results', and prefaced by an introductory chapter narrating and analysing the events of 1848–51. As before, it began with the economy, then went on to society and politics, before covering the rural and urban worlds, social class, science, culture and the arts in the second part of the book. Its geographical scope was wider than before, reflecting the expanding impact of the 'dual revolution' in the period covered.[8] The focus was European, as the historian of Victorian Britain J. F. C. Harrison noted, but the context was global.[9]

The most brilliant and combative of all the reviews of the book was a lengthy discussion in the *Times Literary Supplement* by the American economic historian David Landes, author of a superb study of technological innovation and its impact in the Industrial Revolution, *The Unbound Prometheus* (1969). He began in dashing style:

I love to read Eric Hobsbawm. He knows so much; he reads everything; he translates German poetry into English rhyme; and whatever he writes about, he has something important to say. I also disagree with him a lot, so that reading one of his books or articles is like a good game of squash: you come away tired but invigorated and feeling virtuous for the effort.[10]

Landes detected innumerable examples of bias in the book's coverage. Processes that others might regard as positive, such as the legalisation of trade unions, or the great migrations of poor and persecuted Europeans across the Atlantic to the Americas, were somehow explained away in the book as aspects of capitalist exploitation. There was no room for idealism: the American Civil War, according to Hobsbawm, was all about the effective exploitation of labour and the freeing up of territory for capitalism, not about the abolition of slavery or the ideal of human freedom and dignity. Business interests were everything. The spread of capitalism to extra-European parts of the world brought only further exploitation (Landes expressed a positive view of the economic effects of colonialism that few would agree with today).

Like other critics, he found fault with the book's neglect, or underestimation, of the force of nationalism, even though it had been recognised by Friedrich Engels, among others. Landes also dissented from the book's explanation of the failure of revolution in 1848 in terms of the bourgeois fear of proletarian revolt, along with the readiness of the peasantry to be bought off by agrarian reform (in fact, Eric's argument has stood the test of time).[11] Even more off-beam was Landes' objection to the book's treatment of nationalism as an ideology, like socialism or Communism (what else, surely, was it?). Landes' rosy-hued vision of factory employers as 'good fathers and providers to their workers' and their employees as 'docile' or even 'obedient, dull and stupid' was already being exploded by numerous studies of worker protest, union organisation, strikes and revolts, running alongside almost as many exposures of the ruthless practices of management intimidation and authoritarianism. Landes had his own biases, which ran directly counter to Eric's:

for him, workers' mass politics ended in 'the equality of terror', while bourgeois politics, in and out of the factory, merely led to 'the inequality of influence'.

'All in all', Landes concluded, '*The Age of Capital* is the portrait of an unpleasant system run by unpleasant people.' It was 'reductionist' and Eric was 'a victim of doctrine'. It was systematically biased, for example in its unalloyed admiration for Karl Marx and its sarcastic treatment of other thinkers, such as the Positivist Auguste Comte. The book was 'too systematic, perhaps even too cerebral' in its treatment of society. Eric's 'people lack the substance that comes with empathy and intimacy'. The book was in the end 'profoundly ahistorical or even anti-historical' and although students and 'intelligent laymen' should indeed read *The Age of Capital*, 'it should be marked HANDLE WITH CARE'. Landes' review might justly be regarded as the response of capitalism's spokesman to capitalism's critic. Beneath the conservative rhetoric, however, he landed some shrewd blows. The book's treatment of gender and the role of women and the family was less than adequate, as Landes suggested. And its palpable hostility to nationalism delivered a less than convincing account of what was, after all, one of the most important political ideologies of the nineteenth century. Eric realised this, and was to return to the subject again in an attempt to deliver a more systematic and more satisfactory treatment.[12]

Landes' assessment of the book's Marxism as 'reductionist' was not shared by other reviewers. In J. F. C. Harrison's opinion, Eric's Marxism was 'worn very lightly indeed; and there is little in the book which most socialists, and many liberals, would not find perfectly familiar and acceptable'. It offered a kind of consensus leftist view with which anyone who was not an out-and-out conservative could be expected to agree.[13] Eric might be a Marxist, Asa Briggs conceded, 'but his is not a crudely deterministic view of history'. As for lack of sympathy with the bourgeoisie, Briggs noted the vividness of Eric's evocation of the material triumphs of the post-1848 decades: 'Even the rawest business-adventurers are given their due' – men such as Henry Meiggs, a corrupt but enterprising entrepreneur in the wild world of nineteenth-century Latin

America: 'Can anyone who have ever seen the Peruvian Central Railway', Eric asked rhetorically, 'deny the grandeur of the concept and achievement of his romantic if rascally imagination'?[14]

There were other criticisms, inevitable with a book of such scale and scope. James Joll, historian of radical movements in the nineteenth century, was surprised by the book's dismissal of religion. 'Both Gladstone and Bismarck', he commented, 'would, I suspect, have disagreed with Hobsbawm's dictum that "compared with secular ideology, religion in our period is of comparatively slight interest, and does not deserve extended treatment"'.[15] Paul Thompson, pioneer of oral history, found another gap in coverage, for, while *The Age of Capital* included a full discussion of high culture and the arts, it provided no more than a brief reference to popular culture, mass sport, or indeed the social life of the working classes.[16]

Perhaps the most common criticism levelled at the book was of what many reviewers saw as its Eurocentrism. The left-wing Welsh historian Gwyn Alf Williams found that 'the global perspective on occasion quavers and crumples'.[17] There was no denying that Eric's knowledge was deepest and broadest on Europe itself. The American historian of slavery David Brion Davis criticised Eric's 'cavalier treatment of American history'.

> Hobsbawm's own discussions of American society are not only thin and distorted, but reflect a common British tendency to envision 19th-century America as an overgrown, monstrous and somewhat exotic former colony – an Australia or Canada gone mad. Although Hobsbawm makes occasional and inaccurate use of some of the best recent historical literature, he clings to a stereotyped and curiously English obsession with America's 'Wild West' and 'robber barons'.

This simply would not do. Eric was missing out on a golden opportunity to explore the development of capitalism on the American continent, and this weakened the book.[18] In fact, of course, Eric was far from parochially Eurocentric in his interests. He wrote about India and Japan as well as Europe and Latin

America.[19] He was interested in the Japanese appropriation of European economic and industrial models in the nineteenth century,[20] and he bemoaned the acceptance of hierarchical social structures in Japanese society.[21] The Eurocentrism of his synoptic histories stemmed from his thesis that industrialisation began in Europe and spread from there to the rest of the world. But his antipathy to America was commented on by many.

Nevertheless, not surprisingly, *The Age of Capital* was greeted in overwhelmingly positive terms by the vast majority of reviewers. It displayed all the virtues that had already become apparent in its predecessor volume. It cemented Eric's worldwide reputation as an historian who combined penetrating analysis with illuminating detail, high-level scholarship with the ability to appeal to a broad readership. It was immediately translated into Italian, French, Portuguese, German, Hungarian, Dutch, Norwegian and Spanish, with other foreign editions, including Greek, Turkish and Arabic, following in due course. The Brazilian edition alone sold ninety-six thousand copies.[22] The book had all the hallmarks of Eric's scholarly maturity – bold generalisation, engaging detail, immense readability, thought-provoking and sometimes epigrammatically expressed hypotheses, breadth of coverage, dazzling erudition and cogent, stylish exposition. Like its predecessor it was quickly recognised as a classic. It was soon produced in a cheap paperback edition, it has never been out of print and it continues to be widely used in teaching more than forty years after its first publication.

II

By the mid-1970s, when *The Age of Capital* appeared, Eric had achieved not only commercial success but also academic recognition. His ascent into the hallowed halls of the Establishment was marked also by his election in 1983 to the Athenaeum Club in Pall Mall, London, the haunt of senior academics and clergymen (it was said to contain more bishops per square yard than anywhere else in the world except the Vatican). It counted among its past members more than fifty Nobel laureates. Women were not allowed to become members until 2002. Election depended on the support of a substantial number of existing members, but there was no system of 'blackballing' by which in some London clubs a single member had been able to veto the application of someone he did not like. Members had to dress formally, as they still do, even for breakfast. By the early 1980s Eric's reputation was such that he was elected without difficulty. The Oxford historian Keith Thomas was startled, 'when I became a member of the Athenaeum, to see seated in the bar this dark-suited figure, half-hidden behind the *Times*'. It was Eric. 'He had', Thomas noted, 'a strong sense of what was or wasn't the establishment and in his way was a bit of a tuft-hunter, certainly an intellectual snob.'[23] As the French labour historian Michelle Perrot perceptively remarked, after having visited Eric in Cambridge, Eric 'the Marxist, who opposed established society, had at the same time a profound respect for the traditions of this British society that had welcomed him into its arms'.[24]

Further recognition came to Eric as the economist Nicholas Kaldor, a prominent adviser to the Labour Party leadership, proposed Eric for an Honorary Fellowship at King's College, Cambridge. 'Many of us', he wrote, 'regard him as the most distinguished economic historian in the country.' He had been bypassed for professorial appointments in Cambridge on more than one occasion, he remarked, 'and there can be little doubt that ideological prejudices played an important role as less distinguished candidates were elected'. Giving him an Honorary Fellowship at King's would, therefore, he added, 'be some sort of acknowledgment, not only of his exceptional intellectual distinction, but that he has been rather hard-done-by by Cambridge'.[25] Kaldor's proposal was accepted by the Fellows of King's, and Eric was elected an Honorary Fellow of the College in 1973. Two years earlier he had been elected a Foreign Honorary Member of the American Academy of Arts and Sciences, along with the London-based ancient historian Arnaldo Momigliano and the violinist Yehudi Menuhin.[26]

In 1976 he was finally elected to a Fellowship of the British Academy, which was, and is, for the arts, humanities and social sciences what the Royal Society is for scientists. Only one or two specialists on modern history were elected to this august body every year, and Noel Annan wrote to Eric congratulating him and giving his opinion that the honour was long overdue.

> I have always admired the way ever since the war that you have met rebuffs by the old Establishment. I thought it was monstrous that you never got a lectureship at Cambridge, still more monstrous that you were not offered the chair in Economic History either at Oxford or at Cambridge, and yet still more monstrous that that whited sepulchre in Birkbeck held up your conferment of title until after his retirement. Amused resignation was your reaction, and you gained the admiration of all your friends by the way you simply went on writing admirable books and articles unperturbed. So many people get eaten up by a sense of injustice and tear themselves to pieces. It is so much to your credit and sense of humour that you did not.[27]

In his typically Establishment style Annan had sent the note even before Eric had received the official notification of his Fellowship. Eric responded warmly:

> You needn't bother to commiserate retrospectively. I have not felt seriously victimized since the end of the '50s, because there were always enough people in whose judgment I had confidence who thought I was good (probably better than I thought myself): you, to name but one. The stuff I did was appreciated in the trade as well as by students etc. For the past six or seven years the formal recognition has come. I didn't really doubt that I'd get a chair eventually, and I haven't really doubted that I'd get the FBA in the end. In fact, it is quite convenient for these things to come later rather than sooner. It avoids that feeling of anticlimax in early middle age, when one recognizes that the climb is at an end. Of course these delays have been so tolerable chiefly because people like yourself were, so to speak, providing moral recognition.

Besides, someone like myself couldn't lose. Being kept out by
the Establishment is an asset for someone who's made his reputation as an outsider. My problem now, that the Establishment
is increasingly clasping me to its international bosom – and
frankly, I am vain enough to like this kind of initial-collecting –
is how to keep my bona fides as an old Bolshevik, itself now a
very fuddy-duddy and respectable role by the standards of the
young insurrectionaries. Still, one cannot escape one's fate, and
there are considerable compensations . . .[28]

In particular, Eric, said Keith Thomas, 'attached a lot of importance to membership of the British Academy'.[29]

Major differences and disagreements have seldom disturbed
the scholarly tranquillity of the British Academy and its affairs.
The one great exception, perhaps, was the row that erupted
over Mrs Thatcher's revelation in Parliament on 5 November
1979 that Sir Anthony Blunt, a Fellow of the British Academy,
Surveyor of the Queen's Pictures, and a leading art historian
whose monograph on Poussin is still the standard work today,
had been a Soviet spy during the war, passing Bletchley Park
decrypts of German radio traffic to the Russians, especially
where they concerned the Eastern Front. The risk he created
in doing so was that their use, for example, during the Battle
of Kursk, might have alerted the Germans to the fact that their
supposedly secret messages were being deciphered, leading them
to change the codes they used and thus making them inaccessible
to the British. More seriously perhaps, Blunt had recruited John
Cairncross as a Soviet spy and he was aware from early on that
Guy Burgess was also working for the Soviet secret service, but
did not reveal to anybody that he knew what either of them was
doing. In 1963, Michael Straight had told the British security
services that Blunt had been a Soviet spy. Blunt had confessed in
return for a promise of immunity from prosecution. MI5 agreed
to keep the matter secret for fifteen years.

By 1979, when this period was up, rumours of his treason were
beginning to circulate, prompting Mrs Thatcher to issue a formal

public statement in the House of Commons exposing Blunt's guilt. Blunt went to ground, hiding in the flat of his former student Brian Sewell and then with his friend the historian James Joll, who was forced to resign from his Chair at the London School of Economics when his role in the affair came to light.[30] All three men were homosexual, and the British media were gripped by an outbreak of homophobia. The home of Eric's friend the art historian Francis Haskell was besieged by reporters suspecting him of harbouring Blunt (Haskell had recently hosted a lecture by him, and had a Russian wife). Blunt was stripped of his knighthood on the orders of the Queen, and deprived of his Honorary Fellowship at Trinity College, Cambridge.[31] Newspaper reporters pointed the finger at the Cambridge Apostles, branding them as a homosexual Soviet spy ring.

Always alert to the objectionable possibility of a witch-hunt, Hugh Trevor-Roper was repelled by the newspapers' hounding of Blunt. It could serve no possible useful purpose, he wrote in the *Spectator*.[32] Encouraged by his public stance, Eric wrote to him privately in March 1980. He could not, of course, speak out at the Academy himself, he told Trevor-Roper:

> Quite apart from being counter-productive or dismissed as biased, people like myself cannot help but be seen as defending their past ... If the Academy is to be stopped from making a fool of itself (and us), then it can be done only by people like yourself. I hesitate to say 'by you', though I am sure your individual voice would carry a great and perhaps decisive weight, since you cannot be suspected of any sympathy for Blunt's past views, and you are on record as condemning his extra-curricular activities, not to mention your personal standing.[33]

Trevor-Roper, who had recently been created a Tory life peer with the title of Lord Dacre of Glanton, agreed with Eric, who told the President of the Academy, the classicist Sir Kenneth Dover: 'To expel a Fellow in any circumstances – has it ever happened before in our Academy? – is a serious step ... To consider

expelling him for reasons which have nothing to do with the cri-
teria which determined his election, is an even more serious step
and requires much heartsearching.' The only legitimate reason
for expulsion was academic misconduct (for example, plagiarism
of somebody else's work), not least because these were grounds on
which Fellows could agree, since they had elected him (or her) on
academic grounds. 'I think the reputation of our Academy and
of this country for civilized behaviour would suffer if we expelled
Blunt, whatever our views of his conduct. Nor do I think I am
alone in this view.'[34]

Nevertheless, the Council of the British Academy voted by a
narrow margin (nine to eight) to bring a motion before the annual
general meeting of Fellows on 3 July 1980 for Blunt's expulsion. The
Fellows rejected it, as they did a motion to censure Blunt without
expelling him, put by Isaiah Berlin and Lionel Robbins. Instead,
they voted by 42 votes to 20, with 25 abstentions, to move on to
the next item of business. This was, as Dover told Fellows on 22
August, 'an absolutely firm, clear and decisive refusal to pronounce
on a person's fitness to be a Fellow in the light of non-scholarly misconduct'.[35] Passions ran high on both sides, and Fellows opposed to
Blunt now threatened to resign if he was not forced to give up his
Fellowship. Jack Plumb was particularly vocal in his condemnation
of the Academy for refusing to expel Blunt and campaigned along
with the nineteenth-century political historian Norman Gash to
reverse the decision.[36] In Eric's view, however, the vote should
have been the end of the business. It was time, he told Dover, for
wounds to be healed, and an appeal should have been made to
the Fellows – both supporters and opponents of expulsion – who
actually had resigned, to rescind their resignations.[37] In his reply
to Eric's letter, Dover pointed out that opinion among the Fellows
was more deeply divided than ever:

> Ever since it was demanded of me last December that I should
> 'give a strong lead' (so, for the expulsion of Blunt) and also
> expected of me that I should prevent the idea of expelling Blunt
> from going any further, I have known that *no* course of action

was open to me, at any stage, which everyone would regard as consonant with my duty.[38]

After the vote, however, Dover now considered himself free to ask Blunt to consider resignation, and, weary of the battle, the former spy obliged, whereupon A. J. P. Taylor, who had sworn to resign his own Fellowship if Blunt was forced to go, carried out his promise and himself left the Academy in protest.[39]

Eric himself, of course, like Blunt, had been kept under surveillance by the security services for many years, although unlike Blunt he had never considered spying for the Soviet Union, nor indeed had he ever been in a position to do so. Like Blunt, he had achieved a status of considerable academic eminence. However, he was, for all that, still sensitive about his reputation on the Left. His long period of surveillance by MI5 had a curious coda in the mid-1980s. In the 1986 novel *A Perfect Spy* by John le Carré (pseudonym of David Cornwell, who had been an intelligence agent for MI5 and then MI6 in the late 1950s and early 1960s), there was a mention on page 233, as Eric pointed out to him after having his attention drawn to it by Noel Annan, among a 'team of British spooks talking to a CIA delegation one "Hobsbawn, seconded from the Security Service". Fortunately he does not reappear and says nothing.' Still, the implication was obvious:

The name is – I can assure you – more consistently misspelt than any other I know. It is also entirely identifiable with a fairly limited number of real persons ... I don't suppose any H will actually regard a fictional membership of MI5 as actual defamation though, speaking as one who has had a file since at least 1942 (at least so I was then told by a friendly chap), it makes me slightly uneasy ... All the same, you might consider calling the man something else in the many subsequent editions of your book.

My question is simply this: how on earth did you hit on the name? Is it an esoteric joke, something dredged up from among subconscious associations, or what? Why is his name mentioned only this once – or did it escape total elimination? All of us who write find unexpected and unintended things slipping onto our prose. I have some idea of how they slip into mine. It is always interesting to discover how they slip into someone else's.[40]

Eric did not directly threaten legal action, but the implication was clearly there between the lines.

Le Carré was quick to respond. This was not the first time he had encountered a real person whose name he had used in one of his spy novels, he said, though Eric was quite right to point out that his own name, however spelt or misspelt, was extremely unusual and therefore easily identifiable. Le Carré therefore denied any particular intention in using the name. He assured Eric that

I've no idea why I chose a name similar to yours, since I have never consciously heard of you, or your namesakes. There was no coy joke . . .[41]

He went on to say that he simply chose names for their musicality and visual impact: Hobsbawm had stood out as different, a way of setting the character apart. While expressing doubt that any legal complaint would succeed, le Carré nonetheless offered, if Eric was particularly distressed, to alter the name in future editions of the novel. However, with more than fifty publishers to contact, he warned this would be 'a bit of a chase'.

It is perfectly possible that he picked up the name from a half-remembered file he had seen while he was working for the intelligence services, and his protestation that he had never heard of Eric cannot be taken entirely at face value.

In his reply, Eric repeated his request that the name be removed from future editions and reprints of the novel:

The actual identification with me has been made (see the review of the book by Noel Annan in the *New York Review* – he also thinks it is an esoteric joke), and I am not pleased at the prospect of jokey conversations on the subject of my putative relations with MI5. We shall never find out whether it is

actionable to put someone who sounds like me into your novel
as a Security official, because it would be both pompous and
ridiculous to try to find out. But it is mildly uncomfortable
to figure as such for someone who, like myself, has an old-
established track record on the marxist left. And it is far from
impossible that among my readers in, say, some Latinamerican
republics (where I am quite well known among the university
public) there are people whose sophistication is not up to yours
and mine. One should never underestimate the capacity of
some readers for literalness.[42]

The exchange ended, however, on a positive note, with Eric
assuring the novelist that he admired his work and could thus 'use
this occasion to send you the fan-letter I have sometimes thought
of writing'. Needless to say, le Carré never made the amendment
to the text that Eric had requested.

III

Eric did not accept every honour offered to him: in 1987 he turned
down the invitation to deliver the Ford Lectures, a prestigious
series held annually at Oxford University, on the grounds that
the lectures were by statute to be on English history, and he was
now working 'on comparative lines'.[43] Still, the mere fact that he
had been asked showed that he was now widely accepted in the
academic world as one of Britain's leading historians. Predictably,
of course, his gravitation towards the Establishment did not please
everybody on the Left. Peter Brown, then Secretary of the British
Academy, remembered an occasion when he went to a lecture with
Eric at the French Institute in South Kensington,

And at the party afterwards someone came up and attacked
him quite violently for having sold out to the Establishment.
He was quite disconcerted, as who mightn't be? – and sheep-
ishly murmured the rather lame excuse that it was best to join

something to change it. It made me smile, for in the settings of the Academy and the Athenaeum, where I saw most of him, so far as I am aware he made not the slightest move to change anything.[44]

Eric was too averse to scheming and plotting to make any attempt to change the august institutions he had now joined.

Far more important for him than any of this was the fact that he had a stable home life and a loving family. The Irish historian Roy Foster, a colleague at Birkbeck and a friend of the family, felt that Marlene's achievement with Eric was 'to lighten him up, and to make very gentle fun of him, when he needed it, and to push the enjoyable things of life – you know, persuading Eric ... to go to a matinée of, I think it was Tristan, when he should have been writing a book. That was a kind of triumph.'[45] Among the frequent guests at Eric and Marlene's house in Hampstead was Claire Tomalin, the literary biographer, who had got to know Eric after she had commissioned work from him as literary editor of the *New Statesman*:

> I was invited up to Nassington Road and met Marlene and I had huge respect, rather awestruck by Eric, and was completely amazed to find that it was a wonderful bourgeois household, very comfortable, very hospitable, full of friends, different friends, not at all what I somehow expected (a rather austere household). And very cheekily ... I said to him, how, being a Communist, how he managed to square this with the sort of life he lived in Hampstead with every comfort and pleasure. And he said to me ... 'If you are on a ship that's going down, you might as well travel first class.'[46]

She was struck by Eric's 'Viennese charm ... this extraordinary way of binding friends to him and never forgetting them, maintaining the warmth and introducing them to each other'. Marlene had the same qualities. They were, Tomalin thought, 'an ideally suited couple ... They had a lot of fun together.'

I think she gave him a sort of warmth, perhaps he hadn't had before. She made it possible for them to entertain all the time, she produced these wonderful meals, you know, 'Oh, just come up for something on Sunday', and enormous amounts of food. She organised the house, she got the garden organised, the cottage in Wales, she took entire responsibility, she gave Eric the setting in which he could live, work, and be happy and comfortable.

Eric was a loyal and committed friend. Claire Tomalin was struck by the fact that he would go to all her husband Michael Frayn's plays and read all her books.

A constant stream of visitors passed through the house. These included colleagues and friends from many countries: in 1976–7, for instance, Carl E. Schorske, Eugene Genovese and Elizabeth Fox-Genovese, Martin Bernal and Charles Tilly from the USA, Madeleine Rebérioux, Patrick Fridenson, Michelle Perrot and Jacques Revel from France, Dieter Groh from Germany, and other guests from Italy, Denmark, Austria, Argentina, Chile and the USSR.[47] In 1980–1 Eric and Marlene entertained some fifty visitors including Emmanuel Le Roy Ladurie (France), Carlo Ginzburg (Italy), Hans Medick (Germany), Romila Thapar (India), Arno Mayer, Immanuel Wallerstein and Eric Foner (USA, separately), Ivan Berend (Hungary), and various scholars from Latin America. Eric and Marlene had already begun holding dinner parties for these and other, locally based friends and acquaintances, making their home at Nassington Road a centre for a cosmopolitan collection of left-wing visitors of all kinds. After dinner parties, his old friend Elise Marienstras noticed, as so many others had done, Eric's impracticality, as everyone went into the kitchen (before dishwashers became common), and 'he didn't know how to do the washing-up but knew how to dry the dishes'.[48] Before meals, he sat in the kitchen and watched a small television there, 'not only the news but also football, tennis. It was always funny to see him watching football with interest, and he knew it, he understood what was going on.'

By the mid-1970s, Eric's children had entered their teens and the usual, in their case mildly, rebellious phase of growing up.[49] Julia did not do well enough in her A levels to get into Sussex to read English, which was her original intention, so she went to the Polytechnic of Central London – now the University of Westminster – to study modern languages, which she hated. She took a year out to work for the student union, fell in love with the union president, Alaric Bamping, whom she subsequently married, and never went back. Eric was 'completely aghast'.[50] Julia felt that her father was more anxious about her future than angry that she had turned her back on academia. She found a job as a researcher in television, much to his relief. Andy's rebellion was somewhat more serious. 'I was just so anti-academia and exams', he remembered, 'and I'd just had it ... I was just very unhappy and confused and I didn't really end up turning up [at school] a lot.' A meeting was held at the school with Eric and Marlene at which it was made clear that if they did not take Andy out of the school, he was likely to be expelled. Eric asked his friend Garry Runciman for advice, and he suggested Branson, a school, as Andy put it, for 'misfits', based near Montreal, in Canada. It was a fee-paying boarding school with a strong emphasis on outdoor pursuits, but Eric and Marlene decided it was the best solution for Andy's situation, as indeed it turned out to be. Eric smoothed the way by getting his former pupil Alan Adamson, who lived near Montreal, to keep an eye on the situation, though, as it turned out, he did not really need to.[51]

The success of *The Age of Revolution* and its effect on his tax affairs prompted Eric to engage an accountant to manage his finances. Rounded off to the nearest pound, his income as a freelance writer, author and broadcaster rose from £1300 in 1962–3 to £19,098 in 1985–6, and £91,557 in 1989–90. Until 1978 his salary outpaced his earnings as a self-employed writer, lecturer and broadcaster, and inflation was doing his income as much damage as it was everyone else's, but, still, these sums were far from trivial.[52] The vast bulk of Eric's earnings as a freelancer came from book royalties; broadcasting and reviewing made up only a small proportion of the whole: in 1987–8, for example, he earned just over £2000 from journalism, a little more than £2200 from lecturing, and nearly £18,000 from royalties and advances on his books.

He owed his new-found prosperity not least to the energy and acumen of his literary agent, David Higham. However, Higham died unexpectedly in March 1978 after a short illness, as Eric was informed by Bruce Hunter, who now took on the task of looking after him at the agency.[53] 'Poor David! No more corner table at the Étoile', Eric exclaimed. 'Still, he got his memoirs in – if a literary agent can't deliver in good time who can? – and he did get well beyond the scriptural distance. Are there any other patriarchs left?'[54] Eric's relationship with Bruce Hunter was initially not an easy one. In October 1983, when Hunter stated his intention of negotiating a contract for a further book of essays on labour history (originally entitled 'More Labouring Men', later *Worlds of Labour*), Eric replied crossly that he had proposed the idea a long time ago and the publishers had 'had it for ages' Why was it taking so long?

To make matters worse, Hunter had referred to his nineteenth-century volumes as works of 'economic history'. Eric continued:

Dear Bruce, I have been associated with Highams since David approached me twenty years ago, when I was far from well known in my field. I owed him a debt of gratitude, and I have not minded paying you commission for doing not very much – since I have been lucky enough to get more offers to write books than I can cope with, and all or most of those international editions on which I rely so much. In fact, in the past ten years or more I have found myself pushing Highams to get better terms than they initially thought they could get. But an author ought to feel that his agent knows and cares about his affairs. Your letter does not suggest that in this case he does.[55]

He felt that the agency had many more lucrative clients than him, especially since he had not published a book for some time, and so it had been neglecting him (in fact, according to Bruce

Hunter, he was one of their top-earning clients).[56] Offers of publication came from him to them, not the other way round. 'And today, when the publication of more books is becoming a matter of more urgent importance to me, as does a survey of my backlist, I find I cannot have much confidence in what you are doing.' So he would be looking for a new agent who would represent his interests more energetically. Bruce Hunter quickly apologised for his reference to Eric's books as 'economic history', and defended himself over the lack of progress of 'More Labouring Men', which he blamed on the publisher.[57] This, coupled with an agreeable lunch, seemed to smooth Eric's ruffled feathers, and he stayed with the agency after all, eventually coming to rely heavily on Hunter's advice.

Despite his success, the scars of Eric's childhood poverty remained. 'Even after his books were selling in millions', Roderick Floud noted, '... I think he was always worried about money'.[58] As Elise Marienstras recalled, 'he was terribly thrifty' and 'looked after every penny'. When he visited Paris, even in extreme old age, when he found it difficult to walk, 'there was no question of taking a taxi: he had to take the Metro'. At his home in Hampstead, Elise noticed that he complained when Marlene bought an expensive item of food: 'Look how dear this brand is, it's cheaper in the other delicatessen.' Yet he was generous to his colleagues, who frequently stayed with him and Marlene, often more than one at a time – 'the two spare bedrooms on the second floor were always occupied'.[59]

His accountants of course did what all good accountants do, and made a variety of suggestions as to how he might reduce the burden of income tax on these earnings. Until the 1990s, there were relatively few opportunities for academics to apply for grants from bodies such as the British Academy and the Leverhulme Trust to give them relief from teaching to carry out research. Nor was Birkbeck a wealthy enough institution to provide its own research funds for travel and subsistence abroad. So, on his accountants' advice, he claimed his research and travel as allowable expenses against his earnings as a freelance author, writer and lecturer. As a freelancer he also claimed expenses for use of telephone, postage, stationery and equipment (typewriter, for example). In addition, like many academics, he also claimed use of home as office, purchase of books for teaching, employment of research assistants, and subscriptions to libraries and periodicals.

The sums he claimed in expenses as a freelancer were very substantial and in many years reduced his tax liability to a fraction of his gross earnings. This was not only because he spent a lot on travel, but also because he regularly paid money to typists, secretaries and research assistants. These were the days when typists were needed to prepare the final versions of books and articles ready for publication, and, given Birkbeck's meagre resources, it was not possible to use university staff to do this. In 1984–5 he employed Dr R. Avery and Ms Susan Haskins as research assistants, and Dr Pat Thane to do some replacement teaching, totalling £1550 in salaries altogether.[60] This was a normal part of Eric's working practice. Eric also claimed 'subsistence in the USA' as expenses against tax. This involved his retaining receipts for food and other basic items, a laborious business but worth it in the end, for the sums were not inconsiderable – £5885 in the tax year 1985–6, for example.

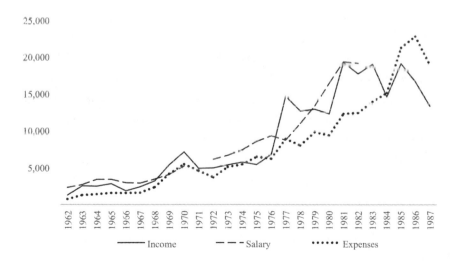

Eric Hobsbawm: salary/pension, freelance income, expenses 1962–1987 (£)

Eric had the usual small sums invested in building societies, banks and life insurance companies (for life insurance and annuities), but in order to deal with foreign earnings he opened bank accounts in France and Switzerland in the early 1980s and in 1984–5 his tax return for the first time recorded investments in companies where the money was handled by his Swiss bank. These included Quebec Hydro and three UK companies (Distillers, M&G Second General Trust and Shell Transport and Trading); his total income in sterling from these investments was £5586 for the year. In 1989–90 his income also included £8000 from renting out property. He held shares in a variety of companies and institutions, though these were all basically savings accounts; Eric did not buy and sell shares or speculate on the stock market, as Karl Marx had in his day.[61]

IV

All the while, Eric was constantly travelling abroad. He kept a careful record of his trips so that he could set the expenses he incurred against tax. In the tax year 1977–8 Eric spent fifty-five days out of the country, going to Paris for a conference (21–23 April), New York City and Cornell, in upstate New York, for lectures (27 April–25 May), Stuttgart, Konstanz and Winterthur for conferences (23–26 June), Paris again to meet his publishers and carry out some research (2–8 November), Vienna for a lecture and to research (14–19 November), Florence for a lecture and an editorial meeting (9–11 December), and South America, from 31 March to 4 April, the last day of the tax year. He remained in South America from 5 to 22 April, in Peru and Brazil, for 'conference, research, publishers, contacts, lectures'. From 11 to 14 June he was in Berlin for a conference, then after a brief return to the UK he was in Germany again from 21 to 26 June, this time in Göttingen and Frankfurt for conferences and meetings with his publishers. He spent 15–18 September in Turin and Genoa on publishing business, 5–7 October in Hamburg at a congress, 20–22 October in Frankfurt for the annual Book Fair, and was then in Paris from 1 to 8, 10 to 15, and 18 to 22 December, lecturing at the École des Hautes Études en Sciences Sociales. A trip to Florence from 9 to 12 February to meet publishers and a further visit to Paris for 'contacts' from 9 to 11 March completed the sixty-one days he spent abroad in the tax year 1978–9.[62] This was a fairly typical year: by now well enough known to merit an entry in *Who's Who*, he listed his recreation there as 'travel'. Friends and colleagues would encounter him in the most unlikely places. Alan Mackay, a distinguished crystallographer at Birkbeck, who had many international connections, described how

> in the summer of 1987 I was on leave in Seoul and I was sitting in a tea room in the centre of Seoul with a Japanese friend, when I noticed a non-Korean figure shambling down the road outside. I could not see a face, but it walked like Eric Hobsbawm. I rushed over and it was indeed Eric, who joined us briefly for a cup of tea. He was on a visit invited by publishers, who nevertheless pirated his books. Eric remarked, of Seoul, that the Soviet Union would have looked like this if the policies of Bukharin had been implemented.[63]

This pattern of almost ceaseless travel was to continue until near the end of his life.

Although he visited Paris several times every year, Eric's personal contacts with France and the French decreased sharply in frequency and duration after the end of his relationship with Hélène Berghauer. Marriage with Marlene, on the other hand, with her long and intimate experience of Italy and her wide circle of friends there, meant that his acquaintance with the country deepened and his contacts there grew in number and importance. There was also a political dimension to this change of orientation. For while the French Communist Party remained mired in the Stalinist orthodoxy that Eric found so arid and distasteful, the Italian Communist Party, shocked by the Soviet invasion of Czechoslovakia in 1968, had built on the example of the liberal, reformist Communism pioneered in Prague to develop a similar set of doctrines, shared by the Communist Party in Spain, that became known in the 1970s as 'Eurocommunism'. Moreover, unlike its British counterpart, Italian Communism was a success story: a mass movement with two million members in the 1950s, and only slightly fewer in the following decades. Nor did it in any way share the British Party's anti-intellectualism.[64]

Primitive Rebels and *Bandits* had aroused considerable interest in Italy because of their coverage of Italian subjects. They were translated into Italian, to be followed by the *Age of* books and, indeed, others. His publisher, Giulio Einaudi, would invite Eric to Turin, where 'he would take (under-royaltied) authors like me to dinner at the opulent Cambio restaurant, unchanged since Cavour had planned the transformation of the Kingdom of Savoy into the Kingdom of Italy at its tables'.[65] Einaudi made sure that every book Eric published with him was discussed intensively in the papers, including the Communist ones. This brought his name to the attention of Communist readers. In the mid-1960s he began to write articles, in Italian, for the Party's monthly magazine *Rinascita*, reported in *L'Unità*, the Communist Party's daily newspaper, on subjects such as 'Illusions and Disappointments of British Trade Unions', 'The Labour Party: Powerlessness and Disappointment', 'London Thinks About What Happens After Wilson', or simply 'Report on the English Left'. This was the first time he had actively commented on British politics, and it began to give him a taste for it. He was frequently interviewed on the condition of the Left in Europe, the terrorism of the IRA (for which he had no sympathy at all, given the Catholic and nationalist impulses behind it), the future of the Italian Communist Party, British elections, and much more besides.[66]

On 1 and 2 October 1975 he recorded a series of interviews with the Italian Communist Party's leading figure on the cultural and economic side, Giorgio Napolitano, continuing the conversation when Napolitano visited London on 19 March 1977. By now the two men had become personal friends, and remained close to the end of Eric's life, by which time Napolitano had become a dominant figure in post-Communist Italy, serving two terms as the country's President. Like many other leading Italian Communists, he had joined the Party during the anti-fascist struggles of the last phase of the war. A native of Naples, as his name suggests, he saw in the Communist Party the most promising way of bringing about the reconstruction and renewal of the Italian south, mired for decades in violence, poverty and corruption. The legacy of Fascism had, he thought, to be overcome by tearing up the social roots of Mussolini's movement, through land reform on the one hand and the creation of a mass, grass-roots democratic political movement on the other.[67]

The Communists in Italy took part in the first post-war government and played a prominent role in local politics and administration.[68] This integration into the national political system propelled them in a reformist and gradualist direction, despite some equivocations in 1956 over the Soviet invasion of Hungary. The Italian road to socialism, the two men agreed, was a democratic road. Shocked by the violent overthrow of the Allende government in Chile in 1973, the Italian Communists struck what they called a 'historic compromise' with the conservative Christian Democrats, supporting their administration and pushing the idea of the Popular Front one step further in the interests of Italian democracy. Eric was particularly struck by the role of intellectuals in the Party. The Party remained wedded to Marxism, but rejected the degeneration of theory into dogma and thought carefully about the way forward for Communism in a world where a proletarian revolution was extremely unlikely. The publication of the interviews as a small book considerably boosted Eric's reputation among Italian Communists.

His profile was enhanced a few years later as his work on banditry and the Mafia in Sicily gained a sudden topicality with the beginning of the *mattanza* ('slaughter'), an outbreak of violence between rival families in the Sicilian Mafia that led to more than 400 deaths and 140 'disappearances' over the next two years. The violence spilled over into a campaign of assassination of policemen, judges and prosecutors, above all those involved in the attempt of the Italian state to bring the *mattanza* to a halt by arresting leading figures in the rival gangs. When Eric was invited in March 1981 to Palermo to address a conference on banditry and the Mafia, therefore, as *L'Unità* reported, he

> found himself to be the object of unexpected interest and atten-
> tion. Four days ... spent among a mainly young or very young
> audience resulted in a series of observations which proved to be
> dramatically topical in a political sense. ... Hobsbawm found
> himself at the centre of a passionate debate regarding a crucial
> problem of civil coexistence in Sicily: the gangster-style assault
> by the Mafia specialising in dealing in heroin, and the new
> relationship between the Mafia and power ... The English
> historian recognised ... [that] the island [of Sicily], which at
> the time of Giuliano's gang had been an observatory for the
> false myth of the new [Robin] Hood, is now devastated – the
> historian claimed – by a serious process of the Mafia's colonisa-
> tion of the state and its institutions which is characteristic of the
> Italian situation as a whole, and by the bloody consequences of
> this process.[69]

In other words, Eric was arguing that the prosecutors, policemen and lawyers who had been trying to contain or even suppress
the Mafia were a minority in their profession: rampant corruption
had put most of the rest of them in the Mafia's pockets. In this he
was undoubtedly right; but eventually the continued assassination
campaign of the Mafia against judicial officials made the pursuit
and prosecution of the hit men and their masters unavoidable, and
several hundred were arrested and sentenced in a series of major
trials in the mid-1980s.[70]

Eric's closeness to the Italian Communist Party gained particular strength from his admiration for the ideas of its leader in
the 1920s, Antonio Gramsci, whose writings had become one of
the impulses behind the political reorientation of the Party in the
1970s. Gramsci had been imprisoned under the Fascists and died
in 1937 shortly after his release on health grounds. During his

imprisonment, he covered the equivalent of some four thousand pages with theoretical reflections of a distinctly unorthodox kind, published in Italian in six volumes from 1948 to 1951. Eric had already begun to study them in the 1950s and acknowledged that they had played a significant part in the development of his approach to history.[71] In 1974, the first publication of his prison notebooks and letters in English provided Eric with the opportunity to write about Gramsci's ideas at length.[72] He described Gramsci as 'probably the most original communist thinker produced in the twentieth-century West'. He had laid greater stress than any other Marxist thinker on the key role of intellectuals in civil society. They were important in creating the 'hegemony', or non-coercive, non-state leadership exercised by the ruling class over civil society, and, similarly, in order to overthrow the ruling class in capitalism, revolutionary movements of the 'subaltern' classes in town and country needed their own intellectuals, whether they were university trained professionals or 'organic intellectuals' who emerged from the working class itself. Communism, Gramsci believed, had to replace the Stalinist system of 'bureaucratic centralism' with a new 'democratic centralism', as Eric, under his influence, had demanded of the British Communist Party during the crisis of 1956. The Italian masses, however, had long been regrettably passive, and it was the duty of the Party and its intellectuals to rouse them and lead them to create their own form of socialist hegemony that would supplant the rule of the bourgeoisie.[73] Eric's enthusiasm for Gramsci meshed with that of the Italian Communist Party itself; both saw Gramsci's ideas as an important impulse behind Eurocommunism.

By this time, Eric had far more to do with the Communist Party of Italy than with the Communist Party of Great Britain. In Italy he was lionised as an important intellectual; in Great Britain he was treated by the Party as something of an embarrassment, if an occasionally useful one. But the significance of his publications in Italian was not just a demonstration of his closeness to the Italian Left. Eric had not previously commented in public on British politics, and his new role as, in effect, the Italian Communist Party's

UK correspondent marked the beginning of a new phase in his writing that would eventually bring him to involve himself directly in the politics of the Labour Party at home.

V

When Eric resumed his regular visits to Paris in the mid-1970s, it was academic interests that brought him there, not personal or political ones. He already knew Fernand Braudel, the commanding figure of the *Annales* school, who described him in 1973 as 'one of my very rare English friends'.[74] For his part, Eric admired Braudel's work, not least for his 'sheer curiosity':

> Historians simply have to be curious about anything they see, particularly the things which are not particularly evident, things by the side of the archives or by the side of sources. And Braudel, a very great historian, once told me, he said historians are never on holiday, on vacation. They are always, so to speak, on the job. Whenever, he said, I get into a train, I learn something. And I think it is very important because this is another way of saying, 'be open to new phenomena'.[75]

Eric's contacts with the *Annales* historians intensified considerably in the following years. In 1974, Georges Haupt, a Holocaust survivor, exile from Communist Romania and historian of socialism, conceived the idea of holding a regular series of international round-table discussions on social history. Clemens Heller, an Austrian-American economic historian, co-founder with Braudel of the Maison des Sciences de l'Homme in Paris, raised the money from German foundations (Eric got to know him well; they generally conversed in German rather than in French).[76] The aim of the seminars was to encourage free discussion, centred on papers but with no expectation of publication.[77] Despite its international ambitions, it was, to begin with at least, an Anglo-French exchange, and Eric considered its value lay not least in allowing him and the other English historians who participated (including Edward Thompson and his wife Dorothy, an historian of Chartism) to get to know French researchers in the field, such as Michelle Perrot, Patrick Fridenson, Madeleine Rebérioux and Maurice Agulhon. The American historical sociologist Charles Tilly would sometimes attend, as would American historians David Montgomery and Joan Scott, the Italianist Louise Tilly (Charles's wife) and the German historian of social democracy Dieter Groh. Not all of them spoke French, and Eric frequently acted for them as an interpreter. The social theorist Pierre Bourdieu was particularly excited by Eric's participation, and the two men became good friends. Michelle Perrot noticed that 'there was a certain opposition, a little bit of rivalry as well, between Thompson and Hobsbawm. Eric Hobsbawm's Marxism was more classical, while E. P. Thompson's was more innovative'; Thompson 'found Eric not sufficiently critical of Marxism and above all of Communism', while Eric found Thompson 'a little bit too polemical'. For Perrot, the moments when they clashed were among the high points of the seminars. The spontaneity and lack of formality of the meetings were what attracted her most. Unlike most colloquia, where participants read prepared papers followed by a short discussion, the round-table sessions provided a forum for genuine, free and fluid discussion. 'Apart from the personal friendships made', Eric noted, 'the intellectual debt I owe to these meetings is substantial, and I think this is so for most of us.'[78]

The meetings were initially concerned with labour history, then moved on to the history of the middle classes. One session was held on women in the working class, another on industrialisation and the family. A focus on the social history of the arts brought in outside specialists such as the American historian of the Viennese fin-de-siècle Carl E. Schorske and Eric's friend the art historian Francis Haskell. Towards the end of the 1970s a group of German social historians based at the Max Planck Institute for History in Göttingen, notably Hans Medick, David Sabean and Alf Lüdtke, introduced an element of social anthropology into the discussions, leading to the attendance of some British anthropologists such as

Jack Goody and Marilyn Strathern. By the late 1970s the circle was beginning to fall apart as its members moved up the academic hierarchy and took on demanding jobs. The meeting at Konstanz, where Dieter Groh was based, was the last, not least because it revealed unresolvable conflicts on the issue of class consciousness between the Marxists and non-Marxists in the group. Taking her aside, Edward Thompson asked Michelle Perrot, 'Do you think we've got anything left to say to one another?' It was clear, she thought, that he did not.

The will to continue was also seriously weakened by the sudden death in 1978, at the age of fifty, of Georges Haupt, who fell victim to a heart attack at Rome airport. As a central figure in the workshops, he seemed somehow indispensable: as Patrick Fridenson recalled, 'we realized that the years we had lived from '75 to '77 would never be rebuilt without Georges Haupt'. Eric continued to be a frequent visitor to Paris, however, and was grateful to the Maison des Sciences de l'Homme for providing him with a desk and a share in an office, allowing him to meet students and discuss matters of common interest.[79] It was, he thought, 'the most important international intellectual meeting-point in Europe and perhaps in the world ... Nobody visits the MSH without taking away a new idea, a new project or a new contact. That has been my experience.'[80]

His admiration for the *Annales* school and its historians did not stop him from being critical of some of their work. Emmanuel Le Roy Ladurie's book *Jasmin's Witch* (published in English translation in 1987) he found, for instance, 'relatively specialised', 'relatively slight', and showed signs of 'having been written in a hurry'. Still, it was 'a fascinating piece of detective-work and, as always, extraordinarily intelligent and stimulating, as well as readable ... I am an admirer of this great historian', he added, and 'disposed to detect the lion's footprint even where others miss it'.[81] He was equally indulgent, at least on a personal level, towards Louis Althusser, who stayed with him and Marlene in 1979 during a short visit to London, ostensibly to attend a seminar, in fact to try and recruit Eric for 'some hare-brained stratospheric initiative', as Eric later recalled. Marlene had to look after him while Eric and Althusser's official host were busy one morning, and Althusser, seeing the Hobsbawms' upright piano, said he had remembered he had come to buy a grand piano; he got Marlene to look up where the nearest saleroom was, and insisted on her taking him there. He bought an immensely expensive concert grand, and told the staff he wanted it shipped to Paris. When his host arrived, he demanded he take him to a car showroom in Mayfair, in order to buy a Rolls-Royce (or possibly a Jaguar). It was with some difficulty that the shops were persuaded not to follow up his orders. After his return to Paris, Althusser's mental state deteriorated even further. On 16 November 1980 he strangled his wife and was taken to a mental hospital; a court subsequently ruled him unfit to stand trial. Eric declared himself 'very sorry for poor Althusser, the Paris strangler. Crazy as a coot, but I'd have predicted suicide rather than manslaughter.'[82]

VI

In 1976 Eric was appointed Andrew D. White Professor-at-Large at Cornell University, a major Ivy League school in Ithaca, upstate New York. The idea behind the professorships was to invite up to twenty world-class intellectuals from across the globe to come to the university for one week in each of two three-year periods with the mandate simply to enliven its intellectual and cultural life. He did his first stint in 1977, landing in New York in late April before flying on a smaller plane to Ithaca, where the campus was located. 'I walked up and down Broadway on the upper west side a bit', he reported, 'and bought myself a <u>marvellous</u> salt beef sandwich to say hello to New York.' Cornell he found 'prettily situated in hills and by a lake. Sort of semi-Austrian scenery but not so tidy.' He stayed in a student hostel, which was 'quite civilized' though the food was 'pretty awful'.[83] He was being worked hard, he told Marlene during his first visit, meeting people, giving lunchtime 'brown bag' talks, and generally socialising with students and colleagues. The campus was nice, however, 'and one gets a fair bit of walking in because the distances are quite large. Fortunately my Welsh experience makes me negotiate the hills without trouble.'[84] The university was something of a cultural island in a rural desert, 'isolated and inaccessible' and almost entirely self-sufficient. He was not surprised that suicide was 'quite common among students and others'.

He socialised with American professors who worked on Europe, and had been out a couple of times with visiting Europeans:

> The Europeans among themselves agree that the Americans are incomprehensible, . . . the most foreign people on earth bar the Japanese. The American's don't know how foreign they are, and see themselves as honorary Englishmen, Frenchmen, Italians etc., but oh boy they are not. The easiest to come to terms with are the New York Jews (who, of course, have tended to marry good Southern belles or New England protestants) because they are just like Woody Allen.[85]

Apart from a visit to Immanuel Wallerstein's seminar in Binghamton, also located in upstate New York, he spent much of his time in the library, reading 'anything that comes into my head'. He was taken out to view the local beauty spots in the hills, but found them 'not very wild' compared to Wales. 'The seminars . . . all merge in my memory into one. The sessions of drinks with colleagues or having meals with them, also (except for the ones in the open air).' He was becoming tired of the receptions organised for him, with all the 'standing up smiling in a fixed manner and trying to remember whether I've met these people before somewhere. I think three weeks will turn out to be quite enough.'[86] On his second visit, he still found life at Cornell 'fairly boring. Downtown Ithaca is not worth going to', he wrote to Marlene during this second stint, 'seems to be getting even more provincial and tatty since I was here last – and there's not much action here on the campus.'[87]

Back in the USA in March 1981, he stopped off first at New York, where he went, for the first time it seems, to the Metropolitan

Opera ('much too big, more of a football stadium than an opera'), finding the production of *Don Carlos* 'Victorian and ultra-lush'. Flying across the States to California, he stayed first in the 'wonderful' Laguna Hotel, on the beach, then had to endure 'three tough days [of] ... boring and irritating, not to say infuriating conferences, lectures, endless talks with colleagues and students, dinners – the whole hellish academic circuit. They mean well, but even when they drive me round to show me Hollywood, they keep talking and asking questions.'[88] To get away from it all, he booked himself into the Miramar, a 'vast motel-resort' in Santa Barbara, recommended by friends, driving there himself. 'It was a restful couple of days, even though I would no more have picked this place than I'd pick the music which switches on automatically when I shut my Hertz rental car.' Though it was warm enough in the Californian spring, he was struck by the fact that 'nobody <u>swims</u> in the ocean. In fact the beach is empty so that one can admire the sea-birds and oil-rigs. People swim in bathing-pools, which are <u>really</u> heated, so that even I go in without shivering and you can stay in for hours. There's nothing to do except swim, and watch colour tv.' He drove back up to Los Angeles to catch a plane north for a lecture at Santa Cruz, still finding America alienating:

> Driving through those meaningless Los Angeles streets, all factories, Holiday Inns, garages and general mess, and along the freeway, listening to sports commentaries I can't understand and mediocre rock-music, is like taking part in some fancy-dress ball. I stop at a gas-station and fill up with petrol (70p a gallon) and feel like somebody trying on a funny mask. I've just had my first chance to wash out shirts, socks and pants, and this, curiously, makes me feel a proper individual – someone who belongs elsewhere and is just visiting, not just on a brief holiday from life ... Funny place, funny people.

After this, he went to San Francisco, then, renting another car, he stayed in a small hotel in Marin County, trying but failing to see the whales pass by in the sea under the cliffs, before going on to visit a grove of huge redwoods, 'an <u>extraordinary</u> sensation to be among these giant trees ... and even more so to be quite <u>alone</u> – because it's 20 miles up an unpaved road'. He continued to marvel at the Americans, noting that one man, a television programme manager, to whom he gave a lift, asked if London 'was a big town or a small town', and spoke in 'psychobabble' all the way.[89]

Latin America he felt he understood better, but what he saw when he next visited was not encouraging. In early April 1978 he arrived in Lima for a conference after a difficult journey involving air traffic computer breakdowns, missed connections and the theft of his duty-free bag.[90] 'Lima', he wrote to Marlene,

> is running down. Neglected, in disrepair, filthy, impoverished. The town centre is awful, though Miraflores [an upmarket city precinct] seems only slightly shopsoiled. Fewer cars around and older ones, a lot more down-at-heel people, new barriadas [shanty towns], and a general air of hopelessness. Oh dear ... when I think of 1971 when there seemed to be an air of very modest hope. The Archivo Agrario (where they put all those hacienda records) is a slum: it has a roof (just) but broken window-panes ... Even an old bourgeois restaurant I used to go to in town, while still working, has the stucco peeling off and nobody puts it right. Nobody has money, for even the middle class are hard pushed.[91]

The country, which was just beginning a transition to democracy from years of military dictatorship, was hit by rampant inflation, which it took some years to get under control. Eric found himself 'overrun by Peruvian students who used to be in London and had to return without finishing their thesis, and now want consultations'.

There were worse places in South America to be, however. Argentina was now under a brutal military dictatorship, which, with the clandestine support of the Americans, arrested, tortured and 'disappeared' tens of thousands of citizens suspected of taking or supporting armed resistance movements. Lima, Eric noted, was 'full of exile [sic] Argentines commiserating with one another'. Things were just as bad in Brazil, where a military dictatorship was still in power, though it was nearing its end. 'My old acquaintance from Brazil, Eulalia Lobo', he added, 'says she is going for a long trip to the Andes (La Paz, Potosi) before returning to Rio. I say: "I'm a bit scared to go on short trips up to those heights". She says: "Well, when I was being tortured in jail I got used to headaches, so I expect I can stand it." Clearly on this continent these days you need to keep a sense of humour noir.'

He was back in South America in 1986, visiting Colombia and staying in the Hotel Tequandama in Bogotá. As he reported to Marlene,

> In this luxury hotel (by local standards) we have just had as guest Ariel Sharon, the Israeli minister, and the place was therefore full of Colombian soldiers & police and the man's own heavies. So full that I bet any terrorist could have got in, since obviously the soldiers & police didn't know each other. Now he's gone and Miss Universe is here. Fewer soldiers, but a greater interest among civilian males. All I can say is that these girls, seen close up, don't seem any better than a lot of what one can see on the streets of London.[92]

In sharp contrast to this, killing continued on the streets 'at a rate which impresses even Colombians', with fifty-seven judges shot dead in four years. Paramilitary death squads were roaming around 'murdering petty criminals, prostitutes, homosexuals and left-wingers'.

Things were not much better in Medellín, where he went next, to attend a conference at the National University of Colombia. This was

> the city which has the record for drug-business and for death-squads who rush round on motorbikes killing any prostitutes, homosexuals, beggars, not to mention 'subversives' they see …

The last development during the 'university week' I was there for, was during a horse-show organised by the Veterinary Faculty on the campus. Since the most enthusiastic horse-breeders and owners, as everyone knows, are the big drug barons, one of them – or rather his father, a huge fat character looking like the Godfather – attended with a troop of bodyguards. A bunch of students, true to Latinamerican manhood, demonstrated against him. The bodyguards took out their guns and fired – luckily only into the air. The students started throwing stones. The Godfather said he'd never been so insulted in his life and threatened to withdraw his horses from the show. The Vice-Rector for Academic Affairs (!) wiped his forehead and tried to calm things down. Twenty rather tricky minutes. The Rector, after a decent interval, called the rest of the horse-show off, as the University was not in a position to guarantee the security of participants. All very different from Birkbeck College.[93]

From here he went on to Mexico, which he also found alarmingly violent: 'People get killed left right and centre, especially in universities.' It seemed to be raining continuously, he reported, and he had been obliged to buy himself an umbrella ('the Mexicans find it inconceivable that there can be an Englishman who has no umbrella'). He had been there before with Marlene and the children, and missed them badly this time. However, he reported to Marlene, 'the tequila is still good'.[94] All in all, his experience of Latin America in the 1980s was far less positive than it had been during his earlier visits. It was to be some time before things began to change for the better.

VII

Foreign travel on a considerable scale did not prevent Eric from engaging with British politics far more closely than he had done before. The change in focus of his political commentary came partly from his reporting on Britain for the Italian Communist press, but also from a greatly intensified relationship with the 'theoretical journal' of the British Communist Party, *Marxism Today*. From time to time he had, to be sure, contributed articles to the magazine through the 1950s and 1960s, but most of them were on historical topics such as 'History and "The Dark Satanic Mills"', 'From Feudalism to Capitalism', 'Karl Marx and the British Labour Movement', 'Capitalist Development: Some Historical Problems', or 'The Labour Movement and Military Coups'.[95] In 1977, however, the editorship was taken over by Martin Jacques, who tried to use the journal as a vehicle of the Eurocommunist tendency in British Communism, but soon had lost hope of converting the Party as a whole and began to turn *Marxism Today* into a general vehicle of debate about the future of British politics. Broadening the basis of contributions and getting well-known people to write for it boosted the magazine's circulation from around two thousand when Jacques took over to twenty-five thousand by the time it closed, following the collapse of Communism, in 1991.

In these circumstances, Jacques naturally thought of asking Eric to contribute to the journal. 'I rang him up one day', he later recalled, 'and . . . introduced myself . . . and I met him for lunch at Birkbeck.' Jacques asked Eric to write on the tenth anniversary of the events of 1968, and he delivered a characteristically wide-ranging piece, seeing it in a 'hugely expansive' way, as nobody else could. In common with many other contributors brought in by Jacques, Eric did not use standard Party jargon or confine himself to standard Party topics. He was, Jacques thought, an 'independent-minded person, who [was] very self-confident about his capacity as a historian, about his capacity as a writer, and, I think, also, politically very self-confident. You know, he wasn't in hock to anyone, or anything.' He was a thinker, not an activist ('I never heard him talk about branch meetings or selling newspapers and all that kind of thing'). Jacques continued to commission articles from Eric until the end of the 1980s. 'Eric was the only author', he recalled, 'whom I never, ever edited.' His pieces always arrived polished-perfect, unlike those of many other contributors.[96]

If, in the eighteen years from 1958 to 1976, Eric had contributed ten articles to the magazine, then, in the following fourteen years, to 1991, he wrote no fewer than thirty. When *Marxism Today* eventually ceased publication in 1991, Jacques told Eric:

You have written some brilliant stuff ... Without you, *MT* would have been in Division III not Division I. And of course, you have been my mentor, my adviser, my support, my inspiration ... When I first came to London I hardly knew you, I just enormously admired your work. I remember our first lunch at Birkbeck, my efforts to persuade you to write (I think the first piece was the one on 68?), to get you to be on the editorial board, and to write and write and interview ... and ... You have been marvellous.[97]

It was through *Marxism Today* that Eric gained a role in British political debate, catapulting the magazine to public prominence in the process. In 1978, Jacques 'stumbled across a lecture' by Eric, advertised in the *Morning Star*, with the title 'The Forward March of Labour Halted?' and asked him for a copy (it was in fact the annual Marx Memorial Lecture, which Eric delivered on 17 March 1978). 'As soon as I saw the title', he remembered, 'I thought, this is exactly the kind of article I want for *Marxism Today*', so he asked Eric if he could publish it, and he agreed. Jacques knew it would stir up a debate.[98] Taking his cue from Gramsci, Eric argued that the 'workerism' of the British labour movement was obsolete. The expansion of the university system in Britain and elsewhere during the late 1960s and early 1970s, with thousands of young lecturers employed to fill the newly available jobs, had created a new body of intellectuals who were critical of capitalist society. 'In Britain, the typical Labour candidate between the wars was a miner or railwayman. Today, he or she is much more likely to be someone described as a "lecturer".' There was a downside to this: the new intellectuals were dangerously inclined to look down on manual workers. But that could be corrected. Intellectuals were in any case essential if the Left was to understand the nature of the crisis of capitalism that had begun with the oil price rise five years before.[99]

Eric pointed out that in the late nineteenth century, the continued expansion of industrial capitalism had led socialists everywhere, including in the United Kingdom, to believe that eventually industrial workers would make up the majority of the population. This belief underpinned the confident growth of trade unions and the labour movement for many decades. But since the Second World War the rise of white-collar work and the expansion of the service sector had led to a relative decline in the strength of the industrial working class. The result was a fall in trade union membership and a decline in the Labour Party vote. 'The forward march of British labour . . . began to falter thirty years ago.' It was time to recognise this and do what was necessary. Eric did not say what that was; his essay made no suggestions for action. But it was clear by implication that he was saying the labour movement and the working class now needed to make tactical alliances with other groups in society and politics if it was ever to achieve power again.[100]

The article unleashed a storm of controversy among the magazine's readers, and indeed far beyond. This was not least because, the following year, a 'winter of discontent' in which trade union militancy, given practical expression in a long series of strikes, alienated large sectors of the general public. A general election held on 3 May 1979 ousted the Labour government led by the centrist James Callaghan and brought the Conservatives to power. Led by Margaret Thatcher, the new government introduced a radical policy of reducing the role of the state in the economy, cutting public spending, deregulating the financial sector and curtailing trade union rights. The post-war consensus was broken, and neo-liberal economics assumed a dominant position in policymaking. Discontent in the Labour Party with the policies of Callaghan led to a sharp lurch to the left. Eric's lecture was in a sense, therefore, the curtain-raiser to a period of deep crisis and self-examination in the labour movement, which to some extent explains the controversy it caused.[101]

Riding on the wings of the storm, Jacques got Eric to conduct a lengthy interview with Tony Benn, who had emerged as a major figure on the Labour Left. Benn had heard of Eric, but was not very familiar with his work: 'Martin Jacques rang', he noted in his diary on 21 May 1980, 'and said Eric Hobsbawm had agreed to interview me in the framework of a seminar at Birkbeck College (of which he is Master) for reproduction in *Marxism Today*. I am looking forward to that very much indeed: to be taken through one's paces by a distinguished Marxist philosopher will be an extremely interesting and demanding experience.'[102] Conducted at Birkbeck, where of course Eric had never been Master, on 15 July 1980, published in October 1980 and running to nine pages, the conversation ranged widely across the political scene. As Eric pointed out correctly, they were in a crisis of the entire political and social order that had grown up since the Second World War. Benn charged that the Labour Party had been content with defending the post-war settlement and the welfare state instead of using them as a springboard for further transformations. A democratic, grass-roots movement was needed to break the stranglehold of the union and parliamentary leadership over the party as a whole, which was preventing it from moving beyond the politics of the post-war era.[103]

Given the influence on him of Gramsci, and the arguments of his Marx Memorial Lecture, it was not surprising that Eric pointed out that a third of blue-collar workers had voted for Thatcher, and it was necessary not only to try and win them back but also to appeal to a far broader spectrum of society, including 'middle-class intellectuals'. However, he did agree that the fault for the decline in membership lay not least with the Labour governments of the 1960s. 'Wilson was I think very nearly the worst thing that has happened to the Labour Party', he observed: he had no really coherent policy, and his government did little more than lurch from crisis to crisis. Its major achievement was the social liberalisation pushed through by Roy Jenkins as Home Secretary. It was necessary to ensure that the next Labour government was a genuinely radical one. 'It's through the Labour Party and primarily through

Labour governments that any social change that is likely to happen in this country is in the first instance going to be achieved', he told Benn, repeating a belief that he had held ever since the mid-1930s. For his part, Benn argued that social transformation would only happen through a decentralisation of power and the democratisation of key institutions, but Eric pushed him to give some concrete content to these concepts. 'I am finding your questions very difficult', Benn told him ruefully, but he did say that what he favoured was a mixed economy in which the big companies were 'publicly owned or publicly controlled', with statutory planning agreements forcing 'the hundred major companies' to be publicly accountable. Eric agreed.

Shortly after the interview was published, the Labour Left scored a major victory following Callaghan's resignation, when Michael Foot was elected leader of the party in November 1980, by a margin of ten votes over his right-wing rival (and Callaghan's favoured candidate) Denis Healey. In response to these developments, on 26 March 1981 four leading Labour moderates, led by Roy Jenkins, but not including Healey himself, resigned to form the new Social Democratic Party, which was soon registering support at the same level as Labour in the opinion polls. In this crisis, the Labour Left put up Tony Benn for the Deputy Leadership of the Party on 27 September 1981. Healey beat him by less than 1 per cent in the election but this only seemed to spur the 'Bennites' on. Internecine political strife now gripped the Labour Party as both radicals and moderates vied for power, with Foot unable to impose any kind of control.

In his 1980 interview with Eric, Benn declared that one of the key differences between the 1930s and the 1980s in Britain was that 'the option of war as a solution to the problem of the slump has been rendered absurd, though not impossible, because of the development of nuclear weapons'. Whether or not it was a solution to the problem of the economic depression, however, it was soon to provide an unexpected remedy for the unpopularity of the Conservative Party. On 2 April 1982, the Argentine military dictatorship under General Leopoldo Galtieri, seeking to reverse its own difficulties at home, mounted an amphibious invasion of the Falkland Islands (or Malvinas), a British sovereign territory in the South Atlantic some way off the Argentine coast, along with the more distant islands of South Georgia and South Sandwich; Argentina had long laid claim to all these islands and their takeover was a popular cause. After a token resistance, the 1680 inhabitants of the Falklands, led by the Governor Sir Rex Hunt, surrendered. The Thatcher government immediately organised an armed naval flotilla, which began steaming towards the islands. By the end of the month the shooting war had begun, with combat aircraft engaging in dogfights over the sea, and two ships, the Argentine cruiser *General Belgrano* and the British destroyer HMS *Sheffield*, sunk with considerable loss of life. British troops landed on the Falklands on 21 May. After fierce fighting on the ground, they had recaptured the islands by 14 June, along with South Georgia and the South Sandwich Islands a few days later. Total loss of life on both sides amounted to just over nine hundred.

The Labour leader Michael Foot instinctively backed the war: as far as he was concerned, this was an unprovoked act of aggression by a military dictatorship which had to be fought, just as Hitler's aggression had to be fought in 1939. Eric was taken in neither by the Thatcher government's deliberate recourse to images of the Second World War, with its 'War Cabinet' and its repeated invocation of Churchill (or 'Winston', as Mrs Thatcher called him familiarly), nor by Foot's unthinking revival of the rhetoric of democratic patriotism he had first espoused in his crusade against Appeasement decades before. In a speech delivered late in 1982 to *Marxism Today*'s 'Moving Left Show', Eric cut through the posturing of the parliamentarians, arguing that the Argentine claim on the Falklands, located off the country's coast, was stronger than that of the United Kingdom, located many thousands of miles away. The Thatcher government had brought the crisis on itself by neglecting the island's defence, withdrawing, on grounds of cost, the one armed ship that had been stationed there, and failing to anticipate the invasion although it had been repeatedly warned by intelligence reports.[104] He recognised, of

Eric met Marlene Schwarz in November 1961 on her return to London after working for the United Nations in the Congo, where this photograph shows her in 1960. She wisely turned down a request from the future dictator Joseph-Desiré Mobutu to give him private English lessons.

Fatherhood transformed Eric's life from the 1960s onwards. Andy was born in 1963 and Julia the following year.

Alan Sillitoe (1928–2010), author of *Saturday Night and Sunday Morning*, and his family, shared a house in Clapham with the Hobsbawms in the mid-1960s. Eric got an émigré Austrian architect to partition it into two maisonettes.

The Cuban revolutionary Ernesto ('Che') Guevara (1928–67), for whom Eric acted as an interpreter during a visit to the island in January 1962 sponsored by the British Cuba Committee. The speech, he said, contained nothing of interest.

Kenneth Tynan (1927–80), theatre critic, the first person to say 'fuck' on British television. He knew Eric from Soho's Downbeat Club and organized the British Cuba Committee with him after the failed American invasion in 1961.

For some years Eric believed Latin America had more revolutionary potential than anywhere else in the world. In 1971 he travelled up into the Peruvian sierra on this pony.

Luiz Inácio Lula da Silva (b. 1945), trade union leader and President of Brazil 2003–2010. He remains immensely popular among workers. His public acknowledgment of Eric's intellectual influence helped propel *Age of Extremes* to the top of Brazil's best-seller lists.

Eric with Ticlia, a stray cat which adopted the family on their return from Latin America in 1971 and stayed until her death fifteen years later. 'She knew Eric was the important one', Marlene said, 'because he made the least fuss over her.'

George Weidenfeld (1919–2016), the publishing impresario who commissioned *The Age of Revolution*. In 1938 he was last man to fight a student duel in Vienna, defeating his much larger Nazi opponent by concealing beforehand the fact that he was left-handed.

Caricature by John Minnion (b. 1949) of the *New Statesman*. Eric was the magazine's jazz critic in the late 1950s and early 1960s, writing under the name 'Francis Newton'. From the 1970s (when this sketch was penned) he contributed political articles under his own name.

Contemplating the abyss: for over two decades, from the late 1960s onwards, Eric and the family spent frequent periods in the Croesor Valley, in Snowdonia, where they enjoyed long walks on the steep slopes of Cnicht, 'the Welsh Matterhorn'.

Eric in 2011, discussing his new book, *How to Change the World: Tales of Marx and Marxism*, before an audience of 1600 people at the Hay Literary Festival, with Tristram Hunt, biographer of Engels and Labour MP for Stoke-on-Trent. The event, sponsored by the *Daily Telegraph*, was held somewhat incongruously in the Barclays Wealth Tent, where Eric gave 'an absolute tour-de-force performance'.

Historians of *Past & Present*, painted in 1999 by Stephen Farthing (b. 1950). From left to right (also in a political sense, as intended by the artist): Eric Hobsbawm, Christopher Hill, Rodney Hilton, Lawrence Stone, John Elliott, Joan Thirsk and Keith Thomas (who was not at all pleased at his positioning).

Eric in his nineties, wearing 'one of those Bolshevik caps' and looking like 'a real revolutionary', according to Keith Thomas.

Eric's grave in Highgate cemetery, 'just to the right of Karl Marx'. At his funeral, the mourners exited the crematorium to the strains of the *Internationale*, the battle-hymn of the Communist movement.

course, that a 'general sense of outrage and humiliation' had gripped the country on all sides, including the Labour Left. But, he observed,

> This upsurge of feeling had nothing to do with the Falklands as such . . . a far-away country swathed in mists off Cape Horn, about which we knew nothing and cared less. It has everything to do with the history of this country since 1945 and the visible acceleration of the crisis of British capitalism since the late 1960s and in particular the slump of the late 70s and early 80s . . . This was a reaction to the decline of the British Empire such as we had predicted for so long.

And he quoted Mrs Thatcher's condemnation 'the waverers and the faint-hearts' who thought 'Britain was no longer the nation that had built an empire and ruled a quarter of the world. Well', she added, 'they were wrong.' The war, Eric concluded, 'didn't prove anything of the kind'. A settlement with Argentina before the outbreak of hostilities had been perfectly possible, but Thatcher had rejected any such idea out of hand.

Typically, Eric noted the incomprehension that had greeted the British military action right across the Continent. 'Most Europeans could not understand what all the fuss was about.' The war had nothing to do with international realpolitik or real material or strategic interests. It had everything to do with British domestic politics. The war was popular because it 'cheered people up' in a dire economic situation, 'as if we had won a World Cup with guns'. The consequences were made clear in the General Election held on 9 June 1983, which the Conservatives won with a massive majority, bringing them more than 60 per cent of the seats in the House of Commons. They won in part because Labour entered the campaign with a hard-left manifesto dubbed by one MP as 'the longest suicide note in history', demanding unilateral nuclear disarmament, the nationalisation of key industries and banks, major tax increases, the abolition of the House of Lords and Britain's exit from what later became the European Union. Thatcher was still reaping the benefits of the 'Falklands effect', of course, but above all, as Eric pointed out, the Conservatives triumphed because the Social Democrats, who pulled in 25 per cent of the vote to Labour's 28 per cent, had split the opposition down the middle, allowing many Conservative candidates to win constituencies, under the British 'first-past-the-post' electoral system, that they might not otherwise have taken.[105]

Michael Foot promptly resigned as Labour Party leader following this crushing defeat and was succeeded on 2 October 1983 by the much younger Neil Kinnock, a Welsh MP and left-winger though not a member of the Bennite faction. The centrist Roy Hattersley was elected Deputy Leader. Analysing the election results for *Marxism Today* in an article entitled 'Labour's Lost Millions', Eric found 'not a glimmer of comfort' in them. Labour's vote had fallen sharply in all social strata; the majority of the working class were now no longer Labour voters. Too many in the labour movement were 'engaged in a civil war rather than in fighting the Right ... To put it brutally, for many [on the Left], a Thatcher government was preferable to a reformist Labour government.' Thatcherism was committed to a reactionary transformation of British capitalism, and indeed of the British political system, and defeating it was 'the condition of survival for a decent Britain'. So, electoral pacts between the Social Democrats, Liberals and Labour were essential, just as the labour movement had to broaden its appeal, become 'more than a class party', abandon sectarianism and recognise that its 1983 manifesto had failed to appeal to the majority even of the working class. Characteristically, Eric urged the party to look to the example of France, where the leader of the Socialist Party, François Mitterrand, had been elected President in 1981, and Spain, where Felipe González, leader of the Socialist Workers' Party, had won a general election in 1982. Neo-socialist parties such as these, and to a degree also the Italian Communist Party, had shown the way, not least by collaborating with other political parties. Unity of all progressive and democratic forces was needed if Thatcher's conservative revolution was to be stopped.[106]

Once more, Eric sparked an impassioned debate within the labour movement. His arguments ran into stiff opposition, especially from Ralph Miliband, a Marxist sociologist and prominent figure in the New Left. In January 1984, Miliband told Eric 'that your attack on the left is mistaken and plays into the hands of people with whom you cannot have anything in common'. He was 'in effect, asking the Left to be quiet and let the Right and Centre run the Labour Party, no doubt with occasional bones being thrown to the Left, as has always been the case in the past'. It was quite wrong of Eric to 'sound the retreat'.[107] In response, Eric maintained that the effect of his writings and lectures in this area since 1978 had been

1) to bring matters into the open which ought to have been discussed on the Left much earlier, and thus to help launch a debate which has been useful .... I should add that this has happened not because I set out to launch a political campaign – I had no such intentions when I gave my original lecture in 1978 from which the whole debate sprang – but because the *sectarians* were outraged by my views and insisted on controverting them, which led other people *on the left* to say 'Wait a minute, the man has put his finger on some very real problems which do cause us difficulties in our work.' My contribution was to help mobilise the non-sectarian left. 2) My views were taken up, with relief, by leading members of the 'soft left' – *not* the right – in the Labour Party, and notably by Kinnock, who quoted them with approval at the Labour Party Conference of 1982, and again that of 1983. I have been called 'Kinnock's favourite Marxist', but not, so far as I am aware, Heal[e]y's or Hattersley's. Now doubtless my views, coming from someone with a fairly lengthy track record of being on the left, have the effect of demonstrating that the word 'left' cannot be monopolised by the 'hard left' of 1980–1983. But unless you take the view that the *only* left was the one which, say, rallied round Benn's campaign for the deputy leadership (which I was one of the very many to regard as ill-advised, unnecessary and disastrous), this is not damaging to the

whole left but only to a particular kind of left. Nor was I in any sense 'sounding the retreat'. On the contrary, I was predicting, accurately as it turned out, that Labour was heading for a rout and favouring a different policy which *could* lead to a resumption of its advance. And indeed since Kinnock's election it has shown marked signs of revival.[108]

Miliband countered by dubbing Kinnock 'Harold Wilson Mark II'. If Benn had won the contest for the Deputy Leadership this would at least 'have strengthened the leftward shift which you welcomed'.[109] For his part, responding to an enquiry by a Ph.D. student in 2002, Eric explained that 'I was for Tony Benn until he threw away his chances of leading a united Labour Party in Jan[uary] 1981 after the party's special conference, choosing instead to make a bid for sole control based on the sectarian left.' He did think his articles 'had some impact, because I was among the first to predict trouble for the Labour Party, and because I was a passionate opponent of the Bennites, but one with an undeniable record on the extreme left. Hence my name and writings were useful to Kinnock.'[110]

Never one to miss an opportunity, especially not one provided by the controversy raging over 'Labour's Lost Millions', Martin Jacques asked the new Labour leader's office to give permission for Eric to interview Kinnock for *Marxism Today*. Kinnock's press secretary Patricia Hewitt told Kinnock this would be 'an excellent opportunity for you to lay out ideas' and also asked the *Guardian* to publish extracts for the opening Monday of the Labour Party Conference.[111] The lengthy exchange of views took place on 3 September 1984, a month before the Labour Party Conference, where Kinnock was due to give his first speech as leader, and was published during the conference itself. The Labour Party, Eric observed, needed a vision of 'a particular kind of Britain', a coherent set of ideas, and – as Kinnock conceded – it had not yet achieved this. In a series of very lengthy replies that confirmed his reputation as something of a windbag, Kinnock deflected the thrust of Eric's questioning by repeatedly attacking Margaret

Thatcher's policies as backward-looking and reactionary. Martin Jacques, who was present wielding the voice recorder, later remembered that 'Eric caught my eye at one point, and we both went, you know, this is going to be a very boring and unrewarding experience'.[112] Eric's response was to point out that Thatcherism meant the dismantling of the post-war settlement and a reliance almost exclusively on the market – 'a sort of bourgeois anarchism' – and he wanted to know what combination of planning, public ownership and private enterprise the Labour leader favoured.[113]

Kinnock reiterated Labour's commitment to renationalise key industries, to centralise planning and to create a national investment bank. The problem was, as Eric pointed out, that it might well be impossible to restore the industries, such as coal and steel, that Thatcher had destroyed. Perhaps, he suggested, typically, a Labour government might look to other European countries, such as France or Sweden, for inspiration? Kinnock did not think other countries were a good example. Eric raised the question of Labour's relationship with the unions, especially the miners' union, then engaged in a bitter dispute with the government that was to end in its total defeat. Kinnock was careful to avoid saying anything critical of the miners' union, though Eric even offered to turn the voice recorder off if he felt the issue was too sensitive to go on the record. But it was clear that the Labour leader felt uncomfortable dealing with the issue of union militancy, which had been exploited to such effect by the Conservative government.[114] For his part, Eric was, in private, sharply critical of the miners' leader Arthur Scargill, whose intransigence and self-aggrandisement had caused the defeat of the strikers, bringing catastrophe to the union movement in general. One of his students remembered an occasion at which 'his contempt for Scargill . . . resounded through a half-hour row with [John] Saville, effectively closing a surprise party for Raphael Samuel on 3 January 1985'.[115]

Altogether the interview failed to pin the Labour leader down to any very concrete statements. It was noticeable that Eric consistently used the first-person plural when talking about the Labour Party in the Kinnock interview – 'we', 'us', 'our'. His identification with it seemed complete, the Communist Party forgotten. By now, Eric had launched a full-scale assault on what he called 'the retreat into extremism' in parts of the labour movement, accusing his critics of lack of political realism (were they, he asked, 'living in the same country – even on the same planet – as most of us?'). Political alliances, Eric declared, invoking the example of the Popular Front governments in France and Spain during the 1930s, did not imply the abandonment of socialism. It was time for the British labour movement to stop being so parochial.[116]

In 1987, not long before a general election, he underlined even more emphatically his belief that defeating Thatcherism, whose unprecedented aim was to destroy the labour movement, was the overwhelming priority. Tactical voting was imperative. Where Liberal or Social Democratic candidates stood the best chance of defeating a Tory, Labour voters should cast their vote in their favour. The Social Democrats were the party of the intelligentsia and the professional classes, and they were naturally more opposed to the Tories than they were to Labour, especially now that Neil Kinnock was steering the Labour Party back towards the middle ground. A social alliance with Labour's core working-class vote was vital. A coalition government with Labour would be the most likely outcome of a strong performance by the centrist parties, committed to social management of the economy, improvements in education and the modernisation of Britain's crumbling infra-structure.[117] These were arguments central to the whole future of the labour movement, and they were enormously influential in the long run. In 1987, however, they failed to have any impact. Tactical voting was not widely practised. The continued division of the anti-Tory vote, combined with the strong recovery of the economy, delivered a result more or less the same as the one which had confirmed Thatcher in power in 1983.

Eric's articles on the Labour Party and its future were gathered together in his collection *Politics for a Rational Left: Political Writing 1977–1988*, published by Verso (New Left Books) in May 1989. In a lengthy review of the book, Ross McKibbin, an Oxford-based historian of twentieth-century Britain and an acute and perceptive observer of Labour politics, noted: 'It is hard not to conclude that the educated classes in Hobsbawm's thinking now play the role once played by the old working class.' As it went on, reproducing essays in chronological order, McKibbin thought that the book's arguments grew increasingly minimalist and tactical. There was nothing particularly Marxist about them. 'It is as though the collapse of those classic labour movements, in which he has invested much of his political and intellectual life, has left his Marxism momentarily rudderless.' In fact the evidence of these essays suggested that 'Hobsbawm today sees "socialism" in practice as a mixed economy with the state having a general supervisory and regulatory function – differing little from the kind of social organization Keynes seems to have envisaged in the *General Theory*'. In similar terms, the political writer R. W. Johnson noted 'the absence of any viable Marxist analysis'. Marxist or not, however, in the longer term Eric's arguments won the day. The hard left, organised in the Trotskyite 'militant tendency', was defeated, and Kinnock persuaded the party to drop policies that alienated voters, such as leaving NATO and Europe, raising taxes and abandoning nuclear weapons. After the crushing electoral defeat of 1987, the third in a row, the Labour Party could not any longer avoid a fundamental confrontation with the problems it faced. Mrs Thatcher had gained new confidence in her mission to transform Britain and destroy the traditional labour movement in the process. Eric noted that she had begun talking, not of her government, but of her 'regime'. This, he suggested, was 'the language of a "New Order" ... the language of an authoritarian one-party government which is systematically setting about creating the conditions for staying that way'. The task of defeating it had become even more urgent than before.[118]

Not long after the 1987 General Election, however, Mrs Thatcher's government began to get into trouble. Unpopular policies such as the introduction of a 'poll tax', which provoked massive demonstrations on the streets of London, added to growing dissension within the government over Europe to put Labour well ahead in the opinion polls. Eric became more optimistic about the chances of a Labour victory at the next election.[119] Thatcher's increasingly strident opposition to European integration led to her overthrow by Conservative MPs in November 1990. Her successor, John Major, exercised a down-to-earth appeal to voters in the General Election in April 1992, while Kinnock overreached himself in staging an excessively slick professional campaign that only put voters off, especially when it stumbled. Armed with a small but serviceable majority, the Conservatives stayed in power while Kinnock was forced to resign in his turn. After a brief interval, the duumvirate of Tony Blair and Gordon Brown rebranded the Labour Party as 'New Labour', broadened its appeal, won back voters who had deserted to the Social (now Liberal) Democrats and won a series of general elections, coming to power in 1997 and remaining in government up to 2010.

'If "New Labour" had intellectual founding fathers,' as Harold Wilson's biographer Ben Pimlott concluded, Eric 'could certainly claim to be one of them.'[120] Perry Anderson, one of the founders of *New Left Review*, thought that insofar as he had any influence on a complex process of change within the labour movement, Eric had brought about a catastrophic defeat for the Left. But he was missing the point. It was not the defeat of the Labour Left that Eric helped bring about – that was achieved above all by Kinnock – but the reorientation of the party towards an appeal to intellectuals in the broadest sense, to professionals and the urban middle classes as well as to its traditional base among the manual working class. His influence here was undeniable. By the early 1980s, as Roderick Floud remembered, Eric 'wasn't, I would say, a political activist in any sense. I mean he was writing, certainly, yes, and he became obviously and increasingly a guru, if he wasn't already, of various groups on the left. But that was the extent of his political activism.'[121] True though it was, that too, in a way, missed the point. Eric's influence was exerted through his writing, above all for *Marxism Today*. As Martin Jacques concluded, 'Eric was by this time seen . . . as . . . an intellectual guru in the Labour Party . . . From being a Communist intellectual he became *the* intellectual of the Left.'[122]

VIII

'I'll be retiring in 18 months', Eric told his former student Alan Adamson in November 1980, 'and I suppose it will be a wrench, after all these years – even though I'll not be short of work to do or places to go to.'[123] Having reached the then statutory age of sixty-five, Eric left Birkbeck on 30 July 1982 and was immediately appointed Emeritus Professor of Economic and Social History, a purely honorific title that carried no obligations but recognised both his academic distinction and his thirty-five years of service to the College.[124] Eric continued to visit Birkbeck following his retirement, to pick up post and meet with old friends and colleagues. But he loved teaching and was frustrated at having to give it up. So, when he was contacted early in 1984 by Ira Katznelson, from the New School for Social Research in New York, with an offer to teach there, he was seriously interested. The New School boasted a history of radicalism dating back to its founding by scholars dismissed from Columbia University in New York for opposing American participation in the First World War. In the 1930s it had provided a refuge for German social scientists forced into exile by the Nazis. Privately funded, it had gone through a period of difficulty in the 1970s but, thanks to generous backing from Dorothy Hirshon, a wealthy widow (her fortune came from a brief marriage to the son of the media mogul William Randolph Hearst), its fortunes were now recovering.

Katznelson, a social scientist who straddled the disciplines of politics, sociology and history, had been hired from the University of Chicago as Dean to build a faculty at the intersection of history and social science. Under his leadership the prominent social-science historians Charles and Louise Tilly were hired in 1984, and as they were casting about for other, comparable figures to attract to New York, Katznelson thought of Eric, who, he knew, had recently retired 'as a result of age – but not as a result of mental infirmity – from Birkbeck'. In contrast to the situation in the UK, there was no mandatory retirement age for academics in the US, so the way was clear for Katznelson to ask Eric to come over. The two men did not know each other, though they had a mutual acquaintance in Ralph Miliband, but, undeterred, Katznelson

> rang him up cold, more or less . . . I said 'Here I am! I'm the new Dean of . . . ' I mean, the name wasn't completely cold to him, but I don't think he even knew that I was at the New School when I rang, and I explained the nature of the project – the ambitions of a new gang that was arriving – and 'might he be interested in coming?' And without asking anything about terms or 'what would you pay me?' or, you know, that, [he] said 'I'd be very interested', and very quickly we consummated a relationship that brought him . . . quite regularly to the institution.[125]

Eric told Katznelson that 'he would relish the chance to continue with teaching, especially at an institution sharing many of Birkbeck's features', including a strong focus on teaching mature and graduate students.[126]

He agreed to teach Master's and doctoral students (who, in the USA, were required to do coursework, unlike in British universities) each Fall Semester, from the beginning of September to just before Christmas. The New School made an apartment available for him to stay in, though it was a different one each year: as Katznelson recalled, one year he lived in a high-rise apartment block that projected on to the East River. It was called 'Waterside – I remember he liked very much having a study in which boats were passing underneath . . . He lived in – typically – in various already furnished accommodation of people on sabbatical.' Arriving in New York in September 1986, Eric was indeed impressed by the Waterside apartment, which was 'magnificent, with a view over the East River and everything'. The Waterside Plaza was 'a sort of island colony with everything – a lovely plaza to sit on, with a view of the Chrysler Building and the UN, and full of small children, the basic shops etc.'. It was an hour and a half's walk to the New School 'and much the same by bus', but Eric did not mind.[127]

He was appointed to two cross-disciplinary committees formed to build up the nexus of historical and social studies at the New School: the Center for Studies of Social Change, led by Charles Tilly, and the Committee on Historical Studies. He was far more than a normal visiting professor:

> It was understood that he would be a recurring visitor, and therefore he had standing as a faculty member. He came to faculty meetings. One of the great features of Eric's time at the New School was how committed he was institutionally, much as he was at Birkbeck; and he talked about Birkbeck and the New School as being very similar. And he was a terrific citizen of the New School ... The full faculty of about seventy – when he first came it was about forty-five or fifty, but it grew to the mid-seventies – met once a month ... to discuss whatever business was at hand. Eric, when he was in residence, was always there, and an active participant. He also helped govern the Center for Social Change.[128]

Less formally, Eric usually went to a Friday afternoon workshop run under the title 'Think and then Drink', in which he was also an active participant.

As Katznelson noted, he socialised a great deal, especially when Marlene, who only came over for relatively short periods, was not there – 'a very vibrant lunch-goer with individual faculty and students – a real player, in the good sense of the term'. Every year, on the fourth Thursday in November, he and Marlene were invited to an annual Thanksgiving Day party thrown by Eric Foner, an American historian at Columbia University whom Eric had taken under his wing years before, when he was researching in London, where, Foner remembered, Eric's seminar had taught him how to do social history. The Foners invited people from abroad, or from places in the USA too distant to travel to from New York, for 'a quintessentially American dinner – turkey etc. (with some Italian dishes thrown in, in honour of my wife's Italian heritage). Of course, Eric's presence meant many interesting discussions of politics.' History figured as well: Foner remembered in particular a conversation one year about female bandits, between Eric and Millicent Hodson, a well-known choreographer and dance historian, famous for her reconstruction of Nijinsky's choreography for the first performance of Stravinsky's *Rite of Spring*.[129]

Along with Charles Tilly, who quickly became a personal friend, he

> offered students a remarkable model of how to be well known and yet be in the trenches, demonstrating less by telling, and more by showing what it means to be a craftsman: how to set high standards, and ... how to do analytical history ... He was open, tolerant of people with – students with – very different perspectives ... He knew something about everything, and he knew a lot about many things. It was hard to find a subject that any graduate student or current faculty member was working on, that somehow didn't touch on things Eric had both knowledge and opinions about.[130]

He was particularly enthused by the students who came to the New School from Latin American countries, and 'helped make them feel at home'. Katznelson felt that Eric 'had such a deep warmth about him. You know, he was just a very warm and caring friend.' Eric enjoyed visiting his old haunts among New York's jazz clubs and bars, sometimes just dropping in for a drink on his own, sometimes taking friends and colleagues. They made him feel nostalgic, awakening memories he could 'only share with others who have had the same past, and I kept thinking of someone like my cousin Denis, as I looked (across the usual Japanese or Korean) at another elderly jazzfan sitting by himself at the bar, listening over a drink'.[131] More often, however, he went to the Metropolitan Opera, especially when Marlene was there to accompany him.[132] He socialised a great deal with his publisher André Schiffrin and his family, and entertained a constant stream of friends and acquaintances passing through. Perry Anderson, then also teaching at the New School, lived for a time in the same apartment block and frequently joined Eric for breakfast.

He was a frequent guest at dinner parties at Bob Silvers' home, usually attended by eminent literary and cultural figures, many of whom wrote for the *New York Review of Books*. On one occasion, after a party thrown by George Weidenfeld in a New York hotel, Eric

> said hello at the bar to Jack (Sir John) Plumb, who once com-missioned Christopher [Hill] and myself to write books for Penguin (Industry and Empire) and is now a rich unhappy old reactionary and lonely gay, staying at the Carlyle and having a drink with Senator Daniel Moynihan and his wife, the Senator looking less gross in real life than on the TV screen, which is unusual and unexpected. George looks gross too. We waffled around. I said why didn't he actually make some concrete pro-posals sometimes. We parted like intimate old friends do.[133]

New York was a dangerous place still in the mid-1980s, before it was cleaned up, the police purged of corruption and large areas 'gentrified', as Eric noted:

> I keep collecting more New York stories. The ultimate one was told to me at Bob Silvers' party by someone. It seems the NY police is in the habit, when they find a dead body (in this instance it was an elderly middle-class lady who had died in her flat) of selling the credit-cards for $50 or 100, then the buyer runs up a bill (in this case some $700) and everybody is satisfied except the credit card company . . . More NY vignette[s]. Ladies talking to each other on the bus: 'They can't throw a man off the bus just because he's drunk and snoring.' 'Well, he didn't do no harm. The ones that cause trouble aren't drunk. My husband got mugged in Brooklyn, they weren't drunk.' 'That's nothing. I got mugged right here on 20th Street.' Not me, however, so far, touch wood.[134]

It would be some time before the streets of New York became safe to walk along.

In 1988 Eric was back teaching at the New School again, though he did not enjoy it as much as before, partly because he was not feeling very well 'or because I can't get a lot of work done, or maybe just because that smell of urine on the steps of the subway is much more obtrusive'. At a dinner thrown by the Schiffrins, he met the young writer Annie Cohen-Salal, whose just-published biography of Jean-Paul Sartre André had commissioned – 'a thin, sharp-faced, rather neurotic and very bright North African Jewish girl, madly anti-zionist, who is staying in NY for a few days with one of Sartre's ex-mistresses (and one of André Breton's ex-mistresses too, for that matter, one of whom Beauvoir used to be madly jealous)'. He took her to the Museum of Modern Art the next day, perhaps relishing the opportunity to spend a morning speaking French. He delivered a lecture at Bard College, at Annandale-on-Hudson, where he found 'the usual ancient German, the usual ex-don from Harvard who couldn't get tenure there and has become much more radical, the usual lady professor anxious to discuss the cultural atmosphere of London' – an air of frustrated ambition hung about them all.[135] This was certainly not the case at the New School. Eric relished the opportunities his position there provided, not just to carry on teaching, but also to mingle and mix on the social scene of New York with some of America's leading intellectuals. He would continue coming to the New School well into the 1990s.

IX

Throughout this period Eric, as before, played a key role on the editorial board of *Past & Present*. The tradition, established on the journal's foundation in 1952, of all members of the board reading all submissions to the journal, continued. Originally designed to ensure the approval of both Marxist and non-Marxist members for all articles accepted for publication, it has the merit of providing would-be contributors with a wide range of views and criticisms of their work. Eric's notes on articles submitted were always trenchantly expressed. He did not like articles written in jargon, even if it was Marxist jargon. He wanted conceptualisation, but at the same time it had to be rooted in empirical research robust enough to justify it. He liked articles to have a comparative dimension. Problems addressed had to be clearly formulated and original, and above all they had to address questions of social change. And they had to deal with causality. Eric read virtually all the contributions, including those that were way outside his own fields of interest, and also had what a later editor, Joanna Innes, called 'an editorial mindset: making suggestions as to which other board members should read a piece, or what might be said to the author in the light of responses received'. As Keith Thomas recalled,

> Eric was a dominating figure at the *Past and Present* Board, apparently omniscient and with strong views on every subject. He wore one of those Bolshevik caps and looked like a real revolutionary. I was struck by his curiously Edwardian habit of saying something important and then seeking approval by following it by 'What what?'

When his friend Francis Haskell joined the board, Eric ceased to lunch with the others and went off to eat with Francis and Larissa Haskell at their house in Oxford's Walton Street, but otherwise his intense engagement with *Past & Present* continued unchanged.[136] In 1987, when he turned seventy, Eric retired from the board, along with Rodney Hilton, prompting a protest from Edward Thompson: 'You ARE *P&P*. We could shed *anyone* else. The work you have done is remarkable, it is difficult to think of any precedent ... I do hope this is a fictional and formal "retirement" only.'[137] It was indeed. Like the other members of the editorial board appointed before a retiring age of seventy was introduced in the 1990s, Eric continued to go to the annual summer meeting of the board well into the 2000s, and contributed actively to its deliberations. And he continued to comment on articles submitted to the journal long after his retirement from the board, giving his opinion on a vast range of periods and subjects. Typically he called for one article in the field of medical history to be 'recast' because 'it stands too close to the subject for non-specialists'. At the other end of the spectrum, he advised against publishing one piece because it was 'high general journalism . . . A shortened version would be good for *Prospect* [a weekly current affairs magazine].' He deployed his enormous range of knowledge to dismiss a good number of contributions as unoriginal, unsurprising, or repeating debates first aired decades before. Purely empirical contributions he vetoed with the comment that they raised no historical questions; where he smelled a whiff of postmodernism he was equally dismissive ('a pointless exercise in seminar methodology' was his comment on one such piece).[138] He was quick to urge shortening of articles he considered overlong ('The last two pages', he wrote of one such contribution, 'do not add much to the argument'). Traditional diplomatic history always aroused his critical faculties ('a footnote to the history of war guilt debates' was his comment on another).[139]

One of Eric's most influential books was an edited volume of papers that came out of a conference organised by the Past and Present Society, the body that now oversaw the publication of the journal. By this time the journal had also established a book series, published by Cambridge University Press. Entitled *The Invention of Tradition*, the volume, edited by Eric together with the Manchester-based African historian Terry Ranger (another member of the editorial board), was accepted for publication in the series by the Syndics of Cambridge University Press in April 1978 on the recommendation of Trevor Aston, the journal's editor. The contract was very far removed indeed from the commercial agreements Eric was used to. No royalties would be paid up to one thousand copies, 10 per cent from there to five thousand, and 15 per cent thereafter, with 7½ per cent for the paperback.[140] The payments were all to be made directly to the Past and Present Society, not to the authors or editors.[141] Progress on putting the book together was slow.[142] Both men objected to the Press's request that they compile the index ('I don't think I have been asked to do my own indexing as author or editor for near-on a generation', Eric observed, though Ranger eventually agreed to do it if he could keep it short and simple).[143] The contract was not issued until 26 April 1982, by which time the royalty rate from one thousand to fifteen hundred copies had been reduced to 5½ per cent and the higher rate payable after five thousand copies had disappeared.[144] The book was eventually published in 1983 and a paperback edition appeared in April 1984.

Eric later recalled that the inspiration for the idea behind *The Invention of Tradition* came to him when, as a student at King's College, Cambridge, he realised that the famous Christmas Service of Nine Lessons and Carols had only been devised a few years before his arrival in the mid-1930s.[145] Unusually for a volume of scholarly essays based on the proceedings of an academic conference, *The Invention of Tradition* was widely reviewed in the press, partly because several of its contributors were well known beyond the academic world, and partly, no doubt, because of its eye-catching title. Almost all of the reviewers contented themselves with registering their surprise and delight at the essays that made up the book, and recounting some of the central arguments and examples it presented. None tried to overturn its central premiss, though the literary biographer and editor of the collected works of Daniel Defoe, P. N. Furbank, who had been introduced into the Apostles by Eric many decades earlier, voiced some scepticism about the concept of 'tradition' as deployed in the book. Surely Eric and his collaborators were confusing it with custom, as for example in the case of the monarch's Christmas radio broadcast. A more plausible candidate was the Scottish tartan kilt, invented in the eighteenth century but now claiming at least implicitly to go back into the mists of antiquity the subject of a rollicking, debunking essay by Hugh Trevor-Roper.[146] Underlying the volume, however, was a deep scepticism about the claim of nations to trace their identity back to a remote past, and what was original about it was in particular its focus on the symbolic means by which they sought to articulate this claim.[147] The problem of nationalism was still preoccupying Eric in the early 1980s, and he was to treat it at greater length, and in a more wider-ranging analysis, shortly afterwards, in his Wiles Lectures of 1985.

X

Although he had long since moved on from the field in which he began his academic career, British labour history, Eric still felt he had something to contribute to it, and in 1984 he gathered together the essays on the subject he had published in *Labouring Men* into a second collection, entitled *Worlds of Labour*, published in 1984. The book's publication gave reviewers the opportunity to assess the impact Eric had made on labour history in Britain. Roy Foster noted correctly that 'Hobsbawm's work is sharply different from the labour historiography that prevailed before he made his mark on it', above all in its 'combination of cosmopolitanism and intellectualism'. This was 'not characteristic of the writers who dominated British labour history before him'. These men were guild socialists, radical liberals, or Christian moralists whose work – such as that of the Hammonds – was 'diffuse and emotional in its analysis and literary in its tone'. Eric's early work 'had a strong effect on this kind of history'. It put the question of exploitation and living standards during the Industrial Revolution back on the agenda, and showed how Marxism was not an instrument of Stalinist dogma but the creation of the mid-to-late nineteenth century, 'no more frightening or apocalyptic than the nostrums of most other economic analysts'. Trade union history, then very much the legal and institutional narrative of the growth of unionism from the Victorian era to the present, was wrenched from its teleology by Eric, and brought into relation with the British economy of its own time, which Eric saw as archaic in many ways, mirrored by the decentralised structure and inveterate reformism of the unions.[148]

The young trade union historian Alastair Reid, while criticising the book's 'outdated' insistence on the clarity of class divisions within English society, echoed Foster in paying tribute to Eric's impact on the discipline, even though this was 'still not fully appreciated by labour historians themselves, who tend to be rather over-antiquarian in their study of labour institutions and events, and consequently neglect the broader context of their inquiries'.[149]

More seriously, however, it was becoming clear that labour history was now entering a period of crisis – terminal crisis, as it was to prove. More than most kinds of history, it had been linked to a particular ideology – socialism – and the cultural and intellectual assumptions behind it. The forward march of labour had halted, and with it the forward march of labour history.[150]

By this time Eric was becoming more relaxed about meeting deadlines and entering into new publishing ventures. There were a number of possibilities, he told Bruce Hunter in 1977, but he was not sure whether he wanted to pursue them all:

> I still have a contract with George W. for a book on 'Revolution'. After that I have a general plan for a book I want to write generalizing the sort of things I discuss in *Primitive Rebels* and *Bandits* into a work on 'Popular Politics before the invention of politics', but that will have to wait for a bit. I could also, at shorter notice, work up another collection of essays or two on the lines of 'Revolutionaries' about various historical subjects, but here again, I'm in no hurry.[151]

In fact, he was in so little of a hurry that neither of the two books he mentioned was ever written, while the collection of essays did not appear until 1998. Of more immediate concern to him was the question of how well his existing titles were doing. *Industry and Empire*, he agreed with Bruce Hunter, was still selling, though not in the USA. Penguin were reprinting it every year in the UK, the German and French editions were still in print, and the latter in particular was, he hoped, benefiting from the fact that 'modern England is on the *programme d'agrégation*'. His hope was not fulfilled. *Industry and Empire* was a failure in France, very quickly superseded by François Bédarida's social history of modern England, a volume very much in the style then popular in the French system, filled with maps and charts, almost as much historical geography as social history.[152] Moreover, *Industry and Empire* was becoming outdated, as Eric was beginning to realise, and needed revising. He asked his former Ph.D. student Chris Wrigley to work through it, correcting the statistics (which certainly needed improving) and going through the existing text (which did not). Wrigley also felt the book needed an extra final chapter covering the most recent period. Eric discussed with him what to include, but then, as Wrigley reported, 'I was pretty well scared out of my wits when he said, "You write it" . . . [But] he read it and said, "This is actually very good", and I nearly died of shock!'[153] In the new edition, *Industry and Empire* acquired the subtitle *The Birth of the Industrial Revolution*, thus acknowledging the imbalance of coverage noted on its first appearance. It continued to be set for economic and social history courses in universities across the UK for many years and is still in use today.

Eric was less pleased with sales of *Bandits*, which he thought Penguin had stopped reprinting. He believed that 'there is a market for this book, which can go on selling modestly and steadily as *Primitive Rebels* has done since 1959'. He wanted Bruce Hunter to see if he could revive it: 'It hasn't got a built-in student sale, unfortunately, but it's readable.' Foreign editions were doing well, as were translations of *Revolutionaries*, except in the USA. (In fact, the Penguin edition was still in print, selling up to two thousand copies a year, with some six thousand in stock.)[154] 'The very recent German edition (poor translation) will probably suffer from the decline in the public for leftwing writings.' *The Age of Capital* had, to Eric's disappointment, not been adopted as a textbook by the Open University (the UK's distance-learning higher education institution, with many thousands of students), but, again, foreign editions were doing well. The main problem was the lack of a paperback edition in the USA: 'It will only sell if it gets into paperback, because that's the only way it will get prescribed in colleges, and that in turn is the only real public I have over there.' What was needed was to find a publisher with 'links with the many radical dons aged 30–[3]5 who would prescribe a Hobsbawm'.[155] It was eventually paperbacked in the USA by Vintage Books, part of the Random House empire.

One reason why the new projects Eric mentioned to Bruce Hunter were set aside was that, even as he was corresponding with him, he was embarking on a major new book. In 1974, even before

The Age of Capital had been published, the chief history editor at Weidenfeld, Andrew Wheatcroft, broached with Eric the idea of a follow-up volume:

> The last of the three nineteenth century volumes in the History of Civilisation has never been filled ... One of the things which impressed me on reading THE AGE OF CAPITAL was the feeling of continuity between it and THE AGE OF REVOLUTION. I did feel there was a unified picture being presented which helped to make much more sense of the period than disconnected studies. This prompted me to wonder whether you would consider taking on the third volume, 1875 to 1914. Clearly, the great attraction from the readers' point of view would be the continuity of approach and the presentation of the century as a whole. I can well see that from your point of view, having done two, the prospect of the third might fill you with horror. It does seem to be a fascinating period which is also relatively sparsely covered. Of course, specialist studies abound, but I have never come across a proper, unifying, study.[156]

Responding to Wheatcroft's suggestion, Eric confessed: 'I'd like to think a bit about your idea ... Hitherto I hadn't actually thought of going on to 1914.'[157] But as he pushed on with *The Age of Capital*, Eric later remembered, it 'became clear to me that I had let myself in for a large analytic synthesis of the history of the 19th century'. The follow-up volume was to become 'the first actually consciously planned volume, *The Age of Empire*'.[158]

In fact, Eric had not been Wheatcroft's first choice to write the late nineteenth century volume in the Weidenfeld *History of Civilization*. He had previously approached Robert Rhodes-James, a Conservative MP and author of a critical book on Churchill, but Rhodes-James turned down the idea – probably a good decision, since he knew relatively little non-British and indeed non-political history and as a Conservative MP did not have the time anyway to carry out a project on this scale.[159] Eric certainly did, but here, too, his approach to writing was relaxed, not least because by this stage in his career he did not feel an urgent need for money any more. He began work on the volume in 1977, as he told Bruce Hunter:

> I have been doing some reading and thinking about the third 19th century follow-up to 'Age of Rev' and 'Age of Cap', but am in no hurry to press on with it. At the moment my royalties are quite satisfactory – a lot of the foreign eds of Age of Cap have come in this year – and most of my other books are in print in various countries. I'd prefer not to rush things. I shall be retiring from the university in 3 years, and that's the time when presumably it would be best to have another boost to my non-pension income. I expect publishers are pressing, but you can say that I'm working on it, which is quite true. That's the next big job.[160]

Nevertheless, from the outset Eric found 'the third 19th century book . . . actually quite an exciting proposition, more fun than Age of Cap[ital]'. He thought that it could lead to packaging all three volumes as a complete set, perhaps with revised editions of the first two (though he never actually did revise them).[161] He began writing *The Age of Empire* in May 1980,[162] and worked steadily through the book during the first half of the 1980s, but it went slowly, and it was not until nearly a decade after he had begun preparing it that he brought the writing to a conclusion. He completed it in 1986 as James S. McDonnell Foundation University Distinguished Scholar at the United Nations University World Institute for Development Economics Research in Helsinki, where he gave some formal and informal seminars, and delivered the typescript of *The Age of Empire* to Juliet Gardiner, his editor at Weidenfeld, just before Christmas 1986.[163]

The book broke with the division of the subject matter into 'developments' and 'results' that had helped structure the first two volumes in the series, and presented the material in a single, long sequence of chapters. In other respects, however, it followed the same pattern of starting with the economy, and continuing with broad, dazzlingly wide-ranging accounts of politics, society and culture. Like the earlier two volumes in the series, it combined

Eric's now customary virtues of readability, analytical penetration and vivid detail and was greeted by the overwhelming majority of reviewers as an instant classic, completing one of the great historical works of the twentieth century. One entirely new feature was the inclusion of a chapter on women. The emergence of women's history during the 1970s had left him, Eric felt, with no choice. But the subject, as Michelle Perrot, herself a pioneer of women's history in France, observed, did not really interest Eric in the end. Indeed, it 'made him ill at ease, because he thought that feminism was challenging the labour movement and challenging Marxism'.[164] In the Marxist tradition, independent feminist movements were a 'bourgeois' distraction from the fight for a social revolution, which, when it was victorious, would be the means by which true female equality would be achieved. Eric found himself in the end unable to escape from this way of approaching the subject.[165] Historians who had worked in the area found the chapter less than satisfactory. Martin Pugh, an expert in the field, noted:

Hobsbawm remains convinced that history is made by people who go out to work. For him women count only in so far as they are part of the labour force, preferably the organized labour force. The most he will concede is that there was in this period a middle-class women's movement, which leads nowhere except in so far as a few of its members were part of the universal movement for socialism. Thus, he concludes, women remained 'outside the history of the nineteenth century'. If this had been written by A. J. P. Taylor the reader would have understood that he was meant to be amused, but in Professor Hobsbawm's Victorian history-for boys it is an apparently earnest judgement.[166]

Even the former Labour Party leader and long-time socialist Michael Foot complained that the book did not go far enough in bringing the feminist movement into the story or describing and accounting for the growth of female independence and assertiveness: 'The New Woman still gets a slightly embarrassed introduction from her gallant if belated sponsor.'[167] More severely, the socialist and feminist historian Catherine Hall criticised Eric's ignorance of recent scholarship on gender and lamented the fact that women were given a separate chapter to themselves, 'while men march through the rest, conquering empires, making revolutions, re-conceptualising the world'.[168] As a pioneer of 'history from below', Eric might have been expected to have taken a different perspective on the part women played in the era he was writing about.

This was not the first time Eric had run into trouble from feminist historians. While he was working on the chapter on women in *The Age of Empire* he had published an article in *History Workshop Journal* on 'man and woman in socialist iconography', using among its illustrations a semi-pornographic etching of a naked woman by the nineteenth-century Belgian artist Félicien Rops, later reproduced in *The Age of Empire*. Eric described it as inspired by socialism, a 'powerful' image of 'the people'. But not only was Rops not a socialist, leading feminists to question why the illustration had been used at all, but Eric had clearly, in the view of the feminists, misinterpreted his drawing. In the next but one issue of *History Workshop Journal*, three feminist historians (including two, Anna Davin and Sheila Rowbotham, who had been supervised as graduate students by Eric) voiced their objections. Eric, they declared, was simply not up with the recent literature on the topic he had chosen to write about. A few issues later, Ruth Richardson, author of an important book on the nineteenth-century Anatomy Acts, roundly condemned Eric's piece, which, she said, had made her profoundly angry:

> Rops's image is not 'powerful' – it is absurd, prurient, shallow and contemptible. What angered me so deeply about Professor Hobsbawm's article, then, was that it purported to offer a non-sexist examination of socialist iconography. Instead, it reproduced at least one profoundly sexist image, which cannot even be called socialist. Not only was this image reproduced uncritically, but the commentary on it compounded its sexism.[169]

Reviewers were right to point to the inadequacy and, beneath the surface, the insincerity of Eric's chapter on women. In the end, it was too radical a departure from the Marxist approach to history for Eric to take seriously. He did not reply to Richardson and his other feminist critics and reproduced the piece without comment or amendment in a later collection of his work.

The age of empire was also the age of imperialism, and a number of critics noted that the book did not follow the classical theories of Lenin or Rosa Luxemburg that posited the overproduction of capital or, alternatively, the desperate need for raw materials as reasons for the expansion of formal empire with the 'scramble for Africa' and subsequent developments in Europe's relations with the rest of the world. Moreover, as Catherine Hall commented:

> The classical Marxism which underpins *The Age of Empire* is not as classical as it once was ... Gone are the days when class was conceptualized in exclusively economic terms. The bourgeoisie of *The Age of Empire* sharpen their consciousness of themselves as a class on the golf course and tennis court. They recognize each other through their shared class-specific culture rather than their shared relations of production. Workers of the world are similarly united through the shared symbol of the cloth cap.[170]

Yet, noted the conservative American historian of Victorian culture Gertrude Himmelfarb, 'relatively little attention [was] paid to the proletariat' in the book. Most of the chapter on 'Workers of the World' was devoted to working-class organisations, not to working-class life. The same was the case – as in *The Age of Capital* – with popular culture. Himmelfarb also noted the absence of any real discussion of working-class standards of living, perhaps because, she commented tartly, 'the condition of the people, at least in most Western countries, significantly improved in the period covered by this volume, belying the Marxist theory of the "immiseration" of the proletariat'.[171]

The Age of Empire still portrayed class structure and class antagonisms as the fundamental principles of social change, but the

American historian Geoffrey Field argued that the book did not take adequate account of the power and influence of pre-industrial aristocratic elites, a point also made by James Joll in the *New York Review of Books*. Eric's response was that his concern was 'to try to detect the manifestation of the new in history'. This was why he said so little about agriculture in *The Age of Empire*, in contrast to the two previous books in the series.[172] Other critics zoomed in on Eric's hostility to modernist culture. Joll thought *The Age of Empire* considerably underestimated the popularity of Picasso. Vast crowds had attended exhibitions of his work all over the world. So Eric's disdain for modernist art as the largely incomprehensible taste of a tiny elite was misplaced.[173]

Periodisation was another problem. If the starting date of 1875 seemed somewhat arbitrary, then so, to some, did the end point of 1914. For John Campbell, who was just embarking on a career as a political biographer that would include lives of Edward Heath, Margaret Thatcher and Roy Jenkins, the real, implied terminal date of *The Age of Empire* was not 1914 but 1917, which loomed over the horizon at the end of the book without ever actually appearing in it. The book's publication completed 'an arch of faith stretching from one climactic peak to another, across the great bourgeois plain of the mid-century':

> The knowledge that the end of the book will see the holocaust of bourgeois Europe imparts to his analysis an air of grim satisfaction. His subject now is the tensions and contradictions, the 'fissures' in the apparent monolith, the ironies which history – Hobsbawm is a great believer in an impersonal force of history – has in store for the unsuspecting middle classes of the *belle époque*. *The Age of Empire* sees the nemesis of the hubristic society described in *The Age of Capital*.[174]

Yet the impression that the bourgeois liberal hegemony was falling apart was, Campbell charged, only achieved by defining 'bourgeois' narrowly as *haut bourgeois* and liberalism as classical liberalism. 'He sets up a paradigm of "true" capitalism and then treats every departure from that model not as development but as disintegration and decline.' He had set up a 'straw man' in order to be able to dance on his grave. In similar vein, David Cannadine exclaimed: 'How fascinating it is to watch the most cosmopolitan and sophisticated Marxist historian of his day writing what is in effect an elegy for mid-Victorian, middle-class liberalism.'[175]

If Campbell had known more about continental European history in the late nineteenth century, he would have understood that Eric was right to chart the disintegration of liberal politics and culture under the impact of the rise of socialism on the Left and the emergence of nationalist populism and Catholic politics on the Right, taking different forms in different countries, but squeezing out much of the liberal middle from political power by 1914. The disruptive influence of a modernist culture that displaced the old certainties of Realism in art and tonality in music was another death-knell for bourgeois culture. This did not mean, of course, that the bourgeoisie disappeared altogether, or that capitalism was about to become obsolete.[176] But it did mean that capitalism, middle-class hegemony and bourgeois culture were entering a long period of extreme crisis from which they would emerge decades later, in the mid-twentieth century, utterly transformed.

The publication of *The Age of Empire* afforded an opportunity to assess what was now a three-volume history of Europe in the 'long nineteenth century', from 1789 to 1914, another of Eric's conceptual inventions that has exerted a powerful influence on subsequent historical scholarship. Perry Anderson offered one of the most perceptive of all reviews of the trilogy. Like other reviewers, he was hugely impressed by Eric's achievement. All three books, he wrote,

> display the same astonishing fusion of gifts: economy of synthesis; vividness of detail; global scope, yet acute sense of regional difference; polymathic fluency, equally at ease with crops and stock markets, nations and classes, statesmen and peasants, sciences and arts; breadth of sympathies for disparate social agents; power of analytic narrative; and not least a style of remarkable clarity and energy, whose signature is the sudden

bolt of metaphoric electricity across the even surface of cool, pungent argument. It is striking how often these flashes of figuration are drawn from the natural world to which he says he felt so close in his youth: 'religion, from being something like the sky, from which no man can escape and which contains all that is above the earth, became something like a bank of clouds, a large but limited and changing feature of the human firmament'.

Anderson thought although there was 'no clanking of theoretical armour', the treatment was 'classically Marxist in its logic', each volume beginning with the economy, followed by politics, social classes and cultural and intellectual life. The volumes were clear in their left-wing political sympathies, 'but the tang of particular judgments is always individual'.[177]

However, Anderson continued, the sheer scale of Eric's achievement had inhibited criticism. He went on, therefore, to offer what he described as 'a few loose thoughts ... bouncing off these superbly polished surfaces'. He found that the explanatory power of the trilogy declined as it went on. Eric explained the British Industrial Revolution with great power and originality by citing the role of empire in India. But in the next volume the account of the economy became more diverse and less persuasive. As *The Age of Revolution* moved into its account of the 1830 revolution, moreover, its claim that this 'marked the definitive defeat of aristocratic by bourgeois power in Western Europe' was surely premature, otherwise 'what need for the upheavals of 1848?' Beyond this, why did Eric in *The Age of Capital* claim that between 1848 and 1875 'in most countries the bourgeoisie, however defined, plainly did not control or exercise political power'? Had capital triumphed without a concomitant triumph of the bourgeoisie in the realm of politics? The explanatory evasion here was compounded in the book, according to Anderson, by dispersing the great political upheavals of the epoch – German and Italian unification, the Meiji restoration, the American Civil War and so on – across different, unrelated chapters. Nor did the employment of the Gramscian concept of 'hegemony' really succeed in bridging the gap. In *The*

Age of Empire liberalism, capitalism and the bourgeoisie were analytically separate categories. Capitalism did not require bourgeois rule; the bourgeoisie no longer needed liberalism.[178]

Anderson's criticisms were, of course, aimed at the disconnect between classical Marxist theory and the empirical and descriptive elements in Eric's three volumes. Fundamentally Anderson was saying that what Eric was describing as an historian failed to fit what Marx and Engels predicted as political theorists. But that did not necessarily mean he was wrong; it could just as easily mean that they were wrong. Throughout his career as an historian, Eric was pulled one way by his Communist and, more broadly, his Marxist commitment, and another by his respect for the facts, the documentary record and the findings and arguments of other historians whose work he acknowledged and respected. At some points of the three volumes, the former wins out over the latter, but overall it is the latter that prevails.

In defending himself against the charge of focusing too exclusively on Europe, Eric argued, 'I have always tried to take a global rather than a narrowly European view in my 19th century vols. though they were bound to give most space to Europe.' He had, after all, been familiar with the non-European world since his study visit to North Africa before the war:

Even in *The Age of Revolution* I pay attention to the expansion of Islam ... Basically, my books are based on the assumption that the system pioneered in the Atlantic seaboard countries of Europe penetrates and captures the rest of the world and transform[s] it. In the period when, speaking economically, Britain is the core country, the non-European world is particularly indispensable, since (in my view) the peculiarity of British industrialization lay precisely in establishing privileged or symbiotic relations with non-European economies.[179]

More serious, perhaps, was the charge that Eric had failed, yet again, to give adequate weight to the force of nationalism. He was conscious of this deficit, and already at the time of writing *The*

Age of Empire he was thinking more deeply about the problem. His ponderings were soon to bear fruit in one of his most influential publications, *Nations and Nationalism since 1780*.

In the year in which *The Age of Empire* was published, Eric celebrated his seventieth birthday. As Neal Ascherson observed, over the years Eric had 'changed little. The lean, gangling frame, the spectacles, the abundant grey hair, the tendency to open-necked shirts – all that is much as it was, and so is the curious, compelling voice: something of an old-fashioned Bloomsbury drawl, with a *Mitteleuropa* edge.'[180] His productivity had not slowed at all. From the mid-1970s to the mid-1980s he had published two major books, *The Age of Capital* and *The Age of Empire*, a collection of essays, *Worlds of Labour*, a hugely influential edited volume on *The Invention of Tradition*, and innumerable articles, most of them now popular rather than academic. He had become a leading public intellectual in Britain with the debate over 'the forward march of labour halted', and to some extent in Italy too, where he had found a congenial political home in the country's reformist Communist Party. He had reconnected with France, though now his engagement there was more academic than personal. He had retired from Birkbeck but continued to teach in the rather similar environment of the New School in New York. As before, he had travelled extensively, deepening in particular his knowledge of Latin America and freeing himself in the process from the illusions that had accompanied his earlier visits there. His home life with Marlene and the children had settled into an agreeable and stable routine. He had gained financial security and academic and public recognition and entered the ranks of the Establishment. But he had no intention of slowing down at all, let alone quitting. 'He accumulated privileges', his Birkbeck colleague Roy Foster remembered, 'but he liked his outsider status.'[181] In the coming decade, he was to be reminded more than once of his ability to ruffle feathers, arouse heated controversy and challenge orthodoxies.

9

'Jeremiah'

1987–1999

I

In 1988, in a lengthy interview for the Brazilian newspaper *Estado de São Paulo*, Eric enthused about the policies introduced in the Soviet Union by Mikhail Gorbachev, appointed as General Secretary of the Communist Party three years before. Gorbachev's policies of *glasnost* (openness) and *perestroika* (restructuring), Eric declared, disproved the claim that the Soviet Union was totalitarian. The long years during which Leonid Brezhnev had been in power had at least established a welcome period of stability after the upheavals of the Stalin and Khrushchev years, but the consequent corruption and stagnation had made reform unavoidable, and Gorbachev's policies demonstrated finally that a Communist system was indeed capable of changing.[1] Eric's optimism, however, was soon to be confounded. Within a short space of time, economic difficulties which Gorbachev's policies were unable to overcome led to a complete reversal of the Soviet Union's previous foreign policy, as the Soviet leader promulgated what came to be known as 'the Sinatra doctrine' – let the satellite countries of Eastern Europe 'do it their way'. If they wanted to break free from Communism, Russia was not going to object. By the early spring of 1989, popular protests were bringing about the replacement of Communist regimes in every Eastern European country. Barriers to the free movement of citizens across the 'iron curtain' began to be dismantled, culminating in the peaceful opening of the Berlin Wall on that day on which so many crucial events in German history had occurred, 9 November.

As things turned out, this was only the beginning. Free elections everywhere ousted the Communists from power. Market forces began to replace the planned economy across Eastern Europe. In 1990, popular pressure brought about the merger of East Germany with the Federal Republic in the West. An attempt by die-hard Communists to overthrow Gorbachev only brought about the dissolution of the Communist Party of the Soviet Union and Gorbachev's replacement by Boris Yeltsin. By the end of 1991, the Soviet Union itself was gone, and eleven new states had emerged on its former territory. Latvia, Lithuania and Estonia regained their independence, and Yugoslavia was beginning to break up under the centrifugal forces of rapidly intensifying nationalism into what eventually became five new states. In 1992, Czechoslovakia split apart into the Czech Republic and Slovakia. Other states across the world, from Ethiopia to Cambodia, abandoned their Communist ideology. This was the final act in the drama that had begun three-quarters of a century before, in the Bolshevik Revolution of 1917, and it was played out with astonishing speed and finality.

While these startling events were unfolding, Eric was at a conference in Uppsala, where over lunch some young Swedish social historians asked him what he thought would be the consequences of the collapse of Communism. The French historian Patrick Fridenson, who was present, vividly remembered his reaction and the shock it caused:

> They expected – given their idea of Eric's freedom of thought – that he would be supporting what was happening. Eric was as cold as ice; and this I will remember till my very last days . . . He said: 'With the Soviet Union you have had peace; you are going to have war.' And he went on for maybe fifteen minutes, which – at a meal – is very long. The young Swedish historians,

who were admirers, were absolutely mad – did not dare to contradict him – but he could see ... the gap increasing between
himself and the Swedish historians. I was completely shocked ...
But of course he was right. We had wars. We had lots of wars
in the East.[2]

Eric recognised immediately that 'the socialism born of the
October Revolution is dead'. The global struggle between socialism and capitalism was over: capitalism had won. The Left was
in full retreat. 'The fall of the Soviet-type system, about which all
illusion had long gone, is less significant than the apparent end
of the dream of which it was the nightmare version', he wrote in
1990. It was the end of Leninism, but not the end of Marxism, he
declared hopefully.[3] But Marxist political parties everywhere collapsed or transformed themselves into moderate forms of Social
Democracy. The Italian Communist Party adapted to the new
situation in 1991, changing its name to 'Democratic Party of the
Left', at the cost of losing many of its more hard-line adherents.
In the longer run, as Eric observed in 2010, it 'lost both its sense
of the past and its sense of a future'.[4] The British Communist
Party had already broken up into Eurocommunist and Stalinist
groups, and now effectively ceased to exist, putting an end to
Eric's lifelong membership. *Marxism Today* was another casualty
of the dissolution as it ran out of money with the collapse of its
funding body.

The political order in the newly independent states of East-
Central and Eastern Europe was, Eric considered, inherently
unstable. 'The prospects for liberal democracy in the region must
be poor, or at least uncertain. And the alternative, given the
unlikelihood of a return to socialism, will most likely be military
or right-wing or both.' Few of Eric's political prognoses were more
prescient than this one, even though it took some years to be
fulfilled. A quarter of a century later, Poland and Hungary were
in the grip of right-wing authoritarian regimes, and other states,
including the Czech Republic, looked as if they might well go
the same way. Eric's prediction of wars generated by 'nationalist

rivalries and conflicts' in areas formerly dominated by Communist regimes also turned out to be correct, as violent clashes broke out across Eastern Europe, from Bosnia to Ukraine, Georgia to Moldova. A third prediction was less accurate, however. Perhaps it was the memory of the 1930s and early 1940s that prompted him to think that Germany, now the dominant force on the European continent, had become a threat to peace 'because German nationalism has dangerous unfinished business – the recovery of the large territories lost in 1945 to Poland and the USSR', but this eventuality never came to pass: Germany and the Germans simply were not interested in recovering anything except economic growth, as it slowed down in the effort to absorb the bankrupt economy of the former German Democratic Republic.

On the other hand, his fear of the outbreak of conflict in the Middle East, where 'adventurism' was 'once more back on the agenda', turned out to be more than justified: indeed, almost immediately, in August 1990, the Iraqi dictator Saddam Hussein invaded the small, oil-rich state of Kuwait, from which an American-led military coalition eventually expelled his troops by the end of February 1991.[5] Eric was not a pacifist, but he opposed every war that the Western powers took part in during the final two decades and more of his life. The Gulf War filled him with despair:

> The war is awful. I can understand why the [Labour] front bench, scared that, once again [following the 1982 Falklands War], the Union Jack will be the winding sheet of Labour, wants to avoid anything that makes them sound less patriotic than the government. (The keynote of this miserable present is 'My War is just as holy as yours'). Still, they don't actually have to say 'me too' quite so uncritically. Especially about a war in which they don't believe and which will solve nothing at the cost of unbelievable suffering, incidentally imposed on the excuse that it 'minimises casualties'.[6]

All over the world, Eric thought gloomily, the wider socialist vision was being replaced by 'worse visions and more dangerous dreams, such as religious fundamentalism, nationalist zealotry or, more generally, that racially tinged xenophobia which looks like becoming the major mass ideology of the *fin de siècle*'. Socialists themselves had abandoned the utopian thinking that had driven them for so long. Yet socialism was, or should be, the answer to the two great problems facing the world in the final decade of the century, the 'ecological crisis' caused by rampant and unchecked capitalism and the 'dramatically widening gap' between rich and poor, viewed on a global scale.[7] Two years later, in Brazil to discuss once more the consequences of the collapse of Communism, he declared that the end of the USSR meant that social advances in the West were in jeopardy. The welfare state, he thought, had been built as a reaction to the rise of Communism, an argument that seemed to brush aside what was surely the major reason, namely the cohesive impulses given Western societies by the two world wars. Whatever the consequences of the collapse, however, Eric could only see them as dire.[8]

Interviewed by the journalist Paul Barker for the *Independent on Sunday* in 1990, Eric – 'thin, almost angular', a man who according to Barker 'liked to wrap up an argument with a swift wisecrack and a sudden grin' – took a mellower, less alarmist point of view. The collapse of Communism in Eastern Europe, he said, was to be welcomed for the Czechs and the East Germans and with some reservation the Hungarians. But, he added, again presciently, 'I am not sure that releasing all of the forces which have been kept frozen for up to 70 years is going to be something the rest of the world would welcome.' The collapse of the Austro-Hungarian Empire in 1918 had had 'almost totally negative results'. People might well feel the same about the collapse of the Soviet Union. Chaos might well ensue. More generally, when asked about the achievements, if any, of Communism, he conceded that it had been, if not a blind alley, at least an historical detour. For a number of countries, however, it had encouraged economic growth and development. Socialism in one country – Russia – however had not been a good idea. 'Looking back, it would have been better if they had picked another way.' Stalin's rapid drive for industrialisation had been 'one of the worst things that anybody, capitalist or socialist, has gone for in the twentieth century'. But Russia lacked a civil society, so 'that is the way it was bound to go'. Asked to compare the fall of Communism in 1989–90 with the revolutions of 1848, he described it as 'the People's Autumn, rather than the People's Spring'. He suspected, however, that a rise in nationalism would be the result, and in Russia at least it was an obscurantist force, 'utterly irrational'.[9]

Asked why he had not resigned from the Communist Party long before it fell apart, he told Barker:

I don't like being in the company of the sort of people I've seen leaving the Communist Party and becoming anti-Communist. There are certain clubs of which I would not wish to be a member. I don't wish to be untrue to my past or to friends and comrades of mine, a lot of them dead, some of them killed by their own side, whom I've admired and who in many ways are models to follow, in their unselfishness and devotion. That's a personal view. It's the view of someone who became politicised in 1931 and 1932 in Berlin and who has never forgotten it.

Communism had been a 'dream of general liberation, the liberation of mankind, the liberation of the poor'. Such an ideal had attracted many genuinely good people. It had been worth fighting for. He had a '*real* reluctance', as Garry Runciman expressed it, to put himself 'in a position where he could be branded as somebody who'd lost the faith'.[10]

Eric's gloom about the future deepened as the unravelling of the post-war settlement continued. In May 1992, he observed,

The situation of the world seems to be becoming darker all the time. Once again people are starving and killing each other in large stretches of the world, and the fact that we are not at the moment risking a single nuclear catastrophe should not make us forget how many people can be killed, tortured and otherwise done to death by the more primitive methods which appear once again to be in fashion in large parts of Europe and Asia.[11]

Already in the summer of 1991, violent conflicts had broken out between Serbia and Croatia over rival, extreme nationalist territorial claims, not least in Bosnia. Accompanied by massacres and 'ethnic cleansing' – a euphemism for genocide – they continued until the end of the decade and beyond. Deaths on all sides were estimated at more than 130,000, and over four million people were driven out of their homes. In a later interview, Eric criticised the global community for failing to recognise the danger of war in the Balkans, and declared that it was morally more than defensible to take up arms to defend the Bosnians from the Serbian threat.[12]

Historians, he warned, 'must resist the formation of national, ethnic and other myths, as they are being formed'. Events in Eastern Europe and the Balkans also seemed to Eric to underline his conviction that nationalism was never a force for good. Already on 13 May 1988, in response to a query about his seemingly negative attitude to Irish nationalism from the left-wing Scottish nationalist and labour historian James D. Young, Eric wrote:

I remain in the curious position of disliking, distrusting, disapproving and fearing nationalism *wherever* it exists, perhaps even more than in the 1970s, but recognising its enormous force, which must be harnessed for progress if possible. And sometimes it is possible. We cannot let the right have the monopoly of the flag. Some things can be achieved by mobilising nationalist feelings. Some great triumphs of the left – notably during the anti-fascist period, and in China, Vietnam, would have been impossible if we had not managed to mobilise national feeling for *progress*. I also happen to like some peoples and sympathise with their national feelings, but that's a matter of personal taste: there is something I find pleasant about small nations and their attempt to build or maintain a separate culture, for example, the Estonians or Finns. However, I cannot be a nationalist and neither, in theory, can any Marxist.[13]

Already Eric was distilling his thoughts on nationalism into a short book, *Nations and Nationalism since 1780: Programme, Myth, Reality* (1990), based on his Wiles Lectures at Queen's University, Belfast, delivered in 1985. After an interval in which he completed *The Age of Empire*, he began working on the book around the time he wrote to Young, completing it during a second stay at the United Nations University World Institute for Development Economics Research in Helsinki.[14]

Over the years, his understanding of nationalism had evolved from seeing it as a form of bourgeois class politics to viewing it as a kind of 'identity politics', reflecting the breakdown of class allegiances rather than articulating them.[15] The events of 1990, not to mention what followed, seemed to prove him right. The book, as Eric observed to his editor at Cambridge University Press, Bill Davies, shortly before its publication, 'by the accidents of history, looks like coming out at the very moment when all literate people will be urgently interested in the force which has (it seems) revolutionized eastern Europe and the Soviet Union apparently at [a] moment's notice. This should make the book unusually promoteable/saleable.'[16] Nation-building, indeed, was the order of the day in the early 1990s. Yet the argument, dating back to the early nineteenth-century Italian nationalist Giuseppe Mazzini, that every nation should form a state, was, and always had been, unworkable in ethnic-linguistic terms. No more than a dozen states across the world, leaving aside some island mini-states, could legitimately claim to be linguistically and ethnically homogeneous. The politics of identity held a crude but powerful appeal for people in Eastern Europe who had been denied political education and experience under decades of Communist rule and were searching for certainties in a disoriented world. Language was beginning to replace concepts such as civil rights and constitutions. Such developments, Eric thought, were likely to be a threat to democracy and an encouragement to violence.[17] A period of reflection on the dangers of untrammelled nationalism was surely needed, and Eric hoped that his book would help in the process.

By and large, of course, as he conceded in a lecture delivered to the American Anthropological Association in 1991, historians had done little or nothing to discourage the rise of nationalism. On the contrary, they had always been an essential part of it. 'What makes a nation is the past, what justifies one nation against others is the past, and historians are the people who produce it.' The problem was that historians who engaged in this activity were mythmakers rather than serious students of the past. For Eric, the idea of an ethnicity deeply rooted in a remote past, as posited by nationalist historians, was another example of an invented tradition. Ethnicity did not have to be linked to nationalism (it was not, for example, in the USA), but what was important to realise was that it was mutable rather than fixed. Nevertheless, 'the nation' appeared as the 'ultimate guarantee' when society failed, as with the collapse of Communism. 'No good will come of it', he declared, 'but it won't last for ever.'[18]

Eric was critical of nationalism and identity politics because, as he insisted, 'the political project of the left is universalist'.[19] Nations were artificial constructs. The book demolished every argument ever advanced in favour of the idea that they were not. The oppression of national minorities in every state dominated by one particular national or linguistic group demonstrated, too, that the nation-state did not necessarily provide the best guarantee of civil and political rights, not least for the minority. This was particularly obvious in the course of the construction of 'nation-states' in Europe in the 1920s and 1930s, following the triumph of the principle of national self-determination at the post-war peace conference of 1919.[20] It was hardly surprising that the Irish political scientist Brendan O'Leary, at that time a lecturer at the London School of Economics, thought that Eric departed from his usual scholarly standards whenever he had to pronounce on nationalism. 'Professor Hobsbawm has made it plain that he loathes nationalism.' Contesting this position, O'Leary contended that national self-determination was the only principle that posed a viable, democratic alternative to world empires like those of Stalin and Hitler. (This was, of course, a false alternative: the most successful supranational bodies have not been those that obliterated national sovereignty but those, like the nineteenth-century Concert of Europe or the twentieth-century European Union, that have shared it.)

The idea of the nation, then, was a modern invention that did not necessarily depend on previous ethnic ties. It played a key role in social and political modernisation. Drawing on the work of Miroslav Hroch on nationalism among the smaller European states, Eric went on to take a broad view of the process of nation-building, which he saw as going through three phases: literary, historical and folkloric movements; the politicisation of ethnicity; and the winning of mass support. In the nineteenth century, liberals saw this as the fastest way to achieve civil rights and parliamentary rule, especially where either large authoritarian empires stood in the way, or where small regional despotisms proved the obstacle. However, only large national states were viable, a view Eric implicitly shared with liberals like John Stuart Mill and, indeed, with Marx and Engels themselves.[21]

The fundamental problem nationalism had always posed for Marxists was that it was difficult to explain in terms of historical materialism and hard to reduce to any kind of coherent class analysis. The Austro-Marxist Otto Bauer had tried to reconcile these principles, but without much success. The American political philosopher Michael Walzer argued that *Nations and Nationalism* also failed to overcome this theoretical problem. Rather than tell extended stories, or examine any nationalist movements in depth, its 'examples are like witnesses at a trial, called to the stand, asked a few questions, hastily dismissed: they are not allowed, as it were to speak for themselves. This is historical scholarship with a polemical purpose. Hobsbawm wants us to reach a verdict on nationalism: that its program is wrong, its myths dangerous, its reality ugly.' Why, for example, did he advance the claim that nationalism emerged 'to fill the emotional void left by the retreat or disintegration ... of *real* human communities'? What these real communities were he did not say, nor did he explain how or why they supposedly disintegrated. In the end, all communities were artificial and imagined, and it was no disparagement to say the same of national communities. By dispelling all the myths, the book made the phenomenon of nationalism incomprehensible.

After the unification of Italy, one Italian statesman said: 'We have made Italy, now we have to make Italians'. Why, Walzer asked, then, did Italy succeed in making a nation out of Tuscans, Sicilians and other denizens of the peninsula who in most cases did not even speak Italian, while they did not make Italians out of Libyans and Ethiopians? (The question was not a fair one since it ignored the racism through which Italians, like all other white Europeans, regarded dark-skinned Africans: they had in truth never any interest in treating the inhabitants of the Italian colonies as anything other than subject races.)[22] Walzer went on to question the book's equation of nationalism with chauvinism, but this too was a misplaced accusation: Eric was familiar enough with European history in the nineteenth century to recognise explicitly its liberal and tolerant aspects; that was why, after all, the concept of chauvinism was coined, to differentiate nationalism from xenophobia. Moreover, the liberation of European colonies like India or Indonesia was itself based above all on the ideology of nationalism, as Eric also surely realised, though his book's coverage was limited almost exclusively to Europe. *Nations and Nationalism* was not as crudely hostile to the subject it treated as Walzer and a number of others supposed. Once more, Eric had shown how he could stir up controversy with an historical perspective on a present problem, and the book ranks alongside other major contributions to the literature as the leading statement of a relativist and historical approach to a central problem of modern history.[23]

Nations and Nationalism, published by Cambridge University Press, as it had to be under the rules laid down for the Wiles Lectures, was not a major earner for Eric, but it has never been out of print and it was almost immediately translated into French and published by Gallimard. The terms offered, Eric complained, 'do not seem to be particularly generous, and in this seem to me to be typical of other French publishers. No doubt Gallimard thinks the honour of being published by them compensates for niggardliness.'[24] He did not manage to secure any improvement in the terms, and the book was published in French in January 1992. The terms offered by Campus Verlag, a freestanding academic press, for the German rights were even lower, however, indeed '*extremely* low', as Christine Oram, rights manager at Cambridge University Press, told them, 'for such an eminent author and far below the terms we have accepted for other languages'. The offer was duly improved, and the book appeared in German in the autumn of 1992.[25] By this time, the Italian edition was also out, and being publicised by interviews with Eric in the press.[26] The book was also published in Spain (1991), Indonesia (1992), Croatia (1993), Finland, Greece, Korea and Sweden (1994), Albania and Bulgaria (1996), Hungary, Moldova and Taiwan (1997); it appeared in Portuguese in 1998, Arabic in 1999, Czech and simplified character Chinese in 2000, Japanese and Dutch in 2001, Hebrew in 2006, and Turkish (date uncertain). *Nations and Nationalism* was one of Eric's most influential and widely discussed books, and continues to be a central text wherever the topic of nationalism is taught and debated.

II

Around the time when he was thinking and writing about it, Eric was confronted by nationalism in a directly personal way. In the 1980s, the rise of radical Welsh nationalism, centred on the Welsh-speaking areas of Snowdonia where Eric and his family were renting their cottage, made life increasingly difficult for people who left their properties vacant for a large part of the year, as the Hobsbawms did. Although otherwise, if they had remained unoccupied, they might well have fallen into decay as the local economy continued to decline, the extreme nationalists argued that holiday cottages were destroying local communities by preventing young people from finding a reasonably inexpensive place to live. The most extreme among them, organised in a clandestine group called

Meibion Glynŵr, named after the leader of the final Welsh rebellion against the English, at the beginning of the fifteenth century, launched a campaign of arson against holiday cottages owned or rented by mostly absent English people. Over a period of twelve years, from 1979 to 1991, some 228 holiday cottages, mostly along the North Welsh coast, in Anglesey and Snowdonia, were attacked. There were rumours that some local policemen were sympathetic to the cause. Certainly, only one person was ever arrested during the entire campaign.[27]

Eric and Marlene's worries about the situation, together with the cautious approach of their landlord Richard Williams-Ellis, who was naturally concerned at these developments and had begun leasing his properties to Welsh-speakers where he could, put pressure on them to leave the Croesor Valley for somewhere safer. In 1991 they brought the lease on Parc Farmhouse to an end after fifteen years and with the aid of the advance for Eric's next book they purchased another cottage, Hollybush, much further south, in the Wye Valley, in the hamlet of Gwenddwr, at Erwood, near Hay, where the annual literary festival attracted writers from far and wide. As the letting agent, Jonathan Lovegrove-Fielden of Knight, Frank and Rutley, conceded in a letter to Eric, 'from your angle, it is somewhat less Nationalistic and, therefore, somewhat safer for a second home!'.[28] The new cottage was situated in rolling hills, which afforded less strenuous walking opportunities than the steep and dramatic slopes of Cnicht, and it was better equipped and altogether more comfortable than Parc Farmhouse, far less draughty and with central heating. From now on, Eric and Marlene went regularly to the annual literary festival at nearby Hay-on-Wye, as well as staying in the new cottage at other times of the year. Over time, he became a regular fixture at the festival, as did the dinner parties he and Marlene threw at the cottage for selected participants. As Peter Florence, the festival's Director, recalled in 2012:

> His sessions at the Hay Festival were always thrilling, particularly the combative conversations with Christopher Hitchens and Simon Schama that flare with brilliance and wit. His

riveting argument with Niall Ferguson about the legacy of the Congress of Vienna is the historiographer's equivalent of Fischer vs Spassky. He spoke in perfect Spanish in Segovia, in Italian in Mantova, and his Portuguese was pretty hot too. For all that Eric's long relationship with Hay was driven by his rooting himself and his family up the road in Erwood, it was Eric who started our love affair with Latin America, and who is indirectly responsible for the Hay Festival now being in Colombia and Mexico, and set fair to expand into Chile and Peru in the next two years.[29]

Eventually, Florence appointed Eric as the festival's President, a largely honorific post that paid recognition not only to his close and long-term commitment to the festival but also to his extraordinary prominence in the world of literature as well as the world of history.

Eric took a close interest in the Gwenddwr Show, held on the last Saturday of July every year, and was often to be found 'sitting in the tent with farmers, and having a beer with them'.[30] In 1997, Eric celebrated his eightieth birthday in Gwenddwr (one of a number of such events in a variety of different locations). As his neighbour Richard Rathbone recalled:

> There was a hard-handed son of the soil called Winston – which is an unlikely juxtaposition, Winston and Eric – they shared the birthday together, in the house of, what had been the house of Lord Birt and Lady Birt, Jane Birt, and they shared a platform together on the balcony, and Eric gave a long speech about longevity and longue durée and life and so on, Winston a rather shorter speech. But it was very intimate, they were close friends in a very real way.[31]

At Birkbeck, a day-long conference was held at which past and present members of the History Department, including Roy Foster and myself, read papers touching upon the subjects which Eric had done so much to illuminate over the years. In 1992 Eric had approached the History Department at Birkbeck with a request for an office and associated facilities to help him deal with his ever-growing volume of correspondence, postage, photocopying and so on. The Master of Birkbeck, Baroness Tessa Blackstone, a Labour Party life peer, agreed on condition (as she told me) 'that he talks to the younger members of the Department'. She did not need to have inserted that proviso into the agreement. As Frank Trentmann, a young economic historian who joined Birkbeck as a Lecturer in 1998, remembered,

> his door was always open, no matter how large the mailbag with prestigious invitations, correspondence, books and off-prints from all over the world ... Eric did not care whether you were a junior colleague or a student, as long as you took history seriously. History was a mission, not a job, and he did not let his reputation stand in its way ... When students asked him to come and talk to them, he would do so, long after retirement. Because the argument, like history itself, never stopped. Talking and walking with Eric was like being whizzed away by the spirit of history, as he outpaced the traffic, with his scarf blowing in the wind, and sometimes flying away.[32]

In 2002, Eric's long commitment to Birkbeck was to be recognised when he was appointed President, an honorary position whose duties included awarding degrees at the annual graduation.

Eric's eightieth birthday was celebrated in Italy with an evening podium discussion with Giorgio Napolitano and others in 'a packed Carlo Felice Theatre in Genoa' in late September. Debate centred on issues such as globalisation, which, Eric declared, was unavoidable but did not have to be carried out under neoliberal auspices, and the secessionist movement in northern Italy, which, he felt, had no historical foundations, unlike, say, the nationalist movement in Scotland.[33] Eric's eightieth was also marked by articles in the British press. Keith Thomas, writing in the *Guardian*, noted that Eric was 'probably the best-known living British historian, certainly the one whose work has been translated into the most languages'. He was, to be sure, no 'delver in the archives', but, as 'one of the most powerful minds of our time', he had 'a rare capacity to devise or disseminate new concepts which leave an enduring mark on historical writing'. He was 'a supreme exemplar of that bourgeois culture which he so memorably dissects'.[34] From a more conservative position, the young historian of modern Russia Orlando Figes, himself soon to go to a professorship at Birkbeck, concurred: Eric was 'probably the best known living historian in the world', whose books were read by 'millions' and whose 'erudition', along with the 'brilliant incisiveness of his analysis', would have impressed Marx himself. Figes found some of Eric's opinions 'rather hard to swallow'. It was 'simply wrong', for example, to argue that there was no alternative to the Bolsheviks in October 1917, or to defend as historically necessary the terror they unleashed in the months afterwards. Nevertheless, Figes remained impressed by Eric's astonishing range and convinced by his rejection of postmodernist relativism, then at the height of its influence in university humanities departments.[35]

Just over a month before Eric turned eighty, New Labour, led by Tony Blair, had won a general election by a landslide. Donald Sassoon was at a dinner party in Nassington Road, with Nina Fishman (another of Eric's former Ph.D. students) and her Italian husband, immediately afterwards. 'And we toasted the election of Tony Blair', Sassoon remembered, 'and he refused . . . I or Nina said: "But come on, after all these years of Tory government?" "Ah", he said, "*you* drink." . . . We were all basically finally relieved that a long period of Tory government would come to an end. But he was not taken in.'[36] Yet Blair clearly felt he owed a debt to Eric for the role he had played in laying the intellectual foundations for New Labour. The time was now, surely, right for his achievements as Britain's most internationally famous, influential and widely read historian to receive some kind of official recognition, a recognition he stood no chance of winning under the Conservatives. Keith Thomas, President of the British Academy from 1993 to 1997, was one of a number of senior figures to recommend Eric for a knighthood. Knowing that this might prove difficult for him to accept, however, Tony Blair, as Prime Minister, also held out to him the alternative of appointment as a Companion of Honour (CH), a parallel order established in 1917 to recognise the services in Britain and the Commonwealth of fifty (later sixty-five) individuals who had made distinguished contributions to the arts, sciences, politics, industry or religion. Eric accepted the CH because, he said, his mother would have wanted him to. But he was also impressed by the fact that the left-wing trade unionist and former fighter in the International Brigades during the Spanish Civil War Jack Jones had accepted a CH. 'I couldn't take the K', Eric said to me at the time: 'I could never have looked my old comrades in the face again. CH is for the awkward squad. Any order that has Jack Jones in it is good enough for me, what?' Many noted the symbolism of the fact that at the formal ceremony of investiture at Buckingham Palace, as Eric knelt on the footstool provided for the Queen to put the ribbon with the medal of the Companion of Honour round his neck, a piece of plaster fell from the ceiling onto the floor.[37]

The award provoked predictable howls of protest on the political Right. Andrew Gimson, recently retired parliamentary sketch writer for the *Daily Telegraph*, writing in the conservative magazine *Standpoint*, edited by Paul Johnson's son Daniel, described Eric as a 'Companion of Dishonour', remarking that, had he been a fascist instead of a Communist, he would not have been treated so favourably (hardly necessary to add that, of course, fascism, unlike Communism, was a political creed characterised by anti-intellectualism and made no contribution whatsoever to historical knowledge and understanding).[38] Equally outspoken was Alfred Sherman, a member of the political group Eric most despised, those who had made the journey from committed Communism – Sherman had also fought in the International Brigades during the Spanish Civil War – to bilious and reactionary conservatism (he was an adviser to Margaret Thatcher, who had him awarded a knighthood for his services). In 1983 Sherman had been dismissed from the Centre for Policy Studies, a leading right-wing think-tank, for his racist and generally cantankerous behaviour, and in the

1990s he became a prominent defender of the Serbian cause during the Balkan Wars of that decade.[39] The award, he thundered, had 'occasioned surprise and resentment ... All Hobsbawm offers is last year's slogans.'[40] On the Left, Eric was, of course, accused of selling out to the Establishment. It was, charged James D. Young, all of a piece with his 'white Eurocentric Stalinism', yet another piece of evidence that attested to his fundamental adherence to the forces of order and his rejection of any kind of 'untidy' revolt or rebellion. In a lengthy, all-out attack on Eric's work, Young did not fight shy of bringing the traditional anti-Semitism of the ultra-left into play either, describing Eric as 'English' in inverted commas whenever he mentioned his nationality.[41]

III

Eric had already begun to think about writing a history covering the twentieth century towards the end of the 1980s. It had turned out to be 'the most revolutionary era in the recorded history of the globe', and yet those who, like himself, had lived through it had 'plainly failed utterly to understand, or even – if politicians – to be fully aware of, what was happening'. It was important to understand the period historically and in a genuinely global perspective. And whoever wrote it would need to begin with the mode of production in material life ('Try it any other way and see what you get').[42] Eric's agent Bruce Hunter agreed that it would be logical to extend his history of the period 1789–1914 to cover 'the short twentieth century'.[43] George Weidenfeld became aware of the proposal early on, and in 1987 he told Eric:

> We would like you to consider very seriously writing this major work which, in a magisterial sweep, would be a cultural and social as well as a political appraisal of 'our age', dealing with the last hundred years or so. This is not the moment to prescribe or describe its contents, but I am convinced that such a book would be an enormous world-wide success and I am backing my

conviction by offering you an advance of £100,000 on world rights when we agree on the length and scope of contents.[44]

Over the next several months Eric prepared a synopsis of the new book, sending it to his agent on 28 April 1988.[45]

Rather than sticking with Weidenfeld, however, Bruce Hunter decided to offer the book for auction to a wide range of publishers, with Eric's approval, since it clearly had the potential to be a major success. He sent Eric's synopsis to several of them,

> telling them the competition they are up against ... Hamish Hamilton would not because they have commissioned [a] 20th century history from Norman Stone and while it will obviously be different from yours, they feel that they couldn't do justice to two in the same list and I expect that's right. The following do want to compete with Weidenfeld: Cape, Simon & Schuster, Collins, Sidgwick & Jackson, Heinemann, Michael Joseph and Century Hutchinson and I have sent them all the synopsis and reviews.[46]

The move caused consternation at Weidenfeld. 'Juliet Gardiner', Hunter reported, referring to the company's history editor, 'seems somewhat upset that we are testing the market, and suggested we would find no-one prepared to offer more than they have.'[47] George Weidenfeld told Bruce Hunter that 'he wd. withdraw rather than participate in an auction'.[48] Angrily, he said to Hunter over the phone: 'This is a great mistake – historians have no business writing about the present. He's a historian; he should stick to what he knows about.'[49]

Weidenfeld was still in the running, however, despite his sense of betrayal at being dumped after so long and fruitful a relationship with Eric. Hunter approached Stuart Proffitt, who he thought would have been the ideal editor, but Proffitt at the time was working for HarperCollins, which was owned by Rupert Murdoch, 'and it was simply impossible to think of Eric being published by Rupert Murdoch'. £100,000 was the upper limit for Cape, Collins and

Heinemann, although Century Hutchinson improved the offer to £125,000.[50] This, like the other proposed advances, would, however, be for world rights, and by this stage in his career Eric was a major name in many countries where publishers could be expected to offer considerable sums for translation rights. From this perspective, the best offer was from Michael Joseph and their paperback imprint Sphere, who proposed £65,000 for the British market only, leaving David Higham Associates to negotiate contracts in the rest of the world. Hunter proposed therefore that the auction be reopened for UK and Commonwealth rights only.[51] Michael Joseph increased their offer to £90,000. George Weidenfeld could not match this because he had no paperback affiliation that would allow him to pay full royalties on softcover editions. In any case, he turned down the proposal to restrict his previous offer to UK and Commonwealth rights only.[52]

The upshot was that Eric was offered a contract with Michael Joseph in December 1988. Not only was it financially the best offer on the table, but Hunter also respected the editor who would take charge of Eric's book there, Susan Watt, who was married to David Watt, an 'intellectual journalist', and – not only for that reason – 'would have a good grasp of why Eric was important at least, and of the work'.[53] Cautiously, given Eric's age, the publisher had insisted on including 'death clauses' providing arrangements for the event of Eric being unable to finish the work. Eric was concerned 'that Marlene shouldn't find herself suddenly having to fork out thousands which had been paid in advance. That's taken care of. I suppose I'd better think of a poss. alternative author if I drop out ... ' He signed the contract on 5 December 1988. Meanwhile, he insisted that Pantheon, the American publishing house run by his friend André Schiffrin, publish the US edition, which they duly did.[54]

Writing the history of one's own times is famously difficult. 'The basic thing about history', Eric said in an interview on BBC Radio 3 on 1 November 1994, 'is precisely that you take your distance', and yet if you write about the times you have lived through 'you are too close to it' and 'you find it very difficult to distinguish from your actions and opinions at the time ... If you write about your own lifetime you are writing about something in which you are emotionally involved.'[55] Eric developed these thoughts when he delivered the University of London's flagship history lecture, named after, and endowed by the widow of, a Victorian Bishop of London, Mandell Creighton, a distinguished historian in his own right, in 1993. Speaking to a packed audience in the Beveridge Hall, the largest lecture theatre in London University's Senate House, on 'The Present as History: Writing the History of One's Own Times', Eric told his audience that he had deliberately kept away from the twentieth century in his professional writings, though not in his journalistic ones. In coming to the twentieth century he came from a particular angle – Vienna in the 1920s, Berlin and Cambridge in the 1930s, years full of experiences that shaped his overall vision of the world. As an ordinary soldier in 1940 listening to Churchill voicing the British people's defiance on the radio he knew that he was right, that 'there was an unassuming grandeur about this moment'. Personal experience and memory informed historical judgement in a way that could only happen with the history of one's own time.[56]

In return for an honorarium of £300 the university normally retained the copyright to the Creighton Lectures and the sole right to publish them.[57] Eric was not happy with this condition. He insisted on retaining the copyright, as he wrote to London University's Principal on 13 November 1993, adding: 'If this is unacceptable to the University, I will, of course, return the honorarium to you. Please forgive me if I write, in this instance, as a professional writer and lecturer rather than as a retired teacher in the University of London. I am both, but my income nowadays depends on one.'[58] This was in fact the first time since the lectures had begun in 1907 that anyone had raised the issue of copyright.[59] He was assured in reply that he had the right to republish it as he saw fit and that the university would not stand in his way.[60]

As with his nineteenth-century volumes, Eric adopted a determinedly thematic and analytical approach in his new book. He rejected the chronological structure of another survey that was to appear in 1997, Sir Martin Gilbert's *History of the Twentieth Century*, published by HarperCollins. Eric concluded: "'The facts", whatever they are are not enough, least of all in close chronological sequence. They cry out for overviews and explanation.'[61] When Eric came to consider how he would structure his own history of the twentieth century, he thought at first that he would divide the century into two halves around 1945, presenting it 'as a sort of diptych' in which a calamitous first half was followed by a booming, peaceful and prosperous second. But after working for a couple of years on the project at the end of the 1980s he changed his mind, influenced by the collapse of Communism in 1989, which forced him to see events since 1973 in a gloomier light.[62] He altered the periodisation to a tripartite structure, beginning with 'the age of catastrophe' from 1914 to 1945, then 'the golden age' from 1945 to 1973 and finally the 'landslide' from 1973 to 1991, when 'the world lost its bearings' following the sharp economic downturn caused by a steep rise in world oil prices enforced by the producers.

To help him with the rewriting, he engaged the services of Lise Grande, who in 1992 began taking a Master's degree at the New School for Social Research after working for one of the branches of the Palestine Liberation Organization. She was his last assistant, unpaid but enthusiastic. As she recalled later:

> He would ask me to do two things. He would send me on trips to try and confirm statistically and archivally things that he wanted for the book, so he would have me do that, and then he would say things like 'figure out what happened with the Muslim movement in 1920 in India' . . . And then he would say 'and I'd like to see it in a week'. So then you'd run off in an area that you had absolutely no competence in . . .[63]

When she started out, Eric told her not to ask any questions ('now, don't bother me'), and for the three years she worked with him, Lise Grande did indeed ask no questions: he wanted a researcher, not a co-author. Working with Eric, Grande found, was challenging in many ways. This was the era before the internet and the World Wide Web had revolutionised the search for information; facts and figures had to be obtained from books and articles, often obscure and difficult to get hold of.

Beyond that, she discovered, Eric was finding the process of rethinking his understanding of the twentieth century a very difficult one:

> We shared an office – a little, tiny [one] . . . And one long desk, one long table desk, and I sat at this end, built into the wall, and he sat here, and he typed. And when he got upset he would unroll the paper and he'd wad [it] up. And . . . he would throw the paper at the rubbish bin and of course it would hit me! And you know, I would turn to him, and he would tilt his head back [and] drum [with his fingers] . . . I mean, he was just this sort of cranky, irritable man.

Like almost everyone else who encountered him, she was struck by the variety and extent of his friendships. On one occasion, he sent her out to get some statistics of how many people had emigrated from Poland, 'and of course he would never tell you how to do that', so she went to the Slavic, Baltic and East European Collections at New York Public Library,

> and I'd found the archivist, and we spent hours combing through documents, and we'd gotten all of this, and Eric had been very irritated and said, 'Now, as soon as you get this, hurry up and bring it right to me.' So I went to the flat and when I got there, it was maybe nine o'clock at night, and there was somebody there, and it was a very interesting looking man, and I bring in the documents, and Eric says, 'Yes, thank you', and this very interesting man says, 'Stay and have a cup of coffee', and I looked at Eric, and he clearly did not want me to, and I said, 'No, no, no, thank you, good evening'. And the next day, I asked Eric, 'Who was that?' It was Gabriel García Márquez.[64]

At the end of the three years, Eric gave her a cheque for $1000 and a fulsome tribute to 'the exceptional Miss Grande' in the book's acknowledgements: 'If somebody had told me that Eric had that regard for me, I would not have known it.' Rather than pursue a career in academia, however, Lise Grande followed an invitation from the United Nations to go to Palestine and work there on its behalf. She asked Eric whether this was all right. 'And he said, "Well, you'll never be *very* good as a historian . . . You're all right, but you won't be really outstanding, so I suggest that you go along and take this job."' She took on increasingly senior positions working for the United Nations in the Congo, in Angola, in South Sudan, and in other trouble spots, and served as Deputy Special Representative of the United Nations Assistance Mission for Iraq. She remained in touch with Eric, sending him long letters from various parts of the globe and visiting him in Nassington Road when she was in London.

To help him further with his book on the twentieth century, Eric taught a course on it at the New School. Lise Grande took the course:

> He was clearly at the time rethinking two very big questions, and he used his lectures to explore in a sense his rethinking. So, one of them, he was absolutely preoccupied with how the twentieth century ended in such a barbarous way, why torture re-emerges, why there is mass destruction, why murder and mass murder is allowed . . . And then he was rethinking the way in which real existing socialism imploded . . . The lecture courses really hinged on those things – of course he was talking about everything, but those were the ones he was really pre-occupied with . . . He was morally disappointed and in a way kind of outraged by how it had all gone wrong . . . It was not a neutral course – well, he was never neutral – it wasn't presented neutrally, it was presented with a sharpness and a constant anger and a tinge of disappointment. I remember, both the professors and I remember him being the most upset by what he taught . . . The other point about being his student was his insistence that you choose sides, you're honest, you know. And that you had a responsibility as a privileged recipient of higher education to

choose the right side. So he was very warrior-like as well. He was cranky, warrior-like, determined.

She sensed how he felt a real moral outrage about the re-emergence of torture as a tool of government in countries that had previously abolished it. 'This *insulted* him. You know, there wasn't any of the blasé, well all states behave badly, this is to be expected, we've always done this to each other.'

Working with Eric and attending his seminars and lectures, she felt, helped her in her later career. He gave her an understanding of 'how ideology worked and what it all meant. I could never have done all of that if I hadn't been Eric's student.' Without it, she would not have been able to deal with the civil wars and violent confrontations that faced her in her attempts to get aid convoys through conflict zones:

> You know, in this utterly chaotic, seemingly chaotic world – it's not chaotic. It is understandable. And that was the incredible confidence that you came out [with] from being Eric's student, ... that you could look at that and you could know it. It required systematic application of systems and thoughts and perspective. And he just handed that to you as a student. It was a great gift ... There was that solidity, that what I now understand as an older person, as moral strength and vigour, and he had it in spades, even as a very old man whose whole project had collapsed. And that was the thing about being one of his last students, there was a great poignancy to working with Eric. Because he'd lost, his side didn't win.

As he said, however, in his Creighton Lecture, destroying in a single phrase the vulgar and ignorant but all too common claim that history is written by the victors, 'the losers make the best historians'.[65]

At the very end of 1993, Eric finished the final draft. Bruce Hunter thought it 'very good indeed' but was less certain about the title. He suggested *The Age of Convulsion* or *The Age of Division*. In any event, there should in his view be a subtitle – *The Short Twentieth Century 1914–1991.*[66] But *Age of Extremes* it remained (the definite article was added for later reprints, for the sake of uniformity with the three nineteenth-century volumes). The book was sent by the publisher to a copy editor early in 1994. Concerned about meeting the deadline for publication in October, in time for the Christmas books market, Eric asked for extra staff to be put to work on the book at Michael Joseph, particularly because the illustrations chosen by the publisher were in Eric's view inadequate and needed working on as well.[67] The book duly appeared on schedule.

Age of Extremes received probably more reviews than any other of Eric's works. His notes summarising them run to eight pages of tiny handwriting.[68] Eric's former pupil Neal Ascherson spoke for many when he lauded the book's astonishing range of knowledge. Ever since he had dazzled his undergraduate contemporaries with his erudition sixty years before, Eric had attracted awed comments of the sort Ascherson penned in the *Independent on Sunday*:

> No historian now writing in English can match his overwhelming command of fact and source. But the key word is 'command'. Hobsbawm's capacity to store and retrieve detail has now reached a scale normally approached only by large archives with big staffs. Appropriately born in Alexandria, he is a walking Alexandrian Library of knowledge, above all concerned with the 19th century. At the same time, no symptoms of pedantry have appeared. Quite the contrary: as the years pass, Eric Hobsbawm's gift for startling, often seductive generalizations from his material has only grown. He is a historian, not a novelist, but the engine inside his narrow head is a Rolls-Royce imagination.[69]

By now, Eric's reputation extended far beyond the field of history into the wider reading public as a whole, so that *Age of Extremes* was reviewed by a number of prominent public intellectuals, most notably perhaps Edward Said, a Palestinian who taught at Columbia University in New York and had been a founding father of post-colonial studies with his book *Orientalism*, published in 1978. Said regarded *Age of Extremes* not least as a work of literature. Perhaps predictably, however, he found its approach too Eurocentric, with political developments in the rest of the world viewed as imitations of what was going on in Europe. Non-European thinkers were neglected or ignored, he charged. As a consequence of this narrowing of perspective, *Age of Extremes* seemed unable to convey 'the underlying drive or thrust of a particular era' along with 'the view from within' purveyed by those who experienced it, the oppressed or endangered communities, the subjects of racial or social discrimination, the originators of resistance especially if, like the Islamic movements the book failed altogether to mention, it was religious in inspiration. Its treatment of culture was reductionist, seeing it merely as the product of politics and economics rather than relatively autonomous from them. Eric's view of modernism was no more than a 'caricature'. Overall, however, he considered it a masterwork despite these deficiencies.[70]

As Said's lengthy analysis suggests, the book was pored over in particular detail by writers and thinkers on the Left. In more than forty pages of the *New Left Review* devoted to it, the Swedish Marxist sociologist Göran Therborn paid tribute to the book's awe-inspiring range, but criticised what he saw as the underestimation of nationalism as a force in the defence of democracy, for example in interwar Spain and wartime Norway and other countries, the turgid analysis of social change ('an area where the great historian's sparkling narrative prose fails him'), and finally, again, the book's obstinate Eurocentrism. The contribution of the comparative political sociologist Michael Mann was more critical. While finding the book hugely impressive ('other general histories of the twentieth century appear plodding, bitty or ideological by comparison'), he thought it could have benefited from a greater interweaving of the big picture with Eric's own life experiences. The book also spent too little time on democratic socialism, and failed to deal adequately with fascism as a gendered phenomenon, an outbreak, to put it bluntly, of disgruntled masculinity. On Soviet Russia, Mann thought Eric took too rosy a view of the Bolshevik Revolution and its immediate aftermath. Like other critics, Mann was taken aback by Eric's gloomy prognosis of the future: 'he and the twentieth century are ageing and he doesn't like it'. Finally, he did not think the book's periodisation either helpful or convincing: 'Hobsbawm has perhaps become trapped by his historian's predilection for Age metaphors.'[71]

Kevin Davey, in *Tribune*, the magazine of the Labour Left in the UK, was also critical of the book's 'cultural conservatism', which condemned post-war poetry, painting and music and 'the decline of the classical genres of high art and literature'. There was 'some truth in his clumsy and rather conventional formulation that the arts anticipated the social breakdowns that followed', but it by no means told the whole story.[72] Similarly, the left-wing Scottish writer and editor Angus Calder sensed 'an ungovernable nostalgia for days when the realist novel and the symphony were fundamental to civilisation' behind 'Hobsbawm's dismissive opinions about rock music, TV and post-1945 painting and literature'. And he found it 'disappointing that a man who has written so well in the past about jazz can allege that Simenon is the only detective writer who can be taken seriously as literature – what about Raymond Chandler? Chester Hines?' Like others, he could point easily enough to gaps in Eric's coverage – in this case 'the music of Mapfumo and the poetry of Serote', not omissions, perhaps, that everyone would have thought of singling out.[73]

Writing in the *Times Literary Supplement*, Ross McKibbin noted in particular the ideological distance Eric had travelled since his early days as a Communist. 'This book has no Marxist teleology; at least, no dialectical one.' Yet the book was still bound together by a fundamentally Marxist approach that made it a 'total history' in which everything was interconnected and was led back in the end to the history of 'capitalism and its fearsome dynamic'. 'The whole structure was framed, though not necessarily determined, by the material basis of society.' Further to the left, Perry Anderson agreed that '*Age of Extremes* is Hobsbawm's masterpiece'. Its break with the earlier trilogy on the nineteenth century was, he noted, marked in particular by 'the complete disappearance from sight of the bourgeoisie, which – unlike chess, drugs or football – does not even rate an entry in the index. Did it vanish historically in August 1914?' Anderson asked rhetorically. Leaving this thought to one side, Anderson moved on to the book's periodisation. Essentially, he observed, the three subdivisions of the 'age of extremes' were economic, the first marked by insufficient demand, the second by effectively managed demand, the third by excessive demand. Without fundamentally challenging this tripartite division, Anderson did suggest that it applied only to certain parts of the world, not, for example, to China, where it was easy enough to argue that the 'Golden Age' was in fact an age of man-made famine and economic disaster, from the civil war through the catastrophic Great Leap Forward to the calamities of the 'cultural revolution', and the decades since the early 1970s had not been an age of stagnation but of unparalleled economic growth. Wars and civil conflicts in Korea, Vietnam, the Middle East, Indonesia and Africa from the 1950s to the 1970s killed perhaps thirty-five million people. 'The global kill rate dropped steeply during the Landslide', Eric's third period, accounting for the deaths of possibly five million people. Eric's 'angle of vision ... in Vienna, Berlin and London' had led to a neglect of East Asia, to the book's cost.[74]

Reflecting this fundamentally European perspective, Eric had also in Anderson's view neglected the twentieth-century history of the United States, compounding this by avoiding any cross-section of Western society as a whole, and in particular any account at all of the Western bourgeoisie. 'The index contains twice as many entries for the USSR as for the USA, but the disparity of attention is actually more marked than this', Anderson charged, because, while the Soviet Union received three full analyses, America received none. Thus in Eric's account of the twentieth century, the 'centrality of the loser makes the relative marginalization of the winner all the more pointed'. By omitting the bourgeoisie and in particular the American bourgeoisie, '*Age of Extremes* offers a decapitated portrait of contemporary society'. Moreover, its negative view of the most recent period of global history ignored the undoubtedly positive development of the worldwide spread of democracy, in which the number of democratic states on the planet more than doubled between 1973 and 2000, a process already well under way at the time when Eric wrote his book, not least in Latin America, which should at least have given him pause for thought. While Eric's account of the collapse of democracy and the rise of various forms of totalitarianism between the wars was a tour de force, he offered no comparable treatment of the reconstruction and spread of democracy after the war.[75]

More towards the centre and right of the political spectrum, the American journalist Christopher Caldwell located the book in the tradition of A. J. P. Taylor, E. P. Thompson and others, as 'one of those great English historians who write to polemicize as well as instruct. It's a style', he continued, 'that is not so much enlightening as invigorating, demanding not just patient attention but alert engagement – and Hobsbawm's history of the twentieth century is one of the last major books we'll receive from that grand tradition.'[76] Eric's old friend Eugene D. Genovese, in a lengthy review in the American magazine the *New Republic*, celebrated him as 'one of the few genuinely great historians of our century'. Genovese's increasingly conservative political position was reflected in his praise for Eric's attack on 'the contemporary rage for personal liberation'. His book, Genovese thought, destroyed one shibboleth of the Left after another, including 'the irrationality of radical feminist theory and, by extension, of much of the claptrap that now passes for radical social theory'. Paradoxically, Genovese made the book seem rather conservative by singling out these aspects.[77]

Perhaps the most critical reviewer was Tony Judt, a specialist on twentieth-century French socialism. Judt thought that 'Eric Hobsbawm's history of the twentieth century is the story of a decline of a civilization, the history of a world which has both brought to full flowering the material and cultural potential of the nineteenth century and betrayed its promise ... There is a Jeremiah-like air of impending doom about much of Hobsbawm's account.'[78] Judt paid tribute to Eric's admission at various points in the book that he had been wrong in his judgement of events. But on the big issues Eric did not seem to have changed his mind since the 1930s. He described the defence of the Spanish Republic in the Civil War as a pure and unalloyed cause, ignoring the baleful role of the Communists in undermining it. He insisted that the October Revolution in Russia in 1917 was a mass popular uprising, ignoring all the research that had demonstrated that it was a coup led by a small and determined minority. He missed the revolutionary qualities and even more the revolutionary impact of fascism, especially during the war. 'Real existing socialism' in post-war Eastern Europe merited a mere six pages out of six hundred, with only a single paragraph on the show trials of the fifties. His neglect of states such as Hungary, Poland, Romania and Czechoslovakia led him virtually to ignore the ruthless and murderous process of Stalin's seizure of power in these states in the late 1940s and early 1950s. Judt ended by accusing Eric of playing down Stalin's reign of terror in the 1930s. Overall, he 'missed, in his version of the twentieth century, the ruthlessly questioning eye which has made him so indispensable a guide to the nineteenth'.

Niall Ferguson regretted that while the Left had this brilliant survey at its disposal, the Right, to which he declared his own unambiguous allegiance, possessed no equivalent ('where is *our* history of the 20th century? Where is *our* Hobsbawm?').[79] Another, less generous right-wing British historian and biographer, Andrew Roberts, found the book so biased as to be 'useless to the general reader' and thought it was nothing but 'rot' written by an 'extremist'. Even readers of the *Daily Telegraph* would have found a knockabout polemic of this kind too crude for their tastes.[80] Another young neocon of the Thatcher generation, Daniel Johnson, damned *Age of Extremes* in similarly robust terms as 'one-sided', based on 'incredible sophistry'. He hoped that Martin Gilbert, Churchill's official biographer, would deliver a less ideological account of the century, though in the event it turned out to be a chronicle rather than a history, as Eric observed in reviewing it.[81] The Canadian postmodernist conservative Modris Eksteins complained

> that Hobsbawm's most acerbic comments are saved not for Hitler or Stalin or Mao or Pol Pot, the mass murderers of our century, but for people like John F. Kennedy ('most overrated'),

Henry Kissinger ('brutally insincere'), Richard Nixon ('most unpleasant') and for the United States as a whole. The U.S. is not surprisingly, blamed for the Cold War, for subsequent political instability in many parts of the world, for environmental degradation, and for unparalleled vulgarity: If our century has had an evil empire, Hobsbawm seems to be saying, it has been the U.S. one, the home of modern capitalism.[82]

Such hostile responses, Bruce Hunter thought, writing from the point of view of a professional literary agent, were not entirely unwelcome: public controversy about a book always did wonders for sales.[83]

In response to these criticisms, Eric insisted that his book was 'an attempt to *rethink* the positions of a lifetime, not to justify them. It is a bizarre, almost an absurd misunderstanding to see it primarily, or in any significant way, as a defence of the communist position, or even more absurd, a pro-Soviet position.' Sweeping assertions along these lines were based on a wilful misreading of the text. Eric defended his argument that Stalin's Soviet Union had saved the West by pointing out that the alliance was only a temporary one. Most readers had accepted this position. As for his alleged failure to deal adequately with Auschwitz, he asserted that this was because he did not believe that such horrors could be adequately imagined. It was perhaps ironic that he spent more space on 'the terrible things done by Stalin and Mao than on Hitler's horrors' but this was 'because there can be no doubt about what a Jewish historian feels about the Nazi genocide, whereas a Marxist historian may be misunderstood if he does not clearly put on record his rejection of the horrors perpetrated in the name of his own cause. Nevertheless', he conceded, 'it would probably have been better to say as much against Hitler as against Stalin', especially in the light of recent research that showed the involvement of ordinary Germans in the genocide.[84]

However mixed the reviews might have been, the book was an immediate commercial success, helped by Eric's appearances on radio and television in the run-up to publication.[85] It seemed to readers to make sense of a puzzling and chaotic period. Advance extracts were serialised in the *Independent on Sunday* and book club rights were sold for £10,000. Ever alert to the advent of new technology, Eric asked Bruce Hunter whether it was 'possible to advertise the book & publish extracts on INTERNET (international computer network)' – he had just been to a course on how to use the internet and how to email.[86] 'The pre-publication reception in Britain is better than I'd hoped for', Eric told Bruce Hunter on 12 October 1994.[87] The guest list for a launch party organised by Michael Joseph included a mixture of historians and intellectuals of various political persuasions, journalists and broadcasters, and old left-wingers.[88] Within a few days of its publication on 27 October 1994, *Age of Extremes* reached number six on the *Sunday Times* bestseller list.[89] The trade magazine the *Bookseller* recorded it at number fourteen on the official bestseller list on 28 November 1994.[90] The book won the Silver PEN award for non-fiction, and Eric was also awarded the Wolfson Foundation History Prize for his entire oeuvre in 1997, only one of seven occasions on which such an award was made (the chairman of the judges, Keith Thomas, had some difficulty in persuading Leonard Wolfson, Chairman of the Trustees, who had the final say, to approve the awarding of the prize to a man with political views diametrically opposed to his own, but he prevailed in the end).[91]

Within a few years, *Age of Extremes* was translated into some thirty languages. Eric went carefully through the Italian translation and supplied the publisher with a long list of corrections.[92] He also checked over the translation of the German edition, which was reviewed more widely and at greater length than any other, including the British, and was the subject of a dozen or more discussions and reviews broadcast on German radio stations.[93] Many German reviewers were struck by the book's pessimistic tone, regarded as strange in a country that had only recently been reunified and was continuing on the peaceful and prosperous path it had embarked upon in the 1950s.[94] Among other things, it was widely noted that the book was a good deal less Marxist than many of Eric's earlier works. As the journalist Franziska Augstein noted: 'In the *Age of*

Extremes he has abandoned categories in which he has thought for his entire life. Thus he does not use the category "class" in his depiction of the twentieth century ... Even his idea of the class struggle, bolstered by social and cultural theory, hardly plays a role in his latest book.'[95] The German edition sold eleven thousand copies in its first month of publication, January 1996, and many thousands more in the following months.[96]

But it was in Brazil that *Age of Extremes* chalked up its greatest success. Since the late 1980s, Eric's ties with the country had become particularly close. He had been invited in 1988 to take part in conferences marking the centenary of the freeing of the slaves by Doña Isabel, the Regent of Brazil, and his reputation in the country, especially since the restoration of democracy in 1985, was such that his arrival on 8 June 1988 made front-page headlines in the daily paper *Folha de S. Paulo*. Accompanied by Marlene, he went to Rio de Janeiro and São Paulo, speaking on racism and workers' movements in nineteenth-century Europe (*Age of Empire* was published in Brazil in August 1988). He stayed with his publisher, Marcus Gasparian, in his São Paulo home. On one occasion, Gasparian recalled later, he was driving Eric and Marlene to Barra do Saí, a beach in São Paulo state. They were stopped by a policeman, for no particular reason, but Marcus had forgotten to bring his driver's licence. He had with him, though, that day's *Folha de S. Paulo*, on the cover of which there was a large photo of Eric. He explained who Eric was, and the policeman, glancing at Eric's unmistakable features, let them go without further comment. This was, Eric remarked, the first time that being an historian had earned him any favours from the police.

He was back in 1992, when he met the socialist trade union leader and future President Lula da Silva.[97] The two men struck up an immediate rapport, and Lula bought and read every one of Eric's books as they appeared in Portuguese translation. Another friend was Fernando Henrique Cardoso. An historical sociologist, academic and public intellectual, Cardoso had been an Associate Director of Studies at the École des Hautes Études en Sciences Sociales in Paris in the late 1960s: 'I remember being with Eric and Alain Touraine', he said in an interview, 'wandering through the "barricades" in Paris in May 1968 (there was a big conference on Marx at UNESCO and we both participated).' In 1994 Cardoso was elected President of Brazil with a large majority, and invited Eric to take part in a seminar in Brasilia, the capital.[98] Cardoso also invited Eric to his official inauguration in 1995, as well as, later, to Buckingham Palace when he was a guest of the Queen, and the Sheldonian Theatre in Oxford when he received an honorary degree. Eric, he said, was an important influence on his thinking, an acknowledgement shared publicly by his successor a few years later.[99]

The publishers of the Brazilian edition of *Age of Extremes* had arranged for Eric to travel there with Marlene in 1995 to 'make his book a big success here'.[100] With the public endorsement of the President, it certainly was. *Age of Extremes* topped the bestseller lists in Brazil in 1995, not just the non-fiction but the general lists, including all books of every kind. Altogether sales of the book in Brazil reached the astonishing figure of 265,000. In total, sales of all Eric's books in the country even before *Age of Extremes* were estimated at some six hundred thousand. The book's extraordinary success in Brazil gave Eric the status of a celebrity whenever he visited the country.[101] A few years later, when Peter Florence was visiting the country, as he recalled,

I went to Parati on the Amazon rainforest coast to help the great Bloomsbury publisher Liz Calder set up the festival that became FLIP. I went into the local bookshop and asked in a faltering mash of Portuguese and Tourist who the best-selling English language writer in Brazil was. The bookseller smiled broadly and said 'Enrique Hobsbawm.' 'No, no,' I said, puzzled. Obviously I must've used the wrong word. 'Sorry. I mean who sells the most books in Brazil?' Same smile, same reply. Non-plussed, but delighted . . . Brazilian readers went crazy for Eric. So I emailed him from the one internet café in town and explained where I was and asked if he'd come . . . The President sent his Minister of Culture, Gilberto Gil, to welcome Eric to the town and inaugurate the festival with the entire Brazilian media in tow. There was music, and speeches and ideas. And the kind of superstardom that makes things happen and changes lives.[102]

All in all, *Age of Extremes* was Eric's most successful book, and did more than any other to boost his reputation on a global scale. It was certainly translated into more languages than any other of his works. Western European languages, where Eric's name was already familiar, tended to come first. But French was not among them, a fact which in due course sparked a major public controversy not only in France but in other countries as well.

IV

The controversy began, in a sense, not in France itself but in America. In 1989, Eric delivered a series of three lectures at Rutgers University, New Jersey, on the occasion of the bicentenary of the French Revolution. Expanding the lectures into a book, *Echoes of the Marseillaise,* published the following year, Eric mounted an impassioned defence of the traditional Marxist interpretation of the Revolution. The Revolution, its memory and its consequences, he argued, not only dominated nineteenth-century European politics but also had a global impact.[103] 1917 in Russia was full of such parallels, as Trotsky's history of the Bolshevik Revolution showed. The desire to avoid, or emulate, the Jacobin Terror of 1793–4, the reaction of Thermidor, or the creation of Napoleon's military dictatorship, had a material effect on the political behaviour of those involved in subsequent revolutions.[104] For Georges Lefebvre's generation of French historians, the struggle against fascism, the resistance to the Nazi occupation and the Vichy regime, and the fight for democracy took nourishment from the celebration of the Revolution of 1789.[105]

It was this tradition against which the writers of the 1980s and 1990s such as François Furet, a former Communist himself, were reacting. In a series of publications, beginning already in the 1970s,

Furet had rejected what he called the 'revolutionary catechism', the standard Marxist or neo-Jacobin account which accorded long-term social and economic origins to the Revolution, saw it in terms of class struggle and celebrated the popular uprisings which drove it on. The Terror of 1793–4, he argued, was not a deviation from the earlier phases of the Revolution but their logical conclusion. Overall the Revolution had set back the French economy and society by decades. Its long-term effects, insofar as there were any, had been overwhelmingly negative. In *Echoes of the Marseillaise*, Eric pilloried 'the absurdity of the assumption that the French Revolution is simply a sort of stumble on the long, slow march of eternal France'.[106] France's late economic modernisation, in the post-war years, had destroyed the social world of the post-revolutionary era and rendered 1789 irrelevant for a new generation of historians. Men like Lefebvre came from humble backgrounds and retained their roots in an 'unreconstructed, ancient, pretechnological France' that went back to the eighteenth century and beyond. By contrast, the revisionists represented the new upper middle class created by economic modernisation. No wonder they rejected the ideas of 1789 in favour of elitism and neo-liberalism.[107]

The bicentenary of the Revolution was celebrated with due pomp and circumstance in France, but it was impossible to conceal the fact that, with the decline and fall of Communism, the Revolution itself no longer seemed to have the significance it once possessed. Moreover, Eric thought, what Furet was rejecting was not just 1789 but also 1917. In this, he was soon proved right, for in 1995 Furet published an all-out attack on Communism: *Le Passé d'une illusion: essai sur l'idée communiste au XXe siècle* (it was published in English translation in 1999 as *The Passing of an Illusion: The Idea of Communism in the Twentieth Century* by Chicago University Press). As soon as the book appeared, Eric was invited to take part in a debate in the magazine *Le Débat* of its central theses by Pierre Nora, Director since 1977 of the École des Hautes Études en Sciences Sociales, home of the *Annales*, and a pioneer of studies of French historical memory, who knew Eric from the seminars in Paris they had taken part in some years before.

At this point, Eric had not read Furet's book, and had doubts about the other proposed participants in the written debate, who included Ernst Nolte and Renzo De Felice, both of whom he regarded as ultra-conservative 'defenders of fascism'. He suggested adding a couple of 'liberals' to the roster of participants. But 'in principle', he told Nora, 'I'll go with it' (*en principe, je marche*).[108] Eric did indeed write a response to Furet. It appeared in number 89 of *Le Débat*. Furet had tried to equate Communism and fascism, he said, but he had qualified this so much that not a great deal was left in the end. As for anti-fascism, he pointed out that Furet's criticisms ignored the existential nature of the fascist threat in the 1930s and early 1940s which forced the Left and the liberal centre into an alliance and brought Communist Parties millions of new adherents since they were by far the most committed and active of fascism's opponents. He conceded that 'the communist movement was indeed based on an illusion', but this did not invalidate its behaviour in building an anti-fascist popular front in the 1930s.[109]

Nora's position at Gallimard made him by far the most important figure in non-subsidised French history publishing. Either the 'Library of Social Sciences' or the 'Library of Histories', both edited by him, would have been a natural place for *Age of Extremes* to appear in French, as had many other translated works, some of them very lengthy. Nora had already organised a French edition of *Nations and Nationalism* and Eric, reporting to him that *Age of Extremes* had received a rapturous reception in the UK even from the conservative press ('I confess I have some difficulty in getting used to reviews that begin with the words "This marvellous book"'), pointed out that, while it was being translated into all the languages of the European Union, the French rights were still up for grabs. He therefore asked his agent to send a copy to Nora, 'as a gift of friendship' if nothing else, but clearly in the hope that Nora would arrange for it to be published in French.[110] Nora received the book and wrote to Eric in May and again in July 1995 to tell him he was reading it 'with great interest and admiration', and though 'the translation would be no small business', he thought that there was no equivalent in French so there was certainly an opening for it in the market.[111] Yet he refused to commit himself. After several months had passed without any formal offer, Eric began to lose patience. He rejected an offer of help from the French Communist Party ('I think at this moment the last thing I need to help along the publication of *Age of Extremes* in French is a formal identification with the CP'). But by January 1996 he was complaining that 'Nora is still stringing me along. He rang the other day and had a long talk with Marlene, about how difficult it all was/might be. The book would be savaged by the critics when it came out etc, and they'd never get their money back bla bla bla ... Let's see whether he will now nerve himself to turn the book down officially. Still, I have a suspicion he may actually have a bad conscience if/when he does.'[112]

Nora did indeed turn the book down. As he explained on 24 January 1996, though it was a book of high quality, which he would have loved to have translated and published, there were two serious obstacles to this aim being achieved. The first was the cost of translation, which would push up the price to a level that would make the book difficult to sell. The second was ideological. 'You risk inviting bad reviews from the *Left* itself, because the tenor of the times – as far as the communists! – is not what one hears in your book.' He did not fear criticism from historians, he feared criticism from those who were politically close to Eric. Perhaps there could be a discussion with Furet in the pages of *Le Débat*.[113] Eric, however, rejected the idea. 'I would like at all costs to avoid my book ... being considered by this placement as a simple anti-Furet. Anyway, my book is far from a defence of communism ... '[114] Meanwhile, the idea of publishing a French translation of *Age of Extremes* was being rejected by one publisher after another. Albin Michel turned the book down because the company had just signed Marc Ferro, a leading modern historian of the *Annales* school, for a history of the twentieth century (it never appeared).[115] Publishers cited the poor sales of *The Age of Revolution* in French, which had only amounted to 3700 copies. There were other examples of a similar sort. But only in Eric's case was there an element of 'ideological sectarianism' in the rejection.[116] The Holocaust had moved to the centre of public cultural memory in the 1990s, yet, as Nora (who was Jewish) told Elise Marienstras, Auschwitz only received a solitary mention in the book. Eric 'wasn't interested at all in the Shoah', she thought: 'He put it to one side, just as he did with the gulags.' For a man of his sweeping, global vision, she added, the Jews were only one set of victims of a war in which more than twenty million people had been killed.[117]

Fayard also rejected the book. Eric was even more irritated by their behaviour than he was by Nora's: 'After refusing for a long time to put anything [on paper] about their decision', he wrote in 1999, 'even to admit that they had taken any decision, we now have two equally implausible explanations.' One was from an anonymous editor 'who almost certainly had not read the book in English', and decided 'that it was no good', while the other was from the director-general of the firm, who declared that the translation would cost too much and that even if someone had covered these costs the book would still have been published at a loss. 'Taking the director's own figures', Eric noted, 'I calculate that the deficit they were prepared to envisage would have been covered by the sale of 400 extra copies.'[118]

When Ania Corless, from Eric's agency, David Higham Associates, visited Paris to take up the issue with Olivier Bétourné, the number two at Fayard, she reported that he was 'embarrassed', but insisted once more that the costs of translation and production would have simply been too high.[119] Although the company had published Eric's previous works, neither Bétourné nor the editor-in-chief Denis Maraval accepted *Age of Extremes*, leading one commentator to suggest complicity with Furet in the matter.[120] It was hardly surprising that Eric was becoming irritated. As he asked rather pointedly in his letter to Nora rejecting the idea of a debate with Furet: 'would it not be a little absurd to present and discuss a book in *Le Débat* which the journal's readers would have no possibility of reading in their own language, but only in English, German, Italian, Spanish, Portuguese, Dutch, Danish, Swedish, Greek, Chinese, Japanese, Korean and Russian, not to speak of Albanian?'[121]

In the end, there was a discussion in *Le Débat*, but not directly of Eric's book: in the issues of March–April 1996 and January–February 1997 Eric summarised the central arguments of *Age of Extremes*, while Furet countered them with the assertion that Nazism and Stalinism had more similarities than differences. In his own contribution to the 1997 symposium, Nora claimed that financial difficulties had prevented the book's publication in French, though French intellectuals also found Eric's partisanship for 'the revolutionary cause' to be embarrassing and had chosen in the end to ignore it. The row reached the French press. *Le Monde Diplomatique*, a left-wing monthly that also appeared in more than a score of foreign editions, was particularly forthright in its condemnation of the French publishing industry. 'Newcomers to dissident points of view', declared the paper, 'will have to learn English. Or one of the nineteen other languages that editorial McCarthyism has not yet contaminated.' Eric's own take on French publishers was equally ironic. 'They're putting up the drawbridges', he remarked, 'and imagining themselves the embattled centre of civilization. Not translating my book simply underlines the uniqueness of the French.'[122]

Finally, an agreement was reached with Éditions Complexe, a small independent publishing house based in Brussels and specialising in history and literature.[123] Its Director, André Versaille, 'heard the rumours coming from Paris, and I didn't hesitate for a single moment'. Why were the French refusing to bring it out? he was asked.

Rather than censorship [he replied], I prefer to speak of an outmoded intolerance common to conventional and politically correct Parisian circles. In fact, the question is whether one thinks one can be both a Marxist and a historian nowadays. On that matter, the responsible French editors reply that Marxism isn't in the contemporary atmosphere any more. In *their* atmosphere, we should more properly say! It's all the same a little shocking to see how a little intellectual elite is deciding what's good or not for the French public.[124]

As the Paris-based Italian historian Enzo Traverso commented, surely it was the duty of publishers also to 'resist the atmosphere of the times': if this were not the case, then Pantheon Books would never have published criticisms of McCarthyism in the early 1950s, Einaudi would have remained silent during the Fascist years in Italy and German exiles would not have published a word between 1933 and 1945.[125] Writing in *Le Monde*, the critic Philippe-Jean Catinchi declared that the book had indeed become 'a symbol of resistance to an ideological hold [over French publishing] of which Pierre Nora, editor at Gallimard and director of the periodical *Le Débat*, is the incarnation'.[126] It was not irrelevant, besides, that Nora was Furet's brother-in-law. Certainly, noted the journalist Robert Verdussen, *Age of Extremes* was characterised by a certain indulgence towards Communism; its detractors were not always wrong in this respect. However, it had an astonishing relevance to its analysis of capitalism and consumerism and the book was worth reading for this alone.[127]

The French translation, carefully checked by Eric, and subsidised in part by *Le Monde Diplomatique*, appeared finally in October 1999.[128] An elaborate programme of radio and television appearances was prepared for the last days of October in Paris, involving public discussions with leading French intellectuals such as Marc Ferro and Alain Finkielkraut, as well as a debate with Pierre Nora, to the latter's credit.[129] On 29 October, addressing a packed audience at the official launch, organised by *Le Monde Diplomatique* in the Grand Amphitheatre of the Sorbonne, in his usual fluent, and by now, according to Bruce Hunter, 'rather old-fashioned French, but beautiful, and perfect, and easily understood', Eric fired both barrels of his polemical shotgun at the French intellectual establishment.[130] His book, he declared,

was published in all the languages of the European Union except one: and in the languages of the former communist states of central and eastern Europe: in Polish, in Czech, in Magyar, in Romanian, in Slovenian, in Serbo-Croat and in Albanian. But until today, not in French. In contradistinction to editors in

Lithuania (3.7 million inhabitants), Moldavia (4.3 million) and Iceland (270,000), editors in France (60 million) do not appear to have deemed it possible or desirable to translate the book into their language.[131]

Yet many of his previous books had been published in French, he pointed out, and some had even appeared as paperbacks. Why then not this one? Eric poured scorn on Nora's claim that anti-Communism in France was currently irresistible because French Communism had been Stalinist for longer than any other. He rejected the view that his retrospective allegiance to the Communist cause fitted badly into the atmosphere of the times. As he had already tried in vain to point out, *Age of Extremes* was not conceived as a defence of Communism, it was a history of the twentieth century. He ended by pointedly thanking not only his publisher and translator but also his 'Parisian friends who in the last few years have proved that not all French intellectuals have viewed with a malevolent eye the fact that their compatriots might read the work of authors who did not enjoy the favour of the fashionable orthodoxies of the nineties'.[132]

The row, which aroused comment far beyond the borders of France,[133] certainly wasn't about money, as he told an Italian newspaper when the Belgian contract had been signed. 'It will flood the Parisian bookshops ... earning more or less the same as the English, German or Italian publishers have, that is to say, a lot. It sounds like a story from the Cold War', he added, incredulously, 'yet it has happened at the end of the century.'[134] And indeed, after such a public and prolonged row – dubbed ironically by one newspaper as 'l'affairette Hobsbawn [*sic*]'[135] – generating considerable publicity even before its appearance, the book was bound to be a success in France, especially since *Le Monde Diplomatique* had opened a subscription list on which five thousand people had already enrolled themselves before the book was even out. It shot immediately onto the bestseller lists and was reprinted three times within a few weeks, selling forty thousand copies by the middle of November and prompting Eric's

Belgian publisher to commission French translations of some of his other books.[136]

Predictably, there was a good deal of criticism, much of it aggressive or even dismissive in tone. One review accused Eric of doing little more than writing a lengthy justification of his career as a Communist and described his polemic against Furet and Nora as an act of 'cultural terrorism' that recalled the show trials of the 1950s.[137] Another, after declaring that all Communist Parties had been tools of Moscow, advised readers to 'consider our new and our old progressives with the ironic indulgence that their impoverished justifications merit'.[138] Other reviewers, however, were more positive, and importantly Eric's publishers had managed to persuade several newspapers and journals to carry extracts from the book.[139] Some years later, however, the French edition got into a different kind of trouble as André Versaille left Complexe to set up on his own, and tried to take *Age of Extremes* with him, since Complexe were no longer selling the book. As Ania Corless noted in June 2008, however, this attempt to move the book to Versaille's new company elicited no response initially apart from legal threats accusing her of an 'abusive breach of contract'. No money had been received from Complexe since 2000. Yet Complexe were now demanding compensation from Eric in person because he had approved moving the book to the new company. 'It seems to me', Ania Corless wrote somewhat tartly to Complexe, 'that rather than the author being required to pay compensation, it is Éditions Complexe who should be paying money that is rightly due.' What Corless dubbed a 'ridiculous situation' was eventually resolved by Versaille, who generously paid Eric the missing royalties.[140]

V

The publication in England of *Age of Extremes* provided the occasion for two public broadcasts, no doubt organised by Eric's publishers. The first of these was *Desert Island Discs*, a popular and much-loved series that has been running since 1942, in which a prominent individual was asked to imagine that they had been cast away on a desert island with a gramophone and eight records. It was up to them to choose the eight, as well as a book (not the Bible or Shakespeare, which, it was assumed, the castaway already had), and a luxury, and in between extracts from the chosen pieces they were interviewed about their life and work. Eric's appearance on the programme was recorded on 24 January 1995 and transmitted on 5 March the same year, to coincide with the book's publication. His choice consisted of three jazz pieces – Charlie Parker's 'Parker's Mood', Billie Holiday's 'He's Funny That Way' and a piece by the Kenny Barron Trio – and five classical extracts, from Bach's Cantata number 80, 'Ein feste Burg ist unser Gott', which Eric chose because of its combative and optimistic nature; the first movement of Schubert's Quintet in C; the minuet from the last act of Offenbach's operetta *Orpheus in the Underworld*; the aria 'Casta diva' from Bellini's opera *Norma*; and Mahler's *Das Lied von der Erde*, where he asked for the final passage to be played, in which an alto voice fades away into eternity.[141] Jazz, while still important to him, thus, as always, occupied only a relatively small place in his musical life. As a luxury he chose a pair of binoculars with which to watch the birds, and as his book he picked a volume of poems in Spanish by Pablo Neruda, whom he had got to know in Chile many years before.

The presenter, the broadcaster Sue Lawley, focused above all on Eric's political beliefs, addressed him distantly as 'Professor Hobsbawm', and made no mention of his writings as an historian. She was unremittingly persistent in her questioning about Eric's political record, and the programme turned into an interrogation. If there had been a chance of bringing about the Communist utopia, then would it have been worth the sacrifice of millions of lives? she asked. Yes, he replied unhesitatingly, just as victory over Hitler in the Second World War had surely been worth the sacrifice of millions of lives. But he had not known about the true extent of Stalin's murderous purges in the 1930s, and if he had come across any reports of them he would not have believed them anyway (as, indeed, he had accepted Walter Duranty's denials of the Ukrainian famine at the time). It was clear that the dream had failed. Why did he still want to belong to the Communist Party after 1956 if he disapproved of so much of what it believed in and so much of what it had done in the past? Eric did his best to answer the increasingly hostile questioning from the normally anodyne Lawley, and reminisced about his time in Paris and Italy when introducing the records, but the atmosphere was frosty and listeners learned very little about Eric or his life. 'It's too bad', the economic historian Maxine Berg told Eric, 'that this programme ... had so little to ask you about your history writing, and so much about your politics.'[142] In the end, listeners were bound to wonder why Eric had been invited onto the programme at all.

He was also the subject of a lengthy television interview by the Canadian writer and public intellectual Michael Ignatieff, conducted a few months earlier. Here again, he came close to confessing that he still thought the Communist utopia worth the sacrifice of the millions killed in its name. The passage needs to be read carefully, as much for what Eric does not say as for what he does:

IGNATIEFF: In 1934, millions of people are dying in the Soviet experiment. If you had known that, would it have made a difference to you at that time? To your commitment? To being a Communist?

HOBSBAWM: ... Probably not.

IGNATIEFF: Why?

HOBSBAWM: Because in a period in which, as you might imagine, mass murder and mass suffering are absolutely universal, the chance of a new world being born in great suffering would still have been worth backing ... The sacrifices were enormous; they were excessive by almost any standard and excessively great. But I'm looking back at it now and I'm saying that because it turns out that the Soviet Union was not the beginning of the world revolution. Had it been, I'm not sure.

IGNATIEFF: What that comes down to is saying that had the
radiant tomorrow actually been created, the loss
of fifteen, twenty million people might have been
justified?

HOBSBAWM: Yes.

But, of course, as Eric admitted, the radiant tomorrow had not
been created. His apparent defence of the mass murders carried
out in Stalin's name was based on a hypothetical statement, not on
what had actually happened.[143]

Eric found Michael Ignatieff's television interview with him
'deeply hostile'.[144] This view was shared by the programme's producer, David Herman, who apologised to Eric, saying he was 'sorry
that the final programme had a more confrontational edge than the
original interview'. *The Times* commented that it was very tough but
Eric emerged from it well. But, of course, the editor had chosen the
most dramatic, or in other words, the most aggressive sections from
what was originally a much lengthier discussion, since they made
the best television. 'The programme', Eric wrote to Herman, 'was
not intended as a bullfight, even one in which the bull managed to
hold his own. I don't think it was fair to either Michael or me, let
alone to the book which was its ostensible subject. Still', he added,
'a surprising number of people saw it, and some went out to buy
the book, so I suppose I must thank you for some effective publicity.
And those who court publicity must pay a price.'[145]

The two interviews reflected a new, post-Cold War hostility
among growing numbers of journalists to the Communist cause,
which was easy enough to criticise now that it had been defeated.
'I am now being interviewed so often', Eric complained in June
1997, 'that I have what might be called "interview fatigue".'[146] Yet
he reacted to interviewers like Lawley and Ignatieff with unfail-
ing courtesy as he defended his lifelong political allegiance to the
principle, though not the practice, of Communism. His faith in the
cause, he confessed, had made him reluctant to criticise it:

While I hope I have never written or said anything about the

Soviet Union that I should feel guilty about, I have tended to avoid dealing with it directly, because I knew that if I had, I would have had to have written things that would have been difficult for a communist to say without affecting my political activity and the feelings of my comrades. This is also why I chose to become a nineteenth-century historian rather than a twentieth-century one. Thus I didn't want to be involved in debates that would either have taken me over onto the other side, or have brought me into conflict with my conscience as an academic.[147]

Yet he conceded that the suffering and death inflicted by Stalin could not 'be anything but shameful and beyond palliation, let alone justification', not least in view of the fact that the promised utopia never arrived and was never likely to:

I have never tried to diminish the appalling things that happened in Russia, though the sheer extent of the massacres we didn't realise … In the early days we knew a new world was being born amid blood and tears and horror: revolution, civil war, famine – we knew of the Volga famine of the early '20s, if not the early '30s. Thanks to the breakdown of the west, we had the illusion that even this brutal, experimental, system was going to work better than the west. It was that or nothing.

It had indeed been an illusion, but people needed to think themselves back into the dark days of the 1930s, when the choice seemed increasingly to be Communism or fascism, and in that situation, nobody who thought rationally could have preferred the latter.

VI

Once he had finished *Age of Extremes*, Eric moved his teaching at the New School from twentieth-century history onto other subjects. He taught a course on 'Historiography and Historical Practice: Revolutions: Meanings and Methods of Historians' at the New

School in the Fall Semester of 1993, with assistant instructor Aldo Lauria-Santiago. The course aimed to explore how historians explained and conceptualised revolutions of one kind and another in Europe and Latin America since the seventeenth century – a theme that would have appeared in the book on revolutions he had once signed up to write. The students had to write critical reviews of the assigned work and also an extended historiographical essay. He also taught a course with Louise Tilly, dealing with historical epistemology and methodology, assigning work by E. H. Carr, Max Weber, Fernand Braudel, Georges Lefebvre and others on topics such as Marxist analysis, historical sociology, ethnography, labour history, family history and so on. The ten students who handed in their evaluations rated the course well above the average of 3 on a scale of 1 to 5, with a mean of 4, and declared themselves willing to recommend the course to their peers. One commented that the course was rather fragmented though 'the instructors were quite good scholars' (meaning very good scholars).[148] In 1994 he taught a kind of amalgam of the two courses with Margaret Jacob, an historian of science.[149]

He also ran a weekly research seminar at the Center for Studies of Social Change with Charles ('Chuck') Tilly. As his research assistant Lise Grande, who attended it regularly, recalled,

A lot of people had come to the New School to be with Eric. So in the seminar you would have what we referred to quite derisively as the N[ew] Y[ork] U[niversity]-type people [historical sociologists], all sort of around Chuck. Jeff Goodwin [NYU sociologist] was there and Theda Scokpol [Harvard sociologist] would come down from Cambridge [Mass.], so there was that kind of crowd there. And then you had all these left-wing students who came from Peru and, you know, from Malawi, and they were all there to study with Eric. You had another part of the faculty, the anthropologists, who were all preoccupied with postmodernism and signifiers and all that. Eric was very derisive of it. If any of them applied to be in his seminar he was, like, 'Once you're serious, you want to talk about something real, then you can come in.' So those people were kept at bay, but the real battle was between what he found to be an overly institutional-focused neutral sociology embodied by [Chuck Tilly] – he respected Chuck enormously, but he felt that was a diminishment of the great questions of the day . . . What a gift to be there.[150]

'So many people wanted to come', she recalled, 'that seminar was packed.' Eric's standards were notoriously high: he did not suffer fools gladly, and could be hard on participants in his courses who he felt did not come up to scratch. In private, however, he took great pains over the weaker students. 'So you saw this kind of extraordinary effort to maintain a very high public standard, and then the generosity and kindness of the person who you dealt with day in and day out.'

In 1995, Eric announced that he was going to give up his teaching at the New School after one more semester.[151] 'Staying for a complete semester had been quite a strain recently – especially on Marlene, who can't drop her work to come to NY for four months. I'm now 78 and am told by the medicals that I have to cut down a bit. So that's what I propose to do.'[152] The Dean, Judith Friedlander, offered a reduced appointment involving three to four weeks each Fall Semester for three years, a public lecture each time, and a graduate seminar, all for a total of $20,000 plus expenses.[153] Eric agreed.[154] That year, he taught a reduced course at the New School on 'The West in Global Perspective'. He returned for the following two years to do the same, before finally retiring altogether.[155]

He continued his active social life while he was in New York. A particular high point was a dinner party thrown by the Mexican novelist Carlos Fuentes on 11 November 1998 to celebrate his seventieth birthday. Other guests included the critic and essayist Susan Sontag, the historian Fritz Stern, the playwright Arthur Miller and the political scientist Richard Sennett.[156] Arthur Schlesinger Jr, who had known Eric from the days when they were both at Cambridge in the late 1930s, was also there, and recorded the occasion in his diary:

On Monday night we had a really good dinner party – Carlos Fuentes ... and Sylvia, Edna O'Brien, Murray Kempton and Barbara Epstein, Aubrey (Abba) and Susie Eban, Eric Hobsbawm, Brian and Sidney Urquhart, Ronald and Betsy Dworkin. It was a tremendous success. Much general conversation: Eban on Israel and the Palestinians, 'There is a tunnel at the end of the light' ... Eric describing the three breakdowns of the 20th century, 1918, 1945 and 1989, of which, he claimed, the last was the worst. His measure seemed to be industrial output which, he said, recovered much faster after the two world wars than it is recovering today. I said that 1918 seemed worse in its psychological shocks – the end of European self-confidence, the rising doubts about democracy, the emergence of fascism and communism. Eric still insisted that 1989 was the worst. Murray Kempton whispered to me, 'the last Stalinist.' True in a way, though I remain fond of Eric.[157]

But by this time Eric's years of teaching at the New School were coming to an end. There were a number of reasons apart from age why he did not try to renew his contract after 1998.

To begin with, the atmosphere in the academic world, at least in America, was no longer one he found congenial. Judith Friedlander noted Eric's 'total impatience with political correctness. He didn't mince words.'[158] On occasion, this could get him into trouble. A student complained (anonymously, needless to say) to her about what he or she considered his 'racist humour' in remarking during his class on Nationalism, Ethnicity and the State: 'Well let's call the spade [probably: a spade a spade]. I hope you will forgive me this very small joke, but speaking of African Americans ... ' This, the complainant thundered, was 'appalling' and a 'naked abuse of intellectual privilege and legitimacy'. A few lines later the single remark had become plural ('racially insulting comments'), though no other example was provided.[159] It is difficult, however, to see how the use of the term 'spade' could have been intended as a racial slur, given its use in the jazz world of the 1950s where Eric had learned it: the complaint (which was without consequences) showed how carefully one had to tread in the minefield of American racial politics in the 1990s. Not that Eric was particularly bothered by this. As Friedlander recalled, 'his strong commitment to seeing the world historically through a class analysis blew holes in the essentialism of the rising hegemony of "cultural relativism". For those foolish enough to take it on, they got it between the eyes.'[160]

By 1997–8 Eric felt that the New School was no longer what it had been when he had joined over a decade before. In the mid-nineties it had gone through some financial difficulties and had to make savings. The management relocated the Committee on Historical Studies from its dilapidated but agreeable premises to an ugly new building with restricted hours of access. Charles Tilly, in his wife's words, was 'so upset about the lack of support for the Center [for Studies of Social Change] and [the Committee on] Historical Studies' that he resigned in 1996 and took a Chair at Columbia University. Margaret Jacob also left for the University of Pennsylvania.' This left Louise Tilly, Chair of the Committee on Historical Studies, desperate to find people to teach the courses.[161] In fact, as she told Eric, the Committee was 'being drastically downsized, and although I will still have a small budget, basically it is being folded'. It was clear 'that there is not much support among the faculty for Historical Studies as we conceived it'.[162] Moreover, the staff shortage had been made worse by the sudden and unexpected death of one of the faculty members. Louise Tilly had approached Eric early in 1996 with a view to filling at least part of the gap, and he had agreed to the Dean's formal request to continue teaching for the time being.[163]

With the loyalty to his friends that was so typical of him, Eric was outraged by these changes. When the New School threw a party in 1997 for his eightieth birthday, Jonathan Fanton, as President, and Judith Friedlander, as Dean, gave brief speeches in Eric's honour. Friedlander, perhaps incautiously, praised him for 'always speaking his mind, for refusing to play by the rules'. For Eric, this was too good an opportunity to miss. 'After I finished', Friedlander recalled,

Eric rose and blasted Jonathan and me for having destroyed Historical Studies and chased his dear friend Charles Tilly from the New School ... This was not the occasion in conventional society to discuss Chuck's very upsetting departure, and, needless to say, the circumstances surrounding Chuck's decision were a great deal more complicated than what Eric's accusation implied ... Eric, faithful Eric, accepted Chuck's side of the story without ever coming to speak to me or Jonathan. And he used his eightieth birthday party to let us know how he felt about it.[164]

Charles Tilly's motives were indeed far from simple; quite apart from anything else, his move to Columbia was in part prompted by his decision to separate from his wife, and continuing to work with her in the same department would have been difficult. In fact, the Committee on Historical Studies survived, as did its faculty, who currently number nine, with a larger number of affiliated teachers.

Eric's loyalty could also be observed in the continuation of his friendship with the American Marxist historian Eugene D. Genovese, author of brilliant Gramscian studies of slavery and slave ownership in the antebellum South, despite Genovese's sharp move to the right at this time, despite even his conversion to Catholicism. A key influence on Genovese's change of position was a bitter controversy involving his wife, Elizabeth ('Betsey') Fox-Genovese, also an historian, who was undergoing a similar transition, ending by becoming perhaps America's leading 'conservative feminist'. In 1992 she was fired by Emory University from the directorship of its Women's Studies Program, of which she was the founder. The programme, Eugene complained, was now being 'handed over to those deemed politically correct'.[165] On hearing of the university's failure to support Fox-Genovese, Eric was outraged.

I would have hoped that a) even feminists who don't agree with Betsey appreciate her contribution, not to mention her distinction; and b) that Emory would have had the nerve to resist the extremes of p.c. The trouble about feminism, or whatever trend in feminism is at the moment orthodox, is that nobody – right or left – in a democracy wants to get on the wrong side of half the voters. However lunatic the views of those who claim to speak in their name – and I know of no intelligent person anywhere in politics who will not privately admit that much of that stuff is plain silly – nobody wants to risk being tagged an enemy of women ... You may say, realistically – I've said so myself tactfully (but not tactfully enough to avoid being tagged as a known 'anti-feminist') – that you won't get a majority of women voting for compulsory one-parent lesbianism, or whatever the slogan may be. However, in democracies with notoriously low political participation ... even crazy feminists are feared, because they might actually control packets of votes which might turn out to be vital ... None of this makes what has happened to Betsey other than totally intolerable. She has my profoundest sympathy.[166]

Ultimately Eric saw the kind of feminism he thought was represented by Betsey's critics as an outcome of 1968, which had regrettably replaced the traditional Left with new social movements ('feminism, greens, rainbow coalitions, gays/lesbians etc') that were 'the opposite of marxist' since what they offered was 'radicalisation, mindless, libertarian and often basically individualist (i.e. anti-social)'. '1968 radicalism provided and provides no basis for progressive politics', he concluded.[167] Here was another reason for Eric's decision to bring his period at the New School to an end.

VII

Back at home in England, Eric's life continued in what had by now become a regular routine. He spent much if not most of his time writing, well into his eighties. He described the process of writing and research in 1997, in response to an enquiry from William Palmer, a professor at Marshall University in the USA who was preparing his book *Engagement with the Past: The World War II*

Generation of Historians, published in 2001. London was exceptionally well provided with great libraries, Eric told Palmer, but when
he was out of the country lecturing or at conferences he was often
close to good library resources too – an indication of how he spent
his free time when he was abroad, probably a necessity if he was
ever going to finish any of his books, given the amount of travelling
he undertook. Deadlines helped give his preparations a sense of
urgency, and sometimes he was able to use research assistants. 'I've
built a lot of my books on courses of lectures, mainly to students.'

> Though I belong to the filing-card generation, I've never felt
> comfortable with cards. For research I've used a combination
> of files on specific subjects, fairly elaborately indexed notebooks
> with what until recently was a pretty good memory. For a book
> I'd get out the relevant notes from my old research-files, do a
> lot of ad hoc reading, and start writing, surrounded by piles of
> books and notes. I usually start drafting early, and read to fill
> in the gaps in knowledge or argument. I rarely draft in the final
> order of chapters. In what order they are written, varies.[168]

There was a lot of crossing-out and changing during the writing process. 'When I wrote on a typewriter, as I have done since
undergraduate days, I used to start pages, half-write them, tear
them out – the usual thing.'
His experience of journalism, starting many decades ago with
his school magazine, gave him an innate sense of how to pace his
writing to fit the required length.

> Getting a feel for length is a help to good writing. Writing a lot is
> essential. And, in my view, remembering that you are trying to
> make yourself clear to readers who are not necessarily experts.
> Writing to impress other academics is easy. I've tried it from
> time to time, but once one has an established position it isn't
> necessary any more.

The historians Eric admitted to admiring were mostly

French – Marc Bloch, the medievalist Georges Duby, Georges Lefebvre, Fernand Braudel – but he also acknowledged the greatness of the English legal historian F. W. Maitland. However, he confessed, 'I haven't developed my prose-style by reading historians, though there have been some very stylish ones in Britain. I've always regarded Bernard Shaw as a model of what an intelligent man can do with prose: I had to read all his writings for my doctoral thesis.' And he was lucky, he wrote, in having worked at Birkbeck, where teaching only took place from six to nine in the evening and so left the days free for writing and research.

> I read at any time libraries or archives are open or books are available, but I am usually too tired to write in the evenings. Morning is my best time, which raises problems as I am not an early riser. However, it takes a few weeks to get into a book. When I have got into top gear, is probably the only time I can go on writing into the night. I used to smoke a pipe while I wrote, but not for a good many years. When I run dry I go for a walk, into a library, or give up till next day.

The evenings were for socialising, or relaxing in front of the television or reading a book, or in one of the dinner parties he and Marlene regularly threw at Nassington Road.

The children, Andy and Julia, both born in the 1960s, had by now grown up and were forging careers and building lives of their own. In 1993, after working as a researcher in television, Julia set up a PR firm, with Sarah Macaulay, an old school friend.[169] Known as Hobsbawm Macaulay Communications, it mostly had clients on the Left, including the Labour Party, the *New Statesman* and several trade unions. Through her work, Sarah Macaulay met, and became the partner of, the Labour Party politician Gordon Brown, Shadow Chancellor of the Exchequer for most of the 1990s, and Chancellor from the moment when Labour won the General Election of 1997. They thus became part of Eric and Marlene's social circle. One evening, Eric's former student and research assistant at the New School, Lise

Grande, flew in from Tajikistan, where she had been working for the United Nations, and arrived late for dinner at Nassington Road. She came into the middle of a lively conversation at the dining table about the Maastricht Treaty (1992), which had laid the foundations for further steps towards European integration, including the creation of a monetary union. She was particularly taken with the knowledgeable and competent contributions of one of the participants in the conversation, a Scotsman whom everyone called Gordon:

> He's describing the Euro and the currency and all of this, and I found this all very interesting, so at the end I said: 'My God, that's really extraordinary. I've never understood that. What is it you do, Gordon?' And the whole table, including Eric, burst into laughter, and . . . Gordon Brown says 'I'm the Chancellor of the Exchequer', and Eric's response was brilliant: he says, 'Well, probably we can safely say that this is the first time in many years that anyone would call the Chancellor of the Exchequer competent!'[170]

Sarah Macaulay and Gordon Brown married in 2000, and Brown remained Chancellor until he succeeded Tony Blair as Prime Minister in 2007. Julia moved on to found the knowledge networking company Editorial Intelligence.

Andy Hobsbawm joined a rock band, Tin Gods, after leaving school, then worked for a magazine publisher before moving into digital media and forming a company, Online Magic, in 1995. After it was taken over by Agency.com he worked for the new owners, becoming chairman of the European operations and then, some time later, co-founding the sustainability non-profit Do The Green Thing and internet of things software company Everything. Eric bought a flat for Andy for £30,000 early in 1990, and sought ways of minimising the tax consequences of the gift, perhaps as 'an interest-free loan which could be diminished every year by the allowable amount of gifts to him'.[171] Andy repaid him at a rate of £100 a month, though he still occasionally had to ask Eric for money to pay his tax bills until he became successful in his new career.[172] Both Andy and Julia wrote; Andy was new media correspondent for the *Financial Times* for a while, and Julia produced three books on life-work balance, communications and networking.

In the meantime, Eric's son with Marion Bennathan, Joss, had completed his A levels and taken an American Studies degree at the University of Sussex, after which he studied acting in Philadelphia then returned to the UK to train as a drama teacher. He forged a successful career in theatrical production and education, working closely with school students, especially in London's East End, where he created the Theatre Lab and founded his own company, Present Moment.[173] Before these achievements, Joss had been a difficult teenager. He had been told at the age of fourteen that Eric was his father, and this seems for a time to have blown him off course. He moved out of home at the age of sixteen to live with his girlfriend Jenny Corrick, also sixteen, marrying her in 1976; they had a daughter, Ella, and a son, Matthias, despite Eric's strong advice to put off having children because it would interfere with their studies. The relationship did not last, ending in divorce. In 1991, Joss wrote to Eric informing him that the secret of his own parentage had somehow leaked out to his own children: 'Matty and Ella asked if I knew who my biological father was so I told them the story. I know that, in the past, you have wanted to see them. I also know that I, like my mother before me, have worried that the resemblance might be noticed.' They were Eric's first grandchildren. So now there was no obstacle to Eric contacting them, though he did not need to feel responsible for them in any way, and the children did not feel any need for a replacement grandfather. 'They understand', Joss added, 'that your own children don't know about me, or them, and why.'[174]

He continued:

There is a certain irony in the fact that they find out at more or less the age I did. However, the information is clearly of less immediate significance for them than it was for me. I told them, after much thought and discussion with Jenny, for various reasons. The thought of them finding out accidentally was unimaginably ghastly. It is also, simply, something about me which it seems right and proper that they should know, in the same way that we all know things about our parents' childhoods and experiences. Partly, too, it was for me. The concealment and secrecy left me with feelings of guilt and shame which it has taken me years to begin to come to terms with. (These feelings were and are irrational, but that's not the point. Of course, Mum and Dad had no intentions of making me feel like that. Equally obviously, you had no part in it.) Telling Ella and Matty is part of my healing process, an assertion that I have nothing to be ashamed of. As I said to them, they should think of it as having more to do with the peculiar nature of their grandparents' relationship.

Joss Bennathan died of cancer in 2014 at the early age of fifty-six, leaving a strong legacy in the field of theatre education, among other things through his book *Making Theatre: The Frazzled Drama Teacher's Guide to Devising* (2013).[175]

Eric's sister Nancy and her husband Victor had moved many years before to the West Country, where she had become secretary to Peter Walker, a Conservative Member of Parliament and sometime Minister. Later, they had moved again, to Menorca, for their retirement.[176] A heavy smoker, Nancy had suffered lung problems for some time, and in 1990 she fell seriously ill. Victor summoned their daughter Anne to care for her, but her condition worsened and within a few months she was dead. Their son Robin remembered phoning Eric to give him the news: 'I was the one who had to tell him that my mother had died', he said, and 'he burst into tears. I was quite stunned, I remember going out to the 'phone box, "I've just got to tell you Mum's died" and he went into floods of tears.' 'And coincidentally we were on the same flight to go to the funeral, except he was in first class and ... when we got to Palma, we had a couple of hours' break, and I went, "Oh, First

Class, Eric," and he went, "I couldn't get an ordinary ticket!"' It was the Easter break, and the standard class seats had all been booked. When they arrived, Anne thanked Eric for coming. 'I just had to say goodbye to her', he said. Despite the very different trajectories their lives had taken, they were still tied together by the close emotional bonds forged by their childhood years and the early death of their parents.[177]

VIII

Appropriately enough, Eric celebrated his eightieth birthday by publishing a lengthy introduction to a new edition of *The Communist Manifesto*, issued by Verso (New Left Books) to mark the 150th anniversary of the tract's first publication. But this was no ordinary reprint. Surprisingly, perhaps, the book quickly attracted a great deal of attention, and reached number three on the bestseller list of the *Village Voice*, the house magazine of New York's Greenwich Village. Perhaps this was because the book appeared in 'a stylish new edition' which aimed 'to make Karl Marx and Friedrich Engels the latest in radical chic'. It was issued in a smart matt-black cover with a glossy red flag filling most of the available space, and the title, authors and editor (Eric) in elegant white lettering below.[178] An ironically phrased news release from the Associated Press news agency, sent to more than 250 American newspapers and magazines, noted that twenty thousand copies had been printed, with the aim of capitalising on a feeling 'on Wall Street that the party can't go on forever':

'With a handle attached, the book could make a snazzy accessory to a designer dress', says Simon Doonan, creative director of Barneys. 'One could sashay toward the new millennium, the 19th-century words of Marx and Engels dangling at one's side.' Doonan is toying with the idea of featuring the 'Manifesto' – along with red lipsticks – in the window as 'conceptual art'. His assistants are looking for the right lipstick – preferably with a Russian-sounding name. With communism gasping around the

world, 'It's OK to look at the book as camp', he says. Around
Wall Street, the very capital of capitalism, the Borders bookstore
at the World Trade Center plans to give the book center display
in the front of the store. Barnes & Noble will likewise market the
'Manifesto' at its 483 superstores as 'a storefront feature'. The
new edition was designed by two trendy, Soviet-born, New York
artists known as Komar and Melamid. With crimson end pages
and a ribbon marker of the same color, 'it's elegant enough to
grace a coffee table', [Colin] Robinson [of Verso] says. That's
not quite what its authors had in mind.[179]

Robinson told another reporter that 'the tome is slim enough
to fit into the pocket of a Donna Karan dress "without ruining
the line"'. 'Consumers of the world, unite!' ran the headline in
the report: 'We have nothing to lose but our credit cards.'[180] 'Karl
Marx', another reporter declared, 'has become a cuddly, kitschy,
innocuous object of fun, nostalgia and irony', not unlike the iconic
poster of Che Guevara, once to be found on every student's wall
and now used among other things to promote Swatch watches,
skis and the like.[181]

Left-wing critics were not amused. The new edition commercialised and trivialised revolutionary ideas, emasculating their
radicalism in the process, they charged. Barbara Ehrenreich,
biographer of Rosa Luxemburg, decried the 'sybaritic classes' of
New York 'mincing about with their designer copies'. The *Manifesto*,
she declared, had become 'an accessory, a stocking-stuffer, a badge
of consummate capitalist cool'. Still: 'At a mere 96 pages, you can
think of it as a greeting card, or even a kind of wake-up call, for
that special person in your life – such as, for example, your boss.'[182]
Why shouldn't the Left use modern commercialism to propagate
its ideas? others asked. 'Marx was hardly busting anyone's chains
sandwiched in the basement political-science section between
Herbert Marcuse and Charles Murphy, but damn it, he was gathering dust with *dignity*.' Maybe it was time to brush him off and
put him out again into the marketplace of ideas.[183] Reviewers were
indeed struck by the book's contemporary resonances:

The world described in the *Manifesto* is the world of electronic
fund transfers and maquiladoras, of banks merging and
Indonesian sweatshops sending Nikes to Van Nuys, of the
International Monetary Fund compelling Korea to discharge
its workers, of the management of Mercedes relocating its plants
to cheaper climes, forcing Germany to lower its wages. It is, in
short, the world of 1998.[184]

Or, to put it another way, at the height of the massive wave of
globalisation that followed the fall of the Berlin Wall, the *Manifesto*,
if its principles were adjusted to the new structure of global capitalism (not too hard a task), had a new and undeniable relevance
in the present day.[185]

So widespread was the publicity given to the new edition that
the *Sacramento Bee* found it necessary to publish a list of '19 myths
about Marx', beginning with what it evidently thought was a
common belief that 'Marx was Russian', continuing with further
misconceptions such as the claim that 'Marx sent spies to start the
Russian revolution'.[186] Together with a new deal with a major US
publisher, W. W. Norton, the reissue boosted Verso's profits and
joined the house's edition of Che Guevara's *Motorcycle Diaries* on the
bestseller lists.[187] Perhaps, too, some people who bought the book
actually read it and thought about its ideas and did not just have
it peeping out of the top of their Gucci handbags: 'Marx's Stock',
declared the *New York Times*, 'Resurges on a 150-Year Tip'.[188] The
publicity attending the 150th anniversary and the reissue of the
Manifesto certainly did a good deal to underline the relevance of
Marx's analysis of capitalism to the 1990s and perhaps also fuelled
the anxieties that were building up towards the end of the millennium. 'Marx's view of free enterprise', reported one commentator,
'is now being echoed by many businessmen who would rather be
flogged than labeled Marxists.'[189]

The book was a huge success in the UK as well as in America.
However, Eric's agent discovered more than twelve years after
publication that Verso had failed to pay Eric any of the royalties
he was due. Hardly any of their books generated any significant

income, so perhaps this was merely due to an oversight. 'It does', the David Higham agency told them, 'seem an unfortunate habit of Verso's that whenever you had a success it's the author who gets penalized.' In June 2011 they replied with some embarrassment, admitting that 'this is of course a great aberration on Verso's part, and one that we're keen to put right. The amount concerned is substantial (£20,678.19). Unfortunately, Verso is not in a position to pay the entire amount in full, immediately.' Perhaps he would be willing to accept an initial payment of £10,000 with the rest following in instalments? Eric's agent was sceptical: 'I am getting the usual sob story of how they can't afford to just pay over a lump sum like this in one go', he told Eric. But Eric, who was well aware of Verso's financial difficulties, proposed instead that the payments be made in four tranches of just over £5000 each, a suggestion accepted with relief by the publisher.[190]

Eric also published a collection of twenty-one of his essays on problems of historiography, with the title *On History* – he taught his last courses at the New School as part of preparations for the book. He signed a contract for it with his old publisher Weidenfeld & Nicolson, though the paperback rights went to Abacus, part of the Little, Brown Group. The collection included a number of discussions of Marxism and history, the *Annales*, 'identity history' and postmodernism. One of the longest and most penetrating reviews of the collection came from the pen of Eric's old antagonist Hugh Trevor-Roper, now in his mid-eighties. Trevor-Roper paid tribute not only to Eric's erudition and sophistication, but also to the influence of Marx on historians in general:

> He gave to our subject a new organizing philosophy and gave it at a time when it was most needed: when the material of history had become overwhelming and previous historical philosophies were running dry. His influence has been immense and fruit-ful: some of the most stimulating of modern historians have responded to it, directly or indirectly.[191]

Of course, he added, Marx picked up on, and in some ways

distorted, broader currents of German historical and philosophical thinking, as indeed did the *Annales* school, which *On History* duly acknowledged with a generosity denied to such thinkers as Tocqueville or Weber. Still, while Soviet Communism solidified the Marxist tradition into a sterile orthodoxy, 'in the West it flowed freely, mingling with other currents: a fertilizing stream'. In the end, Trevor-Roper thought that Eric's Communism could and should be separated from his Marxism, which, 'as a contribution to historical philosophy', might 'continue, revised and modified, to enrich our studies'.

Further critical analysis of *On History*'s approach to the theory and practice of historical research and writing was provided by the medievalist John Arnold, who pointed out that Eric's claim in the book (referring to the misuse of history for purposes of nationalist mythmaking and aggression) that 'the sentences typed on apparently innocuous keyboards may be sentences of death' was an example of the postmodernist claim that language constructs reality which elsewhere in the book Eric spent so much time deriding.[192] In fact, of course, Eric's lifelong fascination with language, his frequent lists of words belonging to new worlds he was discovering, his analysis of the invention of national languages as tools in the formation of national consciousness, all pointed to the fact that he was lumping together extreme and moderate versions of postmodernism in his condemnation of a discourse-based approach to historical writing: in his own practice as an historian, he repeatedly demonstrated that language constructed reality, though it did not, however, replace it.

The collection was translated into fifteen languages. Reviewing the German edition, Jürgen Kocka noted that 'As an historian, Hobsbawm was far removed from the Party Marxism of the Communists. One would be hard put to find even the traces of dogmatism.' He had, Kocka continued, for a long time dismissed the basis-superstructure scheme as mere 'vulgar Marxism' – a view shared by many reviewers; indeed, the British historian Paul Smith's discussion of the book in the *Times Literary Supplement* was carried under the headline 'No vulgar Marxist'.[193] As Kocka observed, cultural history fascinated Eric far too much to allow him to apply crude economic determinism to the past. He had always respected the facts, but the advent of postmodernist hyper-relativism had led to a change from an earlier, critical view of history as a backward discipline because of its fixation on the facts, to a tendency, increasingly pronounced in the 1990s, to declare that historical evidence must be the foundation for historical investigation.[194]

These views also emerged in *Uncommon People: Resistance, Rebellion, and Jazz* (1998), the long-planned follow-up to *Revolutionaries* (1973), and published by Weidenfeld & Nicolson, with a paperback edition produced once more by Abacus. His second collection of non-academic essays demonstrated yet again Eric's alienation from the student rebellion of 1968, his disapproval of the preoccupation of young radicals with sex and his rejection of the development of popular culture since the advent of the Beatles.[195] Without any real unifying theme, and eclectic in its coverage, the book did not do as well as his earlier works, and only appeared in half a dozen foreign languages, though that was still many more than the vast majority of history books published in the UK. The title *Uncommon People*, as John Horne, a Dublin-based historian of modern France, pointed out, 'pays tribute to a classic of British working-class history from which it also marks its distance'. (The work in question was G. D. H. Cole and Raymond Postgate's *The Common People* (1938).) Eric's new book reframed that classic's central argument, that ordinary people and popular movements were the real narrative of British history.

Many reviewers were startled by Eric's hostility in the collection to avant-garde art and music, also expressed in his Walter Neurath Memorial Lecture in 1998, on what he called the decline and fall of the twentieth-century avant-gardes. Here he argued that modern painting had lost its way because it was tied to traditional modes of production, in particular to the idea of the single artwork produced by a single creator, while the real artistic revolutions had come from mass advertising and from cinema. 'A real world, flooding every waking hour with a chaos of sounds, images, symbols, presumptions of a common experience, had put art as a special activity out of business.' The most original artwork produced between the wars, he declared, was the London Underground Map.[196] The lecture revealed a persistent blind spot in Eric's mental and emotional world, one that seemed to have become even more marked since the days when he had regarded Picasso as a great artist.

By the time *Uncommon People* was published the twentieth century was drawing to a close, and in January 1999 the journalist Antonio Polito suggested to Eric a long interview, or series of interviews, in Italian, on 'the end of the century'.[197] The interviews took place shortly after, and were published in English the following year as *The New Century*. Eric used the opportunity to castigate the growth of social inequality, the weakness of global institutions, the decline of political ideology, the degradation of the environment, the disorientation of the Left, the depoliticised, the young, the isolation brought on by a vanishing sense of social solidarity, and much more besides. The future of the public sphere, he concluded, 'was obscure. That is why, at the end of the century, I cannot look to the future with great optimism.'

How far was Eric's perspective still framed by Marxism? When asked by Polito what Marxism was, Eric replied that above all, it 'suggests that, in having understood that a particular historical stage is not permanent, human society is a successful structure because it is capable of change, and thus the present is not its point of arrival'. As Noel Malcolm not unfairly commented in a lengthy review for the *Sunday Telegraph*, 'Most ordinary readers will be blinking at that remark, either because it is a statement of the obvious, or because it does not clearly mean anything at all.' What happened, he asked, to class struggle? What happened to economic determinism? Instead, *The New Century* portrayed the driving forces of history as above all ideological. If Eric condemned the United States as an imperialist power and ascribed this to the long-term impact of the revolutionary ideology of the Declaration of Independence, it was 'to arrive at a Marxist conclusion', Malcolm noted, 'from a radically non-Marxist direction', deriving American

policy in the twenty-first century not from 'the economic imperatives of an advanced stage of capitalism' but from 'the ideas that
buzzed around in the heads of various bewigged gentlemen in the
1770s'. Eric seemed to have 'lost his ideological bearings ... One
can only wonder, therefore, how much guidance he really has to
offer us about the events of the century to come.'[198] Indeed, the
book looked back as much as, perhaps even more than, it looked
forward. Once again, he had to come to terms with his lifelong
commitment to the idea of Communism:

> Like many other communists, I never agreed with the terrible
> things that happened under [the Soviet] regime. But if you think
> that communism is something greater than the history of the
> backward countries in which it happened that communists got
> to power, then that history is not reason enough to abandon the
> chosen cause. Do I regret it? No, I don't think so.[199]

He had spent much of the decade justifying his political choices,
in books, articles and interviews, on radio and on television. As
the century came to an end, it was time, Eric felt, to look back
on his life and career at greater length. The next book he wrote,
yielding to the entreaties of his friends and colleagues, was to be
his autobiography.

10

'National Treasure'

1999–2012

I

'My editor', Eric told Elise Marienstras during a visit to Paris towards the end of the 1990s, 'is insisting absolutely that I write my autobiography, so, good, I'll do it, though I have no idea how.'[1] He put together a formal proposal, however, and sent it to Bruce Hunter. After a good deal of negotiation, the contract for Eric's memoirs went to Michael Joseph, which had been an imprint of the Penguin Books empire since 1985, for an advance of £90,000. They had already published *Age of Extremes*, much to the irritation of Weidenfeld & Nicolson, and it had been such a success that they were keen to secure Eric's memoirs as well. George Weidenfeld tried again to lure Eric back. But in the end, 'Weidenfeld', as Bruce Hunter reported, 'after all don't feel they can compete with Michael Joseph.'[2] This was, in effect, the end of his long relationship with George Weidenfeld. The fame he had acquired as an author in the 1990s had caused him to outgrow it.

A contract was duly drawn up. But in May 2000, as Bruce Hunter reported, 'Michael Joseph have now said to me that they are no longer the right publishers for this book.' Although they continued to bring memoirs onto the market, they were now concentrating on more commercially exploitable ones by stars from the worlds of showbiz and sport. Eric was not unhappy with this decision, since his original editor, Susan Watt, who had steered *Age of Extremes* successfully through the publication process, was no longer with the company and he did not want to work with more junior people. Besides, one particular editor had recently been making headlines and arousing Eric's admiration: Stuart Proffitt, now at the Penguin Press. Indeed, Hunter had initially thought he would make the ideal editor for *Age of Extremes*, but for the fact that he was working for Murdoch-owned HarperCollins. But in 1998, Proffitt, then in his mid-thirties, had resigned from HarperCollins because Murdoch had personally forced the company to spike the memoirs of Hong Kong's last colonial governor, Chris Patten, on the (unacknowledged) grounds that they were too critical of the Chinese, whom Murdoch wanted to keep onside. Proffitt was Patten's editor and created a major media storm by his angry and very public resignation in the face of what he saw as a betrayal by the company's owner. Eric's request for Proffitt to edit his memoirs was readily acceded to. It was a good choice. Proffitt was a meticulous editor and did much to improve the book in a lengthy series of meetings and exchanges of correspondence with Eric over the following months.

Eric completed the first draft relatively quickly, since by the time he came to write the book he was no longer teaching, and he was free from many of the other commitments that had slowed down his writing earlier in his career. The memoirs did not require much research; for much of the time Eric could rely on his own memory, supplemented by consultation of his early diaries and other documents, and, in any case, he had just completed *Age of Extremes*, on the same period and based on wide reading and research, so the background material was already there and did not need updating. Despite the rapidity with which he completed it, however, Eric found his memoirs 'the hardest book to write. How could I interest readers in an unspectacular academic life?' So he aimed the book at young readers who wanted to know something of what 'the most extraordinary century in history' was like, and also to 'those old enough to have passed through some of its passions, hopes, disillusions and dreams'.[3]

Not surprisingly, Stuart Proffitt found the first draft was 'in one way, a rewriting of *Age of Extremes* from the personal perspective'.[4] He felt that the memoirs said far too little about Eric's personal views, feelings and experiences. 'It was an outward-looking rather than inward-looking book.' So he felt that his task as Eric's editor was 'to ask him to reflect *internally* a bit more'. The book was about 'the public man, and the public life. So I tried to get him to say a bit more of the more intimate things; didn't get very far ... It wasn't very easy to have intimate conversations with Eric, it wasn't easy at all.'[5] The first draft, Proffitt felt, also failed to convey to readers exactly why Eric had been a Communist all his life. '*Why* is socialism, indeed communism, the best way of organising the world?' he asked Eric. 'There's an opportunity here for a substantial ideological statement: you are surely better qualified than almost anyone to make it, and there could be no more appropriate place than your autobiography.' Eric was too defensive about his convictions, he thought: he needed to make 'a major *positive* statement ... Attack in these circumstances really might be the best form of defence!'[6] Proffitt got Eric to admit that his lifelong adherence to Communism was 'a tribal matter' more than anything else. Eric had committed himself to the ideals of the October Revolution as a teenager and remained loyal to them all his life. 'I felt at that point that I had really got to the heart of the man', Proffitt concluded, 'and that he was saying what his life had been about, and this was clearly the deep core of his belief, and I hope we got it into the book.'

Meanwhile, Proffitt sent numerous queries and requests for clarification to Eric where he felt statements needed further explanation, or sounded 'self-congratulatory', which might go down well in France, he thought, but not in Britain, where a display of modesty was the way to earn respect. He wanted more on Marlene's background, and told Eric that the description of a dinner as 'agreeable' 'makes you sound like Roy Jenkins!' After demanding more intimate personal details, he rowed back when Eric confessed that he 'introduced Marlene to both the coil and the pill' – 'will people want to know this?' he asked rhetorically.

He was also uneasy about Eric's mention of his illegitimate son, Joss Bennathan: 'My instinct', Proffitt wrote, 'would be either to say nothing at all, or to say more. As it is this will just prompt speculation and perhaps press enquiry.' In places the text needed 'tightening' or even a few cuts, but on the other hand he asked for a longer discussion of the US and its current policies, especially since it looked like President George W. Bush was going to invade Iraq (as he did, alongside Britain, on 20 March 2003). He also wanted some restructuring of some of the chapters, and asked for substantial cuts to the material on Eric's family and relatives (in the end, an entire chapter on this subject was excised). Eric, Proffitt charged, too often sounded 'chippy', filled with resentment, especially about his marginalisation by the British authorities during the war, and this would not make a good impression on his readers. At various junctures he also needed to make his attitude to the 'Party line' clearer. More radically, Proffitt wanted the concluding section in the draft transposed to the opening section, since it told readers why they should be reading the book. It did not make much sense to place it at the end ('if readers have got this far they won't need telling').[7] Eric duly obliged.

He gave Proffitt a lot of trouble over the jacket design and illustration. Publishers tend to want a picture of the author on the front cover of an autobiography, but Eric rejected all the photographs he was shown because he felt they made him look ugly (his embarrassment about his appearance, first evident in his teenage diaries, persisted to the end). For his part, Proffitt turned down Eric's own suggestion of a painting by Paul Klee that seemed to have nothing at all to do with the subject of the book. In the end, he chose a black and white photograph of Eric from his later life. 'Of all the pictures of you which we've looked at', he told Eric, 'this is the one which has had easily the best response. We had it displayed (very large!) on the stand in Frankfurt [Book Fair] where it was much, favourably, commented upon. I particularly like the half-shadow effect', he added, 'and the way that your face is off to the side. I think the overall effect is very striking.' He conceded that Eric had not wanted a photograph of himself on the cover, but insisted that 'this is the way we can best publish and sell the book'.[8] In such matters, the publisher generally has the last word. And, as in all cases of books that mention living people, they would also have the last word on what, if anything, had to be taken out for legal reasons. Penguin's legal department, at that time embroiled in a major defamation action brought against them by the Holocaust denier David Irving, was more worried than usual about possible libel suits, and checked who among the many people mentioned in the book was still alive. The lawyers questioned the typescript's allegations about the Kennedy family's mob connections, the supposed corruption of Mayor Daley (and by possible implication, his son, also Mayor) of Chicago, and suggested putting in qualifying words ('seemingly', for example) in passages towards the end of the book on the invasion of Iraq. But, all in all, they felt there was little to worry about, and changes made for legal reasons remained at a minimum.[9]

The book was published in 2002 as *Interesting Times: A Twentieth-Century Life* – the title, added by Eric at a relatively late stage in the publishing process,[10] being an allusion to the supposed ancient Chinese curse, 'may you live in interesting times' (a saying first reported by the British ambassador to China in the 1930s but not documented in any older sources, either in China or anywhere else). In German the irony was removed and the book was called *Dangerous Times*.[11] The chapters of the autobiography were originally going to be in chronological order, with titles such as 'Portrait of a reluctant Englishman (London 1933–6)', 'An uninteresting war', 'Writing history: becoming well-known and why', 'A respectable Professor (1970s)' and 'A part-time New Yorker' on the 1980s and 1990s. Chapters on individual countries were to be integrated into the structure: 'France and the French (general, but tied on to 1950s)', 'Looking for primitive rebels: Italy and Spain (1951–60)', and so on.[12] By the time it was published, however, Eric had changed his mind, and the final part of the book is structured thematically, with chapters on the different countries he had got to know well, affording opportunities for analysis that a more chronological approach might not have done.

Proffitt was happy with the book's structure and thought it

would be a great success. Certainly every effort was made to promote it. Penguin launched the book at a party in their grand offices on one of the upper floors at 80 Strand on 1 October 2002, in London, with speeches by both author and editor and a crowd of friends, well-wishers and newspaper and magazine correspondents. Eric presented the book ten days later at the Cheltenham Literary Festival and then again in conversation with Peter Hennessy at the Purcell Room in London's South Bank Centre on 16 October. He went to Heffers bookshop in Cambridge on 24 October to promote the book, and interviews were arranged on BBC2's *Newsnight*, Radio 3's *Nightwaves*, Radio 4, Radio 2 and the World Service.[13] By 5 December 2002 the book had been reprinted several times, and thirteen thousand copies of the hardback edition had been sold.[14] The memoirs appeared in sixteen foreign languages, with the best sales, as was now the norm with Eric's books, in Brazil, where more than twenty-seven thousand copies were sold.[15]

Interesting Times was very extensively reviewed in the press and media, thanks not least to the fame Eric had garnered with the huge success of *Age of Extremes*.[16] The relatively impersonal tone of much of the narrative was widely commented on; in the end, Stuart Proffitt was right when he confessed that he had failed to make the book more intimate. The most revealing chapters covered Eric's childhood and adolescence, while a more impersonal tone took over once he got to Cambridge. Particularly in his discussion of his career as a Communist, as Perry Anderson pointed out in a perceptive review, 'we' tended to replace 'I', involving a 'suppression of a subjectivity' that should have illuminated the nature of his commitment in some kind of 'interior synthesis'. One might, of course, respond by pointing out that Communism is a collective movement in which human individuality has to be sublimated in a devotion to the Party and the cause, so it is not surprising that the word 'we' comes into the narrative more frequently at this stage.[17] Still, Anderson had a point.

Tony Judt categorised Eric as a romantic whose nostalgia for the élan of the Communist movement in Weimar Berlin coloured all his writing on Communism, even on the drearily conformist GDR.

Judt admired Eric's consistency in remaining in the Party, but this did not, he thought, come without a cost. 'The most obvious damage is to his prose. Whenever Hobsbawm enters a politically sensitive zone, he retreats into hooded, wooden language, redolent of Party-speak.' And, Judt went on, his commitment also damaged Eric's historical judgement. For instance, he referred to Khrushchev's 1956 speech as 'the brutally ruthless denunciation of Stalin's misdeeds' but called those misdeeds themselves neither brutal nor ruthless. Acknowledging Communism's mistakes was one thing, but, Judt charged, 'Hobsbawm refuses to stare evil in the face and call it by its name; he never engages the moral as well as the political heritage of Stalin and his works'.

Eric knew Judt, especially through being in New York at the same time during the late 1980s and 1990s (Judt held a professorship at New York University). They admired each other's work, though Eric characterised him as 'an academic bruiser', a passionate advocate rather than a dispassionate scholar.[18] But there was something of the Inquisition about Judt's shrill exhortations to Eric to recant or be damned. Anthony Sampson, the doyen of 'condition-of-Britain' literature, was more balanced: 'It is Hobsbawm's self-questioning that gives this book a constant element of surprise and vigour and makes it an exceptional political memoir.'[19] In both *Age of Extremes* and *Interesting Times*, indeed, we have the gripping and moving sight of a lifelong Communist struggling in old age to come to terms not only with the political failure of the cause to which he had devoted the best part of his life, but also to reach some understanding of why it had failed and how much damage it had done.

In many reviews of his autobiography, Eric detected a revival of Cold War thinking since the mid-1990s, largely caused by a new 'moral discourse of absolute good and evil' that had come into vogue after the destruction of the Twin Towers in New York by Islamist fundamentalist terrorists on 11 September 2001:

A few years ago my history of the 'Short 20th Century' was not received as a work of propaganda or ideological justification even by conservatives – anyway outside France. Today things are different. Within the past few weeks someone has concluded from my autobio that 'we must be disgusted by Eric Hobsbawm' (Johann Hari in Indep on Sunday) and someone else . . . cites me as a classic justifier of evil: 'Eric Hobsbawm, for instance, with his elaborate rationalisations of the millions killed in the name of the communist ideal to which he himself subscribed' (Times 2, 13/1/03). I won't bother to comment on these opinions. This sort of thing does indicate a revival of the kind of talk which regards communism and everything connected with it as an evil so evidently absolute that anyone who has ever sympathised with it must be either regarded as deliberately evil, choosing the cause of Satan over God, or too ignorant or half-witted to know the difference: a knave or a fool.[20]

But some reviews were more considered. Richard Vinen, a London University professor who had started off as an historian of France but switched to writing books about modern British history, began by questioning Eric's self-presentation 'as a marginal figure who was kept out of jobs by his political views'. It was only his failure to secure an Oxbridge professorship to which he was implicitly referring; in fact, of course, he had a full-time academic post at Birkbeck from 1947 all the way to his retirement, though it was for some decades possible to argue that as an evening college for part-timers it was hardly part of the academic mainstream. 'The English historical profession in the twentieth century', Vinen suggested, 'was dominated by lone scholars who operated outside established institutions. The best historians – Lewis Namier at the beginning of his career, A. J. P. Taylor at the end, E. P. Thompson for most of his career – have often not even had university jobs.' This was, of course, a very selective list: one could point to many equally good historians who did, starting with Christopher Hill, who became Master of Balliol. The Oxford historian Adrian Gregory put it slightly differently, remarking that Eric was 'ultimately most comfortable on the edges of things, not quite outside events, not even quite outside the establishment, but [at] a self-imposed distance', a position Gregory thought was ultimately an ideal one for the historian to occupy.[21]

Nevertheless, there was some truth in Vinen's argument that Eric had 'always been an institutions man. He has spent almost all his adult life in universities. He must have been among the first major British historians of the modern period who bothered to complete a Ph.D., and he has been an assiduous frequenter of conferences.' He was, Vinen continued, 'in a strange way, a very English figure', a member of gentlemen's clubs like the Apostles, the British Academy and the Athenaeum:

> Even Hobsbawm's much-vaunted cosmopolitanism fits into an English identity. The English Establishment has always had a soft spot for people, like Hobsbawm's friend Isaiah Berlin, who can explain foreign ideas in elegant English prose. Hobsbawm's appeal to the English middle classes – the sweeping and confident assertions, the casual deployment of vast erudition and the evocation of an exotic European culture – might be compared, not entirely frivolously, to that of Elizabeth David.

The comparison was a striking one: Elizabeth David introduced post-war England to French and Italian cooking in a series of beautifully written and technically uncompromising (though entirely workable) recipes featuring authentic foreign cuisine and sometimes hard-to-obtain original ingredients, in a way a sort of culinary counterpart of Eric's historical writing.

Vinen also noted that Eric's talents were recognised sooner by commercial publishers than by university presses. His fame as a writer spread quickly, and '*Primitive Rebels* is even cited by one of the characters in Tom Wolfe's *Bonfire of the Vanities*' (a vast satirical novel on New York in the 1980s), where the term is applied to a leader of the civil rights movement in the city. Vinen thought that 'Hobsbawm was driven into an interesting engagement with social history by a flight from the awkward questions that might have been raised by political history'. He was on shakier ground, perhaps, when he observed: 'The relative insignificance of the CPGB helped to make Hobsbawm significant.' The Party did not really think that 'intellectuals provided it with its only real influence', as Vinen claimed – in fact, it despised intellectuals, and Eric's relations with it were always fraught with difficulty. In the end, politics provided the red thread that ran through the book, so it was hardly surprising that so much of Eric's personal and emotional life was left out. But Marlene for one was not dismayed. 'The unwritten parts are always the best', as she wrote in a postcard to Eric while he was in New York on the occasion of their wedding anniversary.[22]

II

By the beginning of the new century, Eric's life had long since settled into a steady pattern. Most of the time, he worked at Nassington Road, reading as voraciously as ever and writing a continuous stream of articles, essays and journalistic pieces. In 2008, a photograph by Eamonn McCabe appeared of Eric's study, in a series of weekly features in the *Guardian* Saturday magazine on writers' rooms, alongside an explanatory text by Eric himself. The study was lined from floor to ceiling with books, except for a clear space occupied by a photograph of Billie Holiday. Substantial piles of papers tottered precariously on every horizontal surface, squeezing his laptop, on which he now did all his writing, into a tiny space on one of his desks, over which loomed an adjustable lamp. There was little to disturb him, he told McCabe: although he had a record player in the room, 'I hardly ever listen. Music imposes itself too much.'

> I work in what used to be our son Andy's room on the top floor of a Hampstead semi. The room has changed dramatically since it went from teen-age to old-age use, except insofar as it still looks chaotic, though in a different way. Indeed, much of it is: piles of research notes, print-outs, writings, unanswered letters, money stuff, and newly-arrived books, all retrieved by a no-longer-reliable memory. Because I am a historian who works

surrounded by multiple papers, they tend to accumulate on the surface of my two desks round the laptop without which I could no longer function, having been shamed into the computer-era in the late 1980s by my students in New York.

This was emphatically a working room, with no space for socialising. Most of the books crowding the shelves behind the desk were foreign editions of his own works, which served, 'in moments of discouragement, as a reminder that an old cosmopolitan had not entirely failed in 50 years of trying to communicate history to the world's readers. And as an encouragement to go on while I still can.'[23]

Eric and Marlene continued to hold their now-legendary dinner parties at Nassington Road. 'He would open the door', Nick Jacobs remembered, 'and he would be holding a gin and tonic and a stick, doing it all at once, and he was a wonderful host ... Marlene did the cooking, and Eric helped, served round, and he always seemed to be doing the washing-up afterwards ... Eric always did the coffee, the traditional thing, the washing-up and feeding the washing-up machine.'[24] Some guests looked askance at the very traditional division of roles between Eric and Marlene and thought it rather 'Germanic'.[25] But Eric's attitude to women was not really Germanic; the early influence of his mother, an independent author and translator, also told against that view; rather, his attitude towards women is more likely to have been formed by his experience of the jazz world, once he had got over the idea of a comradely political marriage that had proved so disastrous for his relationship with Muriel Seaman: a world in which women were 'chicks', the appendages of players ('cats') but not their equals. In any case, what attracted him to Marlene in the first place, apart from her beauty, charm and intelligence, was not the fact that she was not a fully paid-up member of the writing set or the Establishment, but the breadth of her cultural interests, her cosmopolitanism, her command of French and Italian and her adventurous experiences working for the United Nations in the Congo. As for the dinner parties, Eric's lifelong and notorious impracticality fortunately precluded his taking a role in doing the cooking or preparing the dishes.

Conversation at the dinner table, according to Nick Jacobs, centred on 'political gossip, I would say . . . I don't think that Eric wanted to have serious talk at dinner parties.'[26] But Eric's editor at Penguin, Stuart Proffitt, who also attended these dinners, thought that Eric

> didn't have much small talk . . . There's about twenty seconds of 'how are you?' and then it's 'so how are we going to get out of this mess we're in?' He wanted to cut to the chase straight away. He wanted to talk about present politics, world politics. The quality of his information from around the world, in extreme old age – this must have been when he was ninety-three, ninety-four, something like that – but he knew exactly what was going on all over the world. I mean, he was like a sort of one-man Economist Intelligence Unit; it was really, really extraordinary. And he expected you to be able to engage on that level immediately. So, you know, no slacking![27]

Roy Foster put it slightly differently: conversation tended to focus on 'gossip . . . not social or sexual, not Proustian gossip, but gossip about literary stuff, bad reviews people would get . . . It was metropolitan, literary . . . classic north London, but with a cosmopolitan touch.'[28] 'Their home', as the Indian historian Romila Thapar remembered, 'became a kind of centre where people from all over the world of a radical bent of mind would come' – radical, that is, in an old-fashioned, often Marxist sense. 'No evening was ever dull.'[29] Roy Foster remembered 'Marlene, at one of the bigger dinner parties, around Christmas, coming into the sitting room or dining room, wherever the main company was in, and saying, "I'm so sick of being surrounded by disillusioned Communists! I want to talk about something else!" So clearly the disillusioned Communists had gathered in one of the other rooms and she'd come into where the more frivolous liberals were, and we were frivolous liberals I guess.'[30]

By now, Eric was beginning to outlive his contemporaries. 'All I seem to do', he said to me around this time, 'is go to memorial services these days.' 'I am beginning to feel like a historical monument', Eric told the French history scholar Douglas Johnson on 19 June 2002. He was particularly dismayed by the death of Rodney Hilton on 7 June that year. 'True', he noted, 'the 1930s generation of Marxist historians had proved fairly long-lived, but it is getting very thin by now.' Edward Thompson had died in 1993, Christopher Hill died ten years later. Eric's friend the art historian Francis Haskell died in 2000. Victor Kiernan, somewhat older than Eric, survived as long as he did, dying in 2009 at the age of ninety-five. Raphael Samuel had succumbed to cancer at a much younger age in 1996. Eric's cousin Denis Preston, the well-known record producer, had passed away in Brighton many years before, on 21 October 1979, bringing a long friendship based on a shared love of jazz to an end.[31] Another cousin, Ron Hobsbaum, died in 2004: he had moved back to London in the 1990s and lived not far from Eric and Marlene, and so the two families had renewed their relationship on a more frequent basis than before.[32] To some extent, Eric filled the gaps they left in his life with a group of younger friends and their partners: Leslie Bethell, Roderick Floud, Roy Foster, Martin Jacques, Nick Jacobs, Stuart Proffitt, Richard Rathbone and others.

Surprisingly, perhaps, he was on friendly terms with Niall Ferguson ('right wing but unfortunately not dumb', as Eric called him).[33] 'He is', he wrote on another occasion, 'an enormously talented man who has done extremely interesting work but who could never resist the temptation of being a provocateur.' His most recent book, *The War of the World: History's Age of Hatred* (2006), was 'scandalous', Eric thought, particularly for its 'dangerous amateur socio-biology'. 'I am sorry', he added, 'because he is a clever and charming man and we get on quite well together.'[34] Ferguson's fascination with the problems of economic determinism provided the common ground on which they met. Eric's pocket diary records a dinner with him on 23 June 2004 among other occasions.[35] The London-based historian of Africa Richard Rathbone, whom he had met through being neighbours in Wales, was surprised by their mutual admiration, which he put down to Eric's gratitude for the praise Ferguson had lavished on his work. Rathbone was even more shocked when Eric talked in positive terms of Prince Charles, because of his charitable work, and said that monarchism was the best system he could think of for the United Kingdom. He admired the Conservatives for their pragmatism and their attitude of just getting on with the job. 'The feet of clay did poke out from underneath the majestic robe from time to time', the resolutely left-wing Rathbone commented acerbically.[36]

Eric and Marlene continued to travel to their Welsh cottage two or three times a year, staying a week at a time, always visiting at the time of the Hay Literary Festival. He and Marlene held an annual lunch party at the cottage during the Hay Festival, 'for the passing authors who were lifelong friends – Amartya Sen and Emma Rothschild; Claire Tomalin and Michael Frayn; Sir John Maddox and his wife, the writer Brenda Maddox', as Julia later recalled, 'and Tom Stoppard, who apparently based the Red Cambridge don in his play *Rock 'n' Roll* on my dad'.[37] Eric eventually transferred his vote to the Brecon and Radnorshire parliamentary constituency, which included his cottage in Gwenddwr. It was, he told Fritz Lustig in 2005, 'and remains a marginal constituency, but one where effectively the anti-Tory vote must be Liberal-Democrat, so I don't have to vote for Blair in any shape. Marlene, who votes for Glenda Jackson in Hampstead, has no problems: Glenda's record is good on the [Iraq] war and all else.' Hampstead was a safe Labour seat by this time, and his vote was not needed there.[38] It carried more weight in Brecon and Radnorshire, and indeed the constituency, which voted Conservative in 1992, fell to the Liberal Democrats five years later.[39]

As this suggests, Eric had long since become disillusioned with the New Labour government of Tony Blair; indeed, he had been sceptical about its radicalism from the very start. Blair, he wrote in 2005, was 'systematically planning to move the government to the right ie: in the direction of a market society ... Most people in the party would prefer Brown, who represents a more social democratic tradition, but he is weak.'[40] Blair, he told me once, was 'Thatcher in trousers'. Interviewed in 2007, shortly after the replacement of Tony Blair as Prime Minister by Gordon Brown, who had become a personal friend, Eric struck an uncharacteristic note of political optimism:

> Where Blair went wrong worst was Iraq. At some stage a guy who began as a brilliantly intuitive election-winning politician discovered that he had a calling to save the world by armed inter-vention, and he had it even before he got on to the Americans. Second worst is the complete forgetting that government is for ordinary people. The idea that the only thing that counts are the people who have managed to seize the opportunity in a free market and become rich and famous and celebrated, and to build the values of your society on that – this I think has been Blair's fault; perhaps unconsciously he's been biased in that way. Gordon Brown will be an enormous improvement, at least for those of us who have found it impossible to support the Labour Party in the last Blair period. He has a sense of the traditions of the Labour movement, and above all a sense of social justice and equality.[41]

However, Brown's options were circumscribed by the constraints of globalisation. A return to the old social democratic or Labour Party governments that unfolded economic and social policies in relative isolation from the rest of the world was no longer possible. 'The real problem for Gordon and for everyone else is precisely how this globalization can be detached from a completely free capitalism, which is bound to end in enormous difficulties.'

With advancing age Eric began to decline interviews, recollect-ing, perhaps, his bruising experiences at the hands of Sue Lawley and Michael Ignatieff in the 1990s, though the promotional interviews for *Interesting Times* had gone smoothly enough. Asked in 2007 if he would agree to taking part in a BBC programme called *The Interview*, which involved a half-hour one-to-one question-and-answer session, he said he was too busy, despite the fact that previous interviewees had included such internationally famous figures as UN Secretary-General Kofi Annan, musician Daniel Barenboim and novelist Toni Morrison.[42] By contrast, he was quite happy to talk for Jewish Book Week about Karl Marx, who had just been named by Radio 4 listeners as their favourite philosopher of all time.[43] He still made his views known, on occasion, in British and indeed international politics on issues on which he felt strongly enough. Earlier on, he had been, with Perry Anderson and Raphael Samuel, to the Palestinian Bir-Zeit University on the West Bank, in Ramallah, occupied by the Israelis since the Six-Day War in 1967. It was a sobering experience, he wrote, to live under military occupation: gun-toting Israeli soldiers and settlers were everywhere: 'Guns . . . are the identifying mark of those who rule.' Everywhere there was arbitrariness and fear. People stayed off the streets after dusk. Students and occasionally faculty members were arrested and held without trial in undisclosed locations. 'Constant harassment is the daily small-change of arbitrary rule.' The Israeli regime did not even 'claim to offer Palestinians anything except expropriation, emigration or subjection'. Even more depressing was the fanaticism of the ultra-religious Israeli settlers, who regarded the expansion of Israel and the expulsion of the Arabs as divinely ordained. Some years later, in conversation with me, Eric used the term 'low-level ethnic cleansing' for what was going on, and had been ever since 1948.[44]

Eric had long been suspicious of Zionism, not least because he regarded it as a form of nationalism. It had not succeeded by its own efforts: 'But for Hitler, an independent Israel would probably not exist', he had written in 1987.[45] In a letter to the *Times Literary Supplement* on 13 February 2003 he condemned the policies of the right-wing Israeli government under Ariel Sharon. Eric thought it 'important for Jews who are not Zionist to say in public that belonging to our community does not imply support for Israel's policies or indeed, for the nationalist ideology behind them'.[46] Two years later he signed a letter to the *Guardian* with seventy-four other academics condemning 'Israel's long and brutal occupation of Palestine', including its 'violation of academic freedom' on the West

Bank. The signatories, while not opposed to the boycott of Israeli higher education institutions called for by Palestinian academics, considered that it 'needs to be more carefully thought out'. The letter ended with an appeal for help to be offered to Palestinian academics and the demand that 'Israeli academia has to account for its role in this situation'.[47]

Eric was far from being indiscriminately hostile to the State of Israel, however. 'He was both a fierce critic', Ira Katznelson thought, 'and had his own set of loyalties, which were in part Jewish.' He had

> a sense of – with all his criticisms – of appreciation: that this was a site of rescue, at a time when very few places – there weren't many options, as it were. So that aspect of the experience of Palestine–Israel, I think he took in, and had a sense that one would have to be a kind of – not a phrase he would have used – moral cretin not to recognise that the community living there, in part, came out of a history which he shared in a modest – in a different way.[48]

At the end of 2008, Arab–Israeli tensions erupted once again into open war in the Gaza Strip, where the Israeli government responded to a constant barrage of rockets fired by the ruling Hamas organisation onto civilian targets across the border by bombing the area and sending in ground troops to wipe out the rocket bases. There was the inevitable 'collateral damage' inflicted on civilians. Eric joined with others on the Left to condemn the 'barbarism' of the Israeli military action. It made a lasting solution of the problem more difficult than before, he thought. And it also had wider ramifications:

> Gaza has darkened the outlook for the future of Israel. It has also darkened the outlook for the nine million Jews who live in the diaspora. Let me not beat about the bush: criticism of Israel does not imply anti-semitism, but the actions of the government of Israel occasion shame among Jews and, more than anything

else, they give rise to anti-semitism today. Since 1945 the Jews, inside and outside Israel, have enormously benefited from the bad conscience of a Western world that had refused Jewish immigration in the 1930s before committing or failing to resist genocide. How much of that bad conscience, which virtually eliminated anti-semitism in the West for sixty years and produced a golden era for its diaspora, is left today?[49]

It was unusual for Eric to speak, as he did when addressing the Middle Eastern tangle, explicitly and openly as a Jew. But as Elise Marienstras noted, 'He never concealed the fact that he was Jewish. It was quite normal for him, it was part of his life, and yet, at the same time, being Jewish meant for him simply the fact that he had Jewish parents, and the fact that he had lived life as a Jewish child in Vienna and Berlin.' Many of his friends were Jewish, she added, but Jewishness was for him a part of his identity just as being born and brought up as a Catholic or Protestant was for other people. In the end, perhaps, it didn't matter that much. He did not care much for national or religious minorities or indeed for the survival of minority languages such as Yiddish, she thought, a language to which she and her husband felt committed by their Eastern European background. 'Would it matter if Yiddish disappeared?' he asked her rhetorically: 'A heap of small languages are disappearing, it's normal.' What mattered for Eric, she thought, was class, not nationality or religion: building a society of equals where everyone had the same rights as individuals was important.[50]

III

Eric's cultural life in London continued to be an active one. Despite his public image as a jazz fan, he loved opera, especially Italian opera: Roy Foster remembered him giving 'lyrical descriptions of listening to "Casta Diva" on Italian terraces'. He lived not far from the pianist Alfred Brendel and, Foster recalled, 'the

Hobsbawms used to go to Brendel concerts and sometimes back to Brendel's place afterwards'. Shared interests in the visual arts lay behind his friendship with the great photographer Henri Cartier-Bresson, whom he had first got to know in Paris in the 1950s. His appointments diaries record visits with Marlene to the Wigmore Hall, the city's premier chamber music venue, on frequent occasions, more frequent indeed than his visits to Ronnie Scott's jazz club, up to January 2011, and to the Royal Opera House at Covent Garden. He went to a play at the Young Vic on 9 March 2010, an exhibition at the Tate Gallery on 27 October 2008 and a concert at the Royal Festival Hall on 22 February 2006.[51] But such expeditions were by now becoming more tiring for him. In 2005 Nick Jacobs was at the house in Nassington Road and on an impulse asked Eric if he would like to come with him to an exhibition at the National Maritime Museum in Greenwich on Napoleon and Wellington:

> I think he was in a state when he didn't go out unaccompanied. And he said, 'I don't think that's really my kind of thing' ... And Marlene said, 'But you're a historian, aren't you? Isn't it something you should go and see?' And Eric said, 'Oh, ok.' And we went by boat, and he seemed to have thoroughly enjoyed the boat trip down there, and he was fascinated by the exhibition, which was wonderful, and had, for instance, the suit – beautiful blue suit – that Napoleon wore at the Battle of Marengo. Amazing. It had been dry-cleaned, I'm sure! And then he said, 'You know, I think I've had enough.' I think he was talking physically and not intellectually. And we came back on the boat. But it was a thoroughly pleasant day, and it was easy being with Eric, I would say. [52]

Eric continued to attend the *London Review of Books* Christmas Party, where, on his final visit, in 2010, he sat rather grandly on a chair in a corner of the overcrowded LRB bookshop to receive anyone who wanted a chat with him, as many did.

Eric's foreign trips continued intermittently, but most of them were now fairly brief, a few days at most. His visits to Paris were still relatively frequent though he now always went with Marlene, usually staying at the Hôtel L'Angleterre in the rue Jacob: he was there in March and October 2000, June 2003, June and November 2004. Nor did age and infirmity prevent him from travelling further afield, usually to deliver lectures, to Turin in May 2000, the Salzburg Festival in August 2000 and Mantua in September 2000, Lausanne in January 2002, New York for a week in May 2002, Italy again for five days in November 2002 and again for a longer period in March–April the following year, Venice in February 2003, Spain in April 2003, Italy in July 2003, Brussels in October 2003 and Munich and Berlin in November 2003. The next year he was in Pisa in January, going to Los Angeles for a fortnight almost immediately afterwards. But on 14 June 2005 he complained to Bruce Hunter that 'owing to age, my travels to give lectures abroad are now very restricted'.[53] This was particularly the case with transatlantic travel. As he told the Canadian-German historian and jazz musician Michael Kater in May 2005, 'As I am getting rather old (eighty-eight in June) I am cutting down on travelling across oceans though I have not become entirely sedentary.'[54]

His final transoceanic journey was in December 2004, to India, 'the most fascinating and the most miserable country imaginable'. The gap between rich and poor was more visible than ever. 'At the same time the present government is encouraging (the new Prime Minister reminded me that I had examined his economic history paper when he was at Cambridge in the 1950s).'[55] He delivered a number of lectures, and took part in a podium discussion with Indian historians, chaired by Romila Thapar, at the India International Centre on 14 December. As Shahid Amin remarked, 'Like a lot of us middle-aged historians who are here, we were brought up on Penguin Books and Christopher Hill/Eric Hobsbawm/Edward Thompson.'[56] And – his last major public appearance in France, and a signal honour for any historian, let alone a British one – he was invited to deliver a lecture, in French, to the French Senate on 22 September 2008 on the subject of

'Europe: Histoire, Mythe, Réalité'.[57] The event was a huge success, and he received a standing ovation.[58] An edited version appeared in the French daily *Le Monde* the next morning.

In 2005 he was in Turin for a meeting of elder statesmen sponsored by Mikhail Gorbachev. From 4 to 6 March, more than a hundred retired world leaders and politicians were there. 'I can recall no experience like it', Eric declared: 'Historians rarely find themselves in the presence of their subjects en masse ... It is an unexpected sight, like visiting Madame Tussauds and finding that the wax models have been replaced by the originals.'[59] Towards the end of the month he went to Potsdam; then to Salzburg, again for the Festival, and then Venice in October and Rome in November; and finally Rome from 18 to 21 November 2010, his final outing abroad. He travelled with Marlene to Paris several times to spend two or three days, often during the Christmas holidays, with Maurice Aymard and his family, and then Elise Marienstras and her husband. He travelled on the Eurostar train through the Channel Tunnel, a more convenient and agreeable way than flying, and stayed in Paris from 13 to 15 December 2002, 21–25 December 2005 and 7–11 December 2007, spending a good deal of time with the Marienstrases.[60] 'One was *en famille*', as Elise remembered: 'Just the four of us ... Really like a family. The feeling of being old, of having traversed the whole of this life and of having known each other for so long, and of feeling such warmth towards one another ... It was good.'[61]

With Marlene he was enjoying a new role as the grandfather of some very small children: 'We are having a good time with all these little ones', he commented in July 2005.[62] As Julia recalled:

He engaged in the lives of all of us, his two sons and his daughter, his nine grandchildren, and his young great-granddaughter. He always asked me avidly 'How's business?' during each visit, enjoying my tales from the front line of capitalism. He celebrated every entrepreneurial step forward but was always a bit anxious, leaving answerphone messages saying: 'It's Dad. Just checking in to see how you are. Don't overdo it. Kiss, kiss.' My dad, the academic historian and giant of 'the left', and me, his degreeless, politically plural daughter who loves doing business.

In June 2007 he celebrated his ninetieth birthday. He was on sparkling form, recalling that when he had recently been at Heathrow, he had been relieved to see on the departures board the notice displaying 'delayed', and then even more relieved when it said 'cancelled'. The Austrian Embassy in London held a concert in his honour, at which a string quartet played works by Mozart, Haydn, Mendelssohn, Schubert, Grieg and Shostakovich.[63] At his ninety-fifth and final birthday party in June 2012, as Claire Tomalin recalled, 'he spoke to us then at length with verve and wit, his spirit undimmed by physical pain. As he joked about living to see the failure of capitalism I looked round and saw how he had become part of the English establishment and I thought, "Eric is a magician".'[64] Elise Marienstras found him on this occasion 'very physically diminished'. He was 'there like on a throne. He was being pushed around in a wheelchair and one had to stand in a queue to go and embrace him.' The party was held at the headquarters of the Royal Institute of British Architects in Portland Place. 'The tables were named after operas; there was a seating plan before you entered the room.' The meal was sumptuous. But 'one knew well that he was close to the end, and there was this kind of reverence towards him, it was very curious'.[65] Honours and awards continued to be showered upon him. He received a testimony of appreciation from the German Foreign Minister Joschka Fischer (described by the German ambassador as 'a great admirer of your work').[66] In 2008 he was made an Honorary Member of the Society for the Study of Labour History, whose President he had been since Edward Thompson's death.[67] In 2006 he was elected, very belatedly, to the Royal Society of Literature. In 2000 he was presented with the Ernst Bloch Prize, awarded by the city of Ludwigshafen for outstanding contributions to European culture with a philosophical basis; in 2008 he was granted honorary citizenship by the city of Vienna and in the same year the Bochum History Prize for Economic and Social History. He received honorary degrees from too many different universities to name, from Montevideo to Prague; and, perhaps most importantly, he won the Balzan Prize, awarded in 2003 for an outstanding contribution to European History. As Keith Thomas remembered:

> I was partly responsible for getting him the Balzan Prize. It was an immensely controversial decision and some of the committee members were never reconciled to it. Those who had memories of the DDR, about which Eric has said something favourable, were particularly incensed. They were not encouraged when, Eric being too unwell to come to the ceremony, Julia came to Berne to accept the prize, ostentatious[ly] wearing a pair of bright red shoes.[68]

The prize was worth three-quarters of a million Swiss francs, and half of it had to be devoted to a research project. Eric chose 'Reconstruction in the Immediate Aftermath of War: A Comparative Study of Europe, 1945–50', based in Birkbeck, with two post-doctoral research fellows paid with the prize money, and four workshops or conferences. His involvement was necessarily limited, but the project went well, and produced a number of significant publications in the following years.[69]

IV

Interesting Times, published when he was eighty-five, was Eric's last book. 'I can't write books any more', he told me at the time: 'I don't have the intellectual stamina.' Perhaps so, but stamina or no, it is difficult to retain the long-term perspective needed to research and write a lengthy book, a project that usually takes five years or more, when you are nearing ninety years of age. As he approached his tenth decade, he was 'visibly slowing down, although I'm still writing the odd lecture/article/review. I fear', he told Victor

Kiernan in June 2006, 'I no longer have the energy for another book but I'm hoping to put together various published, unpublished and possibly unwritten shorter pieces into the odd volume.'[70] A prolific writer of articles, both academic and journalistic, Eric had amassed a vast collection of shorter pieces, and he now decided he wanted to concentrate on republishing these in a series of book-length collections. Indeed, feeling intimations of mortality as he entered his nineties, he intended these volumes to continue to appear long after his death. He had originally asked Nick Jacobs to act as his literary executor along with Chris Wrigley, but now he felt he needed someone who could handle the business side of the publications, and he asked Bruce Hunter, who agreed. Wrigley, Hunter thought, 'would bring the historical/editorial skill and I would, I expect, slow him down, in the sense of leaving sufficient gap between books to allow them to sell, have a sense of what order books should be published in, and encourage him to publish only the first-rate material, not fee[l]ing that every scrap must come out'.[71] Eric concurred: 'Your letter has taken a great weight off my mind. Both Marlene and I thank you very much.'[72]

Eric was energised by the idea of publishing a series of collections of his articles and essays. According to Wrigley,

> He had fairly grandiose plans of volumes – I think he was talking of nine or eleven volumes of essays. I mean, I gulped: however loyal I am, I would have thought seven might have been pushing it, but I think Bruce thought five was pushing it . . . I read all . . . the unpublished stuff and made a listing . . . but I did it pretty fast and read the whole lot over several days, and the repetition became apparent I obviously think there are some things that he quite liked that wouldn't be up for reprinting.[73]

The sequence of essay collections that Eric published in his final decade bear witness to the accuracy of Wrigley's observations and the prescience of Hunter's apprehensions: they are generally rather uneven in quality, and often lack any real coherence. On the other hand, they also contain some real gems, some of which had never previously seen the light of day. While Eric's earlier essay collections, including *On History* and *Uncommon People*, had been published by Weidenfeld & Nicolson, these later volumes appeared with Little, Brown, largely because the firm could paperback them under its Abacus imprint without Bruce Hunter having to negotiate the paperback contracts separately, as he had done with the two earlier books.[74]

In the first of these new collections, *Globalisation, Democracy and Terrorism* (2007), Eric reprinted mostly recent work, including unpublished lectures, denouncing globalisation not merely because it increased inequality but also because, with its misleading rhetoric of human rights and democratisation, it too often acted as a cloak for the 'megalomania' of American foreign policy. The rapid spread of transnational capitalism and the global media was confronting nation-states with unprecedented challenges. Liberal democracy might have elbowed aside the military dictatorships so characteristic (at least in Africa and Latin America) of the second half of the twentieth century, but it was ill equipped to resist the power of globalisation.[75] Despite its rather hastily slung together contents, the book was swiftly translated into eleven foreign languages, the Brazilian edition, as always now, being the most successful in terms of sales.

On Empire: America, War, and Global Supremacy was published in 2008 by The New Press, a non-profit-making publishing house set up by Eric's friend André Schiffrin in the early 1990s after he had been ousted from Pantheon by its parent company, allegedly because it was failing to reach its profits targets. At just under a hundred pages, it was the shortest of Eric's late essay collections, presenting a mere ten pieces, all written between 2000 and 2006. The major focus of the collection was again on the decline of democracy, as elected institutions were being nullified by a global capitalism that was out of control. Conventional institutions were powerless in this situation. 'More nonsense and meaningless blather is talked in Western public discourse today about democracy and specifically about the miraculous qualities assigned to governments elected by arithmetical majorities of voters choosing between rival parties, than about almost any other word or political concept.'[76] Democratic governments in post-Soviet Ukraine, for example, or in strife-torn Colombia had not brought any notable improvements in either standards of living or civil order.[77] Here was late Hobsbawm at his most pessimistic, seeing nothing but darkness in the future.[78]

The last book Eric published during his lifetime was *How to Change the World: Marx and Marxism 1840–2011*, a collection of his essays in the field from the previous few decades, again produced by Little, Brown. The idea had initially been mooted by Gregory Elliott, author of a critical assessment of Eric's political thought, to Tariq Ali, a long-term Marxist who was a director of Verso. Tariq reported to Eric that everyone at Verso was 'excited about this proposal, as we feel that this book would be a heavy-hitting response to what will without doubt be next year's orgy of self-congratulation and triumphalism (orchestrated by the European Union and its cultural apparatuses) to mark the twentieth anniversary of the collapse of the Berlin Wall and Communism'.[79] However, although Eric was said to be 'enthusiastic', Verso's financial offer was 'a long way below what would be acceptable'. Verso had too little money to compete with more commercial publishing houses (indeed, the firm around this time asked its authors to forgo royalties altogether to help keep it afloat).[80] The book was eventually published by Little, Brown in 2011. The subtitle had originally been *Tales of Marx and Marxism*, but Eric did not like this. 'His view', as his agent reported, 'is that he was never very keen on "Tales" as a descriptor, suggestive as it is of fiction.'[81]

Its appearance was held up in part by the state in which the original typescript was delivered to the publisher, 'being made up', as Richard Beswick, Eric's editor at Little, Brown complained, 'of photocopied pages from a variety of different publications and electric-typewritten pages, with many typographical mistakes, handwritten amendments, chunks of text missing, different styles for notes in each chapter, details missing from the notes or additional notes needed, and so on'.[82] The numerous corrections and amendments Eric made to the copy-edited text and the proofs in the end came to almost half the cost of the typesetting. Eric agreed to pay £740 towards the additional costs, in the circumstances a reasonable enough compromise.⁸³ One American publisher thought that '*How to Change the World* is a tough assignment in terms of relaunching him here in the US'.⁸⁴ Eric considered that in the USA the book's readership would 'certainly be almost exclusively in the universities'.⁸⁵ The book was turned down in the USA by Basic Books, Public Affairs, Pantheon and Simon & Schuster, but was eventually taken up by Yale University Press, who were willing to pay a relatively modest advance (for Eric) of $10,000.⁸⁶

By the time it appeared, in 2010, however, the context had changed entirely from the one initially sketched out by Tariq Ali. For on 15 September 2008, the collapse of the Lehman Brothers bank in New York triggered a massive global economic downturn. Any triumphalism over the end of Communism in 1989 was now forgotten. In the context of a worldwide economic and financial crisis, Eric declared, the time had come to take Marx seriously again. But the title was perhaps rather misleading: 'Anyone looking for advice on how to foment revolution', the philosopher Alan Ryan pointed out, 'or even on how to cast their next vote, is not going to find it here.'⁸⁷ Still, it posed some crucial questions. Was Marx perhaps right after all in his analysis of the causes of the downfall of capitalism? A new book on the subject by the world's best-known and most widely read historian might provide some answers. And, indeed, for many it did: the book topped the bestseller list at the *Guardian* online bookshop in January 2011, knocking Andrea Levy's novel *Small Island* into tenth place.⁸⁸

Only a few months before his ninety-fifth birthday, Eric was still working on two books, including *When the Tsunami Struck: What Happened to Western Culture?* and *Politics before Politics*, a collection of essays which, however, involved translating some of the pieces from the German, which he was unwilling to do. The former dealt with European bourgeois culture and what Eric thought of as its demise in the twentieth century; its title was changed to *Fractured Times*. The latter was a projected edition of more of his writings in the area of 'primitive rebels'.⁸⁹ He put the second one aside and worked hard on the first, though he was, as he wrote in March 2012, stuck in hospital. It was eventually published in 2013.[90] In this book, Eric returned not merely to the cultural world of his youth, but also to his fascination with its Jewish heritage. He had occasionally written about the role of the Jews in Central European politics and culture before, but here his deep knowledge and love of nineteenth- and early twentieth-century Central European Jewish culture came out clearly in the best pieces in what was, like his other late volumes of essays, a rather uneven collection.[91] The Austrian satirist Karl Kraus took pride of place here, but many others featured too. Undermined by democratisation, technological change and the advent of consumerism, bourgeois culture, Eric argued, was also destroyed by Hitler's extermination of the Jews who played such a central part in its creation in the course of their political and social emancipation in the nineteenth century. *Fractured Times* was thus in large part a requiem for a vanished world.

Other collections of his essays continued to appear intermittently in the following years,[92] but one book project did not come to fruition. Between 2006 and 2012 Hans-Ulrich Obrist, a Swiss art historian and artistic director of the Serpentine Gallery in London, conducted a series of talks with Eric as part of an extensive programme of interviews with leading cultural figures, including the architect Zaha Hadid, the singer and painter Yoko Ono and many others. Some were published as books, others in the Berlin cultural magazine *032c*. When Obrist expressed an interest in publishing the interviews with Eric in book form, Chris Wrigley read through the text and was not keen. 'To begin with', he reported, 'it makes pleasant enough reading. It is rather like being at dinner with Eric, the best of conversations.' But after the opening section, 'it goes downhill'. There was too much repetition, and many points that Eric had made better elsewhere. 'From page 48 on, it is of no interest to the public and would serve Eric's memory very ill, in my opinion, to publish it.' Over half of the twenty-five thousand words would need to be deleted. He recommended to Bruce Hunter that Verso's offer of publication should be turned down. Eventually a drastically shortened version appeared in *032c*.[93]

V

Eric's health had held up through the 1990s, although on 14 June 1994 he was obliged to write to the *Evening Standard* complaining: 'You report that Julia Hobsbawm (London's top 400, 10 June) is the daughter of "the late historian, Eric". If your report is correct, the present letter, which proves that there is life beyond the grave, should be headline news.'[94] Emma Soames, the responsible editor, replied straight away, telling Eric that she was 'deeply apologetic that we killed you off'.[95] But his final years were marked by increasing infirmity. These were, as Marlene described them to me, 'the hospital years'. His problems began in 2001, when he had to have two operations at the Royal Free Hospital in Hampstead, on 6 September and 2 November, to remove a cancerous growth from the lower part of his left leg.[96] The operations were successful, but he now also began to develop prostate problems, kept under control but still worrying.[97] He recovered from these and became more optimistic over the next few years. 'Though we are testing the capacities of the National Health Service in all sorts of ways', he wrote in July 2005, 'it passes the tests rather well – on the whole we are in good enough shape, considering the advancing march of time.'[98] In 2007, however, he developed chronic lymphocytic leukaemia, a slow-acting form of the blood disease which required chemotherapy to bring under control. Still, 'I seem to be holding up quite well in the face of chemotherapy', he reported in June 2007.[99] The chemotherapy continued long-term. 'My medical problems have returned to being manageable', he wrote in June 2009, 'after a couple of months earlier on this year when the treatment of my brand of leukaemia – chronic but in principle controllable – went wrong. This has now been stabilized and the prospect seems good though it will probably limit such activities as foreign travel a bit more than I am used to. It is a bit depressing since until recently I also felt I didn't have very much to complain about.'[100]

Still, Eric now began to think about what was to happen to his voluminous papers after his death. He had kept all of them, in a mass of boxes, folders, files, notebooks and ring-binders filling every spare space in a room on the top floor at Nassington Road, making it difficult even to get through the door. In 2006 Eric had asked Bruce Hunter for his advice on what to do with them. 'I am inclined to think', he wrote, 'that if they are worth a serious amount of money the best thing would be to use them as a gift in lieu of death duties or rather to reduce inheritance tax ... In the meantime', he added, 'I have made arrangements to have a full bibliography made of my published writings.'[101] Hunter thought that the key point was to keep all the papers together with his working personal library and copies of all his books in one place. 'The value of the archive and library are much lessened if they are incomplete.' In addition, he advised that Eric should

> keep it all under your own control as long as possible. It is not possible to ensure the complete exclusion of prying eyes once the archive is housed in an institution, whatever conditions are made by a donor or seller at the outset. One would intend to keep all scholars away from the papers until an authorized biographer had finished with them and only then to have them made available for outside study. And I have noted that you told me that you did not want any biography of you to appear during your or Marlene's lifetime.[102]

This was one of the few occasions on which Eric misjudged his wife: Marlene knew almost every detail of Eric's life, and was in any case not going to be shocked by any revelations contained in the papers or revealed by a biographer.

Eric let the matter rest for a while, then returned to it after he became seriously ill again, in 2010. But he was now no longer dealing directly with Bruce Hunter at David Higham Associates. In October 2010 Hunter told Eric he was to retire in January 2011. 'Your letter', Eric replied, 'though not unexpected, is a bit of a shock ... After all, we have been working together for a very long time. I shall miss not just your negotiating skills and experience, but, chiefly, your judgment and counsel. Notably about my

future publications ... '[103] As his successor, Hunter recommended
Andrew Gordon, who had worked at Little, Brown, now Eric's
principal publisher, before becoming head of non-fiction at Simon
& Schuster, and had recently joined David Higham Associates.[104]
In the meantime, Eric had decided to gift his papers to the Modern
Records Centre at the University of Warwick, where the archives of
leading trade unions and unionists were housed. The Centre agreed
to take Eric's material, which would be transferred there in batches.
If there was a tax advantage in doing so, they would in due course
be converted into a gift.[105] Eric intended to keep the papers for his
lifetime, since he was still using some of them.[106] On 4 November
2010, Eric told Gordon that he needed to engage someone to catalogue them. Gordon suggested Owen Jones, a young, left-wing
journalist and writer for the *Guardian*. Eric agreed, and Jones was
commissioned with the task.[107] He began to sort the papers, gradually reducing the chaos of the top-floor room at Nassington Road
to some kind of order, though much still remained to be done. By
2016 most of them had been sent to Warwick and catalogued more
elaborately by the archivists.

Early in February 2010 Eric had come down with pneumonia,
a dangerous illness for someone so old. As Julia recalled, when she
picked him up from Nassington Road on 12 February to take him
to hospital,

> He looked barely alive and I knew he felt he was not going to
> make it. 'How are you feeling?' I asked him. 'In very poor shape,'
> he replied. We were all struggling to get him downstairs. But once
> at the bottom he insisted on delaying. With extremely faltering
> moves he fetched a book from the uppermost shelf of the front
> room, above his jazz LPs. This emergency reading book was as
> ever pocket-sized, and was bound in red leather, its print close and
> elegant. It had been given to him as a boy by his beloved 'Mama'
> in Vienna, eight decades earlier. On that occasion, he was very
> much alive a couple of days after the antibiotics kicked in. I called
> his mobile to check in and asked if he needed anything. He had a
> big sweet tooth and I expected him to ask for some fruit jellies, a

favourite, or perhaps some dark chocolate. 'I managed to bring a
most turgid book in with me,' he said apologetically. 'Would you
mind getting me something better?' It turned out that the book he
had picked up, assuming it was the last he would ever hold, was a
German edition of The Brothers Karamazov, and with the crisis
over it was now not to his liking. Knowing his weakness for thrill-
ers – one book wall is covered in the Penguin crime paperbacks
with the green spines, his old Ed McBains and more recently
Elmore Leonards – I brought him in The Girl with the Dragon
Tattoo by Stieg Larsson. It got him through the hospital tedium
and even prompted a rather racy discussion about how much
marital bed-hopping it featured. 'Too much,' he declared.[108]

He recovered, and was discharged on 3 March.
But the illness had weakened him. By now he needed two sticks
to walk. He received physiotherapy and underwent a variety of
tests, visiting the Whittington Hospital in north London on 22 June
2010. He was well enough to go to Wales for the first week of April
and again for the New Year, and even to travel to Rome for a few
days, between 18 and 21 November.[109] In August 2010 he felt fit
enough to accept an invitation to visit the recently opened Museum
of Islamic Art in Doha, Qatar. The Egyptian novelist and social
commentator Ahdaf Soueif, who had founded the Palestine Festival
of Literature two years before, had asked for several well-known
intellectuals to visit the museum and write about either the architecture or one of the paintings, treasures and objects displayed.
The essays would be published in a collection by Bloomsbury. It
was a seven-hour flight in either direction, and the weather would
be very warm. Bruce Hunter considered that 'provided he has his
wife Marlene with him, I do think he would be up to it. He went
to Paris not long ago on the train to do a lecture there. And in the
snow this winter he went by bus from Hampstead, where he lives
high on the hill, to the London Library.'[110] So Eric and Marlene
went, travelling first-class on Qatar Airlines, and avoiding the
heat by moving about in air-conditioned cars and staying in air-
conditioned rooms, like all the other visitors did.

Still, Eric's physical decline was obvious to everyone, perhaps, but himself. He was keen to fulfil a long-cherished ambition to go to Isfahan, in Iran, to view its incomparable treasures of Islamic art, which he loved; he knew some scholars in Iran (he knew them everywhere) and they would have shown him around, but Marlene thought he was too frail and put her foot down, much to his disappointment and annoyance. By this time, his hospital stays were growing more frequent. As Julia later noted:

> A grim routine of psyching myself up for 'the end' through much of 2010, 2011 and 2012 was accompanied by relief when he rallied, force of spirit – both his and my mother's – and modern medicine keeping him alive. But on the periphery of my senses was a lonely tinge of something which felt a bit like let-down: knowing this angst would return, knowing he would die, inevitably, and in the meantime waiting, powerless.[111]

In March 2011 he had a fall, since his left leg was no longer fully able to take his weight even with the aid of walking sticks. The wound in his left leg caused by the operation ten years before opened up and began to ulcerate. Hospitalised on 5 May 2011, he suffered a small deep vein thrombosis during his stay, causing some damage to the left side of his face. He continued writing throughout his time in hospital.[112] He was discharged on 10 May. On 13 May he underwent an angioplasty to widen the veins in his left leg, which brought some improvement.[113] By July 2011 Eric was forced to use a Zimmer frame when he walked, 'since walking with 2 sticks (my usual mode of locomotion) is too slow for distances of more than a few tens of yards', and a stairlift had had to be installed at Nassington Road to take him to the first floor, where Julia's husband Alaric had organised the transfer of the essential papers and books from his study on the top floor so that he could carry on working.[114] Despite his deteriorating health, Eric also made it to the opera at Covent Garden on 16 November 2011 for a performance of Mark-Anthony Turnage's opera *Anna Nicole*, but this was his last cultural outing.[115]

He continued to attend the Hay Literary Festival almost to the very end, revelling in his status as its honorary President, and feeling energised by the invitation to speak to a large audience. As Julia remembered:

> You know, there was this wonderful moment when he was *very* close to death. And ... he spoke in front of a thousand people in the Barclays Wealth tent at Hay, and Mum and I were practically patching him together to be physically ready. You know, he was really poorly. And he stood up – Tristram Hunt was in conversation with him – the hall was packed – a thousand people – in this incongruously named Barclays Wealth tent. And it was, like, a sort of spooky – he just became a forty-five-year-old man, in front of us, on stage. And he just gave this absolute tour de force performance; it was completely wonderful. He was really, really loved at Hay.[116]

At Birkbeck, Eric carried on presiding over degree ceremonies as long as he could, sitting in a chair on the stage of the Institute of Education's Logan Hall and shaking hands with the graduands. When Joan Bakewell was mooted as his successor, she was introduced to him, and 'kind of vetted as a successor. They wanted to know that Eric would be pleased', as she later remembered. They had not met since she had been supervised by Eric as an undergraduate.[117]

Richard Rathbone recalled that Eric never ceased to be adept at uncorking champagne bottles. He went to a dinner at Nassington Road in 2011 or 2012,

> And fizz was open, or I think gin and tonic was what Marlene was dishing out at the time. And he whispered in Marlene's ear, he said he had to go up because he was tired, and he went up on the Stannah Stairlift and what he had said was that he wanted us to have a book from his shelves. And Marlene of course pulled out something. I can't remember whether it was *The Age of Empire* or something – anyhow it was a kind of death gift ... But we went

again and the same offering was made and this time it was his, something very abstruse he had written in pamphlet form, which I didn't understand but ... He had a sense of departure, there was no doubt about that.[118]

As Julia recalled, Eric's thirst for knowledge continued right up to the end. He had been reading unceasingly all his life, and never stopped, not even when he was very ill. On one hospital visit he went without a book. What was he going to do? Julia, as she remembered later,

> had just downloaded *The Hare with Amber Eyes* by Edmund de Waal on to my iPad. So I showed him how to navigate the touch-pad. His long finger traced the words and he muttered softly in something close to wonderment: an ancient E.T. in a world whose modernity was becoming strangely alien. On Sundays towards the end we would visit and I would bring, like contraband, newspapers 'from the Right': the *Sunday Telegraph* and the *Sunday Times* or the *Spectator*. While the children played swingball in the garden he would lay down the *Observer* and read hungrily, enjoying his dislike of their politics and often pronouncing witheringly on David Cameron with his worst criticism: 'He's a lightweight.'

He was always keen to learn what the enemy was up to.

When Lise Grande visited Eric in July 2012, he did not have long to live, but his curiosity was undiminished. She had just been appointed head of the United Nations humanitarian mission in India, and when she told him, he was 'very keen to talk about the role of Congress and what was happening now on the great subcontinent and modernity and all of that'.[119] He continued feverishly preparing *Fractured Times*. But by the late summer of 2012 he was clearly dying. 'I am now physically pretty disabled', he wrote in August 2012 in what may well have been his final letter, to his former student Tyrrell Marris, who had taken him on that memorable sailing trip to Spain over six decades before, 'and even such exercises as looking at French cathedrals are no longer feasible for me. Nor indeed much in the way of physical movement.'[120] He had been experiencing problems swallowing for nearly two years. They became severe, but he refused to be fed artificially, and so, as Marlene reported, 'in the end his weight loss prevented him fighting any infections any more'.

On 24 September 2012 Marlene accompanied him to the Royal Free Hospital for one of the regular blood transfusions he was given for his leukaemia – a process he felt comfortable with, since it allowed him to carry on reading, and he always felt better afterwards. Usually she came to pick him up around 6 p.m. and he would be better but on a hunch she popped in to see him at lunchtime and he seemed to have deteriorated. A staff nurse said, 'I really don't think you should take him home today, he's not well enough – he should spend the night here.' Marlene stayed with him in an annexe to the ward, but the following morning his regular doctors did not appear as usual, and it was clear he was about to be moved into palliative care. As she later recalled:

> The doctor said 'we will keep him as comfortable as we can and we will see how we go day by day'. Up in the ward I phoned Andy and Julia and told them these were the last days. Then I phoned his favourite carer Benny, an Indian lady who loved both communism and Jesus. She shaved him (the nurses had no time for that). He lived another six days and looked pretty good. He had some discomfort but no real pain – all that was taken care of. Of course the grandchildren came and I phoned some friends and organised their visits as best I could. Luckily, one of his best friends, Leslie Bethell, who lives in Rio de Janeiro, was in London at that time. These visits did him good: he was lucid and pretty normal. He died in hospital on 1 October 2012.

'It was a peaceful death', Marlene wrote, 'and he was lucid until the end. But I have learned that one does not really expect the expected and so we were all three of us in total shock.'[121]

Eric's death was reported all over the world, in many countries in the main radio and television news bulletins of the day. He had for some time not only been a respected public intellectual in Britain, but also the world's most famous and widely read historian. Newspapers and periodicals everywhere paid tribute to him in lengthy articles. His death made the main BBC television news bulletin and merited a leader in the London *Times*. The leader of the Labour Party, Ed Miliband, paid tribute to him in a speech at the Party Conference. There was an official letter of sympathy from the President of the Republic of Cyprus: 'His seminal writings proudly take up extensive space in even the most humble of homes, as he had the gift to touch and teach people from all walks of life the world over.'[122] The British media concentrated on his lifelong Marxism and his supposedly unrepentant allegiance to Communism, and radio and television discussions in particular did so to the virtual exclusion of his historical works. A tiny handful of unrepentant Cold War warriors, bravely fighting what they imagined to be the West's cause now there was no real enemy to threaten them, poured vitriol over his grave. The writer A. N. Wilson claimed, in a typically impulsive piece, without bothering to think about the subject, let alone present any evidence, that Eric had 'hated Britain' and suggested he might have been a Soviet spy. His books were little more than propaganda and would not be read in the future. His reputation would 'sink without trace'.[123]

Tributes from serious historians focused rightly on Eric's history books and on the contributions he had made to historical understanding. These included figures on the Right as well as the Left. 'Unlike many continental intellectuals of the left', wrote Niall Ferguson, 'Hobsbawm the historian was never a slave to Marxist-Leninist doctrine. His best work was characterized by a remarkable breadth and depth of knowledge, elegant analytical clarity, empathy with the "little man" and a love of the telling detail.' His four 'Age of' books were, said Ferguson, one of the truly great historical works of the twentieth century. Some Conservative politicians appreciated him as well. After Eric's death, as Julia remembered, she

received a very kind handwritten note from Boris Johnson, recalling a conversation he had recently had with Dad in the green
room at Hay. Boris remarked that my father had looked up at him
from his wheelchair 'as wise as a treeful of owls'. I remembered
that conversation clearly because I had introduced them: he had
made the Conservative Mayor of London squirm a bit by asking
him straight out whether it amused him that he irritated 'quite so
many people in your party quite so much of the time'. I suspect
my father rated Boris Johnson's love of books, if not his politics.[124]

When Julia phoned through a death notice to *The Times*, 'the
young man taking copy on the phone sounded stressed: he asked
me to repeat the credit card number several times and then blurted
out suddenly that he had read history at university and had loved
my father's books'. Phone calls came in from Eric's former students all over the world: Marlene was constantly on the phone
dealing with them for several weeks. Over a thousand messages
of condolence arrived at Nassington Road in the mail. When the
family were out, a postman left a printed note reporting the fact
that he had not been able to deliver the mail, but he had also
scribbled a note saying, 'I liked his work and just wanted to send
my condolences.'

He was, as the journalist and Latin Americanist Richard Gott
remarked, 'a prophet recognized more abroad than at home ... He
could fill a stadium in many parts of the world, but in Britain he
has to be content with lecture halls. He appears more often in the
feuilletons of Europe or America (North and South) than in those of
London. His opinions are sought out more by Italian radio than by
the BBC.' The fame Eric had acquired in Brazil as the author of
the best-selling *Age of Extremes* had ensured that his last books would
also notch up high sales figures. Topping the list was the essay collection *On History* (1997), with 40,700 copies, then came *Interesting
Times* with 27,200 and *The New Century* with the same number.
Globalization, Democracy and Terrorism sold 27,000, *How to Change the
World* 13,000, *Fractured Times* 10,000 and *Echoes of the Marseillaise*
6000.[125] 'In Brazil', Julia reported, 'university students hung out

banners saying "Hobsbawm Vivat".'[126] The former President Lula da Silva sent Marlene a message of condolence:

> I have just received with deep sadness the news of your husband's death, my dear friend Eric Hobsbawm. He was one of the most lucid, brilliant and courageous intellectuals of the twentieth century. Since I first met him many years ago, I received from Eric, as he preferred that I treat him, countless encouragements for the establishment of policies that would give a share of Brazil's wealth and benefits to workers . . . More than a privilege, it was an honor to be a contemporary of Eric Hobsbawm's and to have shared moments with him.[127]

Only the newspaper *VEJA*, which had by now moved far to the right, engaging in a campaign against what it called 'Marxist indoctrination' in Brazil's universities, condemned him as a 'moral idiot' for supposedly defending Stalin. This accusation drew a dignified response from the Brazilian Association of Historians, which defended Eric for 'giving a voice to men and women who did not know how to write, who didn't imagine that their strikes, mutinies or even parties were a part of History'. It called Eric 'one of the most important men of the 20th century'.[128]

Eric's death was front-page news in the daily newspapers on the Indian subcontinent. He was, as Romila Thapar, by now a senior figure among Indian historians, remembered,

> an icon among historians of various ages and schools of thought in India. This was in part because his books by now were required reading in the curriculum of the times, and also because he had been commenting on world events including changes taking place in India . . . In many ways his kind of writing was what we turned to when we spoke of the need to include history among the social sciences. This was a significant change because in colonial times history in India was treated as part of Indology, and the focus was on gathering information rather than on trying to analyze it.[129]

His reputation on the subcontinent was, indeed, huge, and reached far beyond the confines of the academic historical profession. After her final visit to him, Lise Grande had gone straight to India. At first, she had difficulty in getting to see the most influential politicians and senior civil servants, even though she was head of the UN humanitarian mission in the country. But when they found out she had known Eric, all this changed, and the mere mention of the fact that she had been Eric's last student was enough to open all doors to her, including the Prime Minister's. She quickly learned the importance of his name. 'The first thing I would say to somebody was, "I'm Eric's student", and well, in you go.' She secured the backing of the Nobel prizewinning development economist Amartya Sen to set up the UN International Centre for Human Development, in Delhi, and at the opening ceremony, he said: 'The only reason I'm here is ... she knew Eric.' When Lise Grande was invited to dinner with the head of the ruling Communist Party in the south Indian state of Kerala, he started to talk about famous Communists he had known, and, without knowing that she had been Eric's student, told the guests:

'I went on a pilgrimage to London and I went to 10 Nassington Road.' And I turn and I look at him, and he says, 'I stood outside the door, because I wanted to see where Eric Hobsbawm lived.' Brilliant. And he had no idea who I was. This was just a story he was telling to the men, comrades sitting round the table. And then I said, 'Well, you know, actually, I've had dinner there. I know him.'[130]

It was the same in many other countries.

Eric had finalised the instructions for his funeral on 23 November 2009, noting that 'these are not intended to bind my survivors'. He wanted it to be private, though his close friends, including Nick Jacobs, Chris Wrigley and Leslie Bethell, were to be notified, along with all the family in Britain and Chile, and Marion Bennathan, Joss and his children. A notice of his death was to be published in the *Guardian* and possibly *The Times*, and 'for

the information of surviving ancient reds, why not the *Morning Star*'
(the daily newspaper published by what was left of the Communist
Party of Great Britain, or more accurately, its successor organisation). As undertakers, thinking back more than seventy years,
he considered that 'Levertons of Belsize Park did Gretl well', and
indeed they were still in business, as they had been ever since
1789, the year, appropriately enough, of the outbreak of the French
Revolution. They were, he instructed, to organise a service at
Golders Green Crematorium, a secular institution opened in 1902,
following it with burial of his ashes in the plot Marlene had bought
in Highgate Cemetery. The service was to be 'non-religious, but I
would like someone to say the Kaddish, which is said when Jews
die. Ira Katznelson is the obvious man.' At the end of his life, Eric
was acknowledging once again his more than merely residual
Jewish identity. He did not want too many speeches at his funeral.
'In order to avoid complications I'd like only one of my children to
speak. I think it should be Andy. I'd also like Nick Jacobs to speak.
Emma Rothschild? I doubt whether Marlene will want to get up
in public on this occasion.' The music was to be resolutely secular:
the meltingly beautiful trio 'Soave sia il vento' from Mozart's opera
Così fan tutte – 'On your voyage, may the winds be gentle; may the
waves be calm; may all the elements respond to your desires' – and
an extract from the slow movement of Schubert's String Quintet,
an equally moving and sublime piece. Both spoke above all of love
and loss; both had a valedictory quality, the Mozart as the two
heroines say farewell to their lovers as they (supposedly) go off to
war, the Schubert to life itself, as the mortally ill composer hovered
on the brink of death. In sharp contrast, Eric wrote that 'I would
like a recording of the Internationale as I go out', a last reminder
of his lifelong political commitment.[131]

Eric's funeral, held at Golders Green Crematorium in north
London on 10 October 2012, began with a tribute from Roy
Foster, followed by a recorded excerpt from Beethoven's *Archduke
Trio* for violin, cello and piano, opus 97, substituting for the
Schubert. Nick Jacobs then read Brecht's *An die Nachgeborenen*, 'To
Those Born After Us', with its opening line, 'Truly, I live in dark

times', and its regret that 'the goal was far distant; it was clearly visible, though for me it could scarcely be reached'. Eric's grandson, Roman Hobsbawm Bamping, read a passage from *Interesting Times*, followed by a recording of the trio from *Così fan tutte* and a lively address from Andy. Helena Kennedy, a left-wing Scottish lawyer and Labour peeress who was related to Marlene by marriage, read from Eric's 2010 reminiscences about his time as a jazz correspondent in the 1950s. In a tribute to Eric's love of jazz, a recording followed of the Kenny Barron Trio playing 'Slow Grind', Eric's choice on *Desert Island Discs*.[133] At the end, Ira Katznelson remembered, he approached the coffin. '"I'm now going to enunciate the classic Jewish prayer, the Kaddish, at Eric's request", I said. And there was a kind of – you could see some intake of breath, and I simply then recited it.'[132] It was on the programme, so nobody should have been surprised, but perhaps people were taken aback by the introduction of a Jewish prayer into a ceremony that Eric had insisted had to be resolutely secular: the Kaddish is addressed, in Hebrew, to the Deity, though, in the liberal version used at Eric's funeral, it also includes the plea to extend Divine mercy 'to all the sons of Adam'. Eric had asked Katznelson to say the prayer as far back as 2007, when he first made arrangements for his death. 'I, of course', Katznelson recalled, 'remember being both deeply moved, honoured, and surprised, because I would not have, you know, anticipated that that would be one of the things that he would want done at his funeral.' It was in remembrance of his mother, who all those years ago had told him never to say or do anything that would cause him to be ashamed of the fact that he was Jewish. 'So', as Julia noted, 'at the very end when Ira, fresh off the red-eye from Manhattan, read the most important prayer of the Jews, I knew that my Dad – unobservant of the Jewish faith in any way during his life – was keeping true to her wish and her memory now, possibly when it mattered most.'[133]

Among the guests was his old girlfriend Jo, with whom Eric had re-established contact in the mid-1960s and who had settled down and brought up a family of her own. She had visited Eric and Marlene in Clapham and in Hampstead many times over the years, and Eric had helped her financially, especially at Christmas time, since she was always short of money. A shared love of jazz was the continuing bond that maintained their friendship. 'She never felt sorry for herself', Marlene remembered, 'and laughed a lot. She was always good company and was lovely to Andy and Julia, who formed their own bond with her family. It was Julia who told Jo when Eric died.'[135] As the family and guests filed out, to the strains of the Internationale, the body was consigned to the flames, to be cremated. The ashes were given to the family for burial.

A few days later, the family and guests made their way to Highgate Cemetery, as Julia reported:

> The cemetery plot, situated as my husband Alaric wryly pointed out later 'just to the right of Karl Marx', had been freshly dug. We were led up a slim track, slippery and muddy from persistent drizzle ... My mum Marlene had bought the plot in an expensive and expansive act of love several years earlier. . . . My dad was pleased knowing that he would end up there. Highgate Cemetery's east wing is full of iconoclasts from the intelligentsia. I can picture him, glasses pushed up over his high forehead, peering longsightedly at the guide produced by the Friends of Highgate Cemetery Trust about its history, hoovering up the text and filleting it for us in an exact and pithy way. 'Ah yes,' he might say, energised like a freshly charged battery by what he had just read, 'you see what is really interesting about this is . . . ' . . . Earlier, as I was buying a small bunch of flowers to lay on the grave, I had an overwhelming sentimental urge to give my father one last thing to read: it seemed impossible that he would never breathe in ideas again. I bought the *London Review of Books*, which he had regularly contributed to in life and which featured, as it happened, his friend Karl Miller's obituary of him. We laid the copy, fresh and folded, on top, and then the gravedigger finished his work.[136]

Conclusion

'There was something "so whole" about Eric all the time', Marlene wrote afterwards, 'and that is what I miss the most. And his lovely voice. It is worse now without the drama of death and funeral. Even though I do not mind being alone here in the house where I feel his presence.'[1] In the meantime, there was the business of tidying up his affairs to cope with. Eric 'was always very conscious of being significantly older than Marlene', Roderick Floud noted, 'and therefore having a responsibility to order his affairs so that she would be well looked-after'.[2] He had made a will in 1962 'in anticipation of my intended marriage with Marlene Schwarz', leaving everything to her and appointing her sole executrix.[3] Half a century later, on 27 June 2012, however, in the face of imminent death, Eric wrote a new Last Will and Testament, more considered and more detailed than the first. He left Marlene as Executrix, along with her cousin Patsy Blair, and also added his friend Garry Runciman, whom he had approached long before, in 1995. As Runciman recalled, Eric and Marlene were staying with him and his family in the Berkshire countryside at the time, 'and he just said, out of the blue, "would you be prepared to consider ... "' Runciman was surprised, but said 'if you ask me to, I will'. An hereditary peer, sometime member of what later became the Financial Services Authority, and President of the British Academy from 2001 to 2005, Runciman was 'somebody who had experience of public life – the world, as it were', and Eric thought that he 'would be a useful person to have for that reason: dealing with lawyers and accountants'.[4] Bruce Hunter and Chris Wrigley were confirmed as Literary Executors.

Eric left the bulk of his estate to Marlene, and after her death to his children. There were smaller legacies: Eric left a Japanese statue to Marion Bennathan, and a first edition of Karl Kraus's *Die letzten Tage der Menschheit*, originally given to him by his mother, to Nick Jacobs, along with a small legacy to Jo. After discussing the matter with Esra Bennathan, Eric had made joint provision with him for Joss Bennathan and his children. The organisers of July's Gwenddwr show, where he had been such an assiduous attender during the time he had stayed at the cottage that he was elected honorary President, coincidentally (one hopes) in the year when Eve, Andy's daughter, won the prize for the best baby under six months of age, received some money to help the show continue.[5]

Eric had also assumed that his friends would want to stage a memorial event for him, and he had issued a few instructions for this:

> Strictly non-religious. Birkbeck, the College should be consulted. Expect they would want to do something and probably their public relations dept will be helpful. BUT DON'T ACCEPT ANY LOCATION IN BIRKBECK ITSELF, AS THERE ARE NO SUITABLE ONES. If King's wants to do something, that's fine by me, but I do not feel a big deal in the Chapel is our style. Consult Roy Foster on this. Possible speakers: Neal Ascherson, Keith Thomas to speak, if he is willing. And/or (Sir) Ian Kershaw. Tristram Hunt? It would be nice if Gordon Brown were willing to say a word or two or send a message.

In the end, the memorial for Eric was held in London University's Senate House on 24 April 2013. There were tributes from his family and friends, including Roderick Floud, Leslie Bethell, Neal Ascherson and Donald Sassoon, Claire Tomalin, Simon Schama, Frank Trentmann and Martin Jacques, together with a recorded tribute from Giorgio Napolitano. Another memorial was organised by the New School in New York from 4 to 6 in the afternoon on 25 October 2013. At Birkbeck, funds were raised from his friends and former colleagues for some postgraduate scholarships in his name, and a large international conference was held from 29 April to 1 May 2014 to assess his legacy: some of the papers were collected and published under the conference's title *History after Hobsbawm* by Oxford University Press in 2017. Edited by John Arnold, Matthew Hilton and Jan Rüger, it explored the nature and impact of Eric's own work – the subject of a penetrating essay by Geoff Eley – and discussed the various aspects of the historian's craft as it might be expected to develop in the twenty-first century. As so often with Eric, history was bridging the gap between past, present and future.

Few assessments of the nature and significance of his impact as an historian were more honest and balanced than those made by Eric himself in his last years. As he looked back over his life not long before his ninetieth birthday, he felt grateful that he

had the good fortune to belong to a worldwide generation of historians who revolutionized the writing of history between the 30s and the historiographical turn of the 70s of the last century, above all through new connections between history and the social sciences. They were not an ideological school but were engaged in the struggle of historiographical 'modernity' against the old Rankean historiography, whether under the flags of economic history, of French sociology and geography as with the *Annales*, of Marxism or of Max Weber. Why the Marxists played such a key role in England has not yet been explained, but the contribution and influence of the journal they founded, *Past and Present*, ran parallel to the French *Annales* and the German 'Bielefeld school' of societal history. All regarded each other as allies. My historiographical development ran through the Economic History Society of my old teacher Mounia Postan, through the well-known group of Communist historians, also as co-founder of *Past and Present*, and as a member, already in 1950, of the social history section of the International Committee of Historical Sciences founded on the initiative of the French.

My work as a historian is rooted in these groups of colleagues, comrades and friends, and my contribution, e.g. to the rise of so-called social or societal history, cannot be divorced from that of these collectives.[6]

Eric thought his own personal contribution rested first of all in his ability to reach many non-professional historians in many countries with his books. 'I believe I have become probably the internationally best-known British historian, at least since Arnold Toynbee', he said proudly:

I would most like to describe myself as a kind of guerrilla historian, who doesn't so much march directly towards his goal behind the artillery fire of the archives, as attack it from the flanking bushes with the Kalashnikov of ideas. I'm basically a curious or problem-oriented historian who tries to bring fresh perspectives to bear on old discussions by posing new questions and opening up new areas. I've sometimes succeeded in this, even if most of my theses haven't prevailed. What counts is that my chapter on bandits in social rebellions unleashed a huge and mostly critical literature on the history of social banditry. The fact that I approach history intuitively and without much planning has helped me in this respect. For it has sometimes enabled me instinctively to recognise the moment in which certain problems as it were come onto the agenda of [historical] science, and then sometimes to grasp it in a phrase. That's why my work on social rebels gained an almost immediate international reputation among younger historians, sociologists and anthropologists. That's most likely the reason why my little phrase 'The Invention of Tradition' and the book that came out of it is still discussed today. And why my little book on *Nation[s] and Nationalism* is circulating in 24 languages despite its obvious errors.[7]

All the books he had published since the 1950s were still, he noted proudly, in print somewhere or other. He did not care, however, how long they would last. 'Obsolescence is the unavoidable fate of the historian.' The only ones who lasted were those whose output attained the status of literature, like Gibbon, Macaulay or Michelet, and he didn't think he belonged in their company, though one never knew: 'only the future can decide'.[8]

There were the inevitable blind spots in his knowledge. Apart from Algeria and Tunisia, the subjects of his undergraduate dissertation, and South Africa under apartheid, he neither knew a great deal nor cared very much about Africa, certainly not sub-Saharan Africa. Lise Grande noted that when she told him about her own work in South Sudan and the United Nations humanitarian missions in Sub-Saharan Africa, 'he was very uninterested ... He didn't think it was important ... "Well, you know, it's not as if all places are equally important. Some just quite clearly aren't ... " And that was absolutely Africa.'[9] Eric had drawn his cultural attitudes primarily from the Central European and especially Austrian tradition of high culture in which he had grown up. His surveys of nineteenth- and twentieth-century history contained little on popular culture, least of all on the folk cultures to which the great mass of Europeans were bound for most of the period. He repeatedly made his distaste for pop music and post-1968 youth culture apparent. His hostility to the artistic avant-garde of the modern age, indeed to modernism in general, was undisguised. Although in his writings (including, provocatively, a lecture delivered at the Salzburg Festival) he dismissed classical music as the endless, barren repetition of the familiar, and modern music as incomprehensible and irrelevant, in fact he possessed a substantial collection of recordings of the classical repertoire and went frequently to the opera and to concerts. The visual arts continued to be an inspiration throughout his life, ever since as a teenager he had explored the great museums and galleries of London, but his interest seemed to stop somewhere in the 1920s. A third blind spot was the history of women, a product most of all of the Marxist influence on his thinking, which prioritised class over gender and regarded feminism as an irrelevant diversion from the struggle for a social revolution that would bring about the equality of women by itself. Although he did his best, especially in *The Age of Empire*, to make good this deficit, his effort was never more than half-hearted, and in dealing with the topic his usual sureness of touch frequently deserted him.

Eric came to Marxist theory and Communist ideals in Berlin in the early 1930s, where the Communist Party seemed to many young people of his generation to hold out the only hope of defeating Nazism and building a better world. The ecstatic feeling of being part of a great mass movement whose members were closely bound together by their common ideals engendered a lifelong, viscerally emotional sense of belonging that formed a substitute for his shattered family life; before it, for a brief time, the Boy Scout movement had fulfilled a similar function. This feeling lasted, buried deep in his soul, for the rest of his life. In the immediate post-war years it powered his academic work, which was directed towards reconstructing the onward march of the labour movement, carried along by the tides of history. But as he became disillusioned with the realities of Communism, he turned towards marginal and deviant people in his work as much as in his own personal life, following the ending of what he had supposed to be a comradely political marriage to his first wife, Muriel Seaman. His search for a community that provided some kind of emotional equivalent of a family led him for a time to the world of jazz, but he eventually became disillusioned with it. Just at the right time, he entered into his second marriage, with Marlene Schwarz, and with her he built a real, stable and emotionally supportive family life of his own. This new, solid and permanent emotional basis supported his turn to the large-scale historical syntheses that made him famous.

He remained consciously part of a global network of left-wing intellectuals for the rest of his life, gradually coming to combine this with the financial and social accoutrements of success and his ascent into the ranks of the British Establishment. His self-image as a communist intellectual rather than a Communist militant or activist was forged very early on, out of disillusion with the marginal status of the British Communist movement compared to the mass movement of its German counterpart. The idea of

Communism, of belonging to a vast, global, mass movement to bring about a just and egalitarian society, survived in him throughout his life, but during his adult years he seldom willingly followed the Party line, and absorbed, above all in Paris in the 1950s, dissident and unorthodox forms of Marxism, repudiating Party orthodoxy even before he broke with it altogether in 1956. He stayed in the Communist Party right up to the end above all because membership was for him a central part of the identity he had formed as an adolescent; in terms of practical politics, he was always closer to the British Labour Party, even after he transferred his formal political loyalties from the British to the Italian Communist Party. He was never a Stalinist, and his belief that the Left needed to acknowledge the crimes and errors of Stalinism was a central feature in his ideological break with the Party in 1956. His Marxism became more diffuse as he grew older, but it never disappeared altogether, blending in a unique intellectual mix with the many other influences he had absorbed, from Cambridge onwards, on his practice as an historian.

Eric was above all a writer, learning his craft long before he turned to history as a profession. Some of his most vivid writings focused on his own personal experiences, recorded in diaries and letters as well as essays and short stories. He came to the practice of history through literature, having read a vast number of classic works of poetry and fiction in several languages, and this was surely a major part of his global appeal, along with his vast breadth of knowledge, his ability to illustrate historical argument with contemporary anecdote and quotation, and his gift for the telling vignette and the striking phrase. It is for this reason as much as for any other that his work has lasted so long.

There was never, as he remarked in the conference held at Birkbeck to mark his eightieth birthday, such a thing as 'Hobsbawmism' or such people as 'Hobsbawmians', or a specific school of historians whom he gathered around him. 'His unusual combination of theoretical clarity, large generalising capacity and an uncanny eye for suggestive detail', as his friend the American historian Eugene D. Genovese, who died just a few days before

Eric, had noted some years before, 'combined with his staggering breadth of reference across countries, continents and centuries, drawing on sources in a wide variety of languages, made his example difficult if not impossible to follow.'[10] But there was a 'Hobsbawm generation, whose interest in the recent past', as Tony Judt noted, 'was irrevocably shaped by Eric Hobsbawm's writing', who read everything Eric wrote, debated it, absorbed it, quarrelled with it, and profited from it.[11] His influence is thus difficult to pin down because, while it has been very wide, it has also been very diffuse and many-sided. All these are reasons why his books and essays are still read and debated today, and will continue to be read and debated long into the future.

List of Abbreviations

AEC	Army Educational Corps
BBC WAC	British Broadcasting Corporation Written Archives Centre (Caversham)
BULSC	Bristol University Library Special Collections
CCAC	Churchill College Archives Centre (Cambridge)
CH	Companion of Honour
CP	Communist Party
CPGB	Communist Party of Great Britain
CUL	Cambridge University Library
DHAA	David Higham Associates Archive (London)
EJH	Eric J. Hobsbawm
FLA	Fritz Lustig Archive (London)
FLN	Front de libération nationale
HFA	Hobsbawm Family Archive (London)
HRC	Harry Ransom Center (University of Texas at Austin)
IT	*Interesting Times*
KCAC	King's College Archive Centre (Cambridge)
LBA	Little, Brown Archive (London)
LHA	Labour History Archive and Study Centre, People's History Museum (Manchester)
LSE	London School of Economics
MRC	Modern Records Centre (University of Warwick)
NATO	North Atlantic Treaty Organisation
OAS	Organisation armée secréte

PBA	Penguin Books Archive (London)
RJE	Richard J. Evans
SMGS	St Marylebone Grammar School
TB	Tagebuch (diary)
TNA	The National Archives (Kew)
UMA	University of Manchester Archive
UNESCO	United Nations Educational, Scientific and Cultural Organisation
WNA	Weidenfeld & Nicolson Archive (London)
WSA	World Student Association

Notes

Preface

1 EJH, *Interesting Times. A Twentieth-Century Life* (Penguin/Allen Lane, 2002, hereinafter *IT*), pp. xii, xiv.
2 Entretien entre Elise Marienstras et Charlotte Faucher, 27.6.2016 à Paris.
3 MRC 937/8/2/35: Stefan Collini, 'The saga of Eric the Red', *Independent* magazine, 14.9.02.
4 *IT*, p. xiii.
5 MRC 937/7/8/1: 'Rathaus/history', Jan. 2008.

Chapter 1: 'The English Boy'

1 Jerry White, *London in the Nineteenth Century: 'A Human Awful Wonder of God'* (London, 2007), p. 154. For the appalling conditions of life in Poland at this time, see David Vital, *A People Apart: The Jews in Europe, 1789–1939* (Oxford, 1999), pp. 299–309.
2 Interview with Robin Marchesi, 6.12.2016.
3 EJH, *The Age of Empire 1875–1914* (London, 1987), pp. 2 3.
4 HFA: *Daily Telegraph*, 1 July 2005. Another of the older Philip's sons became Reuben Osborn, author of a pioneering study of *Freud and Marx*, published by the Left Book Club in 1937. Eric covered the history of his parents' families in a chapter of *Interesting Times* which his editor, Stuart Proffitt, persuaded him to drop because 'it slowed down the narrative'. He expanded it for readers in his own family, but it has remained unpublished and is currently in the Hobsbawm Family Archive as a sixty-two-page typescript under the title 'Two Families'. For Reuben Osborn, see ibid, p. 42.
5 HFA: 'Family Tree', also for the following.
6 MRC 937/1/6/7: EJH to Brian Ryder, 29.4.96.
7 EJH, *The Age of Empire*, p. 2, also for the following; 'Two Families', p. 35.
8 HFA: Extract from 1901 census.
9 For the background, see David Feldman, *Englishmen and Jews: Social Relations and Political Culture, 1840–1914* (London, 1994).
10 HFA: 'Family Tree'; Lanver Mak, *The British in Egypt* (London, 2012)

11　HFA: Reifezeugnis Nelly Grün, with other school reports.

12　EJH, *The Age of Empire*, p. 2; HFA: 'Family Tree'; *IT*, pp. 2–4, 37–40; MRC 937/7/1/8: letter from (indecipherable) to EJH, 23.11.2001; Archiv der israelitischen Kultusgemeinde, Wien: Geburts-Buch für die Israelitsche Kultusgemeinde in Wien, p. 101, Nr. 1006.

13　MRC 937/7/1/2: Nelly Grün (Hobsbaum) letters, 16.4.15 and 20.4.15; Archiv der israelitischen Kultusgemeinde, Wien: Geburts-Anzeige Nancy Hobsbawm, Nr. 2238; MRC 937/7/1/1: copy of a marriage certificate of Moritz Grün and Ernestine Friedmann, issued 9.4.15 for the wedding of Percy Hobsbaum and Nelly Grün, and Certified Copy of an Entry of Marriage, District of British Consulate-General, at Zurich, Switzerland, 1.5.1917.

14　MRC 937/7/1/2: 8.5.15; Nelly to sisters, 9.5.15.

15　*IT*, p. 2; MRC 1215/17: TB 8.6.35: 'Today's my birthday'. See also MRC 937/1/6/6: Eric's son Andy Hobsbawm to EJH, with birthday wishes, 9.6.1995: 'I know it's a day late, but I went by the official Publisher's Calendar this year. You know, the one where you were born on June 9th!' Many if not most articles and short biographies about Eric, including my own memoir, 'Eric John Ernest Hobsbawm', *Biographical Memoirs of Fellows of the British Academy*, XIV (2015), pp. 207–60, still record his date of birth as 9 June. For Eric's names, see EJH, 'Two Families', pp. 44–6.

16　Thanks to Ron's daughter Angela Hobsbaum, who kindly showed me her father's school name tags. Eric's birth certificate also spells his parents' name with a 'w' and not a 'u', but of course Percy's birth had been officially registered long before the war with the correct spelling: HFA: Certified copy of an entry of birth within the district of the British Consul-General at Alexandria, Egypt.

17　*IT*, p. 3.

18　MRC 937/7 /1/3: Nelly to parents, n.d. (May 1919).

19　'Stories my country told me: On the Pressburgerbahn', *Arena* (1996).

20　*IT*, pp. 3–7. The Golds left for Persia in 1930, where Franz Gold worked for the National Bank, and so they survived Nazi persecution. They returned to Vienna after the war, where all four children entered the acting profession. See MRC 937/7/8/1: Melitta Arnemann to EJH, 8.12.2000.

21　MRC 937/7/1/3: Nelly to Gretl, 17.4.31.

22　Archiv der israelitischen Kultusgemeinde Wien: Geburts-Buch für die isr. Kultusgemeinde in Wien, Nr. 2463; ibid, Trauungsbuch für die israelitische Kultusgemeinde in Wien, 1. Bezirk (Innere Stadt), 228.

23　TNA KV2/3980, 14a: Metropolitan Police, 17.8.42.

24　*IT*, p. 11.

25　Archiv der israelitischen Kultusgemeinde Wien: Geburts-Buch für die isr. Kultusgemeinde in Wien, Nr. 407.

26　*IT*, p. 15.

27　Archiv der israelitischen Kultusgemeinde, Wien: Geburts-Anzeige Nancy Hobsbawm, Nr. 2238.

28　MRC 937/7/8/1: 'Wien 2003 5 Mai. Dankesworte' (speech on the occasion of the granting of the grand gold medal of the City of Vienna). It was more than a slight hint, as I discovered in the late 1990s when recording a joint interview in German about the current and future state of history as a discipline for the

Österreichische Zeitschrift für Geschichtswissenschaften: see 'Die Verteidigung der Geschichte. Ein Gespräch zwischen Richard Evans, Eric Hobsbawm und Albert Müller', *Österreichische Zeitschrift für Geschichtswissenschaften*, Vol. 9, No. 1 (April, 1998), pp. 108–23. Neal Ascherson, who heard him speak at an event in Berlin in 1968, was also surprised at his 'intense Austrian accent' (interview with Neal Ascherson, 26.7.2016).

29   *IT*, pp. 9–11. For Nancy's date of birth, see also TNA KV2/3980, 14a, Metropolitan Police, 17.8.42.

30   Archiv der Fichtnergasse-Schule, Wien, Hauptkataloge der Jahrgänge 1927/28 und 1928/29.

31   *IT*, pp. 20–5.

32   *IT*, pp. 12–25. See Peter Pulzer, *The Rise of Political Anti-Semitism in Germany and Austria* (London, 1964).

33   MRC 937/7/1/3: Nelly to Gretl, 13.8.24, 19.9.24.

34   Ibid: Nelly to Gretl, 23.3.25.

35   MRC 937/7/1/2: Nelly to Gretl, 7.3.25 and 18.3.25.

36   *IT*, p. 3, quoting Nelly to Gretl, 5.12.28.

37   *IT*, p. 31.

38   *IT*, pp. 30–1; Peter Eigner and Andrea Helige, *Österreichische Wirtschafts- und Sozialgeschichte im 19. und 20. Jahrhundert* (Vienna, 1999).

39   See for example Martha Ostenso, *Die tollen Carews. Roman* (Deutsch von Nelly Hobsbaum (Wien, 1928)). The novel had appeared in English the previous year as *The Mad Carews*. Nelly's translation had already sold ten thousand copies by the end of 1928.

40   *IT*, p. 27; Wiener Stadt- und Landesarchiv, BG Hietzing, A4/1-1A: (Leopold) Percy Hobsbaum, Nr. 3543040320: Meldezettel für Haupt (Jahres und Monats) wohnparteien, date stamp 13.5.26.

41   *IT*, p. 14.

42   *IT*, p. 9.

43   *IT*, pp. 30–1.

44   MRC 937/7/1/3: Nelly to Gretl, 11.1.29.

45   *IT*, p. 15. Perhaps because of this, Eric kept the atlas for the rest of his life.

46   MRC 937/7/1/3: Nelly to Gretl, 5.2.29.

47   Archiv der Fichtnergasse-Schule, Wien: Bundesgymnasium und Bundesrealgymnasium Wien 13,: Hauptkataloge der Jahrgänge 1927/28 und 1928/29. His school reports gave his name as 'Erich Hobsbawn'. See also: Landesgymnasium in Wien, 13. Bezirk, Jahreszeugnis Schuljahr 1927/29: Hobshawn, Erich.

48   MRC 937/1/5/2. EJH to Christhard Hoffmann, 18.7.88.

49   Archiv der Fichtnergasse-Schule, Wien: Bundesgymnasium und Bundesrealgymnasium Wien 13: Hauptkataloge der Jahrgänge 1927/28 und 1928/29.

50   *IT*, p. 34.

51   *IT*, p. 2.

52   *IT*, pp. 26–31; MRC 937/7/1/8: Merkbuch für Bekenntnisse.

53   *IT*, pp. 26–9.

54   *IT*, p. 28.

55   Ibid, notes; Nelly to Gretl, 5.2.29, 1.3.29.

56 MRC 937/7/1/2: Nelly to Gretl, 5.2.29.
57 *IT*, p. 27; Wiener Stadt- und Landesarchiv, BG Hietzing, A4/1-1A: (Leopold) Percy Hobsbaum, Nr. 3543040320: Meldezettel für Haupt (Jahres und Monats) wohnparteien, date stamp 13.5.26.
58 Interview with Robin Marchesi, 6.12.16.
59 MRC 1215/15: TB 28.11.34.
60 Archiv der israelitischen Kultusgemeinde Wien: Matrikenamt der IKG Wien, Sterbe-Buch über die in Wien bei der israelitischen Kultusgemeinde vorkommenden Todesfälle, Fol.173, Nr. 392.
61 MRC 937/7/1/2: Nelly to Gretl, 15.2.29.
62 Ibid: Nelly to Sidney, 13.3.29.
63 Ibid: Nelly to Gretl, 24.3.29.
64 Wiener Stadt- und Landesarchiv MA 8: BG Hietzing A4/1-1A: (Leopold) Percy Hobsbaum, gest. 8.2.1929: Meldezettel für Haupt (Jahres- und Monats) wohnparteien, date stamp 13.5.26.
65 MRC 937/7/1/2: Nelly to Gretl, undated.
66 *IT*, pp. 31–2.
67 MRC 937/7/1/2: Nelly to Gretl, 28.4.29; EJH to Sidney, 26.4.29. Otto and Walter were two teenage cousins, both living in Berlin.
68 Ibid: Nelly to Gretl, undated; EJH to Gretl, undated (both June 1929).
69 MRC 937/7/1/3: Nelly to Gretl, 24.5.29; MRC 937/7/1/2: Nelly to Gretl, 1.3.29.
70 MRC 1215/21: TB 24.6.40.
71 TNA KV2/3980, 14a: Metropolitan Police, 20.8.42, p. 2.
72 HFA: EJH, speech at funeral service for Roland Matthew Hobsbaum, n.d.
73 *IT*, p. 35.
74 MRC 937/7/1/2: Nelly to Gretl, 21.7.29. The diary, like all the diaries Eric kept before 1934, has not survived.
75 Ibid: Nelly to Gretl, 5.8.29.
76 *IT*, p. 35.
77 MRC 937/7/1/3: Nelly to Gretl, 24.2.30.
78 Ibid: Nelly to Gretl, 15.5.29.
79 MRC 937/7/1/2: Nelly to Gretl, 6.11.29; MRC 937/7/1/3: Nelly to Gretl, 3.5.29; *IT*, pp. 31–2.
80 MRC 937/7/1/2: Nelly to Gretl, 6.11.29.
81 Ibid: Nelly to Gretl, 9.4.30, 15.4.30, 23.4.30.
82 MRC 937/7/1/3; Nelly to Gretl, 17.1.30.
83 Ibid: 2.3.30, 5.5.30.
84 Ibid: 9.4.30, 11.4.30, 25.4.30.
85 Ibid: 18.4.30.
86 *IT*, p. 33.
87 MRC 937/7/1/3; Nelly to Gretl: 28.4.30, 5.5.30.
88 *IT*, p. 13.
89 Ibid: 5.9.30.
90 MRC 937/7/1/2: Nelly to Mimi, 14.9.30.
91 Ibid: Nelly to Mimi, 28.9.30.
92 Ibid: Nelly to Gretl, 19.9.30, 23.9.30; MRC 937/7/1/3: Nelly to Gretl, 17.1.30.
93 MRC 937/7/1/2: Nelly to Sidney, 11.9.30.

94 Ibid: Nelly to Nancy, 3.11.30.
95 *IT*, pp. 35–7. See also MRC 937/7/1/2: Nelly to Gretl, 20.4.21 (misdated, date uncertain); ibid: Nelly to Gretl, 19.3.31, for Nancy's move to Berlin; MRC 937/7/1/3: Nelly to Gretl, 30.8.30.
96 http://adresscomptoir.twoday.net/stories/498219618/ accessed 2.11.2015.
97 *IT*, p. 36.
98 MRC 937/7/1/3: Nelly to Gretl, 19.9.30.
99 MRC 937/7/1/2: Eric to Gretl and Sidney, 6.2.31.
100 Ibid: Nelly to Gretl, 24.11.30.
101 *IT*, p. 42.
102 MRC 937/7/1/2: Nelly to Gretl, 27.10.30; MRC 937/7/3: Nelly to Gretl, 20.10.30, 27.11.30.
103 Ibid: Nelly to Gretl, 12.12.30.
104 Ibid: Nelly to Gretl, 4.12.30.
105 Ibid: Nelly to Gretl, 12.12.30.
106 Ibid: Nelly to Gretl, 20.12.30.
107 Ibid: Nelly to Gretl, 20.12.30.
108 Ibid: Nelly to Gretl, 20.10.30.
109 *IT*, p. 36.
110 MRC 937/7/1/2: Nelly to Gretl, 1.1.31; MRC 937/7/1/3: Nelly to Gretl, 20.12.30.
111 Ibid: Nelly to Sidney and family, 24.4.31.
112 MRC 937/7/1/3: Nelly to Gretl and Sidney, 6.5.31.
113 *IT*, p. 37.
114 Archiv der israelitischen Kultusgemeinde Wien: Matrikenamt der IKG Wien, Sterbe-Buch über die in St. Pölten bei der israelitischen Kultusgemeinde vorkommenden Todesfälle, Fol. 24, Nr. 145. The official record of the burial gave her date of death wrongly as 16 July; Eric misremembered it as 12 July.
115 *IT*, pp. 26–34, 37–41.
116 MRC 937/7/1/4, *passim*.
117 *IT*, pp. 39–40.
118 MRC 1215/16: TB 13.4.35.
119 *IT*, p. 39.
120 MRC 1215/16: TB 2.5.35; *IT*, p. 39.
121 MRC 1215/17: TB 4.6.35.
122 Ibid: TB 12.7.35.
123 *IT*, p. 41.
124 Wiener Stadt- und Landesarchiv, BG Landstrasse, A4/4/4A: Nelly Hobsbawm, gest. 15.7.1931, Nr. 8066691950: Todesfallaufnahme, 24.7.31. The recording official evidently assumed Nelly's surname from Eric's. See also ibid: BG Hietzing, A4/1-1A: Leopold (Percy) Hobsbaum, gest. 8.2.1929, Nr. 3543040320: Meldezettel für Unterparteien, date stamped 16.11.30. Unusually, the document gives Eric's date of birth correctly.
125 HFA: EJH, 'Two Families', p. 58.
126 Wiener Stadt- und Landesarchiv: BG Hietzing, A4/1-1A: Leopold (Percy) Hobsbaum, gest. 8.2.1929, Nr. 3543040320: Meldezettel für Unterparteien, date stamped 16.11.30.
127 *IT*, pp. 33–5, 51; MRC 937/7/1.2: Nelly to Sidney, 4.3.31.
128 *IT*, p. 48.

129   *IT*, p. 59.
130   *IT*, pp. 49–55.
131   Fritz Lustig Archive (FLA): Fritz Lustig memoirs: 'The
      Prinz-Heinrichs-Gymnasium'.
132   Ibid.
133   *IT*, p. 54. They were not, however, as Eric claimed in his memoirs, addressed
      with the title 'Professor'. On being told that he had got this wrong, Eric
      remarked to Fritz Lustig: 'It just shows you can never rely on unaided
      memory.' See FLA: EJH to Fritz Lustig, 5.3.2003; and *IT*, p. 54.
134   Fritz Lustig, 'PHG-Erinnerungen', *Prinz-Heinrichs-Gymnasium Vereinigung
      ehemaliger Schüler*, Rundbrief Nr. 45, August 1982, pp. 12–18, at p. 17; FLA:
      Fritz Lustig, memoirs: 'The Prinz-Heinrichs-Gymnasium'.
135   'Karl-Günther von Hase', *Prinz-Heinrichs-Gymnasium Vereinigung ehemaliger
      Schüler*, Rundbrief Nr. 49, Feb. 1982, pp. 2–12, at p. 7 (reprint of Hase's
      contribution to Rudolf Pôrtner (ed.), *Mein Elternhaus: ein deutsches Familienalbum*
      (Berlin, 1984). See also *IT*, p. 49.
136   *IT*, p. 55.
137   Ibid.
138   Lustig, 'PHG-Erinnerungen', p. 17.
139   Ibid, pp. 13–14.
140   Margret Kraul, *Das deutsche Gymnasium 1780–1980* (Frankfurt, 1984), pp.
      127–44.
141   Interview with Fritz Lustig, 30.5.2016.
142   Interview with Fritz Lustig, 30.5.2016; Heinz Stallmann, *Das Prinz-Heinrichs-
      Gymnasium zu Schöneberg 1890–1945: Geschichte einer Schule* (privately printed,
      Berlin, 1965), pp. 44–55; *IT*, pp. 49–54. Eric did not realise at the time, or
      for long afterwards, that Schönbrunn was actually a member of the Social
      Democratic Party: FLA: EJH to Fritz Lustig, 5.3.2003. I am most grateful to
      Fritz Lustig for providing me with copies of the school history by Stallmann
      and other relevant publications and unpublished material in his possession.
143   MRC 937/1/3/11: *Extract from the memoirs of Theodore H ('Ted') Lustig (1912–2001)*
      [privately printed], pp. 47–8.
144   Interview with Fritz Lustig, 30.5.2016.
145   Lustig, 'PHG-Erinnerungen', p. 13.
146   MRC 1215/17: TB 12.7.35.
147   MRC 1215/21: TB 16.3.40.
148   *IT* p. 52; Lustig, 'PHG-Erinnerungen', p. 18.
149   MRC 937/1/3/11: *Extract from the memoirs of Theodore H ('Ted') Lustig (1912–2001)*
      [privately printed], pp. 32–6.
150   FLA: Fritz Lustig to EJH, 24.4.95.
151   FLA: Fritz Lustig to EJH, 26.2.2003.
152   Lustig, 'PHG-Erinnerungen', p. 16.
153   FLA: Fritz Lustig memoirs: 'The Prinz-Heinrichs-Gymnasium'.
154   *IT*, p. 53; N. Blumental (ed.), *Dokumenty i materialy*, Vol. 1, *Obozy* (Lodz, 1946),
      p. 117; Martin Löffler, 'PHG-Lehrer: Jüngere Generation', *Prinz-Heinrichs-
      Gymnasium Vereinigung ehemaliger Schüler*, Rundbrief 47 (September 1983), pp.
      17–19. Another Jewish teacher, Rubensohn, emigrated: Stallmann, *Das Prinz-
      Heinrichs-Gymnasium*, pp. 131–5.

155 'Karl-Günther von Hase', p. 7; interview with Fritz Lustig, 30.5.2016.

156 *IT*, p. 52. The Gauleiter, Wilhelm Kube, was appointed to run occupied Belarus during the war and was killed in 1943 by a bomb placed under his mattress by a partisan who had managed to secure employment as a chambermaid in his house. See Ernst Klee, *Das Personenlexikon zum Dritten Reich* (Frankfurt, 2005), p. 346.

157 *IT*, pp. 56–7.

158 Fritz Lustig to EJH, 26.2.2003 (also in MRC 937/1/3/11); FLA: EJH to Fritz Lustig, 5.3.2003; *IT*, pp. 56–7.

159 *IT*, p. 57.

160 Richard J. Evans, *The Coming of the Third Reich* (London, 2003), for details.

161 Klaus-Michael Mallmann, *Kommunisten in der Weimarer Republik. Sozialgeschichte einer revolutionären Bewegung* (Darmstadt, 1996), pp. 94–106. More generally, see Eric D. Weitz, *Creating German Communism, 1890–1990: From Popular Protests to Socialist State* (Princeton, NJ, 1997), pp. 100–87; and Eve Rosenhaft, *Beating the Fascists? The German Communists and Political Violence, 1929–1933* (Cambridge, 1983).

162 Evans, *The Coming of the Third Reich*.

163 Nicolau Sevcenko, 'Hobsbawm chega com "A Era dos Impérios"', *Folha de São Paulo*, 8.4.1988.

164 *IT*, p. 54.

165 *IT*, p. 54.

166 *IT*, p. 47.

167 *IT*, p. 62.

168 *IT*, pp. 56–65.

169 Karl Corino, 'DDR-Schriftsteller Stephan Hermlin hat seinen Lebensmythos erlogen. Dichtung in eigener Sache', *Die Zeit*, 4 October 1996; Karl Corino, *Aussen Marmor, innen Gips. Die Legenden des Stephan Hermlin* (Düsseldorf, 1996); Stephan Hermlin, 'Schlusswort,' *Freibeuter* 70 (1996); Christoph Dieckmann, 'Das Hirn will Heimat. DDR im Abendlicht – Blick zurück nach vorn. Ein aktueller Sermon wider die Kampfgruppen der Selbstgerechtigkeit', *Die Zeit*, 25 October 1996, p. 57; Fritz J. Raddatz, 'Der Mann ohne Goldhelm. Ein Nachwort zum Fall Stephan Hermlin', *Die Zeit*, 18 October 1996, p. 63.

170 *IT*, p. 64; MRC 937/1/5/2: EJH to Stephan Hermlin, n.d.; MRC 937/7/8/1: Stephan Hermlin to EJH, 16.3.65.

171 MRC 937/1/5/2: Karl Corino to EJH, 28.6.2007.

172 Among many useful surveys, see Archie Brown, *The Rise and Fall of Communism* (London, 2009), pp. 56–100, and David Priestland, *The Red Flag: Communism and the Making of the Modern World* (London, 2009), pp. 103–81.

173 *IT*, p. 42.

174 *IT*, p. 60.

175 *IT*, p. 58; MRC 1215/15: TB 27.11.34. See also Felix Krolikowski, 'Erinnerungen: Kommunistische Schülerbewegung in der Weimarer Republik', copy in MRC 937/7/8/1, and Knud Andersen, 'Kommunistische Politik an höheren Schulen: Der Sozialistische Schülerbund 1926–1932', *Internationale Wissenschaftliche Korrespondenz zur Geschichte der deutschen Arbeiterbewegung* 42 (2006), 2/3, pp. 237–55.

176 MRC 937/1/3/11: *Extract from the memoirs of Theodore H ('Ted') Lustig (1912–2001)* [privately printed], pp. 52–3.

177 MRC 937/1/6/2; EJH to Bergmann, n.d.

178 MRC 937/6/1/1: *Der Schulkampf*, Oct. 1932. The editor invited contributions for a December issue, but it is doubtful whether this actually appeared.

179 *IT*, p. 59.

180 *IT*, p. 60. The strike was notorious for the tacit collaboration between the Communists and the Nazis. For a concise narrative see Heinrich August Winkler, *Der Weg in die Katastrophe. Arbeiter und Arbeiterbewegung in der Weimarer Republik 1930–1933* (Bonn, 1990), pp. 765–73.

181 *IT*, p. 60.

182 MRC 1215/17: TB 9.5.35.

183 Annemarie Lange, *Berlin in der Weimarer Republik* (East Berlin, 1987), pp. 1064–7.

184 Quoted in Hermann Weber et al. (eds), *Deutschland, Russland, Komintern: Nach der Archivrevolution: Neuerschlossene Quellen zu der Geschichte der KPD und den deutsch-russischen Beziehungen* (Berlin, 2014), pp. 912–13. For another account of the two demonstrations, see Ronald Friedmann, *Die Zentrale Geschichte des Berliner Karl-Liebknecht-Hauses* (Berlin, 2011), pp. 71–83.

185 *IT*, pp. 73–4.

186 'When I tell my American students,' he wrote in 1994, 'that I can remember the day in Berlin on which Hitler became Chancellor of Germany, they look at me as though I had told them that I was present in Ford's theatre when President Lincoln was assassinated in 1865. Both events are equally prehistorical for them. But for me, 30 January 1933 is part of the past which is still part of my present.' (EJH, 'The time of my life', *New Statesman*, 21.10.94, p. 30). See also EJH, 'Diary', *London Review of Books*, 24.1.2008.

187 Ben Fowkes, *Communism in Germany under the Weimar Republic* (London, 1984), pp. 168–9.

188 MRC 937/4/3/4/1: 'I do not know about Chicago', unpublished short story, also for the following paragraphs below.

189 *IT*, pp. 75–7.

190 MRC 1215/13: TB, 24.7.34.

191 Interview with Robin Marchesi, 6.12.2016.

192 Fowkes, *Communism*, pp. 169–70.

193 'Diary', *London Review of Books*, 24.1.2008.

194 Quoted in Hermann Weber, *Die Wandlung des deutschen Kommunismus. Die Stalinisierung der KPD in der Weimarer Republik* (Frankfurt, 1969), pp. 265–6.

195 'The Guru Who Retains Neil Kinnock's Ear', *Observer*, 9 September 1985.

196 *IT*, pp. 65–75.

197 For a typical example of the erroneous assumption that Eric, unlike most 'German Jews', experienced 'extraordinary good fortune in obtaining a British visa when Hitler took over their country', see Richard Grunberger, 'War's aftermath in academe', *Association of Jewish Refugees Information*, September 1997, copy in MRC 937/1/6/11. Grunberger was himself Jewish, born in Vienna, and came to the UK on a *Kindertransport* as part of a scheme on the eve of the Second World War to bring Jewish children out of Nazi-ruled Germany and Austria. Neal Ascherson, one of Eric's later pupils at King's College, Cambridge, was

under a similar misapprehension, wrongly claiming in a biographical profile that 'he was sent to Britain to escape Hitler' (MRC 937/8/2/22/2: Neal Ascherson, 'The Age of Hobsbawm', *Independent on Sunday*, 2.10.94, p. 21). Noel Annan, one of Eric's undergraduate friends at Cambridge, also wrongly described him as 'a refugee from Hitler' (Noel Annan, *Our Age. Portrait of a Generation* (London, 1990), p. 267). For a particularly error-prone account, see MRC 937/8/2/35: Richard Gott, 'Living through an age of extremes', *New Statesman*, 23.9.02, pp. 48–50.

198   HFA: 'Two Families', p. 57.

Chapter 2: 'Ugly as Sin, but a Mind'

1   TNA KV2/3980, 14a: Metropolitan Police, 20.8.42, p. 2.
2   HMC 937/7/8/1: EJH, speech to the Old Philologians, October 2007. Edgware is several kilometres north of Marylebone, Upper Norwood is even further away, across the river, to the south-east.
3   Every single reference to him in the school magazine, *The Philologian*, spells his name with a u and not with a w.
4   Interview with Angela Hobsbaum, 30.3.17.
5   HFA: EJH, 'Two Families', p. 53.
6   MRC 937/7/8/1: EJH, speech to the Old Philologians, October 2007, also for the following.
7   MCC was, and is, the Marylebone Cricket Club, at whose headquarters at Lord's cricket ground the rules of modern cricket were framed. Long-stop is a position on the cricket field located on the boundary behind the batsman, and there is very little to do there except stop the occasional ball that goes past the batsman and wicket-keeper and carries to the boundary, with or without the assistance of the bat. It is generally reserved in school cricket for unathletic boys with no interest in the game; I occupied it on numerous occasions myself when I was at school.
8   HFA: certificates.
9   MRC 1215/13: TB 14.5.34.
10   Ibid: TB 27.7.34.
11   MRC 1215/14: TB 5.8.34.
12   MRC 1215/15: TB 26/28.10.34; the book Eric read was Eliot's *Selected Essays 1917–1932* (1932).
13   MRC 1215/13: TB 10.4.34, 23.6.34. Taught English at school by Guy Deaton, a Leavis pupil of a later generation, I went through exactly the same sequence of reading in the mid-1960s, also ending up with D. H. Lawrence. For a useful recent biography of Leavis, see Richard Storer, *F. R. Leavis* (London, 2010). For Deaton, see the memoir by my fellow-pupil, the military historian Richard Holmes, 'My Mentor', *Guardian*, 26 August 2006 (online).
14   MRC 1215/15: TB 18–23.11.34.
15   *The Philologian*, Vol. 7, No. 1 (Autumn Term, 1934), pp. 25–6.
16   *The Philologian*, Vol. 8, No. 1 (Autumn Term, 1935), p. 22, for Eric's membership of the committee.
17   HFA: EJH, address at the funeral of Roland Matthew Hobsbaum, n.d.
18   'Debating Society', *The Philologian*, Vol. 6, No. 2 (Spring Term, 1934), p. 56.
19   *The Philologian*, Vol. 7, No. 2 (Spring Term, 1935), p. 57.

20 See Jonathan Haslam, *The Soviet Union and the Struggle for Collective Security in Europe, 1933–1939* (London, 1984), p. 66.

21 MRC 1215/18: TB 12.9.35.

22 *The Philologian*, Vol. 8, No. 1 (Autumn Term, 1935), p. 21.

23 *The Philologian*, Vol. 8, No. 3 (Summer Term, 1936), p. 83.

24 MRC 1215/16: TB 12.7.35.

25 MRC 937/4/3/5/1/1: *The Philologian*, Vol. 7, No. 2 (Spring Term, 1935), pp. 46–7. J. Dover Wilson edited a much-used edition of Shakespeare's plays; A. C. Bradley's *Shakespearean Tragedy*, published in 1904, was still regarded as the greatest work of Shakespearean criticism thirty years later; 'Baconians' were those who thought the plays had been written by the Elizabethan polymath Sir Francis Bacon. In *Macbeth* Shakespeare reveals that Lady Macbeth had one child but does not say how old it was, or if she had any more.

26 MRC 937/4/3/5/1/1: *The Philologian*, Vol. 7, No. 2 (Spring Term, 1935), p. 62; see his report in *The Philologian*, Vol. 8, No. 1 (Autumn Term, 1935), p. 24, whose brevity testifies to its author's indifference to its contents, which were confined to sports matters; also the five lines in *The Philologian*, Vol. 8, No. 3 (Summer Term, 1936), p. 85.

27 MRC 937/4/3/5/1/2: *The Philologian*, Vol. 8, No. 3 (Summer Term, 1936), p. 89.

28 MRC 1215/16: TB 22.6.35.

29 MRC 937/7/8/2: EJH, speech to the Old Philologians, October 2007.

30 Miriam Gross, 'An Interview with Eric Hobsbawm', *Time and Tide*, Autumn 1985.

31 MRC 937/7/8/2: EJH, speech to the Old Philologians, October 2007.

32 Ibid; obituary of Llewellyn Smith in *The Philologian*, 1975/77, pp. 43–6; MRC 937/1/1/4: EJH to James D. Young, 13.5.88.

33 MRC 937/7/8/1: EJH, speech to the Old Philologians, October 2007. *The History Boys*, a play by Alan Bennett, opened in 2004 and featured a homosexual history teacher. It was turned into a film in 2006, starring Richard Griffiths.

34 *IT*, p. xiii.

35 MRC 1215/14: TB 8–10.11.34.

36 MRC 1215/13: TB 4.10.34.

37 MRC 937/7/8/1: second interview with *Radical History Review*, typescript. See also ibid: Rathaus/history, Jan. 2008, where he said he became an historian when he read the *Communist Manifesto*, a statement that, as we shall see, elided many twists and turns in his life story before he actually became an historian in 1946.

38 MRC 1215/15: TB 14/17.1.35.

39 MRC 1215/16: TB 18/20.1.35.

40 Ibid.

41 MRC 937/7/8/2: EJH, speech to the Old Philologians, October 2007.

42 MRC 1215/13: TB 29/30.7.34; MRC 1215/15: TB 29.11.34.

43 MRC 1215/13: TB 15.4.34. The book was Laurence Sterne's *The Life and Opinions of Tristram Shandy, Gentleman* (London, 1759–67).

44 MRC 1215/13: TB 27.5.34. *Tugboat Annie* was an American comedy released in 1933 and starring Marie Dressler and Wallace Beery.

45 Ibid: TB 20.6.34.

46 Ibid: TB 12.4.34.

47 Ibid: TB 27.11.34, 15.4.34; MRC 1215/15: 29.11.34; MRC 1215/16: 5.5.35; MRC 1215/17: 17.5.35.

48 MRC 1215/13: TB 10.4.34.

49 'Eric Hobsbawm's *Interesting Times*: An interview with David Howell', *Socialist History* 24 (2003), pp. 1–15.

50 MRC 1215/13: TB 15.6.34.

51 Ibid: TB 23 and 27.6.34.

52 Ibid: TB 1.7.34.

53 Ibid: TB 14.4.34.

54 MRC 1215/14: TB 9.7.34.

55 Ibid: TB 29.8.34.

56 MRC 1215/13: TB 9.5.34.

57 Ibid: TB 17.4.34.

58 Ibid: TB 14.4.34, 28.5.34.

59 MRC 1215/14: TB 5.9.34.

60 MRC 1215/15: TB 23.10.34. Underlining in original. *Dies irae, dies illa* is a quote from the Latin Mass for the Dead: it refers to Judgement Day, 'that day of wrath'.

61 Ibid: TB 12/17.11.34.

62 Of the vast literature on the various Marxist traditions, George Lichtheim, *Marxism* (London, 1961), is one of the more intelligent accounts, and David McLellan, *Marxism after Marx* (London, 1979), one of the more useful.

63 MRC 1215/13: TB 15.5.34.

64 MRC 1215/14: TB 15/16.7.34.

65 MRC 1215/13: TB 28.6.34.

66 Ibid: TB 26.5.34.

67 Ibid: TB 14.4.34.

68 MRC 1215/15. TB 8.12.34.

69 MRC 1215/13: TB 23.5.34.

70 MRC 1215/14: TB 27.7.34. See Sally J. Taylor, *Stalin's Apologist: Walter Duranty. The New York Times's Man in Moscow* (New York, 1990). It was later claimed that Duranty had written privately to the British Embassy in Moscow claiming ten million people had died in the famine (a startling exaggeration, especially coming from Duranty). There were calls later for his Pulitzer Prize to be revoked. For the real impact of the famine, see Robert Conquest, *The Harvest of Sorrow: Soviet Collectivization and the Terror-famine* (Oxford, 1986).

71 MRC 1215/13: TB 23.1.34.

72 MRC 1215/17: TB 21.9.35.

73 MRC 1215/15: TB 12.11.34.

74 MRC 1215/13: TB 21.4.34; TB 12.5.34; TB 28.4.34.

75 MRC 937/7/8/1: second interview with *Radical History Review* (typescript), p. 4. *Left Review* was a cultural journal set up in 1934 by the British Section of the Writers' International, an organisation sponsored by the Communist International. It ceased publication in 1938.

76 MRC 1215/18: TB 25.9.35.

77 MRC 937/4/3/5/1/2: *The Philologian*, Vol. 8, No. 3 (Summer Term, 1936), pp. 68–9.
78 Ibid, pp. 74–5.
79 MRC 1215/18: TB 27.8.35.
80 MRC 1215/14: TB 6.9.34.
81 http://www.themillforestgreen.co.uk/memory-lane. Accessed 22.4.2016.
82 Interview with Angela Hobsbaum, 30.3.17.
83 Angela Hobsbaum to RJE, 5.5.17.
84 MRC 1215/15: TB 5.1.35.
85 Interview with Angela Hobsbaum, 30.3.17.
86 HFA: EJH, address at the funeral of Roland Matthew Hobsbaum, n.d.
87 'In Camp', *The Philologian*, Vol. 7, No. 3 (Summer Term, 1935), pp. 82–3.
88 HFA: EJH, address at the funeral of Roland Matthew Hobsbaum, n.d.
89 'Devon Fishing', *The Philologian*, Vol. 7, No. 1 (Autumn Term, 1934), pp. 7–9.
90 MRC 1215/16: TB 18/20.1.1935.
91 See Christine L. Corton, *London Fog: The Biography* (London, 2015).
92 MRC 1215/15: TB 18–23.11.34. In Greek mythology, Niobe was turned to stone by Artemis after imprudently boasting of her many and talented children. Ixion was a king who murdered his father-in-law; the act drove him mad, but Zeus took pity on him and transported him to Olympus. He behaved badly here, too, however, and lusted after Zeus's wife Hera (Juno in the Roman version of the myth), so Zeus made a cloud in her image and tricked Ixion into mating with it. From this union ultimately were descended the centaurs. Ixion himself was expelled from Olympus and bound for all eternity to a fiery wheel. A mosasaurus was a seventeen-metre-long aquatic dinosaur. The Dorchester and the Grosvenor were two large hotels.
93 MRC 1215/13: TB 29.7.34.
94 MRC 1215/15: TB 23.10.34.
95 MRC 1215/16: TB 28.11.34.
96 MRC 1215/13: TB 10.4.34.
97 Ibid: TB 23.6.34; MRC 1215/15: 28.11.34, 30.11.34.
98 MRC 1215/13: TB 15.4.34, 15.6.34; MRC 1215/15: 28.10.34.
99 MRC 1215/13: TB 28.5.34.
100 Ibid: TB 21.4.34.
101 Ibid: TB 20.7.34.
102 MRC 1215/15: TB 30.4.34, 28.11.34.
103 Ibid: TB 3.12.34. William Stanley Jevons (1835–1882) developed the concept of marginal utility, offering an alternative to the labour theory of value espoused by Marx.
104 MRC 1215/13: TB 10.4.34. For the state of British Communism at this time and before, see Henry Pelling, *The British Communist Party. A Historical Profile* (London, 1958), pp. 1–72.
105 MRC 1215/13: TB 21.4.34.
106 Ibid: TB 30.4.34.
107 Ibid: TB 5.5.34.
108 Ibid: TB 30.4.34.
109 Ibid: TB 15.5.34.

110 Ibid: TB 30.5.34. For the Olympia Rally, see Stephen Dorrill, *Black Shirt. Sir Oswald Mosley and British Fascism* (London, 2006), pp. 295–7.
111 MRC 1215/15: TB 28.11.34.
112 For the letter, see MRC 1215/16: TB 7.4.35.
113 MRC 1215/13: TB 5.5.34.
114 Ibid: TB 14.4.34.
115 Ibid: TB 29.5.34.
116 Ibid: TB 13.4.34.
117 Ibid: TB 1.6.34.
118 Ibid: TB 31.5.34.
119 Ibid: TB 31.5.34.
120 Ibid: TB 1.6.34, underlining in original.
121 Ibid: TB 31.5.34.
122 Ibid: TB 1/64, 1.6.34.
123 Ibid: TB 15.6.34.
124 Ibid: TB 31.5.34.
125 Ibid: TB 1.6.34.
126 Ibid: TB 2/3.6.34.
127 Ibid: TB 1.6.34.
128 Ibid: TB 9.6.34.
129 MRC 1215/15: TB 3.12.34.
130 MRC 1215/16: TB 7.4.35.
131 MRC 1215/14: TB 26.9.34.
132 MRC 1215/15: TB 26–28.10.34. 'Comintern' was the Communist International.
133 MRC 1215/13: TB 9.5.34.
134 MRC 1215/15: TB 29.10.34–1.11.34.
135 MRC 1215/14: TB 30.10.1934.
136 Alan Willis and John Woollard, *Twentieth Century Local Election Results, Volume 2: Election Results For London Metropolitan Boroughs* (1931–1962) (Plymouth: Local Government Chronicle Elections Centre, 2000).
137 MRC 1215/13: TB 5.5.34.
138 Ibid: TB 18.6.34.
139 MRC 1215/15: TB 30.8.34.
140 MRC 1215/17: TB 18.6.35.
141 Ibid: TB 24.7.35.
142 *IT*, p. 42.
143 MRC 1215/15: TB 12.10.34.
144 Stefan Slater, 'Prostitutes and Popular History. Notes on the "Underworld" 1918–1939', *Crime, History and Societies*, Vol. 13, No. 1 (2009), pp. 25–48; Julia Laite, *Common Prostitutes and Ordinary Citizens: Commercial Sex in London, 1885–1960* (London, 2012), p. 255 n. 95.
145 MRC 1215/16: TB 27.3.35, at midnight.
146 'How sad youth is.'
147 Ibid: TB 27.3.35, also for the following.
148 Ibid: TB 28.3.35.
149 MRC 1215/15: TB 12.10.34.
150 Ibid: TB 27/28.11.34.

151 MRC 1215/13: TB 1.7.34, 3.7.34.
152 MRC 1215/14: TB 8/9.10.34.
153 MRC 1215/15: TB 5.1.35.
154 MRC 1215/16: TB 6/7.1.35.
155 Ibid: TB 8/11.1.35.
156 Ibid: TB 14/17.1.35.
157 Ibid: TB 23/28.1.35.
158 Ibid: TB 1–14.2.35, 15–17.2.35, 28–14.2.35.
159 Ibid: TB 18–24.2.35.
160 Ibid: TB 22.1.35. See also ibid: TB 2–6.2.35. Sir Paul Vinogradoff was a Russian-born historian, exiled under the Tsars for his progressive views, who settled in Britain and became a leading specialist on English medieval agrarian history.
161 Ibid: TB 31.1/4.2.35.
162 Ibid, also for the following.
163 EJH, 'How to Plot Your Takeover', *New York Review of Books*, 21.8.69.
164 MRC 1215/16: TB 18.2–3.3.35.
165 Ibid: TB 13.3.35.
166 Ibid: TB 16.3.35.
167 Ibid: TB 7.5.35.
168 Ibid: TB 13.3.35.
169 Ibid: 29/30.1.35. See Virginia Spencer Carr, *Dos Passos: A Life* (Chicago, 2004), p. 289, for this quotation; also John Dos Passos, *In All Countries* (New York, 1934), a volume that included a favourable account of the Soviet Union.
170 MRC 1215/16: TB 7.4.35, also for the following.
171 MRC 1215/17: TB 29.5.35.
172 MRC 1215/16: TB 31.3.35.
173 Ibid: TB 13.4.35.
174 HFA: EJH, address at the funeral of Roland Matthew Hobsbaum, n.d.
175 MRC 1215/16: TB 21–28.4.35.
176 MRC 1215/17: TB 7.8.35.
177 Interview with Robin Marchesi, 6.12.2016.
178 MRC 1215/17: TB 7.8.35, also for the following.
179 TNA KV2/3980, 14A: Metropolitan Police, 20.8.42.
180 MRC 1215/16: TB 5.5.35.
181 MRC 1215/17: TB 4.6.35.
182 Ibid: TB 24.7.35.
183 MRC 1215/18: TB 20.9.35.
184 HFA: copy in the possession of Angela Hobsbaum.
185 Quoted in Angela Hobsbaum to RJE, 31.3.17.
186 MRC 1215/10: 'Listening to the blues'; Val Wilmer, 'Denis Preston' in H. C. G. Matthew and Brian Harrison (eds), *Oxford Dictionary of National Biography*, 45 (Oxford, 2004), pp. 255–6.
187 MRC 1215/15: TB 29.11.34.
188 MRC 1215/17: TB 4.6.35.
189 HFA: Richard Preston to Marlene Hobsbawm, 25.4.2016 (email).
190 MRC 1215/18: TB 25.9.35.

191 Ibid: TB 8.11.35.

192 A. H. Lawrence, *Duke Ellington and his World. A Biography* (London, 2001), pp. 206–25.

193 MRC 1215/10: 'Listening to the blues'.

194 MRC 1215/16: TB 24/28.1.35.

195 MRC 1215/17: TB 10/11.5.35.

196 Ibid: TB 10/11.5.35, 20.5.35.

197 Ibid: TB 20.5.35, 23.5.35, 29.5.35, 8.6.35.

198 Ibid: TB 4.6.35.

199 Ibid: TB 3.7.35.

200 Ibid: TB 12.7.35.

201 Ibid: TB 20.7.35.

202 Ibid: TB 24.7.35.

203 MRC 1215/18: TB 18.8.35.

204 Ibid: TB 13.9.35.

205 Ibid: TB 18.11.35.

206 Ibid: TB 24.11.35.

207 MRC 1215/15: TB 3.12.34.

208 Ibid: TB 4.12.34.

209 HFA: University of London, Higher School Certificate.

210 EJH, speech to the Old Philologians, October 2007. The explorer was Sven Hedin, who wrote several books on his travels in Tibet, including *Abenteuer in Tibet* (*Adventure in Tibet*, Leipzig, 1904).

211 MRC 1215/10: TB 6.11.35.

212 MRC 1215/17: TB 3.8.35.

213 MRC 1215/18: TB 25.9.35.

214 HFA: 'Eric Hobsbawm's Interesting Times', p. 3.

215 MRC 1215/18: TB 25.9.35.

216 Ibid: 'Es kann losgehen.'

217 MRC 937/7/8/1: 'Scholarships at Cambridge' (newspaper clipping); *IT*, pp. 106–7.

218 MRC 1215/18: TB 29.9.35.

219 Ibid: TB 6.10.35.

220 MRC 1215/19: TB 9.1.36, also for the following.

221 Ibid: TB 9.1.36.

222 MRC 1215/18: TB 25.8.35.

223 Ibid: TB 2–8.9.35.

224 *The Philologian*, Vol. 8, No. 1 (Autumn Term, 1935), p. 10, also for the following.

225 MRC 1215/18: TB 2–8.9.35, also for the following.

226 *IT*, p. 83.

227 MRC 1215/1: EJH to Ron Hobsbaum, 5.7.36, and for the following paragraphs below.

228 Ibid: EJH to Ron Hobsbaum, 13.7.36, also for the following paragraph, below. Ernst Thälmann, the popular leader of the German Communist Party under the Weimar Republic, had been kept since 1933 in a concentration camp, where he was murdered by the Nazis shortly before the end of the war; the slogans the crowd shouted were 'Soviets everywhere' and 'Doriot to the pillory'; the Carmagnole was a French revolutionary song, accompanied by

a dance, ridiculing the pre-revolutionary French regime, and 'ça ira' ('it'll be fine') another song from the early 1790s, rewritten to include the injunction to 'string up the bourgeois from the lamp-post'.

229 Ibid: EJH to Ron Hobsbaum, 20.7.36, also for the following paragraphs.

230 War disabled.

231 Ibid: EJH to Ron Hobsbaum, 20.7.36 and 25.7.36.

232 Ibid: EJH to Ron Hobsbaum, 5.8.36, also for the following paragraphs.

233 Ibid, also Alfred H. Barr (ed.), *Fantastic Art, Dada, Surrealism* (New York, 1936), and the entry on Oelze in Martin Wiehle (ed.), *Magdeburger Persönlichkeiten* (Magdeburg, 1993). There is a sharply delineated character sketch of the artist in Wieland Schmied, 'Schweigende Bilder', *Die Zeit*, 13.6.80, also online. In the drama *Trilogie des Widersehens* (1976) by Botho Strauss, one of the characters is obsessed with mounting an exhibition of paintings by Oelze, which he never actually manages to do. None of the writers on Oelze mentions his alcoholism or drug addiction.

234 Ibid: EJH to Ron Hobsbaum, 5.8.36.

235 MRC 1215/10: 'I always wanted to go to the South of France', and MRC 1215/1: EJH to Ron Hobsbaum, late August 1936. Eric also wrote brief narratives of the trip in French and German, to be found in the same file, which also contain a number of versions of the same. The following paragraphs are based on the English version.

236 *Byrrh* is an aromatised aperitif made of red wine, mistelle and quinine. Tarbes was the name of the village.

237 *IT*, p. 234.

238 MRC 1215/10: 'I always wanted to go to the South of France'.

239 Ibid, and HFA Miscellaneous I: 22.1.43.

240 MRC 1215/10: 'I always wanted to go to the South of France'.

241 *IT*, pp. 338–42.

242 MRC 1215/1: EJH to Ron Hobsbaum, late August 1936, also for the rest of this paragraph.

243 Hugh Thomas, *The Spanish Civil War* (London, 1986 edition), p. 653, for the legend; Paul Preston, *The Spanish Holocaust: Inquisition and Extermination in Twentieth-Century Spain* (London, 2012), pp. 399–400, for the real story.

244 MRC 1215/1: EJH to Ron Hobsbaum, late August 1936.

245 Ibid: EJH to Ron Hobsbaum, 12.9.36.

246 *IT*, p. 133.

247 MRC 1215/1: EJH to Ron Hobsbaum, 12.9.36.

248 *IT*, p. 105.

Chapter 3: 'A Freshman who Knows About Everything'

1 MRC 1215/1: EJH to Ron Hobsbaum, 21.10.36, also for the rest of the paragraph.

2 *IT*, pp. 103–5.

3 MRC 937/7/8/1: EJH to Hiroshi Mizuta, n.d. (March 1998), also for the following.

4 Noel Annan, *Our Age. Portrait of a Generation* (London, 1990), p. 174; Thomas E. B. Howarth, *Cambridge Between Two Wars* (London, 1978), pp. 156–8.

5 MRC 937/7/8/1: 'Private Lives' (typescript): published version in 'Tinker, tailor, soldier, don', *Observer*, 21.10.1979; MRC 1215/1: EJH to Ron Hobsbaum, 21.10.36; *IT*, pp. 108–9.

6 *IT*, pp. 102–3. The 'gyp room' was a small pantry kept in the residences by a College servant known as a 'bedder', who made the students' beds and cleaned their rooms.

7 KCAC: fiftieth anniversary toast by Stuart Lyons CBE, 2012. 'Gibbs' was a large eighteenth-century building, named after its architect James Gibbs. It was located next to the Chapel, standing at right angles to it.

8 KCAC: information from Dr Patricia McGuire. In the 1960s 'The Drain' was replaced by the Keynes Building, an ugly modern structure.

9 MRC 937/1/1/5: EJH to Diana Rice, 23.8.2002.

10 For the memories of a contemporary at Cambridge, see Ralph Russell, *Findings, Keepings: Life, Communism and Everything* (London, 2001), pp. 115–16.

11 TNA KV2/3980: cover sheet and file number 73a, 'Extract from Army Paper' (1940). The army was to register his physical condition as 'A1'.

12 Annan, *Our Age*, p. 267.

13 *IT*, p. 112; Henry Stanley Ferns, *Reading from Left to Right: One Man's Political History* (Toronto, 1983), p. 101.

14 Pieter Keuneman, 'Eric Hobsbawm: A Cambridge Profile 1939', reprinted in Raphael Samuel and Gareth Stedman Jones (eds), *Culture, Ideology and Politics. Essays for Eric Hobsbawm* (History Workshop Series, London, 1982), pp. 366–8, at p. 366 (originally Pieter Keuneman, 'In Obscurity', *The Granta May Week Number*, 7.6.39). The rubric 'In Obscurity' was used for pen-portraits of retiring editors of *The Granta*, to contrast ironically with the magazine's features on more high-profile Cambridge characters (*IT*, p. 106). The Cambridge Union was founded in 1815 and is the oldest debating society in the world.

15 Keuneman, 'Eric Hobsbawm', p. 367.

16 HFA TB 1.8.40.

17 MRC 937/4/3/1/5: EJH 'Mr. Rylands Lectures', *The Granta*, 10.11.37.

18 HFA TB 11.7.40. For a more sympathetic sketch, see Noel Annan, *The Dons. Mentors, Eccentrics and Geniuses* (London, 1999), pp. 170–82.

19 KCAC NGA/5/1/452: Noel Annan to EJH, 21.5.76

20 Annan, *Our Age*, p. 189.

21 MRC 937/4/3/1/5: Keuneman, 'Eric Hobsbawm'.

22 MRC 937/1/1/4: Noel Annan to EJH and Marlene Hobsbawm, 6.2.87. Clapham, Professor of Economic History, was Vice-Provost of King's.

23 Annan, *Our Age*, p. 109.

24 MRC 1215/1: EJH to Ron Hobsbaum, 5.5.37, also for the following.

25 Ibid: EJH to Ron Hobsbaum, 3.2.37.

26 For Eric's admiration of the Byzantinist Steven Runciman, see Minoo Dinshaw, *Outlandish Knight: The Byzantine Life of Steven Runciman* (London, 2016), pp. 85–6 and 592. Runciman was a Fellow of Trinity, but resigned in 1938 on coming into a substantial inheritance. He went on to write a three-volume history of the Crusades, one of the greatest works of history written in the twentieth century. His father, Walter Runciman, was President of the Board of Trade in the National Government.

27 Howarth, *Cambridge Between Two Wars*, p. 141.

28 MRC 1215/1: EJH to Ron Hobsbaum, 3.2.37.
29 MRC 937/4/3/1/5: EJH: 'Mr. Willey Lectures', *The Granta*, 17.11.37, p. 113.
30 *IT*, pp. 106–7; Noel Annan, 'Obituary: Christopher Morris', *Independent*, 1.3.93.
31 *IT*, p. 107. For Saltmarsh as lecturer, see Ferns, *Reading from Left to Right*, p. 122.
32 MRC 937/1/8/1: EJH to Hiroshi Mizuta, n.d. (March 1998).
33 *IT*, p. 107. The term 'Tripos', denoting the degree course and examinations, was derived from the three-legged stool undergraduates had to sit on in the Middle Ages when taking an oral examination. The course and examination had two parts, not three, so that a 'double starred First' meant a starred First Class Honours in each part.
34 Maxine Berg, *A Woman in History: Eileen Power, 1889–1940* (Cambridge, 1996), pp. 187–90.
35 Howarth, *Cambridge Between Two Wars*, p. 200.
36 MRC 937/8/2/35: EJH, 'Old Marxist still sorting out global fact from fiction', *Times Higher Education Supplement*, 10/2 (12.7.02).
37 MRC 1215/1: EJH to Ron Hobsbaum, 3.2.37.
38 Ibid: EJH to Ron Hobsbaum, 5.5.37.
39 Ibid: EJH to Ron Hobsbaum, 20.8.40.
40 MRC 937/1/1/3: EJH to Thomas E. B. Howarth, n.d. (1978).
41 Quoted in Howarth, *Cambridge Between Two Wars*, p. 200.
42 M[ichael] M. Postan, *Fact and Relevance. Essays on Historical Method* (Cambridge, 1971), p. ix, and for his critical but informed view of Marx more generally, ibid, pp. 154–68.
43 MRC 937/8/2/35: EJH, 'Old Marxist still sorting out global fact from fiction', *Times Higher Education Supplement*, 10/2 (12.7.02); 'Panel Discussion: Conversations with Eric Hobsbawm', *India Centre International Quarterly* 34/1 (Spring, 2005), pp. 101–25.
44 MRC 937/1/3/11: EJH to Victor Kiernan, 29.3.2003.
45 Ibid: Victor Kiernan to EJH, 26.2.2003. Kiernan had been recruited to the Communist Party by Guy Burgess in 1933. For his teaching, see Ferns, *Reading from Left to Right*, pp. 76–8. Kumaramangalam also became President of the Cambridge Union.
46 MRC 937/1/3/11: EJH to Victor Kiernan, 29.3.2003.
47 Isaiah Berlin to Noel Annan, 13.1.54, in Isaiah Berlin, *Enlightening: Letters 1946–1960*, ed. Henry Hardy and Jennifer Holmes (London, 2009), p. 422.
48 Carole Fink, *Marc Bloch: A Life in History* (Cambridge, 1989), pp. 103 and 179.
49 Berg, *A Woman in History*, pp. 210–15; Stuart Clark (ed.), *The Annales School: Critical Assessments* (London, 1999); Peter Burke, *The French Historical Revolution: The Annales School, 1929–1989* (Stanford, CA, 1990).
50 MRC 937/4/3/1/5: EJH, 'Prof. Trevelyan Lectures', *The Granta*, 27.10.37. George Kitson Clark, then in his thirties, lectured on nineteenth-century British history and was to make his name as a revisionist historian of the Corn Laws.
51 MRC 937/4/3/1/5: 'E.J.H. Observes', *The Granta*, 17.11.37.
52 MRC 1215/1: RJH to Ron Hobsbaum, 21.10.36.
53 MRC 937/4/3/1/5: 'Union United', *The Granta*, 9.6.37, p. 486.
54 *IT*, p. 111.

55 MRC 1215/1: RJH to Ron Hobsbaum, 21.10.36.

56 Kevin Morgan, Gidon Cohen and Andrew Flinn, *Communists and British Society 1920–1991* (London, 2007), pp. 80–3; Kenneth Newton, *The Sociology of British Communism* (London, 1968), p. 76. 'Donkey-jacketism' refers to the woollen jackets with leather shoulders worn by workers at this time. See Raphael Samuel, *The Lost World of British Communism* (London, 2006), pp. 203–14.

57 Newton, *The Sociology of British Communism*, pp. 67–76; Pelling, *The British Communist Party*, p. 81; Andrew Thorpe, *The British Communist Party and Moscow, 1920–43* (Manchester, 2000), p. 231; C. Fleay and M. Sanders, 'The Labour Spain Committee: Labour Party Policy and the Spanish Civil War', *Historical Journal*, Vol. 28 (1985), pp. 187–97.

58 MRC 937/1/3/11: EJH to Victor Kiernan, 29.3.2003.

59 EJH, 'War of Ideas', *Guardian* Saturday Review section, 17.2.07, pp. 1–6, also for the following.

60 HFA: copy in possession of Angela Hobsbaum.

61 MRC 1215/21: TB 21.6.40.

62 Ibid. See also Martin Kettle, 'Jon Vickers', *Guardian*, 23 June 2008.

63 MRC 937/1/1/4: EJH to Ms Wells, n.d.; 'Cambridge Communism in the 1930s and 1940s', *Socialist History* 24 (2003), pp. 40–78. Christopher Hill and Rodney Hilton were at Oxford in the 1930s.

64 MRC 937/1/6/3: EJH to Brian Simon, n.d. (November 1993); see also *IT*, p. 112.

65 MRC 937/7/8/1: EJH to Jason Heppell, 30.6.97.

66 *IT*, p. 122.

67 TNA KV2/3981, 136b; Extract, 20.5.49.

68 See David Margolies and Maroula Joannou (eds), *Heart of the Heartless World: Essays in Cultural Resistance in Memory of Margot Heinemann* (London, 2002). Eric's contribution to the volume is on pp. 216–19. For Bernal, see EJH, 'Red Science', *London Review of Books*, 9.3.2006.

69 Geoff Andrews, *The Shadow Man. At the Heart of the Cambridge Spy Circle* (London, 2015), pp. 74–9.

70 Vasiily Mitrokhin and Christopher Andrew, *The Mitrokhin Archive*, Vol. I (London, 1999), pp. 82–5; *IT*, pp. 122–4.

71 *IT*, pp. 100–114.

72 Ian Buruma, 'The Weird Success of Guy Burgess', *New York Review of Books*, LXIII/20, 22.12.2016, pp. 77–9.

73 *IT*, pp. 100–114. Among a vast and often sensationalist literature on the 'Cambridge spies', the first port of call for reliable information must be Christopher Andrew's authoritative *The Defence of the Realm. The Authorized History of MI5* (London, 2009).

74 Eric was succeeded in his position by Jack Gallagher, who later became an influential historian of British imperialism.

75 MRC 937/6/1/2: *Cambridge University Socialist Club (CUSC) Bulletin*, 30.11.37; MRC 937/6/1/3: EJH to Brian Simon, n.d. (November 1993); *IT*, pp. 112–13.

76 MRC 937/6/1/2: *Cambridge University Socialist Club (CUSC) Bulletin*, 18.1.38.

77 Ibid, 1.2.38.

78 MRC 937/6/1/2: *Cambridge University Socialist Club (CUSC) Bulletin*: 'How about films?', by EJH.

79   Ibid, 22.2.38: 'The fight about realism in art'.

80   Ferns, *Reading from Left to Right*, pp. 109–10.

81   MRC 1215/21: TB 22.3.40. For the reading group, see Ferns, *Reading from Left to Right*, pp. 102–3.

82   MRC 1215/1: EJH to Ron Hobsbaum, n.d. (October 1937).

83   Ferns, *Reading from Left to Right*, p. 114.

84   MRC 937/4/3/1/5: Pieter Keuneman, 'Eric Hobsbawm'.

85   Ibid: 'Cambridge Cameos – Another Local Figure', *The Granta*, 3.3.37, p. 3: EJH to Diana Rice, 18.8.2002. In his memoirs, Eric seems to me to be unfairly disparaging of *The Granta* in his day (*IT*, p. 113).

86   R. E. Swartwout, *It Might Have Happened. A sketch of the later career of Rupert Lister Audenard, First Earl of Slype, etc.* (Cambridge, 1934).

87   MRC 937/4/3/1/5: 'Cambridge Cameos: The Oldest Inhabitant', *The Granta*, 10.3.37 (clipping).

88   Ibid: 'Cambridge Cameos: Nothing Over Sixpence: Woolworth's', *The Granta*, 21.4.37, p. 351.

89   Ibid: 'Cambridge Cameos: Ties With a Past: Ryder and Amies', *The Granta*, 26.5.37, p. 438.

90   Ibid: Pieter Keuneman, 'In Obscurity', *The Granta May Week Number*, 7.6.39.

91   Ibid: EJH, 'New Writing and a New Theatre: Christopher Isherwood', *The Granta*, 17.11.37, p. 121. Petty Cury was then a run-down and slightly disreputable street in central Cambridge.

92   Ibid: EJH, 'The Stars Look Down, I. Professor Laski', *The Granta*, 26.1.38, p. 215, also for the following lines. Eric returned to the subject of Harold Laski many years later, in 'The Left's Megaphone', *London Review of Books*, Vol. 15, No. 13 (8.7.93), pp. 12–13. See Michael Newman, *Harold Laski: A Political Biography* (London, 1993).

93   Nigel Nicolson (ed.), *The Harold Nicolson Diaries 1907–1963* (rev. edn, London, 2004).

94   MRC 937/4/3/1/5: EJH, 'The Stars Look Down, II. Harold Nicolson', *The Granta*, 2.2.38.

95   Ibid: EJH, 'The Stars Look Down, III. Herbert Morrison', *The Granta*, 9.2.38, also for the following part of this paragraph. George Robey was a famous music-hall singer and comedian.

96   Ibid: EJH, 'The Stars Look Down, IV. J. B. S. Haldane', *The Granta*, 23.2.38, p. 285, also for the remainder of this paragraph.

97   MRC 1215/1: EJH to Ron Hobsbaum, 3.2.37.

98   *IT*, p. 113.

99   MRC 937/4/3/1/5: EJH, 'Crime et Châtiment', *The Granta*, 19.10.38, p. 33.

100 Ibid: EJH, 'The Film Editor Speaks: Guitry', *The Granta*, 2.11.38, p. 69.

101 Ibid: EJH, 'The Film Editor Speaks: Fritz Lang', *The Granta*, 9.11.38, p. 89; and 'The Marx Brothers', *The Granta*, 18.11.38.

102 Ibid: EJH, 'The Year of Films', *The Granta*, 30.11.38, p. 157.

103 Ibid: EJH (ed.), *The Granta New Statesman and Nation: The Weekend Review*.

104 Ibid: EJH (ed.), 'Fifty Years On – Perhaps *The National Granta: For a Pure Cambridge*', 8.3.1989 (i.e. 1939). See also 'Leaves from the Nazigranta', 26.4.39.

105 Ibid: *CUSC Bulletin*, 14.10.38, 18.10.38.

106 Ibid: leaflet dated October 1938.

107 Ibid: *CUSC Bulletin*, 14 and 18.10.38.

108 Ibid: *CUSC Bulletin*, 1.11.38.

109 The classic account remains Robert Conquest, *The Great Terror: Stalin's Purges of the 1930s* (London, 1968). For further evidence, see the same author's *The Great Terror: A Reassessment* (Oxford, 1990).

110 Joseph E. Davies, *Mission to Moscow* (Garden City, NJ, 1941).

111 See Vadim Z. Rogovin, *1937: Stalin's Year of Terror* (Oak Park, MI, 1998).

112 Joseph Redman [i.e. Brian Pearce], 'The British Stalinists and the Moscow Trials', *Labour Review*, Vol. 3, No. 2 (March–April 1958), pp. 44–53; Thorpe, *The British Communist Party and Moscow*, p. 237. See more generally Giles Udy, *Labour and the Gulag. Russia and the seduction of the British Left* (London, 2018).

113 MRC 1215/1: EJH to Ron Hobsbaum, 3.2.37, also for the following. Stalin used the murder of Sergei Kirov, the Party boss in Leningrad, as an excuse to begin the purges.

114 See Sidney and Beatrice Webb, *Soviet Communism: A New Civilisation?* (2 vols, New York, 1936), and, for accounts by British Communists who also accepted the validity of the confessions, Saville, *Memoirs from the Left*, pp. 34–6; Russell, *Findings, Keepings*, pp. 145–8; and Claud Cockburn, *I, Claud* (London, 1957, rev. edn 1967), pp. 262–4.

115 MRC 1215/1: EJH to Ron Hobsbaum, 5.5.37; Chris Wrigley, 'May Day in Britain', in Abbey Paterson and Herbert Reiter (eds), *The Ritual of May Day in Western Europe: Past, Present and Future* (London, 2016), pp. 133–59, at p. 148.

116 MRC 1215/1: EJH to Ron Hobsbaum, 5.5.37.

117 MRC 937/4/3/4/1: 'A Non-Political Affair' (typescript), also for the following.

118 Ibid: 'Passport, Love', by J. Share (EJH), also for the following.

119 Ibid. The girl's real name was Zhenia (HFA Diary Notes: In German, 'Interim Report', 12.11.50, p. 2). He tried to find her again when he went to Paris in August 1950, but could not ('how ridiculous it is', he wrote, 'to look for someone in Paris in August, when everybody's on holiday'). See also MRC 1215/10, notes on the south of France.

120 MRC 937/7/2/1, *passim*, also for the following.

121 MRC 1215/1: EJH to Ron Hobsbaum, 22.8.37, also for the remainder of this paragraph.

122 MRC 937/6/1/4: International Conference of the World Student Association.

123 See Julian Jackson, *Popular Front in France: Defending Democracy 1934 1938* (Cambridge, 1988).

124 MRC 1215/1: EJH to Ron Hobsbaum, n.d. (October 1937).

125 MRC 937/4/3/4/1L: 'The Defeatist' by J. Share (EJH), and for the following, below.

126 *IT*, p. 315.

127 'The Defeatist'.

128 KCAC: information from Dr Patricia McGuire.

129 Interview with Angela Hobsbaum, 30.3.17.

130 MRC 1215/1: EJH to Ron Hobsbaum, n.d. (October 1937), also for the following.

131 Ibid: EJH to Ron Hobsbaum, 6.12.37.

132 For a good account of student Communist activities in Oxford, very similar to

those in which Eric participated in Cambridge, see Denis Healey, *The Time of My Life* (London, 1989), pp. 32–8.

133 MRC 1215/1: EJH to Ron Hobsbaum, 6.12.37.

134 Ibid: EJH to Ron Hobsbaum, 28.1.38, also for the following [this must be misdated, because Eden did not resign until February, so the month of the letter should be February, not January].

135 *IT*, pp. 121–2. Elias was lodging at the time with the German socialist exile Francis Carsten, who worked for the Political Warfare Executive during the war and later became an eminent historian. When Carsten visited the Swiss publisher after the war was over, at Elias's request, he found, as he told me, that its shelves were still lined with copies of Elias's book; not a single copy had been sold.

136 MRC 1215/1: EJH to Ron Hobsbaum, 28.1.38 [i.e. 28.2.38].

137 Ibid: EJH to Ron Hobsbaum, 29.4.38.

138 Ibid: EJH to Ron Hobsbaum, 13.6.38.

139 Centre des Archives Diplomatiques de Nantes, 1 TU/701, Service des Renseignements Généraux de Tunisie, Dossiers Nominatifs, numéro 96: Hobsbawm, Eric Ernest, 24754, also for the following. I am indebted to Dr Daniel Lee for making this document available to me.

140 MRC 1215/1: EJH to Ron Hobsbaum, 3.9.38, also for the following.

141 Andrée Viollis was a non-Communist feminist journalist who was on the editorial board of the Communist evening paper *Ce Soir*, headed by the poet Louis Aragon.

142 Hammamet was a small town just down the coast from Tunis.

143 MRC 1215/1: EJH to Ron Hobsbaum, 9.9.38 (postcard).

144 TNA KV2/3980, cover sheet and file 20x: Eric to D[epartment] E[ducational] Office, 8.11.42.

145 MRC 937/7/4/1: 'Land and Colonisation in North Africa. A Paper read to the Political Society, King's College, on November 28th, 1938. By E. J. Hobsbawm, King's College'.

146 Ibid, p. 16.

147 Ibid, pp. 22–3.

148 Ibid, p. 23.

149 MRC 937/7/4/1: 'Report on a Journey to Tunisia and Algeria made under the Political Science Travel Grant: Some notes of French administration in North Africa' (1938), pp. 1–2.

150 Ibid, p. 22.

151 Ibid, p. 36.

152 For the text, see Max Domarus (ed.), *Hitler: Speeches and Proclamations 1932–1945. The Chronicle of a Dictatorship*, II: *The Years 1935–1938* (London, 1992), pp. 1183–94.

153 MRC 937/7/2/2: TB 2.7.40.

154 Ibid: CPGB 'Political Letter to the Communist Party Membership', 25.4.39.

155 HFA 'Family Tree'; interview with Robin Marchesi, 6.12.2016.

156 MRC 1215/1: EJH to Ron Hobsbaum, 12.6.36.

157 Ibid: EJH to Ron Hobsbaum, 1.7.40.

158 Ibid: EJH to Ron Hobsbaum, 7.4.41.

159 MRC 937/7/8/1: EJH, 'As usual during a World Crisis, a superb day'. Roland Searle later became a celebrated cartoonist.

160 MRC 1215/1: EJH to Ron Hobsbaum, n.d. [12 June 1939], also for the following.

161 Wiener Stadt- und Landesarchiv: Bez. Ger. Hietzing Abt. 1 P 52/1929, dated 24.7.41.

162 MRC 937/6/4/6: Eric to Brian Simon, 15.1.79. Iris Murdoch, an Oxford undergraduate Communist, later became a philosophy don and well-known novelist.

163 Peter J. Conradi, *Iris Murdoch: A Life* (London, 2001), p. 98.

164 MRC 937/6/1/6: Communist Student Party School 1939: Eric Hobsbawm.

165 HFA: Degree Certificate.

166 *IT*, pp. 119–21.

167 MRC 937/6/1/5/1–2: Third International Conference of the World Student Association on Democracy and Nation, Paris, 15–19 August 1939; MRC 1215/1: EJH to Ron Hobsbaum, 12.8.39.

168 MRC 937/1/6/3: EJH to Brian Simon, n.d. (November 1993); MRC 937/7/8/1: 'As usual, during a World Crisis, a superb day'. P. N. Haksar studied at the London School of Economics and after independence joined the Indian Foreign Service, becoming ambassador to Austria and Nigeria and finally principal secretary to Prime Minister Indira Gandhi and the first Vice-Chancellor of the Jawaharlal Nehru University. See his memoirs, *One More Life* (1990).

169 MRC 937/7/8/1: 'As usual during a World Crisis, a superb day'.

170 *IT*, pp. 117–25 (quote on p. 124).

171 MRC 1215/1: EJH to Ron Hobsbaum, n.d. (postcard, postmarked 31.7.39).

172 Ibid: EJH to Ron Hobsbaum, 28.8.39.

173 Ibid: EJH to Ron Hobsbaum, 28.8.39.

174 Ibid: EJH to Ron Hobsbaum, 8.9.39.

175 HFA Miscellaneous I: 1.9.42.

176 MRC 937/7/8/1: 'As usual during a World Crisis, a superb day'. Eric may have been mistaken in his identification of the novelist and painter Wyndham Lewis: according to his biographer, he was not in France at the time, but had already booked tickets for himself and his wife to travel by sea to Quebec, sailing from Southampton on 2 September 1939 (Paul O'Keeffe, *Some Sort of Genius: A Life of Wyndham Lewis* (London, 2000), p. 400).

177 *IT*, p. 126.

178 HFA Miscellaneous I: 10.9.42, also for the following.

179 MRC 1215/1: EJH to Ron Hobsbaum, 8.9.39, and for the following.

180 The punitive terms forced on Germany by the Treaty of Versailles were widely blamed for the rise and triumph of Nazism.

181 For the debates unleashed by the Nazi–Soviet Pact within the leadership of the British Communist Party, see Francis Beckett, *Enemy Within. The Rise and Fall of the British Communist Party* (London, 1995), chapter 6.

182 Quoted in Neil Redfern, *Class or Nation. Communists, Imperialism and Two World Wars* (London, 2005), p. 97.

183 For the arguments and divisions in the top ranks of the Party, see Francis King and George Matthews (eds), *About Turn. The British Communist Party and the Second World War. The Verbatim Record of the Central Committee Meetings of 25 September and 2–3 October 1939* (London, 1990); and John Attfield and Stephen

Williams (eds), *1939: The Communist Party of Great Britain and the War. Proceedings of a Conference held on 21 April 1979, Organised by the Communist Party History Group* (London, 1984), especially the documentary Appendices. For the role of Moscow in the upheaval, see Thorpe, *The British Communist Party and Moscow*, pp. 246–9, 256–60.

184 See Robert Edwards, *White Death: Russia's War on Finland 1939–40* (London, 2006).

185 *IT*, p. 154; Raymond Williams, *Politics and Letters: Interviews with New Left Review* (London, 1979), p. 43.

186 MRC 937/6/1/2: *War on the USSR?* Produced by the University Socialist Club, Cambridge. Published by the University Labour Federation.

187 *IT*, pp. 152–3.

Chapter 4: 'A Left-Wing Intellectual in the English Army'

1 See Roger Broad, *Conscription in Britain 1939–1963: The Militarization of a Generation* (London, 2006).

2 TNA KV2/3980: cover sheet and file number 73a: Extract from Army Paper.

3 MRC 1215/28: Introduction to British Army, Cambridge, February 1940, also for the following.

4 Ibid. Slope Arms.

5 MRC 1215/21: TB 6.3.40, 8.3.40.

6 Ibid: TB 12.3.40.

7 Ibid: TB 15.3.40. 'Weapons training,' noted Eric's Cambridge contemporary Ralph Russell, himself from a lower-class but rural background, 'was full of sexual and smutty innuendo' (Russell, *Findings, Keepings*, p. 171).

8 MRC 1215/21: TB 10.3.40.

9 Ibid: TB 14.3.40.

10 Ibid: TB 15.3.40.

11 Ibid: TB 18/19.3.40.

12 Ibid: TB 8.3.40.

13 Ibid: TB 6.3.40.

14 Ibid: TB 6.7.40.

15 Ibid: TB 29.4.40.

16 Ibid: TB 6.3.40.

17 Ibid: TB 10.3.40, 24.3.40.

18 Ibid: TB 8.3.40.

19 Ibid: TB 8.3.40.

20 Ibid: TB 15.3.40.

21 Ibid: TB 6.3.40.

22 MRC 1215/28: May–June 1940, numbers 12–14.

23 MRC 1215/21: TB 8.3.40.

24 Ibid: TB 12.3.40, 14.3.40, 8.4.40.

25 Ibid: TB 16.4.40; MRC 1215/22: TB 26.2.41.

26 Ibid: TB 11.2.41, 26.2.41.

27 Ibid: TB 19.2.41.

28 Ibid: TB 20.2.41.

29 MRC 1215/28: Notes on army language. Notts was short for Nottinghamshire.

30 Ibid: Rhyming slang.

31 Ibid: Some other slang expressions.

32 Ibid: Current sayings in the Company.

33 Ibid: Obscene slang.

34 MRC 1215/21: TB 9–12.4.40.

35 Ibid: TB 15.3.40.

36 MRC 1215/22: TB 12.2.41. The Shadow was an American detective, created by Walter Gibson. The character featured in a popular radio series in the 1930s, starring Orson Welles, and formed the basis for a comic book published from 1940 to 1942, when it closed because of paper shortage. See Thomas J. Shimfield, *Walter B. Gibson and The Shadow* (Jefferson, NC, 2003).

37 MRC 1215/21: TB 20.4.40.

38 Ibid: TB 20/21.3.40.

39 Ibid: TB 25.3.40.

40 Ibid: TB 23.3.40.

41 Ibid: TB 2.4.40.

42 Ibid: TB 3.4.40.

43 Ibid: TB 3.4.40.

44 Ibid: TB 4–7.4.40.

45 Ibid: TB 6.3.40.

46 Ibid: TB 23.3.40.

47 Ibid: TB 29.4.40.

48 Ibid: TB 27.3.40.

49 Ibid: TB 31.3.40.

50 Ibid: TB 16.3.40

51 Ibid: TB 11.3.40. William L. Trotter, *The Winter War: The Russo-Finnish War of 1940* (5th edn, Stanford, CA, 2002), pp. 235–9. For the 'Party line' at this time, see Neil Redfern, *Class or Nation: Communists, Imperialism and Two World Wars* (London, 2005), pp. 95–9, and Thorpe, *The British Communist Party and Moscow*, pp. 159–61.

52 MRC 1215/21: TB 11.3.40; similar, much briefer remarks in TB 29.3.40.

53 Ibid: TB 12.3.40.

54 Ibid: TB 9.4.40.

55 Ibid: TB 29.4.40.

56 Ibid: TB 9–12.4.40.

57 Ibid: TB 29.4.40.

58 Ibid: TB 9–12.4.40.

59 MRC 1215/22: TB 11.2.41.

60 MRC 1215/21: TB 16.4.40.

61 Ibid: TB 17–18.4.40.

62 Ibid: TB 19.4.40.

63 Ibid: TB 22–28.4.40.

64 MRC 1215/22: TB 12.2.41.

65 Army food was normally eaten off tin rather than china plates.

66 MRC 1215/21: TB 2–3.5.40.

67 Ibid. Eric subsequently claimed that he had been turned down because he was a member of the Communist Party, but other known Party members, notably

his fellow historian Christopher Hill, secured appointments in the Intelligence
Corps without difficulty (FLA: Fritz Lustig to EJH, 11.6.2003).

68 *IT*, p. 111.
69 MRC 1215/21: TB 2–3.5.40, 3–9.5.40; see also TB 17.5.40.
70 Ibid: TB 5.5.40.
71 Ibid: TB 10.5.40.
72 MRC 1215/1: EJH to Ron Hobsbaum, n.d. (late September 1940).
73 Ibid: EJH to Ron Hobsbaum, n.d. ('Monday evening').
74 MRC 1215/21: TB 11.5.40.
75 Ibid: TB 25.5.40.
76 Ibid: TB 17.5.40, 25.5.40.
77 MRC 937/4/3/4/1: unpublished typescript, in red, also for rest of paragraph.
    There is no date but references to fens, dykes and the like make it clear the
    location was Norfolk and therefore the date was 1940.
78 MRC 1215/1: EJH to Ron Hobsbaum, n.d. ('Monday evening').
79 MRC 1215/21: TB 17.5.40.
80 Ibid: TB 17.5.40; *IT*, pp. 159–60.
81 MRC 1215/28: 'Very often one doesn't notice' (typescript).
82 *IT*, pp. 159–60; MRC 1215/21: TB 17.5.40.
83 Ibid: TB 15.6.40, 24.7.40.
84 MRC 1215/1: EJH to Ron Hobsbaum, 10.6.40.
85 MRC 1215/21: TB 17.6.40.
86 MRC 1215/1: EJH to Ron Hobsbaum, 10.6.40.
87 MRC 1215/21: TB 15.6.40, 17.6.40.
88 Ibid: TB 17.6.40.
89 MRC 1215/1: EJH to Ron Hobsbaum, 1.7.40, also for the following.
90 Thorpe, *The British Communist Party and Moscow*, pp. 265–7.
91 MRC 937/8/2/22/2: Martin Walker, 'Old comrades never say die', *Guardian*,
    15.10.94, p. 29.
92 MRC 1215/1: EJH to Ron Hobsbaum, 1.7.40.
93 MRC 937/7/2/2: TB 26.6.40.
94 Ibid: TB 2.7.40.
95 See Richard J. Evans, *The Third Reich at War* (London, 2008), pp. 231–4.
96 MRC 937/7/2/2: TB 24.6.40.
97 MRC 1215/1: EJH to Ron Hobsbaum, 1.7.40.
98 MRC 937/7/2/2: TB 6.7.40.
99 Ibid: TB 2.7.40.
100 Ibid: TB 6.7.40.
101 Ibid: TB 26.6.40.
102 Ibid: TB 2.7.40, 8.7.40, 4.8.40.
103 Ibid: TB 4.8.40.
104 MRC 1215/1: EJH to Ron Hobsbaum, 20.8.40. Hermann Goering was the
    head of the German Air Force, the Luftwaffe.
105 MRC 1215/21: TB 1.4.40.
106 Ibid: 12–14.4.40.
107 MRC 1215/23: TB 22.1.43.
108 MRC 937/7/2/2: TB 2.7.40.
109 MRC 1215/28: TB 15.3.41 and MRC 937/4/3/4/1: 'On the same side of

the road he saw Taylor' (unpublished short story dealing with an injured and disfigured serviceman); 'A Very Dishonest Guy' (unpublished and tightly organised conversation piece whose punchline is the revelation that the three beautiful girls whose photo is set beside the bed of one of the men are not his girlfriends, as the hut supposes, but his sisters); 'The Armed Guard', an unpublished, rather rambling story dealing with a soldier who goes absent without leave; 'Ted', abandoned drafts for a story about a malingerer and spiv, which appear to have been torn out of Eric's diary for 1941 (pp. 55–71 and 143–9); 'The Letter', a more coherent manuscript on diary paper, featuring the collective composition of a letter home; and 'Guard in Winter', another manuscript, complete this time, describing the tedium of guard duty; all of these are rather incoherent drafts.

110 MRC 1215/29: 'Pause im Krieg'; 'Kriegspause II'; 'Ritter Tod und Teufel, oder Die Unmilitärischen'. ('43') – 'Before us, the cowardly, the nervous, hangs/A coloured uniform of bravery,/Into which they often force our limbs. . . . We are small,/The times are great.'
111 MRC 1215/29: 'Pause im Krieg' I and II (April 1942).
112 Ibid: 'Bedingtes Gedicht'; 'Anfang 1942' ('Die Zukunft rettet uns'); 'Halb Weiss halb rot', 24.1.43; 'Uebergang'.
113 Ibid: 'Theorie ohne Praxis'; also 'Predigt', where he imagines the unity of theory and practice dozing, half asleep.
114 Ibid: 'On the First of May/Red carnations in our buttonholes/The witnesses of birth and death/the first and last array' ('Die Strasse'); in 'Lied' ('Song') he wrote of the 'doubtful peace' to come, while 'hard times begin'.
115 Ibid: 'Nazis im Fruehjahr'.
116 MRC 937/7/2/2: TB 11.7.40.
117 MRC 1215/1: EJH to Ron Hobsbaum, 1.2.41.
118 Ibid: EJH to Ron Hobsbaum, 7.4.41; MRC 1215/22: TB 15.2.41.
119 MRC 1215/1: EJH to Ron Hobsbaum, 6.11.40.
120 Ibid. EJH to Ron Hobsbaum, 1.2.41.
121 MRC 1215/22: TB 10.2.41.
122 Ibid: TB 11.2.41.
123 Ibid. TB 4.3.41.
124 MRC 1215/1: EJH to Ron Hobsbaum, n.d. (March 1941, with addendum 7.4.41).
125 MRC 1215/22: TB 8.3.41, 11.3.41, 12.3.41, 14.3.41.
126 Ibid. TB 10. 2. 41
127 Ibid: TB 20.2.41.
128 Ibid: TB 27.2.41.
129 Ibid: TB 25.2.41.
130 Ibid: TB 17.3.41, 21.3.41, 22.3.41, 23.3.41, 25.3.41, 7.4.41 and MRC 1215/1: EJH to Ron Hobsbaum, n.d. (March 1941, with addendum 7.4.41). None of these novels was a particularly easy read. Presumably by this time he had finished *War and Peace*.
131 MRC 1215/22: TB 23.2.41, 1.3.41.
132 Ibid: TB 18.2.41.
133 Ibid: TB 19.2.41.
134 Ibid: TB 22.2.41.

135 Ibid: TB 23.2.41.
136 Ibid: TB 7.4.41.
137 Ibid: TB 19.2.41, 20.2.41.
138 Ibid: TB 22.2.41.
139 MRC 1215/1: EJH to Ron Hobsbaum, n.d. (March 1941, with addendum 7.4.41).
140 MRC 1215/22: TB 23.2.41.
141 MRC 1215/1: EJH to Ron Hobsbaum, n.d. (March 1941, with addendum 7.4.41); John Macleod, *River of Fire: The Clydebank Blitz* (London, 2010).
142 MRC 1215/22: TB 12.3.41.
143 MRC 1215/1: EJH to Ron Hobsbaum, n.d. (March 1941, with addendum 7.4.41) and 25.4.41.
144 Ibid: EJH to Ron Hobsbaum, n.d. (May 1941, headed '560 Field Coy Reg, Croxteth Hall, West Derby, Liverpool 12').
145 Richard Whittington-Egan, *The Great Liverpool Blitz* (Liverpool, 1987).
146 MRC 1215/1: EJH to Ron Hobsbaum, n.d. (May 1941, headed '560 Field Coy Reg, Croxteth Hall, West Derby, Liverpool 12'), also for the following.
147 Ibid: EJH to Ron Hobsbaum, 8.7.41.
148 MRC 937/1/1/4: EJH to Tom Pocock, 14.7.81.
149 MRC 1215/1: EJH to Ron Hobsbaum, 8.7.41, also for the following.
150 Richard Bennet (ed.), *The Bedside Lilliput* (London, 1950), contains an anthology of contributions from the years 1937–49.
151 EJH, 'Battle Prospects', *Lilliput*, 1 January 1942, pp. 43–4.
152 EJH, 'It Never Comes Off', *Lilliput*, 1 March 1942, p. 212–14.
153 MRC 1215/1: EJH to Ron Hobsbaum, 13.8.41.
154 MRC 1215/23: TB 1.9.42.
155 *IT*, pp. 156–7.
156 MRC 1215/1: EJH to Ron Hobsbaum, n.d. (March 1941, with addendum 7.4.41).
157 Ibid: EJH to Ron Hobsbaum, 18.9.41, also for the following. Archie White, *The Story of Army Education, 1643–1963* (London, 1963). For White himself, see *IT*, p. 164.
158 MRC 1215/1: EJH to Ron Hobsbaum, 18.9.41.
159 Ibid: EJH to Ron Hobsbaum, 18.9.41. An eisteddfod is a Welsh-language cultural festival featuring in particular music and poetry. Such events were surprisingly common in the British armed forces during the war: my own father was chaired as a bard in an eisteddfod held in his RAF unit in southern Italy in 1945.
160 Ibid: EJH to Harry Hobsbaum, 27.9.42.
161 See Helen Fry, *The King's Most Loyal Enemy Aliens: Germans Who Fought for Britain in the Second World War* (Stroud, 2013), which also includes an interview with Fritz Lustig.
162 Interview with Fritz Lustig, 30.5.2016.
163 Ibid. See also MRC 937/1/6/6: Fritz Lustig to EJH, 24.4.95, and EJH to Fritz Lustig, 30.4.95, also for the following.
164 'The Germans who bugged for Britain', *Jewish Chronicle*, 10.5.2012.
165 MRC 937/6/4.2: *Dieppe and the Don* (London, August 1942); *The Second Front: Six Objections answered by the Daily Worker* (London, 1942).

166 TNA KV2/3980, 12a: Eric to John (Gollan), 3.8.42, also for the following.
167 MRC 1215/1: EJH to Harry Hobsbaum, 27.9.42.
168 See S. P. Mackenzie, 'Vox populi: British army newspapers in the Second World War', *Journal of Contemporary History*, Vol. 24 (1989), pp. 665–82; and MRC 1215/18, 31: 'Wall-Newspapers. By Sgt. Inst. E. Hobsbawm A. E. C.', a survey of wall newspapers with suggestions on how they should be put together and presented.
169 TNA KV2/3980, 11a: Col. Alexander to Special Branch, 17.7.42.
170 Ibid: 8a, Complaints against Instructors A.E.C., 10.7.42.
171 Ibid: 65: 'Note on the Case of No. 2003227 Sgt. Eric John HOBSBAWM, A.E.C.' The acronym 'I.A.E.C.' referred to the other Instructors of the Army Educational Corps.
172 Ibid: 12a, Eric to John (Alexander?), 3.8.42, also for the following.
173 Ibid: 65: 'Note on the Case of No. 2003227 Sgt. Eric John HOBSBAWM, A.E.C.'; also 73a: Extract from Army Paper, and 8a: Complaints against Instructors A.E.C.
174 Ibid: 16x: Extract Y Box 2128, 24.8.42, also for the following.
175 TNA KV2/3980: 65: 'Note on the Case of No. 2003227 Sgt. Eric John HOBSBAWM, A.E.C.'
176 MRC 1215/23: TB 30.8.42.
177 Ibid: TB 10.9.42.
178 Ibid: TB 12.9.42, also for the following.
179 Feliks Dzerzhinsky was the first commander of the Soviet political police, the Cheka, and executor of the post-revolutionary 'red terror' in Russia.
180 TNA KV2/3980: 25a, 30.9.42.
181 MRC 1215/1: EJH to Ron Hobsbaum, 10.10.42.
182 Andrew, *The Defence of the Realm*, p. 173. For a scathing assessment of the social attitudes and assumptions of the intelligence services see Hugh Trevor-Roper, *The Philby Affair: Espionage, Treason, and Secret Services* (London, 1968).
183 TNA KV2/3980: 21/22, 13.9.42.
184 MRC 1215/1: EJH to Ron Hobsbaum, 13.8.41.
185 TNA KV2/3980: 23a, 16.9.42.
186 Ibid: 31a, 14.12.42.
187 Ibid. 20x. Eric to D[epartment] E[ducational] O[ffice], 8.11.42.
188 Ibid: 34, 12.2.43, p. 2.
189 Ibid: 29y, 23.11.42 and 39z, 25.11.42.
190 Ibid: 33, 20.12.42.
191 MRC 1215/28: Wartime Notes: 'Very often we don't notice' (typescript). 'Capstan' was a popular brand of cheap cigarettes with a very high nicotine content.
192 MRC 1215/23: TB 22.1.43.
193 MRC 1215/1: EJH to Ron Hobsbaum, 9.1.43, also for the following.
194 Ibid: EJH to Ron Hobsbaum, 21.2.43; HFA: Degree Certificate, 6.2.43. See also TNA KV2/3981, 149b: Confidential report, 22.11.50.
195 TNA KV2/3980: 371, Extract from file number PF 211, 764, 19.3.43. 'Jack' was the alias of David ('Danny') Gibbons, a Scottish Communist and Spanish Civil War veteran who had been appointed the previous year to organise Party work in the armed forces.

196 Ibid, p. 2.
197 MRC 1215/1: EJH to Ron Hobsbaum, 18.4.43.
198 TNA KV2/3980: 65: 'Note on the Case of No. 2003227 Sgt. Eric John HOBSBAWM, A.E.C.'
199 MRC 1215/1: EJH to Ron Hobsbaum, 18.4.43.
200 Ibid: EJH to Ron Hobsbaum, 21.2.43.
201 Beckett, *Enemy Within*, pp. 94–5.
202 Copies in MRC 937/6/1/2; also MRC 1215/1: EJH to Ron Hobsbaum, 30.6.43.
203 http://www.andrewwhitehead.net/blog/category/ram-nahum; *IT*, p. 112; Sally Vickers, 'I felt he wasn't my real father', *Guardian*, Family Section, 12 November 2012. Freddie had told her daughter of the affair when Sally was young, leading to her conviction that she was in fact Ram Nahum's daughter, though she was not. 'Mouse' died in 2008. For an eyewitness report of the bombing, see Theodor Prager, *Bekenntnisse eines Revisionisten* (Vienna, 1975), pp. 56–8.
204 TNA KV2/3981, 152a: Special Branch, 5.12.51.
205 *IT*, pp. 166, 176–7.
206 MRC 1215/23: TB 31.1.43.
207 MRC 1215/23: 1.9.42.
208 Ibid: 2.9.42.
209 Ibid: 7.9.42, p. 2.
210 MRC 1215/23: TB 29.11.42.
211 MRC 1215/1: EJH to Ron Hobsbaum, 21.2.43.
212 MRC 1215/29: Poems: 'Lied'.
213 Ibid: Poems: 'Du bist wie eine blanke schwarze Strasse' (Mitte July 43).
214 Ibid: Poems: 'Das Mädchen' (7/42).
215 Ibid: Poems: 'Im Frieden' ('At Peace'): 'Only between our close bodies lay, numbing and aroused like fresh hay, peace, memory, the future.'
216 MRC 1215/23: TB 23.2.43.
217 Ibid: TB 7.7.43 [correct date: 7.5.43], also for the following.
218 MRC 1215/1: EJH to Ron Hobsbaum, 18.4.43.
219 TNA KV2/3980: 73a: Extract from Army Paper.
220 MRC 1215/1: EJH to Ron Hobsbaum, 4.5.43.
221 Ibid: EJH to Ron Hobsbaum, 30.6.43.
222 Interview with Angela Hobsbaum, 30.3.17; HFA Angela Hobsbaum, 'R M Hobsbaum Naval Career' (typescript).
223 MRC 1215/1: EJH to Ron Hobsbaum, 30.6.43.
224 Ibid: EJH to Ron Hobsbaum, 7.8.43.
225 TNA KV2/3980: 65: 'Note on the Case of No. 2003227 Sgt. Eric John HOBSBAWM, A.E.C.'
226 Ibid: 47a: Secret and Personal, 1.5.44.
227 Ibid: 50a: Sgt. Instructor Eric John Ernest HOBSBAWM.
228 MRC 1215/1: EJH to Ron Hobsbaum, 30.6.43.
229 MRC 1215/29: 'Verne Citadel, Portland, 1943'. The Verne Citadel, located on the highest point of the island, was used for gun emplacements and batteries.
230 Ibid: 65: 'Note on the Case of No. 2003227 Sgt. Eric John HOBSBAWM, A.E.C.'

231 Ibid: 43d: From Col. R. E. Pickering, Commander IOW Sub-District, 31 May 1944.

232 TNA KV2/3980: 78/79, 8/12.1.45.

233 Ibid: 55d: Holborn 4079, 29.8.44.

234 Ibid: 43d, Holborn 4071, 2.7.44.

235 MRC 1215/28: 'The foreigner', pp. 1–2.

236 Ibid, pp. 4–5, also for the following.

237 Ibid, pp. 6–7.

238 TNA KV2/3980: 61, 17.11.44.

239 Ibid: 61a, Milne report, 17.11.44. The Cairo Forces Parliament, in which Communists and Trotskyists played an important role, voted in favour of many socialist measures it wanted to be taken after the war, including the nationalisation of the banks. See Andy Baker, *The Cairo Parliament, 1943–4: An Experiment in Military Democracy* (Leigh-on-Sea, Essex, 1989).

240 TNA KV2/3980: 62, 18.11.44.

241 Ibid: 67, 24.11.44.

242 Ibid: 69, 4.12.44.

243 Ibid: 94, phone tapping report of the Labour Research Department, 31.5.45.

244 Ibid: 78/79, 8/12.1.45.

245 Keith Jeffery, *MI6. The History of the Secret Intelligence Service 1909–1949* (London, 2010), p. 561.

246 MRC 937/1/1/4. EJH to Tom Pocock, 14.7.81. Moss Taylor-Samuels won the seat from a long-standing Conservative MP, and held it for the next three elections before his death in 1957; the seat remained Labour until the Conservative victory at the 1970 General Election. My father, who was stationed in Italy, always maintained that servicemen voted Labour out of annoyance at not being demobilised as soon as the war was over.

247 LHA CP/IND/MISC/12/1: Papers of Christopher Meredith: EJH to Meredith, 23.8.45, 13.12.45, also for the following.

248 CUL UA BOGS 1/1951, File 123: W. J. Sartain to EJH, 8.12.45.

249 Ibid: Morris to Sartain, 26.12.45

250 Ibid: Postan to Sartain, 22.12.45.

251 HFA: Certificate of Transfer to the Army Reserve, 3.4.46.

252 TNA KV2/3981, 116a, 16.1.46, 117a, 28.1.46 and handwritten letter from George Cholmondley, Commander, 10 Civil Resettlement Unit, to Bailey, 16.1.46; CUL UA BOGS 1/1951, File 123: EJH to the Secretary, Board of Research Studies, Univ. of Cambridge, 15.1.46.

Chapter 5: 'Outsider in the Movement'

1 MRC 937/7/8/1: 'Paperback Writer' (typescript, 2003), p. 1.

2 MRC 937/1/1/4L EJH to Graziano, 1.12.80, also for the following.

3 'Panel Discussion: Conversations with Eric Hobsbawm', *India Centre International Quarterly* 34/1 (Spring, 2005), pp. 101–25.

4 EJH, interview with Pat Thane and Elizabeth Lunbeck, in *Visions of History* (Mid-Atlantic Radical Historians' Organization, New York, 1983), pp. 29–44.

5 *IT*, p. 121.

6 CUL UA BOGS 1/1951, File 123: Postan to W. J. Sartain, 29.1.46; Eric

Hobsbawm, 'Fabianism and the Fabians 1884–1914' (University of Cambridge Ph.D., 1950), Preface.

7   Ibid, p. 2.
8   Ibid, p. 1.
9   Ibid, p. 7.
10 Ibid, p. 166.
11 Ibid, p. 103.
12 Ibid, pp. 109, 112–14, 155–7.
13 Ibid, pp. 43, 168.
14 CUL UA BOGS 1/1951, File 123: EJH to W. Sartain, Secretary of the Board of Research Studies, 15.1.50, also for the following.
15 Ibid: W. J. Sartain to EJH, 24.12.49.
16 Ibid: Postan to Sartain, 8.3.50.
17 Ibid: W. J. Sartain, Secretary of Board of Research Studies, to EJH, 3.4.50; EJH to Sartain, 1.4.50.
18 Ibid: Examiners' Reports on thesis submitted for the degree of Ph.D. entitled 'Fabianism and the Fabians, 1884–1914', by E. J. E. Hobsbawm, 24.11.50: (1): By Mr. R. C. K. Ensor.
19 Ibid: (2): By Professor D. W. Brogan.
20 Ibid: Brogan and Ensor report, n.d. Brogan and Ensor were both subsequently knighted for their services to scholarship.
21 Ibid: Recommendation by Degree Committee, 1.12.50.
22 HFA: Degree Certificate, 27.1.51.
23 CUL UA BOGS 1/1951, File 123: Sartain to R. J. L. Kingsford, Cambridge University Press, 18.12.50; Kingsford to Sartain, 16.12.50.
24 LSE Library, Tawney papers, 6/11. See Lawrence Goldman, *The Life of R. H. Tawney: Socialism and History* (London, 2013), pp. 280–1.
25 Goldman, *The Life of R. H. Tawney*, pp. 276–7.
26 MRC 1215/21: TB 22.3.40.
27 KCAC NGA/5/1/452: Note by Noel Annan on Eric Hobsbawm.
28 MRC 937/7/8/1: 'Rathaus/history', Jan. 2008, pp. 3–4.
29 KCAC/4/11/1/Hobsbawm.
30 KCAC/4/11/2/8/3-5: Professor R. H. Tawney's and Professor T. S. Ashton's Reports on Mr. E. J. E. Hobsbawm's Dissertation 1949 'Studies in the "New" Trade Unionism (1889–1914)': Professor Tawney's Report, also for the following.
31 MRC 937//2/11: Herbert Kisch, 'Hobsbawm and *The Age of Capital*', *Journal of Economic Issues*, XVI/1 (March 1982), pp. 107–30, at p. 107, recalling the lecture, which the author had attended 'as a freshman and as a veteran just back from the war'.
32 KCAC/4/11/2/8/3-5: Professor Ashton's Report.
33 EJH, 'Trends in the British Labor Movement since 1850', *Science and Society*, XIII/4 (Fall, 1949), pp. 289–312.
34 John Saville (ed.), *Democracy and the Labour Movement. Essays in Honour of Dona Torr* (London, 1954), pp. 201–39.
35 EJH, 'The Labour Aristocracy: Twenty-Five Years After', *Bulletin of the Society for the Study of Labour History*, Vol. 40 (1980), revised and expanded in EJH, 'Debating the Labour Aristocracy', in his *Worlds of Labour: Further Studies in the*

History of Labour (London, 1984), pp. 214–26; also 'The Aristocracy of Labour Reconsidered', ibid, pp. 227–51, and 'Artisans and Labour Aristocrats', ibid, pp. 252–72.

36 MRC 937/1/6/1: Tawney to EJH, 4.11.49; EJH to Tawney, 8.11.49.

37 MRC 937/1/3/11: EJH to Victor Kiernan, 19.3.2003.

38 KCAC/39/1/17: Minute Book of the Cambridge Conversazione Society, 11.11.39.

39 MRC 937/7/8/1: 'Apostles' (typescript).

40 William C. Lubenow, *The Cambridge Apostles, 1820–1914: Imagination and Friendship in British Intellectual and Professional Life* (Cambridge, 1998).

41 KCAC/39/1/17: Minute Book of the Cambridge Conversazione Society, 11.3.39, 17.7.43.

42 MRC 937/1/6/5: EJH to Miranda Carter, 11.7.94, in response to Miranda Carter to EJH, 5.7.94. See Miranda Carter, *Anthony Blunt: His Lives* (London, 2001); MRC 937/7/8/1: 'Apostles' (typescript).

43 Annan, *Our Age*, p. 236.

44 MRC 937/7/8/1: 'Apostles' (typescript), also for the following.

45 *IT*, pp. 186–90.

46 Annan, *Our Age*, p. 236.

47 MRC 937/7/8/1: 'Apostles' (typescript, undated).

48 KCAC/39/1/17: Minute Book of the Cambridge Conversazione Society, 29.6.46, 21.10.46, 4.11.46, n.d., 2.12.46, 3.2.47, 17.2.47; *IT*, pp. 186–90; MRC 937/7/8/1: 'Apostles' (typescript, undated).

49 KCAC NGA/5/1/452: EJH to Noel Annan, n.d. (February 1948).

50 HFA: 'Two Families' (unpublished typescript), pp. 23–6.

51 *IT*, pp. 177–8.

52 International Tracing Service (ITS) archive, US Holocaust Memorial Museum TID 525.312-3: Ministère des Anciens Combattants et Victimes de la Guerre, Bureau des Déportés to ITS (Bad Arolsen), 9.1.59; Viktor Moritz Friedmann, Elsa Friedmann; Serge Klarsfeld, 'Memorial to the Jews Deported from France 1942–1944: Convoy 62, November 20, 1943'; Etan Dror to ITS, 26.7.57; Serge Klarsfeld, *Memorial to the Jews Deported from France, 1942–1944* (Paris, 1983), 'Convoy 62, November 20, 1943'; EJH, 'Two Families', pp. 23–5.

53 MRC 937/1/1/1: Gertruda Albrechtová to EJH, 29.3.64; MRC 937/1/5/2: Gertruda Albrechtová to EJH, 10.10.04.

54 Val Wilmer, 'Denis Preston' in H. C. G. Matthew and Brian Harrison (eds), *Oxford Dictionary of National Biography*, 45 (Oxford, 2004), pp. 255–6; HFA: Richard Preston to Marlene Hobsbawm, 14.9.2016 (email).

55 Interview with Robin Marchesi, 6.12.2016; 'Captain Victor Marchesi', *Daily Telegraph*, 13.2.2007.

56 Interview with Robin Marchesi, 6.12.2016, also for the following. See Stephen Haddesley (with Alan Carroll), *Operation Tabarin. Britain's Secret Wartime Expedition to Antarctica 1944–46* (London, 2014). Victor continued to work in biological warfare for some time after the war (ibid, p. 227).

57 Communication from Jeremy Marchesi, 21.11.2016.

58 John L. Gaddis, *The Cold War: A New History* (London, 2005).

59 TNA KV2/3981: Walter Wallich to EJH, 4.7.45.

60 BBC WAC RCONT 1: EJH to Far Eastern Talks Dept, 1.8.47.

61 *IT*, pp. 174–9.
62 TNA KV2/3981, 129: 12.7.48.
63 MRC 937/1/1/4: EJH to Arno Mayer, n.d. (Nov. 1987/Jan. 1988), also for the following. Eugen Kogon's *Der SS-Staat. Das System der deutschen Konzentrationslager* (Munich, 1946), translated into English as *The Theory and Practice of Hell* (New York, 1950), was the first major study of the camps, based on a synthesis of personal experience and historical scholarship. Eric clearly read it on publication.
64 MRC 1215/1: EJH to Ron Hobsbaum, 7.4.41.
65 TNA KV2/3980: 94a, E. Shelmerdine to Mr Sams, MI5, 2.5.45.
66 Ibid: 94a, 12.5.45. For the position, see E. Shelmerdine, Head of Staff Administration, BBC, to MI5, 26.4.45, filed under the same number.
67 Ibid: 89, D. Osborne to Miss Shelmerdine (BBC), 23.4.45.
68 Ibid: cover sheet number 93, 8.5.45.
69 BBC WAC RCONT 15: note: 'Please keep this on top'.
70 BBC WAC RCONT 1: EJH to Director of Talks, Third Programme, 11.12.46.
71 Asa Briggs, *Sound and Vision: The History of Broadcasting in the United Kingdom* IV (Oxford, 1979), pp. 65–7.
72 Isaiah Berlin (ed. Henry Hardy and Jennifer Holmes), *Enlightening. Letters 1946–1960* (London, 2009), p. 794. Kallin is not mentioned in Asa Briggs's official history of the BBC.
73 BBC WAC RCONT 1: Talks Booking Requisition (Anna Kallin to A. A. Talks, 13.1.47).
74 Ibid: EJH to Anna Kallin, 13.2.47.
75 Ibid: Anna Kallin to EJH, 20.2.47, also for the following.
76 Ibid: N. G. Luker to EJH, 9.7.47.
77 Ibid: Anna Kallin to EJH, 20.2.47.
78 Ibid: Talks Booking Requisition, Anna Kallin to A. A. Talks, 17.3.47.
79 Ibid: EJH to Anna Kallin, n.d.; Anna Kallin to EJH, 14.5.47; EJH to Anna Kallin, n.d. (June 1947).
80 Ibid: Talks (Live or Recorded) Retrospective, 25.11.47.
81 Ibid: Lionel Millard to Mr Boswell, Talks Booking Manager, 15.5.48.
82 Ibid: Ronald Boswell to EJH, 10.6.47.
83 Ibid: EJH to Anna Kallin, n.d. (July 1947).
84 *IT*, p. 424 n.11.
85 House of Lords Debates, 29 March 1950, vol. 166 cc607-61, at 611–12.
86 BBC WAC RCONT 1: Talks Booking Requisition: Mr Steedman to Eur. Prog. Ex., 20.1.53. Unfortunately the talk has not survived in either written or recorded form.
87 Ibid: Michael Stephens to EJH, 4.2.53; Talks Booking Requisition, Michael Stephens to Talks Booking Manager, 26.2.53.
88 Ibid: Mary Somerville to Michael Stephens, 16.2.53.
89 Ibid: Michael Stephens to EJH, 17.2.53.
90 Ibid: Lorna Moore to C. T. 'Confidential', 10.3.53.
91 Ibid: Anna Kallin to EJH, 6.10.53.
92 Ibid: J. C. Thornton note 'D. S. W.' 22.3.54, also for the following.
93 Ibid: Anna Kallin to EJH, 26.3.54.
94 Ibid: Ronald Boswell to EJH, 30.3.54.

95 Ibid: EJH to Anna Kallin, 8.4.54.
96 Ibid: Ronald Boswell to Talks Booking Manager, Talks Booking Requisition, 30.9.54. These talks were often tailored to fit into the intervals of live broadcast concerts. Eric received a fee of twenty guineas for the Nestroy talk: Ronald Boswell to EJH, 27.1.55.
97 MRC 937/4/3/1/8: EJH, 'The Viennese Popular Theatre', *Times Literary Supplement*, 11.2.55, pp. 81–2.
98 Ibid: EJH, 'Little Man on Guard', *Times Literary Supplement*, 27.4.51.
99 *IT*, p. 176; for life in Gloucester Crescent in the 1980s, essentially unchanged except for the personnel, see Nina Stibbe, *Love, Nina: Despatches from Family Life* (London, 2013).
100 BBC WAC RCONT 1: EJH to Anna Kallin, n.d.; Anna Kallin to EJH, 14.5.47 ('I hope you and your wife have settled down in your beautiful house'); FLP: EJH to Fritz Lustig, 30.4.95; KCAC NGA/5/1/452: EJH to Noel Annan, n.d. (February 1948).
101 Eric Hobsbawm, 'Portrait of a Neighbourhood', *Lilliput*, 1.4.47, pp. 310–16. The LNER was the London and North-Eastern Railway; the LMS was the London, Midland and Scottish Railway.
102 Ibid. His other post-war contribution to the magazine was a brief biographical sketch of the Regency politician 'Humanity Dick' Martin, pioneer of laws against cruelty to animals: EJH, 'Dumb Friends' Friend', *Lilliput*, 1.5.48, pp. 64–5 'Spiv' was contemporary slang for a flashily dressed man dealing in black market or stolen goods.
103 TNA KV2/3981, 148a: Cambridge.
104 *IT*, pp. 181–2; EJH, 'Red Science', *London Review of Books*, 9.3.2006.
105 CUL UA BOGS 1/1951, File 123: EJH to Sartain, n.d. (August 1947); Sartain to EJH, 21.7.47.
106 Ibid: Sartain to EJH, 8.10.47.
107 Ibid: Postan to Sartain, 29.10.47.
108 Ibid: Oakeshott to Sartain, 26.11.47; Sartain to EJH, 8.10.47; EJH to Sartain, 19.10.47; Sartain to EJH, 22.10.47; Sartain to Postan, 22.10.47; Postan to Sartain, 29.10.47; EJH to Sartain, n.a. [November 1947].
109 HFA Diary Notes: in German, 13.1.51, also for the following.
110 Ibid: 'Interim Report', 12.11.50, p. 2; Marlene Hobsbawm email, 4.7.17. Eric did not mention the abortion in his 'Interim Report', probably because if it had been discovered at the time, he and Muriel might well have been prosecuted.
111 HFA Diary Notes: in German, 'Interim Report', 12.11.50, p. 3, also for the following.
112 MRC 937/1/3/11: Evelyn Pear to EJH, 21.1.2003.
113 Ibid: EJH to Evelyn Pear, 29.1.2003.
114 *The Great Soviet Encyclopedia* (Moscow, 1979), entry on 'Historical Congresses: International'.
115 MRC 937/8/2/35: EJH, 'Old Marxist still sorting out global fact from fiction', *Times Higher Education Supplement*, 10/2 (12.7.02).
116 HFA Diary Notes: in German, 'Interim Report', 12.11.50, p. 4.
117 HFA Diary Notes: in German, 14.12.50, also for the following.
118 Ibid, 16.12.50.
119 KCAC: information from Dr Patricia McGuire. I am grateful to the present

occupant of the rooms, Mr James Trevithick, for showing me round and explaining what they must have been like in the years immediately after the war.

120 HFA Diary Notes: in German, 14.12.50, also for the following. The Provost was Sir John Tressider Sheppard, a classicist who retired from his post in 1954, whom Eric heartily despised ('one of the few people in my life for whom I came to feel genuine hate', *IT*, p. 108); Donald was Donald Beves, Tutor in French, who kept in touch with France 'by touring its restaurants during vacations with friends in his Rolls-Bentley' (ibid); Scholfield was Alwyn Faber Scholfield, retired Keeper of the University Library; John Saltmarsh was an eminent medieval economic and social historian; Arthur Cecil Pigou by the 1950s had retired from his Chair in Economics because of ill health and was reportedly becoming a recluse. All of them were unmarried, and lived in College.

121 HFA Diary Notes: in German, 28.12.50.

122 Neil O'Connor, 'Tizard, Jack', *Oxford Dictionary of National Biography*.

123 HFA Diary Notes: in German, 31.12.50, p. 3.

124 Augustine of Hippo, *The City of God*, Part V, Chapter 18.

125 HFA Diary Notes: in German, 30.12.50, p. 1.

126 Alan Rusbridger, 'Hedi Stadlen. From political activism in Colombo to new insights on Beethoven', *Guardian*, 29.1.2004.

127 HFA Diary Notes: in German, 6.1.51.

128 Ibid, 2.1.51, p. 1; ibid, 3.1.51, p. 2. My parents took the *Daily Telegraph* and I remember being impressed by the intellectual power of Stadlen's writing.

129 Ibid, pp. 2–3, also for the following. J. D. Bernal was an active Communist who taught and researched crystallography at Birkbeck; Maurice Dobb was a Communist economist at Cambridge.

130 Ibid, 12.1.51, pp. 1–2.

131 Ibid, 11.1.51, p. 1.

132 Interview with Robin Marchesi, 6.12.2016.

133 HFA Diary Notes: in German, 12.1.51, p. 2.

134 TNA KV2/3981, 163: report on Eric HOBSBAWM 23.5.51.

135 TNA KV2/3981, 165a: Extract from file PF 211.764. The official title of the magazine included *The Nation*, which it had taken over some time before, but it was usually known simply as the *New Statesman*.

136 MRC 937/7/2/3. Spanish notebook, pp. 1–2.

137 Ibid, pp. 9–10.

138 Ibid, p. 11.

139 Ibid, 20.3.51, 25.3.51 (bullfight), 27.3.51 (beggars, Boy Scouts).

140 Ibid, 20.3.51.

141 Ibid, 21.3.51.

142 Ibid, 22.3.51.

143 Ibid, 23.3.51.

144 Ibid, 27.3.51.

145 Ibid, 24.3.51.

146 Michael Richards, 'Falange, Autarky and Crisis: The Barcelona General Strike of 1951', *European History Quarterly*, Vol. 29 (1999), No. 4, pp. 543–85.

147 TNA KV2/3983: Extract from S.B. report re Winifred Thelme VENESS, suspected Communist sympathiser, 1953, mentioning HOBSBAWM.

148 Archivio della Scuola Normale di Pisa: EJH to Delio Cantimori, 27.6.51 (in French). See EJH, 'Obituary: Delio Cantimori 1904–1966', *Past & Present*, No. 35 (Dec. 1966), pp. 157–8.

149 Archivio della Scuola Normale di Pisa: EJH to Delio Cantimori, 4.8.51.

150 Ibid: EJH to Delio Cantimori, 12.9.51.

151 EJH Wartime Notes: 'The foreigner' (typescript), p. 3.

152 *IT*, p. 346, which dates the visit to 1952, although the correspondence with Cantimori makes it clear that the trip took place the previous year.

153 HFA: Muriel Hobsbawm to EJH, 12.6.52.

154 Victoria Brittain, 'Jack Gaster', *Guardian*, 13 March 2007.

155 HFA: EJH to Jack Gaster, n.d. (June 1952).

156 TNA KV2/3982: intercepted copy of letter from Gaster to EJH, 6.1.53. MI5, as so often, was not quite up with the situation, reporting in October 1953 that 'the indications are that Mrs. HOBSBAWM is no longer in sympathy with Communism' (TNA KV2/3982: David H. Whyte, copy of report on Thistlethwaite, 19.10.53).

157 HFA: Certificate of making Decree Nisi Absolute (Divorce), 9.3.53.

158 Maya Jaggi, 'A Question of Faith', *Guardian*, 20 September 2002. Most accounts wrongly give the date of the divorce as 1951.

159 Tyrrell G. Marris, 'Letter: Peter Marris', *Guardian*, 21.7.2007.

160 MRC 937/1/6/23: EJH to Tyrrell Marris, n.d. (August 2012, Eric's last known letter before his death), and Tyrrell Marris to EJH, 4 and 17.8.2012.

161 MRC 937/4/3/4/1: 'On the river' (English typescript, on blue paper), also for the following paragraphs, below.

162 The account was one of a number of memoirs Eric wrote up as a story, changing some of the details, including some names, in case, perhaps, they were discovered among his papers, or maybe with a view to publishing them at some point, but as far as one can judge keeping closely to the actual sequence and detail of events. See also the set of diary notes he compiled on the trip and used as the basis for the narrative; here he uses the names Marí and Salud for the girls but calls the Spanish boys Paco and Antonio (MRC 1215/25: Seville).

163 Louis-Antoine de Bougainville was an eighteenth-century French navigator and explorer, who landed on Tahiti in 1767 and claimed it for France. His account of the island portrayed it as a natural paradise inhabited by noble savages.

164 MRC 937/1/6/23: EJH to Tyrrell Marris, n.d., and Tyrrell Marris to EJH, 4 and 17.8.2012; MRC 1215/25, 'Segelfahrt' and diary notes (the notes are headed 'Quiros' but clearly refer to the brothel where Salud worked; Eric and the boys did not go to Quiros, which is in Asturias, far inland).

165 Marlene Hobsbawm email, 4.7.2017.

166 'Eric John Ernest Hobsbawm', *King's College, Cambridge, Annual Report* 2015, pp. 81–6.

167 TNA KV2/3983: 'Lascar': Meeting of the National Student Working Committee, 3.4.56 (transcript of monitored conversation at Communist Party headquarters).

168 MRC 937/4/3/1/7: EJH, 'The New Threat to History', *New York Review of Books*, 16.12.93, pp. 62–4.

169 'Eric John Ernest Hobsbawm', *King's College, Cambridge, Annual Report* 2015, pp. 81–6.

170 Interview with Joan Bakewell, 22.7.16, also for the following.
171 MRC 937/1/1/6: Tam Dalyell to EJH, 14.4.2005. See also Tam Dalyell, *The Importance of Being Awkward: The Autobiography of Tam Dalyell* (London, 2011). He later became a prominent Labour back-bencher in the House of Commons.
172 Nicholas Wroe, 'Romantic Nationalist', *Guardian*, 12 April 2003.
173 Interview with Neal Ascherson, 26.7.2016, also for the following.
174 See Tom Wells, *Wild Man: The Life and Times of Daniel Ellsberg* (London, 2001).
175 'The *SRB* Interview: Neal Ascherson', *Scottish Review of Books*, 3.8.2014.
176 Interview with Neal Ascherson, 26.7.2016, also for the following.
177 MRC 937/1/3/11: EJH to Ivan Avakumovic, 21.1.2004.
178 Ibid. See the brilliant obituary essay by David Cannadine, 'John Harold Plumb, 1911–2001', *Proceedings of the British Academy* 124, *Biographical Memoirs of Fellows* III (2005).
179 Interview with Sir Geoffrey Lloyd, 22.3.17, also for the following.
180 Interview with Neal Ascherson, 26.7.2016.
181 MRC 937/7/8/1: 'Apostles' (typescript, undated).
182 ibid: *Guardian* 'Diary' 7.5.85; ibid, 'Apostles' (typescript, undated).
183 *IT*, p. 101.
184 TNA KV2/3981, 181: report on Dr E. HOBSBAWM.
185 Ibid, 152a.
186 Ibid, 87: Ext. from B.L.F. source report, 20.6.52.
187 TNA KV2/3982: General Headquarters Middle East Land Headquarters 'Extract' 19.10.53. For May, see his entry in the *Oxford Dictionary of National Biography*. The report mentions a 'FAITH' who, it says, was 'ERIC's girl friend'. This was Faith Henry, a literary scout for Coward-McCann, part of the Putnam Group. Among other books she secured for them was John Le Carré's *The Spy Who Came in from the Cold* (1963). In her thirties, she was glamorous and attractive, but despite several meetings with him she did not manage to secure the rights to any of Eric's books. Extensive enquiries among survivors and descendants of her circle have failed to turn up even the slightest hint of a sexual relationship, and there is no mention of her in any of Eric's papers (interview with Bruce Hunter, 26.7.2016). This appears to be one of a number of instances in which MI5 leapt to unjustifiable conclusions. On another occasion an MI5 report described Eric as 'a Dutch Jew' (TNA KV2/3982: 'Secret ... from an established and reliable source', 16.12.52).
188 TNA KV2/3981, 152b: B.1, 28.12.50.
189 HFA Diary Notes: in German, 14.12.50.
190 *IT*, p. 183 and n.10.
191 MRC 937/7/8/1: EJH to David Howell, 25 April 2003, and enclosure. A copy of Eric's Party autobiography (along with, presumably, copies of many others) was obtained by an MI5 agent who succeeded in infiltrating the family where the records were kept by posing as a tenant, as part of Operation Party Piece, and can be found in his MI5 file: TNA KV2/3983: 'Autobiography'; see Andrew, *The Defence of the Realm*, pp. 400–1.
192 TNA KV2/3981, 140a: Extract, 28.9.49.
193 HFA Diary Notes: in German, 28.12.50.
194 *IT*, pp. 191–6.
195 MRC 937/4/6/1: *Listener*, 27.1.49.

196   Interview with Neal Ascherson, 26.7.2016; interview with Sir Geoffrey Lloyd, 22.3.2017.
197   Gioietta Kuo, *A Himalayan Odyssey* (Milton Keynes, 2002); interview with Gioietta Kuo, 28.7.2018.
198   TNA KV2/3982: J. H. Money to D. N. Whyte (copy), 19.10.53.
199   Doris Lessing, *Walking in the Shade* (London, 1997), p. 23.
200   TNA KV2/3981, 127a: Extract, 5.5.48.
201   Ibid, 180: Extract from file PF 211764, 29.5.52.
202   *IT*, p. 190.
203   MRC 937/4/6/1: Letter to *Manchester Guardian*, 29.7.1950, and letter to Arthur Clegg (draft), 8.5.1953; letter to *The Times*, 21.5.1960.
204   TNA KV2/3982: N. Dabell to Miss N. E. Wadeley (copy), 14.4.53.
205   TNA KV2/3981, 128c, 27.9.48.
206   Ibid, 130a, 5.1.49, and 128d, 8.12.48.
207   Ibid, 152b: B.1, 28.12.50 and 144a, Extract P.F.211764, 18.4.50.
208   Ibid, 166a: EJH to Dorothy Diamond, 23.6.51.
209   Ibid, 172a: J. L. Vernon to Col. M. F. Allan, 3.1.52.
210   Ibid, Vernon to Allan, 10.6.52.
211   *IT*, p. 101.
212   Straight, *After Long Silence*, pp. 102–7, 229–30. The Smith Act, or Alien Registration Act to give it its proper title, was passed in 1940. It made advocating the overthrow of the United States government a criminal offence and was the basis for the indictment and imprisonment of eleven leading members of the Communist Party in 1949. The Act was later repealed and a number of the convictions ruled unconstitutional by the Supreme Court. See Richard W. Steele, *Free Speech in the Good War* (New York, 1999).
213   TNA KV2/3981, 146: Extract P.F.211763, 26.7.50. Isaiah Berlin also ran into trouble with Michael Straight, whom he considered to be a particularly malicious spreader of false rumours; 'Straight his name but not his nature' (Isaiah Berlin to Arthur Schlesinger, 27.8.53, in Berlin, *Enlightening*, pp. 386–7).
214   *IT*, pp. 192–4.
215   MRC 937/8/2/23/1: Didier Eribon, 'Ma passion du XXe siècle', *Le Nouvel Observateur*, 22–27/10/99, pp. 136–8 [interview with EJH].
216   LHA CP/CENT/CULT/05/11: Committee minute book 1946–51: minute 10.4.48.
217   John Saville, Christopher Hill, George Thomson and Maurice Dobb (eds), *Democracy and the Labour Movement. Essays in honour of Dona Torr* (London, 1954).
218   MRC 937/1/3/11: EJH to Susan Edwards, 12.12.2003.
219   Ibid, also Dokumentationsarchiv des österreichischen Widerstandes, 50120: Korrespondenz Steiner: Hobsbawm, Eric, 1957–1994: EJH to Herbert Steiner, 6.3.57.
220   Antony Howe, 'Dona Torr', *Oxford Dictionary of National Biography*, for further details on Torr.
221   MRC 937/6/2/1: Lines of Development: Statement and discussion on the Content of the History Course in the Secondary School (1948).
222   MRC 937/6/2/2: The Communist Party Historians' Group – a statement on the present position (January 1952), also for the rest of this paragraph.

223   LHA CP/CENT/CULT/05/11: Committee minute book 1946–1951: minute of 26.9.47.
224   MRC 937/1/6/6: EJH to Raphael Samuel, n.d. (August 1994). See also Saville, *Memoirs from the Left*, pp. 87–9.
225   Ibid: Historian's [*sic*] Group. 16th and 17th Century Section, 8.9.48.
226   MRC 937/6/2/2: Historians' Group (19th Cent.) Conference to be held at Marx House Sunday, June 6th, 1948; EJH 'A Note on Kuczynski's Statistics' and covering letter, undated, to Dona Torr. Jürgen Kuczynski published *A Short History of Labour Conditions under Capitalism in Great Britain* in 1946.
227   MRC 937/6/2/1: Notes for Discussion on 'A People's History of England', p. 18.
228   MRC 937/6/2/2: three sets of typescript notes on 'Reformism and Empire' and 'Suggestion for Conference on "Labour and Empire"'. His focus on nineteenth-century radicalism prompted a special meeting, held in Birmingham on 28 June 1953 (MRC 937/6/2/2: 'Discussion on Radicalism').
229   LHA CP/CENT/CULT/05/11: Committee minute book 1946–1951: minute of 14.1.50.
230   Ibid: minute of 3.9.52.
231   Ibid: minutes of 14.11.54 and 20.2.55.
232   LHA CP/CENT/CULT/08/02: Report on the work of the Historians' Group, December 1954.
233   MRC 937/6/2/3: 'Introduction – The General Law of Capitalist Development', p. 1; and additions; full text, typed with handwritten notes.
234   MRC 937/6/2/3: Section XI: Changing Character of the empire after 1880. Discussion. See also, in the same file, and EJH handwritten notes, 'Period 1830–1880', discussion on 'Nature and Character of Bourgeoisie'.
235   Ibid: Session Thirteen: Concluding report and discussion (Friday afternoon, 16th July, 1954). Further copies of the lectures by EJH in LHA CP/CENT/CULT/10/01: Papers of Bill Moore.
236   MRC 937/1/2/12: Edward Thompson to EJH, 23.11. no year (1963).
237   Ibid: Edward Thompson to EJH, 25.10. (1975). See David Parker (ed.), *Ideology, Absolutism and the English Revolution: Debates of the British Communist Historians, 1940–1956* (London, 2008); EJH, 'The Historians' Group of the Communist Party', in Maurice Cornforth (ed.), *Rebels and their Causes* (London, 1978); Harvey J. Kaye, *The Education of Desire: Marxists and the Writing of History* (London, 1992); Raphael Samuel, 'British Marxist Historians', *New Left Review* 120 (1980), pp. 21–96.
238   TNA KV2/3982: Pierre Vilar to EJH, 18.10.52 (copy of intercepted letter).
239   Archivio della Scuola Normale di Pisa: EJH to Delio Cantimori, 13.7.52.
240   TNA KV2/3982: 'Note', 12.11.53.
241   LHA CP/CENT/CULT/05/11: Committee minute book 1946–1951: minute of 29.8.54.
242   MRC 1215/26: Moscow Diary. In his memoirs, Eric preferred to put the emphasis on Stalin's smallness, wondering how someone so tiny could have wielded such power.
243   *IT*, pp. 197–201; TNA KV2/3983: 'British Historians in Moscow', Extract from Summary of World Broadcasts – Part I – USSR.
244   HFA Diary Notes: in German, 6.1.50.

245 I am indebted to Mr Andrew Morris for this information.
246 EJH, Christopher Hill and Rodney Hilton, '*Past & Present*: Origins and Early Years', *Past & Present* 100 (August 1983), pp. 3–14, also for the following.
247 Archivio della Scuola Normale di Pisa: EJH to Delio Cantimori, 31.1.52.
248 Ibid: EJH to Delio Cantimori, 8.1.52; see also TNA KV2/3982: Cantimori to EJH, 18.11.52 (copy of intercepted letter).
249 Archivio della Scuola Normale di Pisa: EJH to Delio Cantimori, August 1955.
250 MRC 937/7/8/1: EJH to unnamed correspondent, n.d.
251 HFA Diary Notes: in German, 16.12.50.
252 MRC 937/8/2/23/1: Didier Eribon, 'Ma passion du XXe siècle', *Le Nouvel Observateur*, 22–27/10/99, pp. 136–8. See also Panel Discussion: Conversations with Eric Hobsbawm', *India Centre International Quarterly*, 34/1 (March 2005), where Eric describes the *Annales* school as the French equivalent of the British Marxist Historians' group.
253 'Introduction', *Past & Present* 1 (February 1952), p. i.
254 MRC 937/8/2/23/1: Pierre Goubert, 'Marxiste à l'anglaise', *Le Monde*, 28.10.99, p. 32.
255 Jacques Le Goff, '*Past & Present*: Later History', *Past & Present* 100 (August 1983), pp. 14–28.
256 MRC 937/7/8/1: EJH to unnamed correspondent, n.d., pp. 3–4.
257 EJH, 'The Machine Breakers', *Past & Present* 1 (February 1952), pp. 57–70.
258 MRC 937/6/2/2: Communist Party Historians' Group, Sixteenth and Seventeenth Centuries Section, 8.3.52. Eric did not belong to the Section but sometimes attended its meetings. See also Parker (ed.), *Ideology, Absolutism and the English Revolution*.
259 EJH, 'The General Crisis of the European Economy in the 17th Century', *Past & Present* 5 (May 1954), pp. 33–53, and 6 (November 1954), pp. 44–65.
260 MRC 937/8/2/1: Frédéric Mauro, 'Sur la "crise" du XVIIe siècle', *Annales ESC*, XIV/1 (1959), pp 181–5. This led to an invitation to Eric to read a paper at the École des Hautes Études en Sciences Sociales, the institutional headquarters of the *Annales* in Paris, which was then published in the journal: 'En Angleterre: Révolution industrielle et vie materielle des classes populaires', *Annales ESC*, 17 (1962).
261 H. R. Trevor-Roper, 'The General Crisis of the 17th Century', *Past & Present* 16 (November 1959), pp. 31–64; Trevor Aston (ed.) *Crisis in Europe 1560–1660: Essays from Past & Present* (Oxford, 1965); Geoffrey Parker and Lesley Smith (eds), *The General Crisis of the Seventeenth Century* (London, 1978).
262 MRC 937/7/8/1: 'The Cold War and the Universities' (typescript, New York, 13.11.97), p. 4.
263 Postan to Tawney, 3.1.51, quoted in Goldman, *The Life of R. H. Tawney*, p. 280.
264 EJH, Christopher Hill and Rodney Hilton, '*Past & Present*: Origins and Early Years', *Past & Present* 100 (August 1983), pp. 3–14.
265 MRC 937/8/2/22/2: Neal Ascherson, 'The Age of Hobsbawm', *Independent on Sunday*, 2.10.94, p. 21.
266 HFA: Troup Horne to EJH, 16.2.50.

Chapter 6: 'A Dangerous Character'

1 *The Great Soviet Encyclopedia* (Moscow, 1979), entry on 'Historical Congresses: International'.
2 Archivio della Scuola Normale di Pisa: EJH to Delio Cantimori, 16.11.54.
3 Maxine Berg, 'East-West Dialogues: Economic Historians, the Cold War, and Détente', *Journal of Modern History*, Vol. 87, No. 1 (March 2015), pp. 36–71.
4 EJH, 'George Rudé: Marxist Historian', *Socialist History Occasional Pamphlets* 2 (1993), pp. 5–11, at p. 11.
5 Archivio della Scuola Normale di Pisa: EJH to Delio Cantimori, Summer 1955. On the letter, the date has been altered by hand to 1952. But in 1952 Eric was living in King's College, Cambridge, not in Gordon Mansions, the address given at the top of the letter; he did not live there until his Fellowship at King's came to an end, which was in the late summer of 1954.
6 Interview with Robin Marchesi, 6.12.2016, also for the following.
7 Interview with Angela Hobsbaum, 30.3.17.
8 Val Wilmer, 'Denis Preston' in H. C. G. Matthew and Brian Harrison (eds), *Oxford Dictionary of National Biography*, 45 (Oxford, 2004), pp. 255–6. I remember being taught to read from this book as a small child in the early 1950s.
9 TNA KV2/3983: Extract from Special Branch Report on Louis Frank MARKS; *IT*, p. 219.
10 Ibid: Metropolitan Police (Special Branch) report, 27.5.55, reporting his departure to France ('It was noticed that his passport contained several "iron curtain" visas').
11 *IT*, p. 329.
12 MRC 937/1/2/10: Hélène Berghauer to EJH, 18 May (no year, probably 1953).
13 Dan Ferrand-Bechmann, 'À propos de Henri Lefebvre et Henri Raymond: Témoignage pour l'histoire de sociologie', *Socio-logos,* put online on 28 March 2007, consulted 30 May 2017, http://socio-logos.revues. org/902/2007; Jack Robertson, *Twentieth-Century Artists on Art: An Index to Writings, Statements, and Interviews by Artists, Architects, and Designers* (2nd edn, London, 1996), p. 110.
14 Entretien entre Elise Marienstras et Charlotte Faucher, 27.7.2016.
15 *IT*, pp. 328–9. Lucien Goldmann was a French-Romanian sociologist and philosopher who sought a new, more flexible, less dogmatic ideology as a way out of what he regarded as the crisis of Marxism in the 1950s. Roland Barthes was a literary theorist who at this time was writing a column on French popular culture for a Parisian magazine, collecting the articles for his anthology *Mythologies,* published in 1957; in 1960, he founded a centre for the study of communication together with Edgar Morin, another sociologist and philosopher, heavily involved in the wartime Resistance, who was drifting away from his original adherence to Marxist doctrine at this time.
16 Entretien entre Maurice Aymard et Charlotte Faucher, 27.7.2016; Entretien entre Michelle Perrot et Charlotte Faucher, 20.9.2016; Patrick Fridenson, notes on Eric's French publications by Charlotte Faucher.
17 Francis Newton, 'St.-Germain Soprano', *New Statesman*, 15.9.56, p. 310.
18 Francis Newton, 'Parisian Jazz', *New Statesman*, 12.7.58, p. 44.
19 Interview with Robin Marchesi, 6.12.16.

20 *IT*, pp. 328–30; Entretien entre Elise Marienstras et Charlotte Faucher, 27.7.2016.
21 MRC 937/1/2/9: Hélène to EJH, 16.3.56; note headed 'Paris, 23'.
22 Ibid: Hélène to EJH, 25.11.54.
23 Ibid: Hélène to EJH, 9.11.56, for one example of a visit to London by the Raymonds. Gioietta Kuo (interview, 28.7.2018) remembered meeting the couple in Eric's rooms at King's.
24 TNA KV2/3982: copy of intercepted letter from Hélène to EJH, 27.11.52.
25 Ibid: copy of intercepted letter from Hélène to EJH, 14.10.52.
26 MRC 937/1/2/9: 'Les Amants', H. Raymond.
27 Ibid: Hélène to EJH, 14.5.53. The sonnet continues: 'I love thee to the depth and breadth and height/My soul can reach'.
28 Ibid: Hélène to EJH, 26.7.52.
29 Ibid: Hélène to EJH, 28.3.57.
30 Ibid: Hélène to EJH, 5.5.58.
31 Ibid: Hélène to EJH, 5.5.58.
32 Ibid: Hélène to EJH, 19.7.60.
33 Ibid: Hélène to EJH, n.d, headed 'lundi 4'.
34 Entretien entre Elise Marienstras et Charlotte Faucher, 27.7.2016. Hélène's brother Henri Berghauer, asked what he knew of her relationship with Eric, said he had met Eric with her several times but did not know about their affair; since at this point in the interview he had not been informed by the interviewer of the affair, it follows that he must in fact have known about it (Entretien entre Charlotte Faucher et Henri Berghauer, 20.9.2016).
35 Jim House and Neil MacMaster, *Paris 1961: Algerians, State Terror, and Memory* (Oxford, 2006).
36 Interview with Neal Ascherson, 26.7.2016.
37 *IT*, pp. 329–30.
38 MRC 937/1/2/10: Hélène to EJH, 24.1.62.
39 Ibid: Hélène to EJH, n.d. ('Le 12 Mai').
40 Ibid: Hélène to EJH, 15.2.65.
41 MRC 937/1/2/9: Hélène to EJH, 17.10.85.
42 MRC 937/2/6/3: Henri to EJH, 15.7.92.
43 *IT*, p. 320.
44 MRC 937/1/3/1: Summary of correspondence between EJH and Hutchinson; 'The Rise of the Wage-Worker' (synopsis).
45 Ibid: Ruth Klauber to EJH, 10.11.53.
46 Ibid: 'Summary of Correspondence between EJH and Hutchinsons', Letter from Cole, 28.11.53.
47 Ibid: EJH to Cole, undated; Cole to EJH, 7.12.53; EJH to Cole, undated; Hutchinson to EJH, 21.1.54, with contract
48 Ibid: EJH to Ruth Klauber, 7.8.55.
49 Ibid: 'Summary of Correspondence between EJH and Hutchinsons', Letter from Cole, 25.10.55.
50 *IT*, pp. 184–5.
51 MRC 937/1/3/1: EJH to Jack Gaster, 26.10.55.
52 Ibid: EJH to Ruth Klauber (draft, undated).
53 Ibid: 'Summary of Correspondence between EJH and Hutchinsons'.

54 Ibid: EJH to Ruth Klauber, undated, probably December 1955.

55 Ibid: EJH to Ruth Klauber, 9.3.56.

56 Ibid: 'Some Hutchinson's University Library Books'.

57 Ibid: 'Statement by the author', also for the following.

58 Ibid: EJH to Ruth Klauber, 22.3.56, also for the following.

59 Ibid: Birkbeck & Co. to Gaster and Turner, 17.4.56.

60 Ibid: Jack Gaster to EJH, 25.4.56.

61 *IT*, p. 184.

62 MRC 937/1/3/1: EJH to W. H. Chaloner, undated.

63 Edwin Chadwick, *Report on the Sanitary Condition of the Labouring Population of Great Britain* (London, 1832, reprinted with a Foreword by Michael W. Flinn, Edinburgh, 1972); John L. and Barbara Hammond, *The Town Labourer 1760–1832: The New Civilisation* (London, 1917).

64 John Harold Clapham, *An Economic History of Modern Britain* (3 vols, Cambridge, 1926–8); Thomas S. Ashton, *The Industrial Revolution, 1760–1830* (The Home University Library, London, 1948).

65 EJH, 'The British Standard of Living, 1790–1850', *Economic History Review* X (1957–58), reprinted with additions in his *Labouring Men: Studies in the History of Labour* (London, 1964), pp. 64–104; 'The Standard of Living During the Industrial Revolution: A Discussion', *Economic History Review* XVI (1963–4), pp. 119–34, followed by a response from Hartwell on pp. 397–416; see also *Labouring Men*, pp. 120–57.

66 Arthur J. Taylor (ed.), *The Standard of Living in Britain in the Industrial Revolution* (London, 1975), including a 'Postscript' by EJH on pp. 179–88.

67 MRC 937/1/2/12: Edward Thompson to EJH, 23.11. no year (1963), also for the following.

68 EJH, 'Organised Orphans', *New Statesman*, 29.11.63.

69 Support for Eric's argument, using health and nutrition statistics, was furnished by Roderick Floud, *Height, Health and History: Nutritional Status in the United Kingdom, 1750–1980* (Cambridge, 1990). The debate, however, rumbles on even in the twenty-first century.

70 For an illuminating and moving portrayal of this kind of sectarian Communist, see David Aaronovitch, *Party Animals: My Family and Other Communists* (London, 2016).

71 *IT*, pp. 201–4.

72 Beckett, *Enemy Within*, pp. 130–3.

73 MRC 937/6/2/2: Implications of 20th Congress for Historians, 8.4.56; Reply from Harry Pollitt, 13.4.56; Resolutions passed at the quarterly committee meeting of the Historians Group, held at the Party Centre on 6th April 1956; LHA CP/CENT/CULT/05/11: Committee minute book 1946–1951: minute of 8.4.56.

74 Harry Pollitt, 'The 20th Congress of the C.P.C.U. – and the role of Stalin', *World News*, Vol. 3, No. 18 (5.5.56), pp. 278–81, 285.

75 John Saville, 'Problems of the Communist Party', *World News*, Vol. 3, No. 20 (19.5.56), p. 314.

76 LHA CP/CENT/CULT/05/11: Committee minute book 1946–1951: minute of 27.5.56.

77 TNA KV2/3983: EJH, 'Labour Unity', *World News*, 16.6.56.

78 Ibid: 'Lascar' phone tap 18.6.56.
79 MRC 937/6/4/3: undated draft.
80 TNA KV2/3983: 'Lascar: Top Secret', n.d., Temple Bar 2151 wiretap 21.6.56; 'Lascar' 21.6.56 wiretap, also for the following.
81 Ibid: 'Extract' transcript of bugged conversation at Party headquarters, 22.6.56.
82 Ibid: EJH, 'Communists and Elections', cutting from *Daily Worker*, 30.7.56.
83 Edward Thompson, 'Winter Wheat in Omsk', *World News*, Vol. 3, No. 26 (30 June 1956), pp. 408–9.
84 George Matthews, 'A Caricature of Our Party', *World News*, Vol. 3, No. 26 (30 June 1956), pp. 409–10.
85 Quoted in Pelling, *The British Communist Party*, p. 171; see also Matthews, *The Shadow Man*, pp. 189–99.
86 Pelling, *The British Communist Party*, p. 173.
87 LHA CP/CENT/CULT/05/11: Committee minute book 1946–1951: minute of 7.7.56.
88 Ibid: Committee minute book 1946–1951: minute of 8.7.56; see also LHA CP/CENT/CULT/11/02: EJH to Alf Jenkin, 1.7.56.
89 James Klugmann, *History of the Communist Party of Great Britain*, I: *Formation and Early Years, 1919–1924* (London: Lawrence and Wishart, 1969) and II: *The General Strike 1925–1927* (London: Lawrence and Wishart, 1969). Eric savaged these volumes in 'Problems of Communist History', EJH, *Revolutionaries: Contemporary Essays* (London, 1973), pp. 3–10. For the background, see Andrews, *The Shadow Man*, pp. 197–9.
90 'Statement by the Executive Committee of the Communist Party on *"The Reasoner"*', *World News*, Vol. 3, No. 46 (17 November 1956), p. 726.
91 *IT*, pp. 205–14; Paul Lendvai, *One Day That Shook the Communist World: The 1956 Hungarian Uprising and Its Legacy* (Princeton, NJ, 2008); György Litván, *The Hungarian Revolution of 1956: Reform, Revolt and Repression, 1953–1963* (Harlow, 1996).
92 EJH, 'Could it have been different?', *London Review of Books*, 16.11.2006.
93 Editorial, *World News*, Vol. 3, No. 45 (10 November 1956), p. 713.
94 MRC 937/6/4/3 Communist Party 1956: Cutting from 'Daily Worker', 9.11.56 (EJH: 'Suppressing facts').
95 *IT*, p. 205.
96 'Rally Round the Party', *World News*, Vol. 3, No. 47 (24 November 1956), p. 756.
97 Pelling, *The British Communist Party*, p. 175.
98 Saville, *Memoirs from the Left*, p. 116.
99 TNA KV2/3983: Betty Grant to Edwin Payne, 12.11.56 (copy of intercepted letter).
100 Ibid: Extract from T/C on TREND o/g call from PETER to RALPH at CHQ 7535, 15.11.56.
101 *New Statesman*, 18.11.56 (correspondence column); TNA KV2/3983: Copy of Telecheck on Temple Bar 2151, Communist Party H.Q.
102 MRC 937/6/4/3: EJH, 'Improving Party Democracy', *World News*, 13.10.56.
103 TNA KV2/3983: Secret: Temple Bar 2151, Communist Party H.Q. Incoming: 22 November 1956 (wiretap).

104   Ibid: 'Lascar' Extract, 4.12.56. Reuben Falber shortly afterwards was appointed Assistant General Secretary of the Communist Party of Great Britain, in which capacity he regularly collected suitcases of cash from the Soviet Embassy (Leonard Goldman, 'Reuben Falber', *Guardian*, 6.6.2006).

105   LHA CP/CENT/CULT/05/11: Committee minute book 1946–1951: minute of 25.11.56.

106   TNA KV2/3983: Betty Grant to W. E. Payne, 3.12.56, copy of intercepted letter, also for the following.

107   LHA CP/CENT/ORG/18/06: Fractional Activity, 1956–1957: memo of 7.12.56. Chimen Abramsky, born in Minsk, was an expert in antiquarian Jewish books, which he collected avidly, and a serious Marx scholar; with Henry Collins, he published *Karl Marx and the British Labour Movement* (London, 1965). He was Raphael Samuel's uncle by marriage. He eventually left the Party in 1958 and embarked on a career teaching Jewish Studies. For a wonderfully evocative memoir, see Sasha Abramsky, *The House of Twenty Thousand Books* (New York, 2015).

108   LHA CP/CENT/CULT/05/11: Committee minute book 1946–1951: minute of 9.12.56.

109   MRC 937/6/4/3 Communist Party 1956: EJH to George Matthews, 10.12.56.

110   Ibid: Matthews to EJH, 19.12.56.

111   LHA CP/CENT/ORG/18/06: Fractional Activity, 1956–1957: memo of 7.12.56.

112   George Matthews, 'Lessons of a Letter', *World News*, Vol. 4, No. 2 (12 January 1957), pp. 24–6, 32.

113   EJH: 'Three Alternatives Face Us', *World News*, Vol. 4, No. 4 (26 January 1957), pp. 61–2 (the illiterate heading was inserted by a sub-editor; Eric would never have spoken of 'three alternatives').

114   Joan Simon, 'Communist Criticism and the Intellectual', *World News*, Vol. 4, No. 8 (23 February 1957), pp. 125–6.

115   TNA KV2/2886: Joseph Peter Astbury ('Lascar'): Discussions after National University Staffs Committee AGM, held 26/27 Jan. 1957. Astbury was a Cambridge contemporary of Eric's, and also an Apostle. He joined the Party in 1936 and was known to have passed nuclear secrets to the Russians through an intermediary. Arnold Kettle was a university teacher of English literature (see Martin Kettle, 'What MI5's records on my father tell us about the uses of surveillance', *Guardian*, 27.7.2011). Ron Bellamy was a full-time Party worker; Brian Simon was an educationalist.

116   Beckett, *Enemy Within*, pp. 135–8.

117   Pelling, *The British Communist Party*, pp. 169–86.

118   LHA CP/CENT/ORG/18/06: Fractional Activity, 1956–1957: memo of 7.12.56.

119   EJH, 'Some Notes about the *Universities and Left Review*', report to Communist Party Executive Meeting, 10–11.5.1958, in LHA CP/CENT/EC/05/08, cited in Andrews, *The Shadow Man*, p. 203.

120   Andrews, *The Shadow Man*, p. 205.

121   LHA CP/CENT/ORG/18/06: Fractional Activity, 1956–1957: memo of 7.12.56.

122 TNA KV2/3985: 'Lascar' Extract 12.11.58 (conversation recorded by listening device at CPGB headquarters).

123 Ibid: 13.11.58.

124 Ibid: 15.12.58.

125 Ibid: 2.1.59.

126 Ibid: 31.3.59.

127 Ibid: 5.5.59.

128 Ibid: 5.5.59.

129 Ibid: 3.6.59.

130 Ibid: 9.6.59.

131 Ibid: 2.6.59, p. 20.

132 Ibid: 5.6.59.

133 Ibid: 10.6.59 (352a and 357a).

134 Ibid: 'Lascar', 5.8.59. Evidently MI5 bureaucrats still felt in 1959 that it was indelicate to spell out in full the swear word 'bloody' even in a report stamped 'TOP SECRET'.

135 Ibid: 9.11.59.

136 Ibid: 4.1.60.

137 Ibid: 1.2.60.

138 Ibid: 13.5.60.

139 TNA KV2/3986: 'Lascar', monitored conversation, 15.1.62.

140 TNA KV2/3985: PA. in P.F. 211,764, HOBSBAWM, signed P. F. Stewart, 24.3.60.

141 Ibid: Copy of minute on PF.74.102, by R. Thistlethwaite, 24.3.60.

142 MRC 937/6/4/6: EJH to Brian Simon, 15.1.79.

143 *IT*, p. 202.

144 TNA KV2/3986: 'Lascar', monitored conversation, 18.11.60.

145 MRC 937/1/2/1: Marion Bennathan to Eric, 1 July (no year, probably 1964).

146 Ibid: Marion to Eric, 'Birmingham, 13th March' (1960).

147 Ibid: Marion to Eric, from Queen Elizabeth Hospital, Tuesday, no date (3.4.58).

148 Ibid: Marion Bennathan to Eric, undated (1957).

149 Ibid: Marion Bennathan to Eric, undated (1958).

150 Ibid: Marion to Eric, postmarked 1959.

151 Ibid: Marion to Eric, 13.5.60; also undated, typed letter mentioning the trial for obscenity of Penguin Books for publishing D. H. Lawrence's *Lady Chatterley's Lover*, which took place in late September and early October 1960.

152 *IT*, p. 221.

153 Ibid, p. 81.

154 EJH, 'Diary', *London Review of Books*, Vol. 32, No. 10 (27.5.2010), p. 41.

155 Martin Niederauer, 'Kein Manifest! Hobsbawm an die Frage von Herrschaft und Befreiung im Jazz', in Andreas Linsenmann and Thorsten Hindrichs (eds), *Hobsbawm, Newton und Jazz. Zum Verhältnis von Musik und Geschichtsschreibung* (Paderborn, 2016), pp. 111–30. See also Christian Brocking's essay in the same volume, 'Distinktion, Kanon, Transgression: Wie Musik den Wunsch nach gesellschaftlicher Veränderung ausdrücken, implizieren und bewirken kann', pp. 131–50. The charge, in the same volume, by Daniel Schläppi, 'Hobsbawm reloaded. Oder wie sich Francis Newton der improvisierten Musik des beginnenden 21. Jahrhunderts hätte annähern können', pp. 151–200, that Eric

had a conservative classical conception of genius and its cult in his attitude to bandleaders like Ellington and Basie, which blinded him to the collective nature of jazz music (pp. 165–6), does not convince. See Eric's encomium to the Duke's 'peculiarly anarchically controlled symbiosis with his musicians' which 'produced music which is *both* created by the players *and* fully shaped by the composer' (Francis Newton, 'The Duke', *New Statesman*, 11.10.58, p. 488). Eric wrote on jazz under the pseudonym 'Francis Newton'.

156 Francis Newton, 'Requiem for an Art', *New Statesman*, 11.8.61, p. 192, also for the following.

157 Francis Newton, 'On the Assembly Line', *New Statesman*, 1.9.61, p. 281, one of the most brilliant of Eric's essays in cultural criticism at this time.

158 Francis Newton, 'No Red Squares', *New Statesman*, 16.3.62, p. 390.

159 Timothy W. Ryback, *Rock Around the Bloc: A History of Rock Music in Eastern Europe and the Soviet Union* (Oxford, 1990); Josef Skvorecky, *Talkin' Moscow Blues* (London, 1989); David Caute, *The Dancer Defects. The Struggle for Cultural Supremacy during the Cold War* (Oxford, 2003), pp. 441–67.

160 Quoted in Kevin Morgan, 'King Street Blues: Jazz and the Left in Britain in the 1930s–1940s', in Andy Croft (ed.), *A Weapon in the Struggle. The Cultural History of the Communist Party in Britain* (London, 1998), pp. 123–41, at p. 148.

161 Sam Aaronovitch, 'The American Threat to British Culture', *Arena: A Magazine of Modern Literature*, Vol. 2 (June–July 1951), No. 8, p. 4, cited in Philip Bounds, 'From Folk to Jazz: Eric Hobsbawm, British Communism and Cultural Studies', *Critique: Journal of Socialist Theory*, 40 (2012) 4, pp. 575–93.

162 Francis Newton, 'Traditional', *New Statesman*, 24.10.59, pp. 538–40. In the seventeenth century the fenmen known as the 'Wisbech tigers' had fiercely resisted the draining of the fens around the East Anglian town. See also Bounds, 'From Folk to Jazz'. Wisbech is a town in the middle of the Norfolk fenlands.

163 Morgan, 'King Street Blues', p. 148.

164 TNA KV2/3985: monitored conversation, 27.5.59.

165 TNA KV2/3983: 'Eric John HOBSBAWM', 239b, 126.1.55.

166 BBC WAC RCONT 1: Anna Kallin, Talks Booking Requisition, to Talks Booking Manager, 2.12.55.

167 Ibid: EJH to Anna Kallin, 17.3.55.

168 Ibid: EJH to Anna Kallin, 3.3.55.

169 BBC WAC RCONT 1: Leslie Stokes quoting Thomas Crowe, 'Announcer's Comment', 26.2.56.

170 Ibid: EJH to Anna Kallin, 19.2.56.

171 Ibid: Anna Kallin to EJH, 19.3.56.

172 Ibid: EJH to Anna Kallin, 27.3.56.

173 Ibid: Anna Kallin to Talks Booking Manager, Talks Booking Requisition, 10.1.57. The talk led to a protest from the Gramophone Department of the BBC, which felt it should have been consulted (ibid, Donald Maclean to Anna Kallin, 23.5.57).

174 Ibid: Talks Booking Requisition, Anna Kallin's secretary to Talks Booking Manager, 21.5.62; EJH to Anna Kallin, 16.4.62; Anna Kallin to EJH, 13.4.62, adding that she wanted to meet Bloch 'in my private capacity to pay tribute to a great man'.

175 Ibid: 'Talks (Live or Recorded) P. T. T. – Talks Meeting', n.d.

176 *IT*, p. 225; EJH, 'Diary', *London Review of Books*, Vol. 32, No. 10 (27.5.2010), p. 41.

177 *IT*, p. 225.

178 MRC 937/8/2/3: 'Dr Hobsbawm is Mr Newton', unattributed clipping.

179 Chris Wrigley, *A. J. P. Taylor. Radical Historian of Europe* (London, 2006), pp. 233–8.

180 Francis Newton, 'Band Discord', *New Statesman*, 25.1.58, pp. 102–3.

181 Francis Newton, 'Significant Sims', *New Statesman*, 17.11.61, p. 757.

182 Colin MacInnes, *Absolute Beginners* (London, 1960, paperback edition 2010), p. 83. The novel was made into a film in 1986 with the same title, starring David Bowie, Patsy Kensit, Steven Berkoff and Mandy Rice-Davies. It was panned by the critics and bombed at the box office, leading to the collapse of the previously successful British production company Goldcrest Films.

183 MacInnes, *Absolute Beginners*, p. 173.

184 EJH, 'Diary', *London Review of Books*, Vol. 32, No. 10 (27.5.2010), p. 41, also for the following.

185 HFA: membership card, expiry date 31.12.64. See Sophie Parkin, *The Colony Room Club* (London, 2013).

186 *IT*, pp. 226–7; EJH, 'Diary', *London Review of Books*, Vol. 32, No. 10 (27.5.2010), p. 41. For an atmospheric account of the clubs and their denizens, see Daniel Farson, *Soho in the Fifties* (London, 1987).

187 Francis Newton, 'The Wild Side', *New Statesman*, 8.4.62, p. 500.

188 Francis Newton, 'How about Playing, Gypsy?' *New Statesman*, 3.2.61, p. 191, also for the following.

189 Francis Newton, 'Basie', *New Statesman*, 6.4.57, p. 438.

190 Francis Newton, 'God', *New Statesman* 17.5.63, p. 768.

191 Francis Newton, 'After Armstrong', *New Statesman*, 30.6.56, p. 760.

192 Francis Newton, 'No Time for Thrushes', *New Statesman*, 13.2.60, p. 218.

193 Francis Newton, 'Mahalia', *New Statesman*, 14.4.61, p. 598; 'Annie Ross', *New Statesman*, 17.1.64, p. 90.

194 Francis Newton, 'The Uncommercials', *New Statesman*, 17.8.57, p. 198; 'Atoms for the Juke Box', *New Statesman*, 22.3.58, pp. 374–5; 'Masked Man', *New Statesman*, 24.11.61, p. 807.

195 Francis Newton, 'Too Cool', *New Statesman*, 16.1.60, p. 68.

196 Francis Newton, 'The Quiet Americans', *New Statesman*, 7.12.57, p. 774; 'MJQ', *New Statesman*, 6.10.61, p. 487; and 'Three plus Basie', *New Statesman*, 13.4.62, pp. 539–40. The Modern Jazz Quartet was an established four man combo of piano, vibraphone, drums and bass that purveyed a cool and unemotional form of blues-influenced instrumental music.

197 Francis Newton, 'Hornrimmed Jazz', *New Statesman*, 1.3.58, p. 266. Dave Brubeck wore horn-rimmed spectacles; also 'Masked Man', *New Statesman*, 24.11.61, p. 806.

198 Francis Newton, 'Miles Away', *New Statesman*, 21.5.60; again in 'Jazz and Folk Records', *New Statesman*, 17.3.61, p. 447.

199 Francis Newton, 'Reluctant Monk', *New Statesman*, 5.5.61, pp. 725–6.

200 Francis Newton, 'Errol Garner', *New Statesman*, 1.6.62, p. 807.

201 Francis Newton, 'Band Call', *New Statesman*, 23.8.58, pp. 220–1.

202 Francis Newton, 'Manhattan Solo', *New Statesman*, 2.7.60, pp. 12–14, also for the following.

203 Francis Newton, 'Back to Grassroots', *New Statesman*, 23.5.59, p. 723.
204 Logie Barrow, 'Anatomising Methuselah' (unpubl. typescript).
205 Francis Newton, 'Mr Acker Requests', *New Statesman*, 17.11.60, p. 736.
206 Francis Newton, 'Too Much Jazz?', *New Statesman*, 12.10.57, pp. 458–9.
207 Francis Newton, 'Band Discord', *New Statesman*, 25.1.58, pp. 102–3.
208 Francis Newton, 'Nothing is for Nothing', *New Statesman*, 5.12.59, pp. 796–7.
209 Francis Newton, 'Mr Granz Makes Music', *New Statesman*, 10.5.58, pp. 600–1. See also 'News from everywhere', *New Statesman*, 3.12.60, p. 876, for a review of a 'Jazz at the Philharmonic' event at London's Festival Hall.
210 EJH, 'Diary', *London Review of Books*, Vol. 32, No. 10 (27.5.2010), p. 41; David Kynaston, *Modernity Britain: Opening the Box, 1957–59* (London, 2013), pp. 169–82.
211 EJH, 'Diary', *London Review of Books*, Vol. 32, No. 10 (27.5.2010), p. 41. Cleo Laine became a well-known jazz singer and married the bandleader John Dankworth.
212 Francis Newton, 'Denmark Street Crusaders', *New Statesman*, 27.9.58, p. 409.
213 Francis Newton, 'The Trend Guessers', *New Statesman*, 21.12.57, pp. 852–3.
214 Francis Newton, 'Pied Pipers', *New Statesman*, 16.2.57, p. 202.
215 Francis Newton, 'Beatles and Before', *New Statesman*, 8.11.63, p. 673, and 'Stan Getz', *New Statesman*, 20.3.64, p. 465.
216 Francis Newton, 'Bob Dylan', *New Statesman*, 22.5.64, p. 818. *Reader's Digest* was an American family magazine containing anodyne and stylistically bland fiction and 'human interest' stories. Bob Dylan went on to win the Nobel Prize in Literature for 2016.
217 Francis Newton, 'The Cats in Italy', *New Statesman*, 28.9.57, pp. 378–80.
218 Francis Newton, 'Palm Court', *New Statesman*, 31.1.64, p. 180.
219 MRC: 'Popular Culture and Personal Responsibility. Verbatim Report of a Conference held at Church House, Westminster, 26th–28th October, 1960' (typescript), pp. 124–5.
220 Francis Newton, 'Bix', *New Statesman*, 11.8.56, p. 160.
221 Francis Newton, 'Post-mortem', *New Statesman*, 27.7.57, pp. 112–14.
222 Francis Newton, 'People's Heroin', *New Statesman*, 3.3.61, pp. 358–9.
223 Francis Newton, 'Travellin' All Alone', *New Statesman*, 15.8.59, p. 191.
224 MRC 937/1/4/2: Joseph Losey to EJH, 24.8.59.
225 Frank Mort, *Capital Affairs: London and the Making of the Permissive Society* (New Haven, 2010); Paul Willetts, *Members Only: The Life and Times of Paul Raymond* (London, 2010).
226 Francis Newton, 'Any Chick Can Do It', *New Statesman*, 24.3.61, p. 436, also for the following.
227 MRC 927/1/4/2: EJH to Bill Randle, 3.9.61.
228 Francis Newton, 'New Thing', *New Statesman*, 28.5.65, p. 85; 'The Man and the Boys', *New Statesman*, 25.3.66 (Eric's last article for the *New Statesman* as 'Francis Newton').
229 Francis Newton, 'Duke', *New Statesman*, 21.2.64, p. 308; 'Ellington and Ella', *New Statesman*, 18.2.66 (reprinted in the issue of 25.4.2013, p. 141, under Eric's own name).
230 Francis Newton, 'New Thing', *New Statesman*, 28.5.65, p. 855.
231 Francis Newton, 'Doldrums', *New Statesman*, 29.3.63, p. 469,
232 EJH, *The Jazz Scene*, 1989 edition, Introduction, pp. vii, 22.

233 *IT*, p. 226.

234 BULSC DM 1107/5190: Tom Maschler to Reg Davis-Poynter, Managing Director, MacGibbon & Kee, 13.10.58.

235 EJH (Francis Newton), *The Jazz Scene* (London, 1989 [1959]), pp. v, 275–80.

236 EJH, *The Jazz Scene*, pp. 239–40, 271–4. See also Francis Newton, 'Lonely Hipsters', *New Statesman*, 23.11.62, p. 754, describing British jazz-lovers as 'mainly working-class'.

237 EJH, *The Jazz Scene*, pp. 256–7.

238 MRC 937/8/2/3: Ramsden Greig, 'The Jazz Bohemians are missing', *Evening Standard*, 26.5.59.

239 Francis Newton, 'The Cautious Critics', *New Statesman*, 9.11.57, p. 604.

240 MRC 937/8/2/3: Benedict Osuch, 'Jazz Scene: a must!', *Jazz Today*, undated clipping, p. 12.

241 Ibid: Clancy Segal, 'That Remarkable Noise', *New Statesman*, 30.5.59, p. 768.

242 BULSC DM 1107/5190: John White to Penguin Books, 10.7.69; Peter Wright to John White, 15.7.69.

243 Francis Newton, 'Status Seeking', *New Statesman*, 26.9.59, p. 392.

244 DHAA BH 2009: Payment advice, 4.12.08.

245 Tony Coe, 'Hobsbawm and Jazz', in Raphael Samuel and Gareth Stedman Jones (eds), *Culture, Ideology and Politics. Essays for Eric Hobsbawm* (History Workshop Series, London, 1982), pp. 149–57.

246 HFA: Folder 11: Diaries/Autobiographical Writings: Notes re JM (1962), also for the following. A 'blower' was a telephone.

247 'Gamine' is waif-like; 'frech' is cheeky.

248 Interview with Lois Wincott, 20.9.2016.

249 Entretien entre Elise Marienstras et Charlotte Faucher, 27.7.2016.

250 MRC 1215/5: Interview notes: Catania.

251 Anna Maria Rao, 'Transizioni. Hobsbawm nella modernistica italiana', *Studi storici* 4, ottobre–dicembre 2013, p. 768.

252 MRC 937/7/8/1: 'Rathaus/history', Jan. 2008, pp. 4–5.

253 UMA USC/63/1/3: minutes of meeting of University Press Committee, 13.2.58, also for the following.

254 MRC 937/4/3/1/8: EJH, 'Voices of the South', *Times Literary Supplement*, 21.10.55, pp. 613–14. The village was the setting for Vittorio de Seta's classic film *Banditti a Orgosolo* (1960).

255 For the Mafia, see also ibid: EJH, 'Transatlantic Racket', *Times Literary Supplement*, 21.9.62.

256 *Visions of History* (New York, 1983), pp. 3–44, at p. 33.

257 MRC 937/8/2/2: John Roberts, 'The Losers', *Observer*, 3.5.59.

258 Ibid: Denis Mack Smith, 'The Meaning of Bandits' [clipping, no attribution], also for the following.

259 MRC 937/1/3/7: EJH to 'Mr Yoken and friends', n.d. (1995?).

260 HRC B39: David Higham Associates, 387–388: David Higham to EJH, 24.11.59.

261 Interview with Bruce Hunter, 26.7.2016.

262 TNA KV2/3983: EJH, 'Marx as Historian', *New Statesman*, 20.8.55, and typescript copy of EJH letter 24.9.55.

263 Isaiah Berlin to the editor of the *New Statesman*, 25.9.55, in Isaiah Berlin,

Enlightening: Letters 1946–1960, ed. Henry Hardy and Jennifer Holmes (London, 2009), pp. 499–500.

264 Adam Sisman, *Hugh Trevor-Roper. The Biography* (London, 2010), pp. 263–6. For the controversy, see *New Statesman*, 6, 20 and 27 August, 10 and 24 September, 1, 8, 15, 22 and 29 October 1955. For the visa, *IT*, pp. 389–90.

265 TNA KV2/3985: EJH to Joan Simon, 10.5.60 (intercepted letter).

266 Ibid: Ext. from T/C on Tom McWHINNIE, 16.5.60.

267 TNA KV2/3985: John Lawrence to H. G. M. Stone, British Embassy, Washington, 20.5.60.

268 EJH, 'The Economics of the Gangster', *Quarterly Review*, 604 (April 1955), pp. 243–56.

269 *IT*, pp. 397–402, also for the following.

270 Francis Newton, 'The Sound of Religion', *New Statesman*, 8.10.60, pp. 522–4.

271 *IT*, Chapter 22, *passim*.

272 EJH, 'Cuban Prospects', *New Statesman*, 22.10.60, reprinted in Leslie Bethell (ed.), *Viva la Revolución! Eric Hobsbawm on Latin America* (London, 2016), pp. 29–33, and 'Introduction', pp. 2–3. Estimates of the number of executions carried out by the Castro regime between 1959 and 1970 vary wildly, but none is lower than two hundred. *When the State Kills: The Death Penalty v. Human Rights*, Amnesty International Publications (London, 1989), puts the figure at just over two hundred from 1959 to 1987. See more generally Jonathan C. Brown, *Cuba's Revolutionary World* (Cambridge, Mass., 2018).

273 TNA KV2/3986: 'Report: International Affairs Committee', 1.11.60 (a very full report on Eric's lecture, which the MI5 agent present found 'really interesting').

274 MRC 937/4/6/1: *The Times*, 23.4.61; also *New Statesman*, 21.7.61.

275 Kenneth Tynan to David Astor, 1.4.61, in Kathleen Tynan (ed.), *Kenneth Tynan: Letters* (London, 1994), p. 264.

276 MRC 937/1/6/5: EJH to Andrew Weale, 21.4.94. See also the MI5 report, noting that a demonstration planned for Trafalgar Square had been cancelled: TNA KV2/3986: 18.4.61.

277 TNA KV2/3986: 9.5.61.

278 MRC 937/1/6/5: EJH to Andrew Weale, 21.4.94.

279 TNA KV2/3986: 'Lascar' – Note for file, pp. 211, 764 HOBSBAWM, no. 394a. For Arnold Kettle, see Martin Kettle, 'What MI5's records on my father tell us about the uses of surveillance', *Guardian*, 28.7.2011.

280 TNA KV2/3986: monitoring transcript 9.2.62.

281 *IT*, pp. 255–6.

282 TNA KV2/3986: Extract from MI6 report, 2.3.62.

283 Francis Newton, 'Rumba Patriotica', *New Statesman*, 26.1.62, pp. 138–9, also for the following.

284 John Lahr (ed.), *The Diaries of Kenneth Tynan* (London, 2001), p. 137.

285 Tracy Tynan, *Wear and Tear: The Threads of My Life* (New York, 2016). Loyal to a fault, Eric later defended Tynan, whose growing obsession with sex was beginning to attract hostile comment, against accusations of misogyny (MRC 937/4/6/1: letter to *The Times*, 6.2.1976).

286 Interview with Robin Marchesi, 6.12.16.

287 Entretien entre Elise Marienstras et Charlotte Faucher, 27.6.2016.

288 Interview with Marlene Hobsbawm, 6.6.2013, email Marlene Hobsbawm to RJE, 30.12.2016, and associated notes by Marlene.

289 MRC 937/1/3/11: EJH to Richard Koenig, 19.11.2004; Marlene Hobsbawm notes, and interview 6.6.2013 and 30.12.2016, also for the following; Walter Schwarz, *The Ideal Occupation* (London, 2011), pp. 9–11, and Marlene Hobsbawm, *Conversations with Lilly* (Canterbury, 1998), pp. 37–8.

290 Entretien entre Elise Marienstras et Charlotte Faucher, 27.6.2016.

291 Interview with Marlene Hobsbawm, 6.6.2013, and emails Marlene Hobsbawm to RJE, 30.12.2016 and 6.8.2017, and notes.

Chapter 7: 'Paperback Writer'

1 MRC 937/7/8/1: 'Paperback Writer' (typescript, 2003), p. 3. Walter Carruthers Sellar and Robert Julian Yeatman, *1066 and all That: A memorable history of England, comprising all the parts you can remember, including 103 good things, 5 bad kings, and 2 genuine dates* (London, 1930), a satire on conventional school history textbooks with their outdated moralising and their obsession with facts and dates.

2 MRC 937/7/8/1: 'Paperback Writer' (typescript, 2003), pp. 3–4 (the pagination differs between the two copies in the file).

3 Ibid: 'Rathaus/history' Jan. 2008, pp. 5–6.

4 George Weidenfeld, *Remembering My Good Friends. An Autobiography* (London, 1994), pp. 243–5; *IT*, p. 185.

5 MRC 937/7/8/1: 'Rathaus/history/', Jan. 2008, p. 6.

6 Ibid: 'Paperback Writer' (typescript, 2003), pp. 4–6.

7 MRC 937/4/3/1/8: EJH, 'The Language of Scholarship', *Times Literary Supplement*, 17.8.56, p. viii.

8 Ibid: 'A New Sort of History: Not a Thread but a Web', *Times Literary Supplement*, 13.10.61, pp. 698–9.

9 EJH, 'Where are British Historians Going?', *Marxist Quarterly*, 2/1 (January 1955), pp. 27–36.

10 MRC 937/7/8/1: second interview with *Radical History Review* (typescript), p. 4.

11 Annan, *Our Age*, p. 267.

12 Hans-Ulrich Wehler, *Deutsche Gesellschaftsgeschichte 1815–1845/49: Von der Reformära bis zur industriellen und politischen 'Doppelrevolution'* (Munich, 1987), covering the 'German dual revolution' in industry and politics. The concept also inspired university history courses in many countries.

13 Georges Lefebvre, *1789* (Paris, 1939); *La Révolution Française* (2 vols, Paris, 1951 and 1957).

14 EJH, *The Age of Revolution: Europe 1789–1848* (London, 1962), p. 82.

15 Ibid, p. 84.

16 Ibid, p. 84.

17 MRC 937/1/2/12: Edward Thompson to EJH, 23.11 (1962).

18 MRC 937/1/5/2: Ernst Fischer to EJH, 20.6.63.

19 Victor Kiernan, 'Revolution and Reaction 1789–1848', *New Left Review* 19 (April 1963), pp. 69–78.

20 MRC 937/1/1/1: Rondo Cameron to EJH, 20.11.62.

21 MRC 937/8/2/4: J. L. Talmon, 'The Age of Revolution', *Encounter*, September 1963, pp. 11–18.

22 Ibid: Prof. G. R. Potter, 'Monarchy under the microscope', *Sheffield Telegraph*, 29.12.62. For similar remarks on Wellington, see the sarcastic review (in the same file) by the philosopher Anthony Quinton, later a Conservative peer, 'Fixing the Blame for Social Evil', *Sunday Telegraph*, 18.11.62.

23 Ibid: Max Beloff, 'Progress through Upheaval', *Daily Telegraph*, 25.1.63.

24 Ibid: T. Desmond Williams, 'The Barricade Mind', *Spectator*, 28.12.62.

25 Ibid: 'Freeing the Middle Class', *Times Literary Supplement*, 11.1.63.

26 Ibid: A. J. P. Taylor, 'Umbrella Men, or The Two Revolutions', *New Statesman*, 30.11.62.

27 Ibid: A. J. P. Taylor, *Observer*, 23.12.62.

28 Ibid: Peter Laslett, 'The new revolutionism', *Guardian*, 30.11.62, also for the following.

29 Ibid: Ernst Wangermann, 'The Age of Revolution', *Marxism Today*, March 1983, pp. 89–92.

30 Dokumentationsarchiv des österreichischen Widerstandes, 50120: Korrespondenz Steiner: Hobsbawm, Eric, 1957–1994: EJH to Herbert Steiner, 29.10.62, for the departure date.

31 TNA KV2/3987: 'Top Secret' 020/1/E1/N10, dated 18.1.63.

32 Ibid: letter to H. M. Gee, 22.1.63.

33 Bethell (ed.),*Viva la Revolución!*, pp. 4–5. This volume reprints a number of the essays referred to in the following pages.

34 MRC 937/7/8/1: EJH 'South American Journey', *Labour Monthly*, July 1963, pp. 329–32, also in *Viva la Revolución!*, pp. 34–9.

35 Francis Newton, 'Bossa Nova', *New Statesman*, 21.12.63, pp. 910–11. *Billboard* and *Cashbox* were two popular American music magazines.

36 MRC 937/7/8/1: EJH, 'South American Journey', *Labour Monthly*, July 1963, pp. 329–32.

37 MRC 937/1/5/4: Pablo Neruda to EJH, 10.6.65.

38 MRC 937/4/3/1/6: EJH, 'Latin America: The Most Critical Area in the World', *Listener*, 2.5.63, also in *Viva la Revolución!*, pp. 43–50.

39 BBC WAC RCONT 1: EJH (from Santiago de Chile) to Anna Kallin, 6.12.62.

40 BBC WAC RCONT 12: Note appended to EJH to Anna Kallin, enclosing synopsis, n.d.

41 EJH, 'Latin America: The Most Critical Area in the World'.

42 MRC 937/4/3/1/6: EJH, 'Social Developments in Latin America', *Listener*, 9.5.63, pp. 778–9, 806, also in *Viva la Revolución!*, pp. 51–8.

43 TNA KV2/3987: 'Mr Hobsbawm's Visit to Latin America', 23.5.63.

44 Ibid: '3. Mr Eric Hobsbawm'.

45 Ibid: 'Lascar': IDRIS COX and JACK WODDIS with Visitor (Eric HOBSBAWM), 1.4.63.

46 Interview with Neal Ascherson, 26.7.2016.

47 EJH, 'Peasant Movements in Colombia' (1969), in *Les Mouvements Paysans dans le Monde Contemporain*, ed. Commission Internationale d'Histoire des Mouvements Sociaux et des Structures Sociales, 3 vols, Naples, 1976, Vol. III, pp. 166–86, also in *Viva la Revolución!*, pp. 196–221.

48 EJH, 'A Hard Man: Che Guevara', *New Society*, 4.4.1968, also in *Viva la Revolución!*, pp. 264–70. One of these short-lived military regimes was led by the left-winger J. J. Torres, himself overthrown in 1971: I recall a party thrown

by ex-student members of his government at St Antony's College, Oxford, in 1972, at which the song 'Hasta Siempre, Comandante', with its promise that Guevara would triumph over death, was sung more than once.

49 EJH, 'Guerrillas in Latin America', in Ralph Miliband and John Saville (eds), *The Socialist Register 1970* (London, 1970), pp. 51–63, and 'Latin American Guerrillas: A Survey', *Latin American Review of Books*, Vol. 1 (1973), pp. 79–88, also in *Viva la Revolución!*, pp. 271–95.

50 EJH, 'What's New in Peru', *New York Review of Books*, 21.5.70. See also EJH, 'Generals as Revolutionaries', *New Society*, 20.11.69.

51 EJH, 'A Case of Neo-Feudalism: La Convención, Peru', *Journal of Latin American Studies*, Vol. I (1969), No. 1, pp. 31–50; EJH, 'Peasant Land Occupations: The Case of Peru', *Past & Present* 62 (February 1974).

52 EJH, 'Peru: The Peculiar "Revolution"', *New York Review of Books*, 16.12.71. See also the exchange on Peruvian 'Indians', *New York Review of Books*, 15.6.72.

53 EJH, 'Latin America as US Empire Cracks', *New York Review of Books*, 25.3.71.

54 EJH, 'A Special Supplement: Chile; Year One', *New York Review of Books*, 23.9.71.

55 HFA: EJH to Marlene, 22.10.1969.

56 These lengthy articles are reprinted in *Viva la Revolución!* along with other pieces noted above.

57 EJH, 'Dictatorship with Charm', *New York Review of Books*, 2.10.1975.

58 'Preste atenção em Campinas', *VEJA*, 4.6.1975; Luiz Sugimoto, 'Sobre Hobsbawm, que veio à Unicamp duas vezes', Unicamp news release, 1.10.2012; MRC 1215/4: notebooks on Latin America 1969 and 1975.

59 Marlene Hobsbawm notes.

60 HFA: Richard Preston to Marlene Hobsbawm, 25.4.2016. Denis subsequently took Eric on a brief business trip to Spain, where Eric acted as translator in negotiations with Spanish musicians. Denis's son Richard suspected that 'this was as much a chance for the two of them to hang out, drink a few beers and put the world to rights'.

61 Julia Hobsbawm, 'Remembering Dad', *Financial Times*, 19.8.2013.

62 BULSC DM1107/A898: EJH to Plumb, 24.8.64.

63 http://www.britishlistedbuildings.co uk/101115734-97-larkhall-rise-sw8-clapham-town-ward; HRC B-40: David Higham Associates 806: change of address notice.

64 Interview with Marlene Hobsbawm, 16.10.2016.

65 WNA 'The Age of Capital': 'Accounts', 31.7.71; WNA 'The Age of Capital': change of address notice, 30.7.71.

66 MRC 937/1/1/3: EJH to Elizabeth Whitcombe, 11.6.73.

67 Marlene Hobsbawm to RJE, 9.9.2017 (email). I remember on one occasion in the 1990s seeing Michael Foot on the bus, looking rather frail, being greeted by the passengers and looked after solicitously by the conductor.

68 Interview with Neal Ascherson, 26.7.2016.

69 MRC 927/1/1/2: Marlene Hobsbawm to Lubomir Doruska, 23.5.73.

70 Interview with Richard Rathbone, 15.12.2016.

71 Charlotte Faucher, entretien avec Elise Marienstras, 27.7.2016.

72 Interview with Andy and Julia Hobsbawm, 11.7.2016, also for the following.

73 Interview with Roderick Floud, 14.9.2016.

74 Julia Hobsbawm, 'Remembering Dad', *Financial Times*, 19.4.2013, also for the following.

75 MRC 937/1/6/3: Andy Hobsbawm to EJH, n.d. (1993).

76 Interview with Andy and Julia Hobsbawm, 11.7.2016.

77 *IT*, pp. 233–9. My own grandfather was a slab dresser, splitting and shaping the rock into roof-slates, at a slate quarry in the area, and I remember visiting the ruins of the once-thriving industry in the 1950s, along with the tracks of the disused narrow-gauge Corris Railway.

78 Interview with Robin Marchesi, 6.12.2016; interview with Andy and Julia Hobsbawm, 11.7.2016.

79 MRC 937/1/1/3: EJH to H. Morris-Jones, n.d. (May 1975).

80 HFA: Marlene Hobsbawm notes; Marlene to RJE, 6.9.2018.

81 Julia Hobsbawm, *Fully Connected: Surviving and Thriving in an Age of Overload* (London, 2017), pp. 109–10, also for the following.

82 HFA: 'Welsh Cottage: Parc Correspondence', copy of lease.

83 MRC 937/1/1/3: Marlene Hobsbawm to Christian Rasmussen, 4.7.73.

84 HFA: EJH to Marlene, n.d. (1973). The railway was the Welsh Highland Railway, a narrow-gauge line that was not to be reopened until 2011.

85 Interview with Andy and Julia Hobsbawm, 11.7.2016.

86 Interview with Robin Marchesi, 6.12.2016.

87 Interview with Angela Hobsbaum, 30.3.2017.

88 Interview with Andy and Julia Hobsbawm, 11.7.2016, amended 8.9.2018.

89 Marlene Hobsbawm to RJE, 9.9.2017 (email).

90 MRC 937/1/2/2: Joss Bennathan to EJH, 30 July 1973; MRC 937/1/6/3: Joss Bennathan to EJH, 29.10.91.

91 MRC 937/1/6/3: Joss Bennathan to EJH, 29.10.91.

92 Ibid: Joss to Eric, 25.1.74.

93 Interview with Roderick Floud, 14.9.2016.

94 Marlene Hobsbawm notes.

95 Charlotte Faucher, entretien avec Elise Marienstras, 27.7.2016.

96 Interview notes: Charlotte Faucher and Marie-Louise Heller, 28.8.2016.

97 MRC 937/1/1/5: Pat Robinson to EJH, 19.1.2001. The 'Big Rock Candy Mountain' was a dreamland in which food and drink were freely available and nobody had to do any work.

98 Alan E. Montgomery to RJE, 26.3.2013.

99 MRC 937/1/1/5: Alan Webb to EJH, 14.9.2002.

100 MRC 937/1/1/4: EJH to Graeme Shankland, n.d. (1984).

101 Romila Thapar, unpublished reminiscences of EJH.

102 John Arnold to RJE, 18.3.2013, and enclosures (including notes by Edward Glover).

103 Pat Stroud to RJE, 25.3.2013 and 11.6.2016.

104 Interview with Lois Wincott, 20.9.2016, also for the following.

105 Peter Archard to RJE, 7.6.2016, and enclosures (including analysis of frequency of topics set for examinations in the course).

106 Peter Archard, 'A world of connections', *BBK Connect*, August 2001, p. 5.

107 MRC 927/1/1/6: John Person to EJH, 7.5.2008.

108 Geoffrey Crossick to RJE, email, 5.9.2017.

109 Interview with Chris Wrigley, 5.10.2016, also for the following.

110 Interview with Donald Sassoon, 20.10.2016, also for the following.
111 Youssef Cassis, interview with Grazia Schiacchitano, n.d.
112 MRC 937/7/8/1: Pip Sharpe to EJH, 28.3.2007.
113 Annan, *Our Age*, p. 267 (footnote).
114 TNA KV2/3985: 'Lascar', monitored conversation 8.12.59.
115 MRC 937/7/8/1: 'The Cold War and the Universities' (typescript, NY, 13.11.97), pp. 3–4.
116 Donald Sassoon, 'Eric Hobsbawm, 1917–2012', *New Left Review*, 77, Sept.–Oct. 2012. I remember being told by a tutor at Oxford around the same time that Thompson's book *The Making of the English Working Class* had probably set back the development of English history by twenty years.
117 See the long and detailed history by Negley Harte, 'The Economic History Society 1926–2001', http://www.history.ac.uk/makinghistory/resources/articles/EHS.html, accessed 30.1.2018.
118 KCAC: NGA/5/1/452: EJH to Noel Annan, 18.9.66, also for the following; thanks also to Dr John Thompson, St Catharine's College, Cambridge, who was a Lecturer in History at University College London in the 1960s. The French historian Alfred Cobban was resolutely anti-Marxist. Eric also rejected tentative approaches from Harvard, Yale, Berkeley and Stanford in the course of the 1970s, on the grounds that he and his family were too firmly rooted in London (correspondence in MRC 937/7/4/4).
119 Keith Thomas, typescript notes on EJH. In 1980, when I was teaching at Columbia University, Stephen Koss, who had just returned from a Visiting Fellowship at All Souls, told me that he had seen one of the Fellows, on perusing the list of guests invited to dinner, summon the butler and say, 'I see there's a *woman* dining in tonight. I'll have supper in my room!' Later, the College successfully made the transition into the twentieth century.
120 MRC 937/1/1/2: Raymond Carr to EJH, 18.12.69.
121 Ibid: Michael Flinn to EJH, 6.5.70; HFA: Ronald Tress to EJH, 23.3.70 and accompanying documents.
122 Interview with Roderick Floud, 14.9.2016, also for the following.
123 MRC 937/8/2/5: A.F. Thompson, 'Ingenious Marxman', unattributed clipping; Margaret Cole, 'So unfair to the Fabians', *Tribune*, 8.1.65; A.J.P. Taylor, 'Men of Labour', *New Statesman*, 27.11.64; Asa Briggs, 'Mapping the world of labour', *Listener*, 3.12.64, pp. 893–4; Lionel Munby, 'Caviar to the working man', *Daily Worker*, 5.11.64.
124 MRC 8/2/5. George Lichtheim, 'Hobsbawm's Choice', *Encounter*, March 1965, pp. 70–4. After producing a series of masterly studies of Marxist and socialist theory, Lichtheim, a freelance scholar who lodged with the eminent German historian Francis Carsten in London, committed suicide at the age of sixty-one when he believed he had nothing more to say, ignoring the pleas of those who thought he was still at the height of his powers 'with a Roman imperviousness to argument' (EJH, 'George Lichtheim', *New Statesman*, 27.4.73).
125 For a positive appreciation of its contribution to labour history, see E.P. Thompson's review in the *Times Literary Supplement*, 31.12.1964.
126 BULSC DM1107/A898: Memorandum of Agreement, 21.6.61.
127 Ibid: Plumb to Pevsner, 16.5.61; Plumb to Pevsner, 12.5.61.

128 Ibid: Pevsner memo, 26.5.61.
129 Ibid: Jacqueline Korn (David Higham Associates) to Pevsner, 15.8.61, and Pevsner to Higham, 9.8.61.
130 Ibid: Korn to David Duguid, 17.1.63.
131 Ibid: Korn to Pevsner, 1.7.63.
132 Ibid: Pevsner to Plumb, 13.12.63.
133 Ibid: Pevsner to Higham, 13.7.64.
134 HRC B-42 David Higham Associates 722: EJH to Miss Korn, 24.8.64.
135 BULSC DM1107/A898: EJH to Plumb, 24.8.64.
136 Ibid: Pevsner to Korn, 28.8.64.
137 Ibid: Peter Wright (history editor, Penguin) to EJH, 21.5.65.
138 Ibid: Bruce Hunter to Dieter Pevsner, 29.12.65.
139 Ibid: Peter Wright to EJH, 8.2.66.
140 Ibid: Peter Wright to Anthony Burton (Weidenfeld & Nicolson), 2.11.66.
141 Ibid: Peter Wright to EJH, 24.10.66. The file also contains correspondence with Christopher Hill about his own contribution to the series.
142 Ibid: Briefing Notes, 26.11.66.
143 Ibid: Julian Shuckburgh to Peter Wright, 16.11.67.
144 Ibid: Julian Shuckburgh to Peter Wright, 26.1.68; Dieter Pevsner to David Higham, 9.4.68.
145 MRC 937/8/2/7: E. P. Thompson, 'In orbit over the Empire', *Times Literary Supplement*, 27.2.69, p. 202, points out that this argument simply repeats that of the earlier book, albeit with a few more details.
146 Ibid. See also the review by Asa Briggs, 'What Was, What Is', *New York Times Book Review*, 3.11.66, in the same file.
147 Ibid: David Rubinstein, 'History which makes sense', *Tribune*, 14.6.68, also for the following. 'The dismal science' was the Victorian writer Thomas Carlyle's term for economics, especially because of the dire predictions of the population theorist Thomas Malthus.
148 Ibid: A. J. P. Taylor, 'Greatness and after', *Observer*, 25.5.68.
149 Ibid: Harold Perkin, 'As Lenin sees us', *Guardian*, 19.4.68. That rare beast, a conservative social historian, Perkin always turned up to social history conferences in an immaculately pressed suit, while the rest of us wore jeans and sweatshirts.
150 Ibid: typescript letter from EJH to Frau Harder (Suhrkamp Verlag, his German publishers), 3.12.68.
151 For an (overwhelmingly positive) assessment, see EJH, 'The Rioting Crowd', *New York Review of Books*, 22.4.65.
152 MRC 937/1/3/11: Olwen Hufton to EJH, n.d. (January 2003); EJH to Olwen Hufton, 15.1.2003; also Judith Adamson to RJE, 28.6.2017.
153 MRC 937/1/6/6: EJH to James Friguglietti, 10.2.94; see also EJH's contribution to the memorial for Rudé, 'George Rudé: Marxist Historian: Memorial Tributes', *Socialist History Occasional Pamphlet* 2 (1993), pp. 5–11.
154 MRC 937/1/1/1: Rudé to EJH, 22 March 1962, also for the following. Lefebvre's classic study focused on the 'Great Fear' of 1789, in which French peasants attacked their seigneurs' châteaux and in many cases burned them to the ground.
155 First published in 1971 and reprinted in Edward Thompson, *Customs in Common* (London, 1991), pp. 185–258.

156 Eric Hobsbawm and George Rudé, *Captain Swing* (London, 1973 [1969]), esp. pp. xi–xvi, xxii (also for a reply to criticisms by the many reviewers of the book).

157 A. J. P. Taylor, 'Revolt of the secret people', *Observer*, 9.2.69. See also John Lawrence Hammond and Barbara Hammond, *The Village Labourer 1760–1832: a study in the government of England before the Reform Bill* (London, 1911).

158 MRC 937/8/2/9: J. H. Plumb, 'Farmers in Arms', *New York Review of Books*, 19.6.69, pp. 36–7.

159 Richard Cobb, 'A very English rising', *Times Literary Supplement*, No. 33, 524 (11.9.69), pp. 989–92.

160 Keith Thomas, typescript notes on EJH. *Religion and the Decline of Magic* was also paperbacked under the Peregrine imprint of Penguin Books.

161 HRC B-40 David Higham Associates 806: David Higham to EJH, 10.12.65

162 HRC B-41 David Higham Associates 1028: EJH to David Higham, 16.11.67.

163 Ibid: David Higham Associates 1043: David Higham to EJH, 20.11.67.

164 Ibid: David Higham to EJH, 30.11.67.

165 Ibid: David Higham to EJH, 14.10.68.

166 MRC 937/8/2/8: Anton Blok, 'The Peasant and the Brigand: Social Banditry Reconsidered', *Comparative Studies in Society and History*, 14/4 (September 1972), pp. 494–503.

167 EJH, 'Armed Business', *New Statesman*, 12.6.64, p. 917.

168 HRC B-41 David Higham Associates 1117: Bruce Hunter to EJH, 14.8.69.

169 Ibid 84: EJH to Hilton Ambler, 7.3.70.

170 Ibid: Hilton Ambler to J. S. Stutter, 23.12.69.

171 DHAA BH 2009: Jessica Purdue to Marigold Atkey, 25.6.09 (email printout).

172 Pascale Baker, *Revolutionaries, Rebels and Robbers. The Golden Age of Banditry in Mexico, Latin America and the Chicano American Southwest, 1850–1950* (London, 2015), p. 4.

173 Published by Wesleyan University Press, Middletown, Connecticut.

174 EJH, 'From Social History to the History of Society', *Daedalus* 100 (1971), 1, pp. 20–45; also in EJH, *On History* (London, 1997), pp. 20–45, and Felix Gilbert and Stephen Graubard (eds), *Historical Studies Today* (New York, 1972).

175 US Department of Justice; Federal Bureau of Investigation (Washington, DC): 105-161920: Eric John Ernest Hobsbawm, memorandum of 7.4.67.

176 Ibid: US Immigration Visa 7.10.66: Applicant at London.

177 Ibid: Assistant Commissioner Adjudications, 9.1.67.

178 Ibid: Eric John Ernest Hobsbawm, 7.9.67; *IT*, pp. 388–91.

179 Ibid: L. Patrick Gray III (Acting Director, FBI) letter of 8.8.72.

180 MRC 937/4/3/1/8: EJH, 'The Cultural Congress of Havana', *Times Literary Supplement*, 25.1.68, pp. 79–80 (signed article).

181 *IT*, pp. 256–7.

182 KCAC NGA/5/1/452: Annan to Sir John Henniker-Major, 22 October 1968, also for the following. The suave and elegantly besuited Sarvepalli Gopal, whom I knew when I was a graduate student at St Antony's College, was himself, ironically, notorious for his own 'imprudent dealings with women'.

183 *IT*, p. 365. Mohan joined Mrs Gandhi's government but died tragically in an air crash in 1973.

184 HFA: EJH to Marlene, n.d.

185 Romila Thapar, unpublished reminiscences of EJH.

186 HFA: EJH to Marlene, 21.12.68.

187 Ibid: EJH to Marlene, 26.12.68, and for the following.

188 TNA FCO 61/581, *passim*: there is an online blog summary of these documents at http://blog.nationalarchives.gov.uk/blog/hobsbawm-unesco-and-notorious-communists/, accessed 1.8.2017.

189 BBC WAC R51/1213/1: 'Personal View', 4.1.72 [misdated, as sometimes happens in early January, to the previous year]; ibid, Adrian Johnson to Ed. D. T. P. (R), 19.1.72.

190 BBC WAC: Scripts card index.

191 MRC 937/4/3/1/6: EJH, 'Terrorism', *Listener*, 22.6.72.

192 Ibid: EJH, 'Shop Stewards', *Listener*, 27.7.72.

193 Interview with Claire Tomalin, 8.3.2017.

194 MRC 937/3/4/1/6: 'Why America Lost the Vietnam War', *Listener*, 18.5.72, pp. 639–41.

195 Ibid: 'The "Listener" has recently carried two articles on the Vietnam War – by Eric Hobsbawm and Anthony Lewis. Radio 3 commissioned this talk by Dennis Duncanson, which is in part a response to Eric Hobsbawm's broadcast', *Listener*, 20.7.72, pp. 77–9.

196 US Department of Justice: Federal Bureau of Investigation (Washington, DC): 105-161920: memoranda of 19.5.69, 18.9.70, 26.10.70, 19.1.71, 3.12.70, 3.4.73.

197 Ibid: Memo of 18.9.70.

198 HFA: EJH to Marlene, 4.5.73.

199 Ibid: EJH to Marlene, 6.5.73.

200 Ibid: EJH to Marlene, 13.5.73.

201 Ibid: EJH to Marlene, n.d., also for the following.

202 Ibid: EJH to Marlene, 27.8.1975.

203 Isaiah Berlin, *Building. Letters 1960–1975* (ed. Henry Hardy and Mark Pottle, London, 2013), p. 47 (Berlin to Robert Silvers, 9 February 1972). Berlin had previously made it clear that he respected Eric as an historian even if he disagreed with his politics (ibid, p. 378, Berlin to John Fulton, 4 March 1963).

204 MRC 937/8/2/6: 'Marx and Sons', *Times Literary Supplement*, 18.2.65.

205 MRC 937/4/3/1/8: EJH, 'Marx in Print', *Times Literary Supplement*, 9.5.68.

206 MRC 935/1/3/4: 'Marx: summary of talks between LW and Progress re edition of Marx and Engels'; *Marx/Engels Collected Works*, 50 vols, London, 1975–2004 and various foreign-language editions.

207 Interview with Nick Jacobs, 16.8.2016 amended 8.9.2018.

208 MRC 935/1/3/4: EJH to David McLellan, 7.11.69, and for the following.

209 Ibid: Eric to Tom Bottomore, 8.11.72. After the collapse of Communism in 1989–90, the International Institute for Social History, an Amsterdam-based archive that housed the Marx-Engels papers and many other socialist records, particularly German, took over the project's administration, and Eric played a role in raising funds for the continuation of the enterprise. The existing team in Moscow liaised with new editorial groups in Denmark, France, Japan and the USA. Eric continued to sit on the editorial board. (MRC 937/1/5/1: EJH letter, 9.1.99).

210 MRC 937/4/3/1/8: EJH, 'Marxism without Marx', *Times Literary Supplement*,

3.12.71, reviewing Louis Althusser, *Lenin and Philosophy and Other Essays* (London, 1971).

211 EJH, 'A Difficult Hope', *New Statesman*, 1.3.74.

212 *IT*, pp. 211–15.

213 EJH, 'In Search of People's History', *London Review of Books*, 19.3.1981, also for the following.

214 MRC 937/1/6/1: Eric to Raph Samuel, 13.5.69.

215 Ibid: EJH to Samuel, 22.5.69.

216 MRC 937 1/1/4: EJH to Stan Shipley, n.d. (c.1977).

217 David Cannadine, 'Down and Out in London', *London Review of Books*, Vol. 3, No. 13 (16 July 1981), pp. 20–1.

218 MRC 937/1/6/2: EJH to Joanna Innes, 11.6.1991; MRC 937/1/6/3: EJH to P. Sweeney, Prosecution Section, Companies House, n.d. (1991).

219 *IT*, pp. 215–17.

220 Quoted in Beckett, *Enemy Within*, p. 167.

221 'Comrades if the whole people did as we do?'; MRC 937/4/3/1/8: EJH, 'Commentary', *Times Literary Supplement*, 16.5.68, p. 511.

222 EJH, 'Birthday Party', *New York Review of Books*, 22.5.69.

223 Entretien entre Elise Marienstras et Charlotte Faucher, 27.6.2016 à Paris.

224 Interview with Neal Ascherson, 26.7.2016.

225 MRC 927/1/1/1: EJH to Truman, 22.7.68.

226 EJH, '1968: Humanity's Last Rage', *New Statesman*, 12.5.2008, p. 33.

227 Reuben Falber, 'The 1968 Czechoslovak Crisis: Inside the British Communist Party', http://www.socialisthistorysociety.co.uk/czechoslovak-crisis/; EJH, '1968: A Retrospect', *Marxism Today*, May 1978, pp. 130–6.

228 EJH, *Revolutionaries: Contemporary Essays* (London, 1973), pp. 216–19.

229 MRC 937/8/2/10: 'Bending the bars', *The Economist*, 1.9.73, p. 93. The title referred to the opening of the review, which portrayed Eric as imprisoned within the cage of his Marxist ideology: 'even if he bends the bars at times to seize on a flower in the field outside, that cage is always there'.

230 Ibid: Tom Kemp, 'Mr Hobsbawn [*sic*]: the sophisticated apologist', *Workers Press*, 2.7.73, pp. 8–9. Gerry Healy's Trotskyist sect was mainly known by virtue of the fact that its members included the actors Vanessa Redgrave and her brother Corin.

231 Ibid: David Halle: 'Spent Revolutionaries', *Congress Bi-Weekly*, 21.6.74, pp. 18–19.

232 Ibid: Arnold Beichman, 'Political', *Christian Science Monitor*, 28.11.73. At the time, the Soviet authorities were indeed consigning dissidents to mental hospitals or allowing them to emigrate, if they were Jewish, to Israel.

233 'Post-mortem on a bloody century', *Financial Times*, 9.10.94.

234 MRC 937/8/2/10: Steven Lukes, 'Keeping Left', *Observer*, 22.7.71, p. 31.

235 WNA, 'The Age of Capital': copy of Leszek Kolakowski, 'Hobsbawm's Choice', *New Statesman*, 27 July 1973.

236 MRC 937/1/3/2: 'Epochs of England, 13.10.64'.

237 Ibid: Eric to Paul Thompson, undated (1974).

238 Ibid: EJH to George Weidenfeld, 30.4.1975.

239 WNA, 'The Age of Capital': George Weidenfeld to David Higham, 23.3.66.

240 HRC B-41 David Higham Associates 186: notes 'Hobsbawm' (yellow paper), n.d. (1971/72).

241 Ibid: David Higham Associates 1043: Note on a Book on Revolution by E. J. Hobsbawm.

242 Ibid: Tom Maschler to Hilary Rubinstein, 2.7.68; David Higham to EJH, 19.7.68; and David Higham to Hilary Rubinstein, 9.9.68.

243 Ibid: David Higham, Note of a phone conversation re Eric Hobsbawm, 1968.

244 Ibid: David Higham Associates 1117: Harold Ober Associates to Bruce Hunter, 12.8.69.

245 Ibid: EJH to Robert F. Fenyo, 23.3.69; Robert F. Fenyo to EJH, 3.12.68.

246 HRC B-41 David Higham Associates 1117: EJH to Robert F. Fenyo, 23.3.69.

247 Ibid: Robert F. Fenyo to EJH, 22.4.69.

248 Ibid: EJH to Bruce Hunter, 25.8.69.

249 HRC B-39 David Higham Associates 387–388: Robert P. Fenyo to EJH, 4.11.70.

250 US Department of Justice: Federal Bureau of Investigation 105-161920: Memo of 18.10.70.

251 HRC B-39 David Higham Associates 387–388: David Higham to Ivan Van Auw, Jr., 25.11.70.

252 Ibid 387–388: Telegram, 22.2.71, et seq.

253 HRC B-41 David Higham Associates 1117: EJH to David Higham, 10.2.69.

254 Ibid: David Higham to EJH, 13.19.69.

255 Ibid. David Higham Associates 338: David Higham to Ivan Van Auw, 19.3.71.

256 Ibid: EJH to David Higham, 1.10.69.

257 WNA, 'The Age of Capital': EJH to Julian Shuckburgh, 19.11.70.

258 Ibid: Bruce Hunter to Julian Shuckburgh, 12.8.71.

259 HRC B-39: Higham and Associates 387-388: 'Hobsbawm' (notes), 1972 and following correspondence.

260 Ibid: David Higham to EJH, 3.1.72, 3.2.72, 25.2.72, 6.7.72, etc.

261 HRC B-41: David Higham Associates 121: David Higham to EJH, 22.7.71 and 19.4.71.

262 Ibid: David Higham Associates 186: David Higham to EJH, 12.12.72.

263 HRC B-43: David Higham Associates 1437: Bruce Hunter to Prentice-Hall, 6.2.87.

264 MRC 937/7/5/2/2: Royalty statements 1961–69; MRC 937/7/5/2/3: Royalty statements 1970–75. When I started as a university lecturer in 1972 my salary was £1760 a year before tax.

265 MRC 937/4/3/1/8: EJH, 'Pop Goes the Artist', *Times Literary Supplement*, 17.12.64.

Chapter 8: 'Intellectual Guru'

1 WNA, 'The Age of Capital': 'Retyped pages'; see also Susan Loden to EJH, 17.2.76, and EJH to Susan Loden, 24.2.76, 25.2.76, and subsequent correspondence, in WNA, file on 'Permission Letters'.

2 WNA, 'The Age of Capital': Andrew Wheatcroft to EJH, 3.6.74.

3 HRC B-39 Higham and Associates 387–388: Notes from 1971 (?) stamped XDH: 'Sequel to the Age of Revolution contract att. (working title)'.

4 WNA, 'The Age of Capital': Susan Loden to Philip Gatrell, 27.7.77.

5 Ibid: Editorial Production, 28.1.75 and picture research letters.

6   MRC 937/2/11: J. F. C. Harrison, *Victorian Studies*, Summer, 1977, pp. 423–5.

7   Ibid: Herbert Kisch, 'Hobsbawm and *The Age of Capital*', *Journal of Economic Issues*, XVI/1 (March 1982), pp. 107–30, at pp. 126–7; see also James J. Sheehan, 'When the world bowed to the power of capital', *Chicago Daily News*, 20.3.76.

8   MRC 937/2/11: David Goodway, 'Victors and Victims', unattributed, undated clipping.

9   Ibid: J. F. C. Harrison, review in *Victorian Studies*, Summer, 1977, pp. 423–5.

10   Ibid: David Landes, 'The ubiquitous bourgeoisie', *Times Literary Supplement*, 4.6.76, pp. 662–6, also for the following.

11   See my *The Pursuit of Power: Europe 1815–1914* (London, 2016).

12   For Eric's generous review of Landes' own next book, *Revolution in Time: Clocks and the Making of the Modern World* (Cambridge, MA, 1983), see EJH, 'On the Watch', *New York Review of Books*, 8.12.1983.

13   MRC 937/8/2/11: J. F. C. Harrison, in *Victorian Studies*, Summer, 1977, pp. 423–5.

14   WNA, Permission Letters; Asa Briggs, 'Around the world in 300 pages', *Books and Bookmen*, March 1976, pp. 13–14.

15   MRC 937/8/2/11: James Joll, 'Charms of the Bourgeoisie', *New Statesman*, 21.11.75, pp. 645–6.

16   Ibid: Paul Thompson, 'Progress at a price', *New Society*, 6.11.75, pp. 328–9.

17   Ibid: Gwyn A. Williams, 'Passepartout', *Guardian*, 13.11.75.

18   Ibid: David Brion Davis, 'The Age of Capital', *New York Times Book Review*, 9.5.76, pp. 27–9.

19   MRC 937/4/3/1/7: EJH, 'The Lowest Depths', *New York Review of Books*, 15.4.82, pp. 15–16.

20   Ibid: EJH, 'Vulnerable Japan', *New York Review of Books*, 17.7.75, pp. 27–31.

21   Ibid: EJH, 'The Lowest Depths', *New York Review of Books*, 15.4.82.

22   Brazilian sales figures estimated by Marcus Gasparian, of Eric's Brazilian publisher Paz e Terra (interview).

23   Keith Thomas, unpublished typescript on EJH.

24   Entretien entre Michelle Perrot et Charlotte Faucher, 20.9.2016.

25   KCAC NK 4/18/5: Nicholas Kaldor to David Landes, 7.11.73.

26   HFA: American Academy of Arts and Sciences: New Members Elected, May 12, 1971.

27   KCAC NGA/5/1/452: Noel Annan to EJH, 21.5.76. The 'whited sepulchre' was R. R. Darlington, the Professor of Medieval History and permanent Head of the History Department at Birkbeck. There is another copy of the letter in MRC 937/1/1/3.

28   KCAC NGA/5/1/452: EJH to Noel Annan, 22.5.76.

29   Keith Thomas, unpublished typescript on EJH.

30   Michael Howard, 'Professor James Joll', *Independent*, 18.7.1994.

31   Miranda Carter, *Anthony Blunt: His Lives* (London, 2001).

32   Hugh Trevor-Roper, 'Blunt Censured, Nothing Gained', *Spectator*, 25.11.1979. p. 11.

33   EJH to Trevor-Roper, n.d. (March 1980), quoted in Sisman, *Hugh Trevor-Roper*, p. 450.

34   MRC 937/1/2/5: British Academy Anthony Blunt: EJH to Kenneth Dover, n.d.

35 Ibid: Kenneth Dover circular, 22.8.1980.
36 Carter, *Anthony Blunt*, pp. 491–3; Kenneth Dover, *Marginal Comment: A Memoir* (London, 1994), pp. 212–20.
37 MRC 937/1/2/5: EJH to Dover, n.d. [August 1980].
38 Ibid: Dover to EJH, 2.9.1980.
39 Kathleen Burk, *Troublemaker. The Life and History of A. J. P. Taylor* (London, 2000), pp. 339–43.
40 MRC 937/1/1/4: EJH to David Cornwell (John le Carré), n.d. (May 1986).
41 Ibid: David Cornwell (John le Carré) to EJH, 27.5.86.
42 Ibid: EJH to David Cornwell (John le Carré), 5.6.86, also for the following.
43 Ibid: EJH to C. H. Lloyd, Secretary to the Board of Electors to the Ford Lectureship, 10.7.87.
44 Peter Brown to RJE, 14.9.2014 (email).
45 Interview with Roy Foster, 5.10.2016.
46 Interview with Claire Tomalin, 3.3.2017, also for the following.
47 MRC 937/7/5/1/2: Income and expenditure details, 1976–7.
48 Entretien entre Elise Marienstras et Charlotte Faucher, 27.7.2016, also for the following.
49 Interview with Andy and Julia Hobsbawm, 11.7.2016, also for the following.
50 Interview with Roderick Floud, 14.9.2016.
51 Correspondence kindly supplied by Judith Adamson.
52 MRC 937/7/5/1/1, also for the following.
53 HRC B-42 David Higham Associates 531: Bruce Hunter to EJH, 31.3.78.
54 Ibid, David Higham Associates 602: EJH to Bruce Hunter, 7.6.78. David Higham's memoirs were published the following year under the title *Literary Gent.*
55 HRC B1-3 David Higham Associates 1141: EJH to Bruce Hunter, 14.10.83, also for the following.
56 Interview with Bruce Hunter, 26.7.2016.
57 HRC B1-3 David Higham Associates 1141: Bruce Hunter to EJH, 20.10.83.
58 Interview with Roderick Floud, 14.9.2016.
59 Entretien entre Elise Marienstras et Charlotte Faucher, 27.7.2016.
60 MRC 937/7/5/1/2: Travel and expenses 1984–5.
61 HFA: Share certificates. Eric's income as a freelancer, though significant, in no way compared to that of A. J. P. Taylor, whose earnings in the 1970s were more than three times greater (Burk, *Troublemaker*, pp. 406–7).
62 MRC 937/7/5/1/2: accounts for 1977–8 and 1978–9 in response to letter from Dawn & Co., Accountants, 8.12.1980, and for the following, annual statements to the accountants.
63 Alan Mackay to RJE, 23.3.2013. Nikolai Bukharin was leader of the 'Right Opposition' in the Soviet Communist Party in the 1920s and a proponent of the New Economic Policy, which allowed a limited amount of private enterprise to take place. He was purged by Stalin and executed in 1938. See Stephen F. Cohen, *Bukharin and the Bolshevik Revolution* (Oxford, 1980).
64 EJH, 'Poker Face', *London Review of Books*, 8.4.2010.
65 EJH, 'An Assembly of Ghosts', *London Review of Books*, 21.4.2005.
66 Mario Ronchi, 'Storia politica ideologia: "I Ribelli"', *L'Unità*, 26.10.1966; 'Illusioni e delusion: dei sindicati Britannici', *L'Unità*, 22.9.1967; 'Labour Party:

impotenza e delusione', *L'Unità*, 13.10.1967; 'Londra pensa al dopo Wilson', *L'Unità*, 31.5.1968; 'Le radici dell'utopia', *L'Unità*, 11.7.1968; 'Rapporto sulla sinistra inglese', *L'Unità*, 3.1.1969; 'Lettra da Londra', *L'Unità*, 4.1.1970; 'Perché Wilson ha perso la partita', *L'Unità*, 26.6.1970; Enzo Santarelli, 'Vecchio e nuovo anarchismo', *L'Unità*, 1972 (on 1968); Fausto Ibba, 'Intervista: lo storico inglese Eric J. Hobsbawm parla dell'attualità', *L'Unità*, 31.5.1984. These are mostly summaries of longer articles by or about Eric in the Communist Party's monthly magazine *Rinascita*. In addition, the newspaper carried reviews of Eric's books as they appeared in Italian.

67 EJH, *The Italian Road to Socialism: An Interview by Eric Hobsbawm with Giorgio Napolitano of the Italian Communist Party* (translated by John Cammett and Victoria DeGrazia, New York, 1977), also for the following.

68 See the series of comic sketches by Giovanni Guareschi, centred on a village priest, Don Camillo, and his local rival, Peppone, the Communist mayor, symbolising the coexistence of Christian Democracy and Communism at the local level in post-war Italy: for example, *The Little World of Don Camillo* (New York, 1950).

69 'Quattro giorni di incontri e viaggi con lo storico Eric Hobsbawm', *L'Unità*, 26.3.1981, p. 5. Giuliano was an early postwar Sicilian bandit who featured in *Primitive Rebels*.

70 For an overview of the 'Second Mafia War', see John Dickie, *Cosa Nostra. A History of the Italian Mafia* (London, 2004).

71 EJH, in *La Repubblica*, 27.4.2007.

72 EJH, 'The Great Gramsci', *New York Review of Books*, 4.4.1974, reviewing Quintin Hoare and Geoffrey Nowell Smith (ed. and trans.), *Selections from the Prison Notebooks of Antonio Gramsci* (London, 1971), and Lynne Lawner (ed. and trans.), *Letters from Prison by Antonio Gramsci* (London, 1973), also for the following. See also EJH, 'Gramsci and Political Theory', *Marxism Today*, July 1977, pp. 205–12.

73 See also EJH, 'Should the Poor Organize?' *New York Review of Books*, 23.3.1978.

74 Archives Fondation Maison des Sciences de l'Homme, Paris: Fonds Fernand Braudel, correspondence active générale: Fernand Braudel to EJH, 19.11.1973.

75 'Panel Discussion: Conversations with Eric Hobsbawm', *India International Centre Quarterly* 31/4 (Spring, 2005), pp. 101–25 (corrected).

76 Interview notes: Charlotte Faucher and Marie-Louise Heller, 28.8.2016.

77 Entretien entre Michelle Perrot et Charlotte Faucher, 20.9.2016, also for the following.

78 MRC 937/7/7/4/6: Personal experience at the MSH: by E. J. Hobsbawm FBA (n.d., late 1980s).

79 CUL Press 3/1/5/989 Hobsbawm. EJH to William Davies, 22.12.81.

80 MRC 937/7/7/4/6: Personal experience at the MSH: by E. J. Hobsbawm FBA (n.d., late 1980s). Interview with Patrick Fridenson, n.d., who pointed out that Braudel, then in his late seventies, did not attend the meetings, the topics also being far removed from his own interests, but often met the participants informally and gave the workshops his seal of approval.

81 MRC 937/1/1/4: EJH to Mr Price, n.d. (1986/7).

82 EJH to Alan Adamson, 25.1.1981 (courtesy of Judith Adamson); Elisabeth Roudinesco, 'Louis Althusser: the murder scene', in eadem, *Philosophy in Turbulent Times* (New York, 2008), p. 113; *IT*, pp. 215–16.

83 HFA: EJH to Marlene, 28.4.1977.
84 HFA: EJH to Marlene, Cornell, 6.5.1977.
85 HFA: EJH to Marlene, Cornell, 1.5.1977.
86 HFA: EJH to Marlene, Cornell, 8.5.1977.
87 HFA: EJH to Marlene, 20.9. n.d.
88 HFA: EJH to Marlene, 1.4.1981.
89 HFA: EJH to Marlene, n.d. (from Thunderbird Lodge, Chico).
90 HFA: EJH to Marlene, 2.4.1978.
91 HFA: EJH to Marlene, 5.4.1978, also for the following.
92 HFA: EJH to Marlene, 23.9.1986, also for the following.
93 HFA: EJH to Marlene, 30.9.1986 (year given by mention of the new airport at Medellín, which was completed in 1985).
94 HFA: EJH to Marlene, 26 July (year uncertain).
95 Respectively, in *Marxism Today* May 1958, pp. 132–9; August 1962, pp. 253–6; June 1968, pp. 166–72; August 1967, pp. 239–43; and October 1974, pp. 302–8.
96 Interview with Martin Jacques, 16.8.2016.
97 MRC 937/1/6/3: Martin Jacques to EJH, 29.2.91.
98 Interview with Martin Jacques, 16.8.2016.
99 EJH, 'Intellectuals, society and the left', *New Society*, 23.11.78, reprinted in *New Statesman*, 16.4.2007, p. 62, to mark Eric's ninetieth birthday.
100 EJH, 'The Forward March of Labour Halted?' *Marxism Today*, September 1978, pp. 279–86.
101 EJH, 'Past Imperfect, Future Tense', *Marxism Today*, October 1986, pp. 12–19.
102 Ruth Winstone (ed.), *Tony Benn: Conflicts of Interest. Diaries 1977–80* (London, 1990), p. 596.
103 'Eric Hobsbawm interviews Tony Benn', *Marxism Today*, October 1980, pp. 5–13, also for the following.
104 EJH, 'Falklands Fallout', *Marxism Today*, January 1983, pp. 13–19, also for the following. The best short study is by Lawrence Freedman, author of the official British history of the war, and Virginia Gamba-Stonehouse, writing from the Argentine side: *Signals of War: Falklands Conflict 1982* (2nd edn, London, 1991).
105 David Butler et al., *The British General Election of 1983* (London, 1984); EJH, 'Labour's Lost Millions', *Marxism Today*, October 1983, pp. 7–13, also for the following.
106 See also EJH, 'The State of the Left in Western Europe', *Marxism Today*, October 1982, pp. 8–15.
107 MRC 937/1/1/4: Ralph Miliband to EJH, 3.1.84. Miliband put forward his arguments in public in his article 'The New Revisionism in Britain', *New Left Review*, 1/15, March–April 1985.
108 MRC 937/1/1/4: EJH to Ralph Miliband, 9.1.84.
109 Ibid: Ralph Miliband to EJH, 19.1.84; also EJH, 'Labour: Rump or Rebirth?' *Marxism Today*, March 1984, pp. 8–12.
110 MRC 937 8/2/18: EJH to Tzu-chen Yang, 28.2.02. See also Ruth Winstone (ed.), *Tony Benn: Free at Last: Diaries 1991–2001* (London, 2002), p. 130 (18.8.1992), for an example of Neil Kinnock quoting Eric.
111 CCAC/KNNK 17/25: Patricia Hewitt to Neil Kinnock, n.d., 'RE: *Marxism Today* interview with Eric Hobsbawm'. See Eric Hobsbawm, 'The Face of Labour's Future', *Marxism Today*, 28/10, October 1984, pp. 8–15.

112 Interview with Martin Jacques, 16.8.2016.

113 CCAC/KNNK 17/25: Sidekicks Services to the Media: Neil Kinnock Interview, Full Transcript, pp. 1–12. For the published version, see EJH, 'The Face of Labour's Future: Eric Hobsbawm interviews Neil Kinnock', *Marxism Today*, October 1984, pp. 8–15.

114 CCAC/KNNK 17/25: Sidekicks Services to the Media: Neil Kinnock Interview, Full Transcript, pp. 13–33.

115 Logie Barrow, 'Anatomising Methuselah', unpublished typescript. Samuel's fiftieth birthday was on 26 December 1984.

116 EJH, 'The Retreat into Extremism', *Marxism Today*, April 1985, p. 7.

117 EJH, 'Snatching Victory From Defeat', *Marxism Today*, May 1987, pp. 14–17; and EJH, 'Out of the Wilderness', *Marxism Today*, October 1987, pp. 12–19, also for the following.

118 EJH, 'No Sense of Mission', *Marxism Today*, April 1988, pp. 14–17; EJH, 'Ostpolitik Reborn', *Marxism Today*, August 1987, pp. 14–19 (interview with the leading German Social Democrat Peter Glotz).

119 EJH, 'Another Forward March Halted', *Marxism Today*, October 1989, pp. 14–19.

120 MRC 937/8/2/29: Ben Pimlott, 'Marx of weakness, Marx of woe', *Independent on Sunday*, 29.6.97, pp. 28–9.

121 Interview with Roderick Floud, 14.9.2016.

122 Interview with Martin Jacques, 16.8.2016.

123 EJH to Alan Adamson, 18.11.1980 (copy courtesy of Judith Adamson).

124 HFA: J. R. Stewart to EJH, 30.7.82. In October 1985 Eric was elected an Honorary Fellow of Birkbeck (HFA: George Overend to EJH, 30.10.85).

125 Interview with Ira Katznelson, 23.8.2016, also for the following.

126 Ira Katznelson, 'Hobsbawm's 20th Century. A Memorial Event', The New School, 25.10.2013 (typescript).

127 HFA: EJH to Marlene, 22.9. [1987].

128 Interview with Ira Katznelson, 23.8.2016, also for the following.

129 Eric Foner to RJE, 29.7.2016 (email).

130 Interview with Ira Katznelson, 23.8.2016, also for the following.

131 HFA: EJH to Marlene, 18.11.1987.

132 HFA: EJH to Marlene, 16.9.1986.

133 HFA: EJH to Marlene, n.d. Daniel Moynihan, the Senator for New York, had served both the Kennedy and Nixon Administrations.

134 HFA: EJH to Marlene, 23.11.1906.

135 HFA: EJH to Marlene, 12.11. [1988].

136 Joanna Innes, 'Eric Hobsbawm as *Past & Present* Editor', unpublished paper for 'After Hobsbawm' conference, 1.5.14; Keith Thomas, unpublished typescript on EJH.

137 MRC 937/1/2/12: Edward Thompson to EJH, 4.7.87.

138 MRC 937/1/1/4: EJH to Paul [no surname], 23.12.86.

139 All comments collected in MRC 937/7/4/11.

140 CUL, Press 3/1/5/989 Hobsbawm: William Davies to EJH, 25.4.78.

141 Ibid: Memorandum of Agreement, 26.4.82.

142 Ibid: Terence Ranger to William Davies, 24.12.81.

143 Ibid: EJH to William Davies, 22.12.81.

144 Ibid: Memorandum of Agreement, 26.4.82.

145 *IT,* p. 103.

146 MRC 937/8/2/13: P. N. Furbank, '"The kilt was invented by a Quaker in 1730"', *Listener,* 1.3.84.

147 Ibid: Colin McArthur, 'Culture as Power: A New Analysis', *Cencrastos,* 16 (1984).

148 MRC 937/8/2/14: Roy Foster, 'Master of Exceptions', *New York Review of Books,* 5.12.85, pp. 44–6.

149 Ibid: Alastair Reid, 'Class and Organization', *Historical Journal,* 30/1 (1987), unpaginated proof.

150 Ibid: Jeffrey Cox, 'Labor History and the Labor Movement', *Journal of British Studies,* 25/2 (April 1986), pp. 234–41.

151 HRC David Higham Associates 531: EJH to Bruce Hunter, 30.11.77.

152 Interview with Patrick Fridenson, n.d. Bédarida's excellent book was translated into English and updated in 1991 as *A Social History of England 1851–1990.*

153 Interview with Chris Wrigley, 5.10.2016.

154 HRC B-42 David Higham Associates 602: Penny Bruce to EJH, 28.6.78.

155 Ibid: EJH to Bruce Hunter, 7.6.78.

156 WNA, 'The Age of Capital': Andrew Wheatcroft to EJH, 15.11.74.

157 Ibid: EJH to Andrew Wheatcroft, 21.11.74.

158 MRC 937/7/8/1: 'Rathaus/history', Jan. 2008, p. 6.

159 WNA, 'The Age of Capital': Andrew Wheatcroft to EJH, 28.11.74.

160 HRC B-42 David Higham Associates 531: EJH to Bruce Hunter, 30.11.77.

161 MRC 937/1/6/24: page from undated letter.

162 HRC B-42 David Higham Associates 843: Penelope Bruce to EJH, 8.5.80.

163 HRC B-43 David Higham Associates 1335: Bruce Hunter to EJH, 22.12.86.

164 Entretien entre Michelle Perrot et Charlotte Faucher, 20.9.2016.

165 See Richard J. Evans, *Comrades and Sisters: Feminism, Socialism and Pacifism in Europe, 1870–1945* (London, 1987).

166 MRC 937/8/2/15: Martin Pugh, 'Imperial motives', unattributed clipping, 3.11.87.

167 Ibid: Michael Foot, 'A new world', *Guardian,* 23.10.87, p. 15.

168 Ibid: Catherine Hall, 'Twilight hour', *New Statesman,* 20.11.87.

169 EJH, 'Man and Woman in Socialist Iconography', *History Workshop Journal,* No. 6 (Autumn, 1978), pp. 121–38; Ruth Richardson, '"In the Posture of a Whore"? A Reply to Eric Hobsbawm', *History Workshop Journal,* No. 14 (Autumn, 1982), pp. 132–7; other articles in *History Workshop Journal,* No. 8.

170 MRC 937/8/2/15: Catherine Hall, 'Twilight hour', *New Statesman,* 20.11.87.

171 Ibid: Gertrude Himmelfarb, 'The Death of the Middle Class', *Wall Street Journal,* 14.3.88, p. 24.

172 Ibid: Geoffrey Field, 'The Longest Century', *Nation,* 20.2.1988, pp. 238–41; James Joll, 'Goodbye to All That', *New York Review of Books,* 14.4.1988, pp. 3–4; EJH response in Nicolau Sevcenko, 'Hobsbawm chega com "A Era dos imperios"', *Folha de S. Paulo,* 4.6.1988.

173 Joll, 'Goodbye to All That', pp. 3–4.

174 MRC 937/8/2/15: John Campbell, 'Towards the great decision', *Times Literary Supplement,* 12–18.2.1988, p. 154, also for the following.

175 Ibid: David Cannadine, 'The strange death of liberal Europe', *New Society,* 27.10.87, pp. 26–7.

176   Ibid: F. M. L. Thompson, 'Going down with the band playing and the rich in evening dress', *London Review of Books*, 7.7.1988, pp. 12–13; in a more vulgar form, H. G. Pitt, 'Loyal to Marxism', *London Magazine*, February 1988, pp. 93–6, affirming the durability of capitalism ('a brisk walk across the park from Westminster for a rather expensive lunch in Piccadilly will reassure one that the expected earthquake is yet to come').

177   MRC 937/8/2/22/1: Perry Anderson, 'Confronting Defeat', *London Review of Books*, 17 October 2002, pp. 10–17, also for the following.

178   Ibid, pp. 10–11.

179   MRC 937/1/6/1: EJH letter, 16.5.86.

180   MRC 937/8/2/22/2: Neal Ascherson, 'The age of Hobsbawm', *Independent on Sunday*, 2 October 1994.

181   Interview with Roy Foster, 5.10.2016.

Chapter 9: 'Jeremiah'

1   Paulo Sérgio Pinheiro, 'Eric Hobsbawm: Espelho de um mundo em mutaçao', *Estado de São Paulo*, 12.6.1988, pp. 80–1.

2   Interview with Patrick Friedenson, n.d. (2016).

3   'The End of the Affair, A Roundtable Discussion', *Marxism Today*, January 1990, pp. 40–5.

4   EJH, 'Splitting Image', *Marxism Today*, February 1990, pp. 14–19; EJH, 'Poker Face', *London Review of Books*, 8.4.2010.

5   EJH, 'Goodbye To All That', *Marxism Today*, October 1990, pp. 18–23.

6   MRC 937/1/6/2: EJH to Chris Wrigley, 4.2.1991.

7   EJH, 'Lost horizons', *New Statesman*, 14.9.1990, pp. 16–18.

8   'Finda URSS ameaça conquistas sociais', *Folha de S. Paulo*, 11.12.1992; 'Hobsbawm revê socialismos "após a queda"', *Folha de S. Paulo*, 10.12.1992.

9   Paul Barker, 'Waking from History's Great Dream', *Independent on Sunday*, 4.2.90, also for the following.

10   Interview with Garry Runciman, 26.7.2016.

11   MRC 937/1/6/3: EJH to Vicente Girbau León, 14.5.92.

12   MRC 937/8/2/25: 'Gerechter Krieg', *Frankfurter Allgemeine Zeitung*, 27.7.95.

13   EJH to James D. Young, 13.5.88, quoted in 'Eric J. Hobsbawm: "Communist" Historian, Companion of Honour and Socialism's Ghosts', from *New Interventions*, Vol. 10, Nos 3–4 (2001) online at https://www.marxists.org/history/etol/writers/young/hobsbawm/index.htm. James D. Young, whose political allegiance shifted seemingly continuously between various groupuscules of the Scottish far Left, was a bald, burly, red-faced and angry little man who was accustomed to refer to himself as 'the Departmental Bolshevik' when I was his colleague in the History Department at Stirling University in the 1970s, although in reality he knew very little about Bolshevism.

14   MRC 937/1/1/4: EJH to UNU/WIDER, 9.4.87.

15   John Breuilly, 'Eric Hobsbawm: nationalism and revolution', *Nations and Nationalism*, 21/4 (2015), pp. 630–57.

16   CUL, Press 3/1/5/989 Hobsbawm: EJH to William Davies, 20.1.90.

17   EJH, 'Dangerous exit from a stormy world', *New Statesman*, 8.11.1991, pp. 16–17.

18 EJH, 'Whose fault-line is it anyway?', *New Statesman*, 24.4.1992, pp. 23–6, reprinted from *Anthropology Today*, February 1992.
19 EJH, 'The nation is Labour's for the taking', *New Statesman*, 3.5.1996, pp. 14–15.
20 MRC 937/8/2/20: Eugen Weber, 'Imagined communities', *Times Literary Supplement*, 26.10–1.11.1990, p. 1149.
21 Ibid: Brendan O'Leary, 'Hobsbawm's Choice', *Times Higher Education Supplement*, 19.10.1990.
22 Ibid: Michael Walzer, 'Only Connect', *New Republic*, 13.8.90, pp. 32–4.
23 Ibid: Carl Levy, in *Labour History Review*, 56/3 (1991).
24 CUL, Press 3/1/5/989: Hobsbawm: EJH to Christine Oram, 24.4.90. Cambridge University Press held world rights in the book, a standard feature of all the Wiles Lectures publications; Eric's agent secured foreign editions by negotiating contracts then passing them onto the press.
25 Ibid: Hobsbawm: Christine Oram to Frank Schwoerer, 8.6.90.
26 'Il disoreine organizzato. Intervista con lo storico Hobsbawm. Il future del mondo: Balcanizzazione globale?', *L'Unità*, 14.4.1991.
27 http://www.bbc.co.uk/news/uk-wales-39281345, accessed 2.12.2017.
28 HFA: Welsh cottage; Parc correspondence: Lovegrove-Fielden to EJH, 5.7.91.
29 Peter Florence, 'Eric Hobsbawm turned history into an art', *Daily Telegraph*, 5.10.2012. At this time the newspaper was sponsoring the Hay Festival.
30 Marlene Hobsbawm to RJE, email, 1.6.2018.
31 Interview with Richard Rathbone, 15.12.2016. John Birt was Director-General of the BBC from 1992 to 2000. According to others present, Eric's speech was in fact not very long at all.
32 Frank Trentmann, 'Living history', *BBK: Birkbeck Magazine*, issue 31 (2012), pp. 8–9.
33 MRC 937/7/6/1–2: 'Festa a Genova per gli 80 anni del grande storico inglese'.
34 MRC 937/8/2/29: Keith Thomas, 'Myth breaker', *Guardian* review section, 10.7.97, p. 16.
35 Ibid: Orlando Figes, 'Revolution in the head', *The Times*, 5.6.97, p. 41.
36 Interview with Donald Sassoon, 20.10.2016. Eric told Tony Benn in June 1998: 'Blair has no connection with socialism at all; he doesn't know what it means, he's just interested in power.' (Ruth Winstone (ed.), *Tony Benn: Free at Last: Diaries 1991–2001* (London, 2002), pp. 487–8, 21.6.98.)
37 Interview with Garry Runciman, 26.7.2016; Keith Thomas, unpublished typescript on EJH.
38 Andrew Gimson, 'Eric Hobsbawm: Companion of Dishonour', *Standpoint*, November 2012 (http://www.standpointmag.co.uk/node/4691/full).
39 'Sir Alfred Sherman', Obituary, *Daily Telegraph*, 28.8.06.
40 Alfred Sherman, 'Last year's slogans', *Spectator*, 25.7.98, and for the following.
41 Young, 'Eric J. Hobsbawm' (as in note 13 above).
42 MRC 937/4/3/1/8: 'The Missing History – A Symposium', *Times Literary Supplement*, 23–29.6.89, p. 690.
43 MRC 937/7/8/1: 'Rathaus/history', Jan. 2008, p. 6.
44 MRC 937/1/1/4: George Weidenfeld to EJH, 21.4.87.
45 HRC B-43 David Higham Associates 1528-1529: EJH to Bruce Hunter, 28.4.88.
46 Ibid: Hunter to EJH, 24.5.88. Stone never produced the promised work. Hunter had evidently comissioned reviews of the synopsis.

47   Ibid: Bruce Hunter to EJH, 10.6.88.

48   Ibid: Bruce Hunter pencil note, 14.6.88.

49   Interview with Bruce Hunter, 26.7.2016, also for the following.

50   HRC B-43 David Higham Associates 1528-1529: Bruce Hunter to EJH, 10.6.88.

51   Ibid: Bruce Hunter to EJH, 17.6.88.

52   Ibid: Bruce Hunter to EJH, 27.6.88.

53   Interview with Bruce Hunter, 26.7.2016.

54   HRC B-43 David Higham Associates 1528-1529: A. Goff to EJH, 1.12.88; reply 5.12.88.

55   'Eric Hobsbawm: A Historian Living Through History', *Socialist History*, 1995, pp. 54–64 (transcript of interview on BBC Radio 3 'Nightwaves', 1.11.1994).

56   Virginia Berridge, 'The present as history: writing the history of one's own time, Eric Hobsbawm (1993)', in David Bates et al. (eds), *The Creighton Century, 1907–2007* (Institute of Historical Research, London, 2009), pp. 277–94. The lecture was summarised in Eric's article 'The time of my life', *New Statesman*, 21 October 1994, pp. 29–33.

57   MRC 937/1/6/3: Peter Holwell to EJH, 11.11.93.

58   Ibid: EJH to the Principal, University of London, 13.11.93.

59   Ibid: Peter Holwell to EJH, 16.11.93.

60   Ibid: Peter Holwell to EJH, 17.12.93.

61   EJH, 'Facts are not enough', *New Statesman*, 8.8.97, pp. 48–9. Martin Gilbert was my tutor for twentieth-century European history at Oxford, and focused on improving my written English, ignoring my arguments altogether ('you'll change your mind by the time you get to Finals anyway').

62   MRC 937/8/2/22/2: EJH, 'The time of my life', *New Statesman*, 21.10.94, pp. 29–33.

63   Interview with Lise Grande, 15.12.2016, also for the following.

64   Novelist, winner of the 1982 Nobel Prize in Literature.

65   I attended the lecture and remember this as a particularly striking moment in it.

66   HRC B-44 David Higham Associates 2289: Bruce Hunter to EJH, 5.1.94.

67   Ibid: EJH to Susan Watt (Michael Joseph) 21.3.94 (copied to Bruce Hunter), and Bruce Hunter to EJH, 24.3.94.

68   MRC 937/8/2/22/2: 'Crits' (handwritten notes).

69   Ibid: Neal Ascherson, 'The Age of Hobsbawm', *Independent on Sunday*, 2.10.94, p. 21.

70   Ibid: Edward Said, 'Contra Mundum', *London Review of Books*, 9.3.95, pp. 22–3.

71   MRC 937/8/2/22/1: Göran Therborn, 'The Autobiography of the Twentieth Century', *New Left Review* 214 (November/December 1995), pp. 81–90; Tom Nairn, 'Breakwaters of 2000: From Ethnic to Civic Nationalism', ibid, pp. 91–103; Michael Mann, 'As the Twentieth Century Ages', ibid, pp. 104–25.

72   Ibid: Kevin Davey, 'Age of Conservatism', *Tribune*, 16.12.94.

73   Ibid: Angus Calder, 'Angry account of a century ending in chaos', *Scotland on Sunday*, 30 October 1994.

74   Ibid: review by Ross McKibbin, *Times Literary Supplement*, 24.10.94; Perry Anderson, 'Confronting Defeat', *London Review of Books*, 17 October 2002,

pp. 10–17, at pp. 12–13; also MRC 937/8/2/36: Stephen Kotkin, 'Left behind', *New Yorker*, 29.9.03.

75 Ibid: pp. 13–14. Similar points in MRC 937/8/2/22/1: Michael Barratt Brown, 'In Extremis: The Forward March of Hobsbawm Halted', *Spokesman* (1995), pp. 95–102. The London-based journalist Thomas Nowotny found the book's pessimism distinctly non-Marxist (review in *Österreichische Zeitschrift für Geschichtswissenschaft* 2/99, no pages given: copy in MRC 937/8/2/29.

76 MRC 937/8/2/22/1: Christopher Caldwell, in *American Spectator*, June 1995, pp. 58–61. Neal Ascherson also noted how the book upended conventional depictions of the period (MRC (937/8/2/22/2: Neal Ascherson, 'The age of Hobsbawm', *Independent on Sunday*. 2.10.94, p. 21).

77 MRC 937/8/2/22/1: Eugene D. Genovese, 'The Squandered Century', *New Republic*, 17 April 1995, pp. 38–43.

78 Ibid: Tony Judt, 'Downhill All the Way', *New York Review of Books*, 25.5.1995, pp. 20–5, also for the following.

79 MRC 937/8/2/22/2: Niall Ferguson, 'How Stalin saved the West', *Sunday Telegraph*, 23.10.94.

80 Ibid: Andrew Roberts, 'An inadvertent history lesson', *Daily Telegraph*, 29.10.94.

81 Ibid: Daniel Johnson, 'History man who plays with extremes', *The Times*, 15.10.94. Not only Johnson but also the historian of ideas Michael Biddiss saw in the book's tripartite division of the century, ending in a prophecy of decline, a parallel with Spengler's *The Decline of the West* (MRC 937/8/2/22/2: Michael Biddiss, 'Four Ages of Modern Man', *Government and Opposition*, 30/3 (1995), pp. 404–11).

82 Ibid: Modris Eksteins, 'Hobsbawm's book on 20th century extraordinary', *Toronto Globe and Mail*, 29.4.95, C25.

83 Interview with Bruce Hunter, 26.7.2016.

84 MRC 937/8/2/23/2: EJH 'Comments on discussion of Eric Hobsbawm: The Age of Extremes' (typescript); MRC 937/8/2/22/2: Freedman review and Hobsbawm response, typescripts. Eric was probably referring to Christopher Browning's book *Ordinary Men: Reserve Police Battalion 101 and the Final Solution in Poland* (New York, 1993), when he mentioned 'recent research'.

85 HRC B-44 David Higham Associates 2289: Bruce Hunter to EJH, 25.10.94.

86 Ibid: Telephone message re. *Age of Extremes*, EJH to Bruce Hunter. I encountered Eric shortly before, on his way out of Birkbeck to attend the course.

87 Ibid: EJH to Bruce Hunter, 12.10.94 and 11.8.94, and Ali Groves to EJH, 25.8.94.

88 Ibid: Marlene Hobsbawm, invitation list, 23.9.1994.

89 Ibid: Ali Groves to EJH, 7.11.94.

90 Ibid: Ali Groves to EJH, 28.11.94.

91 HRC B-45 David Higham Associates 180: Catherine Rutherford to William Miller, 7.3.95, and my own recollection of the event.

92 Ibid: EJH to Ania Corless, 28.3.95 and attached pages.

93 MRC 937/1/6/9: Eginhard Hora (Hanser Verlag) to EJH, 2.2.96.

94 See among many examples MRC 937/8/2/25: Ludger Heidbrink, 'Die Alternative ist Finsternis', *Süddeutsche Zeitung*, 17.3.76.

95 Ibid: Franziska Augstein, 'Mann ohne Club: Hobsbawm und seine Epoche', unattributed and undated article, 18.1.93.

96 MRC 937/1/6/9: Eginhard Hora (Hanser Verlag) to EJH, 2.2.96.

97 MRC 1215/7: 'Lula'.

98 MRC 937/1/6/6: EJH report, 8.2.95

99 Email interview via his grandson, Pedro Cardoso Zylbersztajn. Alain Touraine was Director of Research at the EHESS.

100 HRC B-45 David Higham Associates 180: Luiz Schwarz to Ania Corless, 23.2.95.

101 Figures from Companhia das Letras, Eric's publisher in Brazil, and Marcus Gasparian, son of Eric's first publisher in Brazil, Paz e Terra.

102 Peter Florence, 'Eric Hobsbawm turned history into an art', *Daily Telegraph*, 5.10.2012. FLIP, the Festa Literária Internacional de Parati, was, and is, Brazil's largest literary festival.

103 EJH, *Echoes of the Marseillaise: Two Centuries Look Back on the French Revolution* (London, 1990), pp. 1–31.

104 Ibid, pp. 33–66.

105 Ibid, pp. 67–90.

106 Ibid, p. 92.

107 Ibid, pp. 91–113.

108 HRC B-45 David Higham Associates 180: EJH to Pierre Nora, 1.3.95, EJH to Ania Corless, 1.5.95; MRC 937/1/6/7: Pierre Nora to EJH, 24.3.95. Renzo De Felice was author of a multi-volume biography of Mussolini which many critics considered too favourable to its subject; Ernst Nolte had argued on many occasions that Nazism was an understandable, even in part justified reaction to the threat of Communism.

109 MRC 937/4/3/2/1: EJH 'History and Illusion' typescript. See also Furet, 'Sur l'illusion communiste', proof article, same file.

110 HRC B-45 David Higham Associates 180: EJH to Pierre Nora, 1.3.95.

111 Ibid: EJH to Ania Corless, 1.5.95, MRC 937/1/6/6: Pierre Nora to EJH, 11.7.95.

112 MRC 937/1/6/9: EJH to Ania Corless, 11.1.96.

113 MRC 937/1/6/8: Pierre Nora to EJH, 24.1.96.

114 MRC 937/1/3/13: EJH to Pierre Nora, 5.2.96.

115 MRC 937/1/3/12: Richard Figuier letter to David Higham Associates, 4.4.97

116 MRC 937/8/2/23/1: Philippe-Jean Catinchi, 'Décapant et polémique, le XXe siècle d'Eric Hobsbawm est publié en français', *Le Monde Diplomatique*, 28.10.99, p. 32.

117 Entretien entre Elise Marienstras et Charlotte Faucher, 27.6.2016 à Paris.

118 MRC 937/8/2/23/1: EJH, 'Damned before they published', *New Statesman*, 18.10.99, p. 41.

119 MRC 937/1/3/12: Ania Corless to EJH, 10.6.97; Olivier Bétourné to Boris Hoffman, 3.6. 97.

120 MRC 937/8/2/23/1: Philippe-Jean Catinchi, 'Décapant et polémique, le XXe siècle d'Eric Hobsbawm est publié en français', *Le Monde*, 28.10.99, p. 32.

121 MRC 937/1/3/13: EJH to Pierre Nora, 5.2.96.

122 MRC 937/8/2/23/1: 'Communisme et fascisme au xxe siècle', *Le Débat*, March–April 1996; 'Sur l'histoire du xxe siècle', *Le Débat*, January–February

1997; and see especially Pierre Nora, 'Traduire: nécessité et difficultés', pp. 93–5 in the latter issue. Brief commentary in MRC 937/8/2/22/2: 'Furet vs Hobsbawm', *Newsletter – Committee on Intellectual Correspondence*, Fall/Winter 1997/98, p. 10, and Adam Shatz, 'Chunnel Vision', *Lingua Franca*, November 1997, pp. 22–4. See also Ruggiero Romano, 'Une Étrange Anomalie', *Revue européenne des sciences sociales*, XXXV (1997), 109, pp. 176–9; Thierry Denoël, 'Le livre interdit', *Le Vif/L'Express*, 22.10.99, pp. 36–7.

123   MRC 937/1/3/12: EJH to André Versaille, 24.1.99.

124   MRC 937/8/2/23/1: Thierry Denoël, 'Le livre interdit'.

125   Ibid: Enzo Traverso, 'Des livres, du marché et de l'air du temps', *Quinzaine Littéraire*, 8.99, pp. 13–14.

126   Ibid: Philippe-Jean Catinchi, 'Décapant et polemique' (as in note 120 above).

127   Ibid: Robert Verdussen, 'Hobsbawm et son XXe siècle', *La Libre Culture* [Belgium], 3.11.99, p. 3.

128   MRC 937/1/3/12: EJH to André Versaille, 29.7.99; Gabrielle Gelber to EJH (fax), 16.7.99.

129   Ibid: 'PARIS: Lancement de *l'Age des Extrèmes*: PLANNING'; MRC 937/8/2/23/1: 'Lancement de l'Age des Extrèmes: AGENDA'. Eric's speech at the Sorbonne repeated his Creighton Lecture ('le siècle des extrêmes', ibid, *Res Publica* 23); MRC 937/2/117 for the typescript) with additional remarks on the French publishing scene; HRC B-44 David Higham 68 R15382 (3rd acquisition): Ania Corless to André Versaille, 9.9.99.

130   Interview with Bruce Hunter, 26.7.2016.

131   MRC 937/8/2/23/1: EJH, '"L'Age des extrêmes" échappe à ses censeurs', *Le Monde Diplomatique*, 9.99, pp. 28–9, also for the rest of this paragraph.

132   Ibid.

133   Ibid: Ismael Saz, 'Dos autores y un destino. Furet, Hobsbawm y el malhadado siglo XX', *Eutopías 2a época: Documentos de trabajo*, Vol. 135 (Valencia, 1996); 'Historikerstreit: Hobsbawm gegen Furet', *Frankfurter Allgemeine Zeitung* Feuilleton, 13.7.95; Bernado Valli, 'Eric Hobsbawm la Francia lo mette all'indice', *La Repubblica*, 8.4.97; further selection of French and other reviews, and extracts in the press, in MRC 937/8/2/24.

134   Ibid: 'Hobsbawm: perche i francesi mi hanno ritutato', *L'Unità*, 12.9.1999.

135   MRC 937/8/2/23/1: 'l'affairette Hobsbawn', *Livres hebdo*, 8.10.99. See also MRC 937/8/3/34: 'L'affaire Hobsbawn', *Libération*, 9.9.99.

136   MRC 937/8/2/23/1: 'Top Livres Hebdo', *Le Journal de Dimanche*, 14.11.99 (*Age of Extremes* stood at number two on the non-fiction list, behind a book on corruption in French public life). See also other bestseller lists in the same file (the book was at number four on 'Les Stars du Marché' in *Le Soir*, 10–11.11.99); Antoine Frodefond, 'Le 20ème siècle vu par Eric Hobsbawm: un livre dérangeant en France', *La Dépêche du midi (Dimanche Quinzaine Littéraire)*, 11.11.99; HRC B-44 David Higham Associates 68 R15382 (3rd acquisition): Ania Corless to Agence Hoffman, 10.11.99.

137   MRC 937/8/2/23/1: Jacques Nobécourt, 'Un Marxist recompose le XXe siècle'.

138   Ibid: Jean-Pierre Casanova, 'Les habits neufs du progressisisme. Une étrange interpretation du XXe siècle, selon Eric J. Hobsbawm'.

139   See the various publications in MRC 937/8/2/23/1.

140 DHAA Trans 2009 2/2: Ania Corless to Jeanine Windey, 15.5.08, and to George Hoffman, 17.6.08.

141 MRC 937/1/6/7: BBC – *Desert Island Discs*: *Prof. Eric Hobsbawm.*

142 Ibid: Maxine Berg to EJH, 7.3.95.

143 *The Late Show*, BBC Television, 24 October 1994.

144 MRC 937/1/1/6: EJH to Ivan Avakumovic, 30.3.2007.

145 MRC 937/1/6/5: David Herman to EJH, 25.10.94; EJH to David Herman, 29.10.94.

146 MRC 937/7/8/1: EJH to Jason Heppell, 30.6.97.

147 Eric Hobsbawm (in conversation with Antonio Polito), *The New Century* (translated from the Italian by Allan Cameron, London, Little, Brown, 2000 [1999]), pp. 158–9.

148 MRC 937/7/4/8: Fall 1988 Student Course Evaluation.

149 Ibid: course outlines.

150 Interview with Lise Grande, 15.12.2016, also for the following.

151 MRC 937/1/6/6: Judith Friedlander to EJH, 13.1.94.

152 Ibid: EJH to Judith Friedlander, 15.6.95.

153 MRC 937/7/4/8: Judith Friedlander to EJH, 11.6.96.

154 Ibid: EJH to Judith Friedlander, 4.3.96.

155 Ibid: Michael Hanagan to EJH, 9.5.96.

156 Ibid: note by EJH, 11.11.1998.

157 Arthur M. Schlesinger, Jr, *Journals 1952–2000* (London, 2008), pp. 807–8. Carlos Fuentes was Mexico's leading and much-translated novelist; Edna O'Brien a leading Irish novelist; Ronald Dworkin a legal philosopher, an American who had taught at Oxford; Brian Urquhart a retired British Army officer and Undersecretary-General of the United Nations (he devised the light-blue helmet colour for UN peacekeeping troops); Abba Eban a former Israeli Foreign Minister; Murray Kempton a Pulitzer prizewinning American journalist who lived with Barbara Epstein, co-founder and co-editor of the *New York Review of Books*.

158 Judith Friedlander to RJE, 2.8.2016 (email).

159 MRC 937/1/6/4: 'A concerned student' to EJH, the Dean and the Head of Department, 11.10.94.

160 Judith Friedlander to RJE, 2.8.2016 (email).

161 MRC 937/7/4/8: Louise Tilly to EJH, ? 4.96; Judith Friedlander to RJE, 2.8.2016.

162 Ibid: Louise Tilly to EJH, 4.5.96.

163 Ibid: EJH to Judith Friedlander, 4.3.96.

164 Judith Friedlander to RJE, 2.8.2016 (email).

165 MRC 937/1/6/3: Eugene D. Genovese to EJH, 3.6.92.

166 Ibid: EJH to Eugene D. Genovese, n.d. (1992).

167 Ibid: Eugene D. Genovese was the author of, among other books, *Roll, Jordan, Roll: The World the Slaves Made* (New York, 1974) and Elizabeth Fox-Genovese of *Within the Plantation Household: Black and White Women of the Old South* (London, 1988).

168 MRC 937/7/8/1: EJH to Bill Palmer, n.d. (July 1997), also for the following.

169 MRC 937/8/2/37: David Rosenthal, 'Why the Left is right', *Scotsman*, 7.7.07.

170 Interview with Lise Grande, 15.12.2016.

171 MRC 937/1/6/2: EJH to Poole, Gasters, Solicitors, 13.2.1990.
172 MRC 937/1/6/3: Andy Hobsbawm to EJH, n.d. (1993).
173 Joan Walker, 'Joss Bennathan: Obituary', *Guardian*, 9 December 2014.
174 MRC 937/1/6/3: Joss Bennathan to EJH, 29.10.91, also for the following.
175 Joan Walker, 'Joss Bennathan: Obituary', *Guardian*, 9 December 2014. Marion Bennathan died, a victim of Alzheimer's disease, early in 2018.
176 Interview with Robin Marchesi, 6.12.16, and for the following.
177 Information from Anne Marchesi and Marlene Hobsbawm.
178 MRC 937/8/2/32: Anna Davis to EJH, 18.12.97; Ania Corless to EJH, 19.12.97; EJH to Daniela Bernardelle, 19.1.98; *Village Voice Literary Supplement*, July/August 1998.
179 Ibid: Verena Dobnik, '"Communist Manifesto" is making its Marx again', *Associated Press*, 24.3.98.
180 Ibid: Lyle Stewart, in *Hour* magazine (Montreal), week of 26.2.99. Conceptual artists Vitaly Komar and Alex Melamid are reported to have declared: 'We are not just an artist, we are a movement'. See Carter Ratcliff, *Komar and Melamid* (New York, 1988). Donna Karan's dresses, launched in 1984, were intended to inaugurate a dynamic, brightly coloured style of clothing; she later founded 'Urban Zen', a 'lifestyle brand'. Barney's was a store specialising in designer clothing and luxury accessories.
181 MRC 937/8/2/32: James K. Glassman, 'The Invisible Hand of Karl Marx', *Washington Post*, 31.3.98.
182 Ibid: Barbara Ehrenreich, 'Communism on your coffee table', *Salon Online*, 30.4.98.
183 Ibid: James Poniewozik, 'No irony please – we're leftists', *Salon Media Circus*, 13.5.98.
184 Ibid: Harold Meyerson, 'All Left, Half Right', *LA Weekly*, 14.5.98. The Mexican term *maquiladora* denotes a business that imports raw materials for manufacturing, taking advantage of low import tariffs, then re-exports the finished products to the country where the raw materials originate. Van Nuys is a precinct of Los Angeles with a large recreation area; Nike is a brand of sports clothing. Charles Murphy was a theologian.
185 Ibid: Scott Shane, 'Communist Manifesto 150 Years Old', *Hartford, CT, Press Courant*, 1.5.98, among many others.
186 Ibid: David Barton, '10 myths about Marx', *Sacramento Bee*, 20.4.98.
187 Ibid: Calvin Reid: 'Verso: Sales Up: Marketing Marx', *Publishers Weekly*, 2.2.98.
188 Ibid: Paul Lewis, 'Marx's Stock Resurges on a 150-Year Tip', *New York Times*, 27.6.98, Arts pp. 1–2.
189 Ibid: John Cassidy, 'The Return of Karl Marx', *New Yorker*, 27.10.97.
190 DHAA AMG 2011: Tom Penn to Andrew Gordon, 20.6.11 (email printout); Andrew Gordon to Tom Penn, 21.6.2011 (email printout); Tom Penn to Andrew Gordon, 22.6.2011 (email printout); Andrew Gordon to EJH, 20.6.2011.
191 MRC 937/8/2/29: Hugh Trevor-Roper, 'Marxism without regrets', *Sunday Telegraph*, 15.6.97, review section, p. 13, also for the following.
192 Ibid: John Arnold, 'Igniting Marx with pomo sparks', *Times Higher Education Supplement*, 28.11.97, p. 26.
193 Ibid: Paul Smith, 'No vulgar Marxist', *Times Literary Supplement*, 27.6.99, p. 31.
194 Ibid: Jürgen Kocka, 'Marx lebt! Bei Eric Hobsbawm wird die Aufklärung

weise', *Die Welt*, 5.12.98 p. 14. The book appeared in German under the title *Wieviel Geschichte braucht die Zukunft* in 1998, published by the Hanser Verlag, and was very widely reviewed, mostly in similar terms.

195 MRC 937/8/2/35: Richard Gott, 'Living through an age of extremes', *New Statesman*, 23.9.02, pp. 48–50.

196 EJH, *Behind the Times: The Decline and Fall of the Twentieth Century Avant-Gardes* (London, 1998) [a pamphlet with the text of a single lecture].

197 HRC B-44 David Higham Associates 68 R15382 (3rd acquisition): Giuseppe Laterza to EJH, 18.1.99.

198 MRC 937/2/33: Noel Malcolm, 'What a difference a century makes', *Sunday Telegraph*, 26.3.2000.

199 Ibid: Max Wilkinson, 'Confessions of an unrepentant communist', *Financial Times*, 20/21.5.2000, p. v, also for the following.

Chapter 10: 'National Treasure'

1 Entretien entre Elise Marienstras et Charlotte Faucher, 27.6.2016 à Paris.

2 HRC B-45 David Higham Associates 461: Bruce Hunter to EJH, 24.4.96.

3 MRC 937/7/8/1: 'Paperback Writer' (typescript, 2003), pp. 6–7.

4 PBA: *Interesting Times*: Stuart Proffitt to Bryan Appleyard, 27.6.2002 (phrase repeated in numerous letters to other potential reviewers).

5 Interview with Stuart Proffitt at Penguin Books, also for the following.

6 PBA: *Interesting Times*: Stuart Proffitt to EJH, 25.9.2001.

7 Ibid: Stuart Proffitt, notes on chapters 16 to 24.

8 Ibid: Stuart Proffitt to EJH, 13.11.2001.

9 Ibid: Lisa Graham to Stuart Proffitt, 5.8.2002 and 9.8.2002.

10 Ibid: Bruce Hunter to Helen Fraser, 2.5.2000; Helen Fraser to Bruce Hunter, 16.5.2000.

11 Ibid: Publisher's blurb.

12 HC B-45 David Higham Associates 133: Eric Hobsbawm: 'AUTOBIOGRAPHY' (typed list of twenty-four chapters).

13 PBA: *Interesting Times*: Louise Ball to Stuart Proffitt, 6.9.2002.

14 Ibid: Stuart Proffitt to EJH, 5.12.2002.

15 Figures from Companhia das Letras, Eric's publisher in Brazil.

16 See John Callaghan, 'Looking Back in Amazement: *Interesting Times* and the reviewers', *Socialist History*, 24 (2003), pp. 19–25.

17 MRC 937/8/2/35; Perry Anderson, 'The Age of EJH', *London Review of Books*, 3.20.2002, pp. 3–7, also for the following. For similar observations on the impersonal nature of large stretches of the book, see Volker Depkat, 'Die Fortsetzung von Historiographie mit autobiographischen Mitteln', on the website *H-Soz-u-Kult*, 3.11.2003; also the remarks quoted in the Preface, above.

18 EJH, 'After the Cold War', *London Review of Books*. 26.4.2012, an appreciation written after Judt's tragically premature death from motor neurone disease.

19 MRC 937/8/2/35: Anthony Sampson, 'An extraordinary life', *Guardian*, 12.10.2002.

20 Ibid: EJH: 'Cheltenham 2' (typescript), pp. 9–10.

21 Ibid: Adrian Gregory, 'A key witness finally testifies on the 20th century', *BBC History Magazine*, 1.10.2002.

22 MRC 937/1/6/3: Marlene Hobsbawm to EJH, n.d. (Postcard 'Wedding Reception at Home, New York City, 1926').

23 EJH, 'Writers' rooms', *Guardian* Saturday Review, 12.1.2008, p. 3, in LBA: file on *Uncommon People.*

24 Interview with Nick Jacobs, 16.8.2016.

25 Interview with Garry Runciman, 26.7.2016, added comments by Ruth Runciman.

26 Interview with Nick Jacobs, 16.8.2016.

27 Interview with Stuart Proffitt, at Penguin Books.

28 Interview with Roy Foster, 5.10.2016.

29 Romila Thapar, unpublished reminiscences of EJH, 2016.

30 Interview with Roy Foster, 5.10.2016.

31 Val Wilmer, 'Denis Preston' in H. C. G. Matthew and Brian Harrison (eds), *Oxford Dictionary of National Biography*, 45 (Oxford, 2004), pp. 255–6.

32 Interview with Angela Hobsbaum, 30.3.2017.

33 MRC 937/1/1/5: EJH to David Sullivan, n.d. (Nov./Dec. 2004).

34 MRC 1/5/2: EJH to Franziska Augstein, 19.10.2006. Augstein published an extremely hostile review of the book: 'In deutschen Genpool baden gehen. Reisserische Thesen, nichts dahinter: Niall Fergusons Geschichte der Gewalt im 20. Jahrhundert', *Süddeutsche Zeitung* 228 (4.10.2006), p. 25.

35 MRC 937/7/3/43.

36 Interview with Richard Rathbone, 15.12.2016.

37 Julia Hobsbawm, 'Remembering Dad', *Financial Times*, 20 April 2013. Amartya Sen is a Nobel prizewinning development economist and sometime Master of Trinity College, Cambridge; Emma Rothschild, his wife, an economic historian; John Maddox was a science writer and editor; Brenda Maddox is a literary biographer; Michael Frayn and Tom Stoppard playwrights.

38 FLP: EJH to Fritz Lustig, 27.4.2005.

39 MRC937/4/6/1: *Guardian*, 30.4.87.

40 MRC 937/1/2/8: EJH to János Jemnitz, 26.1.2005.

41 MRC 937/8/2/37: David Rosenthal, 'Why the Left is right', *Scotsman*, 7.7.07, also for the following.

42 DHAA: BH 2005: Alice Wilson to Kirsten Lass (email printout), 28.10.05; Kirsten Lass to Alice Wilson, 27.10.05 (email printout).

43 Ibid: EJH to Bruce Hunter, 18.7.05 (email printout) and attachments.

44 MRC 1215/6: typescript, 'On the West Bank', undated.

45 MRC 937/4/6/1: EJH to the *Times Higher Education Supplement*, 10.4.1987.

46 MRC 937/1/4/1: EJH to Bernard Samuels, 19.2.2003.

47 MRC 937/4/6/1: *Guardian*, 19.4.05.

48 Interview with Ira Katznelson, 23.8.2016.

49 EJH, 'Responses to the War in Gaza', *London Review of Books*, 29.1.2009.

50 Entretien entre Elise Marienstras et Charlotte Faucher, 27.6.2016 à Paris.

51 MRC 937/7/3/39-49: visits to the Wigmore Hall on 7.10, 13.10 and 16.10.2010 and 14.11.2011 for example.

52 Interview with Nick Jacobs, 16.8.2016.

53 DHAA BH 2005: EJH to Bruce Hunter, 14.6.05 (email printout).

54 MRC 937/1/1/6: EJH to Michael Kater ?.5.2005.

55   MRC 937/1/1/6: EJH to Ivan Berend, n.d. (Jan. 2005). Manmohan Singh, who graduated in economics from Cambridge in 1957, was Congress Party Prime Minister for ten years from 2004.

56   'Panel Discussion: Conversations with Eric Hobsbawm', *India International Centre Quarterly* 31/4 (Spring, 2005), pp. 101–25.

57   DHAA BH/AW 2008: Bruce Hunter to Hannah Whitaker, 25.09.08 (email printout), EJH to Bruce Hunter, 25.09.2008 (email printout) and invitation card.

58   Entretien entre Elise Marienstras et Charlotte Faucher, 27.7.2016 à Paris.

59   EJH, 'An Assembly of Ghosts', *London Review of Books*, 21.4.2005.

60   MRC 937/7/3 39-46 (pocket diaries, 2000–2007).

61   Entretien entre Elise Marienstras et Charlotte Faucher, 27.6.2016 à Paris.

62   MRC 937/1/1/6: EJH to Michael Kater, 4.5.2005; EJH to Debbie Valenze, 1.7.2005.

63   Julia Hobsbawm, 'Remembering Dad', *Financial Times*, 20 April 2013; information from Marlene Hobsbawm; speeches and congratulations in MRC 937/7/6/3-4. His speech at the Austrian Embassy party is included in the file.

64   Interview with Claire Tomalin, 8.3.2017.

65   Entretien entre Elise Marienstras et Charlotte Faucher, 27.7.2016.

66   MRC 937/1/1/6: Thomas Matussek to EJH, 6.7.2005.

67   Ibid: Malcolm Chase to EJH, 19.11.2007.

68   Keith Thomas, unpublished manuscript on EJH. Eric eventually spoke at a Balzan Prize event held at the University of Zurich on 16 June 2004 (MRC 937/7/7/21).

69   http://www.balzan.org/en/prizewinners/eric-hobsbawm/research-project-hobsbawm.

70   MRC 937/1/1/6: EJH to Victor Kiernan, 9.6.2006.

71   DHAA BH/MA 2010: 'Eric Hobsbawm meeting with AMG, 04/11/2010'.

72   Ibid: EJH to Bruce Hunter, 5.10.10 (email printout).

73   Interview with Chris Wrigley, 5.10.2016

74   Interview with Bruce Hunter, 26.7.2016.

75   EJH, 'Democracy can be bad for you', *New Statesman*, 5.3.2001, pp. 25–7, originally delivered as the Athenaeum Lecture in London.

76   Quoted in MRC 937/8/2/37: Bill McSweeney, 'A constant communist', *Irish Times*, 21.7.07.

77   Ibid: John Moore, 'A weak-kneed theory', *Morning Star*, 23.7.2007.

78   Ibid: Noel Malcolm, 'If there are two conflicting ways of putting America in the dock, Hobsbawm will happily go for both of them', *Sunday Telegraph*, 1.7.2007; he thought the essays were full of contradictions.

79   DHAA BH/MA 2008: Tariq Ali to EJH, 30.7.2008.

80   DHAA BH/MA 2006: Tariq Ali to EJH, 2.7.2008; EJH to Bruce Hunter, 2.7.2008; Sebastian Budgen to Bruce Hunter, 16.7.2008 (email printout), and Bruce Hunter to Sebastian Budgen, 15.7.2008 (email printout). As a Verso author, I was among many who agreed to forgo my royalties at this time.

81   DHAA AMG 2011: Andrew Gordon to William Frucht, 20.4.2011 (email printout).

82   DHAA BH/MA 2010: Richard Beswick to Bruce Hunter, 10.11.2010 (email printout).

83   Ibid: Bruce Hunter to Richard Beswick, 15.11.2010 (email printout).
84   Ibid: Clive Priddle to Bruce Hunter, 22.10.2010 (email printout).
85   Ibid: EJH to Marigold Atkey, 6.9.2010 (email printout).
86   DHAA AMG 2011: Bruce Hunter to EJH, 23.11.2010 (email printout).
87   MRC 937/8/2/40: Alan Ryan, 'Karl's Way', *Literary Review*, March 2011.
88   Ibid: 'Little, Brown: Bestsellers', 29.1.11.
89   DHAA BH/MA 2010: 'Eric Hobsbawm meeting with AMG', 04.11.2010.
90   DHAA AMG 2012: EJH to Andrew Gordon, 9.3.12 (email printout).
91   EJH, 'Homesickness', *London Review of Books*, 8.4.1993.
92   At the suggestion of the Cambridge Latin Americanist David Brading, Eric was already considering publishing a collection of his essays in the field as early as 2008, and this appeared posthumously in 2016, edited by Leslie Bethell under the title *Viva la Revolución! Eric Hobsbawm on Latin America*.
93   DHAA AMG 2012: Chris Wrigley to Bruce Hunter, 7.12.12.
94   MRC 937/1/6/6: *Evening Standard*, 14.6.94 (clipping sent by Julia Hobsbawm).
95   Ibid: Emma Soames to EJH, 13.6.94.
96   MRC 937/7/3/40: pocket diary for 2001.
97   Ibid.
98   MRC 937/1/1/6: EJH to Debbie Valenze, 1.7.2005.
99   FLA: EJH to Fritz Lustig, 20.6.2007.
100 Ibid: EJH to Fritz Lustig, 15.6.2009.
101 DHAA BH/AW 2006: EJH to Bruce Hunter, 5.10.06. The bibliography, an invaluable guide to Eric's published writings, was compiled by Keith McLelland.
102 Ibid: Bruce Hunter to EJH, 29.09.06.
103 DHAA BH/MA 2010: EJH to Bruce Hunter, 1.10.10 (email printout).
104 Ibid: Bruce Hunter to EJH, 30.9.2010.
105 Ibid: Bruce Hunter to EJH, 4.10.10 (email printout).
106 Ibid: 'Eric Hobsbawm: Papers', 19.3.10.
107 Ibid: 'Eric Hobsbawm meeting with AMG,' 04.11.2010.
108 Julia Hobsbawm, 'Remembering Dad', *Financial Times*, 20 April 2013.
109 MRC 937/7/3/48: pocket diary for 2010.
110 DHAA BH/MA 2010: Bruce Hunter to Kathy Rooney, 23.8.10 (email printout).
111 Julia Hobsbawm, 'Remembering Dad', *Financial Times*, 20 April 2013.
112 DHAA BH/MA 2010: EJH to Marigold Atkey, 3.5.10 (email printout); EJH to Bruce Hunter, 17.2.10 (email printout).
113 HFA: 'Brohi': Karim Brohi to EJH, 14.5.2011.
114 FLA: EJH to Fritz Lustig, 1.7.2011.
115 HFA: Brohi: Julia Hobsbawm to EJH, Marlene, Andy, 26.4.2011 (email); MRC 937/7/3/49: pocket diary for 2011.
116 Interview with Julia and Andy Hobsbawm, 11.7.2016.
117 Interview with Joan Bakewell, 22.7.2016.
118 Interview with Richard Rathbone, 15.12.2016
119 Interview with Lise Grande, 15.12.2016.
120 MRC 937/1/6/23: EJH to Tyrrell Marris, n.d. (between 5 and 16 August 2012).
121 HFA: 'Brohi': Marlene to Karim Brohi, 23.1.13; Marlene Hobsbawm to RJE, 31.8.2018.

122 DHAA AMG 2012: Demetris Christofias to Marlene Hobsbawm, 1.10.12.
123 A. N. Wilson, 'He hated Britain and excused Stalin's genocide. But was the hero of the BBC and the Guardian a TRAITOR too?', *Daily Mail*, 2.10.2012.
124 Julia Hobsbawm, 'Remembering Dad', *Financial Times*, 20.4.2013.
125 Figures from Companhia das Letras, Eric's publisher in Brazil, and Marcus Gasparian, son of Eric's first publisher in Brazil, Paz e Terra.
126 Julia Hobsbawm, 'Remembering Dad', *Financial Times*, 20.4.2013.
127 'Foi uma honra ser contemporâneo e ter convivido com Eric Hobsbawm', diz Lula em mensagem à viúva do historiador. INSTITUTO LULA, October 1st 2012. Since then Lula has been convicted of corruption following the overthrow of the left-wing government of his successor, but he remains a hero to Brazilian workers.
128 'A imperdoável cegueira moral de Eric Hobsbawm', *VEJA*, 4.10.2012: http://veja.abril.com.br/entretenimento/a-imperdoavel-cegueira-ideologica-de-eric-hobsbawm/. For the rejoinder of the Association of Brazilian Historians, see 'Historiadores repudiam matéria da Revista Veja sobre Eric Hobsbawm', http://www.revistaforum.com.br/2012/10/10/historiadores-repudiam-materia-da-revista-veja-sobre-eric-hobsbawm/.
129 Romila Thapar, unpublished reminiscences of EJH, 2016.
130 Interview with Lise Grande, 15.12.2016.
131 MRC 937/7/8/8: Provisional Notes on My Funeral; also for the following paragraph.
132 Interview with Ira Katznelson, 23.8.2016.
133 Ibid: Funeral programme.
134 Julia Hobsbawm, 'Remembering Dad', *Financial Times*, 20.4.2013.
135 Marlene Hobsbawm to RJE, 9.9.2017 (email).
136 Julia Hobsbawm, 'Remembering Dad', *Financial Times*, 20 April 2013.

Conclusion

1   FLP: Marlene Hobsbawm to Fritz Lustig, 10.12.2012.
2   Interview with Roderick Floud, 14.9.2016.
3   HFA: certificates.
4   Interview with Garry Runciman, 26.7.2016, also for the following.
5   HFA: Instructions for funeral and memorial, also for the following.
6   MRC 937/7/8/1. 'Rathaus/history', Jan. 2008, pp. 7–8.
7   Ibid, p. 10.
8   Ibid, p. 11.
9   Interview with Lise Grande, 15.12.2016.
10 See Eugene D. Genovese, 'Squandered Century', *New Republic*, 17.4.1995.
11 Tony Judt, 'Downhill All the Way', *New York Review of Books*, 25.5.1995.

List of Illustrations

Plate section one

Giorgio Napolitano. Giorgio Lotti/Mondadori Portfolio via Getty Images
Jean-Paul Sartre. Ullsteinbild/Ullsteinbild via Getty Images
Die Erwartung by Richard Oelze. Oelze, Richard (1900–1980): Expectation, (Erwartung), 1935–36. New York, Museum of Modern Art (MoMA). Oil on canvas, 32⅛ × 39⅝″ (81.6 × 100.6 cm). Purchase. 27.1940 © 2018. Digital Image, The Museum of Modern Art, New York/Scala, Florence
Eric in 1955, by Peter de Francia. © The Estate of Peter de Francia, courtesy of James Hyman Gallery, London. Gift of Julia Hobsbawm to the Birkbeck Eric Hobsbawm Scholarships Fund

Plate section two

Marlene Schwarz in the Congo, 1960. Courtesy of Marlene Hobsbawm
Eric with Andy and Julia. Courtesy of Marlene Hobsbawm
Alan Sillitoe. © Hulton-Deutsch Collection/CORBIS/Corbis via Getty Images
Ernesto 'Che' Guevara. Joseph Scherschel/The LIFE Picture Collection/Getty Images
Kenneth Tynan. Carl Mydans/The LIFE Picture Collection/Getty Images
Eric in the Peruvian sierra, 1971. Courtesy of Marlene Hobsbawm
Luiz Inácio Lula da Silva. Michael Kappeler/AFP/Getty Images
Eric with Ticlia. Courtesy of Marlene Hobsbawm
George Weidenfeld. © Tim Mercer/Mary Evans Picture Library
Caricature by John Minnion. Lebrecht Music & Arts/Alamy Stock Photo
Eric in the Croesor Valley. Courtesy of Marlene Hobsbawm
On stage at Hay Literary Festival, 2011. Ben Wyeth/Alamy Stock Photo
Historians of *Past & Present*, painted in 1999 by Stephen Farthing. © National Portrait Gallery, London
Eric in his nineties. © Gaby Wood/Telegraph Media Group Ltd 2018
Eric's grave in Highgate cemetery. Alastair Wallace/Shutterstock

Index

Owen, Wilfred 81
Oxford: Eastgate Hotel 429; Walton Street 529
Oxford, University of 93, 161, 266; All Souls College 429; Balliol College 91, 92, 619; Bullingdon Club 147; Ford Lectures 487; Jesus College 429; New College 260; Nuffield College 381; Ruskin College 459; St Antony's College 430, 717–18n48; Sheldonian Theatre 579
Oxford University Press 438, 657; *Oxford History of England* 244

Paetzel, Dr 25
Pageant of History (series) 441–2
Paignton, Devon 63
Paine, Thomas 100, 194
Palermo 498
Palestine 33, 239, 256, 568, 595, 627; Bir-Zeit University, Ramallah 627; Festival of Literature 643
Palestine Liberation Organization 566
Palmer, William, *Engagement with the Past: The World War II Generation of Historians* 598–9
Pantheon Books 435, 439, 472, 564, 586, 636, 638
Papen, Franz von 31, 36, 39, 76
Papon, Maurice 328
Paraguay 409
Paratı, Brazil 579
Parc Farmhouse, Snowdonia 416, 557
Paris viii, 79, 94–106, 151, 156–9, 157, 170, 172–3, 276, 425, 494, 495, 631, 632, 643; Boulevard Kellermann 324; Boulevard Montparnasse 234; Boulevard Saint-Michel 172; Boulevard Sebastopol 150; Buffalo Stadium 99–100; Café Flore 324; Casino de Paris 95–6; Le Chat Qui Pêche 325; Club St Germain 325; Comic Opera 101; Commune 80; La Coupole 325, Les Deux Magots 325; Dome café 104–5; École des Hautes Études en Sciences Sociales 495, 578–9, 581; École nationale supérieure des Beaux-Arts 324; Folies Bergère 95–6; Hôtel Ambassador 157; Hôtel L'Angleterre, rue Jacob 631; International Conference of the World Student Association 157; Jardin du Luxembourg 95; labour movement in 96–7; Latin Quarter 463; Left Bank 459; Louvre 102; Les Macédoines 158, 159; Maison des Sciences de l'Homme 500, 502; mass revolts in 438; Montmartre 95, 102, 255; Montparnasse 95, 104–5; Neuilly 99; Opera 100; Peace Accords (1973) 452; Place Vendôme 177; Porte St Denis 101; La Rhumerie 324; Rue Gay-Lussac 463; Rue d'Ulm 463; Sainte-Chapelle 95; La Samaritaine (department store) 107; Sorbonne University 392,

586; Stock Exchange 101; student demonstrations in (events of May 1968) 462–3, 579; Westminster Bank 177; Winter Velodrome 114; World Exposition 157
Parker, Charlie, 'Parker's Mood' 589
Parkhurst, Isle of Wight 233
Pärt, Arvo 357
Pascal, Roy 137, 147
Pash, Herbert 147
Passchendaele 66
Past & Present: A Journal of Scientific History 315–20, 329, 441, 449, 460, 461, 528–30, 657
Past and Present Society 530
Patten, Chris 613
Patterson, Garran 393
Payne, Edwin 344
Paz e Terra (publisher) 444
Peabody, Corporal 188
Peace Council 161
Peacock, Ronald 381
peasants 476; in Colombia 406; in Latin America 407; in Mexico 443; in Peru 425
Péguy, Charles 115
Penguin Books 375, 429, 432–5, 440, 441, 527, 533, 534, 612, 631; crime paperbacks 643; Pelican (non-fiction imprint) 432–3; Penguin Press 614, 616, 617, 623
Pennsylvania 425
The Pentagon Papers 297
Pepys, Samuel 56
perestroika 545
Perkin, Harold, *The Origins of Modern English Society, 1780–1880* 437
Perrot, Michelle 480, 489, 501, 502, 537
'A Personal View' (BBC radio series) 451
Perth 207
Peru: Central Railway 478; EJH in 394, 405–6, 494, 506, 507; peasants 425; students from 593
Perugia 286
Peter, Haller 19
Petronius, *The Satyricon* 81
Pevsner, Dieter 433–4
Philadelphia 602
Philby, Kim 137, 221, 238
Philippines 256
The Philologian (school magazine) 50–1
Picasso, Pablo 60, 525, 540, 610; *Guernica* 157
Pickthorn, Kenneth 125
Pieck, Wilhelm 57
Pigou, Arthur Cecil 277
Pimlott, Ben 522
Pisa 631
Place, Francis 250
Plamenatz, John, *What is Communism?* 381
Plas Brondanw, Croesor Valley, Wales 415
Plato 78
Platten, Corporal Reggie 190

782 *Eric Hobsbawm: A Life in History*